Fallen Is Babylon

THE NEW TESTAMENT IN CONTEXT

Friendship and Finances in Philippi
THE LETTER OF PAUL TO THE PHILIPPIANS
Ben Witherington III

Walking in the Truth: Perseverers and Deserters
THE FIRST, SECOND, AND THIRD LETTERS OF JOHN
Gerard S. Sloyan

Church and Community in Crisis
THE GOSPEL ACCORDING TO MATTHEW
J. Andrew Overman

Letters to Paul's Delegates
1 TIMOTHY, 2 TIMOTHY, TITUS
Luke Timothy Johnson

Embassy of Onesimus
THE LETTER OF PAUL TO PHILEMON
Allen Dwight Callahan

Community of the Wise
THE LETTER OF JAMES
Robert W. Wall

To Every Nation under Heaven
THE ACTS OF THE APOSTLES
Howard Clark Kee

Fallen Is Babylon

THE REVELATION TO JOHN

Frederick J. Murphy

THE NEW TESTAMENT IN CONTEXT
Howard Clark Kee and J. Andrew Overman, editors

TRINITY PRESS INTERNATIONAL
Harrisburg, Pennsylvania

Copyright © 1998 by Frederick J. Murphy

All rights reserved. No part of this book may be reproduced, stored in a retrieval system, or transmitted, in any form or by any means, electronic, mechanical, photocopying, recording, or otherwise, without the written permission of the publisher.

Trinity Press International, P.O. Box 1321, Harrisburg, PA 17105

Trinity Press International is a division of the Morehouse Group

Library of Congress Cataloging-in-Publication Data

Murphy, Frederick James.

Fallen is Babylon : the revelation to John / Frederick J. Murphy.

p. cm. – (The New Testament in context)

Includes bibliographical references and index.

ISBN 1-56338-152-4

1. Bible N.T. Revelation – Commentaries. I. Title.

II. Series.

BS2825.3.M86 1998

228′.07 – DC21 98-9598

98 99 00 01 02 10 9 8 7 6 5 4 3 2 1

For Rebecca and Jeremy, our children,
Of whom we are so proud,
And who bring us so much joy

Contents

Part II
THE FIRST CYCLE OF ESCHATOLOGICAL VISIONS (4:1–11:19)

Part III
THE SECOND MAJOR CYCLE OF VISIONS (12:1–22:5)

Preface

In recent years there has been a new interest in the Jewish roots of Christianity. Although many Christians have believed that Jesus intended to found a new religion and that the earliest Christians were self-consciously constructing that new religion, most critical scholars would now challenge that understanding. Jesus was fully a Jew, and recent research on the historical Jesus and on the movement that had its origins in him takes that fact seriously. Many of those who joined the movement in its earliest days after Jesus' death thought of themselves as belonging to a group within Judaism. This renewed interest in the Jewishness of Jesus and the Jewishness of earliest Christianity is one of the most fruitful and exciting currents in contemporary New Testament scholarship. It has led to a more accurate appraisal of many early Christian texts, and it has also contributed substantially to modern christologies.

Professor J. Andrew Overman, who wrote the commentary on the gospel of Matthew for this series and who serves as one of the series editors, considers that gospel the product of a Jesus-centered Jewish group in conflict with emerging formative Judaism (Overman 1996; see also Saldarini 1994). The author of Matthew saw himself as defending the true Judaism. Like Matthew, the author of Revelation seems to have been a Jewish Christian who saw following Jesus not as separating him from Judaism but as making him a true Jew. He was an apocalyptic seer, one who saw visions of the destruction of the satanic order that had the Roman political establishment at its center. He saw Jesus as God's agent for that destruction. Jews and Christians who were more at home in the Roman Hellenistic world and who disagreed with his apocalyptic brand of Christianity incurred his condemnation as being in league with Satan. In predicting the fall of Rome, John saw himself as a prophet in the line of the Israelite prophets who declared Babylon's doom.

Allusions to the Hebrew Bible, especially the prophetic books, permeate Revelation.

Although my degree is in the New Testament and Christian origins, I have until now written primarily about second temple Judaism and its texts. But I have been particularly fascinated by the Jewishness of Jesus and the Jewish matrix of Christianity. The story of Christianity's birth from Judaism is complex and intriguing, and there is much that we still do not understand fully. I am happy for this opportunity to write about a New Testament book that has its origins in that time when the distinction between Judaism and Christianity was not nearly as clear as it is now.

The groundwork for this commentary was laid in spring 1994, when I wrote an article on recent research on the book of Revelation and another on the state of the study of apocalypses and apocalypticism (Murphy 1994a, 1994b). That semester was funded by a grant from the College of the Holy Cross, for which I am very grateful. I wish also to thank my colleagues in the Department of Religious Studies at Holy Cross for their constant support, professional and personal. It is hard to imagine a better group of people with whom to carry on the work of studying and teaching about religion. I am privileged to be able to teach students who are wonderfully intelligent, hard working, and good willed. They have helped me keep the basic questions alive, and teaching them has given me much personal fulfillment over the years.

My admiration for and reliance on the work of Professor Adela Yarbro Collins of the University of Chicago are evident throughout this book. I am very grateful to her for her generosity in reading parts of the manuscript and making helpful suggestions, and I am thankful for the kind encouragement she gave me in this project. Thanks also to Professor Alan Avery-Peck, Kraft-Hiatt Professor of Judaic Studies at Holy Cross, who read the introduction and conclusion. I have benefited tremendously from his characteristically incisive and constructive comments, and I deeply enjoy his marvelous sense of humor. I thank my friend John Stansky for reading the manuscript from the point of view of an educated and interested layman. Professor J. Andrew Overman is a friend and a colleague from whom I have learned much. I thank him and Hal Rast of Trinity Press International for their patience and support as they waited for the manuscript of this book.

This book is dedicated to my children, who continue to give depth and meaning to my existence. Watching them grow into the wonderful human beings they are has given me untold pleasure. My wife, Leslie, has shown unstinting patience and support, even when I have given her good reason not to do so. She deserves a great deal of credit for anything that I have managed to accomplish in my work, and I offer her my heartfelt thanks. Finally, I would like to close this preface by honoring the memory of my father, James F. Murphy, who died in June 1997, when this book was in its final stages of preparation. He was a good man, and I miss him very much.

Structural Outline of Revelation

- Descriptive Title (1:1–3)
  - Epistolary Frame (1:4–6)
    - Prophetic Sayings (1:7–8)
      - Inaugural Vision (1:9–3:22)
      - Eschatological Visions (4:1–22:5)
        - Heavenly Throne Room Vision (4:1–5:14)
          - First Great Cycle of Eschatological Visions (6:1–11:19)
            - Seven Seals (6:1–8:5)
            - Seven Trumpets (8:6–11:19)
          - Second Great Cycle of Eschatological Visions (12:1–22:5)
            - Seven Unnumbered Visions (12:1–15:4)
            - Seven Bowls (15:1; 15:5–16:21)
              - Babylon Appendix (17:1–19:10)
            - Seven Unnumbered Visions (19:11–21:8)
              - New Jerusalem Appendix (21:9–22:9)
    - Prophetic Sayings (22:6–20a)
  - Epistolary Frame (22:20b–21)

Abbreviations

Abbreviations for biblical books are as found in the *Journal of Biblical Literature.* The biblical translation used is the New Revised Standard Version (1993).

AB	The Anchor Bible
ABD	*Anchor Bible Dictionary*
Abr.	Philo, *On Abraham*
ANRW	*Aufstieg und Niedergang der römischen Welt*
Ant.	Josephus, *Jewish Antiquities*
Ap.	Josephus, *Against Apion*
Apoc. Abr.	*Apocalypse of Abraham*
Apoc. Pet.	*Apocalypse of Peter*
Asc. Isa.	*Ascension of Isaiah*
2 Bar.	*2 Baruch* (Syriac *Apocalypse of Baruch*)
BASOR	*Bulletin of the American Schools of Oriental Research*
Bib	*Biblica*
BR	*Biblical Research*
BZNW	Beihefte zur Zeitschrift für die neutestamentliche Wissenschaft
CBQ	*Catholic Biblical Quarterly*
Eph.	Ignatius, *Letter to the Ephesians*
HCSB	*HarperCollins Study Bible*
Herm. *Sim.*	Hermas, *Similitudes*
HeyJ	*Heythrop Journal*
Hist.	Tacitus, *Histories*

HUCA	*Hebrew Union College Annual*
IDBSup	*Interpreter's Dictionary of the Bible Supplement*
Int	*Interpretation*
JBL	*Journal of Biblical Literature*
JSNT	*Journal for the Study of the New Testament*
JSNTSup	Journal for the Study of the New Testament Supplement Series
Jub.	*Jubilees*
J.W.	Josephus, *The Jewish Wars*
LCL	Loeb Classical Library
NIB	*New Interpreter's Bible*
NovT	*Novum Testamentum*
NRSV	New Revised Standard Version
NTS	*New Testament Studies*
Odes Sol.	*Odes of Solomon*
Pss. Sol.	*Psalms of Solomon*
1QM	*War Scroll* (Qumran)
1QpHab	*Pesher on Habakkuk* (Qumran)
1QS	*Community Rule* (Qumran)
San.	*Sanhedrin*
SBLSP	*Society of Biblical Literature Seminar Papers*
Sib. Or.	*Sibylline Oracles*
T. Dan.	*Testament of Daniel*
T. Jos.	*Testament of Joseph*
T. Jud.	*Testament of Judah*
T. Levi	*Testament of Levi*
T. Moses	*Testament of Moses*
T. Naph.	*Testament of Naphtali*
WUNT	Wissenschaftliche Untersuchungen zum Neuen Testament
ZNW	*Zeitschrift für die neutestamentliche Wissenschaft*

Introduction

Despite a title that promises clarity and insight, Revelation is one of the strangest and most difficult to understand of all biblical books. Perhaps the biggest obstacle to understanding is that modern readers do not share its original contexts – historical, social, religious, literary, and so on. This commentary aims at illuminating Revelation by situating it in these contexts. It is fitting, therefore, that the commentary be part of a series that stresses the contexts in which the New Testament writings were produced and first read.

Revelation's Historical and Social Context

Roman Power and Symbols

Much of what we have to say on Revelation's historical and social context is included in the following sections on author and date, as well as in the commentary on specific passages. But since some basic notion of the circumstances under which the book was written is essential to everything that follows in this book, we briefly state at the outset what those circumstances were. Revelation was written sometime in the second half of the first century B.C.E. in or near the Roman province of Asia, what is today western Turkey. When it was written, the entire eastern Mediterranean region belonged to the Roman empire. Thus the political system in place was colonial in nature. Although native officials remained important, because through them the Romans ruled and regulated local life, the gigantic and powerful Roman military and political machine could never be far from people's attention. There was a symbiosis between local elites and Rome that found expression in the Roman imperial cult. Asian cities displayed their loyalty to Rome in typical Eastern fashion by paying homage both to the goddess Roma and to the cults of individual Roman emperors, living and dead. Conversely, Rome and its emperors showed favor to local elites by allowing various manifestations of the imperial cult in their cities (see Price 1984; Jones 1980).

Revelation's author, John, was a "seer," one who claimed to have *seen* visions from God on the island of Patmos, a small rocky island in the Aegean Sea just off the western coast of Asia Minor, modern Turkey. John tells us he was sent to the island as punishment for his Christian activity, although the precise nature of his offense is left unstated. John writes a book that takes the form of a letter to be circulated to seven churches in important cities near the coast of western Asia Minor, in the area constituting the Roman province of Asia. The contents of the visions are cryptic and at times bizarre, but they clearly involve disapproval of the Roman empire and its political and religious claims. The seer wishes to influence his audience's attitude toward Rome and toward their social environment. Recipients of the book are meant to see through Rome's fraudulent claims and to recognize God's absolute sovereignty over themselves and over the entire universe. For the seer, Rome enjoyed its success not because of its piety toward its gods and the gods of others, as Romans claimed, but because Satan had granted power and authority to Rome. God's sovereignty is incompatible with Rome's claims, most clearly represented for him through worship of the emperor and the goddess Roma in local cultic spots in Asia. The seer believes that Christ's death initiated God's defeat of Rome and Satan. Since Christ's death, Christians have been engaged in that same battle with Satan and Rome. The seer anticipates God's imminent victory and the establishment of God's reign on earth, expressed in God's descent to earth with Christ to reign forever.

The sociology of knowledge has taught us that the way a group of people looks at itself and its place in the world constitutes its "symbolic universe," its worldview (see Berger and Luckman 1963). Basic convictions about the natural and social world are inculcated in members of any society beginning at birth. For most within any society, this basic worldview is simply self-evident, and it affects the way institutions and customs are formed and maintained. When Revelation's author says that it is Christ and not the emperor who rules the world, when he portrays the cosmic power behind Roman hegemony as Satan and not Rome's gods, and when he portrays civic life in Asia as corrupt and to be avoided instead of a system which Jews and Christians can engage and live in comfortably, he attacks the worldview of the majority of Asia's inhabitants. The messages to the seven churches (chapters 2–3) demonstrate that many Asian Christians do not fully share the author's way of looking at things. Through his book, John seeks to reinforce those Christians who share his view of the world, and to win over the others. John's attempt to adjust the perceptions of his audience is the driving force of Revelation.

Early Christian Context

The more we know about early Christianity, the more information we will have about Revelation's early Christian context. This introduction addresses key topics in early Christianity relevant to the study of Revelation. As we proceed through the commentary, we will frequently draw on other early Christian texts, particularly those from the New Testament, in order to shed light on Revelation.

Scholars are accustomed to trying to prove the literary dependence or independence of texts, but we will not limit ourselves to those texts (from the Hebrew Bible, the New Testament, or elsewhere) upon which Revelation definitely depends, nor will we be interested only in the question of direct influence. Rather, we will draw from any texts that allow us to understand the kinds of Christian traditions and issues shared by Revelation and other early Christian works. Only in this way can the context of Revelation be fleshed out and come alive for the modern reader.

John and Judaism

In its beginning, Christianity was not clearly distinct from Judaism. Jesus was a Jew, as were his followers. The earliest Christians were also Jews. It took some time for the church to become an entity clearly distinguishable from Judaism. At the time Revelation was written, that process was still underway. (For one reconstruction of this complicated process, see Dunn 1991.) Our author seems to have been a Jewish Christian who saw the church as the true Judaism. Thus he can refer to Jews who do not believe in Christ as the "synagogue of Satan" composed of those "who say that they are Jews and are not" (2:9; 3:9). The heat of these words comes from the seer's investment in his own Jewish background.

Our author's Jewishness is manifested in his immersion in the Hebrew Bible, as well as in his very language, which, although Greek, is heavily influenced by Hebrew. He appropriates biblical symbols to express his understanding of God, the church, and their enemies.

Hellenistic Environment

The author lived in the Roman Hellenistic world. The word "Hellenistic" is applied to the world of the eastern Mediterranean, starting with the conquests of Alexander the Great between 333 and 323 B.C.E. Alexander's conquests led to an extensive interaction of cultures which affected Judaism profoundly and into the midst of which Christianity was born. Over the course of the last two centuries B.C.E., the Romans assumed hegemony over the lands bordering the eastern Mediterranean. Because many of the same cultural factors were at work in the Roman period as in the Hellenistic era, many scholars speak of Roman Hellenism. In this book the terms "Hellenism" and "Hellenistic" are used in a broad way that includes the Roman period.

Two influences from the general Hellenistic world are particularly evident in Revelation. The first has to do with a widespread myth we shall refer to as the combat myth. This myth takes many forms, but its basic pattern is a struggle between two divine figures over sovereignty and kingship. One of those figures is often in the form of a monster, frequently a sea-monster, who sometimes has the form of a dragon or some other serpent-like shape. The monster represents the forces of chaos that rise against the forces of order. The combat myth is found in many cultures, often being employed to explain the origin and maintenance of creation. It is also present in many places in the Bible, in the form of allusions and passing references rather than as an extended narrative. Revelation's author assumes familiarity with the basic pattern of the combat myth in one form or another, and he expects it to evoke in his audience strong feelings about the struggles in their own lives as well as in the larger events around them. He seems to have deliberately combined elements from various forms of the combat myth. The combat myth and its influence on Revelation have been studied by Yarbro Collins in *The Combat Myth in the Book of Revelation.* We will have ample opportunity to refer to the combat myth and to Yarbro Collins's work in the commentary below.

A second Hellenistic influence on Revelation involves astrology, an important pursuit in the ancient world generally, and during the Hellenistic period in particular (Martin 1987). The ancients felt that their lives were influenced by forces beyond their control, including the stars, thought to be heavenly beings who influenced earthly events. To be able to read the sky was to know about the forces controlling human life. Bruce Malina studies ancient astrology and its influence on Revelation. He notes astrology's importance for the Hellenistic world and its widespread influence in Judaism during the Hellenistic and Roman periods and afterwards (1995, 14–18). His analysis of Revelation "is based upon the premise that the author of the book of Revelation, the prophet John, has his initial, ecstatic vision while considering the vault of the sky.... As he considers the sky, he observes various phenomena and interacts with various sky entities. What he reports, then, derives from perceptions of the vault of the sky and beyond" (1).

Christians in the Roman Empire

Revelation seems to expect a worldwide persecution of Christians soon to be unleashed by Rome. Christians today are likely to think that from the time that Christianity arrived on the scene, the Romans tried to stamp it out through relentless persecution. The popular image is of Christian martyrs being thrown to the lions in the Coliseum, Rome's great stadium. Examination of the sources for the first century does not support such a picture. This section paints a more accurate picture of Christians' status in the empire, so as to construct a more accurate background for Revelation. The picture that will emerge is one of sporadic and scattered actions against Christians, not of a concerted effort by Romans or provincials to root out Christianity.

In the ancient world, religion, politics, kinship, and economics were intertwined. The political order was seen as divinely sanctioned. Conflicts between different nations were seen as clashes between gods. Success in life, political or economic, depended to some extent on piety. Life in the cities involved participation in the cults of the local gods, as well as support of cults that symbolized the connection of the city to the wider empire, such as the imperial cult. Then as now, religion was big business, whether it be the silversmith guilds of Ephesus that made shrines of Artemis or the temple-state of Judea into which sacrifices, tithes, and taxes flowed from Jews living far and wide. Polytheism was the rule, Jews and Christians being the notable exceptions. Worship of one god did not preclude service to another. One's primary religion was not usually a conscious choice; it flowed from where one was born, into what people, and into what family.

It is not difficult to see how Christianity might disrupt life in the ancient world. It required real conversion that entailed not only dedication to a new God but also rejection of the old ones. It could and did split families and often made it difficult to continue in one's trade, if that involved participation in any religious cult, which it frequently did. Refusal to worship the city gods might raise fears that the gods would be angered. Refusal to worship the empire's gods and to take part in the imperial cult aroused suspicion of disloyalty and was considered to be dangerous to the state because the refusal might anger the gods and imply hostility to the state. This background is an aid to understanding the possible reasons for hostility to Christians (see St. Croix 1963, 1964; Sherwin-White 1964), but it does not mean that Christians were always hated and persecuted. The evidence does not support that.

Revelation is particularly concerned with the Roman imperial cult. Most Roman emperors of the early empire were uncomfortable with being worshiped as divine, but ruler worship was a feature of the eastern Mediterranean. When the Romans took over that region, emperor worship became a means whereby Eastern subjects could express their loyalty and receive imperial favors in return. The only emperors in the early empire who seem to have taken this worship seriously were Caligula and Nero. Augustus allowed his Eastern subjects to set up temples to him, but only if they were also dedicated to the goddess Roma. Roman sources say that Domitian, under whom Revelation was probably written, also took worship of himself seriously, but some now attribute those claims to a desire to denigrate Domitian so as to win the favor of Trajan, who ruled after him (after the brief reign of Nerva; see below on Domitian). Whatever the attitude of individual Roman emperors, the imperial cult was offensive in the extreme to Revelation's author. We shall note his references to it as we proceed. His abhorrence of the cult is clearly expressed in his use of a word usually translated "worship" (*proskyneô*) throughout the book. The word refers to an act of ritual prostration, common for ancient Eastern rulers, but introduced to Rome by Caligula. For the author of Revelation, only God is to be worshiped. In chapter 13, he condemns the worship of the beast, which symbolizes the Roman empire and Nero. Many commentators have argued that the occasion for the writing of Revelation was an insistence that all residents of the empire worship the emperor, but there is no evidence that such a general constraint was ever imposed in the period in question.

New Testament Evidence

We look first to the New Testament itself, the earliest Christian writings, for evidence of persecution. The general picture that emerges is not of a church hounded by Roman authorities but of a group that hoped for good relations with the empire, hopes that were not always disappointed. We also see a church that sometimes, but not always, encountered hostility from its neighbors, but a hostility that was not official persecution. As we shall see, this picture corresponds to what we find in Roman sources as well.

Indications of persecution in the synoptic gospels (Matthew, Mark, and Luke) are confined primarily to the apocalyptic discourses (Matthew 24; Mark 13; Luke 21). The gospels picture Jesus delivering a discourse shortly before his death, a discourse predicting the eschaton (the end of the world as we know it) and events preceding it. The information about persecutions in these discourses is generalized and stylized, and it says little about specific persecutions. The persecutions envisaged may be a traditional description of the sufferings expected before the endtime and so have little evidentiary value.

Paul attests to resistance he met in his ministry. In 2 Cor 11:21–33 he defends his ministry, stressing the suffering he underwent in carrying it out. This passage is not evidence of general persecution of Christianity by the Romans. Paul says explicitly that he has been punished by the Jews five times with thirty-nine lashes. The stoning Paul received was also a Jewish punishment. Later on, Paul mentions danger from his own people. All of this must be seen in the context of problematic relations between Jews and Christians, particularly in the first century. The lashings were official punishments meted out by synagogal authorities because Paul was seen to violate the law or disturbed public order in the Jewish community.

Acts of the Apostles, written by the same author as the gospel of Luke, is in the form of a history of the early church. Debates still rage about its value as a historical account, but it does provide at least one first-century Christian's perception of what the church's place in the world ought to be. Acts is influenced by Luke's desire to portray Jews' rejection of Christianity as a rejection of their own heritage and of God's fulfillment of the promises to their ancestors and by his attempt to show that Romans were either sympathetic or neutral to Christians. But Luke is plausible when he presents the earliest missions as being carried out primarily by Jewish Christians. He is also plausible when he says that Christian missions to Jews often resulted in clashes between Christians and Jews. Romans and other local officials would have reacted to such clashes insofar as they disrupted public order, but they would also have seen them as intra-Jewish problems. Luke has one Roman proconsul, Gallio, say to Jews who complained to him about Paul, "If it were a matter of crime or serious villainy, I would be justified in accepting the complaint of you Jews; but since it is a matter of questions about words and names and your own law, see to it yourselves; I do not wish to be a judge of these matters" (Acts 18:14–15).

Acts also contains many narratives depicting Christians' conflicts with Gentiles. In Acts 16, Paul incurs the ire of the owners of a slave-girl in Philippi who had a spirit of divination; Paul drives out the spirit, thus ruining their profits. The owners drag Paul and his companions before the city authorities, who punish them with flogging and imprisonment. Later there is a riot in Ephesus when Paul's preaching interferes with the business of silversmiths who make shrines to the goddess Artemis (Acts 19:23–41). The town clerk breaks up the riot with the threat of punishment. He suggests that the rioters use the courts if they have legitimate charges. Nothing is said of any court action, and Paul leaves the city soon afterwards. In both Philippi and Ephesus, Paul's preaching causes practical economic problems that in turn lead to local unrest. In both cases the authorities have no option but to take notice, but they do so because of specific disturbances, not because Christianity itself is illegal.

Paul's writings show that he does not see the empire's officials as inherently anti-Christian. Quite the contrary. In Romans he says,

> Let every person be subject to the governing authorities; for there is no authority except from God, and those authorities that exist have been instituted by God. Therefore whoever resists authority resists what God has appointed, and those who resist will incur judgment. For rulers are not a terror to good conduct, but to bad. Do you wish to have no fear of the authority? Then do what is good, and you will receive its approval; for it is God's servant for your good. But if you do what is wrong, you should be afraid, for the authority does not bear the sword in vain! It is the servant of God to execute wrath on the wrongdoer. Therefore one must be subject, not only because of wrath but also because of conscience. (Rom 13:1–5)

It is hard to imagine a sharper contrast of attitudes toward the Roman empire than the one between Paul and Revelation.

Hebrews was written sometime in the last third of the first century C.E. The author (who was not Paul) writes to Christians encountering opposition in their environment. He says to them, "In your struggle against sin you have not yet resisted to the point of shedding your blood" (Heb 12:4). He says:

> After you had been enlightened, you endured a hard struggle with sufferings, sometimes being publicly exposed to abuse [*oneidismois*] and persecution [*thlipsesin*], and sometimes being partners with those so treated. For you had compassion for those who were in prison, and you cheerfully accepted the plundering of your possessions. (Heb 10:32–34)

The word translated "persecution" here, *thlipsis,* occurs in Rev 1:9; 2:9, 10, 22; and 7:14. In early Christian literature it often means eschatological affliction, the sort of troubles attending God's definitive intervention in history and the final defeat of his enemies. Eschatological afflictions need not entail death. Hebrews defines the troubles as imprisonment and confiscation of property. The text does not clarify the precise charges that led to such measures, but the author, and presumably the addressees, take them to be related to their faith.

Another New Testament source of some help in determining the nature of persecution of the early Christians is 1 Peter (see Elliott 1981). Its attribution to Peter is questioned by most scholars. The letter is addressed to the Christians of five Roman provinces in Asia Minor, including Asia, and it claims to have been written in Rome. It was probably written sometime in the last third of the first century C.E. The letter exhorts its readers to proper conduct in the face of adversity, and it acknowledges that they have undergone "various trials [*peirasmois*]" (1:6). It remains vague on the nature of these trials, but no mention is made of death. It attributes hostility to Christians to the misunderstanding that Christianity involves evildoing of some kind:

> For the Lord's sake accept the authority of every human institution, whether of the emperor as supreme, or of governors, as sent by him to punish those who do wrong and to praise those who do right. For it is God's will that by doing right you should silence the ignorance of the foolish. As servants of God, live as free people, yet do not use your freedom as a pretext for evil. Honor everyone. Love the family of believers. Fear God. Honor the emperor. (2:13–17)

In chapter 3, the readers are told,

> Now who will harm you if you are eager to do what is good? But even if you do suffer for doing what is right, you are blessed. Do not fear what they fear, and do not be intimidated, but in your hearts sanctify Christ as Lord. Always be ready to make your defense to anyone who demands from you an accounting for the hope that is in you; yet do it with gentleness and reverence. Keep your conscience clear, so that, when you are maligned, those who abuse you for your good conduct in Christ may be put to shame. (3:13–16)

In the next chapter, the letter suggests a reason that the Christians are maligned: "You have already spent enough time in doing what the Gentiles like to do, living in licentiousness, passions, drunkenness, revels, carousing, and lawless idolatry. They are surprised that you no longer join them in the same excesses of dissipation, and so they blaspheme" (4:3–4). The classification of all Gentiles as extravagant sinners is hyperbole, but this sort of argument was common in the Hellenistic world and is found in Jewish and Christian polemical literature: Accusations of idolatry and sexual immorality are common in Jewish and Christian polemical literature against Gentiles and non-Christians.

The word translated "blaspheme" here means to "injure the reputation of," "revile," "defame." Its object is not necessarily God, but is more often humans (see Rom 3:8). The author suggests that the reason that the Christians are "blasphemed" or "spoken against" is that they once lived the life of their detractors. When they separated themselves from their former lifestyles, they attracted criticism. The social situation to which this attests is a local one where conversion to Christianity disrupts previous social relationships on a local level, symbolized by separation from worship of the common gods and from accepted sexual mores.

This letter counsels good conduct so that those who oppose the Christians might be won over to seeing them as good. It is crucial to the author that he separate the public perception of Christianity from the impression of criminality. He tells his readers, "If you are reviled for the name of Christ, you are blessed, because the spirit of glory, which is the Spirit of God, is resting on you. But let none of you suffer as a murderer, a thief, a criminal, or even as a mischief maker" (4:14–15). Christians suffer primarily because they are thought to do evil things, but their good conduct ought to disprove that misconception. Since the emperor's task is to reward the good and punish the evil, he or his representatives can eventually vindicate Christians if they do good. This view of the emperor is consonant with that of Paul in Romans 13.

Roman Sources

A major persecution of Christians took place under the emperor Nero in 64 C.E. In that year a fire destroyed much of Rome. Rumor had it that Nero himself had started the fire, perhaps so that he could carry out urban renewal projects he had in mind. Nero blamed Rome's Christians for the fire, subjecting them to horrendous tortures. The Roman historian Suetonius mentions this only briefly and with apparent approval: "Punishments were also inflicted on the Christians, a sect professing a new and mischievous religious belief" (*Nero* 16.2). The Roman historian Tacitus takes a different view:

> To suppress this rumor [that Nero started the fire], Nero fabricated scapegoats — and punished with every sort of refinement the notoriously depraved Christians (as they were popularly called).... First, Nero had self-acknowledged Christians arrested. Then, on their information, large number of others were condemned — not so much for incendiarism as for their antisocial tendencies.... Despite their guilt as Christians, and the ruthless punishment it deserved, the victims were pitied. For it was felt that they were being sacrificed to one man's brutality rather than to the national interest. (*Annals* 15.44)

The Christians were punished not for their religion but for arson. Nero needed a scapegoat to distract attention from himself. The Christians were prime candidates because they were generally disliked. This implies that before Nero's persecution they had lived in Rome, had grown into a community big enough to draw Nero's attention, and had made an impression on the public. Neither Tacitus nor any other Roman writer says that the Christians had been persecuted before or that it was illegal to be a Christian. To be sure, Tacitus has a low opinion of Christians, and in this he agrees with Suetonius. Any sect that had for its founder one who had been executed by a Roman governor, probably for political reasons, would hardly be respected by Romans. But the "superstition" survived.

Tacitus calls Christianity a "superstition." The term was applied by upper-class Romans to all forms of religion that they considered excessive, silly, or dangerous to the established order (Hodgson 1992). The proper conduct of public religion helped to maintain the fabric of society. Religious threats to that order were called superstitions. The degree to which the Roman social and political order reacted against superstitions depended on many things, including the political climate, economic conditions, social stability, personalities, and so on. The charge of superstition could be used to strengthen other charges. Indeed, although Judaism was tolerated and sometimes even defended by the Roman order, Roman writers sometimes called Judaism a superstition. After Christianity became the official religion of the Roman empire under Constantine in the early fourth century C.E., Christians routinely referred to religions that were non-Christian and non-Jewish as superstitions.

The Romans were particularly hostile toward superstitions imported from elsewhere. As time went by, the fact that Rome was the center of the empire made it a magnet for immigrants from all over the Mediterranean, and they brought with them their cultures and religious practices. Roman authors denigrated these new arrivals and their offensive ways. Often the only sanction against superstition was satire, ridicule, and ostracism, but that could escalate, given the right situation, as it did under Nero. But Tacitus does not approve Nero's cruelty and says that public opinion saw Nero as serving his own depraved ends rather than the "national interest."

There is no evidence that Nero issued any general edict outlawing Christianity in general. This is clear from another document that is crucial in determining the attitude of the Roman empire toward the early Christians. It is a letter written by Pliny the Younger around the year 112, from Bithynia, a Roman province just north of the province of Asia. Pliny was the governor of Bithynia, and local residents were denouncing Christians to him. He writes to the emperor Trajan for guidance about what to do (Downing 1988).

Pliny's letter shows how a Roman governor looked at Christianity about twenty years after Revelation was written, in a province that shared a border with Asia. Pliny confesses ignorance on how to deal with Christians. Despite his long and distinguished public career, he had never been present at the interrogation of a Christian and does not even know whether being a Christian in itself should be punished or whether proof that some other crime has been committed is necessary. He notes that some crimes are associated with the name "Christian," but he does not name them. From other sources, we know that Christians were accused of cannibalism (perhaps because they ate the body and blood of Christ in the eucharist), incest (possibly because they called each other "brother" and "sister"), and atheism (they refused to worship the gods). Pliny's question recalls 1 Peter, whose readers are warned not to commit any crimes, so that if they were to suffer, it would be clear that they did so for the name of Christ. Many whom Pliny interrogates insist that they have committed no crime. Pliny and 1 Peter make clear that Christians were looked down upon because of the crimes that people associated with the "superstition."

When Pliny executes Christians, he does so not because they are Christians but because they stubbornly resist the power of

Rome. Whether or not it is a crime to be a Christian, people ought to renounce Christ when ordered to do so by the Roman governor. Pliny offers the accused a chance to escape punishment by having them do things no Christian would do—invoke the gods, offer wine and incense to a statue of the emperor, and curse Christ. Offerings to the emperor recall the imperial cult. Refusal to offer before the emperor's statue is represented not as the cause of persecution but as a way of determining one's willingness to submit to Roman authority.

The last paragraph of Pliny's letter reveals what may be the real reason that Christians are being denounced. Christianity has spread rapidly in Bithynia, and the result has been the abandonment of the temples, lack of interest in public religious festivals, and a downturn in the market for meat sacrificed to idols. The general thrust of these disclosures is that Christianity is adversely affecting the religious, social, and economic life of the province. Temples, religious feasts, and sacrifices help to make up the social fabric of the ancient world. They have political, economic, and cultural consequences. One does not disturb that order without strong reactions, particularly from the local citizens who are hurt by the changes.

Trajan's response to Pliny is informative. There is no universal rule for dealing with Christians. They are not to be sought out. This argues strongly against the idea that Rome opposed Christianity as such. Christians were to recant only if they were publicly accused. But that of course implies that Christianity was causing a public disturbance, which always attracted the attention of the Roman authorities. Lack of social stability was a menace to Roman rule. Trajan discourages anonymous accusations. Such accusations proliferate and can be used to attack personal enemies. Rome itself had witnessed such abuse often in the past. Trajan is wise enough to reject witch-hunts.

Because the traditional date for Revelation is late in the reign of the emperor Domitian (81–96 C.E.), many have sought evidence that Domitian conducted a substantive persecution of Christians. There is really no evidence for that. There are indications that he was given to self-exaltation, such as being called "lord and god." Such an attitude, along with the imperial cult that the seer would have observed in Asia, would certainly make Domitian a villain in our author's eyes. But the case has been made by classical scholars that Domitian's picture as gleaned from Roman sources is not entirely trustworthy. Many of the sources in question were written during Trajan's time, when denigration of Domitian's rule to flatter Trajan was commonplace. Reading between the lines of the Roman writers, many scholars reconstruct the period of Domitian in a way that reflects far more favorably upon that emperor. This case has been put strongly by Leonard Thompson (1990), who examines the relevant evidence. The conclusion is that Domitian was no worse than most other Roman emperors when it came to issues of importance for Jews and Christians, and he was considerably better than Caligula and Nero. For someone with our author's views, Domitian or any other Roman emperor was quite bad enough to merit his complete condemnation, especially when the emperor was seen through the lens of the imperial cult in Asia Minor.

The Evidence from Revelation

Does Revelation itself provide evidence of a wide-scale persecution of Christians in the Roman empire or even in the province of Asia? The answer must be no. Revelation certainly envisages a tremendous eschatological battle to take place soon between God and Rome, and by the time that battle takes place, Rome will have persecuted the Christians. It sees signs of that coming crisis in the present. However, none of this implies that there has already been a widespread persecution of Christians.

There are only two concrete examples of persecution in Revelation. The first is the banishment of John the seer to the island of Patmos. John merely says that he was on Patmos "because of [*dia*] the word of God and the testimony of Jesus." Some have questioned whether that is really an instance of persecution, since John might mean that he went to the island to preach the word. There is no direct evidence that Patmos was used for exile by the Romans. However, the Greek word *dia* is never used in Revelation in the sense of "for the purpose of," but always indicates the cause of an effect. So it is likely that John was sent to Patmos as a result of his preaching. Furthermore, Patmos was a small and sparsely populated island, hardly a prime spot for a mission, unlike the seven cities of Asia. It is likely that John was banished to Patmos in an act of repression by either Roman or local officials.

The second case of persecution concerns Antipas, who is called "my witness, my faithful one, who was killed among you, where Satan lives" (2:13). The word for "witness" here is *martys*, from which the English word "martyr" is derived. In later Christian tradition the word came to mean one who died for the faith, but it had not yet acquired this meaning in Revelation. Generally speaking, a witness was one who publicly testified to the gospel. That public stance could result in death in certain circumstances, but it need not necessarily do so. Unfortunately, the text offers no more details. From John's point of view, Antipas died as a witness to the faith. The Romans may have seen it differently. Perhaps they thought him guilty of some other crime.

The most direct evidence that Revelation offers for its immediate historical context must be sought in the messages to the seven churches in chapters 2 and 3. It is in these letters that the author makes specific references to the churches' concrete circumstances. This is where the reference to Antipas's death occurs. But the messages lack evidence of actual persecution. The Christians of Smyrna are warned that some of them will be thrown into prison "for ten days," apparently a symbolic number (2:10). In 3:10 the author speaks of "the hour of trial [*peirasmos*] that is coming on the whole world to test [*peirazô*] the inhabitants of the earth." Both passages refer to the future. What is remarkable about the letters in the context of this discussion is that they are far more concerned with differences within the Christian community than they are about any threat from without.

Persecution is alluded to several times in the eschatological visions beginning in 4:1. At the opening of the fifth seal the author sees under the heavenly altar the faithful who had been killed and who pray to God for vengeance. God tells them that they must wait until the preordained number of martyrs are killed. The faithful under the altar may be the Neronic martyrs, or they be future martyrs. The same ambiguity exists for every other mention of martyrdom in the rest of the book, because the eschatological visions are stylized and use traditional language and because it is not always clear whether they refer to the past, present, or future.

Conclusion

There is no question that the Christians had their problems in the first century, but widespread, systematic persecution by the Roman empire was not one of them. The disaster under Nero was the closest one comes to a major persecution. But the reasons for that persecution and its limited nature do not permit wide-ranging conclusions about the situation in Asia, either during Nero's reign or afterward. The sources surveyed here support the idea that actions against Christians in the first century were sporadic, local, and did not entail the deaths of large numbers, except for Nero's persecution.

Most Christians in the first century were not subject to public punishment. When that did occur, it was most often in the form of afflictions short of death. Frequently it meant being held in low esteem by their neighbors or suffering prejudicial treatment in matters of commerce and property. Pliny's profession of ignorance of Christians and of official Roman positions with regard to them undermines the picture of a Rome dedicated to Christianity's eradication. Texts such as Paul's letter to the Romans, Luke-Acts, and 1 Peter demonstrate a positive attitude toward Roman authorities by some first-century Christians.

Apocalyptic Context: Genre and Worldview

Genre: Apocalypse

Adela Yarbro Collins rightly says that Revelation's literary form is the key to its interpretation (1979, x). A work's literary form, its genre, alerts the reader to how the work should be read. We read novels differently from histories, newspaper articles differently from personal letters, poetry differently from social science textbooks. When texts do not conform to what we expect of them, we are surprised and often frustrated. For most modern readers, reading Revelation is a unique experience. They have never read a book like this before, foreign to their world in both form and content. Since they cannot fit it into any familiar category, they may dismiss it as cryptic, disturbing, or irrelevant. Alternatively, they may read it in inappropriate and even destructive ways, perhaps turning it into a weapon in some cause or other quite foreign to the concerns of the book. Throughout history, Revelation has been used against opponents to label them diabolical and to make simplistic and absolute distinctions between people of differing views.

Our first task, then, is to locate Revelation in its proper literary environment. What kind of book is it? Revelation belongs to a category of ancient literature called "apocalypse," a genre which in fact takes its name from Revelation. In the nineteenth century scholars noted a large number of Jewish and Christian texts dating to the last few centuries before the common era and the first centuries of the common era that were similar to each other in form and content. Among these texts are Daniel in the Hebrew Bible and Revelation in the New Testament. All of these books are revelatory literature; that is, they claim to impart or tell the story of a direct revelation from the supernatural world. Scholars adopted the first word of Revelation, the Greek word *apokalypsis* (revelation), as the name for the entire genre. In the ancient world, the word "apocalypse" actually became the designation for such works, but not until after the time of Revelation (see Smith 1983). In modern English the text that is the focus of this study is called either The Apocalypse or Revelation. As the commentary proceeds, we shall draw numerous comparisons between Revelation and other apocalypses, especially between Revelation and the other biblical apocalypse, Daniel, upon which it draws extensively.

Revelatory genres abounded in the ancient world. The ancients believed that their lives were affected or even controlled by unseen forces, on both large and small scales. Superhuman forces were crucial, whether it be to the fate of individuals or of nations. Magical documents, political prophecies, astrological texts, and the like were common. Apocalypses are a subset of revelatory literature (on apocalypses and apocalypticism in general, see Collins 1984; Murphy 1994a, 1996). The following definition of the genre is widely accepted:

> "Apocalypse" is a genre of revelatory literature with a narrative framework, in which a revelation is mediated by an otherworldly being to a human recipient, disclosing a transcendent reality which is both temporal, insofar as it envisages eschatological salvation, and spatial insofar as it involves another, supernatural world. (Collins 1979, 9)

Yarbro Collins offers the clearest statement of the purpose of apocalypses. They are "intended to interpret present, earthly circumstances in light of the supernatural world and of the future, and to influence both the understanding and behavior of the audience by means of divine authority" (1986, 7).

The revelation in apocalypses usually takes place through visions (things seen) and/or auditions (things heard) that are then explained by an otherworldly figure, usually an angel. The often bizarre nature of the visions indicates their origin in the supernatural world. The word "eschatological" is a key term in the definition. The Greek word *eschaton* means "end." Eschatology is teaching or information about the end of the world as we know it. The word "eschatological" therefore does not necessarily refer to the world ceasing to exist. It does point to a definitive change in the way things are.

The books of the biblical prophets contain a type of eschatology in which God intervenes in history to punish the wicked, reward the good, and rearrange matters on earth so that they conform to the divine will. Apocalyptic eschatology goes farther. John J. Collins (1974) demonstrates that in apocalyptic eschatology death is transcended in some form or other. The idea of resurrection apparently entered Judaism through apocalypticism. The first clear statement in the Bible concerning resurrection is in the apocalyptic book of Daniel, written around 165 B.C.E. (see Dan 12:2–3). Apocalypses also frequently anticipate cosmic changes. Sometimes they speak of the passing away of heaven and earth and the ascent of the righteous to heaven. Other apocalypses depict the reconstitution of life on earth on fundamentally different terms, with Satan gone, for example, and perhaps with death abolished (P. D. Hanson 1976).

The degree of emphasis on the spatial or temporal aspects of the revelation differs from apocalypse to apocalypse. Some are more interested in events to happen soon, and revelations about the unseen world serve that interest by revealing those events. Others evince minimal interest in cosmic upheavals and eschatological events and focus rather on conveying information about the unseen world itself. In all apocalypses, both aspects are present.

The book of Revelation is most interested in events soon to occur that will result in the defeat of Satan and his agent Rome. It expects a general resurrection, a last judgment, the punishment of the wicked in a lake of fire, the passing away of the present heaven and earth, the coming of a new heaven and earth, and the eternal presence of God among humans on a new earth. The point of it all is the reassertion of God's absolute sovereignty over the entire cosmos and particularly over the earth and humans. This is necessary because Satan, having been ejected from heaven, has given his authority to Rome, and most of the world has pledged allegiance to this puppet power. Everything that Revelation discloses about the unseen world asserts God's sovereignty, now exercised in heaven, and soon to be realized fully throughout creation.

Apocalypses generally fall into two types, those in which the recipient of the revelation makes an otherworldly journey and those with a review of history under the guise of prophecy given supposedly by an ancient hero. Apocalypses with a review of history frequently concentrate on eschatological events to which history is said to lead. Those with the otherworldly journey often show more interest in esoteric knowledge about the universe, especially about aspects of it otherwise inaccessible to humans. Revelation contains an otherworldly journey and no real review of history, but its interests are not in speculative knowledge but in eschatology.

Despite its place in the scholarly conception of the genre, some argue that Revelation is not an apocalypse at all. Four main reasons are put forth for excluding it from the genre. It has no review of history; it is not pseudonymous; it has an epistolary framework; and it calls itself a book of prophecy. The lack of a review of history is no problem, since many other apocalypses contain no such review. Almost every other apocalypse is pseudonymous, meaning that the one by whom it claims to be written is not the true author, but Collins notes that the purpose of pseudonymity was to "enhance the prestige and authority of the work" (1977, 331). This was necessary in early Jewish contexts, where prophecy was in decline. Early Christianity experienced what it interpreted as an intense presence of the Spirit, a sign of which was a revival of prophecy. Collins concludes, "Insofar as pseudonymity was due to the decline of prophecy, the Christian author of Revelation was free to dispense with it" (331).

The third and fourth arguments can also be discounted. True, Revelation does have an epistolary introduction and conclusion (1:4–6; 22:21). (The adjective "epistolary" comes from "epistle," meaning "letter.") But the presence of elements of another genre does not argue against the classification of Revelation as an apocalypse, for apocalypses have always been recognized as containing disparate elements. They can also occur as subsections of texts that are of another genre.

The concept of literary genre that is sometimes assumed in these discussions is too rigid. A. Fowler (1982) shows that genres are born, develop, and die, all the while interacting with other genres. Scholars often refer to Revelation as an "apocalyptic letter," which is accurate, as long as this means not only a letter with apocalyptic features but a letter that also belongs to the apocalyptic genre. It should be noted that although Rev 1:4–8 and 22:21 frame the book as if it were a letter, there is a descriptive title at the head of the book (Rev 1:1–3) which formally takes precedence over that epistolary frame. This title begins, "The revelation [*apokalypsis*] of Jesus Christ," and reads almost as a definition of the genre. Placed where it is, it governs the entire book, including the letter elements.

The final objection to considering Revelation an apocalypse is that it claims to be prophecy (1:3; 22:7, 10, 18, 19). As we shall see in a moment, the seer does consider himself a prophet, even the equal of the biblical prophets, although he never applies the term explicitly to himself. This does not change the fact that what he writes has the form of an apocalypse. Elisabeth Schüssler Fiorenza notes that we cannot draw a firm line between prophecy and apocalypse at this period. Early Christian prophets were eschatological and apocalyptic in outlook. Schüssler Fiorenza says that Revelation "must be valued as a genuine expression of early Christian prophecy whose basic experience and self-understanding is apocalyptic" (1985a, 140).

Worldview: Apocalypticism

Apocalypses share a basic worldview, called "apocalypticism," which is expressed in many different ways from text to text. One of its fundamental elements is that there is an unseen world that determines what happens in the seen world. Inaccessible by ordinary means, the unseen world can be known only through direct revelation by a supernatural figure. The visions granted to the seer are often mysterious, even dreamlike, and are in need of explanation. Allusions to real events, places, and persons are often vague. But knowledge encoded in the visions often entails awareness of imminent events that will change the world definitively. Such knowledge makes it possible for those with whom it is shared to be ready for the change and to survive it.

Some or all humans (depending on the apocalypse) have a continued existence after death. Jewish and Christian apocalypses see God in ultimate control of the cosmos, and insight into God's rule and plans enables those who know about them to have proper attitudes and engage in proper behavior so that they will be rewarded after death. Those without that knowledge and who therefore do not please God will either go out of existence or suffer punishment after death.

Also typical of apocalypticism is dualism, seeing things in terms of binary opposites. On the cosmic level, this can be God against Satan, for example, and on the social level it can express itself as one community with a particular set of beliefs and practices that sees itself as radically different from and opposed to the rest of humanity.

Many, but not all, apocalypses express dissatisfaction with the world as it is. Daniel and Revelation have this characteristic, as do other Jewish apocalypses written at the same time as Revelation, such as 4 Ezra, *2 Baruch,* and the *Apocalypse of Abraham. First Enoch,* which combines previously independent apocalypses, also fits. The view of such works is that the world is not as it should be. God's will does not prevail, but such a situation cannot exist indefinitely. Something must change. God will reassert divine sovereignty, and soon. Indeed, those who have true understanding of the universe recognize that despite appearances, God is already in control and has a plan for changing the universe so that it conforms to his will. One can understand the present age only through knowledge of the unseen world that controls it. The vast majority of humans, who lack this special knowledge, are deceived by appearances, for things are not as they appear. Thus Revelation is a profoundly ironic book. Its author believes that only he and those who see the world as he does understand the way things are. Everyone else lives in illusion.

Apocalypses project an individual's or a group's experience onto a cosmic screen (Collins 1984). The group or individual then sees its own experience in the light of cosmic dynamics. Revelation's seer sees the conflict between the Roman empire and faithful Christians as part of a larger battle between God and Satan. Both battles are depicted by drawing on a combat myth that spans most cultures of the ancient world. In apocalypses in general and Revelation in particular, concrete experience is expressed in cosmic and mythic terms. The resultant texts can be applied anew to many other situations.

Apocalypticism involves mythological thinking. But scholars of religion do not use the term "myth" as does modern society in general, for whom myth is something by definition false. Myths are narratives about another time and place involving supernatural figures, but those narratives interpret everyday existence, expressing profound convictions and feelings about the world that cannot be expressed as well by any other medium. In this sense, the modern world has its own myths, too, and humans cannot dispense with myth as a fundamental way of thinking about the world. Bernard Batto (1992, 40), discussing the adaptation of myth in ancient Babylonia and Assyria, provides a summary of the function of myth that also pertains to the Hellenistic period, and even to modern myths:

> Each of these authors consciously and deliberately adapted prior mythic stories and motifs, and created new ones as well, as they crafted their own new literary compositions. Such conscious and deliberate extension of older mythic symbols to new political realities and changing intellectual conceptions is precisely what I mean by mythopoeic speculation. This was more involved than just the creative mind of a poet at work in composing a literary masterpiece, a kind of literary inspiration from the muses, so to speak. Rather, these Babylonian prophets—and later, Assyrian editors—were involved in rethinking the basic values of humankind as understood from their societies' perspectives, what we would call philosophizing or theologizing. However, they did their reflective thinking not through syllogistic reasoning or philosophical categories but through the medium of mythic narrative.... Even today, reading in translation, one can still experience something of the universal appeal of these ancient compositions as a quest after the most profound human questions.

Apocalypticism as defined in the previous paragraphs was widespread in early Christianity and Judaism. Many of the texts from that period either are apocalypses or contain apocalyptic elements. Revelation is the only New Testament apocalypse, but elements of an apocalyptic worldview are found in Paul, the synoptic gospels (Matthew, Mark, Luke), and even the gospel of John. Some see in Hebrews a combination of Platonic and apocalyptic concepts.

Revelation stands out from other Jewish and Christian works of its time not because of its apocalyptic outlook but because of the relentless way it uses the apocalyptic genre to attack Rome and its claim to legitimacy and sovereignty. As myth, Revelation supplies basic patterns that can help readers in many different times and places to decipher the significance of their own experience and to see a broader significance in it.

Numbers in Revelation

A striking feature of Revelation is its use of numbers (on this, see Yarbro Collins 1974, 1996). This should be seen in the context of numbers' significance for the ancient world in general. Many philosophies and religions considered numbers key to understanding the universe. The followers of Pythagoras were known for their interest in numbers, and this interest influenced Plato and many who followed him.

Numbers are used for several purposes in apocalypses. Periodization of history is common, in which all history is divided into a fixed number of periods – seven, ten, or twelve, for example. Because of such periodization, it is often said that apocalypses engage in calculating the time of the eschaton precisely. In fact, most Jewish and Christian apocalypses show no interest in such precise calculations (Hartman 1976). Rather, they periodize history simply to demonstrate that history is ordered and that God controls it. Apocalyptic authors usually show their audiences that they live at the end of times and that the eschaton is near. The numbers they offer are almost always purposely vague and hard to relate to specific times (Daniel 12:7, 11–12 seems to be an exception). Periodization also demonstrates that the course of history is determined by God and so is inexorable. This is meant to be a source of hope to the righteous, of threat to the wicked, and of warning to all others.

A second major use of numbers is to show that the cosmos is ordered. For example, many works specify the number of heavens, three and seven being the most common. Other examples are four corners of the earth, sometimes associated with four winds and the four directions, twelve gates through which the sun passes in each of the twelve months, and so on. God is the source of this order, and the order often carries eschatological and moral significance.

Revelation's use of numbers is unusual in two respects. The first is that numbers dominate the book to a degree not seen in other apocalypses. Second, in many cases it is difficult to decide why the author chose certain numbers. Our discussion of the use of numbers in specific passages is found in the commentary. We limit ourselves here to some general observations.

The use of numbers to reveal the structure of history is not common in Revelation. Unlike many apocalypses, it makes no attempt to periodize the broad sweep of history. However, like most other Jewish and Christian apocalypses, Revelation is interested not in calculations of when the end will occur but in the fact that the end is determined by God and is imminent for the audience contemporary with the author. Chapter 17 speaks of seven kings. However one identifies these kings, and the suggestions have been many because of the vagueness of the references, the text clearly speaks of the early Roman empire. It considers the end to be near, but nothing more specific than this can be said. Three other time indications are drawn directly from Daniel and characterize the present period of distress for the church as foreordained and temporary (11:2, 3; 12:6), but again they do not allow a precise calculation of the end, nor do they encompass the whole of history.

The use of numbers to describe the structure of the cosmos is also rare in Revelation. Revelation's heaven apparently has only one level. It does speak of four corners of the earth in 7:1. Given the predominance of numbers throughout the book, it is remarkable that they are used only minimally to organize time and the cosmos.

A third use of numbers found in Revelation is gematria (using the numerical value of letters to convey or discover hidden meanings). Hebrew and Greek did not have an independent set of characters as numerals, so letters stood for numbers. Any word or name could be transformed into its numerical equivalent. Revelation 13 contains a famous instance of gematria, where the beast's number is said to be 666 and is called "a human number." Many commentators take this as a reference to Nero, a position we shall defend, but the nature of gematria makes any reference inherently ambiguous.

The most common use of numbers in Revelation is to structure the book itself. In this connection, the number seven is by far the most common in the work. Yarbro Collins notes that seven is commonly used as a structuring principle by both Jewish and Christian sources around the time of Revelation, but while in other works it is implicit, Revelation makes it explicit (1996, 119–20). There are seven spirits before God; the one like a son of man has seven stars in his hand; there are seven messages to seven churches; the visions come in groups of seven, sometimes explicitly numbered (seals, trumpets, bowls) and sometimes not; there are seven beatitudes in Revelation; and so on.

Many commentators claim that seven is the number for completeness in antiquity, so that when the seer writes to seven churches, for example, he writes symbolically to the universal church. Yarbro Collins shows that there is very little evidence that seven bore this meaning generally (1996, 122–27). Nonetheless, seven was indeed an important number in the ancient world. Yarbro Collins (1996, 97) believes that by the second century B.C.E. "there was probably a well-developed Pythagorean speculative tradition on the number seven." Such speculation would have been especially useful to Jews, for whom the week consisted of seven days, the seventh of which was the sabbath. The most famous Jewish philosopher of the Roman imperial period, Philo of Alexandria, combines Jewish and Greek ideas in his writings, and he attests to the importance of reflection on numbers in general and on the number seven in particular. He even wrote a treatise called "On Numbers." Yarbro Collins notes, "Philo's discussion of the number seven very clearly emphasizes its role in the order of the cosmos," so that observance of the sabbath "is a way of conforming one's life to the cosmic order" (1996, 99).

Yarbro Collins offers many examples of the prevalence of numbers in Jewish and early Christian apocalypses (1996, 99–114). The numbers seven and twelve are especially prominent, probably because of their importance in measuring "microtime," that is, weeks and years. "Macrotime," the broader sweep of history, is analogous to microtime. In addition, numbers describe the order of the cosmos. Particularly prominent in Jewish texts is what Yarbro Collins calls "sabbatical logic" (1996, 75–76). This term applies to Jeremiah's prediction that the exile of the Jews to Babylonia in the sixth century B.C.E. would last seventy years and to many subsequent reinterpretations of his prophecy to comment on the entire second temple period, often said to be seven times seventy, or four hundred ninety years (Knibb 1976).

There seems to be no single reason that the number seven is so prominent in Revelation. Yarbro Collins cautions that the reason for the use of seven must be determined anew for each context in the work. For example, there are probably seven stars in the hand of the son of man in chapter 1 because of the seven planets. The seven lights on the candelabrum (menorah) in the temple probably account for there being seven torches before

God in chapter 4. But other uses of seven, for example, the seven seals, trumpets, and bowls, have no precise parallels. Rather, the author has a predilection for seven because of its overriding importance in Hellenistic circles as well as in Jewish writings in general and apocalypses in particular.

The second most important number in Revelation, twelve, was probably chosen for similar reasons. It was prominent in the Hellenistic world because of its association with the twelve months of the year and the signs of the zodiac. It was particularly appropriate in Jewish and Christian contexts because of the twelve tribes of Israel and the twelve apostles. The number thus suggests that cosmos and community are related in a harmonious whole in conformity with God's plan (Yarbro Collins 1996, 134).

Revelation's author writes of ultimate realities and of the true meaning of history and of the universe. His liberal use of numbers such as seven and twelve symbolizes that the visions he recounts reveal this true meaning. Central to Revelation is the sovereignty of God and the defeat of Satan and his puppet, Rome. Yarbro Collins refers to the insights of a previous scholar, Mathias Rissi, when she says, "They [numbers] make visible the will of God and Christ which stands behind and directs all events. They are, as it were, the net in which the Satanic forces are captured, surrounded and confined on all sides" (1996, 137).

Revelation's Literary Context

Revelation's Biblical Context

The literary context within which Revelation must be read includes more than just apocalypses. More than any other New Testament book, Revelation draws upon and depends upon the Hebrew Bible, what Christians call the "Old Testament." The "Bible" of the early Christians was what we know as the Old Testament. Obviously, when the New Testament books were being written, there was no such thing as the New Testament in the sense of a fixed collection of sacred books. Unless otherwise specified, throughout this commentary the noun "Bible" and the adjective "biblical" refer to the Hebrew Bible, not to the combination of the Old and New Testaments that Christians now call the Bible.

The Bible is a major element of our author's literary and symbolic world. He reads his own experiences and observes his environment through its lenses. It provides much of his imagery, mythology, and language. He sees himself in the mold of a biblical prophet, and he takes up the traditions preserved in the Bible and uses them to express the word of God anew for his own world. The author does not simply "apply" the Bible to his own day, for the Bible deeply influences the way he sees things in his own time. John was a living symbol of what recently has been called "intertextuality," the insight that neither texts nor authors live in isolation and that everything is connected to everything else. In a sense, John was controlled by his images, symbols, and narratives as much as he controlled them. He was caught in a web of meaning that determined the way he experienced the world. This means that fully appreciating how Revelation is connected to the Hebrew Bible will not be a simple matter of listing references and possible echoes. Indeed, attempts to categorize the ways in which John consciously uses scripture and to find specific biblical allusions must recognize that everything John says is influenced by the Bible in some way. Still, John transforms the biblical material into something new in the light of his own historical and social situation and his own experiences, visionary and otherwise.

Despite John's rootedness in the Bible, there is not a single direct quotation of the Bible in Revelation, although many passages verge on direct quotation. This fascinating combination — heavy dependence on the Bible but no direct citation of it — is a technique evident in many other apocalypses as well. It necessitates spending a good deal of time tracing some of the almost innumerable parallels and echoes of the Bible in our text. Not to do so would be to miss the rich texture the author has created out of the strands and colors of the biblical literature with which he is so deeply engaged. Commentators often use metaphors to describe the way in which Revelation uses biblical and extrabiblical traditions. George Caird compares Revelation's use of traditional images to the effect a kaleidoscope has on familiar objects. They are still recognizable, but they have been combined and transformed to produce something new and fascinating. Caird also compares Revelation to a rainbow that can be ruined if we look only at its individual colors, a process he calls "unweaving" the rainbow. Perhaps at points this commentary is guilty of unweaving, but it is our hope that looking carefully at the individual colors will lead to a deeper appreciation of the entire rainbow as well.

In a classic study of Revelation, Austin Farrer uses the figure of a rebirth of images, a figure that provides him with the title of his book. He notes that the basic symbols that provide meaning for humanity periodically become transformed and take on new and generative life. He suggests that Christ so powerfully gave rebirth to Israel's images that the process resulted in the birth of Christianity. This way of speaking is helpful, as long as it does not imply a supercessionist theology, in which Christianity promotes itself by denigrating Judaism. Supercessionist theology maintains that Christianity is the fulfillment of Judaism, so that when Christianity came into being, Judaism was obsolete. This can even affect historical study, as when historians of earliest Christianity paint Judaism as empty and legalistic, in contrast to Christianity, which embodies the best of earlier Israelite, and especially prophetic, religion. Both Judaism and Christianity are religions of the book, and both lay claim to what is essentially the same sacred literature, so supercessionist theology has often made its argument through scripture. Farrer is right that integral to Christianity's birth was a powerful transformation of Judaism's symbols, but if that view is combined with the theological argument that now Judaism has been surpassed, it becomes problematic. It ought to be noted that in recent years many mainstream Christian churches have rejected supercessionist theology.

The present commentary elucidates Revelation's biblical context not only by pointing out parallels and supplying lists of allusions but also by quoting biblical passages, sometimes at length, and spending time explaining them and how the author uses them to create something new. At times that can be painstaking and detailed work, but the increase in appreciation of the author's artistry, of his deep knowledge of and engagement with the sacred text, and of the many complex resonances of his final narrative is well worth the effort. We counsel the reader to be patient and to be willing to read "in detail," for the author of Revelation has indeed written "in detail." Furthermore, attention will often be drawn to other Jewish and Christian texts in which some of the same use of biblical images appears. This is not to say that John copies other authors or that they copy him. Rather the point is to become aware of a general context in which the Bible was being used by many

Christians and Jews as a way of understanding themselves and their own present.

Revelation and Noncanonical Literature

The Bible is by far the strongest literary influence on Revelation, but it is not the only one. There is a large body of literature written around the time of Revelation and in the centuries just before and after which supplies us with other comparative material. This material is not within the canon of scripture, so it is called noncanonical or extrabiblical. Much of that material has been collected together and translated into English under the title *The Old Testament Pseudepigrapha* (Charlesworth 1983–85). The collection contains many apocalypses, as well as many texts with apocalyptic elements.

The collections of Sibylline oracles are one of the most important groups of texts for our purposes. These are collections of a kind of prophetic writing produced at different times and places. The oracles are cryptic prophecy in verse, often with heavy political content. The Sibyl was a traditional female prophetic figure in the Hellenistic world. The texts that interest us are the ones written by Jews and Christians. Since some of these were written during the Roman period, they deal with some of the same issues as does Revelation, for example, Roman rule. Another important text is *1 Enoch,* a composite document in the form of an apocalypse whose parts were written between the third century B.C.E. and the first century C.E. *First Enoch* furnishes numerous parallels to Revelation: angelology, reward and punishment in the afterlife, and many other items. Fourth Ezra and *2 Baruch* are Jewish apocalypses roughly contemporary with Revelation (Stone 1990; Murphy 1985a). While these texts attest to a conceptual and symbolic world shared by their authors, one cannot claim with confidence that Revelation manifests a literary dependence on any one of these texts as it clearly does on the Bible. The Bible is a sourcebook shared by all of these authors, and it is the bedrock on which our author stands. But in the present work we frequently refer to and at times quote some of these extrabiblical documents so as to shed light on Revelation. Our aim is to elucidate Revelation's context by examining other works which view the world in ways similar to the ways our author does and which use the Bible in analogous ways.

"Decoding" Revelation's Images

A problem every interpreter of Revelation faces is the degree to which the book's images should be correlated with aspects of the real world, past, present, or future. Many interpreters have even sought to show that Revelation's images relate in detail to events in the interpreters' own times (Wainwright 1993). Application of Revelation to the present continues unabated today. Reviewing this history of interpretation, one is struck by how strange and idiosyncratic many of these interpretations now appear. But one also notices how pliable Revelation's images are, since they indeed can be used to interpret so many disparate situations over the centuries. For example, Martin Luther and some other Protestant commentators interpreted the beast of chapter 13 as the papacy. Not to be outdone, some Catholic commentators "discovered" that the number of the beast, 666, was an encoded way of alluding to Luther (Boring 1989, 48). More recently, the ten kings of Revelation 17 have been seen as the European Economic Community or, alternatively, OPEC, the Organization of Petroleum Exporting Countries. More recently still, David Koresh interpreted the seven seals of Revelation to refer to him and his community of Branch Davidians at Waco, Texas. This must raise doubts about whether this is how the book's author meant it to be interpreted, or whether the book in fact reveals specifics about future events at all. Identification of particular figures and events in Revelation with specific people and occurrences outside the text is bound to be subjective in the extreme, convincing primarily to those already convinced on other grounds.

One image in Revelation that has been subjected to many different interpretations is the kingdom of Christ that lasts for a thousand years (20:4–6). This is often spoken of as the "millennium," a word that comes from the Latin words for "thousand," *mille,* and "year," *annus.* This passage has received more attention than is warranted by its function in Revelation, as we shall explain in the commentary. But one can legitimately ask whether the author intended a literal messianic kingdom to precede the definitive defeat of Satan (20:7–10) and the coming of God's kingdom to earth. General categories of interpretation of this passage have received names appropriate to their specifics. Premillennialists believe that Christ will come before the millennium; postmillennialists hold that he will arrive after his faithful have ruled for the thousand years; and amillennialists hold that no literal kingdom is meant. "Chiliasts" (from the Greek for "thousand," *chilias*) is a name usually applied to early Christians who expected a literal kingdom to come soon. Such an expectation could supply hope to those living under adverse conditions by envisioning a future world in which they would be rewarded. Some Christian writers opposed the chiliastic interpretation, but Wainwright (1993, 30–31) observes that chiliasm was popular until Constantine made Christianity the official religion of the Roman empire, thus bringing to an end Roman persecution of Christianity (and, unfortunately, setting in motion Christian persecution of other religions). Wainwright suggests that chiliasm was a reasonable view that "met the needs of Christians who lived under the threat of persecution amid the dangers of war," although he recognizes that other responses were also possible under such circumstances. An example is Origen, who read Revelation in a nonliteral way, despite the fact that his father was martyred and he himself faced the same fate. Writing after the time of Constantine, Augustine espoused the view that the millennium was realized in the church itself, and so was coterminous with church history.

Another basic approach to Revelation's images is called preterist. This view says that to the extent that the seer's images can be applied to concrete persons or events or institutions at all, they refer to things and people in the seer's own world. Any future expectations in the book refer to things the author expected to happen soon in his own time, as his repeated use of the word "soon" indicates (see commentary, especially on 1:1; 2:16; 3:11; 6:11; 11:14; 22:6, 7, 12, 20). This viewpoint characterizes this commentary. This is not to say that the book has nothing to say to us today. It is only to claim that the author was writing for his own time and that he expected the final battle, the general resurrection, the last judgment, and the coming to earth of God's kingdom to happen soon, well before the twentieth century.

This raises the problem of how literally the seer means his images and of whether he intends for them to be correlated with events, institutions, and persons outside the text. The book of Revelation addresses the specific situation within which the seer lived. At the same time, the seer saw that situation in the context of a much broader cosmic struggle. These two things — rootedness in a real historical situation and transcendence of that situation—must be held together. On the one hand, Revelation's imagery does reflect the author's concrete historical situation, but it cannot be reduced to an allegory of it or a coded way of referring to that situation. On the other hand, Revelation does not represent only an exotic way of expressing timeless truths. There are certainly allusions in the text to specific persons, places, and events in the author's world. To the extent that those can be determined, we shall try to do so. But those allusions are woven into the visions and cannot be simply separated from them. Some have suggested that the author's references to the world outside the text were purposely made opaque so as to hide its true meaning from any enemies who might stumble across it. This is unlikely. These images would not fool the seer's contemporaries. Rather, they make the circumstances of the seer's world part of a larger, mysterious universe whose realities can be expressed only through mythological and poetic means. There is a complex interaction between the seer's everyday world and the symbolic universe he inhabits. This commentary seeks to do justice to that complexity.

Author

Pseudonymity

Who wrote the book of Revelation? This may seem a strange question to modern readers. In our world, a book is usually written by a person (or group of persons) who wishes to be known, receives credit for the book, and is cited by name in subsequent works. In the modern context, the question about who wrote a particular biblical book can sound somewhat conspiratorial, as if by asking the question one were raising doubts about the book's value, authenticity, inspired status, honesty, and so on.

Modern ideas of intellectual ownership do not always apply to ancient Jewish and Christian writings. Authorship of biblical books, as well as of many other ancient books, is often obscure. Although legend once attributed the first five books of the Hebrew Bible to Moses, those books do not claim to be written by him, nor do modern scholars think that they were. Similarly, no author claims responsibility for the Deuteronomistic History (Joshua, Judges, 1–2 Samuel, 1–2 Kings). Some psalms are attributed to David, but many are anonymous. The writing prophets, those who left written oracles in their own names, had their works altered over the years — new oracles pertaining to new situations were added; older oracles were edited; and so on.

The New Testament is not immune from difficulties in determining authorship. The four canonical gospels were written by different people at different times in different places, and they were originally anonymous. Their attribution to specific authors was added when the gospels were collected together. Of the thirteen letters attributed to Paul in the New Testament, only seven are accepted as authentic by virtually all scholars (Romans, 1–2 Corinthians, Galatians, Philippians, 1 Thessalonians, Philemon). The rest (Ephesians, Colossians, 2 Thessalonians, 1–2 Timothy, Titus) may not be by Paul. They are pseudonymous; they have a false (Greek: *pseudos*) name (Greek: *onoma;* see Meade 1987; Metzger 1972).

John

On one level, the answer to the question about who wrote Revelation is clear, surprisingly clear for a biblical book. Revelation begins with what might be called a descriptive title (1:1–3). The book is a revelation given by God to Jesus, who in turn passes it on to "his servant John" through an angel. John bears witness to this revelation, "even to all that he saw." There is also an epistolary introduction in which the writer is identified as "John." In 1:9, John again identifies himself by name as he begins to narrate his inaugural vision. In 22:8, John identifies himself one last time: "I, John, am the one who heard and saw these things." He is also the one who wrote them down, as is clear from his position as sender of the revelatory letter (1:4), as well as from his being told to write down his visions (1:11, 19; 2:1, 8, 12, 18; 3:1, 7, 14; 14:13; 19:9; 21:5; cf. 10:4).

Revelation, then, claims that John is its author and the recipient of the visions contained in it. But could Revelation be pseudonymous? Almost every other apocalypse, Jewish or Christian, from the third century B.C.E. to the second century C.E., is pseudonymous. Jewish apocalypses are commonly attributed to ancient heroes and sages, thereby lending the apocalypses authority, and they frequently contain features associated with those ancient heroes. There are apocalypses in the names of people such as Ezra, Abraham, Baruch, and Moses. Christians wrote apocalypses in the names of their heroes, such as Peter and Paul. But the author of Revelation does not use any information about any known "John" that reinforces his message. Indeed the author says little about himself. The very confusion of both ancient and modern authors about which John could be meant argues against pseudonymity, since, for the ascription of a book to a false author to be effective, the reader must know who the alleged author is. There really is no evidence that "John" is a pseudonym.

Given that the author's real name is probably "John," which John is meant? "John" had been a common Jewish name since the Babylonian exile (587 B.C.E.), and there were several men with this name in early Christian traditions. The most famous was John the Baptist. Josephine Massyngberde Ford attempts to connect Revelation with this John but finds no supporters for her position (1975). A view popular in antiquity was that John the apostle wrote Revelation. The earliest witness for this view is Justin Martyr, a second-century apologist who was martyred in Rome in 165 C.E. Justin lived for a time in Ephesus, home to one of the seven churches of Revelation. The view is also espoused by Irenaeus, who grew up in Smyrna, home to the second of the seven churches, and then moved to Lyons in Gaul (now France), where he became bishop. Irenaeus knew Polycarp, a bishop of Smyrna who was martyred at around the middle of the second century. Writing in around 180, Irenaeus claims that John the apostle wrote both the gospel of John and the book of Revelation (on the relation of the gospel of John and Revelation, see Schüssler Fiorenza 1985b). He says that he had listened to Polycarp and others who had met John the apostle in Asia Minor.

In the middle of the third century, Dionysius, bishop of Alexandria, argued that the gospel and letters of John could not have been written by the same person who wrote Revelation since the former are anonymous whereas the latter is not, and because of marked differences in the Greek of the documents. Dionysius's analysis is supported by modern research, which finds the gospel of John and Revelation to be quite different in terms of content as well. Although there are intriguing connections between Revelation and the gospel of John, the contacts must be explained otherwise than by positing a common author. So if the gospel of John was written by the apostle, then Revelation was not. However, the gospel itself is anonymous, and few think that it was written by the apostle (Brown 1979).

There is also a chronological argument against apostolic authorship for Revelation. If the date of 95–96 C.E. is accepted for its writing, a date advocated below, then John the apostle would have been quite elderly by that time. Further, Christian tradition speaks of the martyrdom of John son of Zebedee, perhaps before 70 C.E.

The strongest argument against apostolic authorship is internal to Revelation itself. The author never speaks of himself as an apostle. Although he is anxious for his audience to receive his writing as authoritative, he never claims membership in Jesus' inner circle or apostolic standing within the church. Further, Revelation says that the apostles' names are written on the twelve foundations of the city. This sort of thing was said after the apostolic period was over. For example, in Eph 2:20 the apostles are said to be the foundations of the new temple that is the church. Ephesians was not written by Paul, but was written after his death. Its exaltation of the apostles contrasts sharply with Paul's own attitude toward those who were apostles before him, seen in such places as Galatians 2–3 and 1 Cor 15:10. In 1 Cor 3:9, Paul refers to the church as "God's building," and in 3:11, he says, "No one can lay any foundation other than the one that has been laid; that foundation is Jesus Christ."

If, then, the author of Revelation is neither John the Baptist nor John the apostle, are there other candidates? Dionysius of Alexandria suggested John Mark, who briefly accompanied Paul and Barnabas on a missionary journey, but Dionysius argued against his own suggestion on the grounds that John Mark did not travel with them all the way to Asia Minor, site of Revelation's churches. There is nothing to tie him to Revelation. Papias, who in the early second century was bishop of Hierapolis, which was close to Laodicea, home to one of the seven churches, says that he used to question anyone who knew any of the apostles or others with access to reliable oral tradition from Jesus. He supplies a list of names of such people, and in that list there are two Johns mentioned, one who seems to have been the apostle and the other whom he calls "the presbyter." This leads some to suggest that the author of Revelation was John the Presbyter (*presbyteros* is Greek for "elder"). For a time, this was a common view even among modern scholars. However, there is no real evidence to connect Revelation to this presbyter, and even if there were, next to nothing is known about him. So we conclude that we simply do not know who wrote Revelation.

John's Social Location

While we cannot identify a specific individual through the name John, information from the book does enable us to speak about the seer's "social location," his position in society. That position can be approximated by combining hints in the book with what we know generally of his historical and social context.

The social role that sheds most light on John is that of prophet. While John never explicitly calls himself a prophet, it is clear that he considers himself one (Boring 1992, 498, points out that Paul does not claim to be a prophet, but he acts like one). He receives direct revelation from God that he passes on to the churches in the form of a book. The prologue (1:1–3) ends with a beatitude that starts with the words, "Blessed is the one who reads aloud the words of the prophecy." Before the final prophetic saying (22:20) and epistolary blessing (22:21) is the following warning: "I warn everyone who hears the words of the prophecy of this book: if anyone adds to them, God will add to that person the plagues described in this book; if anyone takes away from the words of the book of this prophecy, God will take away that person's share in the tree of life and in the holy city, which are described in this book" (22:18–19). John self-consciously writes a book of prophecy, which makes him unique among the known prophets of earliest Christianity but similar to the biblical writing prophets (see Ruiz 1989).

Prophecy was widespread in earliest Christianity and has continued to play a role of varying intensity throughout the history of Christianity. A useful definition is the following: "The early Christian prophet was an immediately-inspired spokesperson for God, the risen Jesus, or the Spirit, who received intelligible oracles that he or she felt impelled to deliver to the Christian community or, representing the community, to the general public" (Boring 1992, 496). "Immediately-inspired" means that the prophet receives revelation directly from God or Jesus.

It is a common misapprehension that prophecy is primarily prediction, and that has led to many applications of the "predictions" contained in Revelation to later times, events, and persons. It is true that there is prediction in prophecy, whether one looks at the Hebrew Bible or early Christian prophecy, but the focus of prophecy is to affect the audience's present behavior and attitudes. Prophecy reveals God's judgment on human affairs and discloses God's will. Biblical prophets sometimes make their prophecies conditional – the punishment predicted will transpire only if the audience does not repent; if they do, then good will come. In apocalypses the issue of prediction becomes more acute, since they often seem to foretell quite specific occurrences associated with the inexorable march of history to its final climax. Throughout history, interpreters of Revelation have used such predictions in the book to "prove" that their own times were the final times and that their own enemies were God's enemies. But the substantial amount of actual prediction in Revelation serves primarily to illumine the true nature of power in the present and so to reveal the true nature of things. This is not to deny that Revelation predicts specific eschatological events, but its purpose is not to convey detailed information about them.

Yarbro Collins suggests that Revelation's images are pointers, not roadmaps. They say something important about God's relation to the world and what is to happen in the future, but they do not intend to lay out in detail the exact course of future events. Any attempt to extract such a roadmap from Revelation distorts the text and ultimately makes it less than it is. Revelation's main interest is in affecting its readers in the present, so that they are ready for God's judgment. Even when it does convey specific information about eschatological events, it presents those events as imminent for the audience. They are to happen *soon.*

Early Christian prophecy was seen as a result of the presence of the Spirit in the community. For Paul, the presence of the Spirit in the church results in a number of gifts (*charismata* in Greek), including tongues, healing, teaching, and so on (1 Corinthians 12–14). In 1 Corinthians 14 he holds up prophecy as one of the most important gifts, since it conveys God's word to the community in intelligible form. In Paul's various lists of spiritual gifts, prophecy is the only constant (1 Cor 12:8–11, 28–30; 13:1–2; Rom 12:6–8; see Boring 1992, 498). For Luke, the outbreak of prophecy in the church was due to an eschatological outpouring of the Spirit promised in Joel 2:28–32 (Acts 2:17–21). Although most sources attest to the belief that the entire Christian community possessed the Spirit, it is also clear that there were specific individuals within the community who were known as prophets and who stood out as such. Both sides of the equation, that all have the Spirit and that not all are prophets, are present in texts such as 1 Corinthians 12–14 and Acts of the Apostles.

It is not surprising that a phenomenon in which an individual speaks for God should lead to conflict within the church. The same was the case regarding the prophecy depicted in the Hebrew Bible. In Deuteronomy 18, Moses warns the Israelites that there will be false prophets and provides a way to test them; in Jeremiah 28, the prophet Hananiah accuses Jeremiah of not prophesying accurately, and Jeremiah returns the compliment; in 1 Kings 22, the prophet Micaiah ben Imlah prophesies in opposition to four hundred other prophets. The same is true in the early church. In 1 Thess 5:19–22, Paul instructs the Thessalonians, "Do not quench the Spirit. Do not despise the words of prophets, but test everything; hold fast to what is good; abstain from every form of evil." The Didache, a Christian document perhaps from the area of Syria around the late first century B.C.E., urges acceptance of wandering prophets, but it also demands a critical assessment of them.

Studies of early Christian prophets have frequently seen two main types, community and wandering prophets. David Aune refines this by dividing wandering prophets into three further categories: (1) those who left their home churches and went elsewhere to fulfill a particular task (as did Agabus, Judas, and Silas in Acts 11:28; 15:32; 21:10); (2) circuit prophets who regularly visited a specific group of churches (perhaps John, the seer of Revelation); and (3) prophets whose itinerant lifestyle embodied ideals of homelessness and detachment from family, friends, and possessions (e.g., the prophets described in the Didache; see Aune 1981, 27). Yarbro Collins (1984, 35) cautions against a strict division between community and wandering prophets, given the amount of mobility among early Christians. She continues, "Nevertheless, if not pressed too far, the distinction is probably a useful one; by means of it we can distinguish prophets who at particular times were occupied primarily with local and trans-local ministries, respectively. The distinction is especially important in the light of evidence that at least some wandering prophets had an ascetic life-style."

The coincidence of a traveling lifestyle, ascetic practice, and association with specific churches may occur in John, the seer of Revelation. John writes to seven churches which form a rough circle, and the order in which they are mentioned in 1:11 and in chapters 2 and 3 traces that circle in a clockwise direction. He does not claim a particular office. His message will gain acceptance only if his audience believes that he did indeed receive visions in which God and Jesus communicated directly with him. John is known to the churches, as is evident from the lack of any introduction of himself. The epistolary introduction to Revelation begins simply, "John to the seven churches that are in Asia" (1:4). John knows particulars about each church he addresses. All these facts support Aune's view that John is a kind of circuit prophet whose circle consists of the seven churches.

Many try to be more specific about John's social location and that of the seven churches. Yarbro Collins traces a certain line of analysis beginning in 1927 when Carl Clemen suggested that John's churches were sectlike groups (1984, 35–37). In 1966, A. Satake proceeded further along such lines when he saw the absence of any mention of bishops and deacons in Revelation and the prominence of prophets as evidence that in the seven churches' organization prophets predominated, similar to the situation of the earliest churches in Palestine. That structure was allegedly changed by James when he assumed control of the Jerusalem church, but the earlier structure continued in small groups that eventually migrated to western Asia Minor, probably due to the war in Palestine between the Jews and Romans (66–73 C.E.). Satake's hypothesis is weakened at both ends (Palestine and Asia Minor) when it is recognized that the reconstruction of the earliest Palestinian church organization rests on slim evidence and that there is little reason to suppose that one can deduce the organization of the Asian churches on the basis of Revelation. There is no evidence that leads to the conclusion that John's churches were small, sectarian groups. As will be seen from an analysis of the messages to the seven churches in Revelation 2–3, it is much more likely that they were what might be called mainstream churches, comprised of persons of a variety of viewpoints, social classes, and attitudes toward non-Christian culture.

Aune convincingly explains the absence of bishops and deacons from the pages of Revelation. He considers John a wandering prophet who gained a hearing by resting the authority for the revelation squarely on its divine origin. He addresses this revelation directly to the community itself, not to its leaders. At the same time, since John was a wandering prophet, he depended on the support of the churches, including their leaders, for sustenance. "The absence of any criticism of local officials may be partially understood as a desire not to alienate those upon whom he might someday be dependent" (Aune 1981, 26).

If John is a wandering prophet writing to mainstream churches in major Asian cities, churches in which he is known and can expect a hearing but in which he holds no office, other questions arise. Are there groups within those churches that have a special affinity with John or that owe him particular allegiance? Does he have followers in those churches? There is no direct evidence on which to base an answer to these questions. However, John is known by these churches, writes them an apocalyptic letter (which would have to be delivered by some trusted colleague sympathetic to his point of view), and knows their histories. He entirely approves of Smyrna and Philadelphia, and partially of Ephesus and Pergamum. Even the churches of Thyatira and Sardis contain members of whom he approves. Only Laodicea receives no word of approval from him. There are certainly those in the churches who share his views, and in some churches (Smyrna and Philadelphia) they are in the majority. There is no evidence that his sympathizers form a coherent group easily separable from the churches as a whole.

Is John the head of a circle or school of prophets? Are there community prophets of whom he is the leader or who are especially influenced by him? These are much-disputed questions. Answers to them focus on the terms "prophet" and "servant." Some take the word "servants" in 1:1, 22:6, 9, and 10:7 to refer to Christian prophets. Some commentators go still further and refer to a prophetic "school." The terms "group" and "circle" are rather vague and leave the door open for a variety of interpretations. "School" is somewhat more precise in that it implies an identifiable group engaged in a regular and disciplined way of teaching, learning, writing, rewriting, interpreting, and so on (Stendahl 1968; Schüssler Fiorenza 1985a, 85–113). Yarbro Collins carefully reexamines the evidence and concludes that it is insufficient for the decision that John is in touch with a prophetic group in the churches, much less that he is its leader. She also takes issue with the idea that Revelation bears the marks of having been influenced by a prophetic school. She claims that there is no instance of the use of "prophet" in Revelation that clearly refers to Christian prophets. All uses can just as easily refer to prophets from the Hebrew Bible. The author makes no clear distinction between the people of God in its manifestations as Israel or followers of Christ. Christian prophecy is in continuity with that of the Hebrew Bible. God is the God of the spirits of the prophets, be they Jewish or Christian. In 2:9 and 3:9 the author even seems implicitly to claim the name "Jew."

Yarbro Collins finishes her treatment of the social location of Revelation's author with the observations that he is probably Jewish, and from Palestine. She bases her conclusions on the following evidence. He assumes that those who follow Jesus are continuous with Israel, even to the extent of implying that those in the churches are the true Jews (2:9; 3:9). The form that the author's anti-Roman feeling takes is similar in several ways to the fourth book of the Sibylline Oracles, which is Jewish, dates to about 80 C.E., and probably comes from the Jordan Valley or perhaps Syria. Revelation's author does not insist that the Torah be kept by Christians, but his insistence on avoidance of fornication and food sacrificed to idols is similar to the injunctions to Gentile Christians contained in the letter of the Jewish-Christian church in Jerusalem as recorded in Acts 15. Evidence gleaned from his rather odd Greek points to the probability that the author knew Hebrew or Aramaic, which it is unlikely that a Diaspora Jew would know (see Mussies 1980; Yarbro Collins 1984, 47). Charles (1920) documents the heavy Semitic influence on John's Greek, and G. Mussies demonstrates that the author avoids syntactical constructions that constitute Semitisms in the Septuagint but that do not have a counterpart in his contemporary Hebrew or Aramaic. Yarbro Collins attributes this strange Greek not to an inability to use proper Greek but to cultural pride. John uses the language of the eastern empire, but his strange usage is a form of resistance to the culture it carries.

Date

Clues about the date of Revelation are both external and internal to the text. The existence of Revelation is attested to in several sources. Andreas of Caesarea, a commentator on Revelation writing in the sixth century, says that Papias, bishop of Hierapolis, near the seven cities in the early second century, knew Revelation. The first direct witness to its existence is that of Justin Martyr in about 135. Revelation played an important role in the spirit-filled, prophetic form of Christianity called Montanism, in the second century. The most important second-century witness to Revelation is Irenaeus. Writing about 180, he claims that the revelation described in the book was received by John the apostle at the end of the reign of Domitian (81–96 C.E.). Irenaeus spent his youth in Smyrna and claims to have received information about the author of Revelation from Polycarp of Smyrna. In the section on authorship, we rejected Irenaeus's identification of the author as the apostle John, so his claim about the date should then also be treated with caution. His testimony ought to be accepted only if it conforms with internal indications of date. Later witnesses, such as Victorinus of Pettau, who wrote a commentary on Revelation in around 300 C.E., and Eusebius, the main early church historian who wrote at about the same time, support Irenaeus's date, but they may rely on him or on a common tradition, so they are not necessarily independent witnesses.

The author of Revelation does not specify when he receives his vision, except to say that it happened on the Lord's day. Given the cryptic nature of the book, it is difficult to find internal clues for its date. The discussion of the date by Yarbro Collins (1984, 54–82) is balanced and complete, and we follow it here. She discusses internal indications of date under the following topics: the name Babylon, the seven kings of Revelation 17, the Jerusalem temple, Domitian and the Christians, and the messages to the seven churches. Of these five topics, we deal with the first three here. Domitian is discussed above under "Christians in the Roman Empire," and the messages to the seven churches are dealt with in the commentary.

The designation of Rome as Babylon is strong evidence that Revelation was written after the destruction of the Jerusalem temple by the Romans in 70 C.E. The reason for the identification of Rome with Babylon is that in 587 B.C.E. the Babylonians destroyed Jerusalem and its temple, leaving lasting scars in Israel's consciousness. It is not surprising that it became the paradigm through which to interpret the equally devastating disaster suffered by the Jews in 70 C.E. Two Jewish apocalypses — 4 Ezra and *2 Baruch* — written at around the turn of the second century focus on the second destruction by speaking of it within the fictional setting of the first destruction. For these documents, "Babylon" is Rome. In *Sib. Or.* 5:143, 159, Rome is also called Babylon, in the context of a passage about the downfall of Nero and the destruction of Jerusalem.

Revelation also means Rome when it says "Babylon." The seer

Figure 1

	A	B	C	D	E	F	G	H
Julius Caesar (101–44 B.C.E.)	1	1						1
Augustus (31 B.C.E.–14 C.E.)	2	2	1	1				2
Tiberius (14–37 C.E.)	3	3	2	2				–
Gaius (37–41)	4	4	3	3	1			–
Claudius (41–54)	5	5	4	4	2			3
Nero (54–68)	6	6	5	5	3	1		–
Galba (June 68–January 69)	7	–	6	–	4	2	1	–
Otho (69)	8	–	7	–	5	3	2	–
Vitellius (69)		–	8	–	6	4	3	–
Vespasian (69–79)		7		6	7	5	4	4
Titus (79–81)		8		7	8	6	5	5
Domitian (81–96)				8		7(8)	6	6
[Neronic Antichrist]							–	7(8)
Nerva (96–98)							7(8)	

himself says that the name Babylon, written on the head of the great prostitute, is a "mystery" (17:5). An angel volunteers to disclose the "mystery" of the woman. The woman sits on a beast with seven heads, and the angel says that the seven heads are "seven mountains" (17:9). He also says that the woman is "the great city that rules over the kings of the earth" (17:18). Rome was known for its seven hills and was the center of a "worldwide" empire. The angel also supplies a second interpretation of the seven heads: "Also, they are seven kings, of whom five have fallen, one is living, and the other has not yet come; and when he comes, he must remain only a little while. As for the beast that was and is not, it is an eighth but it belongs to the seven, and it goes to destruction" (17:9b-11). This short passage has received much close scrutiny over the years because it appears to give specific data by which Revelation can be dated. Nonetheless, the eight kings cannot be correlated with emperors in such a way that a clear date is established.

Aune has compiled a chart (see figure 1) that is of great help in following the arguments for the various interpretations of the seven kings (*HCSB,* 2330). The letters at the top of the chart represent specific interpretations.

The seven kings have been interpreted in four basic ways

(Yarbro Collins 1984, 59–60). (1) The seven kings are listed consecutively and include all Roman emperors from the beginning of the empire to the time of the author; the list begins with the first (interpreted as either Julius Caesar or Augustus), and the author writes under the sixth. (2) The seven kings are listed consecutively, but the author does not really write under the sixth, either because he is using an earlier source or because he wishes to make the work appear as if it had been written earlier than it actually was. (3) This is not a consecutive listing, but is a selective list, the principle of selection being different depending on the interpreter. (4) The number is purely symbolic, so it cannot be correlated with actual emperors.

Yarbro Collins shows that the first option results in insurmountable difficulties. The most straightforward application of this option would begin the list with Julius Caesar. He is the first of the emperors in a work called *The Twelve Caesars,* written by the Roman Suetonius under the emperor Hadrian in the early second century. He is also the first emperor in three Jewish sources—*Sib. Or.* 5:12–51; 4 Ezra 11–12; and Josephus's *Ant.* 18 §§32–33. Starting with Julius Caesar and counting consecutively, the sixth emperor would be Nero (column A in Aune's chart). In that case, the author writes under Nero and expects that the reign of the next emperor will be short (which it was; Galba ruled only about seven months) and that the one after that would be Nero again. This would satisfy those who think that Revelation was written during a time of great persecution of the Christians, for Nero persecuted the Christians after the great fire of Rome in 64 C.E., as explained above. However, it would mean that Revelation was written before the destruction of Jerusalem. We have seen above that it is most probable that the name Babylon was applied to Rome because, like Babylon of old, it destroyed Jerusalem and its temple, and that did not occur until 70 C.E.

Other commentators contend that although Julius Caesar is considered the first emperor by several ancient authors, it was really Augustus who began imperial rule in earnest. A. A. Bell (1979) is a forceful advocate of this view, using as evidence the Roman writer Tacitus (*Hist.* 1.1; *Annals*). But beginning with Augustus instead of Julius Caesar makes the sixth emperor Galba, who ruled from June 68 to January 69, so it would still date Revelation to before 70, which is again contradicted by the use of the name Babylon (Aune's column C).

Other interpreters do not count the three emperors Galba, Otho, and Vitellius, because these emperors ruled only for very short times during the turmoil that followed Nero's death in 68. Of these interpreters, some then begin the list with Julius Caesar (column B) and others with Augustus (column D). If we begin with Julius, then Nero is still the sixth emperor, so the objection based on the name Babylon still holds. If Augustus is treated as the first emperor, then the sixth emperor becomes Vespasian. The problem with this solution is that there is no strong rationale for discounting Galba, Otho, and Vitellius as emperors. They are included by Suetonius in his treatment of the twelve Caesars, and they are also in the Jewish lists found in *Sib. Or.* 5:12–51 and 4 Ezra 11–12. The Roman senate recognized each of them as emperor in turn.

The second option Yarbro Collins presents is that the author does not write under the sixth king. That could be because, like other writers of apocalypses, he wishes to make it seem as if the work was written earlier than it was in fact. In other apocalypses, this goes along with attribution of the apocalypse to some ancient seer who then "predicts" events which for the actual author are already past. This lends the apocalypse authority. But it is highly unlikely that this is the case with Revelation. If it were, it would be the only instance in the book where such antedating occurs. This short and somewhat obscure passage located in the seventeenth of twenty-two chapters could hardly then lend authority to the book as a whole. Further, "John" is not a pseudonym, as we have shown above.

Another possibility is that the author is using a source written under the sixth emperor, either incorporating it unaltered into his work or reinterpreting it. This would account for the author's not writing under the sixth emperor, and it would not necessitate the sort of fictional predictions associated with pseudonymity.

Yarbro Collins's third option is that the list of seven is selective, and it is this option that she finds most persuasive. She suggests that Caligula is the first king. John was a Jewish Christian, and the reign of Caligula was traumatic for Jews. He tried to erect a statue of himself in the temple at Jerusalem, and disaster was averted only because he was assassinated before the deed was done. Galba, Otho, and Vitellius had extremely short reigns and did not affect Jews and Christians in any discernible way. The first six emperors would then be Caligula, Claudius, Nero,

Vespasian, Titus, and Domitian, the last of whom was on the throne at Revelation's writing. Yarbro Collins supports her solution, a selective list of emperors, with the observation that the eagle vision in 4 Ezra singles out emperors who are particularly feared or hated when it depicts the three Flavians (Vespasian, Titus, and Domitian) as three heads of the eagle, whereas they are also three of the twelve kings represented by the eagle's wings (4 Ezra 11–12).

Turning to the fourth of Yarbro Collins's four interpretive options listed above, we must ask whether the number seven is purely symbolic. There is no question that seven is a number heavy with significance for Revelation. The clearest principle of organization in the book is the number seven. On the one hand, then, the seven-headed beast may have influenced the idea that there are seven kings. On the other hand, this does not mean that there is no correspondence between the seven kings of Revelation 17 and some real Roman emperors. When 4 Ezra 11–12 speaks of twelve emperors, for example, it is clear that it has in mind specific emperors.

The last issue to be treated under the topic of date is the Jerusalem temple. In Rev 11:1–2, it appears that Jerusalem's temple is still standing, so that would indicate a date before 70 C.E. But Yarbro Collins argues that it is unlikely that John wrote 11:1–2. It is most likely a source incorporated by the author (see commentary).

In summary, Justin gives us solid evidence of Revelation's existence by about 135 C.E., and he assumes it was written substantially earlier than his own time, since he attributes it to John the apostle, while Revelation's use of the name "Babylon" for Rome strongly suggests a date post-70 C.E. This leaves about a forty year spread during which Revelation could have been written. After this detailed discussion, there seems to be no reason to reject the date given by Irenaeus.

Structure

As one reads a text as complex as Revelation, it helps to have an idea of its overall structure. But anyone seeking a clear picture of Revelation's structure soon confronts a large number of proposals. To some extent, determination of the structure of any biblical book is problematic, because the earliest manuscripts did not have such rudimentary guides to reading as punctuation and capitalization, much less paragraph and section markers, section headings and tables of contents. Nonetheless, general agreement on structure can often be reached when indicators in the text provide pointers to how the author divided the work. Revelation is rich and complex, featuring numbering, cross-references, contrasting parallelism, reuse of the same or similar images in the same or different ways, and so on. There are, indeed, almost *too many* indications of structure in the book. The result is that even today, almost two thousand years after its writing, scholars continue to propose new analyses of Revelation's structure, but there is still no general consensus on many aspects of its principles of organization.

The following pages seek not just to lay out a structure but also to disclose the reasoning and assumptions that underlie it. The best discussion of Revelation's structure is found in Yarbro Collins's book *The Combat Myth in the Book of Revelation* (1976, 5–55). We follow her discussion closely throughout this section and for the most part adopt her conclusions. Her analysis combines Farrer's division into six series of seven elements each (seven messages, seals, trumpets, bowls, and two sets of seven unnumbered visions) with Günther Bornkamm's view of the book as two great cycles of visions, the first cryptic and the second recapitulating and clarifying the first (1937). She modifies the proposals of both scholars somewhat. She also adds the observation that several passages serve to interlock larger sections.

Framing Elements

Epistolary elements frame Revelation, making it formally a letter. Revelation 1:4–5a contains the indication of addressee and writer familiar from Paul's letters. This is followed by a doxology (an ascription of praise; 1:5b-6), as is found in Paul's letter to the Galatians (1:4–5). The book concludes with a blessing typical of a Pauline letter (Rev 22:21). Unlike Pauline letters, this is a circular letter, meant to be read not just in one church but in seven (1:4). The seven messages to the seven churches contained in chapters 2 and 3 have sometimes been considered originally independent letters to each of the seven churches, later incorporated into Revelation (Charles 1920, 1:43–47). This is unlikely. The messages are not letters in form, nor do they claim to be letters. Their formal uniformity and their close connections with other parts of Revelation indicate that they were written for their present contexts. They strengthen the impression that Revelation is a circular letter because each message addresses the particular situation of the church addressed but is meant to be heard by all of the churches, as the concluding formulas demonstrate.

A short prayer for the coming of Jesus (22:20b) intervenes between his statement that he is coming soon and the final epistolary blessing (22:21). This sort of prayer also occurs in 1 Cor 16:22. Bornkamm (1969, 171–72) believes that such liturgical formulas both in Paul and Revelation show that both are to be read in liturgical gatherings, a context also suggested by Rev 1:3, which blesses the one who reads Revelation aloud and those who hear it.

Revelation is both an apocalypse and an apocalyptic circular letter. But those designations explain only a small portion of its structural features. Another element common to prologue and epilogue is the occurrence of prophetic sayings (1:7–8; 22:6–20a). Those in 1:7–8 foreshadow Christ's second coming (1:7), which brings about the complete sovereignty of God over the entire cosmos, and they contain God's statement of his identity, itself a claim to sovereignty (1:8). Thus a major theme of the visions to follow is stated at the outset—God's sovereignty exercised through Christ. The prophetic statements at the end of the book (22:6–20a) are mostly put in the form of words of Christ and serve to legitimate the content of the visions.

General Structure of 1:9–22:5

Although we generally follow Yarbro Collins with respect to structure, we diverge slightly from her concerning the relation of 1:9–3:22 to the rest of the book. We follow her in seeing two great cycles of visions in Revelation (see below), but rather than take 1:9–11:19 as the first great vision cycle, we break out 1:9–3:22 as the inaugural vision that lays the groundwork for all of the visions that follow. The elaborate introduction of this section that specifies where and when John receives the vision is unparalleled in the rest of the book. Further, the content of 1:9–3:22 is very different than the subsequent visions. After describing in detail the supernatural figure that John encounters, it addresses the present situations of the churches in relatively concrete language. The visions from 4:1 on deal with the eschatological events soon to happen to the whole universe. The inaugural vision of 1:9–3:22 constitutes a commissioning of the seer to prophesy not just about the visions in 4:1–11:19 but also about the subsequent visions in the book. So 1:9–3:22 is best seen as an introduction to all of Revelation's subsequent visions. Thus 1:9–22:5 is in three sections—an inaugural vision in 1:9–3:22 and two great cycles of visions, the first in 4:1–11:19 and the second in 12:1–22:5.

In line with our comments on the role of 1:9–3:22 as an introduction to the whole work, we see chapters 4 and 5, the heavenly throne room scene, as governing not only the seals and trumpets but also the second great vision cycle. Chapters 4 and 5 are an elaborate scene allowing the audience to experience all that follows as coming from God on the heavenly throne. No such scene precedes the second cycle, which begins abruptly with 12:1. The second great cycle is interlocked with the first through the appearance of the beast in 11:7 as well as by the commissioning of the seer in chapter 10 to prophesy about the contents of the second great vision cycle. The commission is delivered by "another mighty angel," which associates the scene with that of chapter 5, where a "mighty angel" asks who is worthy to open the sealed scroll.

The Number Seven as an Organizing Principle

The seven messages to the churches comprise the first of four numbered series of seven. The other three series are the seven seals, the seven trumpets, and the seven bowls. In addition to these series, Farrer discerns two other series of seven visions, these unnumbered. The first unnumbered series occurs between the seven trumpets and the seven bowls, and the second comes between what are called the Babylon appendix (17:1–19:10) and the new Jerusalem appendix (21:9–22:9). Yarbro Collins accepts the hypothesis that there are two unnumbered series, as do we. Therefore the bulk of the visions in Revelation take place in six series of seven items each. They are as follows:

Seven messages to the churches	2:1–3:22
Seven seals	6:1–8:5
Seven trumpets	8:6–11:19
First unnumbered series of seven	12:1–15:4
Seven bowls	16:1–21
Second unnumbered series of seven	19:11–21:8

Recapitulation

So far the analysis of Revelation's structure seems fairly straightforward. The question now becomes how the series of seven contained in the visions of eschatological events are related. Charles holds that the book's visions are chronologically arranged. One follows from the other, and taken together they trace the course of the eschatological events to its conclusion in the establishment of God's reign on earth. But even Charles recognizes that the book cannot bear that construction in its present form. For example, when he finds that he cannot discern a "logical" order in 20:4–22:21, he is reduced to saying, "The traditional order of the text exhibits a hopeless mental confusion and a tissue of irreconcilable contradictions" (1920, 1:1). He then resorts to source theories that account for repetitions and contradictions by ascribing them to unrelated sources. In addition, he rearranges and emends the text freely to arrive at what he believes makes sense, which he then accepts as the original text. Even these techniques do not solve all problems for him, however, so he suggests that the author died before finishing his work and that the work was completed by "a faithful but unintelligent disciple" (1920, 1:1). Yarbro Collins comments, "When such machinations are necessary to maintain a theory, the viability of that theory is highly questionable" (1976, 11).

Many commentators besides Charles resort to source theories to explain the repetitions, parallels, and contradictions in Revelation (see the analysis of Boismard 1965 in Ruiz 1989, 27–61). Such an approach was especially popular in the nineteenth and early twentieth centuries, when it was assumed that in their original form, ancient documents must have made "sense," meaning that they would conform to the standards of organization and presentation normal today, and when it was believed that corrupted texts could be reconstructed by application of those standards. Most commentators now see Revelation as a unity for the most part, because most of the book displays consistent language, style, and thought.

If Revelation is for the most part a unity, as we think it is, then we must posit some form of recapitulation to explain the repetitions and parallels throughout the work. Many of Revelation's earliest interpreters thought it contained recapitulation, but during the heyday of source criticism the theory was less popular.

Bornkamm revived it, and Yarbro Collins uses it systematically in her structural analysis. She defines recapitulation simply as "describing the same events several times in different ways" (1976, 8). That is, later passages in Revelation cover the same ground as earlier passages, sometimes from a different point of view, sometimes with further developments, sometimes with different images. There is no simple linear plot to follow through the visions. Throughout the commentary we shall note ways in which later passages recapitulate earlier ones.

Yarbro Collins demonstrates that a basic pattern appears in the five series that deal primarily with the future. The elements of the pattern are, "(1) persecution, (2) punishment of the nations or judgment, and (3) triumph of God, the Lamb and his followers or salvation" (1979, xiii). This pattern addresses the central problems in Revelation — the hostility of the world to faithful Christians, and Roman rule which is antithetical to God. These circumstances posed severe practical and theological problems for John and those who thought as he did. This pattern assures them that persecution is not the final word. The time is coming when the faithful will be vindicated, their oppressors punished, and the reign of God established on earth.

Yarbro Collins (1979, xiii) supplies the following list of the occurrence of these three elements in each of the series:

1. The seven seals
   - persecution 6:9–11
   - judgment 6:12–17
   - triumph 7:9–17

2. The seven trumpets
   - allusion to persecution 8:3–5
   - allusion to judgment 9:15
   - triumph 11:15–19

3. Seven unnumbered visions
   - persecution 12–13 (especially 13:7–10)
   - judgment 14:14–20
   - triumph 15:2–4

4. The seven bowls
   - persecution 16:4–7
   - judgment 16:17–20
   - triumph 19:1–10

5. Seven unnumbered visions
    persecution 20:9
    judgment 20:9–15
    triumph 21:1–22:5

Yarbro Collins does not include the first series in this analysis, but all three elements of the pattern are represented there as well. Persecution is mentioned in 2:10, 13, and 3:10, and is implied in the reference to the conquerors at the end of each message; punishment is implied in 2:26–27 and perhaps in 3:9 and in the reference to the conquerors; and reward is mentioned at the end of each message.

Two Great Cycles of Visions

Bornkamm thinks that the sealed scroll of chapter 5 cannot be read until all seals are broken, so he considers that disclosure of its content begins at 8:2 and ends at 22:6. He sees two parallel sections, 8:2–14:20 and 15:1–19:21. Arguing from parallels between the two parts, such as the obvious parallel between the content of the trumpets and the bowls, he sees the second main passage as recapitulating the first. He argues that whereas the first passage is cryptic and vague, the second passage covers the same material with more detail and clarity.

Yarbro Collins accepts the basic idea that the first part of Revelation is vaguer than the second and that the second part clarifies the first, but she shows convincingly that Bornkamm's division of the text is unlikely. Instead she argues for a break between 11:19 and 12:1. She sees 1:9–11:19 as a closely knit section. Revelation 4:1 begins a new section, but it has close contacts with the inaugural vision in 1:9–3:22, as we note in the commentary. Further, 4:1–11:19 is unified by various means. The heavenly throne room scene in chapter 4 includes the giving of a sealed scroll to the Lamb (representing Christ) in chapter 5, and the opening of the seals begins in 6:1. The seventh seal is opened at the beginning of chapter 8, and part of its contents is the coming forth of seven angels to blow seven trumpets. Thus the seven seals are securely tied to the seven trumpets. The trumpets conclude in 11:19. Then there is a new beginning in 12:1, with no formal link to the seventh trumpet. This clean break between 11:19 and 12:1 must be the division between the first and second great sections of Revelation. Therefore the first great cycle of visions consists of 1:9–11:19, and the second is made up of 12:1–22:5. The visions of 12:1–22:5 do indeed cover much of the same territory as do those of 1:9–11:19, and they do so with greater specificity and clarity. We agree with Yarbro Collins in seeing a break between 11:19 and 12:1 which divides two great cycles of eschatological visions, but, as explained above, we think it best to take 1:9–3:22 as an inaugural vision that introduces all of 4:1–22:5.

The seventh trumpet is a remarkably complete statement of the pattern Yarbro Collins traces in the five series of seven. Revelation 11:15–19 contains a proclamation of the coming of the kingdom of God and the messiah (triumph), an announcement that God's wrath has come against the nations (punishment), that reward has come to the righteous (triumph), and that the destroyers (persecution) will be destroyed. For all practical purposes, the book has reached its conclusion, and nothing more needs to happen. A clean break after 11:19 is therefore natural.

Interlocking Sections

Yarbro Collins (1976, 16–20) notes the device of interlocking that ties the sections of Revelation together. Passages which interlock the sections look both forward and backward. We discuss those in more detail in the commentary, but here we note the chief ones. The messages to the seven churches (chapters 2–3) are the first example. They look back to the epistolary introduction which marks Revelation as a circular letter to the seven churches (1:4), and they are also part of the inaugural vision, and so look forward to the visions to come. Similarly, 4:1 refers back to the figure that appears to John in chapter 1 and alludes to the command he gives John to write what is to come in the future (1:11), and it also introduces the eschatological visions to follow.

Yarbro Collins turns next to the transition between the seven seals and the seven trumpets (8:1–5). Part of the result of the opening of the seventh seal is the introduction of the trumpets series, thus firmly interlocking the two series. There is also a liturgical interlude (8:3–5) in which an angel takes fire from the altar, the same altar beneath which are the martyrs who pray for vengeance in the fifth seal (6:9–11), and throws it on the earth, a foreshadowing of the plagues to be hurled on the earth from heaven in the first four trumpets (8:7–12). The prayers of the faithful are mentioned in both 6:9–11 and 8:3.

There are still other interlocking passages. In 11:7, in a section (10:1–11:14) placed between the sixth and seventh trumpets, a beast appears from the abyss that foreshadows the beast in the second major cycle of visions (see especially chapters 13 and 17). Revelation 15:2–4 is the seventh of the unnumbered visions beginning with 12:1, but it occurs within a chapter that introduces the bowls series. Thus it ties the two series together just as the liturgical interlude in 8:3–5 ties the seals and trumpets together. The bowls series (15:1; 15:5–16:21) is closely linked to what follows, in that the seventh bowl describes the fall of Rome, elaborated in the Babylon appendix (17:1–19:10) that follows, and the Babylon appendix is parallel to the new Jerusalem appendix (21:9–22:9), thus tying the second unnumbered series of visions (19:11–21:8) into the rest of the book. Yarbro Collins makes the case that the open scroll given by the angel to the seer in chapter 10 symbolizes the content of the visions contained in the second great cycle (12:1–22:5). There are many more ways in which the parts of Revelation are connected. Indeed the entire book is held together by a web of such connections, and we shall note many of them in the commentary.

Structure and Meaning

Yarbro Collins's analysis yields a structure that allows the reader to experience Revelation as a coherent whole. But it does make reading the book a frustrating experience for anyone seeking a clear map of future events, because such a structure makes it impossible to turn the book into a series of clear predictions of concrete events. Charles's emendations make Revelation a book more susceptible to such use, but the book still refuses to provide clear predictions. Rather Revelation's purpose is to offer solace and hope to those alienated from Roman rule and local culture by repeating the pattern of persecution, punishment of the persecutors, and triumph of God and the faithful, so that it determines how the audience of the book sees the world.

Such repetition is common in other apocalyptic and prophetic works of the time (see Yarbro Collins 1976, 43–44). An excellent example is the biblical apocalypse Daniel, which so deeply influences Revelation. The same series of events is described in four passages in Daniel: 7:1–18, 19–27; 8:1–25;

10:12–12:3. Yarbro Collins concludes that in each of the apocalypses she lists the real point is not in the details of each of the variations of the basic story, but rather in the pattern embodied in each variation. Repetition makes the pattern more apparent. For Revelation, the pattern represents "the movement from persecution to salvation through combat." She cites two important students of myth, Paul Ricoeur and Claude Lévi-Strauss, who find recapitulation and repetition to be central to mythic language in general.

The function of a book like Revelation is not just to convey information. Rather it is to effect a change in the way the audience perceives the world and its basic attitude toward it. This is both cognitive and emotional. Mythic images, especially when replayed in variations, evoke deep-seated feelings that express humanity's most profound fears and hopes. They do so in a manner that is more poetic than informational. By setting up these deep resonances in the audience, the book of Revelation changes their perception of the world.

Introductory Verses

Chapter One

Prologue (Descriptive Title; 1:1–3)

Ancient books often begin with a few words about their authors and content, as does Revelation (1:1–3; see Luke 1:1–4; Acts 1:1–5; Josephus, *Ant.* 1 §§1–26). It is difficult, however, to find a precise parallel for the way Revelation begins. Phrases such as "descriptive title" (Yarbro Collins 1979, 4) and "titular summary" (Boring 1989, 64) have been coined to try to characterize 1:1–2. Charles (1920, 1:5) speaks of the tripartite nature of 1:1–3: the verses disclose the source of the revelation, outline its content, and pronounce a blessing on those who read it, hear it, and keep it.

The openings of prophetic books furnish intriguing comparisons, particularly given John's prophetic consciousness and his extensive use of the Bible. These comparisons are the more striking when we widen our view for a moment to include all of Rev 1:1–9. The following are the openings of some prophetic books:

> The vision of Isaiah son of Amos, which he saw concerning Judah and Jerusalem in the days of Uzziah, Jotham, Ahaz, and Hezekiah, kings of Judah. (Isa 1:1)
>
> The word of the LORD that came to Hosea son of Beeri, in the days of Kings Uzziah, Jotham, Ahaz, and Hezekiah of Judah, and in the days of King Jeroboam son of Joash of Israel. (Hos 1:1)
>
> The words of Amos, who was among the shepherds of Tekoa, which he saw concerning Israel in the days of King Uzziah of Judah and in the days of King Jeroboam son of Joash of Israel, two years before the earthquake. And he said: "The LORD roars from Zion, and utters his voice from Jerusalem; the pastures of the shepherds wither, and the top of Carmel dries up." (Amos 1:1–2)

Each of these prophetic passages offers parallels to Rev 1:1–9. They all begin with a self-identification of the prophet, as does Revelation, and a notification of the time when the prophecies were received, which correlates with Rev 1:9. The book of Isaiah styles itself as an account of a "vision" Isaiah "saw." John claims to write "all that he saw" (1:2). Hosea records the "word of the LORD" that came to him. John names the revelation he receives the "word of God" (1:2). After his self-identification, Amos begins with an oracle containing the essence of the message of the entire book (1:2). That corresponds with the prophetic saying and the divine oracle contained in Rev 1:7–8 (Schüssler Fiorenza 1991, 39). In the prophetic books, these introductions are in the third person, whereas in the rest of the books God or the prophet speaks mostly in the first person. The same is true of Revelation. These parallels suggest that John sees himself as a prophet like the biblical prophets. This is confirmed by John's reference to his book as "the words of the prophecy" in 1:3 (cf. 19:10; 22:7, 10, 18, 19).

At the same time, Rev 1:1–3 demonstrates the apocalyptic character of Revelation. The entire work is called in Greek an *apokalypsis* (1:1), meaning "revelation" or "unveiling" of what has hitherto been hidden. The occurrence of *apokalypsis* as the first word of this book led to its adoption as the title of an entire genre of ancient literature (see introduction under "Genre"), but it is unlikely that the author meant it so here, since it had never been used as such before. Rather, *apokalypsis* describes the nature and function of Revelation. It is a *revelatory* work. It is meant to "show" something that would otherwise remain unknown. The verb "to show" (*deiknymi*) occurs here and at other key points in the work (4:1; 17:1; 21:9, 10; 22:1, 6, 8). What is "shown" is the immediate future, "what must soon take place" (1:1). The visions in chapters 4 to 22 present that future as eschatological. An otherworldly dimension is introduced by the mention of an intermediary angel, a feature common in apocalypses. A note of urgency is sounded with the information that the future events described in Revelation are to take place "soon" (1:2) and by the final words of the blessing: "For the time is near" (1:3).

These initial verses (1:1–3) legitimate all of Revelation. They claim that John is not the source of what follows. The revelation is given by God to Jesus Christ, who gives it to an angel to deliver to John. John merely witnesses to the revelation. The title of the work is not "Revelation of John" but "Revelation of Jesus Christ."

To reject the revelation is to repudiate God and Jesus, to whom God entrusted the revelation. At the end of the book, Jesus himself bears witness to the truth of Revelation (22:6-7, 16, 20). Because of the divine origin of Revelation, it must be preserved free of alteration. It closes with solemn warnings to that effect: "I warn everyone who hears the words of the prophecy of this book: if anyone adds to them, God will add to that person the plagues described in this book; if anyone takes away from the words of the book of this prophecy, God will take away that person's share in the tree of life in the holy city, which are described in this book" (22:18-19).

Revelation is theocentric. The book is called the revelation of Jesus Christ, but it is God who gives Jesus that revelation, and he gives it to him so that Jesus might send it to John through an angel and so that John might in turn convey it to the churches. This five-part chain of transmission — God, Jesus, angel, John, churches — guarantees the truth of the revelation. At the same time, it expresses God's mysteriousness and his distance from humans. Although God accomplishes what happens on earth, he does so through intermediaries. God says little in the book, and even actions that originate with God are often spoken of as coming from the throne, or announced through an angel, or some similar device. This combination of a distant and mysterious God with the effectiveness of God's eschatological action is typical of apocalypticism. The use of an angelic intermediary is also typically apocalyptic, although angels' interpretive function is usually more extensive than is evident in Revelation. God's transcendence throughout Revelation makes the book's ending the more remarkable, for chapters 21 and 22 picture God on earth and portray an intimate relation between God and the saved at the end.

Jesus Christ "makes known" (Greek: *sêmainô*) the revelation by sending it by his angel to John (1:1). The verb *sêmainô* occurs only here in Revelation. It occurs only five other times in all of the New Testament, but four of the five uses are helpful as background to the revelatory use of the term in our text. In John 12:33, 18:32, and 21:19, it signifies Jesus' cryptic allusion to his own death. In Acts 11:28, the verb indicates a prediction by the Christian prophet Agabus. The most notable parallel to Revelation's use of the verb is found in the Septuagint version of Daniel 2, where it refers to God's revelation to Daniel of a vision and its interpretation, the revelation involving the disclosure of events to come (Dan 2:23, 30, 45). All of these elements—the cryptic nature of the commission as in John's gospel, the prophetic prediction as in the case of Agabus, and the apocalyptic revelation of future events—are present in Revelation's use of *sêmainô*. In Rev 1:1, the revelation is given to John so that he might convey it to God's "servants." The revelation is not complete until that happens.

God gives "the revelation of Jesus Christ" to Jesus, who imparts it to John, who then testifies to "the word of God and to the testimony of Jesus Christ, even to all that he saw" (1:2). The "revelation of Jesus Christ," the "word of God," the "testimony of Jesus Christ," and "all that he [John] saw" are essentially the same. They designate the same reality as is encompassed in the "words of the prophecy" in 1:3, meaning the book of Revelation itself. There is no clear distinction between the specific revelation contained in Revelation and the word of God in general. John's prophecy is not a subset of Christian revelation. It is identical with it.

For John, the "testimony of Jesus" is twofold. First, Jesus bore witness to the sovereignty of God during his earthly life, for which he was put to death. Second, the visions in Revelation are a continuation of Jesus' witness to God's sovereignty. Jesus testifies to the truth of Revelation in 22:20: "The one who testifies to these things says, 'Surely, I am coming soon.' " The two aspects of Jesus' testimony are of a piece. Jesus' earthly testimony establishes the possibility of Christians opposing the blasphemous forces arrayed against God and God's faithful as Jesus himself opposed them. Christian testimony is made possible first by Jesus' original testimony, which constituted Christians as God's loyal people, and then by the revelation Jesus sends through John (and angels), which discloses the necessity of opposing the satanic forces.

John's concept of the "word of God" is influenced by the Bible. There the word of God is active and effective. God creates the world with his word (Genesis 1). The divine word as mediated through the prophets accomplishes what it predicts. As Isaiah says, "So shall my word be that goes out from my mouth; it shall not return to me empty, but it shall accomplish that which I purpose, and succeed in the thing for which I sent it" (55:11). For John, God's word in the sealed scroll accomplishes what it describes as the scroll is unsealed. God's and Jesus' oracles occur at key points in the book as solemn words that are effective. Generally speaking, all of Revelation is an effective word from God that accomplishes what it describes.

The first of seven beatitudes in Revelation is in 1:3 (the others are 14:13; 16:15; 19:9; 20:6; 22:7, 14). All of the beatitudes define the boundaries of the Christian churches as John believes they should be. This is characteristic of beatitudes as a form. They are a didactic tool defining proper conduct and attitude. Jesus adopted this form in a forceful prophetic critique of society. Shocking beatitudes like "Blessed are you poor, for yours is the kingdom of God" (Luke 6:20) imply that the kingdom does not belong to the rich. Luke adds the woe, "But woe to you who are rich, for you have received your consolation" (Luke 6:24). Through this beatitude, Luke's Jesus turns society on its head. Those usually considered unhappy are called happy; those usually considered happy are warned of impending disaster. Revelation fits into this prophetic tradition. For John, the powerful are about to fall; the oppressed are to be vindicated. The world is not as it appears. The blessed are those who "keep" the "words of the prophecy" (1:3), not those who persecute the faithful. Those who believe the prophecy are blessed, because only they know the universe from God's viewpoint and are in a position to be on God's side in the struggle between God and Satan.

There is a similar beatitude at the end of the book: "Blessed is the one who keeps the words of the prophecy of this book" (22:7), so the beatitudes in 1:3 and 22:7 frame the whole of Revelation. A couple of verses after the beatitude in 22:7, an angel calls himself "a fellow servant with you and your comrades [brothers] the prophets, and with those who *keep* the words of this book" (22:9). The verb "to keep" is common in Revelation in this connection, as is the verb "to hold." Hearers are exhorted to "keep" or "hold" the prophecy of this book, the witness of Jesus, the commandments of God, and so on. Such language suggests that the audience is in jeopardy of *not* holding on to the truth, an impression bolstered by the messages to the churches of chapters 2 and 3. It also suggests that what is to be "held" is not simply information or doctrine. It is a moral stance, a way of life, that must be guarded against the encroachments of the evil world.

The beatitude assumes a situation where the church gathers for a public reading of Revelation. Nehemiah 8:2 mentions a public reading of the Torah, and New Testament documents attest to public reading of scripture in Jewish contexts (Luke 4:16;

Acts 13:15). Both Col 4:16 and 1 Thess 5:27 imply that Paul's letters were read in a gathering of the church, and 1 Tim 4:13 refers to public reading of scripture. Such public reading is of course necessary where literacy is low, as in the ancient world, but it is also appropriate to the sort of liturgical gatherings indispensable to communal life then and now. The numerous liturgical elements of Revelation make reading it aloud particularly appropriate (see Vanni 1991).

There are two additional biblical allusions in 1:1-3. God is said to inform his servants about what must soon take place, recalling Amos 3:7: "Surely the LORD does nothing, without revealing his secret to his servants the prophets" (cf. Revelation 10). "Servants" in 1:1 refers not just to Christian prophets but to all faithful Christians, and Christians are given information about what must soon take place through Revelation, characterized as a book of prophecy. The phrase "what must soon take place" may also be an allusion to the book of Daniel, where Daniel says, "There is a God in heaven who reveals mysteries, and he has disclosed to King Nebuchadnezzar what will happen at the end of days" (Dan 2:28).

For Revelation, what is revealed is what *must* take place (*dei genesthai*). The course of future events has already been determined by God. The prophets usually believe that impending punishment can be averted by repentance. Apocalyptic prophecy believes that future events will unfold as God has decreed regardless of human activity. The Greek verb *dei* ("it is necessary") is repeated eight times in Revelation, indicating the determinism typical of apocalypses.

There are numerous points of contact between Revelation's prologue (1:1-3) and its epilogue (22:6-21), thus forming an inclusio for the entire book. An inclusio is a frame. Something is repeated at the beginning and end of a passage, thus setting off the passage as a unit. We have already drawn attention to the similar beatitudes in 1:3 and 22:7 exhorting the audience to "keep" "the revelation." In both 1:1-2 and 22:6-7, God is seen as the source of the revelation. In both, the revelation comes to John through an angelic intermediary. In both places, what is revealed is "what must soon take place." In 1:2, John is called God's "servant" who conveys the revelation to God's "servants," and he describes his book as a "prophecy" (1:3). In 22:6, God is called the "God of the spirit of the prophets," and he sends his angel to "show his servants what must soon take place." In 1:2, the revelation is termed the "testimony of Jesus Christ." In 22:16, Jesus refers to the "testimony" he sends to the churches, and in 22:20, Jesus is the one who "testifies" to these things. Twice in 1:1–3 and once in 22:6 the author says that the book's visions concern imminent events. Interpretations of Revelation that make it a prediction of distant future happenings ignore these indications. The end is near. Everything up to and including the binding of Satan will happen soon.

When the beatitude in 1:3 says that the time is near, it uses the word *kairos* for "time." In New Testament usage, this Greek word frequently indicates a temporal point that is of particular significance in God's plan. When Revelation claims, "The time is near," it echoes the eschatological tone evident in many parts of the New Testament, including the message attributed to Jesus. Jesus' first words in the gospel of Mark are, "The time [*kairos*] is fulfilled, and the kingdom of God has come near; repent, and believe in the good news" (1:15; cf. 13:33; Matt 8:29; 1 Cor 4:5; see Ford 1975, 374, on *kairos*). Revelation also concerns the coming of God's kingdom to earth, and it sees that coming as near.

Chapter Two

Epistolary Opening (1:4–8)

Sender, Addressees, Greeting (1:4–5a)

Revelation 1:4–6 has the form of the opening of a typical Pauline letter. Paul's letters begin with noting the sender and addressees, and then sending greetings. There usually follow a brief prayer and thanksgiving. Revelation 1:4–5a contains the first three elements—sender, addressees, greeting. Revelation is like Paul's letter to the Galatians in that there is no prayer and thanksgiving, unusual for Paul. Paul does include a brief doxology in Gal 1:5, as does Revelation in 1:5b–6. A doxology is direct praise of God, and so it is a form of prayer, but somewhat different from Paul's usual form.

John's mention of the sender and addressees is quite terse. In contrast to most letters of Paul, where Paul, in identifying himself as the sender, takes the opportunity to characterize himself in a way that enhances his authority, John simply gives his name. John is undoubtedly known to his audience, so he does not need to identify himself, but of course the same would apply to Paul. John's terseness in referring to himself in 1:4 accords with his avoidance of applying to himself any title whatever throughout the book. The authority that John expects Revelation to carry comes from the fact that it is divine revelation.

John addresses his apocalyptic letter "to the seven churches that are in Asia" (1:4). Asia means the Roman province of Asia, located in the western part of Asia Minor (present-day Turkey). Like Paul, John uses the word "church" to denote the local church. We learn later that John writes to these churches because he is instructed to do so by Jesus (1:11). That later reference lists the churches by name. They are Ephesus, Smyrna, Pergamum, Thyatira, Sardis, Philadelphia, and Laodicea. It is not by chance that there are seven churches. As noted earlier, the number seven permeates Revelation. Most commentators take it to mean completion, so that in writing to seven churches, John in fact addresses all churches. Yarbro Collins questions whether there is any solid evidence that seven means completion and looks instead to the widespread use of seven in the ancient world (see introduction under "Numbers in Revelation").

Revelation 1:4b–5a is the letter's greeting. In contrast to its sender and addressees, which are unexpanded, here Revelation freely expands the Pauline formula. It begins in a way that is precisely parallel to Pauline letters: "Grace to you and peace from . . . " "Grace" is a common word in Pauline letters, but in Revelation it is used only here and in 22:21, a verse which imitates the closing of a Pauline letter. "Peace," used by Paul in the greetings at the beginning and ending of his letters as well as in his descriptions of the new relationship to God in Christ, appears only here and in passing in 6:4. In Rev 1:4–5, grace and peace come from God, the seven spirits before God's throne, and Jesus. The author thinks of himself as a mediator between God and Jesus, on the one hand, and the churches, on the other (Yarbro Collins 1979, 7).

Some commentators consider 1:4b–5a a trinitarian formulation, although no one claims that the full trinitarian doctrine defined centuries later is completely present here or that there is thought of three persons in one God, coequal and coeternal, with the Holy Spirit processing from the Father and the Son. But it is misleading even to speak of an early form of trinitarian thought here, for the seven spirits are not an expression for the Holy Spirit. There is no clear conception of a Holy Spirit in Revelation, even in the biblical sense. The identity of the seven spirits will be discussed below. It is true, however, that Revelation expresses a high christology. Jesus is seen as close to the Father in function and authority, although the supremacy of God the Father is preserved.

The author's predilection for threes is reflected in the three entities from whom grace and peace come, God, the seven spirits, and Jesus. God is characterized as follows: "From him who is [*ho ôn*] and who was and who is to come," another threefold formulation. The biblical root of this designation of God is found in Exodus 3. There God reveals the divine name to Moses. The significance of names was deeper in the ancient world than in the modern, and it was frequently thought that one's name contained something of one's person. Knowledge of someone's name conferred a degree of power over that person. This was particularly true of the names of supernatural beings. In revealing his name to Moses, God was to some degree revealing himself.

Because of the importance attached to disclosure of the divine name, Exodus 3 shows signs of repeated expansion and reworking. Most relevant to Revelation is God's first answer to Moses' question about the divine name: "God said to Moses, 'I am who I am.' " This is an effort to decode the divine name "Yahweh" found in the Hebrew Bible by deriving it from the Hebrew verb "to be" (*hyh*). The Septuagint (LXX), a translation of the Jewish scriptures into Greek, translates it, "I am the one who is" (*egô eimi ho ôn*). "The one who is" is in the form of the present participle of the verb "to be" with the definite article (*ho ôn*). The first part of God's title in Rev 1:4, "who is," is the same Greek construction (*ho ôn*). This designation of God is also found in the LXX of Jer 1:6; 14:3; 39(32):17; Wisd 13:1 (Ford 1975, 376; she also points to Philo, *Abr.* 121; *Quod Deus* 69; and Josephus, *Ant.* 8 §350, as well as rabbinic and targumic literature; see also Charles 1920, 1:10).

A similar designation for God is also found in non-Jewish authors. The most frequently adduced example occurs in the Greek author Pausanias of the second century C.E., who mentions an inscription that reads "Zeus was, Zeus is, Zeus will be" (for other examples, see Charles 1920, 1:10–11). Revelation differs from both Jewish and Gentile examples in that the third element of the title is not "who will be" but "who is to come." This alteration allows the title to incorporate two aspects of God — God's eternity and God's involvement in history. The past and present uses of the verb "to be" signify God's eternity, and the shift from the verb "to be" to the verb "to come" implies that God has a dynamic relation to the world which is about to change. God is distant, but God will soon visit the world. As George Caird says, "It sets the church's coming ordeal against a background of God's eternity, but it also brings God down into the arena of history" (1966, 16). The eternal God is about to visit his creation, and his coming will radically change everything.

The second member of the triad from whom grace and peace come is "the seven spirits who are before his [God's] throne." There are two major interpretations of these spirits. The more unlikely one is that they are a sevenfold expression of God's own presence or that of the Holy Spirit. The text usually used to support such a reading is Isa 11:2, where God's Spirit is defined in terms of six qualities that in later interpretation became seven (see Charles 1920, 1:11). A more likely proposal is that the seven spirits are independent supernatural beings that belong to God's heavenly entourage. If so, they are probably angels and are best seen as the seven angels (archangels) associated with God in various texts.

This sort of triple formulation of God, Jesus, and the angels is found in other eschatological contexts. For example, Luke 9:26 speaks of the arrival of the Son of Man "when he comes in his glory and the glory of the Father and of the holy angels." Similarly, 1 Tim 5:21 gives a solemn warning "in the presence of God and of Christ Jesus and of the elect angels."

The biblical text standing behind the seven spirits of Rev 1:4 is found in Zechariah 4. There the prophet has a vision of "a lampstand all of gold, with a bowl on the top of it; there are seven lamps on it" (4:2). An interpreting angel later identifies the seven lamps for the prophet: "These seven are the eyes of the Lord, which range through the whole earth" (4:10). This passage from Zechariah is very influential in John's vision, as we will see later (see our comments on the lampstands in 1:12–13 and on the two prophets in chapter 11). The origin of Zechariah's image is the menorah, the lampstand with seven lamps found in God's temple (Exod 25:31–40; 37:17–24). To decide how Revelation uses the image, it is useful to look elsewhere in the book for passages that shed light on the seven spirits.

Later in chapter 1 there is a vision of the cosmic Christ. John sees Jesus surrounded by seven golden lampstands, holding seven stars in his hand (1:12, 16). In 1:20, Jesus informs the seer that the lampstands are the seven churches and the stars are "the angels of the seven churches." In 3:1, Jesus is described as "the one who has the seven spirits of God and the seven stars." The throne vision of chapter 4 includes mention of "seven flaming torches, which are the seven spirits of God" in front of God's throne (4:5). In 5:6, Jesus is presented as a lamb with seven horns and seven eyes, "which are the seven spirits of God sent out into all the earth." The collection of these passages does not allow a clear identification of the seven spirits. It also warns us that the imagery of Revelation is fluid, for in 4:5 the seven spirits are torches burning before God's throne, and in 5:6 they are the Lamb's eyes, which, like the eyes in Zechariah 4, roam the earth. The fact that these spirits can be sent out into the world, that they are spoken of in parallel with God and Jesus in 1:4–5, and that they are paralleled with the seven stars (angels) in 3:1 indicates that they are independent supernatural entities, closely associated with God and Jesus but subordinate to them. This makes it unlikely that they are merely a sevenfold expression for God or God's Spirit.

The seven spirits are paralleled with the seven stars in 3:1. This raises the possibility that the spirits are angels, since 1:20 says that the stars in Jesus' hand are angels. Charles (1920, 1:13) notes that stars are angels in *2 Enoch* 30:14; 86:1, 3, and that stars are conscious beings capable of disobedience in *2 Enoch* 18:13–16; 21:1–6. Angels are not often called spirits, but there are instances of such usage. Hebrews 1:7 quotes Ps 104:4 to the effect that "God makes his angels winds," where "winds" is the same word as "spirits" in both the Hebrew and Greek versions of the psalm and in the Greek of Hebrews. In Heb 1:14, the author asks, "Are not all angels spirits in the divine service, sent to serve for the sake of those who are to inherit salvation?" *Jubilees* 2:2 closely associates angels and spirits. (See also 1 Kgs 22:21–23, where the spirit is apparently an angel [see Charles, 1920, 1:13].)

There are instances of seven angels in Jewish documents. In Tobit, a Jewish work from the fourth or third century B.C.E., an angel declares, "I am Raphael, one of the seven angels who stand ready and enter before the glory of the Lord" (12:15). Ezekiel may refer to these seven angels when he pictures seven supernatural figures who serve as God's agents to punish Jerusalem in Ezek 9:2. *First Enoch* 20 names the leading angels; in some manuscripts there are six, but others have seven. Later in *1 Enoch,* reference is made to "the seven first snow-white ones," which appear to be angels (90:21). In *T. Levi* 8:2, Levi has a vision in which he is clothed in the priestly garments by seven figures in white garments, apparently angels. The ultimate origin of the seven supernatural beings in God's entourage in all these texts is probably to be found in ancient Near Eastern conceptions. Charles (1920, 11–12) mentions in particular the seven Babylonian astral deities.

It is not surprising that John mentions God's angelic entourage at this early point in his book. Angels are intimately involved in the action to follow. God and Jesus share absolute sovereignty over all creation, and angelic intermediaries aid them both in revealing what is to take place and in accomplishing it.

The third entity from whom grace and peace come is Jesus

Christ. He bears three titles, corresponding to three stages in Jesus' work. He is "faithful witness" in his death, "firstborn of the dead" in his resurrection, and he then becomes "ruler of the kings of the earth." The noun "witness" (*martys*) always occurs in Revelation in association with death. It is applied to Jesus (here and in 3:14) and to Antipas, who is said in 2:13 to have given his life for the faith. It is applied to two unidentified witnesses in 11:3, who also are put to death. In 17:6, a prostitute, symbolizing Rome, is said to be "drunk with the blood of the saints and the blood of the witnesses of Jesus." Revelation was written to encourage its recipients to resist Hellenistic culture and Roman rule by their style of life as well as by public confession in the context of a trial, when necessary. They must be willing to die, if such witness leads to death. Jesus is the prime example of such witness to the death, and the fact that he was raised gives hope to those who follow in his footsteps. Although in Revelation the noun "witness" (*martys*) has not yet achieved the technical meaning of one who dies for the faith as it will in later Christian history, its meaning is tending in that direction (Trites 1973).

The adjective "faithful" modifies "witness" in Jesus' title here (1:5) and in its other two uses, applied to the slain Antipas (2:13) and to Jesus (3:14). In 2:10, members of the church at Smyrna are exhorted in the face of persecution to be "faithful until death."

Jesus' second and third titles are "firstborn of the dead, and the ruler of the kings of the earth." In Rev 3:14, Jesus is spoken of as the beginning or origin (*archê*) of creation (see our commentary on 3:14). The same collocation of resurrection, sovereignty, and being the beginning of creation is found in the christology of Colossians. The hymn in Colossians 1 speaks of Jesus as "the firstborn from the dead, so that he might come to have first place in everything" (Col 1:18). Earlier in the hymn, Jesus is "the firstborn of all creation" (Col 1:15), assuming the sort of wisdom christology contained in John 1:1–18 (cf. Heb 1:6; 12:23).

The third title is "ruler of the kings of the earth." The sovereignty of Jesus as over all earthly authorities is an expression of God's sovereignty over the world and sounds a major theme in Revelation. To those outside of Christianity, Caesar seems to rule, and the Roman empire seems invincible. But Christians, and particularly those with whom John shares his vision, know that things are not as they appear. The true ruler is God, who shares his throne with Jesus. That state of affairs is already manifest in heaven, and it will soon be manifest on earth as well. It is expressed most powerfully toward the end of the vision when Jesus appears at the end of the present era riding on a white horse, bent on striking down the nations and ruling over them, and carrying the names "King of kings and Lord of lords" (19:11-16). Boring (1989, 76) eloquently captures John's intention: "The phrase 'ruler of kings on earth' attributes to Jesus the title claimed by the Roman Caesars, whose claim to sovereignty John wants his readers to see as a false caricature of the real lordship of Christ."

Psalm 89, a messianic psalm in praise of the God who chose David and his lineage to be kings over Israel forever, contains in short space the same elements applied to Jesus in Rev 1:5a—witness, firstborn, and sovereignty. Speaking of David, God says, "I will make him the firstborn, the highest of the kings of earth" (Ps 89:29). Later, God declares, "His line shall endure forever, and his throne endure before me like the sun. It shall be established forever like the moon, an enduring witness in the skies" (89:37). Jesus is the Davidic messiah in Revelation (see 3:7; 5:5; 22:16), so the use of Psalm 89 as a source of titles for him is appropriate. Isaiah 55:3-4 also associates David's rule and sovereignty over the nations with the theme of witness: "I will make with you an everlasting covenant, my steadfast, sure love for David. See, I made him a witness to the peoples, a leader and commander for the peoples." In these biblical examples as in those from Revelation, what is witnessed to is God's sovereignty.

Doxology (1:5b-6)

In Gal 1:3-5 and 2 Cor 1:3-4, Paul substitutes a doxology for the prayer and thanksgiving found at the beginning of his other letters. Revelation's form corresponds to Galatians and 2 Corinthians. Doxology is a form with roots in the Bible. It is a form that expresses the patron-client relationship that models the divine-human relationships in the Bible. God does something for humans that is experienced as favor, not as something owed. In return, humans give honor to God and are loyal to him. This mirrors the everyday human patron-client relationship in the ancient Near East and during the Hellenistic and Roman periods. The ultimate issue in Revelation is loyalty—one must choose loyalty either to God and Jesus or to Satan and Rome. One must give public praise to one or the other, so the doxologies contained in the work are crucial. J. P. M. Sweet puts it well, drawing on Ignatius of Antioch to support his point: "Worship is the true creaturely response of man to God and in itself the defeat of the rebellious powers which were operative in Egypt and Babylon, and now Rome" (1979, 62).

The doxology is addressed to Jesus, attesting to his exalted status. Three activities are predicated of Jesus, corresponding to John's predilections for threes and to the three titles assigned to Jesus in the greeting. Schüssler Fiorenza (1991, 42) points to the doxological form, the use of participles, and the switch from "you" to "us" as indicators that this is a hymnic formulation. Based on her analysis of the language, mentioned below, she concludes that John has taken traditional confessional language, probably from a baptismal context, and reworked it to conform to a Pauline prescript. This exemplifies the author's creative reuse of tradition.

The first two of Jesus' activities in the doxology, "loves" and "freed," are participles, the first in the present and the second in the aorist (the Greek tense expressing a simple past action). The present tense of the first verb, "loves," means that John refers to Jesus' ongoing love for Christians. That love is particularly meaningful to Christians who feel themselves separated from the world and perhaps about to undergo persecution. Schüssler Fiorenza (1991, 42) lists analogous instances of the verb "to love" in the New Testament and observes that they occur in passages that depend on formulations drawn from baptismal contexts (Gal 2:20; 2 Thess 2:16; Eph 1:5–6; 2:4ff.; 5:25ff.). In these instances the verb "to love" is in the aorist, stressing what Jesus has done for Christians in the past. Given the prevalence of the aorist formulation in the New Testament, the author's use of the present is significant as an assurance to Christians of Jesus' ongoing love for them.

Jesus' next activity is that he "freed us from our sins by his blood" (1:5). Emphasis on the blood of Jesus as freeing us from alienation from God is prominent in Pauline circles (Roloff [1993, 26] cites Gal 3:13; 4:5; 1 Cor 6:20; 7:23; 1 Pet 1:18). Schüssler Fiorenza (1991, 42) notes that although the phrase "to him who has freed (*lysanti*) us" is unique in the New

Testament, words from the same root (*lyô*) frequently mean redemption (e.g., *lytron, lytrousthai, apolytrôsis*) and are associated with "blood" (Rom 3:24–26; Eph 1:7; Heb 9:12; 1 Pet 1:19). Both baptismal and eucharistic contexts have been suggested for such formulas; in either case, we again see John dependent on Christian tradition. A textual variant substituting "washed" (*lousanti*) for "freed" (*lysanti*) may have resulted from a scribe hearing a baptismal formulation behind the phrase. By Christ's blood, Christians have been freed from the world of sin. A reminder of the price of that liberation makes sense in a book which exhorts its listeners to be willing to pay a similar price for maintaining that freedom. In 12:11, the liberating benefit of Christ's blood can be accessed only by those willing to shed their own blood: "But they have conquered him [Satan] by the blood of the Lamb and by the word of their testimony, for they did not cling to life even in the face of death."

Revelation 1:6 now suddenly shifts from participial forms to the indicative: "and made us to be a kingdom, priests serving his God and Father." The biblical background of this clause is Exod 19:6. In that chapter, God, having freed Israel from Egypt and brought them to Mount Sinai, speaks to Moses and tells him to remind the people that he has freed them. He continues, "Now, therefore, if you obey my voice and keep my covenant, you shall be my treasured possession out of all the peoples. Indeed, the whole earth is mine, but you shall be for me a priestly kingdom and a holy nation" (19:5–6). Revelation 1:6, with its mention of priests, kingdom, and a nation, is the first clear allusion to the exodus in Revelation. The Hebrew reads literally, "a kingdom of priests," whereas Revelation has the somewhat awkward "made us a kingdom, priests," but Revelation's version does correspond to other ancient versions of Exodus (Charles 1920, 1:16). Whether or not it is due to John's reworking of the original reading of Exod 19:6, his use of two nouns is fitting, since he portrays Christians both as kings (5:10; 20:4, 6; 22:5) and priests (5:10; 7:15; 20:4, 6). As kings, they will rule over the earth with Jesus. This will be a reversal of the present, when Christians are ruled by the agents of Satan.

The application of Exod 19:6 to Christians is an implicit claim that it is the church that is now the true people of God (Caird 1966, 17). Revelation fits the general Christian trend of seeing itself as the fulfillment of Judaism. Paul claims that the church is now the Israel of God (Gal 6:16); Matthew says Jesus fulfills

Torah (e.g., Matt 5:17–20); the gospel of John finds in the Christian community the reality only hinted at in Moses' Torah (e.g., John 1:17); Hebrews sees in Christ's death the reality of which the Jewish cult was only the shadow (e.g., Hebrews 9; Boring [1989, 78] also points to Phil 3:3; Jas 1:1; and 1 Pet 1:1, 17).

Exodus 19:6 associates priesthood and kingship, thus connecting what in the twentieth century we often think of as the religious and secular realms. For John and his contemporaries, no such dichotomy holds. Kingship and priesthood go together (1:6; 5:10; 20:6). Priesthood has political consequences, and kingship is closely entangled with religion. The author sees the religious-political phenomenon of the imperial cult as the perfect symbol for the incompatibility of loyalty to God and emperor cult. Worship and loyalty are synonymous. Willingness to witness to God's sovereignty as Jesus did leads to membership in a community that worships God as his priests and shares in the reign of God and Jesus.

The closest parallel to Revelation's collocation of redemption through Christ's blood and establishment as kings and priests occurs in 1 Peter. That letter reminds its readers that they were "ransomed" (the verb used is *lytroô,* a root related to the root *lyô* used in Rev 1:5 for "freed") from their sinful past, "not with perishable things like silver or gold, but with the precious blood of Christ, like that of a lamb without defect or blemish." Later the letter says, "But now you are a chosen race, a royal priesthood, a holy nation" (2:9; see also 2:4). Common to 1 Peter and Revelation are being freed by Christ's blood, Christ being compared to a lamb, priesthood, kingship, and nation. First Peter is often said to draw on a baptismal liturgy, so this strengthens Schüssler Fiorenza's point that Revelation's author draws on baptismal traditions here.

For Revelation, all true Christians are priests. Although Israel had a special priestly caste, language about universal priesthood is possible even within the Hebrew Bible. Isaiah 61:6 says, "You shall be called priests of the LORD, you shall be named ministers of our God; you shall enjoy the wealth of the nations, and in their riches you shall glory" (see commentary on Rev 21:24–26). The use of such language in Isaiah does not imply the abolition of the Levitical priesthood in Israel, but in Revelation it does become part of the polemic against non-Christian Judaism, as becomes still clearer when the new Jerusalem is without a temple because now God is truly present (21:22). That Christians now represent a kingdom implies that where Christians are, there God reigns (Roloff 1993, 26).

The three activities of Jesus in 1:5b–6, loving, freeing, and making a kingdom and priests, are closely connected and can all be read against the backdrop of the exodus story, for God loved Israel, freed them from Egypt, brought them to Mount Sinai, and made them kings and priests. This exodus paradigm of kings and priests undergirds all of Revelation. The kingship of Christ, so emphasized throughout the book, is one that he shares both with his Father and with Christians (see esp. 3:21). The kingship of Christians will be manifest in the future, but it is also a present, hidden fact.

Jesus is praised for having made Christians kings and priests. Christians already share in the kingship of Christ, so things are not as they appear. There is an already and a not yet here that are also typical of Paul, another apocalyptic thinker who insists on the present reality of what is to be made public in the future. The kingship of Christ, shared with Christians, is the message of Revelation. In a sense, the whole of Revelation is contained in this doxology, and what follows is just a detailing of how this kingship will work itself out so that the entire cosmos, the Roman empire in particular, will embody it. G. A. Krodel (1989, 86) expresses it well: "Before he unfolds his futuristic, apocalyptic eschatology, he has articulated the present eschatological existence of his hearers, an existence that contradicts the claims of the world and therefore must be affirmed ever anew in faith and perseverance, in trials and tribulations, in worship and in praise."

Christians have been made priests through Jesus. Priests mediate between God and humanity. They represent God to humanity and humanity to God. Revelation 7:9–17 connects the priesthood of the faithful with the blood of Christ. There John sees Christians who have already come though the great tribulation and who have "washed their robes and made them white in the blood of the Lamb" (7:14). They are gathered around God's heavenly throne, and they "worship him day and night within his temple," so they are priests, since only priests worship within the temple itself. In the thousand-year messianic kingdom, those who will give their lives in loyalty to God will rise with Christ: "They will be priests of God and of Christ, and they will reign with him a thousand years" (20:4). As in 1:6, priesthood and kingship go together in 20:4.

The doxology of 1:5–6 concludes by ascribing "glory and dominion" to Christ (cf. 1 Pet 4:11; 1 Chr 29:11). The same things (in addition to blessing and honor) are ascribed to God and Jesus jointly in 5:13. This makes sense within the context of patron-client relations seen in a political framework. Clients must honor their patron by recognizing the power the patron possesses. Unless the clients publicly recognize that power, the patron's position is in jeopardy. Glory is honor, and glory is ascribed to God throughout Revelation. The word appears sixteen times in this connection. To ascribe glory is also to submit to one's sovereign. When a portion of Jerusalem is destroyed by God, its inhabitants are terrified and so give God glory (11:13). In contrast, despite plagues poured from heaven on rebellious humans, they refuse to repent and give God glory (16:9).

The doxology in 1:5b–6 ends with the word "amen," a Hebrew word found in prayers and liturgies that signifies assent. The entire doxology reminds us that Revelation was meant to be read in the context of Christian worship and is permeated with liturgical elements.

Prophetic Pronouncement and Divine Oracle (1:7–8)

Verses 7 and 8 might seem on first glance to be intrusive in their contexts. The epistolary introduction proper ends with verse 6, and the seer begins a direct communication with his addressees in verse 9. The intervening verses are a prophetic pronouncement (verse 7) and a divine oracle (verse 8). There is no strict parallel for the insertion of prophetic pronouncements or divine oracles at this point in John's formal model, the Pauline letter.

Although Rev 1:7–8 might appear to be intrusive, it is not really so in the context of Revelation as a whole. John calls his book a prophecy (1:3; 22:7, 10, 18–19), and the entire book is based on John's prophetic experiences. As he writes, from time to time the prophetic spirit overwhelms him so that oracles emerge in the text that seem somewhat out of place. Other examples are in 14:13 and 16:15. The two prophetic sayings in 1:7–8 announce the two main themes of the entire book. Verse 7 announces the second coming of Christ, this time as judge of the whole world. This announcement is fulfilled later, particularly in 19:11–21. Verse 8 contains words of God, claiming his sovereignty over the cosmos.

The prophetic pronouncement of 1:7 reads,

> Look! He is coming with the clouds;
>   every eye will see him,
> even those who pierced him;
>   and on his account all the tribes of the earth will wail.
> So it is to be. Amen.

This verse combines Dan 7:13 and Zech 12:10. The author makes extensive use of both Daniel and Zechariah throughout Revelation, but especially of Daniel. Daniel 7 is a favorite source for both Jewish and Christian traditions in our period, and it is the origin of the title Son of Man, so important to the gospels. Although the prophetic saying in 1:7 does not use the phrase "son of man," it borrows the imagery of one coming on the clouds from Dan 7:13, which reads, "I saw one like a son of man [NRSV: 'human being'], coming with the clouds of heaven." Revelation 1:7 combines this with Zech 12:10 (which reads in part, "When they look on the one whom they have pierced, they shall mourn for him, as one mourns for an only child, and weep bitterly over him, as one weeps over a firstborn").

In itself all this is rather cryptic, for Revelation does not say who was pierced, nor why the tribes mourn. But in the context of Revelation, this must describe Christ's second coming. The combination of Dan 7:13 and Zech 12:10 applied to Christ's parousia (second coming) is in Matt 24:30 as well. There are differences between Matt 24:30 and Rev 1:7, for Matthew identifies the one who comes as the Son of Man, and he does not mention piercing specifically. The gospel of John refers to Zech 12:10 in its narrative of the crucifixion, and John does mention the element of piercing: "They will look on the one whom they have pierced" (John 19:37). The gospel of John does not apply the verse to Jesus' eschatological coming, however, but simply to the crucifixion itself. The use of Zech 12:10 in John 19 and the combination of Dan 7:13 and Zech 12:10 in Matt 24:30 show that our author reworks Christian tradition in Rev 1:7.

Revelation 1:7 fulfills an important function in the book. It predicts at the outset the triumphant return of Christ, the one whom Satan and Satan's earthly allies put to death for his witness to God's sovereignty. The entire world will see Christ's return, particularly those who killed him. They will mourn when they see him come. The text does not make clear whether their mourning constitutes repentance or despair. Boring (1989,

80) suggests that the author leaves this purposely vague, so that some will take it as promise and others as warning, depending on their stance toward Christ. Several times in the book the author refers to the repentance of the earth's inhabitants, but they usually fail to repent (9:20–21; 16:9, 11; but see 11:13).

The prophetic pronouncement is followed by the words, "Yes [NRSV: 'So it is to be']. Amen." The words are the Greek and Hebrew words of confirmation, respectively. The Hebrew word is used in liturgical contexts to signal assent to a prayer, as when it confirms the doxology of Rev 1:6 (see also 5:14; 7:12; 19:4; 22:21). A parallel to the use of "amen" in 1:7 occurs in Rev 22:20. In that verse there is a direct statement by Jesus himself that he is coming, followed by the words, "Amen. Come, Lord Jesus!" Those words are a communal response to Jesus' oracle that he is coming, or at least are the response of the author on behalf of the community. The references to Jesus' coming at the beginning and end of Revelation (1:7; 22:20), in each case followed by the word "Amen," constitute yet another element connecting the beginning of the book to the end. In this case the element is one that expresses one of the major themes of the book.

Some take the words "Yes. Amen" to be a response of an actual audience as Revelation is read aloud in the liturgy (implied by 1:3), so that the reading is to some degree interactive (Vanni 1991). Others think that the words are spoken by God himself, for God speaks the next verse (1:8; Schüssler Fiorenza 1991, 44). God thus guarantees that what is spoken of in 1:7 will come to pass. This would be parallel to 14:13, where God's Spirit responds "Yes" to a beatitude spoken by a voice from heaven.

God speaks in 1:8. This is striking, since God speaks directly only here and at the end of the book, in 21:5–8. Here God himself proclaims his sovereignty. That claim is already implied in God's title in the letter's greeting in 1:4, for there God is the one "who is and who was and who is to come," and 1:5 makes it clear that God exercises his sovereignty over human kings through Christ, who is "the ruler of the kings of the earth." But in 1:4–5 it is the seer who speaks, while in 1:8 it is God himself. God says that he is the Alpha and the Omega. Alpha and Omega are the first and last letters of the Greek alphabet. When God speaks at the end of Revelation, he says, "I am the Alpha and the Omega, the beginning and the end" (21:6). So at the beginning and end of the book, God declares himself to be the Alpha and

Omega, the beginning and end of all. God is the origin of creation, as is stressed in the hymn of God's heavenly attendants in the divine throne room scene (4:11) and in the angel's words of 10:6-7. God is also the goal of history, since the entire book concludes with God in the new Jerusalem on earth, surrounded by worshipers.

God's sovereignty is also asserted through the other titles attributed to him in 1:8. He is "Lord God," a title that the Roman writer Suetonius claims was used by the Roman emperor Domitian, the emperor in whose reign Revelation was written. It is God, not the emperor, who truly reigns. The title of God found in 1:4 appears on God's lips in 1:8: "Who is and who was and who is to come." This is another way of saying what "Alpha and Omega" claims. God is the origin and the goal of all. Finally, God calls himself "the Almighty." This is Revelation's favorite title for God. It is a title used only ten times in the New Testament, nine of which are in Revelation (1:8; 4:8; 11:17; 15:3; 16:7, 14; 19:6, 15; 21:22).

The two prophetic pronouncements in 1:7-8 prepare the way for the following visions. The eschatological events in those visions culminate in the coming of Christ and the presence of God and Christ on the throne in the new Jerusalem. The prophetic verses proclaim first the second coming of Jesus (1:7) and then God's sovereignty over all (1:8), but the two things are inseparable. God reigns through Christ (cf. 1:5). God even created through Christ (3:14; cf. Col 1:16; John 1:3). Revelation's high estimation of Christ's status is expressed in many ways throughout the book, and at the end Jesus actually adopts the title God bears in 1:8 and 21:6. In 22:13, Jesus announces, "I am the Alpha and the Omega, the first and the last, the beginning and the end." When the full implications of Rev 1:7-8 are appreciated, they can be seen to contain in summary the main points of Revelation.

Part I

Inaugural Vision: One Like a Son of Man (1:9–3:22)

Chapter Three

The Risen Christ Appears (1:9–20)

Circumstances of the Vision (1:9–10a)

Revelation 1:9–3:22 is an inaugural vision in which the risen Jesus, initially a mysterious figure, first appears to John. In keeping with both prophetic and apocalyptic usage, the seer begins by telling the circumstances under which he received his revelation. Of the prophetic books, Revelation is closest to the books of Isaiah and Ezekiel here, both of which have major visionary experiences narrated at or toward their beginnings (Isaiah 6; Ezekiel 1). Although John identified himself in the letter opening (1:4), he does so again here, again in keeping with prophetic and apocalyptic conventions. The words "I, John" (1:9) are echoed at the end of the book where he reminds his audience that he is "the one who heard and saw these things" (22:8), thus forming yet another frame around the entire vision. Charles (1920, 1:20) compares Revelation's "I, John" with Dan 7:15, 28; 8:1; 9:2; 4 Ezra 3:1; *1 Enoch* 12:3; and so on.

John describes himself as "your brother who share[s] with you in Jesus the persecution and the kingdom and the patient endurance" (1:9). The word translated here as "who share" is actually a noun in Greek, *synkoinônos,* meaning fellow-sharer. This word and related ones (*koinônia,* "fellowship" or "sharing," and *koinônos,* "sharer" or "partner") are used often by Paul to emphasize the unity in Christ of believers or to indicate their sharing in the life of Christ (e.g., Rom 11:17; 1 Cor 9:23; Phil 1:7; see also, e.g., Acts 2:42; Heb 10:33; 1 Pet 5:1; 2 Pet 1:4; 1 John 1:3, 6, 7). The verbal form from the same root is used in Rev 18:4 when Christians are encouraged to come out of Rome so as *not* to share in its sins. John's use of the word *synkoinônos* stresses his partnership with his audience, a close relationship that results from their shared status in Christ. John's use of the word "brother" also underlines his close relationship with his audience. Early Christians called each other brother or sister, a practice found in other religious groups of the time. It is an instance of what anthropologists call fictive kinship, implying a familial model of community.

Although the words "in Jesus" come at the end of this phrase in Greek, all three elements — persecution, kingdom, and endurance — are shared by John and the churches "in Jesus" (1:9). The Greek has only one definite article for all three nouns, tying them closely together. Revelation's usage here is again close to that of Paul, who uses "in Christ" to speak of the unity of Christians who through sharing in the death and resurrection of Christ have attained a new status before God and a new relationship with one another.

The word translated "persecution" here is *thlipsis,* which in the New Testament and in Revelation in particular means suffering associated with the endtime. The final showdown between good and evil associated with the endtime means suffering for those engaged in that battle. That conviction is found in many Jewish and Christian apocalypses. Perhaps the classic expression of it is in Daniel. For Daniel, the climax of history comes when God intervenes through Israel's protective angel, Michael: "At that time Michael, the great prince, the protector of your people, shall arise. There shall be a time of anguish, such as has never occurred since nations first came into existence. But at that time your people shall be delivered, everyone who is found written in the book" (12:1). Although the revealing angel tells Daniel that his people will ultimately be delivered from the anguish, they do not escape it entirely, since the book foretells terrible sufferings for them. The word for "anguish" found in the Septuagint (and Theodotion as well) of Dan 12:1 is *thlipsis,* the word that is so prominent in Revelation.

Early Christians tended to interpret rejection by their environment as eschatological suffering. When our author uses the word *thlipsis,* he has in mind its full eschatological meaning. That is clearest in chapter 7, where he has a proleptic vision of Christians dressed in white and worshiping before God's throne. A heavenly figure (one of the elders) explains to the seer: "These are they who have come out of the great ordeal [*thlipsis*]; they have washed their robes and made them white in the blood of the Lamb" (7:14). The message to the church at Smyrna states that both their present and imminent suffering are *thlipsis* (2:9–10). The seer himself has suffered for his loyalty to God (1:9). Throughout Revelation, the author makes a close connection between Jesus' witness and death and Christians' witness and suffering. Through witnessing even in the face of death, Christians win their place in the kingdom of Jesus and his Father. It is fitting, therefore, that "kingdom" appears with "persecution" in the threefold phrase in 1:9.

The seer often exhorts his listeners to "endurance," which means steadfast loyalty to God even in the face of threats and refusal to submit to idolatrous Rome. "Endurance" is particularly evident in the messages to the churches (2:2, 3, 19; 3:10), and it also occurs in 13:10, where its context is the onslaught of Rome, and 14:12, where it follows a portrayal of the punishments awaiting those who submit to Rome.

To a modern mind it might seem strange that there is any need for a struggle between God and his enemies. After all, God is almighty, an attribute repeatedly mentioned throughout Revelation, so God should be able to win the battle effortlessly. But apocalypticism takes anti-God powers much more seriously than that. Their power is real and is of cosmic proportions. Although God's status ensures final victory, the battle with Satan is real both on the angelic and on the human levels. For a while, the dragon wins, as Yarbro Collins (1979, 11) puts it.

At first glance, it may seem that persecution and endurance belong to the present for the churches, whereas kingdom is future. That ignores the apocalyptic viewpoint, in which things are not as they appear. As was made clear in 1:5, Jesus Christ has already borne witness and maintained his loyalty to God; he has risen; and he is presently "ruler of the kings of the earth." Through those activities he has freed Christians from their sins and already made them a kingdom and transformed them into priests. To be sure, the lordship of Christ and the rule of Christ's followers are not apparent on earth. To all appearances Rome rules, and most humans follow it in awe, obedience, and even worship. But Christians see things as they really are. It is they who submit to the true Lord of lords and King of kings (see 19:16; 17:14), so they already share in that kingdom, evident in heaven, but hidden on earth. Their rule on earth will be fully and publicly implemented in chapter 20, when those killed for the faith will rise to rule with Jesus for a thousand years. Schüssler Fiorenza (1991, 51) puts it well:

> According to John, Christian existence is determined by the conjunction of oppressive eschatological tribulations with the Christian claim to share in the divine empire and royal power of God, which requires consistent resistance and steadfast perseverance. This is the challenge facing Christians as representatives of God's power and empire here and now.

John now informs his audience of the circumstances of his vision. He says that he was "on the island called Patmos because of [*dia*] the word of God and the testimony of Jesus" (1:9). Patmos is a small (about five by ten miles), rocky island in the Aegean Sea, just to the west of the Roman province of Asia. It was about sixty-five miles west of Ephesus, one of the seven cities to which messages are directed in chapters 2 and 3. It was sparsely populated, but it did have a Greek school and shrines to Artemis and Apollo. Some scholars have thought that John went to Patmos in order to preach. It is more likely, however, that he was sent there as a penalty for preaching. Elsewhere in Revelation, the word *dia* (because of) always introduces the cause of something, not its purpose (Charles 1920, 1:22). This interpretation also makes better sense of John's claim that he shares persecution with his audience. Although many have claimed that Patmos was a penal colony, there is no solid evidence for that (Mounce 1977, 75). The Romans often banished to islands those whom they could not execute because of their social standing or did not wish to punish in that way. John probably falls into this category (see Caird 1966, 21–22).

"The word of God and the testimony of Jesus" is John's designation for the content of his vision (1:2, 9). There were quite different ways of understanding Christianity and living it out in the early years of the church, as indeed throughout history. John's view of Christians and their place in the world got him into trouble with the authorities, but John himself tells of Christians within the seven churches who saw things quite differently than he did (chapters 2–3). Such Christians got along well in Hellenistic Asian society. It was perhaps John's opposition to coexistence with that society that drew attention to him, or maybe it was the eschatological tenor of his message with its dire predictions for Rome's fall and the punishment of those, like the Asian aristocrats, who cooperated with it. Yarbro Collins notes, "Christianity as such was offensive to many at the time, but the eschatological character of John's teaching may have been viewed as subversive by authorities" (1990, 1001, where Yarbro Collins refers to MacMullen 1966, 142–62).

John receives his vision while exiled on Patmos. Revelation 1:10 makes the time of the vision still more precise: "I was in the spirit on the Lord's day." This is the first recorded use of "the Lord's day." In the second century it clearly meant Sunday (Charles 1920, 1:23), as it probably does here as well. Paul speaks of "revelations" being received and shared with the community during liturgy (1 Cor 14:26–33), and the liturgy probably happened on Sunday (see 1 Cor 16:2; Acts 20:7; Mark 16:2). Ford (1975, 382) suggests that the Christian "Lord's day" was in conscious imitation of and opposition to "emperor's day."

John says that he was "in the spirit" on the Lord's day. He probably refers to an altered state of consciousness, like a trance (Pilch 1993). John then hears a loud voice like a trumpet behind him. The scenario recalls Ezek 3:12: "Then the spirit lifted me up, and as the glory of the Lord rose from its place, I heard behind me the sound of loud rumbling." Revelation 1:10 and Ezek 3:12 share the references to the spirit and to a loud sound coming from behind the seer. In Rev 1:10, the sound is like that of a trumpet. A trumpet is often associated with the presence of God in the Hebrew Bible. When Moses is on Mount Sinai speaking to God, it is described as follows: "As the blast of the trumpet grew louder and louder, Moses would speak and God would answer him in thunder" (Exod 19:19; see Heb 12:19). The sound of a trumpet accompanies the arrival of Jesus at his second coming in Matt 24:31 and 1 Thess 4:16 (see 1 Cor 15:52). The use of a trumpet in Rev 1:10 foreshadows the seven trumpets of Revelation 8–11.

Appearance of the One like a Son of Man (1:10b–20)

John says he hears a loud voice "like" (*hôs*) a trumpet. This is the first occurrence of the word "like," and it is used an additional fifty-five times in Revelation. It is a word common in vision reports, accompanying the use of everyday categories, like trumpets, to portray ultimately indescribable phenomena. The technique of employing the word "like" or similar words reaches an extreme in Ezekiel's vision of God, a vision that contributes heavily to Revelation 1. Ezekiel's description culminates in the statement, "This was the *appearance* of the *likeness* of the glory of the LORD" (1:28).

In Rev 1:11, John is told to write what he sees "in a book" (*biblion*) and send it to the seven named churches. The seer is frequently commanded to write what he sees (1:3; 2:17; 3:12; 14:1; 17:5), and it is clear that the author intends for the readers to see the book of Revelation itself as the repository of that writing, so that the *biblion* of 1:11 is actually the book of Revelation. The revelation is not to remain private, affecting only the seer, as does Paul's vision in 2 Cor 12:1–6 (but see Rev 10:4). The process of revelation is not complete until the message is heard by the churches to which it is addressed (Yarbro Collins 1979, 6).

One must ask why John (or Jesus, to follow the logic of the work itself) would choose these particular churches to make up the number seven. We know that there were other Christian churches in the same area which are not included on the list. It could be that John had contact with these particular churches and felt them to be under his guidance. John may have been a sort of circuit prophet, traveling between the churches. It is clear from the message addressed to each church that John had specific knowledge of conditions within those churches and wished to address them. The churches formed a circle and lay on main roads in the region. Distribution of John's message would have been easy from these seven strategic locations. Some have suggested that the seven churches were actually located in postal districts (Charles 1920, 1:24–25; Ramsay 1994, 133–41).

Revelation 1:12–20 is a vision of the risen Christ. The vision follows the epiphany form, in which the seer receives a vision, becomes frightened, is told by a supernatural figure not to fear, and then receives a revelation. In verse 12, John turns to "see" the voice speaking behind him. This is analogous to Amos "seeing" God's words in Amos 1:1. John turns and sees seven golden lampstands. This recalls the golden menorah (candelabrum) in the temple (Exod 25:31–40), although in Exodus there is a single lampstand with seven lamps (one in the middle and three on each side), whereas in Revelation there are seven separate lampstands. John's vision also recalls the vision in Zechariah 4, but the image in Zechariah is slightly different from both Exodus and Revelation, for Zechariah sees a single bowl at the top of the lampstand with seven lamps on it (4:2; see our comments on 1:4). Our author transforms the single lampstand of the temple into seven individual lampstands so that Jesus can stand among them. Ford (1975, 382) thinks that the freestanding lamps of the temple's Holy Place may have exerted an influence here. In any case, the seven lamps recall God's presence and indicate that the figure John now sees is closely associated with God.

John next sees a mysterious unidentified figure "like a son of man" standing among the lampstands. In the gospels, "Son of Man" is a title, used with the definite article. In Rev 1:13, it appears without the definite article and is not a title. In Hebrew and Aramaic texts inside and outside the Hebrew Bible, "son of man" means "human." For example, in Ezekiel, God repeatedly addresses the prophet as "son of man." Daniel displays the same usage, for when he sees "one like a son of man" in Dan 7:13, he means simply a figure that looks like a human being. In Dan 10:16, the one like a "son of man" is an angel, and it is likely that Dan 7:13 also describes an angel, probably Michael, Israel's own protecting angel (see 12:1; Collins 1993, 304–10). Two noncanonical Jewish apocalypses roughly contemporaneous with Revelation, 4 Ezra and the Similitudes of Enoch (*1 Enoch* 37–71), develop Daniel's "son of man." They use "son of man" in a nontitular way, but for them the son of man refers to a superhuman messianic figure to come at the end of time. Revelation's usage resembles that of 4 Ezra and *1 Enoch*—it uses "son of man" in a nontitular way to refer to a superhuman messianic figure.

The details of the vision of Jesus in 1:12–16 come primarily from Daniel's vision of an angel in Daniel 10, and of God in Daniel 7. In Daniel 10 Daniel says,

> I looked up and saw a man clothed in linen, with a belt of gold from Uphaz around his waist. His body was like beryl, his face like lightning, his eyes like flaming torches, his arms and legs like the gleam of burnished bronze, and the sound of his words like the roar of a multitude.... Then I heard the sound of his words; and when I heard the sound of his words, I fell into a trance, face to the ground. (Dan 10:5–6, 9)

In describing God in Daniel 7, Daniel says, "His clothing was white as snow, and the hair of his head was like pure wool." The gospel writers draw on Daniel 7 and 10 when they portray Jesus at his transfiguration: "He was transfigured before them, and his face shone like the sun, and his clothes became dazzling white" (Matt 17:2).

As usual, our author does not simply quote scripture or adopt its images wholesale, but rather he creates new images by combining elements from various biblical sources. He begins by saying that the mysterious one like a son of man wears a long robe (*podêrês*) with "a golden sash across his chest." This is the only use of the Greek word *podêrês* in the New Testament. Some commentators take it to refer to the high priestly robe, so that Christ is portrayed as high priest here. But Christ nowhere appears as high priest in Revelation. Christians are said to be priests in 1:6; 5:10; and 20:6, but nowhere is that associated with a priesthood of Christ. The case is different with kingship, for in 20:6 it is said that "they [Christians] will reign with him [Christ] a thousand years." Christ's kingship is shared by faithful Christians. In that same verse it is said that during the thousand-year messianic reign, the risen martyrs "will be priests of God and of Christ." In other words, Christians as priests serve both God and Christ. When the priestly image is used, Christ is put on the divine side of the equation with God, and he receives priestly service—he does not render it. This attests to Revelation's high christology (Bauckham 1993, 54-65).

The one like a son of man is dressed in a manner similar to the angels of Rev 15:6, who are "robed in pure white linen, with golden sashes across their chests." This recalls the angel of Dan 10:5, who was "clothed in linen, with a belt of gold from Uphaz around his waist." The high priest's belt was not made of gold (Exod 39:29; but see Mounce 1977, 78). Our author does not imply that Jesus is a priest, but only that he is a mysterious, supernatural figure, comparable to Daniel's angel and to the angels of Revelation 15 (see also Ezek 9:2, 3, 11).

In John's vision Christ's "head and his hair were white as white wool, white as snow" (1:14). This recalls God in Daniel 7, where God's clothing is white as snow, and God's hair is "like pure wool." It is likely that Daniel alludes to the whiteness of God's hair and that John reads it that way (see Collins 1993, 301-2). In the synoptic gospels, Jesus' clothes are "dazzling white" at the transfiguration. It is striking that whereas the synoptics pick up the element of white clothing from God's portrait in Daniel 7, Revelation picks up the whiteness of the hair. Our author underscores the uniqueness of Jesus. There are many figures in Revelation who have white garments. But Jesus is the only one who is said to have white *hair.* The image is startling. It has nothing to do with age as such, although the original image in Daniel 7 comes from the notion that God is very old, since he is called the Ancient of Days (Dan 7:9). Revelation's concern is to associate Jesus with God closely.

The next features of Jesus come again from Daniel 10. John says of Jesus, "His eyes were like a flame of fire, his feet were like burnished bronze, refined as in a furnace." Daniel says of the angel, "His eyes were like flaming torches, his arms and legs like the gleam of burnished bronze" (10:6). Jesus' flaming eyes may imply his ability to see all, as well as the scorching judgment with which he observes evil (see the repetition of these traits in 2:18 and 19:12). The words of the angel in Daniel 10 are "like the roar of a multitude." The risen Jesus in Revelation also has an impressive voice, "like the sound of many waters," the same expression as is found describing God's coming in Ezek 43:2. Steve Moyise notes that in 19:6 John associates the sound of a multitude with the sound of many waters, perhaps representing a cross reference between Ezek 43:2 and Dan 10:6 (1995, 37). He also observes that the elements shared by Daniel 10 and Revelation 1 occur in roughly the same order in both texts, strengthening the impression that Revelation uses Daniel here.

John now says that Jesus has seven stars in his right hand (1:16). The ancients believed that there were seven planets. When the young son of Domitian died, Domitian struck a coin that pictured his wife, Domitia, as the queen of heaven, and his son playing with seven stars (Sweet 1979, 71). Revelation's image of Jesus with seven stars in his hand may be an allusion to that coin and an implicit critique of it. It is not the Roman imperial family that has cosmic significance, but Jesus. In 1:20, the stars are interpreted by Jesus as the angels of the seven churches. That interpretation is not at odds with seeing the stars as the seven planets or seven stars, since stars could be seen as angels, as we saw in connection with 1:4. Others suggest that the seven stars could be a constellation, such as Ursa Minor (the Little Dipper) or the Pleiades (see Yarbro Collins 1990, 1001; 1996, 106-7). Interpreting the temple cosmically, Philo and Josephus mention the connection of the seven lamps of the menorah with the seven planets, a connection that may have been known to our author as well. In a world in which astrology was widespread and influential, the picture of Jesus holding seven stars in his hand would be powerful. It uses astrological imagery to enhance Jesus' image. The stars may be thought of as controlling human fate, but Jesus controls the stars.

A sharp sword protrudes from Jesus' mouth (Rev 1:16). Here

the author combines two images found in Isaiah. Isaiah 11:4 says that the messianic figure in that passage "shall strike the earth with the rod of his mouth," and in Isa 49:2 the prophet says, "He made my mouth like a sharp sword." These images combine to portray Jesus as one whose very words of judgment carry destructive force. The sword is two-edged, and in Heb 4:12 God's word is compared to a two-edged sword which is "able to judge the thoughts and intentions of the heart." Relevant also is 2 Thess 4:8, where Jesus slays the eschatological adversary "with the breath of his mouth," an image similar to that found in 4 Ezra 13:4, where the eschatological Son of Man destroys his enemies with the burning voice that comes from his mouth (Fekkes [1994, 118] also mentions *Pss. Sol.* 17:24, 35; *1 Enoch* 62:2; and several texts from Qumran). Toward the end of Revelation (19:15, 21), Jesus is depicted as a warrior with a sword coming out of his mouth, so that this image forms another frame for the bulk of the visions.

The depiction of Jesus ends with the observation that "his face was like the sun shining with full force" (1:16). The image matches that of Jesus' transfiguration in the synoptic gospels.

The effect of the epiphany in Rev 1:12–16 is powerful. Jesus has not yet been explicitly identified, although in the next section it will become clear that it is he. The seer faces a supernatural figure with angelic traits, but one that is clearly more than an ordinary angel. The angelic appearance, drawn from Daniel 10, is altered through the addition of traits belonging to God. The author uses elements from the Hebrew Bible, from Christian tradition, and from his Greco-Roman environment to paint the picture of a powerful and frightening Jesus. He is omniscient, with burning and penetrating eyes, and of great strength, with immovable feet. It is just such a Jesus that is needed to comfort Christians who oppose the awesome power of the Roman empire, a power that presented itself in cosmic terms.

Revelation 1:17 constitutes the second part of the epiphanic form, the fearful reaction of the seer. He falls at Jesus' feet "as though dead." Fear and falling to the ground are the typical reactions to the appearance of a supernatural figure, be it God, an angel, or some other entity (Charles 1920, 1:31). Daniel reacts to the angel this way in Daniel 10. Unique to Revelation, however, is the phrase "as though dead." This may be significant for the author, since John is immediately revived by the touch of Christ, the one who was dead and rose. That Christ touches the seer with his right hand should cause no confusion, as if it would be impossible for him to do so with a hand full of stars. That would be to take the vision too literally. The awesome figure of 1:12–16 now interacts with John directly, and the vision accommodates that.

As is usual with the epiphany form, the supernatural figure now says not to fear, identifies himself, and conveys a message. This follows the model of Daniel 10. Christ says that he is "the first and the last." God applies this phrase to himself in Isa 44:6; 48:12. In Isaiah, it fits God's claims that he controls history and so is the only true God, and it occurs in the context of a work, Second Isaiah (Isaiah 40–55), that engages in polemic against the apparently victorious gods of a nation that oppresses Israel, Babylon. Revelation uses the phrase in a similar way. Although it may seem that Rome and its gods control history, in actuality God does so through Jesus.

Charles (1920, 2:220) thinks that "first and last" would call to mind in the hearers a similar title applied to God in Orphic circles and common in many variants in the ancient world. The all-encompassing claim implied in the title "first and last" is like that suggested by God's title in 1:8, the "Alpha and the Omega." Both titles are brought together along with a third in 22:13, where Jesus says, "I am the Alpha and Omega, the first and the last, the beginning [*archê*] and the end." He says this right after promising, "I am coming soon" (22:12). Given that Jesus is called "the origin [or beginning: *archê*] of God's creation" in 3:14, Jesus can justly claim to be the first and the last. He is the beginning of creation, and history will culminate in his second coming. The only other occurrence of the title Alpha and Omega is on God's lips in 21:6, where it also occurs with "beginning and end." Clearly, God and Christ are closely joined in these titles. Christ shares the divine sovereignty, a pattern that permeates Revelation and demonstrates its high christology.

Next, the one like a son of man claims that he is "the living one" (*ho zôn;* 1:18). This simple predication is rich with biblical resonances. God is frequently spoken of as "the living God" in the Hebrew Bible, particularly in contexts where a contrast with other gods is at issue. A *locus classicus* for this is Jeremiah 10, where the prophet ridicules idols as lifeless creations of their makers. In contrast, Israel's God is living and true: "But the Lord is the true God; he is the living God and the everlasting King.

At his wrath the earth quakes, and the nations cannot endure his indignation" (10:10). Jeremiah then extols God as the creator and looks forward to the punishment of the idolaters (10:12–15; Charles [1920, 1:32] also points to Josh 3:10; Pss 42:3; 84:3; etc.).

The mysterious figure now says, "I was dead, and see, I am alive forever and ever" (1:18). The figure must be Christ, who died and rose. The phrase combines the divine attribute of living forever with the reality of Jesus' death. God is the one who lives forever in Rev 4:9, where the heavenly entourage gives glory to God on the throne "who lives forever and ever," and in 15:7 God is again the one "who lives forever and ever." In 10:6, the revealing angel connects the idea of God's eternal life with creation. Sirach 18:1 also combines the ideas of God's eternity and God's creative act: "He who lives forever created the whole universe." *First Enoch* 5:1 says that creatures belong to the one who lives forever. Daniel also speaks of God as "the one who lives forever," although not in conjunction with creation (12:7). It is this rich background in Jewish thought that the author evokes when he applies this divine predication to Jesus. Christians attain endless life, but the phrase "the one who lives forever and ever" with its biblical resonances is reserved to God and Jesus.

Jesus asserts that he has "the keys of Death and of Hades" (1:18). "Hades" is the Greek word for the underworld, and in the LXX it translates the Hebrew word "Sheol." This is not "hell" as we usually conceptualize it, but is rather a place where all go after death (see our comments on 20:14). Death and Hades are personified in 6:8, where Death is the rider of the fourth horse in the fourth seal who is allowed to roam the earth with Hades following him. In 20:13–14, Death and Hades are forced to give up the dead in them and are then thrown into the fiery lake. A similar personification of Death and Sheol appears in Hos 13:14; Ps 18:4–5; and Prov 5:5 (Charles 1920, 1:32 n. 1).

The power over death claimed by John in Rev 1:18 is a sign of divine sovereignty. In the Greco-Roman world, that power belonged to the goddess Hekate (Aune 1987, 484–89). Here, however, it is not Hekate that has power over death, but Jesus. Charles (1920, 1:33) adduces rabbinic texts to the effect that only God has such power. Revelation 1:18 challenges Roman imperial power, which reserved to itself the right to put people to death, a right it apparently exercised in the case of the Christian martyr Antipas, mentioned in the message to the church at Pergamum (Rev 2:13). At the beginning of that message, Christ's possession of a sword is mentioned. The Roman right to condemn to death is expressed in Roman law as the *ius gladii,* the right of the sword. Again, Revelation contrasts appearance and reality. Rome appears to have the power of death, but it is really God and Jesus who hold that power. These contexts recall Paul's statement in 1 Corinthians that Jesus will progressively destroy his eschatological adversaries, conceived of as cosmic opponents, where "the last enemy to be destroyed is death" (1 Cor 15:26). Later in the chapter, Paul addresses personified Death, echoing the words of Isaiah and Hosea (1 Cor 15:54-55; Isa 25:7; Hos 13:14). Again we find that our author's words evoke a theme in Jewish and early Christian thought.

Jesus now commands the seer, "Now write what you have seen, what is, and what is to take place after this" (1:19). These words have often been taken as an outline of the book of Revelation itself. "What you have seen" would be the vision just recounted; "what is" would be the present situation of the seven churches described in the messages of chapters 2 and 3; and "what is to take place" would be the eschatological events contained in the rest of Revelation. Such a neat division does not work (Mounce 1977, 81-82; van Unnick 1962-63; Beale 1992; Michaels 1991). The messages to the churches refer to both present and future events, and the later visions deal with the author's present as well as the future. It is better to interpret "what you have seen" to be a proleptic use of the past tense that assumes that the writing will take place after the visions are complete, so that the visions are in the past when the writing takes place.

As the chapter ends, the supernatural figure supplies the interpretation of a specific element of the vision, the "mystery of the seven stars" (1:20). The reference to the stars as a "mystery" recalls Dan 2:28ff., where the "mystery" is the meaning of the king's dream, a meaning that discloses events to take place. Such a use of "mystery" is common in apocalyptic parlance (see Rom 11:25-26; 1 Cor 15:51-52; Brown 1958a; 1958b). Revelation 1:20 says that the seven stars in Christ's right hand are the angels of the seven churches and that the seven lampstands among which Christ stands are the seven churches themselves (1:20). Speaking of the fact that the cultic lampstands represent the churches, Yarbro Collins (1979, 12) suggests, "The implication is that the Church, the followers of God and the Lamb, is the new, spiritual temple. Since John was writing after the destruction of the Jerusalem temple, it was especially important to understand how the presence of God might be felt in the new situation."

The image of a cosmic, mysterious, powerful Christ who holds the fate of the churches in his hand and who remains close to them is a source of hope for those who think that the forces of Rome are arrayed against them. For those who experience the Roman empire and Hellenistic culture as foreign and inimical, this picture of a Christ intimately engaged with their communities affords an alternative vision of the universe, one in which they are the ones who are close to the ultimate power in the cosmos and are protected by it.

Chapter Four

Seven Messages to Seven Churches (Chapters 2–3)

Overview of the Messages

Chapters 2 and 3 stand out in Revelation in terms of both form and content. They take the form of seven messages to seven churches. Charles (1920, 1:37–42) believes that the messages were originally seven real letters sent by John to each of the churches and later incorporated by him into the book of Revelation. He argues that there is a basic difference of outlook between the messages and the rest of the book. He sees in the messages little expectation of a general persecution to come upon the worldwide church, which is clearly anticipated throughout the rest of the book. Because of similarity of "diction and idiom," Charles still maintains that the messages were written by the same author who wrote the rest of the apocalypse. He speculates that when the author incorporated the "letters" into the apocalypse, he added the attributes of Christ at the beginnings of the messages to tie them to chapter 1 and the references to eschatological reward and punishment at their ends to connect them with chapters 20 to 22; Charles also proposes that John made small insertions such as 3:10 to adapt the letters to the book's viewpoint. Charles is certainly correct in seeing that the messages are tightly tied to the rest of Revelation. But the differences in content between chapters 2 and 3 and the rest of the apocalypse are due to the function these chapters serve in tying the cosmic struggle depicted in the rest of the book to the concrete situations of the seven churches, and not to their previously independent existence, as Charles thinks.

The words addressed to each church demonstrate specific

awareness of the situation of that church. These are real messages to real churches and are evidence that John was familiar with and known to these Christian communities. They show in detail how each church must relate its own situation and behavior to a larger cosmic drama. William Ramsay (1904) and Colin Hemer (1986) believe that they have found allusions in the letters to features peculiar to each church, indicating knowledge by the seer of local features – geographical, legendary, and so on. In many cases their suggestions seem forced, but we do include the more plausible of their ideas. What determines the author's choice of images is his desire to see the local situation in the light of his visions in chapter 1 and of the eschatological consummation. As is clear throughout Revelation, the author also makes liberal use of the Bible to shed light on the churches' present (see Moyise 1995).

There is a close connection between what the churches experience and the cosmic clash between the risen Christ and Satan. The churches' own experience is the embodiment of that struggle for them, and the outcome of their specific struggles is closely tied to the outcome of the cosmic battle. As Boring says, "The church is not spectator to the cosmic battle between God and the forces of evil, but experiences it in its own life" (1989, 92). This fits the apocalyptic mode of making sense of experience. One's experience is projected onto a cosmic screen in which God and Satan collide, and then that screen becomes the background for interpreting one's experience (Collins 1984, 32).

The messages to the seven churches are not in letter form, so the frequent reference to them as the seven letters is incorrect. Their formal features have occasioned much discussion. The messages are remarkably consistent, being made up of the same elements in the same sequence, for the most part. The formal structure of the messages does not have an exact parallel outside of Revelation. This has led to a number of suggestions about the model the author may have used in composing them, but it seems clear that the overall form of the messages is due to the author's creativity (Aune [1990] discusses the options). Most commentators recognize the heavy prophetic element in these messages. We begin by examining what is common to the messages and then treat each message separately. What follows is a brief discussion of the seven constituent parts of the messages.

Constituent Parts

Destination

In each case, the message is to be sent to "the angel of the church" in question. So, for example, the first message begins, "To the angel of the church in Ephesus" (2:1). Commentators offer a number of possibilities for the identification of these angels. Some take the Greek word *angelos* not as "angel," its usual translation, but as "messenger," the original meaning of the word. If "messenger" is the correct translation, then the way is open to various interpretations. Charles (1920, 1:34) notes that the figures have been seen as the carriers of the letters to the churches, delegates from the churches to the seer, officials of the churches or synagogues, or bishops of the churches. Others suggest that they are local prophets with allegiance to John (Schüssler Fiorenza 1991, 52–53). However, each of these interpretations requires taking *angelos* in a relatively unusual sense both in Jewish and Christian literature in general and in Revelation in particular. Although *angelos* can refer to humans in the New Testament (Matt 11:10; Luke 9:52), it more commonly designates angels there. Elsewhere in Revelation, *angelos* always means "angel." Charles (1920, 1:34) notes that this is the way it is used in other apocalyptic works as well.

Charles (1920, 1:34–35) says that if the *angelos* represent angelic entities, as is likely, two possibilities remain. Either they are guardian angels of the churches, or they are heavenly counterparts of the churches, that is, heavenly "ideals" virtually identical with the churches themselves. He opts for the latter alternative. But this particular brand of symbolization is not characteristic of Revelation. Indeed, the work as a whole assumes the independence of the cosmic figures it describes from earthly entities, even though those figures are intimately engaged with earthly persons, institutions, and events. It is better to choose Charles's first option, namely, that the angels are in some sense the guardian or representative angels of the churches. This notion has its roots in the biblical idea that individual nations, including Israel, have supernatural patrons. For example, in Daniel, the archangel Michael is Israel's protector angel (10:13, 20–21; 12:1), who is also called a "prince." He, along with the angel Gabriel, fights the "princes," or heavenly representatives, of Persia and Greece (10:20–21). Still deeper biblical roots for this idea can be found in Deut 32:8-9, where each god is assigned its own nation, the Lord receiving Israel.

It is most likely, then, that the angels to whom the messages are addressed are the heavenly patrons or protectors of the churches. In some sense the angels share responsibility with Christians for the behavior of the churches, for both the approval and the censure resulting from such behavior are addressed to the angels. The close connection between angel and church is expressed in the very language of the messages, which shifts back and forth between the second person singular, indicating the angel of each church, the second person plural, suggesting the Christian congregation, and the third person, speaking of church members. In the commentary that follows, no distinction will be made between what is said to the angel of a church and what is said to that church itself. The two are really one and the same.

Church members know the content of the messages only because they have overheard them being conveyed to their angels (Boring 1989, 87). This closely associates the supernatural and natural planes, an association central to apocalypses in general. What is said to their heavenly representative by the risen Christ is of the utmost importance to the churches and is completely reliable (or in Revelation's terminology, "faithful") and true (cf. 21:5; 22:6).

The author is careful to guard against granting angels any status that would detract from the sovereignty of God and Jesus. He does so in three ways (Krodel 1989, 104). First, the angels have already been identified in 1:20 with the stars that are in Jesus' right hand. Jesus controls them. Second, they share in the approval or censure expressed in the messages. Third, a revealing angel expressly forbids John to worship him in 19:10 and 22:9, ranging himself among the servants of God and Jesus alongside John and his fellow Christians.

The messages are written not to church leaders but to the churches as wholes in the person of the angels. This conforms to the pattern found in Paul's authentic letters. The dearth of terms in Revelation denoting church leaders has often been noted. It has been interpreted in two basic ways. Either John is hostile to church leaders and wishes to bypass them, or he does not wish to confront them in any way. It is also possible that no unambiguous church structure was in place, so that church leadership was still fairly fluid.

Command to Write

This recalls the command to write found in 1:11, 19, where it applies to the whole of Revelation. The author conceives of his book as written prophecy (1:3; 22:7, 10, 18–19). What is conveyed is a revelation from Christ, and since the disclosure of that revelation is prophecy, the commands to write in the messages constitute prophetic commissions in their own right. There is precedent in the Hebrew Bible for prophets conveying their prophecies in writing, such as when Elijah writes a prophetic letter to the king in 2 Chr 21:12–15, or when Jeremiah writes to the exiles in Babylonia in Jeremiah 29, or when God tells Isaiah to commit his prophecy to writing (Isa 8:1; 30:8). In those cases, the writing is itself an act of prophecy. In Isaiah's case, the Lord actually commands him to prophesy through writing. In the same way, Revelation's command to write is a prophetic commission.

Pronouncement Formula

In each of the messages the command to write is followed by the formula *tade legei,* which literally means, "These things says [Christ]." This Greek phrase is used more than 250 times in the Septuagint to translate the first two words of the Hebrew *kh ʾmr yhwh,* often translated, "Thus says the Lord" (Aune 1990, 187). It is a common prophetic formula, often called the messenger formula. It sets off the words to follow as coming directly from God. The phrase is frequent in the Septuagint, but it is rare in Koine Greek (Charles 1920, 1:48). Its rarity may contribute to the solemnity of its tone here.

Self-identification of the Speaker

While the biblical messenger formula identifies God as the speaker of the prophetic words, in Revelation 2–3 Christ is the source. The attributes Christ uses to identify himself are taken for the most part from the vision in chapter 1, but there are other attributes as well. There is often a connection between what is said of Christ and what is said to the churches. As Boring puts it, "The ethical imperative is founded on the christological indicative, the Christian life is founded on the fact and reality of Christ" (1989, 88).

Body

The body of the messages consists of approval and/or censure, warnings about future punishments or promises of future rewards, calls to repentance, and specific commands. Smyrna and Philadelphia receive no censure. Laodicea receives an entirely negative appraisal. The other churches get mixed reviews. Each of these sections begins with the words "I know," stressing Christ's omniscience. Christ knows everything that transpires in the churches, and so his judgment is true. These sections most closely resemble prophetic oracles of judgment and salvation found elsewhere in the Bible.

Call to Listen

In the first three messages the call to listen occurs next, but in the last four it is the last item. The call to listen is identical in all seven messages: "Let anyone who has an ear listen to what the Spirit is saying to the churches." Calls to listen are common in both prophetic and wisdom literature (e.g., Isa 1:10; Jer 2:4; Hos 4:1; Amos 3:1; see Boring 1989, 89). The closest parallels to the calls to listen in Revelation 2–3 are in the gospel parable tradition, for example, Mark 4:9: "Let anyone with ears to hear listen" (see also Matt 11:15; 13:9, 43; Mark 4:23; Luke 8:8; 14:35). The allusion to the gospel tradition is deliberate. A call to listen indicates that the words to which they are attached are of great importance. Understanding Christ's words and acting on them determines one's eschatological fate. There may be a hint here of the apocalyptic theme that only the elect will be able to understand (Yarbro Collins 1979, 14), since the calls imply that not everyone "has an ear." That is certainly the idea in Mark 4, where only the disciples receive the secret of the kingdom of heaven.

Christ's words are "what the Spirit is saying to the churches." Christ and the Spirit are not identified in Revelation, but they are closely related. This is perhaps most strikingly put in 19:10: "The testimony of Jesus is the spirit of prophecy." The words of Jesus come to early Christianity through prophecy, associated with the Spirit. The same sort of close interplay between Jesus' communication with the church and the presence of the Spirit is found in John's gospel (See John 14:16–17, 25–26; 15:26–27; 16:7–15). In a similar vein, Paul can say in 2 Cor 3:17, "The Lord [Jesus] is the Spirit."

Promise of Eschatological Rewards

In the first three messages the promise of eschatological rewards comes before the call to listen, and in the last four messages the call to listen and promise of rewards are reversed. The promises all correspond to aspects of the eschatological fulfillment pictured in chapters 20 to 22, so they help to tie the messages firmly to Revelation's eschatological viewpoint.

Promises are made to the "one who conquers." The word "to conquer" (*nikaô*) is common in Revelation but rare in the rest of the New Testament. In Revelation it is always used in connection with the eschatological battle begun by Jesus and in which Christians are engaged. It denotes Christ's victory over the powers of Satan (3:21; 5:5; 17:14), Satan's temporary victories over Christians (11:7; 13:7), and Christians' participation in Christ's victory (2:7, 11, 17, 26; 3:5, 12, 21; 12:11; 15:2; 21:7), and it once refers to eschatological events that are unclear (6:2). There is some disagreement over whether only martyrs "conquer." Charles (1920, 1:54) holds that this is so. In other words, Christians conquer through their martyrdom. Revelation 3:21 links the Christian's victory closely with Christ's, and 12:11 connects the conqueror's victory with Christ's death and that of the faithful: "They have conquered him [Satan] by the blood of the Lamb and by the word of their testimony, for they did not cling to life even in the face of death." (In the one instance of "conquer" in the gospel of John it is related to Christ's death [16:33].) Caird also thinks that when the verb *nikaô* is used in Revelation it refers to actual martyrdom, but he observes that the things promised to martyrs are also given to anyone who is faithful, even if they are not martyred (1966, 33). He solves this by saying that all Christians must be willing to resist the powers of evil to death, even if not all become actual martyrs. The seer "himself does not know who the martyrs will be; not all Christians will suffer martyrdom, but all must face the prospect of it" (Caird 1966, 33).

The Messages as Wholes

The prophetic elements of the messages are clear in the analysis above, but the author does not rigidly follow models he finds in the prophetic literature. Rather he creates something new, but as he does so he brings the entire biblical prophetic tradition to bear on his own situation. It is worth noting that many of the elements present in the messages are also found together in the prophetic literature. Amos 5 is a good example. It begins with a call to listen (5:1), uses the prophetic messenger formula (5:3), enumerates attributes of the God who gives the oracle (and even does so with reference to stellar constellations in 5:8–9), gives specific instructions on how to behave (5:4–6, 14–15), tells of future punishment and reward (5:3–7, 14–15), describes the sins of the people using the words "I know" (5:10–13), and tells of God's coming (5:16–17). This shows that it is not just individual elements such as the messenger formula that lend a prophetic air to these chapters, but it is also the ensemble of elements that calls to mind the prophets.

Aune (1990, 198–204) offers another paradigm against which to see the messages. He agrees that the Hebrew Bible is a source here, but he insists that we also look to the author's Greco-Roman environment. For him, Revelation's opposition of Christianity and the Roman empire expresses itself in chapters 2 and 3 in the appropriation and transformation of features of imperial decrees. He acknowledges that there is a great deal of variety in such decrees, making the tracing of parallels difficult, but he lists the following as frequent in imperial decrees: the *prooemium* or preface; the *promulgatio* or proclamation, such as "I make known that"; the *narratio* or rehearsal of the "facts of the matter"; the *dispositio* or decision; the *sanctio* that is meant to ensure obedience. Revelation's messages do not contain the *prooemium.* Aune sees a marked similarity between the *narratio* and the parts of the body of the seven messages that describe the situation of the churches. The "I know" language of Revelation recalls the sorts of things the king might say, such as "I have heard," or "I have learned," or even "I know." The specific demands of the body of the messages correspond to the *dispositio* or decision of the decrees. Finally, the eschatological promises of Revelation are like the *sanctio* of the decrees.

In the Bible, God is depicted as a great king, so it is not surprising that there would be similarities between the emperor's edicts and God's oracles. In presenting God's words, biblical prophecy itself naturally contains features that derive from imperial contexts. In ancient Near Eastern cultures, there was a close connection between royal imagery and religious imagery. Gods sounded like kings, and kings sounded like gods. Even as found in the Bible, therefore, prophetic forms provided John with an effective means of countering imperial Rome's claims to authority. But it is also possible that the form of the messages owes something to Roman imperial edicts, as Aune proposes, and that the author expected that connection to be made, since it would support his picture of Rome's pretensions as counterfeit. The ones truly qualified to issue worldwide decrees are God and Christ. This fits with the whole of Revelation, but especially with those many passages that depict God and Christ in royal terms. Revelation has already made reference to God's throne (1:4) and will soon present an elaborate scenario of the heavenly royal court (chapters 4–5).

Each of the seven messages addresses a particular church, but that is not to say that its relevance is limited to that church. At the end of each message is the injunction to "listen to what the Spirit is saying to the churches." Each church must listen to all of the messages and learn from them. Although the seer is most familiar with western Asia Minor, he anticipates a worldwide persecution and a cosmic resolution to the battle between good and evil. He undoubtedly demands the same faithfulness of Christians throughout the world that he requires of the seven churches, so his revelation is of universal significance.

The Opponents of John: Apostles, Prophets, Nicolaitans

In several of the churches the seer faces opposition that probably represents a single movement within the Asian churches. Since the messages supply the clearest hints about the situations the author addresses, they deserve special examination. We begin by collecting the relevant passages.

> *From the message to Ephesus:* "I know that you cannot tolerate evildoers; you have tested those who claim to be apostles but are not, and have found them to be false" (2:2). "You have this to your credit: you hate the works of the Nicolaitans, which I also hate" (2:6).

> *From the message to Pergamum:* "But I have a few things against you: you have some there who hold to the teaching of Balaam, who taught Balak to put a stumbling block before the people of Israel, so that they would eat food sacrificed to idols and practice fornication. So you also have some who hold to the teaching of the Nicolaitans" (2:14–15).

> *From the message to Thyatira:* "But I have this against you: you tolerate that woman Jezebel, who calls herself a prophet and is teaching and beguiling my servants to practice fornication and to eat food sacrificed to idols.... Beware, I am throwing her on a bed, and those who commit adultery with her I am throwing into great distress, unless they repent of her doings; and I will strike her children dead.... But to the rest of you in Thyatira, who do not hold to this teaching, who have not learned what some call 'the deep things of Satan,' to you I say, I do not lay on you any other burden; only hold fast to what you have until I come" (2:20-25).

We have only one side of the argument here. The views of John's opponents have not been recorded. We have a natural sympathy for the biblical account and the biblical authors. But good historical method requires that we take full account of our sources' biases. The treatment of the opponents in the passages cited above is not neutral. It is polemical. Unless we consider the polemic, we will have a distorted picture of the historical situation. John's opponents considered themselves Christians, even apostles and prophets. John's words reveal that these opponents were accepted as such by some whom John respects, such as the church in Thyatira, which tolerates "Jezebel" but is otherwise blameless. Apparently, good Christians could be sympathetic to John's opponents.

It must also be observed that there was much variety in the early church, both in doctrine and in practice. Even a cursory reading of the New Testament shows that internal conflict was typical. The conflict is focused most clearly in disagreements between leading representatives of different positions. It is in this light that we must view John's statements about false apostles, so-called prophets, and those who were influenced by them.

Because of the fluid and evolving nature of authority in the early church, we find numerous references in early Christianity to false authorities and to the necessity of testing all authorities to determine their legitimacy. Paul rails against the "super-apostles" who have invaded the Corinthian church, calling them "false apostles, deceitful workers, disguising themselves as apostles of Christ. And no wonder! Even Satan disguises himself as an angel of light" (2 Cor 11:13-14). Similarly, he terms those in the Jerusalem church with whom he disagrees "false believers secretly brought in, who slipped in to spy on the freedom we have in Christ Jesus, so that they might enslave us" (Gal 2:4). In the same letter he calls Peter, James, and John "those who were supposed to be acknowledged leaders (what they actually were makes no difference to me; God shows no partiality)" (2:6). Paul demands that words of Christian prophets be "weighed" (1 Cor 14:29).

Matthew's Jesus warns of false prophets in the Sermon on the Mount and demands that they be judged by their works (Matt 7:15–20). He also says that many who appear to be good Christians and who prophesy, do miracles, and perform exorcisms in his name will be condemned at the last judgment (Matt 7:21–23). Mark's Jesus predicts, "False messiahs and false prophets will appear and produce signs and omens, to lead astray, if possible, the elect" (Mark 13:22). The Didache, a church order compiled at about the same time as Revelation, supplies criteria by which true prophets can be distinguished from false. Examples could be multiplied. The overall picture is one where disagreements are taken very seriously and where each side believes that God approves of it and condemns its opponents.

Revelation conforms to this pattern of conflict. Thyatira does not share John's view of "Jezebel" and her adherents, and Pergamum, despite its noble character as holding fast to Jesus' name, contains Nicolaitans. We now turn to the specific issues of contention between John and his opponents, to the extent that these can be determined from his terse references to them.

In the message to Pergamum, it is said that there are those who advocate the teaching of "Balaam, who taught Balak to put a stumbling block before the people of Israel, so that they would eat food sacrificed to idols and practice fornication. So you also have some who hold to the teaching of the Nicolaitans" (2:14–15). The phrasing of "So you *also*" makes it probable that the Nicolaitans are precisely those who adhere to Balaam's teaching.

The story of Balaam appears in Numbers 22–24; 31:8, 16. He was a non-Israelite prophet whom the Moabite king Balak summoned to curse Israel when it was encamped in the plains of Moab, before it entered Canaan. The story in Numbers 22–24 is fairly positive toward him, but priestly editors added 31:15–16, in which Moses, angry at his military officers for sparing some foreign women, says, "Have you allowed all the women to live? These women here, on Balaam's advice, made the Israelites act treacherously against the LORD in the affair of Peor, so that the plague came among the congregation of the LORD." Moses refers to the incident narrated in Numbers 25: "When Israel was staying at Shittim, the people began to have sexual relations with the women of Moab. These invited the people to the sacrifices of their gods, and the people ate and bowed down to their gods" (25:1–2). Numbers 25 gives Balaam no role in this episode, but Num 31:16 makes the connection, so that Balaam is blamed for leading Israel to fornication and to eating food sacrificed to idols. In later Jewish and Christian tradition, Balaam is generally a negative figure. He appears in the New Testament here, as well as in 2 Pet 2:15–16 and Jude 11.

Some Christian authors of the first centuries, beginning with Irenaeus, thought that the Nicolaitans took their name from Nicolaus, one of the seven Hellenists appointed to care for Hellenist widows in the Jerusalem church in Acts 6. There is no evidence to support this. It is possible, however, that the name Nicolaitans does come from the name of the founder of the group or a prominent member of it. There is even perhaps a connection between the name Balaam and the appellation Nicolaitans. Later rabbinic tradition (*Sanh.* 105a in the Babylonian Talmud) gives the etymology of Balaam as from *blʿ ʾm,* meaning the one who swallows or overcomes the people (Charles 1920, 1:52). Nicolaus, which comes from the Greek words *nikaô,* meaning "to conquer," and *laos,* meaning "people," would then have a similar etymology. The clever wordplay between Nicolaitans and Balaam would be appropriate given the emphasis in Revelation on conquering. Indeed in the messages containing references to the Nicolaitans, "the one who conquers" is the one who rejects the Nicolaitans. As intriguing as these suggestions are, they remain speculative.

The message to Pergamum accuses the Nicolaitans of teaching fornication and eating food sacrificed to idols, like Balaam. In the message to Thyatira, the Christian prophet "Jezebel" is accused of the same things. It is unlikely that John's prophetic opponent in Thyatira actually bore that name. Jezebel's namesake was a Canaanite noblewoman who married the Israelite king Ahab. She brought her gods with her to Israel and actively promoted their cult (1 Kings 18–19 and 2 Kings 9). She was opposed by the prophet Elijah (1 Kgs 18:1–19:3). Second Kings 9:22 speaks of Jezebel's "whoredoms and sorceries," meaning her idolatrous practices. The names Ahab and Jezebel became infamous in Israelite and Jewish tradition. A Jew or a Christian would hardly be named Jezebel. Rather, the author calls her that contemptuously.

John accuses some in Thyatira of committing adultery with Jezebel. It is not impossible that there was actual sexual immorality being practiced in the Asian churches. But it stretches the imagination to think that "Jezebel" was really carrying on adulterous affairs with a number of people in Thyatira and that the church there tolerated it. Fornication and adultery are frequent biblical images for idolatry, and this is probably the meaning of Jezebel's "whoredoms" in 2 Kgs 9:22. If eating food sacrificed to idols is considered idolatry by the seer, then pairing it with fornication may simply be using two nouns for one idea, a common rhetorical device known as hendiadys. Sexual immorality is used symbolically in chapters 17 and 18 when speaking of Rome and those who cooperate with it. In 9:21, 21:8, and 22:15, fornication is literal, but in each of those cases it is part of a general catalog of vices and receives no individual attention as in chapters 2, 17, and 18.

Alternatively, there may be some real sexual activity by members of the Thyatiran church of which John disapproves. The biblical Balaam was accused of encouraging the mating of Israelite men with foreign women. Perhaps Christians of the Nicolaitan persuasion were marrying non-Christians. In 1 Corinthians 7, Paul deals with whether Christians ought to divorce their non-Christian spouses. The very fact that the question arose implies that some thought such marriages wrong. Paul's answer is that they should not separate, if the unbelieving spouse is content to remain married. Otherwise, divorce is permissible, and the Christian spouse is then free to marry another, provided the new mate is a Christian. For one who does not recognize the legitimacy of marriages between Christians and non-Christians, Paul's advice could appear to encourage fornication. Nicolaitans may have had a view similar to Paul's, and Revelation's author may have taken a stricter view.

That leaves the issue of eating food sacrificed to idols. When Gentiles began to enter the church in substantial numbers, their relation to Torah regulations had to be worked out. Acts 15 gives an account of a meeting in Jerusalem of church leaders, including Peter, Paul, and James, which probably took place in 48 C.E. Paul speaks of the same meeting in Galatians 2. The assembly at Jerusalem decided not to require that newly converted Gentiles observe the Torah. However, they did lay the following obligations on them: "It has seemed good to the Holy Spirit and to us to impose on you no further burden than these essentials: that you abstain from what has been sacrificed to idols and from blood and from what is strangled and from fornication" (Acts 15:28–29). The forbidding of food sacrificed to idols and fornication in these guidelines corresponds to our seer's viewpoint. If the seer was a Jewish Christian recently arrived from Palestine after the destruction of Jerusalem in 70 C.E., he may well have been disturbed by the way that the Asian Christians participated in the culture around them, an engagement that may well have included eating sacrificial food in violation of the decision reached in Jerusalem years earlier. This last requires some explanation.

Most people in the ancient world did not eat meat often (see Theissen 1982, 125–29). It was too expensive. Most meat eating occurred at festivals of the gods or during meetings of trade guilds, business groups, and so on. A wealthy host might serve meat at a banquet. At any of these occasions, it would always be possible that the meat had been offered to an idol. It is a modern misconception that ancient sacrifices entailed completely burning the sacrificial victim. More commonly the meat was eaten by the priests or other participants at the sacrifice, or it was later sold. Of course, Jewish Christians would have developed methods of dealing with this situation, since keeping a distance from non-Jewish cults was in their heritage. But Gentiles were in a different situation. They came from a polytheistic society in which the patronage of one god did not exclude that of another. When Gentiles entered Christianity and took on its exclusivistic demands, they needed to work out ways of relating to their environment that would allow them both to be faithful to their new religion and to continue to maintain social and business contacts in the wider world. They did so in different ways, and differences led to tension. They also did so, at least in the early stages, in contact with Jewish Christians, who themselves had a variety of points of view, ranging from that of Jerusalem's circumcision party that demanded full observance of the Torah for Gentile Christians (Galatians 2; Acts 15:5) to Paul's more liberal view, described below.

Paul gives a relatively detailed treatment of food offered to idols in 1 Corinthians 8–10. In those chapters Paul considers the different circumstances in which Christians might face the problem of eating such food, although he is not as explicit about the situations to which he alludes as one would like. He is clear that under no circumstances may a Christian participate in the worship of idols, which he associates with demons. However, it is permissible to eat meat originally sacrificed to idols and now sold in the marketplace. Christ has broken the power of demons, and the whole earth belongs to God. Those who worship the one true God may partake with thanksgiving of what belongs to God. But Paul warns that not every Christian fully understands this, and those who do not may misunderstand and be scandalized by seeing their fellows eat sacrificial meat. Therefore Paul counsels those who are free because of their superior knowledge to forgo their freedom for the sake of their "weak" brothers and sisters. Love takes precedence over knowledge.

Paul wrote 1 Corinthians in Ephesus, one of the seven churches of Revelation (1 Cor 16:1–9). According to Acts 19, Paul spent about two years there, preaching and teaching both in the city and in the surrounding area. It is probable that the Ephesians were familiar with Paul's views on sacrificial food and found his advice useful as they navigated their way between the demands of Christianity and the realities of their everyday life.

The seer John writes some forty years after Paul's stay in Ephesus. We have already made the case that he arrived in Asia from Jewish Palestine, an area that perhaps did not have a liberal attitude toward such matters as eating food sacrificed to idols. John sees eating such food as idolatry. This fits his negative view of Roman Asian culture in general.

The message to Thyatira, which attacks Jezebel and her followers, speaks of those "who have not learned what some call 'the deep things of Satan.' " Unless there are Satan worshipers in the church, which is highly unlikely, this is probably not what John's opponents call their doctrine. But they may indeed have spoken of "deep things." In 1 Corinthians, Paul speaks of a superior wisdom to which not all Christians have access. He says, "We speak of wisdom, secret and hidden, which God declared before the ages for our glory. . . . These things God has revealed to us through the Spirit, for the Spirit searches everything, even the depths of God" (2:7, 10). John's opponents in Thyatira may be preaching what they call "the depths of God," and our author sarcastically turns that into "the deep things of Satan."

The Message to Ephesus (2:1–7)

For more specifics about each of the seven cities, see Ramsay (1904), Hemer (1986), and the article on each city in the *Anchor Bible Dictionary* or other good Bible dictionaries and atlases. Ephesus was the foremost commercial and cultural center of the Roman province of Asia. It fell under Roman rule in 133 B.C.E., when the kingdom of Pergamum, of which Ephesus was a part, was ceded to Rome by Attalus III, the last of the independent Pergamene kings. Its prominence was due to its strategic location at the mouth of the Cayster River, on a gulf of the Aegean Sea that made it an excellent harbor. Throughout the years the harbor at Ephesus tended to become silted up, causing the city to move several times.

Major Roman roads intersected at Ephesus. It was the location of a large temple to the goddess Artemis that was one of the seven wonders of the ancient world. In this cult, the Earth Mother goddess of western Asia Minor was identified with the Greek goddess Artemis. Artemis corresponds to the Roman goddess Diana. The site of Artemis's temple seems to have originally been a shrine with a sacred tree, and some of Ephesus's coins depict this tree (see Ford 1975, 388; Krodel 1989, 109).

Ephesus was also a center of the Roman imperial cult. As early as 29 B.C.E., Augustus allowed the city to set aside sacred precincts for the cult of Roma and Julius Caesar. Those precincts were within Artemis's sacred enclosure, a situation that reflected the extent to which the imperial cult and loyalty to Rome had become central to Asia's political and religious life. Ephesus later received permission to build temples to the emperors Claudius, Domitian, and Hadrian. Parts of a colossal statue of Domitian are still preserved in the museum at Ephesus.

It is unclear whether Ephesus was the official capital of the Roman province of Asia. Some commentators confidently claim that it was, and others assert just as confidently that Pergamum was the capital. Charles (1920, 60) chooses Pergamum for reasons that will be clarified when we examine that message. Hemer (1986, 84–86) examines the issue but is unable to resolve the question. He suggests that there was a complex interplay between several Asian cities and Rome concerning honor and power and that the Romans used the competition between the cities to their own purposes. All seven cities in Revelation became centers of the imperial cult to one degree or other;

all were sites of Roman legal proceedings; and all were prominent in their own right. That being said, Ephesus was probably the most important city in Asia when all factors are taken into account – economic, political, and religious. It is fitting that Ephesus appears as the first of the seven cities in Revelation.

Ephesus was also prominent in earliest Asian Christianity. Acts 19 says that Paul preached in a lecture hall at Ephesus: "This continued for two years, so that all the residents of Asia, both Jews and Greeks, heard the word of the Lord" (19:10). Acts also states that just before making the trip to Jerusalem that led to his arrest and eventual death, Paul made a major speech to the elders of the Ephesian church (20:17–38). The Pastoral Epistles situate Paul's protégé Timothy in Ephesus (1 Tim 1:3; 2 Tim 1:18; 4:12). Many scholars (perhaps the majority) think Paul's letter to the Ephesians is pseudonymous. It may not even have been addressed to Ephesus originally, since that address is omitted in some of the best manuscripts. There is reason to think that it was composed as a sort of cover letter for a collection of Paul's letters. If so, it is significant that it was eventually associated with Ephesus, providing more evidence of the city's importance to early Christianity. Later tradition associates the apostle John and Jesus' mother Mary with Ephesus. Ignatius, the bishop of Antioch who in the first part of the second century was brought to Rome to be martyred and who wrote letters to various churches along his route, wrote his longest letter to Ephesus.

As with all the churches, the message is addressed to its angel. The identification of the source of the message as the one "who holds the seven stars in his right hand, who walks among the seven golden lampstands" (2:1), alludes to the vision of the one like a son of man in chapter 1 (1:16). The messages that use predications taken from the vision in chapter 1 do so in reverse order of their occurrence in that chapter (Farrer 1949, 70–86). The last verse of chapter 1 interprets the lampstands and the stars, and the first of the seven messages, the one to Ephesus, takes up these elements. Revelation 1:20 says that the lampstands are the churches and the stars are their angels. The vision in chapter 1 and the reference to it in 2:1 imply that Christ is present among the churches and that he has ultimate control and authority over them. Authority over the churches is associated with cosmic rule, as Christ holds the seven stars in his hand (1:16; 2:1).

As in all of the messages, the body begins with the words "I know." The cosmic Christ is intimately acquainted with the realities of the Asian churches. Christ begins in 2:2 on a positive note and says that he knows their "works" (*erga*), "toil" (*kopos*), and "patient endurance" (*hypomonê*). Paul has a similar trilogy of work, toil, and endurance in 1 Thessalonians. He says that he prays for them, "remembering before our God and Father your work [*ergou*] of faith and labor [*kopou*] of love and steadfastness [*hypomonês*] of hope in our Lord Jesus Christ" (1:3). Although the specific circumstances are not the same, the basic meanings of the terms are constant. Together the terms represent the faithful and consistent living out of the Christian life in the face of challenges and obstacles and in the hope of future reward and vindication.

In Revelation, "faith" (*pistis*) means faithfulness to God in the face of opposition. "Works" (*erga*) is a common New Testament term denoting morally significant behavior. When praised, it means activity done in accordance with God's will and on behalf of God and the church. "Steadfastness" (*hypomonê*), often translated "endurance," is the Christian virtue most characteristic of Revelation, because it means not only consistency but strength and courage when one might be tempted to give up because of difficulty and persecution. Schüssler Fiorenza (1991, 51) defines it as "consistent resistance and steadfast perseverance" when subjected to "oppressive eschatological tribulations."

In what follows John specifies what works, toil, and endurance mean in the addressees' circumstances, and in so doing he puns on those terms. First he says, "I know that you cannot tolerate [*bastasai*] evildoers" (2:2). Refusal to tolerate evildoers is made still more specific: "You have tested those who claim to be apostles but are not, and have found them to be false" (2:2). These false apostles are probably identical with the Nicolaitans of 2:6, 15, and the followers of Balaam and Jezebel of 2:14, 20–24. The Ephesians are praised for having resisted this heresy. Ignatius of Antioch also praises the Ephesians for their rejection of heresy (*Eph.* 9.1).

Revelation 2:3 cleverly wraps up Christ's praise of the Ephesians through its use of language: "I also know that you are enduring patiently [*hypomonên echeis:* literally, 'You have patient endurance,' the same word for 'endurance' as in 2:2] and bearing up [*ebastasas:* the same verb as is used for 'cannot tolerate' in 2:2] for the sake of my name, and that you have not grown weary [*ou kekopiakes:* a verbal form of the word for 'toil' used in

2:2, *kopos*]" (2:3). Nothing in 2:3 makes the Ephesians' behavior any more specific. Refusal to "bear" the false apostles constitutes "bearing up for the sake of my name." The Ephesians' "toil" in opposing the false apostles is characterized by their not being "worn out" (*ou kekopiakes*) by that toil (*kopos,* the same Greek root in both instances).

Early on in Christian tradition the inner group of twelve disciples was identified with the term "apostle," so that Christians today speak of "the twelve apostles." Revelation's new Jerusalem has twelve foundations on which are written the names of the twelve apostles, so it knows this usage (21:14; see Mark 3:14). However, the New Testament and other early Christian texts show that "apostle" was applied more broadly. In his list of witnesses to the resurrection (1 Cor 15:6–9), Paul mentions "the twelve" separately from "all the apostles," and he claims to be an apostle both in that list and frequently throughout his letters. Acts 14:14 calls Paul and Barnabas apostles. The term *apostolos* simply means "one sent," and it is applied to traveling missionaries, teachers, and founders of churches. The Didache says that apostles must be tested to see if they are genuine. False apostles are mentioned in 2 Cor 11:1–15.

After praising the Ephesians, Christ criticizes them: "But I have this against you, that you have abandoned the love you had at first. Remember then from what you have fallen; repent, and do the works you did at first. If not, I will come to you and remove your lampstand from its place, unless you repent" (2:5). Although Christ has commended them for their works in 2:2, it now becomes clear that it is not their works in their entirety that deserve approval but only their rejection of false apostles. Ironically, there may be a connection between the Ephesians' opposition toward false apostles and their lack of love.

In the letters purportedly written by Paul to Timothy, leader of the Ephesian church (letters thought by many to be pseudonymous), he encourages Timothy to oppose false teaching. "Paul" stresses the need for a loving attitude toward false teachers: "The Lord's servant must not be quarrelsome but kindly to everyone, an apt teacher, patient, correcting opponents with gentleness. God may perhaps grant that they will repent and come to know the truth" (2 Tim 2:23–25). These words imply that opposition to other Christian teachers *could* lead to alienation and a loss of a loving attitude. Revelation's seer wishes to praise the church for its opposition to false apostles but exhorts it to recover the loving attitude toward the wayward encouraged by the author of 2 Tim 2:23–25.

The Ephesians are told to repent. The word "repent" (*metanoeô*) throughout the New Testament means more than just feeling sorrow for wrongdoing. Its root meaning is to change one's mind, to change one's way of thinking. The corresponding Hebrew term is *shûb,* "to turn." For both the New Testament and Hebrew Bible, repentance means a radical reordering of one's life so that it conforms to God's will. The use of this term in the message to Ephesus reveals the seriousness of the charges against that church. That seriousness is revealed also in the threat leveled against it. When Christ says that he will come and remove the lampstand from its place, it may be simply that the church at Ephesus will lose its preeminence among the churches. However, since the lampstands are not assigned any relative position in the vision of chapter 1, it is more likely that Ephesus will cease to be a church. It looks as if it will be cut off from Christ altogether. Orthodoxy without love is unacceptable. This ordering of priorities recalls 1 Corinthians 13, where Paul says that without love all other Christian virtues and achievements are useless. The threat to move Ephesus's lampstand may be particularly appropriate, since the city was forced to move its location several times due to the silting up of its harbor (Ramsay 1994, 169, 176–78; Hemer 1986, 52–54).

Commentators have been struck by the fact that Christ's coming seems to be conditional in 2:5. Only if the church does not repent will he come. Therefore, the reasoning goes, this cannot mean the parousia, Christ's second and definitive coming. The idea that Christ might come in judgment to a particular church, apart from the parousia, seems to moderate the imminence of expectation of the eschaton, and so this supports Charles's idea that the messages originally had an independent existence, because their eschatology is different from that of Revelation as a whole. Such a conclusion is hardly necessary. Even if it is accepted that Christ might exercise judgment on a particular church before the parousia, this need not mean that the parousia itself is distant. Further, Christ's threat in 2:5 might refer to the parousia itself. The apodosis of the conditional sentence (the "then" part of the "if/then" construction) may include *both* the ideas of coming and removing the lampstand (Krodel 1989, 109). In other words, Christ is saying that if they do not repent, he will come *and* remove the lampstand. Understood is that if they do repent, he will come and reward them, as described in 2:7. This would be consonant with the insistence, apparent in various places in the book, that the anticipated eschatological events are coming soon (1:1, 3; 2:16; 3:11; 22:7, 12, 20).

Revelation 2:6 returns the message to a positive note. The Ephesian church is commended for "hating" the works of the Nicolaitans, as Christ himself hates them. Since the Nicolaitans are the false apostles, 2:6 and 2:2 form a frame for the message. Some Christian readers are surprised by the occurrence of the word "hate" here, but it is not the Nicolaitans themselves who are hated; it is their works. Furthermore, the verb "hate" is used with God as its subject in the Bible to indicate the depth of divine disapproval (Roloff 1993, 45, points to Ps 97:10; Sir 17:26; Matt 13:9; Luke 14:26). Like the biblical God, Revelation's Christ does not tolerate sinners or their deeds.

Revelation 2:7 begins with the exhortation to listen. All of the churches are told to listen to all of the messages. The message from Christ comes through the medium of prophecy, and prophecy is associated with the Spirit, so the message is called "What the Spirit is saying to the churches."

The message to Ephesus ends with the following promise: "To everyone who conquers, I will give permission to eat from the tree of life that is in the paradise of God" (2:7). "The one who conquers" is the one who successfully resists the temptations and hostility of a culture opposed to God. It remains to examine the content of the promise. As already noted, a tree was depicted on Ephesian coinage, and it was probably associated with the cult of Artemis. It is appropriate, then, that our author, in implicit contrast to that idolatrous tree, promises participation in the tree of life to those who resist their environment (Ramsay 1994, 179–81; Hemer 1986, 41–52).

The reference to the tree also recalls Genesis 3. When Adam and Eve eat the forbidden fruit of the tree of the knowledge of good and evil, God expels them from the Garden of Eden, so that they might not "take also from the tree of life, and eat, and live forever" (3:22). In Jewish texts of the later second temple period, the expected setting right of the world, be it conceived in apocalyptic or prophetic terms, was often thought of as a restoration of circumstances that obtained at the beginning of creation, conceived of as a golden age when all was as God willed it to be. Therefore imagery taken from the beginning of Genesis was employed to paint a picture of the endtime. In *1 Enoch*

24-25, for example, one of the features of the end is the transplanting of the tree of life to Jerusalem, to be enjoyed by the elect (Wallace [1992, 658] also notes *T. Levi* 18:10-11; 4 Ezra 7:123-24; 8:52; 1QS 1:3-4; 1QH 8:5-6). According to *T. Levi* 18:11, the eschatological priest "will grant to the saints to eat of the tree of life." Ford cites rabbinic references to the effect that paradise and the tree of life will be present at the end of time (1975, 388). These pages embody the apocalyptic principle that the endtime is like the beginning of creation.

The promises at the end of each message in Revelation 2-3 tie the messages to the eschatological fulfillment depicted in Revelation 20-22. The promise in 2:7 that the one who conquers will eat of the tree of life in "the paradise of God" finds its fulfillment in chapter 22. A river flows through the middle of the eschatological Jerusalem. "On either side of the river is the tree of life with its twelve kinds of fruit, producing fruit each month; and the leaves of the tree are for the healing of the nations" (22:2).

Revelation 2:7 contains the only mention of "paradise" in the book. The Greek word *paradeisos* derives from the Persian word for "garden," used in the Septuagint to translate "Garden of Eden." In postbiblical Jewish literature, it is used to denote the place where the righteous go after death (e.g., *1 Enoch* 60:8; 61:12; *2 Enoch* 8:1; 4 Ezra 7:36; *2 Bar.* 51:10-11), a usage picked up by the New Testament (Luke 23:43; 2 Cor 12:2-4; see Charles 1920, 2:160, for a full discussion of paradise; see also Charlesworth 1992; Hemer 1986, 50-52). Other New Testament sources see its location as heaven, but since Revelation expects God and Christ to come to the new earthly Jerusalem at the eschaton, it is there that paradise will also be found. The basic idea is that the bliss of the original creation will be restored in the endtime.

The Message to Smyrna (2:8-11)

The ancient city of Smyrna lay about forty-five miles north of Ephesus. It was at the tip of a bay that cut deeply into the coast of Asia, on the eastern shore of the Aegean Sea. It was a prosperous and important city at the terminus of a trade route running east through Lydia and into Phrygia along the Hermus Valley. The original city had been located some miles further inland but was destroyed by the expanding Lydian kingdom in around 600 B.C.E.

It was rebuilt by the successors of Alexander the Great around 300 B.C.E. During the three centuries from 600 to 300 B.C.E. the Smyrneans kept their traditions alive and retained their identity. This history makes the emphasis on death and resurrection in the message particularly appropriate (Ramsay 1994, 182, 196–97; Hemer 1986, 61). The city included a hill that was about five hundred feet high on which was built the acropolis. The effect was so striking that some called the acropolis the "crown" of Smyna, which perhaps influenced the crown imagery in the message (Ramsay 1994, 186–88; Hemer 1986, 73–74).

Smyrna had for a long time been an ally of Rome. It sided with Rome in its conflicts with Carthage (265–146 B.C.E.). As early as 195 B.C.E. it had a temple to the goddess Roma. In 26 C.E. it received permission to build a temple to the emperor Tiberius, an honor that had been sought by others as well. It thus became a *nekoros,* a coveted honor meaning that it was a keeper of an imperial temple. At the time of the writing of Revelation, it was a Roman assize city, a site for Roman legal procedures. It vied with Ephesus for the title "first in Asia," which may be why the seer used the title "the first and the last" of Christ here. The origin of the church at Smyrna is unclear. Perhaps it was evangelized by Paul operating out of Ephesus (see Acts 19:10). The letter of Ignatius of Antioch to the church in the early second century assumes that there is a well-organized congregation, including a bishop, elders, and deacons (Mounce 1977, 92).

The messages to Smyrna and Philadelphia are the only two that are entirely positive. They are also the only two in which tension with the Jews is mentioned. The Jews were an important and respected part of the Smyrnean population. Later Christian tradition saw the Smyrnean Jews as hostile to the Christians there. The *Martyrdom of Polycarp* and the *Acts of Pionius* claim that Smyrna's Jews had a hand in the deaths of Polycarp (d. ca. 155 C.E.) and Pionius (d. ca. 250 C.E.). D. S. Potter (1992, 75) thinks that the documents contain accurate information about relations within Smyrna.

The seer thinks that the church to which this message is addressed is about to undergo persecution and that some of its members may die. He writes to prepare them. In this message, Christ fittingly identifies himself as "the first and the last, who was dead and came to life [*ezêsen*]" (2:8), attributes of the one like a son of man in 1:17–18. The biblical background of "the first and the last" is discussed in the commentary on 1:17, and in that context the phrase is also juxtaposed to mention of Christ's death and resurrection. "First and last" is a title applied to God in the Bible signifying his superiority to any other gods, and here it reemphasizes the absolute authority of Christ. Here, as in 1:17, it is juxtaposed to mention of his death and resurrection. Moyise remarks upon the profundity of juxtaposing a divine title expressing eternity with a reference to Christ's death (1995, 30). The reference to death and resurrection is important in this message, for it is clear that its addressees will not be sheltered from physical death, but will rise to everlasting life. Yarbro Collins (1979, 17) notes that seeing in the death and resurrection of Jesus the paradigm for Christian existence "has tremendous power to console." It imparts ultimate significance to Christian suffering.

Death and life are apparent opposites, but things are not as they appear. What the world sees as death, Christians should see as life. Indeed, the author uses a number of opposites in this message that undermine what he sees as a false perception of reality. Ford (1975, 394) presents them as follows:

first	*and*	last
became dead	*but*	came to life
poverty	*but*	in abundance
say they are Jews	*but*	are not
unto death	*and*	crown of life

The body of the message begins, "I know your affliction [*thlipsis*] and your poverty, even though you are rich" (2:9). What seems true about the church at Smyrna, that it is poor, is not true. The word used for "poverty" (*ptôcheia*) usually means destitution (Mounce 1977, 92). The church lives in material poverty, but its poverty hides the true riches it possesses, since it has the approval of the one who bears the title "the first and the last." The one who transcends everything is its protector. Poverty and riches are contrasted with respect to the Laodicean church as well. But the church at Laodicea receives the opposite judgment—it seems to be rich and prosperous, but it is poor (3:17).

It may be that the Smyrnean church is materially poor because of its allegiance to Christ. This recalls Hebrews. We referred to Hebrews 10 in the introduction while discussing persecution of the earliest church. It is helpful to cite a passage from that chapter:

> You endured a hard struggle with sufferings, sometimes being publicly exposed to abuse and persecution, and sometimes being partners with those so treated. For you had compassion on those who were in prison, and you cheerfully accepted the plundering of your possessions, knowing that you yourselves possessed something better and more lasting. (Heb 10:32-34)

Applying this to the church at Smyrna, some propose that being a Christian has brought disapproval on church members so that they can no longer make a decent living (Mounce 1977, 92). Yarbro Collins (1990, 1002) approaches the situation from a different angle when she suggests that many members of the church were recent immigrants from Galilee and Judea, which affected their economic status. Whatever the reasons for its poverty, its material poverty hides the church's true situation. Properly understood, the church is perhaps the richest in Asia because of its absolute obedience to God and Christ.

Revelation's contrast of material poverty and spiritual wealth reflects such contrasts elsewhere in the New Testament. Charles (1920, 1:56) supplies examples. Paul says of himself that he ministers to his churches "as poor, yet making many rich" (2 Cor 6:10). The letter of James asks, "Has not God chosen the poor in the world to be rich in faith and to be the heirs of the kingdom that he has promised to those who love him?" (Jas 2:5). At the end of the parable of the rich fool, Jesus asserts, "So it is with those who store up treasures for themselves but are not rich toward God" (Luke 12:21). Wealth is often spoken of as spiritual rather than material (1 Tim 6:18). Examples could be multiplied. Such language is typical of a group critical of society's values.

In 1:9, John tells all the churches that he shares their "persecution" (*thlipsis*). As explained in the commentary on 1:9, *thlipsis* is a general word denoting the sufferings associated with the endtime, and its use in 1:9 implies that such *thlipsis* now engulfs all of the Asian churches. *Thlipsis* has the same meaning here, but now the seer considers the specific sufferings of the Smyrnean church as part of the eschatological sufferings. Christ says that he knows their affliction (*thlipsis*) and then immediately mentions their poverty (2:9). Then he mentions the "slander" of the local Jews who he says belong to the "synagogue of Satan." Next he says, "Do not fear what you are about to suffer. Beware, the devil is about to throw some of you into prison so that you may be tested, and for ten days you will have affliction [*thlipsis*]. But be faithful until death, and I will give you the crown of life" (2:10). The juxtaposition of these terms — affliction, poverty, slander by the Jews who belong to Satan, and affliction (including prison) brought on by the devil's opposition — supplies hints that allow speculation about what is going on in Smyrna. The seer anticipates trouble for the church. Although there is probably already opposition to the church, particularly on the part of the Jews, the real affliction lies in the immediate future. The Jews seem to be the immediate cause of this affliction, but as in the book as a whole, the real culprit is Satan.

The Greek word translated "devil" is *diabolos,* the word used in the Septuagint to translate the Hebrew word *satan.* Both *satan* and *diabolos* mean "accuser" or "slanderer." In Revelation 12, when Satan is thrown out of heaven, a heavenly voice proclaims, "The accuser of our comrades has been thrown down, who accuses them day and night before our God" (12:10). As will be explained more fully in that context, this depends on the image of Satan in the Bible as the angelic prosecuting attorney in God's court. It is fitting that the author introduces the Greek *diabolos* in the letter to Smyrna — the addressees are likely to face accusers in a Roman court soon, and God sees Rome as Satan's representative on earth. The seer sees prison in the church's future, so the affliction involves the legal authorities.

In ancient Roman society, prison was not a punishment in itself. People went to prison to await trial, to await execution, or to be forced to do something. The seer expects that some Smyrnean Christians will face death. Whether or not this actually comes to pass, they must be ready to be faithful even to the point of dying. The death penalty was a sanction the Roman authorities reserved for their own use. Precisely how and why the Smyrnean Christians face death is not explicit. It is likely that we are to draw a connection between the "slander" of the Jews and the suffering to come at the hands of the authorities. It may be that although Christians initially benefited from the privileges accorded to the Jews — for example, exemption from army service and from participation in civic cults — as it became clear to outsiders that Christianity and Judaism were not the same, Christians were more vulnerable to maltreatment at the hands of their neighbors and local officials. It may also be that there were tensions between Christians and non-Christian Jews that upset the authorities. Some think the emperor Claudius expelled the Jews from Rome because of rioting over a certain Chrestos, possibly a misspelling of Christos, although this view has been challenged recently (see Suetonius, *Claudius* 25.4). In any case, it is plausible that some Jews had a hand in denouncing some Christians to the local authorities, but the exact charges are not stated.

The seer's calling the Jews a "synagogue of Satan" recalls the Johannine Jesus in John 8, who says that his Jewish opponents are children of Satan. There is a major difference between the gospel of John and Revelation here, however. In the gospel, "Jews" is a pejorative term, although its precise meaning is disputed (see Ashton 1985). Here the seer says that the opponents "say that they are Jews but are not" (2:9). This strange claim has led to speculation about who these "Jews" were. Some think that they were Judaizers, Christians who may or may not have been Jewish themselves but who advocated Christian obedience to the Torah. Most believe that they were the non-Christian Jewish community of Smyrna and that they opposed the Christian church there. As far as the seer is concerned, only those Jews who believe in Jesus are truly Jews. Paul makes a similar sort of argument in Romans and Galatians, where he argues on the basis of scripture that the true children of Abraham are those who belong to Christ. But Paul never tries to deny the appellation "Jews" to his kinsmen (although he does refer to Christians as "the Israel of God" in Gal 6:16). Our author goes so far as to deny that his opponents are really Jews, implying that he holds this term in high regard and presumably applies it to himself as truly deserving of it.

The phrase "synagogue of Satan" is unique to Revelation. It occurs nowhere else in Christian or Jewish literature. It may be similar to the phrase "assembly of Belial" in the Dead Sea Scrolls (1QH 2:22), although it is disputed whether Belial ought to be taken as a proper name or as a noun meaning "deceit." Either way, there is a parallel with Revelation. In both cases, those considering themselves the true Israel look with disdain on others who also claim to belong to Israel. Yarbro Collins (1990, 1002) suggests that the conflict between the Smyrnean Christians and non-Christian Jews is more like the sort of intra-Jewish conflict apparent in the Dead Sea Scrolls than like a conflict between different religions, and she suggests looking at the following passages: 1QS 5:1–2, 10–20; 9:16; CD 1:12; 1QM 1:1; 4:9–10; 1QH 2:22. J. Andrew Overman (1990) analyzes the gospel of Matthew in terms of the same sort of intra-Jewish conflict between Christian and non-Christian Jews, a perspective that informs his commentary on Matthew in this series (1996; see Saldarini 1994).

Krodel (1989, 111) believes that the seer was disturbed with the Jews not only because they did not accept Jesus but also because they were comfortable with Hellenistic society in Smyrna. The seer may have disapproved of Jewish accommodation to local culture in Smyrna. Conversely, Smyrnean Jews would have been uncomfortable with John's apocalypticism as well as with his use of their scripture to apocalyptic and Christian ends.

The seer tells the Smyrneans that they will be "tested" (*peirazô*) and that they will have affliction (*thlipsis*) for ten days. Testing and affliction are features of the endtime. The period of suffering attending the final cosmic and human battle between good and evil is a time when the true mettle of humans will be put to the test. It is this eschatological circumstance that is behind the final petition of the Lord's Prayer: "And do not bring us to the time of trial [*peirasmos,* from *peirazô,* 'to test'], but rescue us from the evil one" (Matt 6:13). The "evil one" is probably Satan. The opposition the Smyrneans face is part of this eschatological struggle. That the struggle is worldwide is clear from 3:10, where Christ promises the Philadelphians, "I will keep you from the hour of trial [*peirasmou*] that is coming on the whole world to test [*peirasai*] the inhabitants of the earth." The word *peirasmos* can mean "test" or "temptation," hence the more familiar translation of the Lord's Prayer, "Lead us not into temptation." Caird (1966, 36) comments, "What Satan intends as a temptation, God uses as a test."

"Ten days" is not to be taken literally. It recalls the ten days during which Daniel and his companions were allowed to live the Jewish way of life to see if it hindered them in their service to the Babylonian court (Dan 1:12–13). Ten days is a substantial amount of time, but it is not lengthy. It is certainly short compared to the millennium in which the victorious martyrs reign with Christ (20:4–6; Krodel 1989, 113). Ten is always a negative number in Revelation. Elsewhere in the book it refers to the ten horns on the head of Satan or the beast that represents the Roman empire (Rev 12:3; 13:1 [twice]; 17:3, 7, 12 [twice], 16). The time of testing is limited, recalling the synoptic apocalyptic discourse where Christ says concerning the final afflictions, "If the Lord had not cut short those days, no one would be saved; but for the sake of the elect, whom he chose, he has cut short those days" (Mark 13:20).

Within the body of the message to Smyrna there is a promise to those who resist evil to the point of dying: "I will give you the crown of life [*stephanon tês zôês*]" (2:10). Crown imagery is so widespread in Jewish, Christian, and Hellenistic settings that it is impossible to determine a precise setting from which it might come, but the following suggestions are helpful. The promise of a crown would have been particularly appropriate for the church at Smyrna, since Smyrna's acropolis was spoken of as its crown. The word for crown used in Rev 2:10 is not *diadêma,* the word for a royal crown, but *stephanos,* more often used of the wreath bestowed for victory in the games, the wreath of honor worn by participants in banquets, or a crown given by a grateful city to a benefactor (Hemer 1986, 72). The second-century traveler and writer Pausanias says that Smyrna was famous for its games (Pausanias 6.14.3; Charles 1920, 1:58).

Game imagery in connection to crowns appears in 1 Cor 9:25 and 2 Tim 2:5 (see also Phil 3:14; 1 Pet 5:4; Charles 1920, 1:58–59 offers other Jewish and Christian examples; see Ford 1975, 396). The closest New Testament parallel to this promise is in Jas 1:12: "Blessed is anyone who endures [*hypomenei:* verbal form of the noun *hypomonê,* common in Revelation] temptation [*peirasmon:* the same word used in the Lord's Prayer for the final testing]. Such a one has stood the test and will receive the crown of life [*stephanon tês zôês*] that the Lord has promised those who love him." In both James and Revelation, those who endure and pass the eschatological test will receive the crown of life. Charles (1920, 1:58–59) notes that heavenly beings wear crowns in some texts (cf. *2 Enoch* 14:2; *3 Bar.* 6:1). These contexts, games and heaven, are not mutually exclusive. Indeed, elsewhere in the New Testament winning heaven is equivalent to winning a crown.

The "crown of life" recalls the promise made to the Ephesians that they will eat of the tree of life (2:7). When humans sinned, God decreed death and ensured that humans would not live forever by denying them access to the tree of life (Gen 3:19–24; see Rom 5:12–14; 1 Cor 15:21). When the eschaton comes and all is as God originally intended, humans will no longer die. As Rev

21:4 says, "Death will be no more" (see 1 Cor 15:26). It is fitting that the author stresses the future true life with God to a church he thinks faces physical death. As the book of Wisdom says: "In the eyes of the foolish they seemed to have died, and their departure was thought to be a disaster, and their going from us to be their destruction; but they are at peace. For though in the sight of others they were punished, their hope is full of immortality" (3:2–4).

The message concludes with the usual command to "listen to what the Spirit is saying to the churches" and with a final promise: "Whoever conquers will not be harmed by the second death." The Greek here is emphatic. Christ asserts that the Smyrneans, though not spared physical death, will *not* face the second death. "Second death" is a phrase found in later Jewish texts (Charles 1920, 1:59). In 21:8, the fiery lake in which Satan, the beast, and the false prophet meet their end is called the second death, and all sinners end up there. It means the eternal punishment to be endured by those who are cut off from God. The resurrected Christian martyrs who reign with Christ for a thousand years escape the second death (20:6). For the Smyrneans, the first death is not real, for it leads to escape from the second death and to the attainment of the crown of life.

The Message to Pergamum (2:12–17)

Pergamum was one of Asia's most important cities. It had been the capital of the Attalid kingdom of Asia Minor that was ceded to Rome when King Attalus III died in 133 B.C.E. It may still have been the seat of Roman government at the time of the writing of Revelation, but that is not clear (see comments on Ephesus; Hemer 1986, 82–83). Pergamum was an imposing city. It was built on a one-thousand-foot-high, cone-shaped hill some fifteen miles inland from the Aegean. It dominated the Cayster Valley and was a natural fortress. Its very name means "citadel." It contained a number of important temples, the primary of which were the ones to Zeus, Athena, Dionysus, and Asclepius. It was the first city in Asia allowed to build a temple to a living emperor. In 29 B.C.E. it raised a temple to Augustus and Roma, giving it pride of place in the imperial cult in Asia. It was an assize city, meaning that official Roman judicial proceedings took place there.

The message to Pergamum has several things in common with the one to Ephesus (Yarbro Collins 1979, 18–19). Both begin with attributes of Christ that foreshadow warnings of punishment to the respective churches. Both contain praise and censure of their churches. Both deal with the Christian group called the Nicolaitans. But Ephesus is commended for rejecting this group, whereas Pergamum is criticized for tolerating it.

The message begins with the usual address to the church's angel and the identification of the sender of the message, Christ. The author continues to work his way back through the predications of Christ contained in the vision in chapter 1. The message from Ephesus draws from 1:20; that to Smyrna derives from 1:17–18; and the one to Pergamum comes from 1:16. Christ describes himself as the one "who has the sharp two-edged sword" (2:12). Later in the message Christ threatens to use the sword against the church members, and there he refers to it as "the sword of my mouth" (2:16). In 1:16, it is said of the mysterious one like a son of man that "from his mouth came a sharp, two-edged sword." As noted in the commentary on 1:16, two biblical passages in the background of that verse are Isa 11:4, which says that a messianic figure "shall strike the earth with the rod of his mouth, and with the breath of his lips he shall kill the wicked," and Isa 49:2, in which the prophet declares, "He made my mouth like a sharp sword." The combination of these allusions presents Jesus as a powerful judge whose word divides between good and evil and punishes the evil. Also relevant are Heb 4:12, where God's word is "a two-edged sword" that is "able to judge the thoughts and intentions of the heart," and 2 Thess 4:8, where Jesus defeats the eschatological "lawless one . . . with the breath of his mouth" (see 4 Ezra 13:4; see Fekkes 1994, 116–22).

Christ threatens to use the sword against Christians (2:16). The seer writes this book not just to console and strengthen the faithful but to correct those who have strayed and to bring them back to the truth before it is too late. When the final battle comes, the lines between the good and bad will be already drawn, and it will remain for Christ simply to destroy the evil. In chapter 19, Christ kills his enemies with the sword of his mouth. By this time, if those whom Christ censured in the message to the Pergamene church have not repented, they will be among those whom Christ kills.

The sword imagery fits Pergamum's circumstances (Ramsay 1994, 213–14). The city was central to Roman power in the region, both because of its position in the imperial cult and because of its role in Roman administration, which had the power of capital punishment, called the *ius gladii,* the "law of the sword" (see 20:4 and Rom 13:4). In Romans 13, Paul defends Roman power and warns his readers, "The authority does not bear the sword in vain" (13:4). In Revelation, Christ has the real power of the sword, although the Roman empire's power to decree physical death is not denied. When the messages to Smyrna and Pergamum are looked at together, the first says not to fear death at the hands of the authorities, lest one incur the second death, and the second warns of the sword borne by Christ. That is reminiscent of Jesus' advice in Matt 10:28: "Do not fear those who kill the body but cannot kill the soul; rather fear him who can destroy both soul and body in hell."

The body of the message begins, "I know where you are living, where Satan's throne is" (2:13). Why Pergamum is called the location of Satan's throne is debated. One of the most frequently proposed solutions is that it refers to the massive altar to Zeus on the city's acropolis, visible from a distance. Others have suggested one of the other cults located in the city, especially the one to Asclepius. Asclepius was the god of healing, and his shrine in Pergamum was famous. The symbol of Asclepius was the serpent, a fact that is reflected in the symbol of medicine even today. The author may have connected the cultic serpent with the serpentlike dragon in chapter 12, which is Satan. Still others see the mountain on which Pergamum and its shrines were built as Satan's throne.

Ramsay makes a suggestion that ties the reference to Satan's throne closely to Revelation's main concerns. He sees it as referring to the temple of Augustus at Pergamum (1994, 214–15). In 13:2, the dragon (Satan) gives its throne to the beast (Rome). The throne symbolizes Roman authority, granted to it by Satan. Pergamum stands out in the seer's mind as a center of Roman authority in Asia.

Yarbro Collins combines some of these suggestions in a hypothesis that takes account of the archeological remains at Pergamum (1997). She first notes that mountains were often seen as the thrones of gods or the sites of their thrones in the ancient Near East, in the religion of ancient Israel, and in second temple Judaism (1997, 7–10); and mountains or prominent hills were often the sites of temples and sacred areas. One of the most prominent features of the city of Pergamum was a steep hill that served as its acropolis. Yarbro Collins agrees with those who place importance on the massive altar found on the acropolis, but she adds that it was part of a larger complex that included temples to Zeus and to Athena. She thinks the entire complex, especially the altar and the temple to Zeus, is the referent of the term "throne of Satan." Ancient Jews and Christians often saw the gods as angels or demons, and Yarbro Collins says, "In dualistic apocalyptic contexts, it was a short step from *daimones* (demons) to unclean spirits or demons. In the context of such a perspective, Satan, as the chief of the fallen angels, would correspond to Zeus, the ruler of the gods in Hellenistic religion" (1997, 6). She observes that the seer also says that "Satan lives" in Pergamum (2:13) and that the same verb for "lives" (*katoikeô*) is sometimes used for gods dwelling in their temples.

Yarbro Collins points to a frieze that covered the four sides of the great altar as evidence for her hypothesis. That frieze depicted the combat myth we discussed in the introduction. The frieze represented Zeus's victory over his enemies, a victory that preserved the order of the universe. Visitors to Pergamum would have seen the altar as a representation not only of the mythic victory of Zeus but also of the "stability and dignity of the current dynasty" (Yarbro Collins 1997, 24), originally of the Attalid rulers who built the altar and later of the Romans who inherited the Attalid kingdom. Yarbro Collins notes that Domitian, the emperor under whom we think Revelation was written, was identified with Zeus (1997, 14–15). Yarbro Collins's suggestion for the referent of the "throne of Satan" has the advantage of identifying a highly visible feature of Pergamum that brings together religious symbols with Roman rule, Zeus with the emperor.

Revelation's author takes the combat myth that had been used to bolster the legitimacy of Rome and turns it to the opposite purpose, to prove Rome's illegitimacy. Zeus is not the highest god but the highest demon, Satan. His representative, the emperor, Domitian, sits not on a divine throne but on a satanic one. The true God shares his throne with Christ. Zeus and the emperor, apparent guardians of order, are in fact revolting against the creator and his representative, Christ.

The church members at Pergamum are commended for "holding fast to my name" and for not denying their faith in Christ (2:13). This was despite the martyrdom of Antipas, who was killed among them, "where Satan lives" (2:13). We know nothing about Antipas beyond what Revelation tells us. John sees his death as resulting from his faithfulness to Christ. If the references to Satan framing the mention of Antipas's death allude to official Roman power, this may imply that Antipas was killed according to Roman legal procedures. In both Pliny's letter and the *Martyrdom of Polycarp,* Christians can avoid punishment by cursing Christ. If Antipas was confronted with that same option, that would make sense of the formulation "holding fast to my name" for which the Pergamenes are praised (2:13).

If the references to Satan are more general, then Antipas may have died in a less formal way, perhaps as the result of mob action. Either way, the seer sees his death as the work of Satan and so as related to idolatrous Roman power. The possibility remains open that it is only from the Christian point of view that Antipas has died for Christ's sake. First Peter, also addressed to Christians living in Roman Asia Minor, allows the possibility that Christians will be accused of crimes other than being Christian and advises them to avoid all wrongdoing so that the fact that they suffer for bearing the name of Christian might be undeniable (1 Pet 4:12–19). That Antipas was killed is not proof that being a Christian was itself a crime in Asia at the time of the seer.

It is striking that Antipas is awarded the same title as is given to Jesus in 1:5. Jesus is called "the faithful witness" (*martys*), and Antipas is called "my faithful witness" (*martys*). The Greek word *martys* had not yet attained the technical meaning of one who dies for the faith. Its basic meaning was still "witness" (Trites 1973). But John encourages his audience to be ready to bear public witness even to the point of death, a death he considers likely given the impending tribulation. Just as Christ's witness resulted in his death, so did that of Antipas. That makes Antipas the model Christian, the one who has already done what all other Christians must be prepared to do.

Since the Pergamene church has been faithful to Christ under demanding and frightening circumstances, it is remarkable that the seer now goes on to criticize it. The "few things" that he has against the church really amount to one thing—they tolerate the Nicolaitans, here also called the followers of Balaam, whom he accuses of eating food sacrificed to idols and of fornication. This group and their practices were examined above under the heading "The Opponents of John." The case was made there that what John had against them was their willingness to accept Hellenistic culture to some degree. John sees that as apostasy, but they evidently do not. Their position may even be similar to that of

Paul on the issues in question. The seer is able to bring forward the name of only a single person who was actually martyred in Pergamum, and he criticizes the church as a whole for tolerating the Nicolaitans. It may be only the minority of the church that shares John's harder line. This would explain his willingness to threaten the church with punishment when Christ comes. He says, "Repent then. If not, I will come to you soon and make war [*polemêsô*] against them with the sword of my mouth" (2:16).

The verb "make war" (*polemeô*) occurs in the New Testament only once outside of Revelation (Jas 4:2), but it occurs six times within Revelation, all in connection with the eschatological battle against Satan. In 12:7, it is used twice to describe eschatological warfare when Satan and his angels fight Michael and his angels. In 17:14 and 19:11, it denotes the final battles between the warrior Christ and his enemies. In 13:4, worshipers of the beast marvel, "Who is like the beast and who can fight [*polemêsai*] against it?" It is noteworthy, then, that Christ in 2:16 can speak of coming to "make war" on those whom the Pergamene church, exemplary in its resistance to Roman power, accepts. As was noted with respect to the message to Ephesus (2:5), the apodosis of the conditional sentence, the "then" part, includes coming *and* punishment. We are of the opinion that Christ's coming refers to the eschaton. If they do not repent, then his coming will mean punishment for them.

After the usual command to listen (2:17) comes the promise to the one who conquers. Two things are promised, manna and a white stone (see Hemer 1986, 94–102). Manna is the less mysterious of these two elements. It was the miraculous food God gave the Israelites in the desert after rescuing them from Egypt. Thus it is associated with the exodus, which was a liberation from oppressive political power, and with God's protection of the people. Some Jewish traditions hold that at the end of time God will again give manna to his people (*2 Bar.* 29:8 and *Sib. Or.* 7:149; see Charles 1920, 1:65, for rabbinic references; see also John 6). John draws on this stream of tradition when he promises that his hearers, if they are faithful, will receive the eschatological manna. They will be the heirs of God's protection as in the exodus. It is appropriate that in a message demanding abstention from idolatrous food, the promised reward includes food given by God.

The second part of the promise is harder to interpret. The conqueror will receive a white stone on which is written a "new name that no one knows except the one who receives it" (2:17). Although there are many partial parallels to this image, there is none that is completely satisfying. Questions arise concerning the significance of a stone, whose name is written on it, and the meaning of its color.

Small stones were used for various purposes in the Hellenistic world. They could be used for voting, including voting for a particular verdict in a trial. In that case, white could signify acquittal. They could also be used as tickets of admission to functions. Some feel that the emphasis on food (and so perhaps banquets) in this message – food sacrificed to idols and manna given to the victors – makes the ticket idea plausible. That would not explain the color white or the engraving with a secret name.

An especially helpful comparison is that of amulets, which sometimes took the form of stones engraved with the name of a supernatural entity whose protection the bearer sought. As noted earlier, names had great significance in the ancient world. They were thought to contain something of the essence of their owners, and possession of the name of a supernatural figure gave one some claim on that figure. Following the parallel of amulets, the name engraved on the stone in Rev 2:17 would be that of God or Christ. In chapter 19, it is said that the eschatological Christ "has a name inscribed that no one knows but himself" (19:12), and later in the same passage it says, "On his robe and on his thigh he has a name inscribed, 'King of kings and Lord of lords' " (19:16). That the stone of 2:17 has Christ's name inscribed on it gains support from the observation that the church at Pergamum is extolled for holding fast to Christ's name. The secrecy of the name may correspond to the secrecy of Christ's name in 19:12. Although in chapter 19 only Christ knows the name, this may not apply to the period when the eschatological rewards are given to the faithful. This would explain why the recipient of the name knows what it is in 2:17.

The newness of the name is more problematic. A new name implies some transformation of the name's referent (see Isa 62:2–3; 65:15). The key to this may be in Philippians 2, where it is only after his resurrection that Jesus receives the name "Lord" (Phil 2:9–11). In Rom 1:4, Paul seems to imply that Jesus receives the title "Son of God" because of or from the time of his resurrection. Another possible background to the "new name" is the fact that the Roman senate bestowed on Octavian a new name, "Augustus." The seer could be subtly alluding to the Roman emperor and surpassing him by speaking of the new name given to Christ or to the Christian who "conquers" Rome (Ford 1975, 401).

The whiteness of the stone fits well with the use of white in the rest of Revelation. White appears twenty-one times in Revelation, symbolizing purity, that is, fitness for entering the heavenly world where God is enthroned, and readiness for being part of the new Jerusalem. It represents victory over evil and the joy of communion with God and Christ. The color white figures in the vision of Christ (1:14 [three times]), the white garments of the saved (3:4, 5, 18; 6:11; 7:9, 13, 14), Christ's white horse for the final battle (19:11), the garb of the heavenly army (19:14 [twice]), and the great white throne on which God sits at the end of times (20:11).

The Message to Thyatira (2:18–29)

Thyatira lay about half-way between Pergamum and Sardis on the major road connecting those two cities. Concerning the message to Thyatira, Charles makes the comment, "The longest letter is addressed to the least important of the Seven Cities" (1920, 1:67). Thyatira was built around 300 B.C.E. by the Seleucids, a dynasty begun by one of the immediate successors of Alexander the Great. It was founded as a frontier city to guard a border region of the Seleucid empire. On its coins Thyatira depicted a warrior with ax raised over his head, ready to smash his enemies to pieces, which perhaps influenced the message's characterization of Christians as ones who will smash the nations with a rod of iron (2:26–27; Ford 1975, 405). The city later served as a military outpost for the kings of Pergamum. Its importance had dwindled since the Roman takeover of Asia Minor, and at the time of the writing of Revelation it was not as prominent as Ephesus, Smyrna, and Pergamum. It was not the site of an imperial temple. Thyatira was a city known primarily for trade and craftsmanship of small articles. Acts mentions a convert named Lydia who was "from the city of Thyatira and a dealer in purple cloth" (16:14). She had a house Philippi in Macedonia, across the Aegean from Asia. This attests both to Thyatira's craftsmanship and to its trade connections. Most important as background to the message to the church at Thyatira was the importance of trade guilds in the life of the city (Ramsay 1994, 238), since

Christian members of such guilds would have to face questions of assimilation that were of concern to the seer.

After the initial addressing of the message to the church's angel, Christ identifies himself as "the Son of God, who has eyes like a flame of fire, and whose feet are like burnished bronze" (2:18). This is the only time in the book of Revelation that Jesus is explicitly given the title "Son of God," although God is spoken of as Jesus' father in 1:6; 2:27; 3:5, 21; and 14:1. It is one of the few characterizations of Christ used in the messages not found in the vision of chapter 1. The reason for the explicit use of the title here might be that in 2:26–28 this message uses Psalm 2. In that psalm, God tells the Israelite king, "You are my son, today I have begotten you" (Ps 2:7). This corresponds to other biblical passages where the anointed king (messiah) is called God's son. The most famous is where God tells David concerning his son Solomon, "I will be a father to him, and he shall be a son to me.... Your house and your kingdom shall be made sure forever before me; your throne shall be established forever" (2 Sam 7:14, 16). These passages were important for Christians in their evaluation of the person and work of Jesus. At the beginning of each of the synoptic gospels, Jesus is baptized and receives a vision in which Ps 2:7 is employed to identify Jesus as the Son of God, meaning he is God's anointed eschatological agent who announces and helps to accomplish the defeat of Satan and to establish the kingdom of God. The use of the title in Rev 2:18 draws on that central christological stream, thereby emphasizing Jesus' closeness to God and his role as God's agent with God's authority. In 2:28, he gives Christians authority "even as I also received authority from my Father." As in Psalm 2, Jesus as Son of God rules over the nations and smashes them (as do Christians, empowered by Christ), activities appropriate to the message.

The other attributes of Jesus in 2:18 are also appropriate to the message. Christ's "eyes like a flame of fire" stress his ability to see deeply, and so search the minds and hearts of Christians to judge them (2:23). His "feet... like burnished bronze" symbolize stability and unshakable strength. The seer depends here on Dan 10:6, where the angel's feet were like burnished brass (*chalkos*).

The body of the message falls into three sections. The first contains praise for the church and its works; the second criticizes the church and especially certain members of it for accepting the false prophet Jezebel and her teaching; and the third reverts to a positive tone toward those who do not agree with Jezebel. The alternation of praise and censure is also found in the messages to Ephesus and Pergamum.

Christ begins by saying that he "knows" of the church's "works" and then specifies them: "your love, faith, service, and patient endurance" (2:19). He intensifies his praise by saying, "I know that your last works are greater than the first." In some ways the Thyatiran church is the mirror image of the one at Ephesus. Where Ephesus is praised for rejecting the false apostles, Thyatira accepts them. While Ephesus is blamed for losing the love that it had at first, Thyatira receives praise for its love, included among its works, and is told that those works are even greater than at first. "Faith" in Revelation always means absolute loyalty to Christ, especially when engagement with surrounding culture might mitigate such loyalty. "Service" (*diakonia*) is used only here in Revelation. Elsewhere in the New Testament it denotes many sorts of service to the church, ranging from taking care of the needs of widows (Acts 6) to missionary work. "Patient endurance" (*hypomonê*) has been dealt with already (see comments on Ephesus, esp. on 2:2). It calls to mind the opposition Christians face in trying to be faithful to Christ and is the quality of facing such opposition with steadfastness. Christ's rather sweeping praise of the Thyatirans makes it the more striking when he levels serious criticism at them in the next section.

The seer's main opponent in Thyatira is one whom he calls Jezebel. He says that she "calls herself a prophet [*legousa heautên prophêtin:* literally, saying that she is a prophet]" (2:20). Apparently some in the church accept her as such, while the others at least tolerate her. The construction of using the verb "to say" (*legô*) with the reflexive pronoun to denote something untrue said by someone about him- or herself also occurs in the message to Ephesus, concerning those in the church "saying that they were apostles [*legontas heautous apostolous*]" (2:2). A similar construction occurs in the present message concerning knowledge that some supposedly have of the deep things of Satan, "as they say [*hôs legousin*]" (2:24).

Since John's opponent in Thyatira is a woman, the question naturally arises whether the seer is unwilling to accept female leadership, as is, for example, the author of the Pastoral Epistles (see 1 Tim 2:11–15). The question becomes more acute given the sometimes objectionable female images in Revelation, such as the one usually referred to as "the great whore Babylon" (see chapter 17; see Pippin 1992a, 1992b, 1992c). But if the seer was against female leadership in principle, he never says so. Rather, he objects to Jezebel's teaching.

The nature of Jezebel's offenses is discussed in the section above on John's opponents. She did not call herself "Jezebel" but was called that by the seer because he saw her actions as analogous to the biblical Jezebel. The biblical Jezebel promoted the worship of Baal in Israel and persecuted Yahweh's prophets. Her greatest adversary was the prophet Elijah (see the Elijah allusions in Revelation 11). The seer accuses "Jezebel" of "teaching and beguiling my servants to practice fornication and to eat food sacrificed to idols" (2:20). No specifically sexual sins are described in the Bible's stories about Jezebel, but the revolutionary and soon-to-be-king Jehu says, "What peace can there be, so long as the many whoredoms and sorceries of your mother Jezebel continue?" (2 Kgs 9:22). It is likely that Jehu uses sexual terms to symbolize idolatry, as is common in the Hebrew Bible. In 2:22, those who listen to Jezebel are said to commit adultery with her. It is hardly likely that a church that deserves such praise as is given to Thyatira in 2:19 would tolerate open and multiple adulteries. It is far more plausible that sexual terms are used figuratively here. Similarly Rome is depicted as a "great whore" in chapter 17. Mounce (1977, 104) points out that Israel itself is portrayed as a harlot in Hos 9:1; Jer 3:6; and Ezek 23:19.

In our discussion of John's opponents above, we suggest that there was a single Christian movement with adherents in Pergamum and Thyatira, whose promoters were rejected at Ephesus. The movement advocated eating food sacrificed to idols. The activity labeled "fornication" by the seer either was sexual conduct accepted by some but not others or was simply some act such as eating sacrificial food. The problem regarding eating sacrificial food may have been particularly acute in Thyatira, whose trade guilds were so prominent in the city's life. For Christians to withdraw completely from activities such as guild meetings put them at a disadvantage socially and economically in their world. Participation in such meetings may be what prompted Paul to allow eating food sacrificed to idols unless it caused scandal (1 Corinthians 8–10). It would not be surprising if Jezebel's teaching attracted adherents among those who sought to continue their business and social contacts while remaining faithful to Christ.

Jezebel is said to teach and "beguile" Christ's servants. The word "beguile" or "deceive" is used of Satan (12:9; 20:3, 8, 10), the second beast (false prophet; 13:14; 19:20), and the great harlot (Rome; 18:23), so the company Jezebel keeps puts her on the wrong side of the eschatological battle. Sweet (1979, 94) notes that Jesus predicts widespread deception in the last days, according to Matt 24:5, 11, 24. Christ says of Jezebel, "I gave her time to repent, but she refuses to repent of her fornication" (2:21). The seer may have delivered a warning to Jezebel which went unheeded. The idea that God gives sinners time to repent is known in the New Testament and Hebrew Bible (Wisd 11:23; 12:10, 19; Rom 2:4; cf. *2 Bar.* 12:4; 21:21; 4 Ezra 7:134). Jezebel has not repented, but she doubtless sees no reason to repent. In her own eyes, she does not sin. Revelation's Christ implies that there is no longer time for Jezebel to repent. That time is past. The idea that after a certain point repentance is impossible is expressed in passages such as 4 Ezra 7:33, 82, 113–15; 9:11; *1 Enoch* 62–63, and in the messages to Revelation's churches where God gives time to repent.

Revelation 2:22–23 discloses Christ's plans for Jezebel and her followers. He says, "I am throwing her on a bed, and those who commit adultery with her I am throwing into great distress, unless they repent of their doings; and I will strike her children dead." Jezebel's punishment is ambiguous. The word for "bed" could mean an ordinary bed. The juxtaposition of her being thrown on a bed with mention of those who commit adultery with her is graphically suggestive. As "sexual" sin takes place on a bed, so her punishment will occur on a bed. This is similar to the graphic image of Judah as an unfaithful wife whom her husband punishes by bringing her lovers against her to mutilate and humiliate her (Ezekiel 23). Alternatively, the reference may be to a sickbed (Charles 1920, 1:71–72). The seer may expect actual illness to overtake Jezebel, since the idea of illness as a punishment for sin is known in the New Testament (Mark 2:1–12; John 9:1–2; 1 Cor 11:29–30). A bed could also hint at a deathbed, which would be supported by Christ's claim that he will kill her children. The coordination of sin and punishment recalls the familiar biblical notion that the punishment fits the crime (see Ps 7:15–16; Wisd 11:15–16; Matt 7:2–3; Mark 4:24; Acts 7:41–43; Rom 1:22–32; 2:1; Heb 7:2). There is probably a double meaning in Rev 2:22. Jezebel's new bed will be one of both fornication and sickness.

Christ promises that he will throw those who commit adultery with Jezebel "into great distress [*thlipsin*], unless they repent of her doings," and that he will kill her children (2:22–23). Although it is too late for Jezebel to repent, those who commit adultery with her can still do so. The use of the word *thlipsis* here indicates that the punishment of Jezebel and her followers is part of God's eschatological defeat of satanic powers.

Retribution against John's opponents will be a sign to the entire church that nothing escapes Christ's notice and that no sin will go unpunished. "All the churches will know that I am the one who searches minds and hearts" (2:23), a formulation based on biblical statements (Pss 7:10; 64:6–7; Jer 11:20; 17:10; 20:12; Rom 8:27; 1 Thess 2:4). That each person will be judged according to his or her works is an idea familiar in both Christianity and Judaism, and is common in Revelation (e.g., Rev 18:6, 20; 20:12–13; 22:12; cf. Matt 16:27; Rom 2:6; 2 Cor 5:10).

Revelation's Christ now turns his attention to those who have not followed Jezebel's teaching, which he calls "the deep things of Satan." This phrase has occasioned much comment, from which two major interpretations emerge. One assumes that John's opponents actually claim to know "the deep things of Satan," and the other assumes that this is a sarcastic phrase by which John characterizes her teaching as satanic. The first interpretation does not imply that John's opponents were Satan worshipers. They may have felt able to participate in Hellenistic cults because they were protected by their relationship to Christ. There may have been some who thought that such participation gave them knowledge of Satan and his secrets that would be useful in fighting him (Mounce 1977, 105–6). In 1 Corinthians 10, Paul argues that the Christian sacraments will not protect those who take part in idolatry. Alternatively, the opponents may have belonged to an early form of gnosticism which saw the material world, and therefore its creator, as evil, and which accordingly saw the serpent of Genesis who opposed that creator as good. In the second century, such a group is documented. They are given the name Ophites, taken from *ophis,* meaning "serpent," a name applied to Satan in Rev 12:9 (Mounce 1977, 105; Charles 1920, 1:73). Yarbro Collins (1990, 1002) suggests that the seer's opponents may teach magical formulas by which to control spirits.

The more common interpretation is that it is the seer who calls the group's teaching "the deep things of Satan," not they. They may have claimed for themselves that they knew "the depths," meaning the depths of Christian truth, or more specifically "the depths of God." Paul claims in 1 Cor 2:10 that the Spirit reveals to "mature" Christians the "depths of God." If Jezebel's group claims this sort of knowledge for itself, then the seer may be parodying their claims.

Christ says to those who do not agree with Jezebel's teachings, "I do not lay on you any other burden [*baros*]; only hold fast to what you have until I come" (2:24-25). The Greek word for burden here is the same as is used in the decree of the Jerusalem church in Acts 15:28-29: "It has seemed good to the Holy Spirit and to us to impose no further burden [*baros*] than these essentials: that you abstain from food sacrificed to idols and from blood and from what is strangled and from fornication." The specific word used (*baros*), the idea of a *further* burden not to be imposed, and the context of food sacrificed to idols and fornication connect the two passages. Although John does not quote the Jerusalem decree (as indeed he does not quote scripture), it seems to be in the background (Charles 1920, 1:74). Given the context, holding fast must mean to continue to do the works praised in 2:19, and especially to exercise faithfulness to Christ by rejecting Jezebel and her teaching.

This is the only message that has two promises "to the one who conquers." The first is, "To everyone who conquers and continues to do my works to the end, I will give authority over the nations; to rule them with an iron rod, as when clay pots are shattered—even as I also received authority from my Father" (2:26-28). The word "works" occurs six times in this message, stressing that each Christian will answer for his or her own works (2:23). The hearers face two clear options. Either they will follow Jezebel and do her works or they will do Christ's works (2:26). Those works must be done "until the end."

This promise depends heavily on Psalm 2. Psalm 2 was composed for the coronation of an Israelite king. The king was anointed with oil as a sign of his dedication to his royal position, and so he was a "messiah," which in Hebrew means "anointed one." He is also called the "son of God" (Ps 2:7; see also 2 Sam 7:14). God says to the messiah:

> Ask of me, and I will make the nations your heritage,
> and the ends of the earth your possession.
> You shall break them with a rod of iron,
> and dash them in pieces like a potter's vessel. (Ps 2:8-9)

Revelation 2:26–27 and Psalm 2 share the following elements: authority over the nations, shattering the nations as clay pots, and the messiah as God's son. This language is echoed in 19:15, where the risen Christ comes as a warrior to conquer and rule (see comments on 1:5 and 1:16). In Rev 2:26–27, "everyone who conquers," all faithful Christians, also rule. A share of the faithful in the messiah's rule is common in Christian tradition (Matt 19:28; 1 Cor 6:3; Rev 5:10; 12:5; 19:15).

In Rev 2:26–27, ruling with an iron rod is in synonymous parallelism with the shattering of clay pots. This sort of rule seems rather destructive and seems to contrast with the Greek word for "rule" here (*poimainô*), which can also mean "shepherd," but the same parallel between "rule" (*poimainô*) and "smash" is present in the Septuagint version of Psalm 2 (Charles 1920, 1:75–76). The word for "rod" in Hebrew is *shebet,* which can also mean a royal "scepter." Numbers 24:17, Balaam's prophecy, which predicts that a scepter (*shebet*) will arise out of Israel, and a star out of Jacob, was taken as messianic in both Jewish and Christian circles. In Ps 2:9, written for a royal coronation, the king "smashes" or "rules," depending on the translation, the nations with a *shebet* of iron. This recalls the messianic Isa 11:4 (already seen as part of the background to Rev 1:16 and 2:16), where the Davidic king will "smite the earth with the rod [*shebet*] of his mouth, and with the breath of his lips he shall kill the wicked." The scepter is a rod symbolizing kingship, but it can also be seen as a weapon. Kingly power carries destructive potential. In Revelation, Christ's power will be used to destroy his enemies (esp. in chapters 19–20), or, in the Thyatiran situation, to kill Jezebel's children.

Commentators have pointed out that it makes no sense for destructive power to be given to Christians *after* the final battle between good and evil in chapters 19–20, since then the enemies will already be destroyed, but it is unlikely that Christians will literally have political and military power before the final battle. Therefore, many suggest that Christians actualize their conquest over evil through their suffering and death. This fits the statement in the heavenly hymn of chapter 12, "They have conquered him [Satan] by the blood of the Lamb and by the word of their testimony, for they did not cling to life even in the face of death" (12:11; Caird 1966, 45; Krodel 1989, 129–30; Sweet 1979, 96). Yarbro Collins applies the future to the present: "It is a symbolic expression of the conviction that the persecuted righteous actually are more powerful than the unrighteous rulers — that, in spite of appearances, their righteous lives and testimony have a deeper truth and a deeper meaningfulness" (1979, 23).

Some commentators think that Christians will participate in the final battle between Jesus and Satan depicted in chapter 19. Charles (1920, 1:75) says, "[Verses] 27ab imply the actual destruction of the heathen nations as in xix. 15, and apparently in their destruction the triumphant martyrs (cf. ii. 26, xvii. 14) are to be active agents as members of the heavenly hosts which should follow the word of God, xix. 13-14."

The second promise to the one who conquers is that he or she will be given the "morning star" (2:28). Various interpretations have been offered for this (Mounce 1977, 107, lists six). The morning star is Venus. The morning star can symbolize victory, the victory of light over darkness. Krodel (1989, 130) notes that Venus was "symbol of imperial authority in Roman legions." In 22:16, Christ says, "I am the root and descendant of David, the bright morning star," taking for himself a symbol that is a heavenly body of unique glory. The morning star is juxtaposed with Jesus' Davidic lineage in 22:16.

It is likely that the reward of being given the morning star in 2:28 is associated for the author with the rod (scepter) of 2:27 and that the association derives from Num 24:17, Balaam's prophecy, where the star and the scepter are parallel items representing the rise of a king in Israel (Hemer 1986, 125). This likelihood is strengthened by the mention of Balaam in the message to Pergamum. When Christians are promised the scepter and the star, they are promised a share in Christ's messianic glory.

Astrology and magic were important in the ancient world. Life was dominated by supernatural forces which could be to some degree controlled by magic and predicted by astrology. The promise that faithful Christians would possess the glorious morning star, the star associated with Jesus himself, must have been powerful to citizens of that world. In addition to the associations of the morning star noted above, Yarbro Collins (1976, 81-82) points out that in a fragmentary Canaanite text, a star-god revolts against the main god and is defeated. The rebellion myth is also behind Isaiah 14, where the rebel is the "morning star"; the myth is later applied to Satan (see Revelation 12). Revelation claims Jesus is the real morning star, not Satan. Whereas in Isaiah 14 the morning star tries to usurp God's sovereignty,

Christ legitimately shares in it. Just as the claim that Jesus holds seven stars in his hand asserts his cosmic power and authority, so the possession of the morning star by Christians gives them a power analogous to that of Jesus.

This is the first message in which the injunction to hear what the Spirit is saying to the churches comes last (2:29). The final three messages retain this order. Although many tentative suggestions have been offered for this change of order, none enjoys widespread support. In the first three messages, the command to listen precedes the eschatological promise, thus emphasizing the promise. But the seer may also have wanted to end the entire section containing the messages with the command to listen, and so he had to change the order of the command and the promises at some point. He could have achieved his end by switching the order in the final message, but this central message, the one to Thyatira, was also a logical point for doing it.

We began the exposition of the message to Thyatira by repeating Charles's observation that it was the longest of the messages. In ancient literature, the middle position was often emphatic. This message proves particularly rich in its use of the Bible, especially Psalm 2. The main themes of Psalm 2—God's bestowal of royal authority on his messiah and the exercise of that authority in the destruction of the enemies of God and his messiah—are applied to Christ, and Christ applies them to Christians. This is a microcosm of the book of Revelation as a whole.

The Message to Sardis (3:1–6)

Sardis was located about thirty miles southeast of Thyatira. It was built on the northern side of Mount Tmolus and dominated the Hermus Valley. Its acropolis was on a spur of the mountain and constituted a natural fortress which had never been taken by direct assault. Twice the city was captured when its inhabitants allowed attackers to sneak in. Many think that the references in the message to staying alert draw on those local memories. But injunctions to stay alert are so common in writings of an eschatological nature that we do not know whether the author intended any local allusion here.

Sardis had been a city of great glory when it was the capital of the ancient Lydian kingdom. Croesus, legendary for his wealth, was king of Lydia in the sixth century B.C.E. Sardis became the seat of a Persian satrapy when Lydia was incorporated into the Persian empire in the mid-sixth century, and it subsequently fell under the sway of the Seleucids, the Pergamenes, and the Romans. Although much has been made of its status in the Lydian kingdom as contrasted with its less splendid standing in the Roman empire (Ramsay 1994, 259), pictures of its decline are perhaps overdrawn (Hemer 1986, 134). At the time of the writing of Revelation, it was still a city of some importance, the Roman geographer Strabo calling it a "great city" in 26 C.E. It lay on a major road that came from Susa in the east.

In 17 C.E., Sardis suffered an earthquake. The emperor Tiberius helped it to recover by giving it ten million sesterces and exempting it from taxes for five years. In 26 C.E., Sardis competed for the privilege of building a temple to Tiberius but lost to Smyrna. Sardis was a center of the cult of Cybele, the great Phrygian nature goddess, who was identified with the Greek goddess Artemis. Cybele had a huge temple in Sardis which apparently was never completely finished. Some connect this with the seer's accusation that the works of the church members are not "finished" (Krodel 1989, 132). The wool industry was important at Sardis, and it claimed to be the first place where wool-dyeing was done. Some find a local allusion in the fact that the message to the church at Sardis refers to white clothing. Although there seems to have been an important and well-established Jewish community at Sardis (Josephus, *Ant.* 10 §§259–61), there is no hint of the kind of tension between church and synagogue that is evident in the messages to Smyrna and Philadelphia.

The message to the church at Sardis begins with the usual command, addressed to the church's angel, to write. The one who commands is the one who has the seven spirits of God and the seven stars (3:1). This is reminiscent of Christ's characterization in the message to Ephesus (2:1; see 1:16). Revelation 1:20 identifies the seven stars as the angels of the seven churches. We noted the connection between the seven stars, spirits, lampstands, and torches in our discussion of Rev 1:4 (see also 4:5 and 5:6). The seven spirits of God are supernatural beings, probably angels of God's entourage, who are present before God's throne and who also go out to do God's work in the world. The conception is based on Zech 4:10.

There is not much specificity in the charges the author levels against Sardis, so it is perhaps appropriate that the traits of Christ used here are rather general. In addition to the attributes of Christ that the messages to Ephesus and Sardis share, the following similarities between the two messages have been noted: "Both are censured for a fall from a former position (2:5 with 3:3), both are called upon to remember and repent (2:5 with 3:3), and both promise the victor *zoe* (life) under appropriate figures" (Mounce 1977, 110 n. 4).

The seer's assessment of the church at Sardis is negative, although the charge is cryptic: "I know your works; you have a name of being alive, but you are dead." The word "name" occurs four times in this message (3:1, 4, 5 [twice]). The "name" of the Sardian church is said to be false in 3:1. The church's "name," its reputation, of being alive is undeserved. Once again, things are not as they appear. In 3:4, "names" is used as a synonym for persons, denoting those who are faithful to Christ. In 3:5, the "names" of the faithful will not be blotted out of the book of life. This play on the word "name" reflects on the difference between a false "name" which deceives humans and the true "name" of each person, known by God. In the message to Pergamum, each conqueror receives a "new name" (2:17), corresponding to his or her real status in God's eyes, a status fulfilled in the new Jerusalem.

The terms "alive" and "dead" are not meant literally here but are symbolic for spiritual states, as is common in early Christian literature (Charles 1920, 1:79, adduces 2 Cor 6:9; Jas 2:17; 2 Tim 3:5; Ford 1975, 408, adds Luke 10:24; Col 2:13). Revelation's Christ is saying that most Christians think highly of the Sardian church. They think that the church is "alive," that it has a good relationship with God and is approved by God. The seer sees things differently. The appearance of spiritual health masks spiritual decay and death. Sardis's situation is the opposite of Smyrna's. The latter may soon die, but is promised life. The former is thought to be alive, but is already dead.

It is difficult to know exactly why the author thinks that the Sardian church is dead. There is no obvious sin or fault that has led other Christians to the same conclusion. We have already shown how the activities of the Nicolaitans were approved by some, tolerated by others, and condemned by the seer and the Ephesian church. Since the message does not mention food sacrificed to idols or fornication, it is not likely that these are issues in the church. The author makes major issues of these items in other messages, so he would not be content to refer to them in such a cryptic way here. Nor is there any indication that there are any outside pressures on the church, such as a hostile Jewish community or insistence on emperor worship. The seer's general position is antiassimilationist, so it is likely he thinks that the church in Sardis is not maintaining proper distance from its environment. One can speculate that the church in Sardis gets along well with its non-Christian neighbors, coexists with the important Jewish community, and is not affected by groups such as the Nicolaitans. The seer, who sees Christianity as uncompromisingly opposed to Asian and Roman culture, disapproves of their comfort with their setting, even though he can accuse them of nothing more concrete.

The seer's Christ issues a series of commands to the church, backed up with the threat of Christ's coming. The Sardians are told, "Wake up [*ginou grêgorôn*], and strengthen what remains and is on the point of death, for I have not found your works perfect in the sight of my God" (3:2). The words translated "wake up" literally mean "be alert." The verb *grêgoreô* is frequent in eschatological contexts, being found three times, for example, in Mark's eschatological discourse (13:34, 35, 37). Although 3:1 accuses the church of being dead, we now hear that there are things that are only "at the point of death." The author has apparently exaggerated the situation to shock his audience into action.

The use of the word "strengthen" connotes conflict, for which strength is needed. It is used in Luke 9:51 where Jesus sets his course for Jerusalem, where he will suffer and die. There the Greek literally and rather awkwardly reads, "He strengthened his face to go to Jerusalem." In Luke 22, Peter is told that he will deny Jesus out of fear of the Jewish and Roman authorities. Then Jesus says, "Once you have turned back, strengthen your brothers" (22:32). Other New Testament uses of the word also imply that there is opposition, so strength is needed. If church members at Sardis strengthen their resistance to the corrosive forces that surround them, they can still be saved. If they do that, their works will be "perfect," completed.

The word translated "perfect" here is from the verb *plêroô*, meaning "to complete." The seer is not saying that the church will be approved only if it is completely faultless but that the church members must finish what they started. Their baptism began a process of alienation from this world, its powers, and its values. The compromise they have reached means disloyalty to Christ. Christ assures the Sardians that his judgment is consonant with that of "my God." Christ is in a unique position to claim God as "my God."

The church is ordered to "remember" what it had heard and to obey it. Like the church at Ephesus, the Sardian church was once better than it is. It has fallen from a higher state. It has forgotten what it once heard. This probably refers to the original gospel preached to it, perhaps even to its conversion and baptism as a result of that gospel (see Charles 1920, 1:80; Krodel 1989, 132-33). The very remembrance of that gospel as originally heard and received will bring the church to its senses, for it will be able to perceive the inconsistency between that gospel and its present way of life.

Christ warns that if the church does not "wake up," "be alert," "I will come like a thief, and you will not know at what hour I will come to you" (3:3). The seer at this point draws on Jesus traditions. Matthew's Jesus warns the disciples, "Keep awake [*grêgoreite*] therefore, for you do not know on what day your Lord is coming. But understand this: if the owner of the house had known in what part of the night the thief was coming, he would have stayed awake [*egrêgorêsen*] and would not have let his house be broken into. Therefore you must also be ready, for the Son of Man is coming at an unexpected hour" (24:42-44; cf. Luke 12:39-40). Paul draws on the same traditions when he warns the Thessalonians to "keep awake" (*grêgorômen*) in expectation of Christ's coming, "for you yourselves know very well that the day of the Lord will come like a thief in the night. . . . You, beloved, are not in darkness, for that day to surprise you like a thief" (1 Thess 5:2, 4). The second letter of Peter carries a similar warning: "The day of the Lord will come like a thief" (2 Pet 3:10).

As with the threat of Jesus' coming in the message to the churches at Ephesus and Pergamum, there is some question whether the coming that Jesus speaks of in this message is the eschaton or earlier. We decided in the cases of Ephesus and Pergamum that the author was probably speaking of the eschaton. The same is true here. The command to stay awake and the comparison of Jesus' second coming to that of a thief in the night suggest an eschatological context. Revelation as a whole concentrates on the endtime events, and most references to the coming of Jesus clearly refer to the eschaton.

Verse 4 reveals that there are "still a few persons in Sardis who have not soiled their clothes; they will walk with me, dressed in white, for they are worthy." Up until this point, it has seemed that the whole Sardian church deserves only censure. Now we discover that a few are faithful in the seer's estimation. The faithful seem to be in the minority. The reference to soiled clothes may allude to the white garment worn by those who have just been baptized (Krodel 1989, 133; Yarbro Collins 1990, 1003; Charles 1920, 1:81). The whiteness of the garment represents the newly acquired purity of the wearer. Those who have not soiled their garments have maintained this pure state (cf. Zech 3:4). They remain blameless before God. These are the same ones spoken of in 16:15, who "keep" their robes. Christ speaks of their future glory, anticipating the formal promises made in the next verse to the one who conquers. They will walk with Christ, dressed in white.

"Walking" is a common Jewish metaphor for behavior. The Hebrew word for law, *halakah,* derives from the verb "to walk," *halak.* To walk in the ways of the Lord is to obey God's commands. In Rev 3:4, "walking" itself becomes a reward. It is a symbol for being in Christ's presence permanently. The emphasis here is that one is *with* Christ precisely *in* one's behavior. The use of the word "walk" creates an echo between chapters 3 and 21 and assures the conquerors a place in the new Jerusalem, where the nations walk in God's light.

The promise to the conqueror is in three parts (3:5). The first promises that anyone in Sardis who follows the example of those few who "have not soiled their garments" will, like them, receive white robes. Charles (1920, 1:82–83) tries to show that the white robes refer to resurrection bodies. Whether or not this is correct in every instance in Revelation, it is clear that Revelation's clothing imagery is similar to the references in Jewish and Christian sources to glorious clothing worn by the righteous in heaven (e.g., 2 Cor 5:1–4; *1 Enoch* 62:15–16; 2 Esdras 2:39, 45; *Asc. Isa.* 4:16; 9:9, 17; *Apocalypse of Peter* 3; Herm. *Sim.* 8.2.3; *Odes Sol.* 11:10, 14; 21:2, 3; 25:8; 1QS 4:7–10). Glorious, white garments are the appropriate garb for being in God's presence. Angels are often seen as wearing white robes (Mark 16:5; Matt 28:3; Acts 1:10; Rev 4:4). The promise of heavenly robes is already fulfilled for the martyrs under the heavenly altar (6:11), and the seer has a proleptic vision of triumphant Christians in 7:9, 13, 14 wearing white robes. In 19:8, the bride of the Lamb, the church, is lauded by heavenly beings with the words, " 'His bride has made herself ready; to her it has been granted to be clothed with fine linen, bright and pure' — for the fine linen is the righteous deeds of the saints." As in 3:4, it is those who have proven themselves worthy by their works who will be clothed in white.

The second promise made to the conqueror is that Christ will not blot his or her name out of the book of life. The notion that there are heavenly books is common in the ancient Near East. One cannot point to one single source for this idea, nor to one single idea that covers all the types of heavenly books. Such books are obviously compatible with apocalyptic views of the universe, since in apocalypticism the unseen, heavenly world explains the seen world. As background for heavenly books, Charles (1920, 1:84) points to Exod 32:32-33 (God's book); Ps 69:28 (the book of the living); and Isa 4:3 (everyone who has been recorded for life), each indicating lists of those who belong to Israel and will share in its benefits conferred by God (cf. also *Jub.* 30:22-23). This is analogous to the list of citizens of a city who have full privileges and responsibilities in it. In later Jewish literature the book may be a list of those destined for future, eternal life (Dan 12:1; *1 Enoch* 47:3; 104:1; 108:7), a meaning found also in Phil 4:3; Luke 10:20; and Heb 12:23.

There is the additional notion that human deeds are recorded in heaven and that the books containing these deeds can be used as evidence at the last judgment (e.g., Ps 66:8; Mal 3:16; Neh 13:14; *Jub.* 30:20; Charles 1920, 1:84, supplies a long list). A major example of this is in Daniel 7, where the divine judge takes his seat on the throne in heaven: "The court sat in judgment, and the books were opened" (Dan 7:10). A similar book is mentioned in Mal 3:16: "The Lord took note and listened, and a book of remembrance was written before him of those who revered the Lord and thought on his name" (cf. *Jub.* 30:20). The two types of books, those containing the names of the righteous and those in which good and bad deeds are recorded, are combined in Rev 20:12.

In Rev 3:5, the book of life is that book which contains the list of the righteous. The conqueror avoids having his or her name blotted out of that book. This has its closest parallels in Exod 32:32-33 and Ps 69:28. In Exodus 32, Moses responds to God's decision to destroy Israel by requesting that he himself be blotted out of God's book. God replies that only sinners will be blotted out of the book. Similarly, the psalmist of Psalm 69 prays concerning his enemies, "Let them be blotted out of the book of the living; let them not be enrolled among the righteous" (Ps 69:28). The Sardians have their names in the book now, but they can lose their status. The names of the elect have been written in the book since before the foundation of the world (13:8; 17:8). Those whose names are not in the book end up worshiping the beast (13:8) and going to perdition (17:8), reinforcing the social and ethical dualism typical of apocalypticism. The book of life will be used at the last judgment along with books recording human deeds (20:12, 15). Only those whose names are in the book will gain access to the new Jerusalem to partake in its blessings.

The third part of the promise to the conqueror is, "I will confess your name before my Father and before his angels" (3:5). This is a clear echo of Christ's words found in the synoptic gospels: "Everyone who confesses me before others, the Son of Man also will confess before the angels of God" (Luke 12:8); "Everyone therefore who confesses me before others, I also will confess before my Father in heaven" (Matt 10:32). These passages imply a forensic setting in which Christ acts as a witness. The judgment takes place before God and the angels, as it does in Daniel 7. This impression is strengthened by the use of the word "before" in Revelation. It is a very common word in the book, and it is used most commonly to speak of things happening "before" God's throne. It first appears in 1:4, in connection with "the seven spirits who are before his throne." A striking use is in 12:10, where Satan is the one who accuses Christians "before our God." The message to Sardis concludes with the familiar command to listen (3:6).

The Message to Philadelphia (3:7–13)

Philadelphia was located about thirty miles southeast of Sardis. It lay on a major east-west road, along the route of the official Roman post. The city was founded in the second century B.C.E. by the Pergamene dynasty, the Attalids, for the purpose of spreading Greek culture in the area and as a means of social and political control. It was seen as the gateway to the East, since it lay on the access road to the central plateau of Asia Minor. Like Sardis, it was destroyed in the great earthquake of 17 C.E., and it also received help from the emperor Tiberius. In gratitude, it took on the name Neocaesarea. Later, as an expression of loyalty to the emperor Vespasian, it took on his family name, calling itself Flavia. Some think that this history of changing names influenced the name imagery in the message. Philadelphia did not receive an imperial temple until the early third century C.E., at which time it received the title *neokoros.* The message to Philadelphia is similar to the one to Smyrna in two ways. These are the only two messages that are completely positive toward the churches in question, and only these two messages reflect acute conflict with the local synagogues. In the message to Philadelphia the conflict with non-Christian Jews colors the whole text.

The message begins with the usual command to write. The messenger formula identifies Christ as "the holy one, the true one, who has the key of David, who opens and no one will shut, who shuts and no one opens" (3:7). Holiness is a quality of God throughout the Hebrew Bible (e.g., Isa 1:4; 5:9; 6:3; 40:25; 65:16; Hab 3:3) and in noncanonical Jewish literature (e.g., *1 Enoch* 1:2; 37:2; 93:11). God is by definition holy, as is anyone and anything associated with God or belonging to God. Christianity adopted Judaism's history, scriptures, images, and basic concepts. It worshiped Judaism's God. But it changed the conceptions concerning how God related to the world and the way the world was to relate to God. Inevitably this involved a redefinition of holiness. Jesus is called "the holy one" in Mark 1:24; Luke 4:34; John 6:69; and Acts 3:14, and the "holy servant" in Acts 4:27, 30. Non-Christian Jews would have disputed Christ's holiness, that is, that he belonged to God in the ways Christians claimed.

Christ also declares himself the "true one" (*alêthinos*) in Rev 3:7. In the context of Greek philosophy and religion, "true" is likely to mean "real," whereas in the context of biblical religion, it more often means "trustworthy" or faithful. Both meanings make sense in the context of Revelation. The seer claims to see beyond the appearances of things, which are deceiving, to the way things really are. Jesus is the true mediator between heaven and earth, the real messiah, the one who represents God's action and rule in the world. "True" can also have the meaning "faithful" here. The same Greek word is used a few times of God in the Septuagint (Exod 34:6; Isa 65:16; Ps 86:15), where the Hebrew is *'mt,* or *'mn* (Charles 1920, 1:85–88). The Hebrew root is used to indicate God's trustworthiness or faithfulness to his role in the covenant. Applying "holy" and "true" to Jesus fits the general pattern in Revelation of assigning qualities usually associated with God to him.

This is the first time *alêthinos* is used in Revelation. It appears again in 3:14, where Jesus is called the "faithful and true witness." The association of "true" with "faithful" in 3:14 and the use of both adjectives to modify "witness" put everything into the context of standing against the forces of falsehood opposing Christianity. That is precisely the situation of the churches. As Christ was faithful and true in his witness, so must Christians be. Antipas lived up to this standard in Pergamum (2:13). Jesus is again called faithful and true as he does battle with the satanic armies in 19:11.

The only other figure called both holy and true is God (6:10). The martyrs under the heavenly altar cry out for vengeance against those who killed them, addressing God as "holy and true." All other instances of "true" in Revelation reflect this same polemical background. It is God's ways that are true, not those of the world (15:3). God's ways are not arbitrary, as are those of the Jewish or Roman authorities, but rather they come from God himself, so they are by definition true (16:7; 19:2). John assures the audience that in reading Revelation they have direct access to God's judgments and plans and that the words they read are also "true" (19:9; 21:5; 22:6).

Jesus also identifies himself in 3:7 as the one who has the "key of David, who opens and no one will shut, who shuts and no one opens." This alludes to Isaiah 22, which describes a change in King David's stewards. God says to the old steward concerning the new one, "I will commit your authority to his hand, and he shall be a father to the inhabitants of Jerusalem and to the house of Judah. I will place on his shoulder the key of the house of David; he shall open, and no one shall shut; he shall shut, and no one shall open" (Isa 22:21–22). David's steward controlled access to the king, and there was no appeal from his decisions in this matter. His position was of such prominence that he was called a father to David's subjects. In the later centuries of the second temple period, David's reign was remembered as a golden era. Messianic hopes were built on memories and legends about David's rule. When in Rev 3:7 Jesus claims that he holds the key of David, he lays claim to messianic authority. It is he who controls access to the messianic kingdom, and it is he who directs eschatological events. In 5:5, it is precisely as "the Lion of the tribe of Judah, the Root of David," that Jesus breaks the seven seals of the scroll and sets in motion the eschatological events.

Jesus' claim concerning the key of David recalls the description of Jesus in 1:18: "I was dead, and see, I am alive forever and ever; and I have the keys of Death and of Hades." At two other points in Revelation a key is mentioned. In 9:1, a fallen star is given the key to the bottomless pit, and he releases demonic locusts that afflict humans who do not belong to Christ. In 20:1, an angel uses the key to the bottomless pit to imprison Satan for the thousand-year messianic reign. Although Jesus himself does not directly use the key in these instances, these events are part of the eschatological occurrences caused by opening the seals of the heavenly scroll. Hades, to which Jesus has the key, is related to the bottomless pit.

The body of the message to Philadelphia begins with the familiar "I know." "I know your works. Look, I have set before you an open door, which no one is able to shut. I know you have but little power, and yet you have kept my word and have not denied my name" (3:8). This verse links the body of the message to Christ's attributes in 3:7. Some think that the open door refers to a missionary opportunity open to the Philadelphians (see 1 Cor 16:9; 2 Cor 2:12; Col 4:3). Since the message centers on Jewish-Christian relations, some even see a mission to the Jews in this verse. However, there is no hint elsewhere in the message of such missionary activity. In Acts 14:27, Paul and Barnabas tell of how God "opened a door of faith for the Gentiles," which is closer to Revelation's meaning. Jesus has opened the door of God's kingdom to the Philadelphian Christians. Christ assures them that no one can shut that door. The door remains open to the Philadelphians because they have not denied Jesus' name (3:8).

The key to 3:8 may lie in the next verse: "I will make those of the synagogue of Satan who say that they are Jews and are not, but are lying – I will make them come and bow down before your feet, and they will learn that I have loved you" (3:9). Belief in Jesus as the one who controls access to the messianic kingdom may have become a contentious issue between Christians and the local Jewish community. Local Jews may have declared that the Christians were not members of the covenant community and therefore had the door of the messianic kingdom shut to them. If so, they were wrong, according to John, and their judgment would not affect the real status of the Christians. In time the Jews would come to realize that (3:9).

Jesus' ultimate authority is symbolized by his possession of the key of David in 3:7. In Matthew, Jesus gives the power of the keys to Peter: "I will give you the keys of the kingdom of heaven, and whatever you bind on earth will be bound in heaven, and whatever you loose on earth will be loosed in heaven" (Matt 16:19). Jesus gives Peter the keys because Peter recognizes him as the messiah (Matt 16:15–20), so in both Matthew and Revelation, Jesus' authority is related to his messiahship; it concerns access to the messianic kingdom; and it is symbolized by keys. In both Matthew and Revelation, the broader context is a dispute with non-Christian Jews over this authority of Jesus. In John 10, the centrality of Jesus is put even more forcefully. There Jesus not only has the keys to the door—he *is* the door through which everyone must enter (John 10:7–9), and it is only through him that anyone can come to the Father (John 14:6). The gospel of John is also written in the context of a dispute with non-Christian Jews over who really has access to God. The Philadelphian Christians are powerless (Rev 3:8); the biblical roots of their Jewish neighbors are more obvious; and the Jews themselves reject the messiahship of Jesus. Yet Jesus assures them that it is to them, not to the Jews, that the door has been opened. Christ praises them for keeping his word and not denying his name. Both verbs are in the past tense, which suggests specific incidents. The Philadelphians' refusal to deny Jesus' name fits the idea of a conflict with Jews who deny Jesus the title of messiah.

In a bit of irony that reveals the author's facility with the biblical text, the traditional biblical promise that the Gentiles will eventually acknowledge the Jewish God as the true God and will come to worship in Jerusalem is turned against non-Christian Jews. That biblical promise appears in many passages (and is reflected in Rev 15:4; 21:23–26), but the closest to Revelation is Isa 60:14: "The descendants of those that oppressed you shall come bending low to you, and all who despised you shall bow down at your feet; they shall call you the City of the Lord, the Zion of the Holy One of Israel." In this passage, Israel's Gentile oppressors will bear witness to God's vindication of Israel. But Revelation's author looks for a vindication of Christians that will cause non-Christian Jews to bow to the feet of the Christians. The title of God in Isa 60:14 is "The Holy One of Israel," which may influence the choice of the title "the holy one" for Christ at the beginning of the message (3:7). In the end, the Jews will know that Christ, "the holy one," has "loved" the Christians

(3:9). The special relationship between God and Israel is sometimes expressed in the Bible through saying that God loves Israel (Deut 7:13; 10:14–15). Jesus has assumed God's covenantal role, lover and protector of the people. At the beginning of Revelation, the seer says that Jesus freed the Christians and made them "to be a kingdom, priests serving his God and Father" (1:6), thereby considering promises made by God to Israel at the exodus (Exod 19:5–6) to be fulfilled in the relation between Christ and Christians. It is not so much that God's promises have been transferred to the Christians, but that they are the true Jews for whom God's promises were always meant.

The author does not see the conflict between Christians and non-Christian Jews as a new religion, Christianity, arguing against an old one, Judaism. He calls the opponents in Philadelphia those "who say that they are Jews and are not, but are lying," and calls them a "synagogue of Satan." For the author, who is himself Jewish, the definition of "Jew" has changed. Now the true Jew is the one who keeps the word of Jesus and does not deny his name (see Paul's arguments to the same effect in Rom 2:28–29; 9:6–8). Those who call themselves Jews but do not believe in Jesus are liars. This reasoning is similar to what is found in John 8. There Jesus calls the Jews liars and the children of Satan because they do not accept him.

Of course outsiders saw the members of the synagogue as the real Jews. To the extent that the Christians belonged to the synagogue, they were seen as Jews. When the bond between synagogue and church was broken, the Christians would have had trouble identifying themselves properly in terms that would have been accepted by others. When that happened, as it obviously had in Smyrna and Philadelphia, Christians were left with acute social and theological problems. The social problems stemmed from their status as a new group in a world where newness itself was suspect and from their loss of the protection the Roman empire granted to Judaism. Their theological problems were rooted in the fact that their legitimacy depended to some extent on an interpretation of the Jewish scriptures that most Jews rejected.

Christ now promises: "Because you have kept my word of patient endurance, I will keep you from the hour of trial [*peirasmos*] that is coming on the whole world to test [*peirasai*] the inhabitants of the earth" (1:10). "You have kept" is in the past tense, as were the verbs of "you have kept my word and have not denied my name" in 3:8, so here again there may be specific incidents the author has in mind where the Philadelphians proved themselves faithful. Christ promises to "keep" them from the coming trial, since they have "kept" his word. The test here is another way of speaking of the tribulation (*thlipsis*) soon to come. It is the same word (*peirasmos*) that is usually translated "temptation" in the Lord's Prayer, whose petition "Lead us not into temptation" should be read as an eschatological plea (Matt 6:13). Christ promises to keep the Philadelphians from the test that is coming "on the whole world to test the inhabitants of the earth." Since it is obvious that Christians have suffered and are expected to suffer, even to the point of giving their lives, Christ does not promise that the church will escape suffering. Rather because of its past faithfulness, he will give the church the support needed to survive the coming afflictions. The faithful in the church will be among those who in 7:14 are said to have "come out of the great ordeal [*thlipsis*]." This is similar to the idea in John 17:15: "I am not asking you to take them out of the world, but I ask you to protect them from the evil one [Satan]." Another way of thinking about this is to say that the Christians will have *afflictions,* but they will not experience the coming *wrath* of God.

Christ now promises the church that he is coming soon. In the messages to Ephesus and Sardis, this is a warning. Here it is a promise of deliverance, and he encourages them to "hold fast what you have, so that no one may seize your crown" (3:11). The word used for "crown" here is *stephanos,* which means a reward in an athletic context (see, e.g., 1 Cor 9:25; 2 Thess 4:8), rather than *diadêma,* which would have royal connotations (see comments on the message to Smyrna). The idea is that they have already passed their test (3:8, 10) and have won their crowns. Now they must be diligent, so that when Christ comes they will still possess them. If they give in to pressure, in this case exercised by local Jews, they can still lose their crowns. It is interesting to note that the only other message in which crowns are mentioned as a reward is the one to Smyrna, in which the Jews are also the major opponents.

The promise to the conqueror is appropriate to a message which criticizes non-Christian Jews, for it uses imagery associated with the Jerusalem temple (3:12). Jews would apply such imagery to the real temple (recently destroyed) or to themselves (as did the community of the Dead Sea Scrolls). But Christ promises that it is the Philadelphian Christians who will become pillars in God's temple, never more going out of it. At first glance this seems to contradict 21:22, where there is no temple in the new Jerusalem. But Revelation's images are fluid and can be evocative and expressive as well as referential. The statement in chapter 22 that there is no temple in the new Jerusalem shows that the eschatological order far surpasses what precedes it, since God and Christ will be directly present with the faithful. But the seer can still use temple imagery in this message as another way to express the closeness of the faithful with God at the fulfillment (3:12).

"Pillar" is an image that is widespread over many cultures, stretching into our own. It is not uncommon for us to speak of "pillars of the community." Similarly, Paul speaks of James, Peter, and John as "pillars" of the Jerusalem church (Gal 2:9; see also 1 Tim 3:15). Revelation's use of pillar imagery expresses the high status of the Philadelphians in the new Jerusalem. The use of temple imagery to express social entities is well known from the period in Jewish and Greek sources. The community of the Dead Sea Scrolls spoke of their community as a temple (see Gärtner 1965), and Paul calls the church at Corinth "God's building" (1 Cor 3:10). Ephesians 2:19–22 calls the church God's temple.

Christ promises that the Philadelphians will never have to leave the temple of, as he says, "my God." Christ uses the phrase "my God" three more times in the rest of the promise to the conqueror. The repetition stresses the close relation between Christ and God. He says that he will write on the conquerors "the name of my God, and the name of the city of my God, the new Jerusalem that comes down from my God out of heaven, and my own new name." Inscriptions on temple pillars and walls were common in the ancient world. That God's name is written on their foreheads may reflect the fact that the high priest bore the name of God on the front of his turban (Exod 28:36–38), so they are being portrayed as priests. That the faithful bear God's name connects with 14:1, where the 144,000 have God's name written on their foreheads, and 22:4, where the servants of God who worship God in the new Jerusalem have God's name on their foreheads. In 7:3, the faithful have a seal placed on their foreheads so that they will be spared from God's wrath.

God's name written on the faithful also indicates that they belong to God (cf. Isa 43:7). It is especially important in view of the dualism that pervades Revelation to know who is on God's side. There are two passages in which the wicked are marked by a name on their foreheads. In 17:5, the great whore of Babylon has a mysterious name on her forehead that reveals her essence. In 13:16-18, the name of the beast is written on the hands or foreheads of the beast's followers.

The second item written on the faithful is the name of God's city, the new Jerusalem, whose coming down out of heaven is recounted in 21:2 and whose description occupies the bulk of chapters 21 and 22. The faithful will be permanent citizens of that city where God will dwell, and so they bear its name. Finally, Christ writes his own "new name" on them. All that belongs to God belongs to Jesus, and all that belongs to Jesus belongs to God. God and the Lamb even share the throne at the end of the book. So it is fitting that both of their names are written on the faithful. It is not completely clear what Christ's "new name" means. When Christ rides out to the final battle in 19:11-16, much is made of his name. He is called "the Word of God" and "King of kings and Lord of lords" (19:13, 16). He also has "a name inscribed that no one knows but himself" (19:12). It may be Christ's secret name that is inscribed on the white stone given to the conqueror in the message to Pergamum (2:17).

The message to the church at Philadelphia ends with the usual call to hear what the Spirit is saying to the churches (3:13).

The Message to Laodicea (3:14-22)

Laodicea was a prosperous city situated on the nexus of important trade routes. When it suffered major earthquake damage in 60-61 C.E., it did not need imperial help to recover. It lay about forty miles southeast of Philadelphia on the same road that connected Pergamum, Thyatira, and Philadelphia. Laodicea is the seventh of the seven cities in Revelation, and the road that connected it to Ephesus on the west completed the circuit of the seven cities. Laodicea was known for its locally manufactured black wool from which carpets were made, for its textile industry, for banking, and for its medical school. Each of these features finds an echo in the message. A strategic weakness of the city was its distance from its water supply. Water had to be carried to the city through stone pipes. Laodicea's closest important neighbors were Hierapolis (six miles away) and Colossae (ten miles away). Hierapolis was known for its hot springs, which flowed toward Laodicea. It is suggested that by the time they reached the vicinity of Laodicea they had become tepid, another possible allusion in the message.

The beginning of the church at Laodicea is unknown, but it is mentioned several times in the letter to the Colossians attributed to Paul. The authorship of Colossians is disputed. Regardless of how one decides this question, the letter can still tell us a bit about Laodicea. In Col 4:15, "Paul" asks for greetings to be passed on by the Colossians to members of the Laodicean church. Colossians 4:16 instructs the Colossians to send their letter to Laodicea to be read and to read the letter Paul sent to the Laodiceans. (Only one letter has survived that purports to be Paul's letter to the Laodiceans, and most scholars consider it spurious.) Colossians 2:1 says that Paul works hard for both the Colossians and the Laodiceans. Colossians 4:13 says that Epaphras has worked hard for the churches of Colossae, Hierapolis, and Laodicea. Colossians 1:7 and 4:12–13 may imply that Epaphras was the founder of the church at Colossae, and he may well have founded the churches at Hierapolis and Laodicea as well (although Acts 19:10 claims that all of Asia heard the gospel because of Paul's work, an idealizing view). The close relationship between the churches at Colossae and Laodicea that the letter to the Colossians depicts is quite plausible, given their geographical proximity. It is therefore intriguing that the message to the Laodiceans in Revelation contains several points of contact with the letter to the Colossians, particularly with its christology.

The message to the church of Laodicea is similar to the one to Sardis. In neither message is it possible to be very specific about exactly what is happening in the church, yet these two messages are the two most negative of the seven. Both messages admit that things are *apparently* going well in each of the two churches but assert that appearances are deceptive. In Sardis the author finds "a few persons" who deserve praise. In Laodicea there are not even a few. We know that there were important Jewish communities in Sardis and Laodicea, but the author mentions no conflicts with Jews there, as he does for Smyrna and Philadelphia. It is suggestive that it is the churches whose membership is located in a low social and economic stratum (Smyrna and Philadelphia) that encounter problems with the local Jewish communities, whereas those which are well established in their surroundings (Sardis and Laodicea) have no such problems. This may be because of the well-established nature of the Jewish communities in Asia, a situation attested to by Josephus. Tension between Jews and Christians was always a possibility, given their conflicting claims based on many of the same traditions and scriptures, but such tension may have received an added impetus when combined with class conflict of the sort we have discerned behind some of the messages in Revelation.

After the initial commission to write, Christ is characterized as "the Amen, the faithful and true witness, the origin [*archê*] of God's creation" (3:14). The word "amen" comes from the Hebrew *'mn* (see 1:6-7). "Amen" is used in the Hebrew Bible and the New Testament as a liturgical response signifying agreement with the prayer just uttered. It is used in the gospel of John in an unusual way to furnish a solemn introduction to words of Jesus: "Amen, Amen, I say to you." This usage grows out of its use as agreement, for it serves to confirm strongly something that Jesus is about to say.

To speak of a particular person as the "Amen" is more unusual still, and this has led to various explanations. The Hebrew "amen" comes from the same root as *'emet,* which denotes God's faithfulness to the covenant. The phrase "God of amen" occurs in Isa 65:16, and it is translated in the NRSV as "God of faithfulness." The LXX translates this as *ton theon ton alêthinon,* "the God who is true," which Charles (1920, 1:94) reads as indicating that the LXX interprets Isa 65:16 to mean "the True One," that is, "the One who keeps covenant." If this is the background to Revelation's usage, the title may refer to Christ's faithfulness to churches. Another possibility is related to this one. As was already mentioned, "amen" can be a liturgical response indicating assent. Paul plays upon this meaning in 2 Corinthians when he says, "In him [Christ] every one of God's promises is a 'yes.' For this reason it is through him that we say the 'Amen' to the glory of God" (1:20). Jesus is the fulfillment of God's promises. He is God's saying yes to the human race. Therefore, the "amen," the liturgical "yes," is said in Jesus' name. This suggested background for Rev 3:14 is compatible with the first, which sees "amen" as related to Jesus' faithfulness to the covenant, and it also fits Revelation's view that the entire history of God's dealings with humanity reaches a culmination in the death of Christ, who brings to fruition all the promises to God's people.

Christ is next called "the faithful and true witness, the origin of God's creation" (3:14). These qualities refer back to 1:5, where Jesus is called "the faithful witness, the firstborn of the dead, and the ruler of the kings of the earth." In our discussion of 1:5, we noted the relationship between Christ's being the firstborn of the dead and his universal sovereignty. There is a progression from Jesus' earthly witness resulting in his death, to his resurrection, to his rule. The message to Laodicea contains these same elements. In 3:14, Jesus is called the faithful and true witness, and in 3:21, the promise to the conqueror reminds the audience of Christ's victory, which results in the possession of a throne.

Christ now says that he is the "origin" (*archê*) of creation. The juxtaposition of "origin" and "Amen" in 3:21 may be a subtle interpretation of the title "first and last" in the message to Smyrna (2:8) and in the vision of the one like a son of man in 1:17.

We just noted that the title "faithful and true witness" in 3:14 recalls 1:5, which itself has contacts with the hymn of Colossians 1. Now we find another echo of that hymn in Christ as the origin of creation. Colossians says,

> He is the image of the invisible God, the firstborn of all creation; for in him all things in heaven and on earth were created, things visible and invisible, whether thrones or dominions or rulers or powers—all things have been created through him and for him. He himself is before all things, and in him all things hold together. (Col 1:15-17)

Both Rev 3:14 and Col 1:15-17 reflect wisdom christology, an interpretation of the person and work of Jesus in terms of the personification of wisdom that appears in passages such as Proverbs 8, Wisdom of Solomon 7, and Sirach 24. In those passages, wisdom is present with God at creation. Revelation uses these wisdom resonances to claim that Jesus is Lord of all not only because of his death and resurrection but also because his ascendancy goes back to the beginning of creation and even before. The "*archê* of God's creation" is somewhat ambiguous, just as similar statements about personified wisdom are. It could mean that Jesus was never created and that it was through him that all was created, or it could mean simply that Jesus is the first of God's creatures and that he shares in God's creative function.

The wisdom background of the "origin of God's creation" motif makes us look again at Jesus as "the Amen." Proverbs 8 is one of the wisdom passages that pictures wisdom as present with God at the creation. Proverbs 8:30 says, "Then [at the creation] I was beside him, like a master worker." The word translated "master worker" here is *'mon* in the Hebrew, a word that is close to the Hebrew word for "amen." In Prov 8:22, wisdom declares, "The Lord created me at the beginning of his work, the first of his acts of long ago." L. H. Silberman (1963) notes that in *Genesis Rabbah,* a midrash (ancient Jewish interpretation) on Genesis, the "master workman" (*'mon*) of Prov 8:30 and the "beginning" of 8:22 are both taken as titles for wisdom. Furthermore, in Prov 14:5 and 14:25, wisdom is called the "faithful witness," in both instances the word for "faithful" being taken from the same Hebrew root from which "amen" and *'mon* come. Thus all three titles of Jesus in 3:14—amen, faithful and true witness, origin of God's creation—come from a wisdom context (Proverbs 8 and 14), and two of them are also found together in a midrash on Genesis. The fact that Revelation's creative use of wisdom material parallels that of the midrash reinforces the conviction that Revelation's author is a Jew steeped in sacred scripture and in the interpretation of it current in his own time in Jewish, Christian, and Jewish-Christian circles.

The body of the message to Laodicea falls into four main parts. The first contains a cryptic indictment using hot and cold imagery (3:15-16); the second becomes a bit more specific about the indictment (3:17); the third counsels a certain action (3:18-19); and the fourth is a prophetic declaration (3:20).

Christ begins by telling the Laodiceans that they are neither hot nor cold, so he will spit them out of his mouth (3:15-16). This means that the faith of the Laodiceans is of the dull, routine sort. They are neither on fire with religious fervor nor completely indifferent. Christ will not settle for this type of faith. He would prefer that they make a choice, even if that choice means rejection of him (being "cold"). There may be a local allusion in the temperature imagery here (Hemer 1986, 186-91). Hierapolis had hot springs that cooled to a tepid state as they approached Laodicea. The source of Laodicea's drinking water was some six miles away, so the waters warmed as they traveled far from their source. Laodicea was able neither to profit from the beneficial effects of the hot springs nor to enjoy the coolness of a fresh spring.

Verse 17 makes the accusation more specific. Jesus says, "You say, 'I am rich, I have prospered, and I need nothing.' You do not realize that you are wretched, pitiable, poor, blind, and naked" (3:17). The words imputed to the Laodiceans echo those of the northern kingdom of Israel (Ephraim) when Hosea condemns it: "Ephraim has said, 'Ah, I am rich, I have gained wealth for myself; in all of my gain no offense has been found in me that would be sin' " (Hos 12:8). The Laodicean church is apparently well positioned economically and perhaps socially. The statement "I need nothing" may allude to the fact that the city repaired its earthquake damage without outside assistance (Ramsay 1994, 316; Hemer 1986, 191-96). Like the city of Laodicea itself, members of the church there may have felt that they had all their bets covered. They were financially successful and looked forward to reigning with Christ for all eternity. But Christ has a surprise in store for them. As in all the messages, he begins by saying "I know." This is contrasted with the Laodiceans' ignorance, for Christ says, "You do not know [NRSV: realize] that you are wretched" (3:17; Charles 1920, 1:96). Their material wealth masks spiritual poverty. Their situation is the opposite of that of the church in Smyrna, which is poor and powerless in the eyes of the world but rich in the eyes of God. The words chosen to express this may be especially appropriate to Laodicea. Laodicea was known for banking, medicine, and textiles. Despite this, the church there is poor, blind, and naked (Ramsay 1994, 316-17). Things are not as they appear.

The next section of the message exhorts the church to action (3:18-19). The action recommended matches the indictment. The church's members are in fact poor, so they should "buy" from Christ gold refined by fire. They are naked, and they should buy white robes from him. They are blind, so they should buy eye salve from him so that they might see. The irony here is strong. The church needs the most help in precisely those areas for which it thinks it is doing well.

The gold that Christians obtain from Christ, symbolizing all the riches available in Christ, is "refined by fire" (*pepurômenon*). The refinement of the gold indicates its purity and therefore its high quality. Only by obtaining such gold will the Laodiceans truly be rich. The inferior gold of which they are proud will do them no good. The use of wealth to symbolize what Christians obtain through their relationship with Jesus echoes Colossians, which describes the faith of Gentiles as "the riches of the glory of this mystery" (1:27).

Several times in Revelation there is an implicit contrast between the gold of this world and the gold of God's world. On the negative side, the evil locusts arising from the abyss wear crowns of gold (9:7); idols are made of gold (9:20); the great whore of Babylon is adorned with gold (17:4); and the merchants of the earth bring their cargo of gold and other precious things to the evil city (18:16). On the positive side, the new Jerusalem is measured with a golden rod (21:15); it is made of pure gold (21:18); and its street is pure gold (21:21). The contrast between the two types of gold is reminiscent of Christ's words in Luke 12:33–34: "Sell your possessions, and give alms. Make purses for yourselves that do not wear out, an unfailing treasure in heaven, where no thief comes near and no moth destroys. For where your treasure is, there your heart will be also." Christianity was not unique in contrasting material riches with something else thought to be true riches. Philosophers in the Greco-Roman world did so as well, as did Jewish writers.

Christ enjoins the Laodiceans to buy from him white robes, lest the shame of their nakedness be visible (3:18). We have already discussed, in the context of the message to Sardis, the use of white robes as the proper attire for the resurrected righteous (see comments on 3:5). Paul's usage in 2 Corinthians 5 is similar to that in the message to Laodicea. Paul discusses both the mortal body and the glorified body as dwellings and as garments simultaneously. He says he wishes to leave his present "tent" behind, not because he wishes to be naked, but because he wishes "to be further clothed" (2 Cor 5:4). In neither Revelation nor 2 Corinthians is it fully clear just what it would mean to be naked. Generally speaking, Jews believed not so much in immortality of the soul as in resurrection of the body. The idea of a bodiless soul is rare in Jewish literature of the second temple period, and Paul and our author may mean such bodiless souls when they speak of nakedness. So to receive a white robe means to receive one's glorious resurrection body, a meaning which Charles finds in 3:5 as well (1920, 1:82–83). Here in 3:18, Revelation seems to envisage resurrected bodies for the faithful only. Lack of such a body is a punishment for the unworthy. Nakedness was accepted in Greco-Roman environments. But in Jewish tradition nakedness was shameful and was sometimes used as a symbol of judgment and humiliation (Mounce 1977, 127; he refers to Isa 20:1–4; 2 Sam 10:4; Ezek 16:37–39).

Finally, Christ counsels the Laodiceans to buy from him salve for their eyes that they might see. Again, there is irony here. They think they see very well. They think they judge their own situation rightly, and they consider themselves rich, probably both materially and spiritually. There may be a local allusion to the medical community at Laodicea that thinks it can offer healing salve to those in need. But only Christ has the salve that restores true vision.

To modern ears, it may sound strange that Christ encourages the Laodiceans to "buy" these items from him. The background for this may be Israel's wisdom tradition, which we have already seen to be influential in this message. The book of Proverbs exhorts its readers, "Buy truth, and do not sell it; buy wisdom, instruction, and understanding" (23:23; cf. 17:16). This may originally have referred to fees charged by those who ran schools. The book of Baruch uses the image of buying in a different way when it asks rhetorically concerning wisdom, "Who will buy her with pure gold?" (3:30), meaning that no one can obtain wisdom by purchasing it. Obviously, Christ is not expecting actual money from the Laodiceans, but the author is tapping into the wisdom tradition for its resonances. Wisdom, true understanding of how the world works, was a precious commodity in the ancient world, and different traditions claimed access to it. Apocalyptic traditions used language similar to that used by wisdom circles partly for historical reasons (wisdom played a role in the development of apocalypticism) and partly because wisdom language was widespread in Jewish and Christian circles and was meaningful to inhabitants of the Hellenistic world. Christ identifies himself here as the source of true wisdom and declares that the Laodiceans' "investment" in him would bear fruit.

Christ now urges the Laodiceans to repent because, as he says, "I reprove and discipline those whom I love" (3:19). This echoes Prov 3:11–12: "My child, do not despise the LORD's discipline or be weary of his reproof, for the LORD reproves the one he loves, as a father the son in whom he delights." This is susceptible to two main interpretations. Christ is speaking to a church that seems quite comfortable and so is not experiencing reproof or discipline. One interpretation, therefore, is that when Christ is speaking about those whom he loves, he does not mean the Laodiceans. If he really loved them, they would be suffering like the church at Smyrna, for example. The Laodiceans may even think, wrongly, that Christians who suffer like those at Smyrna are not in Christ's favor (Yarbro Collins 1979, 31). If so, Christ disabuses them of this notion. All of Revelation requires that normal human reasoning must be turned on its head if one is to know how things really are. Those who suffer are those who are in God's favor. Those who are comfortable are suspect for that very reason (cf. Luke 6:20–31). When the Laodiceans repent and become faithful, their suffering will be the badge of authenticity.

Another interpretation of 3:19 is that the message itself constitutes Christ's reproof and discipline. Christ professes his love for the Laodiceans despite their unworthiness. He reproaches them because he loves them, and he urges them to repent.

Revelation does not give explicit clues about which of these two readings is correct. However, the first fits more securely into the book as a whole, a major theme of which is that those who suffer, or are at least willing to suffer, in setting themselves apart from their surrounding culture are the ones in God's favor. This reading is bolstered indirectly by Christ's injunction to "be earnest," which might more accurately be translated "be zealous." The sort of zeal that takes an uncompromisingly prophetic stance against accepted values does not characterize the church at Laodicea.

In Hebrews the author uses Prov 3:11–12 in the same way as does Revelation's author. Persecution is to be received as God's chastisement on those whom he loves (12:5–6). Persecution is not a sign of God's powerlessness or disfavor. It means the opposite of what it seems to mean. It indicates God's love. The parallel between Hebrews 12 and Rev 3:19 is the more significant in the light of the possibly similar situations of the recipients of Hebrews and the Asian churches, as discussed in the introduction above.

Verse 20 is a prophetic pronouncement: "Listen! I am standing at the door, knocking; if you hear my voice and open the door, I will come in to you and eat with you, and you with me." In any culture, eating is full of symbolism. In the ancient Mediterranean world, this was especially so. Because of the symbolic weight of meals, Jesus made eating a major part of his ministry, letting meals represent closeness with God and making them symbols for the messianic age (see 19:9–18, and meal scenes throughout the gospels). Opening the door to Jesus so that he might come in and eat is opening oneself to a close relationship with him, with all that entails. The reason the Laodiceans are not yet ready to eat with Christ is their unwillingness to take on the sufferings that true loyalty to him require. This same juxtaposition of ideas is found in Luke 22:28–30, where Jesus says, "You are those who have stood by me in my trials; and I confer on you, just as my Father has conferred on me, a kingdom, so that you may eat and drink at my table in my kingdom, and you will sit on thrones judging the twelve tribes of Israel" (cf. Matt 19:28). The same logic is apparent in 2 Tim 2:11: "If we have died with him, we will also live with him; if we endure, we will also reign with him."

The usual promise to the conqueror comes in verse 21: "To the one who conquers I will give a place with me on my throne, just as I myself conquered and sat down with my Father on his throne." Jesus is depicted as sitting on the throne with God in Rev 22:1, 3. This image may derive originally from Christian application to Christ of Ps 110:1: "The LORD says to my lord, 'Sit at my right hand until I make your enemies your footstool.' " Revelation 3:21 supplies another echo of Colossians, whose audience is told, "So if you have been raised with Christ, seek the things that are above, where Christ is, seated at the right hand of God" (Col 3:1). Again we have the familiar pattern of royal rule following resurrection. Psalm 110 was very important in Christian exegesis of the Bible (see Matt 22:44; 26:64; Mark 12:36; 14:62; 16:19; Luke 20:42–43; Acts 2:34–35; Rom 8:34; 1 Cor 15:25; Eph 1:20; Col 3:1; Heb 1:3, 13; 7:17, 21; 8:1; 10:12). As usual, Revelation goes further than the rest of the New Testament. The author is not content to assert that Christ sits at the right hand of God. He declares that Christ actually sits on the throne *with* God. This conforms to the tendency in Revelation to attribute to Christ what had previously been asserted of God (Bauckham 1993, 54–65).

Part II

The First Cycle of Eschatological Visions (4:1–11:19)

Chapter Five

Heavenly Throne Room and Heavenly Liturgy (Chapters 4–5)

Narrative Introduction (4:1–2)

Chapters 4 and 5 of Revelation are the very heart of the book. Chapter 4 affords the seer (and so his audience) a glimpse into God's throne room, which teaches him that God retains sovereignty over the universe, despite appearances to the contrary on earth. Revelation 4:1–2 is a narrative introduction to the throne room vision. It signals both continuity and discontinuity with what precedes. Continuity is expressed in several ways. The voice that addresses John is also the voice that he heard speaking like a trumpet in chapter 1, belonging to the one like a son of man. The same Christ who sent the messages to the churches now summons John up to heaven, saying, "I will show you what must take place after this" (4:1). This wording recalls both 1:1, where the purpose of the revelation is "to show his servants what must soon take place," and 1:19, where John is told to write "what you have seen, what is, and what is to take place after this." Revelation 1:1, 19 and 4:1 all echo the similar phrase in Dan 2:45.

Although chapters 4 and 5 are firmly tied to what precedes, they are also a new beginning. The words "after this I looked," which introduce 4:1, usually introduce a "new and important vision" in Revelation (Charles 1920, 1:106; see 7:1, 9; 15:5; 18:1; 19:1). The scene and the type of vision shift. In chapters 1 to 3, John has been on the island of Patmos, seeing and hearing from the risen Christ. He has been given relatively concrete messages for each of the seven churches in their historical peculiarity. But at the beginning of chapter 4, John is told to ascend to heaven to learn "what must take place after this" (4:1). His vantage point becomes the heavenly throne room. He will now be able to see from God's viewpoint, the only truly valid one. "What must take place after this" consists of eschatological events that have their origin in God, so the seer will be able to understand what is really happening on earth when he sees what happens in heaven. This is typically apocalyptic.

Most apocalypses featuring a heavenly journey give more details than does Revelation (see Collins and Fishbane 1995; Himmelfarb 1993). Often an apocalyptic seer records many specifics of the ascent and of the heavenly regions through which he travels. Revelation offers little such description. Our author's intent is not so much to convey knowledge of heavenly geography as it is to assert a close connection between the heavenly and earthly realms. God rules both. Because the seer sees things from heaven's viewpoint, he has an unrestricted view of the entire cosmos.

We begin our explanation of the vision of heaven in chapter 4 with a look at the first chapter of Genesis. There are two creation stories at the beginning of Genesis. Our interest lies with the first (Gen 1:1–2:3). There God creates light on the first day. On the second day, "God made the dome and separated the waters that were under the dome from the waters that were above the dome. And it was so. God called the dome Sky" (Gen 1:7–8). Other translations call the "dome" the "firmament," and the "sky" "heaven." Apparently, before God's creative action, the universe was solid water. God placed the firmament, a bowl-shaped physical barrier, between the waters above and the waters below so as to create dry land for plants, animals, and humans.

When John sees a door opened in heaven in Rev 4:1, the door is in the firmament or dome of heaven. When he is ordered to come up to heaven, he presumably passes through that door, and then he sees God on his throne (4:2). His words recall those that introduce Ezekiel's first vision: "The heavens were opened, and I saw visions of God" (1:1), although Ezekiel mentions no door. Other such visions do mention entrance doors or gates to heaven (see Gen 28:17; *T. Levi* 5:1; 3 Macc 6:18). "Heaven" occurs in the singular in 4:1. Other apocalypses have several heavens — five, seven, or even ten. Paul tells us that he was caught up to the third heaven, where paradise is preserved (2 Cor 12:2–4). A multilayered heaven emphasizes God's transcendence. In *3 Baruch,* for example, the seer is allowed only as far as the fifth heaven and is not permitted to enter the divine throne room.

In Revelation, by contrast, the seer enters the immediate presence of God. John has direct access to the source of all that is to happen (see Charles 1920, 1:108).

When John sees the door opened, he is immediately "in the spirit." John already says in 1:10 that his vision takes place while he is "in the spirit," meaning that he is in a prophetic trance when he receives his vision. It is never said that John comes out of the spirit, so the notice in 4:2 seems superfluous. John may model his presentation on that of Ezekiel here. In chapter 8, Ezekiel is sitting in his house in Babylonia when the "hand of the Lord God fell upon" him. A mysterious "one that looked like a son of man" (NRSV: "like a human being") appears to him. Then the spirit lifts Ezekiel up and brings him to Jerusalem to see visions (8:3–4). Later the prophetic spirit comes upon Ezekiel in Jerusalem and he begins to prophesy (11:5). Some see in this double mention of the spirit in Ezekiel the model for the double mention in Revelation. In Revelation 1, the spirit allows John to see the vision of Christ on Patmos, and in chapter 4, it may transport him to heaven. Revelation is not explicit that the spirit transports John in 4:2, but neither does it offer any other description of his ascent. John may assume that his audience will perceive the analogy with Ezekiel 8 and so understand the spirit's role.

The similarity between Ezekiel 8 and Rev 4:1–3 is broader than the element of transportation in the spirit. In both cases the spirit is associated with visions that are introduced by the words "I saw." In both cases the context includes a mysterious figure said to be like a son of man. Although the specifics of the son of man figure in Revelation 1 come from Daniel 7 and 10, there are also broad similarities between the figures in Ezekiel 8 and Revelation 1 in that they are bright and associated with fire (Ezek 8:2; Rev 1:14–15). In both Ezekiel 8 and Revelation 4, the seer is brought into God's presence. Finally, both chapters allude to an earlier vision; John refers to the trumpetlike voice of Revelation 1, and Ezekiel looks back to his vision of God in chapter 1. The relationship between Revelation 4 and Ezekiel 8 foreshadows the extensive allusions to the book of Ezekiel to follow.

In Rev 4:2, John expresses the heart of his book: "There in heaven stood a throne, with one seated on the throne." The one on the throne obviously is God. "Throne" is one of the most common words in Revelation, occurring forty-seven times and in almost every chapter. "Throne" captures what is at stake throughout the book – sovereignty (see Boring 1986). Who really rules? Who is truly worthy of honor and glory and might? Revelation's answer is univocal. God and the Lamb alone deserve such recognition.

Biblical Texts concerning Visions of Heaven Used by John

John's vision of God is in a long line of such visions in Israelite and Jewish literature. The Bible furnishes examples in 1 Kings 22, Isaiah 6, Ezekiel 1, Zechariah 4, and Daniel 7. Postbiblical examples are *1 Enoch* 14, *2 Enoch, T. Levi* 3–5, *Apoc. Abr.* 18. In later Jewish mystical tradition, the vision of God's chariot-throne (in Hebrew, *merkabah,* thus the term "merkabah mysticism") is central (see Gruenwald 1980). Before analyzing Revelation 4–5, we should acquaint ourselves with the texts on which the author draws. It is clear that he uses biblical texts, especially Isaiah 6, Ezekiel 1, and Daniel 7. Although there is no compelling evidence that he uses any postbiblical text, we shall quote several because they furnish useful parallels to Revelation's visions, being Jewish treatments of the same subjects using the same raw materials. They therefore illuminate the literary and theological context of Revelation. This is not to deny that the seer had his own mystical vision of heaven. But even if he did have such an experience, it was heavily influenced and even formed by descriptions he had read of other such experiences.

The classic appearance of God in the Bible is the theophany at Mount Sinai. The appearance contains several elements typical of a divine appearance—fire, thunder and lightning, a thick cloud, an earthquake, and the sound of a loud trumpet. It is interesting to speculate on the origins of the associations of these elements with a theophany. Human fascination with mysterious and powerful forces of nature, such as volcanoes, thunderstorms, and earthquakes certainly played a role. By the time of the writing of the biblical texts and certainly by the seer's time such associations were conventional.

In Exodus 19, God instructs Moses to climb Mount Sinai to receive the Torah. Because of God's holiness and majesty, no one but Moses is allowed to ascend the mountain when God is present. After suitable preparations are made,

> On the morning of the third day there was thunder and lightning, as well as a thick cloud on the mountain, and

> a blast of a trumpet so loud that all the people who were in the camp trembled.... Now Mount Sinai was wrapped with smoke, because the Lord had descended upon it in fire; the smoke went up like the smoke of a kiln, while the whole mountain shook violently. As the blast of the trumpet grew louder and louder, Moses would speak and God would answer him in thunder. (Exod 19:16, 18-19)

Later, in Exodus 24, Moses, Aaron and his sons, and seventy elders ascend Mount Sinai to seal the covenant with God. "They saw the God of Israel. Under his feet there was something like pavement of sapphire stone, like the very heaven for clearness" (24:10). The "pavement" here, compared to heaven (probably meaning the firmament) for its transparency, is like the sea of glass in Revelation 4, also transparent.

Prophetic and apocalyptic texts develop descriptions of visions of God, God's dwelling place in heaven, and God's intervention in human affairs. Such descriptions use the traditional language of natural phenomena and add such features as precious stones, detailed descriptions of heaven's features, facts about God's heavenly entourage, and even specific details of God's appearance. We frequently refer to Isaiah and Ezekiel in the commentary on chapters 4-5, so here we simply note relevant aspects of those texts, but for the other texts adduced we shall briefly indicate the parallels here.

John's vision of the heavenly throne room is heavily influenced by Ezekiel, who says that he was beside a river in Babylon when

> the heavens were opened, and I saw visions of God.... As I looked, a stormy wind came out of the north: a great cloud with brightness around it and fire flashing forth continually, and in the middle of the fire, something like gleaming amber. In the middle of it was something like four living creatures. This was their appearance: they were of human form. Each had four faces, and each of them had four wings. Their legs were straight, and the soles of their feet were like the soles of a calf's foot; and they sparkled like burnished bronze.... As for the appearance of their faces: the four had the face of a human being, the face of a lion on the right side, the face of an ox on the left side, and the face of an eagle.... In the middle of the living creatures there was something that looked like burning coals

> of fire, like torches moving to and fro among the living creatures; the fire was bright, and lightning issued from the fire. The living creatures darted to and fro, like a flash of lightning. . . . (Ezek 1:1, 4–7, 10, 13–14)

Ezekiel now sees a wheel beside each creature, an allusion to the chariot on which God rides, a feature taken from descriptions of ancient Near Eastern gods but missing in Revelation. The prophet describes the movement of the wheels and creatures. Relevant for our purposes is that each of the wheels is "full of eyes all around" (1:15–21). Ezekiel continues:

> Over the heads of the living creatures there was something like a dome, shining like crystal, spread out above their heads. Under the dome their wings were stretched out straight, one toward another; and each of the creatures had two wings covering its body. When they moved, I heard the sound of their wings like the sound of mighty waters, like the thunder of the Almighty, a sound of tumult like the sound of an army; when they stopped, they let down their wings. And there came a voice from above the dome over their heads; when they stopped, they let down their wings.
>
> And above the dome over their heads there was something like a throne, in appearance like sapphire; and seated above the likeness of a throne was something that seemed like a human form. Upward from what appeared like the loins I saw something like gleaming amber, something that looked like fire enclosed all around; and downward from what looked like the loins I saw something that looked like fire, and there was splendor all around. Like the bow in a cloud on a rainy day, such was the appearance of the splendor all around. This was the appearance of the likeness of the glory of the LORD. When I saw it, I fell on my face, and I heard the voice of someone speaking. (Ezek 1:22–28).

Isaiah 6 is another vision of God that influences Revelation. In that chapter Isaiah recounts the vision he had in the temple that constituted his prophetic commissioning. It begins as follows:

> In the year that King Uzziah died, I saw the Lord sitting on a throne, high and lofty; and the hem of his robe filled the temple. Seraphs were in attendance above him; each had six wings: with two they covered their faces, and with two

they covered their feet, and with two they flew. And one called to another and said:

> "Holy, holy, holy is the LORD of hosts;
> the whole earth is full of his glory."

The pivots on the thresholds shook at the voices of those who called, and the house filled with smoke. (Isa 6:1–4)

Daniel's throne scene is in chapter 7. We quote just those sections of interest as parallels to Revelation 4–5:

> As I watched,
> thrones were set in place,
> and an Ancient One took his throne,
> his clothing was white as snow,
> and the hair of his head like pure wool;
> his throne was fiery flames,
> and its wheels were burning fire.
> A stream of fire issued
> and flowed out from his presence.
> A thousand thousands served him,
> and ten thousand times ten thousand stood attending him....
> I saw one like a human being [literally: son of man]
> coming with the clouds of heaven.
> And he came to the Ancient One
> and was present before him.
> To him was given dominion
> and glory and kingship,
> that all peoples, nations, and languages
> should serve him.
> His dominion is an everlasting dominion,
> that shall not pass away,
> and his kingship is one
> that shall never be destroyed. (Dan 7:9–10, 13–14)

Revelation 4–5 shares many features with Daniel 7. In neither one is God named. Both scenes have numerous thrones in heaven. In both God is surrounded by ten thousand times ten thousand angels. In both scenes a figure approaches God. In Daniel, one like a son of man comes to God on the clouds (cf. Rev 14:14), and he receives "dominion and glory and kingship, that all peoples, nations, and languages should serve him." In

Revelation 5, the Lamb (who in fact is the same as the one like a son of man in chapter 1) comes to God and takes the scroll which makes him master over the endtime events, and he is then said to be worthy to receive, among other things, power and glory and might. In Daniel, all peoples, nations, and languages serve the son of man, and in Revelation the Lamb has won "saints from every tribe and language and people and nation" for God (Rev 5:9; see 7:9; 11:9; 13:7; 14:6; 17:15). The word translated "saints" in Revelation also means "holy ones" (*hagioi*). Elsewhere in Daniel 7, the angels are called "holy ones" and Israel is called the "people of the holy ones" (7:27).

Nonbiblical Texts Useful as Background to Revelation

In *1 Enoch* 14 the seer, Enoch, is caught up to heaven and sees the heavenly throne room:

> As for its floor, it was of fire and above it was lightning and the path of the stars; and as for the ceiling, it was flaming fire. And I observed and saw inside a lofty throne – its appearance was like crystal and its wheels like the shining sun; and [I heard?] the voice of the cherubim; and from beneath the throne were issuing streams of flaming fire. It was difficult to look at it. And the Great Glory was sitting on it – as for his gown, which was shining more brightly than the sun, it was whiter than any snow. . . . No one could come near unto him from among those that surrounded the tens of millions [that stood] before him. (*1 Enoch* 14:17–20, 22)

Elements common to *1 Enoch* and Revelation are the throne, crystal, fire, lightning, a council of angels in constant attendance, whiteness, and praising cherubim.

The *Apocalypse of Abraham* was written at about the same time as Revelation. It contains a vision of God in chapter 18:

> I saw under the fire a throne of fire and the many-eyed ones round about, reciting the song, under the throne four fiery living creatures, singing. And the appearance of each of them was the same, each having four faces. And this [was] the aspect of their faces: of a lion, of a man, of an ox, and of an eagle. Each one had four heads on its body so that the four living creatures had sixteen faces. And each one

> had six wings: two on the shoulders, two halfway down, and two at the loins. (18:3–6).

Like Revelation, the *Apocalypse of Abraham* depends on Ezekiel and Isaiah. The four living creatures bearing the throne come from Ezekiel, and the fact that they have six wings (rather than four as in Ezekiel) and sing praises (instead of merely bearing the throne as in Ezekiel) comes from Isaiah. Like Revelation, this text transfers Ezekiel's eyes in the wheels of the chariot to the four living creatures, but it retains the wheels themselves with their eyes.

Testament of Levi 2–5 is in the form of an apocalypse. The text pictures several heavens:

> The lowest... contains fire, snow, and ice, ready for the day determined by God's righteous judgment. In it are all the spirits of those dispatched to achieve the punishment of mankind. In the second are the armies arrayed for the day of judgment to work vengeance on the spirits of error and of Beliar. Above them are the Holy Ones (angels). In the uppermost heaven of all dwells the Great Glory in the Holy of Holies superior to all holiness. There with him are the archangels, who serve and offer propitiatory sacrifices to the Lord in behalf of all the sins of ignorance of the righteous ones.... There with him are thrones and authorities; their praises to God are offered eternally. (3:2–5, 8)

Common to both the *Testament of Levi* and Revelation are God's heavenly attendants, the angels. Certain chief angels are given the title "archangels" here, and in Revelation certain angels are also singled out. Angels in both texts fulfill priestly duties on behalf of humans. In Revelation, one class of angels sits on thrones, and in the *Testament of Levi* some angels are given the title "thrones." The second heaven in the *Testament of Levi* contains heavenly armies, and Revelation 19 describes heavenly armies that follow the victorious Christ. In both, God's awesomeness is expressed through earthquakes (see Rev 6:12; 8:5; 11:13, 19; 16:18). Both have fire and ice as part of God's arsenal.

John's Vision of God and Heaven (Chapter 4)

John uses Isaiah 6 and Ezekiel 1 extensively. Like the authors of the postbiblical texts cited above, John adapts these texts to his own purposes. John limits his description of God to the terse statement, "The one seated there looks like jasper and carnelian, and around the throne is a rainbow that looks like an emerald" (4:3). One could say that this is a description that is not a description. In Jewish and Christian texts containing trips to heaven, earthly realties are enlisted to describe supernatural realities, but there is often the realization that earthly terms are not adequate to express the supernatural. There are degrees of specificity about such descriptions ranging from reluctance to speak at all to detailed descriptions even of the deity itself. Paul illustrates the former end of the spectrum when he says that when he made his trip to paradise (in the third heaven), he "heard things that are not to be told, that no mortal is permitted to repeat" (2 Cor 12:4). This has a counterpart in Rev 10:4, where the seer is told to keep secret what he hears the seven thunders saying. Ezekiel is freer in his portrayal of God, but he qualifies it with phrases that discourage taking the details too literally: "something like a throne," "the likeness of a throne," "what appeared like loins," and so on. The summarizing sentence that concludes Ezekiel's description is illustrative: "This was the *appearance* of the *likeness* of the glory of the Lord" (Ezek 1:28).

Boring (1989, 103) suggests that Revelation's reluctance to describe God directly is at least partially due to the fact that God exercises dominion through Jesus. The divinity is left somewhat blank, as it were, so that the space can be filled in by what is said about Christ, who is described in detail several times (chapters 1, 5, 19). This impression is fortified by the designation of God simply as the "one seated on the throne" (twelve times).

The numerous scenes throughout Revelation that take place in heaven have aspects of both a royal court and a temple. The clearest expression of the connection between throne and temple is in 7:15, where, speaking of those who have survived the "great ordeal," the seer says, "For this reason they are before the throne of God, and worship him day and night within his temple." This mixture of political and religious elements is natural for the ancients. This is as true for Romans as for Jews. Religious symbolism bolsters and supports the Roman empire, and Revelation uses such symbolism to attack the empire. John's statement that he saw God on the throne is as political as it is religious (Boring 1986). John's scenario of God seated on his throne surrounded by angelic attendants may be modeled on the Roman imperial court, where the emperor heard legal cases, surrounded by his advisers, senators, members of the consular class, and so on (Aune 1983a, 8-9; Yarbro Collins 1990, 1004).

John compares God's appearance to the precious stones jasper and carnelian, and God is surrounded by a rainbow that looks like emerald (4:3). Ezekiel also uses precious stones to describe God and God's entourage (1:16, 26, 27). Revelation's emerald rainbow recalls Ezekiel 1, where God is surrounded by splendor that is compared to a rainbow (1:28). Precious stones, including jasper, carnelian, and emerald, are used to describe the glory of the king of Tyre in Ezek 28:13. The rainbow alludes to Genesis 9, where it is a sign of God's promise never to destroy the earth by a flood again. There is irony in this allusion. The story in Genesis attests to God's grace in allowing a new beginning for human history through Noah after the flood, but it is also a reminder of God's ability to destroy creation in judgment. The flood is used several times in the New Testament as a warning about God's judgment (Matt 24:36-39; 2 Pet 2:5; 3:6; cf. 1 Pet 3:20; Heb 11:7). Thus Revelation's rainbow has connotations of both grace and judgment.

Next come descriptions of two main categories of heavenly attendants, the twenty-four elders and the four living creatures (4:4, 6-11). As befitting a powerful emperor, God is surrounded by supernatural entities occupying various levels in a heavenly hierarchy. In polytheistic cultures, those entities could be thought of as gods and goddesses, as well as lesser attendants. Israel's monotheism transformed those divinities into lesser creatures, angels. In a couple of passages in the Hebrew Bible, the older idea of a council of gods survives. Examples of this are Psalm 82, Deut 32:8-9, and Gen 6:1-4. Passages like these disclose the roots of key apocalyptic concepts, developed in works like *1 Enoch* and Revelation. There is a heaven populated by supernatural figures where decisions are taken and actions performed that determine what happens in the natural world. The ancients see what we call "natural" and "supernatural" as realms of the same universe. One can tour heaven and return, for example, and angels and demons are much more commonly encountered by humans than in our age.

Charles (1920, 1:115-16) suggests that 4:4, which concerns the elders, has been misplaced. This is because he pictures heaven as a series of concentric circles. God is at the center on the throne, surrounded by the four living creatures, who are in turn surrounded by the twenty-four elders, who are surrounded by an innumerable multitude. In 7:9–11 and 19:1–4, the order of the groups is from the outside to the inside – multitude, angels, elders, four creatures, and God at the center on the throne. Charles's picture of the heavenly court is correct, but the mention of the elders first in chapter 4 may indicate a different organizing principle at work. This may be an example of the ancient rhetorical form called "chiasm," from the Greek letter chi, which is in the shape of an "x," also called "ring structure." First the elders are mentioned (4:4), then a throne scene (4:5–9), then the elders again (4:10–11). Thus the structure is ABA'. Such a structure emphasizes the middle element. Here the middle element, the throne scene in 4:5–9, can be seen as a microcosm of the whole of Revelation. In one way or another, everything that follows in Revelation flows from God's throne. From the throne come theophanic elements which later accompany the climaxes of the seal, trumpet, and bowl sections. This means that God is the source of the eschatological events. The seven torches before the throne may be related to the seven angels who carry out the trumpet and bowl series. The glassy sea relates to the only other mention of it, in the victory scene of 15:2, connecting 4:6 to that final victory. Finally, the four living creatures, God's closest attendants, proclaim the meaning of the scene in a doxology using titles of God stressing his power and intent to intervene in human affairs soon.

The identity of the twenty-four elders of 4:4 is difficult to determine. The main question is whether they are angels or humans. Charles (1920, 1:128–29) conveniently summarizes the characteristics of the twenty-four elders. They occupy thrones around God (4:4; 11:16); they wear golden crowns and white garments (4:4); they are called elders and number twenty-four; the seer calls one of them *kyrie,* which means "sir" or "lord" (7:13); they act as interpreters in 7:13; they act as priests in offering to God the prayers of the faithful (5:8); they encourage the seer in his vision (5:5); and they participate in the heavenly liturgy through singing and playing the harp (5:8, 14; 11:16; 19:4).

Aspects of the elders' depiction support the view that they are humans. In 4:4, they are seated on thrones and wear white garments and golden crowns. Each of these items is associated with faithful believers who have conquered (2:10; 3:4–5, 11, 18, 21; 6:11; 7:9, 13–14; 20:4). Ford (1975, 72, depending on Feuillet 1965), observes that angels are not depicted anywhere else wearing crowns, sitting on thrones, or being called elders.

The number twenty-four may come from adding together the number of tribes of Israel and the number of apostles. This would fit with the picture of the new Jerusalem in Revelation 21, where the names of the twelve tribes are written on its gates and the names of the apostles on its foundations (21:12–14). Alternatively, the number may reflect the number of Israelite priestly divisions (1 Chr 24:7–18). Either of these origins for the number twenty-four might be taken to support the identification of the elders as humans. For other suggestions regarding the number twenty-four, see Ford 1975, 72–73.

Charles (1920, 1:129–33) rejects the notion that the elders are humans. He sees them as angelic figures who are part of God's heavenly entourage. He finds that their functions—acting as interpreting figures in the apocalypse, serving as heavenly priests, offering the prayers of the faithful to God, consoling the seer during his vision—are fitting for angels, not humans. Furthermore, in chapters 4 and 5 the eschatological events that will result in the triumph of the righteous are yet to happen. For a connection between angels and thrones, Charles points to the thrones in Daniel 7, which he thinks are there for God's angelic attendants. One might add that there was an order of angelic attendants called "thrones" (see *T. Levi* 3:1–5, quoted above). All in all, it seems most likely that the seer took the elders as angels whose portrayal is strongly influenced by the political/religious imagery that also influenced the depiction of the reward of the righteous elsewhere in the book.

The idea that there are twenty-four elders because of the twenty-four priestly divisions in Israel, an idea supported by Charles, would work even if the elders are angels. This brings to mind the ancient principle, assumed by apocalypticism, that heavenly and earthly realities are intimately linked. The same principle would be at work if the number of elders is related to the twelve tribes of Israel and the twelve apostles. The new Jerusalem in chapter 21 incorporates these two twelves into its very architecture, and the tribes are associated with angels in that same architecture. The fact that the elders have three characteristics also attributed to triumphant Christians—thrones, crowns, and white garments—supports the idea that they are angelic representatives of the unified people of God, both before and after

Christ. That they fulfill both priestly and royal functions also connects them with God's people (1:6; 20:4, 6).

The very fact that John calls the figures "elders" joins them closely to God's people. Elders were an important group in the Jewish community and in many Christian groups. Seventy Israelite elders accompany Moses, the priest Aaron, and Aaron's priestly sons when they ascend the mountain to conclude the covenant with God (Exodus 24; see Isa 24:23).

Before leaving the twenty-four elders, we should mention the possible astrological resonances of the image. The Babylonians designated twenty-four stars, half to the north and half to the south of the zodiac, as "Judges of the All." Yarbro Collins (1990, 1004) says, "If such figures are the prototypes of the 24 elders, their presence and their placement in a circle around the deity symbolize cosmic order and governance." Malina (1995, 93–97) notes that such star-gods, or astral deities, were common in the ancient world and that they varied in number from twenty-four to seventy-two. He says they were known as decans, from the Greek *deka* meaning "ten," since originally there was one decan for each ten degrees of the zodiac. Malina's analysis supplies an additional reason for the author's calling them elders. Both "decan" and "elder" could be used to describe members of councils. This fits with the idea that the twenty-four correspond to the divine council as seen in the Hebrew Bible. It is not necessary to decide between an astrological interpretation and a theological or political one. All of these realms are interrelated in the seer's world. For example, stars were thought to be angels.

The text now returns to the throne, which is the center of the heavenly scene. From the throne there come "flashes of lightning, and rumblings and peals of thunder" (4:5). Such phenomena are typical of theophanies, the parade example being Exodus 19. Because thunder, lightning, and loud noises are typical expressions of God's presence, they occur when that presence is stressed in Revelation. Such phenomena accompany the opening of the seventh seal (8:5), the blowing of the seventh trumpet (11:19), and the pouring out of the seventh bowl (16:18), each of which happens in heaven before God's throne, thus connecting the throne scene of chapter 4 to the climaxes of the seals, trumpets, and bowls. This emphasizes that God is the source of the eschatological events that result in Satan's overthrow and the coming of God's kingdom (see Giblin 1994, 84).

The seer sees seven flaming torches before God's throne and

identifies them as "the seven spirits of God." These are "the seven spirits that are before his throne" in 1:4 who, with the Father and Jesus, greet the seven churches (see commentary there). The author may also be influenced by Ezek 1:13-14, where "torches" move about among the four creatures.

John now tells us that "in front of the throne there is something like a sea of glass, like crystal" (4:6). As usual, several biblical elements come together here. As explained above, in Genesis 1, God separates the primeval waters with a firmament, with waters above it and below it. Thus there are waters above the "firmament" or "sky" (see, e.g., Pss 104:1-4; 148:1-4; *T. Levi* 2:7; *1 Enoch* 54:8; *2 Enoch* 3:3; *Jub.* 2:4). The firmament is transparent. In Revelation, the transparency of the firmament is transferred to the heavenly sea, making it like glass.

Another biblical element feeds into the notion of the crystal sea. In the Jerusalem temple there was a "molten sea," which was a large bronze vessel full of water (1 Kgs 7:23-26). Its original function is uncertain. It may represent the cosmic sea that God conquered in creation and over which he has control. This reflects an ancient myth shared in one form or another by many Near Eastern civilizations. The basic shape of the myth is of an attack on a creator god by a sea-monster, in which the monster is defeated. Caird (1966, 66) notes that the myth has been stripped of its mythical features in Genesis 1, and he supplies other helpful biblical references (Job 9:13; 38:8-11; Pss 74:13-14; 89:10; 104:5-9; Prov 8:27-29; Sir 39:17).

Daniel 7 alludes to this myth when four beasts emerge from the sea, symbolizing four successive empires that oppressed Israel. This notion of the cosmic sea also comes into play in Revelation 13, where the evil beast (Rome and/or the emperor Nero) arises out of the sea, and in Rev 21:1, where the sea goes out of existence at the eschaton. In Rev 15:2-4, the faithful celebrate God's victory and stand beside the glassy sea singing the song of Moses (see comments there).

The "four living creatures" which are "in the midst of [NRSV: around] the throne, and on each side of the throne" (4:6), are among the most fascinating entities in Revelation. Charles (1920, 1:119-123) traces a possible tradition history of these creatures through Jewish literature. They are the superhuman figures closest to God, as is indicated by their somewhat confusing location, both in the midst of (*en mesô*) and around the throne. The Greek word *mesos* always indicates extreme closeness in Revelation. Aside from this verse, only Christ is said to be "in the midst of" the throne (5:6; 7:17; see also 3:21; 22:1, 3). Elsewhere, the four creatures are simply said to be around the throne. John's language here is probably influenced by that of Ezekiel, who uses "in the midst of" three times in his first chapter in connection with the four living creatures (Ezek 1:4, 5, 13).

The depiction of the creatures draws on a range of biblical texts and ancient mythology. In Solomon's temple, the ark of the covenant, symbol of God's presence with the people, was overshadowed by two cherubs who spread their wings over it in a protective manner (1 Kgs 6:24–28; cf. Exod 25:18–21). The most immediate biblical parallels occur in Isaiah 6 and Ezekiel 1 and 10. Ezekiel has "four living creatures" in his theophany, which he also calls "cherubs" ("cherubim" is the Hebrew plural of the word). In Ezekiel's vision, the creatures bear God's chariot-throne (1:15–25; 10:3–5, 18–22; 11:22–23; cf. 1 Kgs 19:15; Pss 18:10; 80:1; 99:1; Isa 37:16). Each creature has four wings and four faces, those of a human, a lion, an ox, and an eagle, each on a different side of its head. They remain silent. In Isaiah 6, God is attended by an unnumbered group of "seraphs" (seraphim), each with six wings. They sing praise to God in a form which has come to be called the "trisagion," from the Greek for "thrice holy": "Holy, holy, holy is the LORD of hosts; the whole earth is full of his glory" (6:3).

Revelation takes the idea of "four living creatures" with four wings and four faces from Ezekiel. The seer alters it by changing the number of wings from four to six to match Isaiah and by distributing the four faces among the four creatures so that each has only one face. Unlike in Ezekiel, Revelation's creatures do not bear the chariot, for God does not move in Revelation. He is enthroned in heaven, and he is the fixed origin of what follows in the book, until he descends to dwell with humanity. This frees the creatures to act individually (15:7). Since they do not perform the function of carrying God around, they take on the role the seraphim of Isaiah 6 fulfill, that of praise. Charles (1920, 1:120–21) notes that this shift of function from carrying to praising conforms to a general trend in postbiblical literature for these creatures. Their song is close to Isaiah's trisagion, with suitable adaptation to Revelation's theology, to be discussed below. In Ezekiel, the rims of the chariot wheels are "full of eyes all around" (1:18; 10:12). This refers to God's omniscience (see

Zech 4:10, where the seven lamps before God are his eyes that "range through the whole earth"). Revelation has no chariot wheels, so it transfers the eyes to the creatures. The eyes may signify the watchfulness demanded of guards. In Gen 3:24, God places a cherub as a guard over Eden so that humankind may not reenter it. Cherubs guard God's throne in *1 Enoch* 71:7. Angels are called "watchers" in *1 Enoch* 1–36 and in Dan 4:13, 17, 23, possibly alluding to a guard function.

The opacity of the image of the four faces leads to speculation about their significance. No one satisfactory answer has been found. The identification of each face with one of the four evangelists is a later development, attested earliest by Irenaeus in the second half of the second century. An interesting proposal is that they refer to four constellations. That would make sense of their being "full of eyes," which could be the stars. Malina offers the fullest treatment of such a possibility (1995, 97–100; see also Charles 1920, 1:122–23). John does not make further use of the symbolism of the four different faces. What is significant for him is that this is an authentic detail of a vision of God on his throne, and as such it is sanctioned by John's main source for such information, Ezekiel.

The four living creatures in Revelation unceasingly sing the song of praise that Isaiah 6 attributes to the seraphim, with significant alterations. Isaiah has, "Holy, holy, holy is the LORD of hosts; the whole earth is full of his glory" (6:3). Revelation changes this to, "Holy, holy, holy, the Lord God the Almighty, who was and is and is to come" (4:8). "Lord God the Almighty" is a suitable translation of "LORD of hosts," the Hebrew of Isa 6:3. The Hebrew is "Yahweh Sabaoth." "Sabaoth" means "hosts" in the sense of a multitude, usually an army. The Septuagint translates this as "LORD Sabaoth" throughout Isaiah, but as "Almighty" (*pantokratôr*) elsewhere in the prophets. John cannot agree with Isaiah that heaven and earth are full of God's glory. The earth is ruled by forces inimical to God. God's glory will fill all creation when God reclaims the earth, which is soon to happen. Meanwhile, John completes the trisagion by repeating (in slightly different order) the formula he introduces in 1:4 (see commentary there). God was, is, and is to come. The formulation asserts God's eternity, while at the same time claiming that God will soon intervene in affairs both human and cosmic.

The hymn in 4:8 is the first of a series of hymns punctuating Revelation. The hymns are sung by heavenly creatures who are in a position to know the true order of things. They offer definitive comments on the meaning of what John witnesses. They function much as the chorus does in ancient Greek tragedy (see *T. Levi* 3:8; *1 Enoch* 39:12–14; 40; *2 Enoch* 21:1).

The text now returns to the twenty-four elders, completing the ring structure opened in 4:4. It does so by having the elders join the praise of the four living creatures. When the creatures give praise, the elders join in the liturgy both through a symbolic action (casting down their crowns before the throne; 4:10) and through their own hymn (4:11). The hymn sung by the elders is a doxology, similar to the doxology with which the seer opens his apocalyptic letter (1:5; see comments there). Doxologies are formal acclamations of praise and support. The emperor also expected such formal acclamations from his subjects. Acclamations of the emperor sometimes included the word "worthy," as is found here in Revelation (Boring 1989, 103; cf. Schüssler Fiorenza 1991, 59). That God is referred to as "our Lord and God" here may reflect the fact that Domitian, under whom Revelation was written, wanted to be addressed by that title, according to one ancient author. The frequency of doxologies directed to God and Christ in Revelation is a function of the continuous opposition the author seeks to create between God's rule and that of Rome.

God had long been pictured as the great king in Israel's liturgy and traditions, so doxologies were not an innovation of our author. A biblical doxology often cited as closest to the ones found in Revelation appears in 1 Chronicles in a long psalm of praise attributed to David:

> Honor and majesty are before him;
> strength and joy are in his place.
> Ascribe to the LORD, O families of the peoples,
> ascribe to the LORD glory and strength. (1 Chr 16:27–28)

In these verses, God is deemed worthy of honor, majesty, strength (twice), joy, and glory. This is formal recognition of God's supreme place in society and the universe. In the two doxologies sung by the heavenly beings in Revelation 4, God is proclaimed to be "worthy" of similar things: holiness, glory, honor, and power (cf. 4:11; 5:9, 12). God's supremacy is also asserted in this passage outside of the doxologies themselves by the designation of God as "the one who lives forever and ever" (4:9–10; cf. Dan 4:34). Chapter 4 ends with the acknowledgment that God is the source of all creation, so that by definition creation owes him thanks for its very existence (4:11).

The twenty-four elders accompany their song of praise with a symbolic action. They "worship" God and throw their crowns down before the throne (4:10). The word translated "worship" by the NRSV is the Greek *proskyneô*. It literally means to prostrate oneself. This action of prostration was very meaningful in the ancient world (Aune 1983a, 13–14). When Alexander the Great conquered the Persian empire in the late fourth century B.C.E., he adopted the Eastern practice of making his subordinates prostrate themselves before him. This did not go over well with his Macedonian compatriots, who were used to a less autocratic form of leadership. The Romans were originally also unaccustomed to such autocratic forms, but when they conquered the eastern Mediterranean, they accepted from their subjects the sort of honor and ceremony customary in that area, including cultic homage. The seer allows only God to be honored in this way. Twice when John attempts to honor an angel with prostration, the angel rebukes him and says such honor is due to God alone (19:10; 22:8–9).

The casting down of crowns may also relate to a symbolic action employed at the imperial court. The Roman historian Tacitus says that the king Tiridates performed this action before Caesar as an act of submission and loyalty (*Annals* 15.29). Although the subordinate is a legitimate king, he is subject to the emperor and places his authority and resources at the emperor's disposal. He can take up his crown again only with the approval of the emperor. These heavenly kings in Revelation 4, the elders, perform this act of ultimate submission to God because God the creator is the one who is truly "worthy" of glory, honor, and power.

So ends chapter 4. Ford (1975, 76–78) points out that visions of the heavenly throne are frequently associated with prophetic missions, as in 1 Kgs 22:19–23, Isaiah 6, Ezekiel 1 and 10, and Revelation itself. That observation applies to all of the visions of heaven discussed earlier, given a certain latitude in the definition of prophecy to include apocalyptic seers, a definition to which our own seer subscribes. Access to heaven and its secrets qualifies the prophets and seers for their role of mediators between God and people. Jeremiah challenges false prophets: "For who has stood in the council of the LORD so as to see and to hear his word?" (23:18). The visit to heaven may not just legitimate the prophet's mission—it can give it content. John's visit to heaven changes his perspective on the world. He now sees things very differently, from heaven's viewpoint. He witnesses God's sovereignty, and in the hymns of praise he hears he understands that all creation depends in an ultimate way on God. The vision lays bare the falseness of Rome's claim to power and authority.

The Lamb Receives His Commission (Chapter 5)

Chapter 4 sets the scene for Christ's commissioning as the one who puts in motion the eschatological events. In chapter 5, Christ is presented in the heavenly court as the one uniquely qualified to inaugurate these events. The chapter divides into three main parts, each introduced by a formulaic phrase "Then I saw" (5:1, 6, 11). In the first part (5:1–5), the seer observes a scroll in God's hand, a scroll sealed with seven seals that no one can open. One of the elders tells the seer that the Davidic messiah is able to open it. In the second part (5:6–10), Christ appears as a lamb and takes the scroll from God. He is then praised in a hymn sung by the four creatures and the twenty-four elders. In the third part (5:11–14), there are two hymns. The first praises the Lamb and is sung by a multitude of angels in heaven. The second praises both God and the Lamb and is sung by every creature in the cosmos. The four living creatures then say "Amen," and the twenty-four elders fall down in worship.

Chapter 5 shows progression in several ways. First, there is a narrative progression from the first part, where one is sought to open the scroll, to the second part, where Christ appears and receives praise for being able to open the scroll, to the third part, where there are hymns of praise to God and the Lamb. Second, there is progression in the content of the hymns. The first praises Christ in some specificity for his redemptive work; the second praises him more generally, applying to him qualities often applied to God in doxologies; and the third joins God and the Lamb together in a doxology. Third, there is a progression in the identity of the singers. The first hymn is sung only by the heavenly attendants closest to the throne, the four creatures and twenty-four elders. The second is sung by a multitude of angels who surround the throne. The third is sung by every creature in heaven, on earth, and in the sea. The scene is then concluded by the first ones to sing, the four creatures and the elders, forming a frame. The final form of progression is the movement from God to Christ to God *and* Christ. The chapter begins with God on the throne, a scene set up by chapter 4 and picked up in 5:1. Then attention shifts to Christ as the one who can open the scroll. Finally the scene ends with a doxology to God and the Lamb together. There is also progress as one proceeds through chapters 4 and 5. The most important progression is from God as the single figure on the throne (4:2) to God and Christ together receiving the homage of the entire cosmos (5:13–14). There is also a progression in the number of qualities mentioned in the doxologies. The one sung to God alone has three; the one to Christ has four; and the one to both has seven.

Chapter 5 begins with the central figure of chapter 4, God seated on the throne. In 5:1, the focus is on a scroll in God's hand. It is "a scroll written on the inside and on the back, sealed with seven seals" (5:1). The scroll has received a great many interpretations, but we concentrate on the most likely (see Ford 1975, 84). The scroll is in heaven. This immediately suggests parallels with heavenly books or scrolls or tablets (see comments on 3:5). The closest parallels to Revelation's scroll are heavenly texts containing information about the future. Biblical examples include Ps 139:16: "In your book were written all the days that were formed for me, when none of them yet existed." In Dan 10:21, an angel, probably Gabriel, tells Daniel, "I am to tell you what is inscribed in the book of truth," and then foretells the future. *First Enoch* speaks of heavenly books that predict the future (81:1–3; 93:1–3; 103:2; 106:19; 107:1; 108:7). The scroll in Revelation contains the eschatological events which are predetermined, determinism being typical of apocalypticism. This does not imply individual predestination, for although the course of events is set, individuals must still decide which side they will choose.

The scroll in Revelation 5 is sealed. Sealing is important in Daniel. The angel Gabriel predicts the future to Daniel in chapter 8, and at the end of that chapter he orders, "Seal up the vision, for it refers to many days from now" (8:26). Daniel receives similar orders in chapter 12: "But you, Daniel, keep the words secret and the book sealed until the time of the end" (12:4; see 12:9). Daniel was written around 165 B.C.E., but within the fiction of the book Daniel lives centuries earlier. The "predictions" of what is to happen between Daniel's time and that of the actual author are really in the past for the writer. This technique is called "predictions after the event" (*vaticinia ex eventu*). Such "predictions" will obviously be correct, and so will lend credibility to genuine predictions. (In fact, when Daniel 11 turns to real prediction, its predictions turn out to be inaccurate [11:40–45; see Clifford 1975].) To maintain the fiction, the author had to explain why Daniel's predictions were unknown until 165 B.C.E. The sealing of the book explains this.

In Revelation the scroll in chapter 5 is also sealed. Unlike in Daniel, this is not because John has been given a prophecy only to be fulfilled centuries hence. The scroll is not an earthly writing to be kept secret, but a heavenly writing, seen in Revelation 5 by a human for the first time. The sealing signifies that God's plan for the endtime was unknown until now and so was incapable of being accomplished until now. In contrast to Daniel, where the seer is told to seal his visions, at the end of Revelation an angel tells John, "Do not seal up the words of the prophecy of this book, for the time is near" (22:10). In Revelation the seer lives in the endtime, so the book containing the eschatological events must be open, not closed. As each seal is broken an eschatological event happens. The scroll is God's detailed plan for the endtime. That plan can be realized only if the scroll is opened. Since only Christ can open the scroll, only he can set the endtime events into motion. By breaking the seals, Christ releases God's word written in the scroll, a word which then becomes effective. God's word is by definition effective, as God says in Isaiah, "My word . . . that goes out from my mouth . . . shall not return to me empty, but it shall accomplish that which I purpose, and succeed in the thing for which I sent it" (55:11). A final point is that seals often signify the guarantee of their owners. If the scroll is sealed by God, then what is within it is authentically God's.

The scroll scene of Revelation 5 recalls a similar scene in Ezekiel. Ezekiel's scroll influences both Revelation 5 and 10, so we consider all three texts in relation to each other. Ezekiel reports the following words of God:

> Open your mouth and eat what I give you. I looked, and a hand was stretched out to me, and a written scroll was in it. He spread it out before me; it had writing on the front and on the back, and written on it were words of lamentation and mourning and woe. He said to me, O mortal [literally: son of man], eat what is offered to you; eat this scroll, and

> go, speak to the house of Israel. So I opened my mouth, and he gave me the scroll to eat. He said to me, Mortal, eat this scroll that I give you and fill your stomach with it. Then I ate it; and in my mouth it was as sweet as honey. (Ezek 2:8–3:3)

Ezekiel is then ordered to prophesy to Israel (3:5). In both Revelation 5 and Ezekiel, the prophet or seer sees a scroll in the hand of a heavenly entity. Both scrolls are written on front and back, signifying the large quantity of material in each. In Revelation 10, the seer sees a "mighty angel" descend from heaven with an open scroll in his hand. The seer is told to take and eat the scroll, which is bitter in his stomach but sweet in his mouth. He is then told, "You must prophesy again about many peoples and nations and languages and kings" (Rev 10:8–11). The sweetness of Ezekiel's and John's scrolls recalls statements in the Bible that God's words and commands are sweet to their recipients (Pss 19:10; 119:103; Jer 15:16, 17). The bitterness in the stomach in Revelation refers to the negative features of what is revealed.

We have seen that the scroll visions in Revelation 5 and 10 both draw on Ezekiel, but this is not the only thing that connects the two chapters in Revelation. Both are scroll visions in which a "mighty angel" plays an important role. In 5:2, the mighty angel asks "with a loud voice, 'Who is worthy to open the scroll or to break its seals?' " In 10:1, "another mighty angel" descends from heaven holding a scroll. These are two of only three "mighty angels" in the book, the last appearing in 18:21 to announce the fall of Babylon (Rome), the main goal of the events in the scroll of chapter 5. In Revelation 10, the seer sees a scroll that "has been opened" (the perfect passive participle, which in Greek refers to a past action that has an enduring effect on the present). This implies that the scroll had previously been closed, an allusion to the sealed scroll of chapter 5. We noted in the introduction under "Structure" that the open scroll contains the second great cycle of visions (12:1–22:5), which themselves are a less cryptic version of the first great cycle of visions (4:1–11:19). Thus the content of the scrolls in chapters 5 and 10 is essentially the same, and one of the central features of those visions is the fall of Babylon/Rome, which the third "mighty angel" announces in 18:21.

The mighty angel of chapter 5 proclaims "with a loud voice."

This phrase is frequent in Revelation, occurring nineteen times. What the angel says concerns the entire cosmos and must be heard everywhere. The angel asks, "Who is worthy to open the scroll and break its seals?" (5:2). The theme of worthiness is repeated in 5:4, 9, and 12, so it helps to tie the chapter together. The chapter's theme is the worthiness of Christ to set the endtime events in motion because of his redemptive work. The word "worthy" is used of God in Rev 4:11, where God is deemed worthy of praise because of his work in creation. Thus the two great moments of creation and redemption are marked with acclamations about the worthiness of God (4:11) and Christ (5:12).

When the angel first asks who can open the scroll, "no one in heaven or on the earth or under the earth was able to open the scroll or to look into it" (5:3). This verse assumes a three-tiered cosmos. The seer weeps because God's plans will not be put into effect. The power of Satan will remain unbroken, and God's sovereignty will be limited. One of the elders comforts the seer saying, "Do not weep. See, the Lion of the tribe of Judah, the Root of David, has conquered, so that he can open the scroll and its seven seals" (5:5). The Davidic messiah, who is of the tribe of Judah, is able to open the scroll. The title "Lion of Judah" derives from Gen 49:9–10, in a chapter where Jacob (also named Israel) blesses his twelve sons. Judah's posterity is to bear kingly rule. Judah is compared to a lion (49:9), and it is said, "The scepter shall not depart from Judah, nor the ruler's staff from between his feet, until tribute comes to him" (49:10). These verses were considered messianic by both Jews and Christians. In a Jewish apocalypse contemporary with Revelation, the seer Ezra has a vision of a lion who condemns an eagle for pride and oppression. The eagle symbolizes Rome and the lion is "the Messiah whom the Most High has kept until the end of days, who will arise from the offspring of David," who will judge the wicked and reward the righteous (4 Ezra 11:36–12:35; see also *T. Jud.* 24:5). "Root of David" means of David's family, and it denotes a hoped-for king who will restore the Davidic line (Isa 11:10; Rom 15:12). Christ himself says in 22:16: "I am the root and descendant of David." A similar Davidic title also based on tree imagery is "branch" (Isa 11:1; Jer 23:5; 33:15; Zech 3:8; 6:12).

The first section of chapter 5 ends with an elder's assertion that the messiah "has conquered" so that he can open the scroll (5:5). In the messages to the seven churches, conquering means resisting Roman power and idolatry to the death if necessary and maintaining loyalty to the true sovereign of the universe, God.

Revelation 5:6 introduces the chapter's second section with the familiar phrase, "Then I saw." There is an intimate connection between 5:5 and 5:6, thus joining the two first two sections of chapter 5. In 5:5, the angel tells the seer that the Davidic messiah will be able to open the scroll, and in 5:6 the seer sees that messiah. But the form that the messiah takes is a shock. David was a king, with royal pomp and power. The comparison of the Davidic messiah to a lion raises expectations of a fierce and warlike entity. But in 5:6, John sees "a Lamb standing as if it had been slaughtered." Jesus is referred to as the Lamb twenty-nine times in the book, making it his main designation. The precise nature of this image of the Lamb has been the subject of much discussion. A central issue is whether the warlike traits of a lion are replaced by the meekness of the Lamb or whether the messiah retains warlike qualities (see McDonald 1996). The answer is not simple. The lion does not become a lamb, nor does the Lamb become a lion. Rather, Revelation's messiah is both. Christ won his victory over Satan and made possible the victory of Christians through his suffering and death. This is nonviolent. But he will also exercise force against the partisans of evil (chapter 19) and will punish them as they deserve. The desire for vengeance voiced by the martyrs in heaven (6:11) will be satisfied. But in this life, both for Christ and for Christians, the victory must be won by suffering and death. Satan must win the battle before Christ wins the war. After that the forces of heaven will be unleashed against Satan and his minions (chapters 19-20).

The origin of the Lamb image is uncertain. As with many images presented by the seer, it probably comes from several sources. The word for "lamb" here, *arnion,* is used in the New Testament only here and in John 21:15, where it refers to Christians. In the Septuagint it appears in Jer 11:19, where the prophet says, "I was like a gentle lamb led to the slaughter." The form *arnion* is diminutive, which some have taken to stress its meekness. The Lamb looks "as if it had been slaughtered." The word for "slaughter" is often (though not necessarily) used in a cultic context, and this calls to mind the slaughter of the Passover lamb. This connection is supported by the hymn sung to the Lamb in this section, where he is described as worthy to open the seals because "you were slaughtered and by your blood you ransomed [literally: bought] for God saints from every tribe and language and people and nation; you have made them to be a kingdom and priests serving our God, and they will reign on earth" (5:9–10; cf. 1:5–6). This recalls Paul's argument exhorting the Corinthians to good behavior because "our paschal [i.e., Passover] lamb, Christ, has been sacrificed" (1 Cor 5:7), later adding "You were bought with a price" (1 Cor 6:20; 7:23). The Passover connection is also made by the reference to the faithful becoming a kingdom and priests. As is explained in our comments on 1:5–6, this language comes from Exod 19:6, where, after rescuing Israel from Egypt in the exodus, God makes them kings and priests.

Another biblical passage influencing our author's presentation of the Lamb is Isa 52:13–53:12, the song of the suffering servant. It furnished Christians with much material for meditating on the suffering and death of Christ. A key verse for Christians was 53:7:

> He was oppressed, and he was afflicted,
> yet he did not open his mouth;
> like a lamb that is led to the slaughter,
> and like a sheep that before its shearers is silent,
> so he did not open his mouth.

This verse is used explicitly of Jesus in Acts 8:32. Another New Testament passage that uses lamb imagery is in 1 Peter: "You know that you were ransomed from the futile ways inherited from your ancestors, not with perishable things like silver and gold, but with the precious blood of Christ, like that of a lamb without defect or blemish" (1:18–19). The specification that Christ was without defect or blemish, typical of sacrificial animals (see the sacrifices throughout the book of Leviticus) and of the Passover lamb (Exod 12:5), and the emphasis on blood recall the Passover lamb. "Ransom" is a price paid to free someone, as, for example, a slave might be ransomed or redeemed by his or her family. Being ransomed by the blood of Christ is a common concept in the New Testament, as we see in 1 Peter, Paul, and Revelation. Paul and Revelation associate this with God's ransoming the people from Egypt in the exodus.

One of the many intriguing points of contact between Revelation and the gospel of John is the depiction of Jesus as a lamb. Twice in the gospel, John the Baptist refers to Jesus as "the Lamb of God" (1:29, 36), and in 1:29 he is the one who "takes away the sins of the world." The Greek word for "lamb" there is *am-*

nos, but the notion that Jesus is a lamb who has freed Christians from sin is common to the gospel and Revelation.

Both the Passover lamb and the lamb of Isaiah 53 are passive. Each is slaughtered, and neither fights back or utters a sound. But there are other sorts of lambs in Jewish literature, and their image is evoked by the statement in Rev 5:6 that the Lamb has seven horns. The horn is a symbol of strength and fighting capability in the Bible. This Lamb has seven of them. Seven is also the total number of horns on the four beasts that arise out of the sea in Daniel 7, and the beast that arises out of the sea in Revelation 13 also has seven horns. Since the Lamb is the antithesis of the beast in chapter 13, he also is portrayed as having seven horns. Other militant sheep are found in Dan 8:20-21; *1 Enoch* 90; and *T. Jos.* 19:8-9.

The Lamb's location is unclear. The text says literally that it was "in the midst of" the throne and "in the midst of" the four living creatures (5:6). There is no problem with picturing Christ on the throne itself. He is certainly there in 3:21 and 22:1, 3. But the double use of the phrase "in the midst of" more likely reflects a Hebrew construction, which would mean that the Lamb is between the throne and the four living creatures (see Charles 1920, 1:140). The Lamb is the closest figure to the throne without actually sitting on it. This makes better sense out of the notice that he "went and took the scroll from the right hand of the one who was seated on the throne" (5:7). The Lamb then engages in the eschatological tasks (chapters 6-20) for which he is commissioned in this chapter, and he finally ends up on the throne with God at the end of the book.

The Lamb has seven eyes, "which are the seven spirits of God sent out into all the earth" (5:6). The eyes are part of the Lamb, but they belong to God, and it is through those eyes, really God's spirits, that God gathers information about "all the earth." These seven spirits are probably the same ones who are before God's throne and who send their greetings to the churches in 1:4 and who are also the seven torches of 4:5. They may also be related to the seven angels of the trumpets and bowls. Their description in chapter 5 again recalls Zechariah 4, where the seven lamps are "the eyes of the Lord, which range through the whole earth" (4:10; see comments on 1:4 and 4:10). The eyes are now part of the Lamb, signifying that God exercises dominion through Christ.

The picture of the Lamb in Rev 5:6 surely taxes the imagination of even the most creative reader. It is often said by commentators that Israelite or Jewish imagination was more verbal than visual. Therefore one should avoid trying to devise a visual image that does justice to every detail of Revelation's description. The same would apply to Daniel and to many other apocalypses. The idea of a lamb with seven horns and seven eyes is bizarre enough. When those seven eyes turn out to be spirits that patrol the earth, the image is more difficult still. And when those spirits are also stationary before God, this adds another problem. On the one hand, it would be a mistake to think that we can dispense with our author's images and arrive at the ideas "behind" them, for the images' evocative power is crucial to Revelation. On the other hand, we cannot expect those images to be completely consistent. They are distorted by the variety of sources the author uses, by the degree to which consistency must yield to the point the author is trying to make, and by the fact that these are images from another world that, although they relate to the earthly world, do not entirely follow its logic.

The Lamb's taking of the scroll from God is a climactic moment. The four living creatures and the twenty-four elders react immediately. They first fall before the Lamb. As they do so, they hold censers whose incense is the prayers of the saints, that is, Christians (the meaning of the word "saints" throughout Revelation). Their action is one of worship, and it is the more remarkable in that it is the very entities who attend God who now worship Christ. They do not need to turn from God to worship Christ because of the Lamb's position in 5:6. They worship Christ as priests. They offer incense to Christ, which is interpreted as the prayers of the faithful. The idea that angelic figures mediate between humans and God in that they present human prayers to God is found in the Jewish works *3 Baruch* 11; *T. Levi* 3:5–7; Tob 12:12, and in the Christian works *Apocalypse of Paul* 7–10 and Origen's *First Principles* 1.8.1 (Charles 1920, 1:145). Prayer is compared to incense and sacrifice in Ps 141:2.

The four living creatures and the twenty-four elders now sing a "new song" to the Lamb. New acts of salvation require new songs to acknowledge them. Psalms contain six examples of this (33:3; 40:3; 96:1; 98:1; 144:9; 149:1). Isaiah also uses the new song motif.

> See, the former things have come to pass,
>   and new things I now declare;

before they spring forth,
I tell you of them.
Sing to the LORD a new song,
his praise from the end of the earth! (Isa 42:9-10)

This usage is comparable to that in Psalms. In Isaiah 65, the newness of God's salvific action seems more radical:

For I am about to create new heavens
and a new earth;
the former things shall not be remembered
or come to mind.
But be glad and rejoice forever
in what I am creating;
for I am about to create Jerusalem as a joy,
and its people as a delight. (Isa 65:17-18)

Although these words do not occur in an apocalypse, they show prophecy taking a turn in the direction of apocalypticism. The prophet speaks in terms of cosmic change and relates that to the re-creation of Jerusalem. So great are the impending events that God's previous actions fade before them.

Most elements of the hymn of God's attendants have been touched on already in this section. The hymn extols the Lamb as the one who is able to open the scroll and thereby set the eschatological events in motion. He can do this because he has been "slaughtered," and by his blood he has ransomed or purchased persons "from every tribe and language and people and nation." This last phrase occurs repeatedly in Revelation with changes only in the order of the words (5:9; 7:9; 11:9; 13:7; 14:6). It echoes similar phrases in Daniel (3:4, 7, 29; 5:19; 6:25; 7:14). In Daniel 3, 5, and 6, the phrase relates to the extensive power of the foreign emperor who rules Israel, and in Dan 7:14, it defines the scope of the authority given by God to the one like a son of man. Thus all of humanity is transferred from the evil empire to God's rule. Such a change is like that in Revelation 5, where Christ has ransomed people from all humanity, thereby transferring them from Satan's realm to God's.

As in 1:5-6, the redemption of the people makes them a kingdom and priests, an echo of Exod 19:6 and so an allusion to the exodus tradition. The manuscripts differ on whether the end of the hymn says that the faithful "reign" (present) or "will reign" (future). It is a principle in textual criticism to accept the more difficult reading, because scribes in recopying a manuscript are more likely to change it in the direction of being more comprehensible rather than less. There is no difficulty in expecting the faithful to reign in the future, after Satan and his representatives have been defeated. Indeed the martyrs do reign with Christ in the messianic kingdom in chapter 20. It is more difficult to understand how Christians can be said to reign at present. But this is really no different from saying that Christ has made them (past tense) a kingdom and priests (1:5–6; 5:9–10). Things are not as they appear. Christians may endure suffering and even death in the present, but the victory is really already won, assured in the Lamb's own victory. John's trip to heaven allows his audience to experience vicariously the victory that they do not yet see on earth (see Gager 1975; Barr 1984).

The last section of chapter 5 also begins with the formula "And I saw" (5:11). John hears "the voice of many angels surrounding the throne and the living creatures and elders; they numbered myriads of myriads and thousands of thousands, singing with full voice" (5:11–12). The word "myriad" literally means ten thousand but is generally used to designate large numbers. The effect is to say that there was an uncountable multitude in attendance on God. Such an assertion is common in heavenly scenes. Revelation echoes the classic scene in Dan 7:10: "A thousand thousands served him, and ten thousand times ten thousand stood attending him" (cf. *1 Enoch* 40:1; 60:1; 71:8). Revelation says that these singers surround the living creatures and the elders, so these latter two groups do not participate in the following hymn. This supports the liturgical feeling of the scenario, where each group speaks or sings at the proper time. It also sets apart the elders and creatures and makes more effective their confirming words and actions that close the chapter in 5:14.

The song of the angelic multitudes is a doxology which declares the Lamb worthy of seven things. All three items in the doxology to God in 4:11 are included—glory, honor, and power. The other four items are wealth, wisdom, might, and blessing. The only other occurrence of the word "wealth" is in 18:17, where merchants marvel that the wealth of Babylon (Rome) is "laid waste." There is nothing wrong with power and wealth in themselves, but they should belong to God and God's representatives. The rather triumphalistic terms in which Christ is described mirror the ways royalty and "great people" of the ancient world were seen.

After the Lamb receives proper recognition from the angelic hosts, another scene of praise is introduced with the words, "Then I heard every creature in heaven and on earth and under the earth and in the sea, and all that is in them, singing" (5:13). Since the four living creatures and the elders respond to this hymn, they probably do not sing here. This is a magnificent and climactic scene. All living creatures in the universe except for God's closest attendants sing a hymn to God and the Lamb, and then the closest attendants deliver the confirming "Amen" accompanied by a final gesture of worship. The doxology acknowledges the power of God and the Lamb together over the entire universe and renders the proper recognition due from clients to the greatest patron imaginable. This is obviously an idealized scene, for Rome and its supporters cannot be among those who worship God and the Lamb. In this sense the scene is proleptic. It anticipates the time when all opposition to God's sovereignty will be overcome.

The four living creatures sing the first doxology (4:8) and say "Amen" to the last (5:14), an appropriate role for God's closest attendants. References to the elders also help to tie chapters 4 and 5 together because the elders are the first of the heavenly attendants mentioned in the vision (4:4), and they perform the closing action (5:14). The order of appearance of the attendants in chapter 4 is elders first and then creatures, and the order of action in 5:14 is creatures first and then elders, creating a chiasm. Chapters 4 and 5 should be read together as a unit. The unit begins with one sitting on the throne alone, and it ends with a doxology to both the one sitting on the throne and the Lamb. This sets the stage for the rest of the book, for it is from that throne, which now means not just divine sovereignty but divine power and authority working through the Lamb, that the rest of what happens flows.

Yarbro Collins (1997, 18–19) shows that the scene and events in chapters 4 and 5 reflect the combat myth that is at the heart of Revelation:

> Chaps. 4 and 5 reflect the genre of the combat myth in the way in which the scene is presented. The relationship between the enthroned deity and the risen Jesus is analogous to that between the administrator-father-gods and

the young-warrior-gods of the ancient Near Eastern combat myths. The divine council in Revelation is also faced with a crisis, symbolized by the impossibility of opening the scroll with the seven seals. This crisis begins to be resolved when the risen Jesus, who is both Lion and Lamb, opens the seals, unleashing cosmic conflict. It will be resolved fully, however, only with the reappearance of the risen Jesus as the mighty Word of God, foretold in chap. 19, when he will engage the enemies of God in the final battle. His victory will lead to his joint kingship with God in the new Jerusalem that will come down from heaven to a new earth.

Chapter Six

The Seven Seals (6:1–8:5)

The Seven Seals as a Whole

In chapters 6 to 8, the Lamb opens each of the seven seals on the scroll, and as he opens each one, eschatological events happen. After the first six seals (chapter 6), there is an extended interlude that occupies all of chapter 7. When the seventh seal is opened at the beginning of chapter 8, it unleashes another series of seven, the seven trumpets. Thus the seals lead into the trumpets, and the trumpets constitute the seventh seal. The seals and trumpets are not discrete, consecutive sets of events. They describe some of the same events from different points of view and with different images. The same can be said of the third series of seven, the seven bowls (chapter 16). According to Yarbro Collins (1990, 1004), "The major themes in each series are persecution of the faithful, judgment of their adversaries, and salvation of the faithful."

Charles (1920, 1:154–61) furnishes important guidelines to the interpretation of the eschatological events contained in the seven seals. He notes that some commentators have employed what he calls the "contemporary historical method." This means that the seals are interpreted as if they refer to specific events in the seer's time, but such interpretation leads to widely divergent identifications for each seal. Attempts to establish a one-to-one connection between each item in the text and events or entities in the world outside of the text cannot be carried through successfully. Although such connections sometimes exist and should be attended to when they are likely, the seer's goal is to contextualize events in a broad symbolic universe so that their ultimate significance emerges. The result is a literary work that is far from being a simple allegory which simply encodes events and generalizes about them.

Figure 2

Matt 24:6, 7, 9ª, 29	Mark 13:7–9ª, 24–25	Luke 21:9–12ª, 25–26	Rev 6:2–17; 7:1 (Numbers refer to seals.)
1. Wars.	1. Wars.	1. Wars.	1. War.
2. International strife.	2. International strife.	2. International strife.	2. International strife.
3. Famines.	3. Earthquakes.	3. Earthquakes.	3. Famine.
4. Earthquakes.	4. Famines.	4. Famines.	4. Pestilence (death and Hades).
5. Persecutions.	5. Persecutions.	5. Pestilence.	5. Persecutions.
6. Eclipses of the sun and moon; falling of the stars; shaking of the powers in heaven.	6. (As in Matt).	6. Persecutions. 7. Signs in the sun, moon, and stars; men fainting for fear of the things coming on the world; shaking of the powers in heaven.	6. (6:12–7:3) Earthquakes, eclipse of the sun, ensanguining of the moon, falling of the stars, men calling on the rocks to fall on them, shaking of the powers of heaven, four destroying winds (cf. Luke 21:25).

Charles's key to the seals is the eschatological scenario contained in Jesus' apocalyptic discourses in the synoptic gospels. Charles lays out the parallels between Revelation and the gospels in figure 2 (1920, 1:158).

There is a close similarity here not only in individual elements but in their order. This is a strong case for contact between Revelation's author and the synoptic tradition, although Charles observes that the precise nature of the contact is uncertain. It is possible that the author knows the gospels, but Charles (1920, 1:158–61) thinks that both the gospels and Revelation depend on an earlier source. Be that as it may, the author of Revelation depends on an already established Christian tradition about the endtime events. That earlier Christian tradition grew out of Jewish expectations as preserved in numerous apocalypses. Most apocalypses expect a time of upheaval heralding the eschaton. A classic statement of this is in Dan 12:1: "There shall be a time of anguish, such as has never occurred since nations first came into existence." Social and cosmic upheaval was to mark the culmination of history, and the ways of expressing that became stereotyped over time.

The first four of the seven seals are closely associated with each other. The pattern in each is the same. As each seal is opened, one of the four living creatures says "Come," and a horseman appears who causes eschatological events on earth. The biblical background of the four horsemen is found in Zechariah. In Zechariah 1, the prophet has a vision of a man on a red horse, behind whom are three other horses, red, sorrel (a yellowish or reddish brown), and white (1:8). The prophet is told, "They are those whom the LORD has sent to patrol the earth" (1:10). The text continues, "Then they spoke to the angel of the LORD who was standing among the myrtle trees, 'We have patrolled the earth, and lo, the whole earth remains at peace.' Then the angel of the LORD said, 'O LORD of hosts, how long will you withhold mercy from Jerusalem and the cities of Judah . . . ?' " (1:11–12). Revelation borrows the following elements from this vision: the four horsemen (although Zech 1:8 mentions one man and four horses, their report to the angel in 1:11 implies that each horse has a rider), the colors of the horses, the fact that the horsemen are sent to perform a mission on earth, and the question "How long?" relating to the need for God to vindicate his people (see Rev 6:10). Zechariah 6 contains a vision in which four chariots, each with horses of a specific color (red, black, white, dappled gray) and each representing the wind from a particular quarter, are sent to patrol the earth. The horses in Revelation symbolize God's action in the world, as do those in Zechariah. The author takes great liberties with Zechariah's symbolism. He usually exercises such freedom, but in this case it is facilitated by the flexibility of the imagery in Zechariah 1 and 6, where the colors change slightly and are presented in two different orders with no strong symbolism attached to each color.

The First Seal (6:1–2)

As the Lamb opens the first seal, one of the four living creatures says "with a voice of thunder, 'Come!' " (6:1). Thunder is usually associated with the divine presence, as we showed when discussing chapter 4. This living creature speaks for God as he summons the first of the four horsemen. It is God, through Jesus and his angelic attendants, who causes the eschatological events to happen.

In response to the creature's call a man appears riding a white horse, carrying a bow, and he is given a crown. The man "came out conquering and to conquer." The identity of the first horseman has been the subject of much discussion. In several ways he resembles the Christ of chapter 19 (for arguments for and against an identification of the two, see Charles 1920, 1:164, and Boring 1989, 123). Both figures ride on white horses and wear crowns. Both conquer their adversaries. The horseman in chapter 6 is told to "come," and Christ is asked to come in 22:17, 20 (see Boring 1989, 123).

The case against identifying the first horseman with Christ is much stronger. For every similarity between the two riders, there is a dissimilarity. Although they both wear crowns, the horseman of chapter 6 wears a *stephanos,* a word usually denoting the crown of victory in athletic contests or warfare. But Christ is said to wear "many crowns," where the word for "crown" is *diadêma,* the word for royal crowns. The weapons of the two figures are different, the horseman of chapter 6 carrying a bow and Christ wielding a two-edged sword that protrudes from his mouth. Both are conquerors, but Christ is portrayed as going to battle against the eschatological enemies of God arrayed for battle, a battle that brings to a definitive end the struggle between good and evil, whereas the other horseman is carrying on a general warfare with no specified enemies, and his activity begins, and does not end, the eschatological events. The activity of the man in chapter 6 is entirely military, whereas when Christ is said to conquer in 3:21 and 5:5, it is his suffering and death that are at issue (but see 17:14). The man of chapter 6 is told to "come" to begin punishing the earth, whereas Jesus is entreated to "come" by a Christian community at prayer, hoping for its final delivery. The strongest argument for not seeing the horseman of chapter 6 as Jesus is that he is closely associated with the next three horsemen who appear when seals two, three, and four are opened. Together these four horsemen bring about the first four eschatological events. It is unlikely that Christ, who is the one who is opening each successive seal in heaven, would make an appearance on earth to carry out just the first of these events.

There is another interpretation of the general resemblances between the two riders of white horses besides seeing them as identical. Both spell doom for the Roman empire. The first horseman rides out to conquer, and subsequent events prove that it is the Roman empire that is conquered. But that conquest is not complete and definitive until Christ rides out on his white horse in chapter 19. What the first horseman begins, Christ finishes. The two form an inclusio that helps to tie all of the eschatological events together and focus them on the defeat of Rome and Satan (Boring 1989, 123).

The first horseman clearly represents war, but there are more specific resonances present. The fact that he carries a bow would have been significant for a hearer in the first century. Only Parthians had mounted archers at this time. Parthia was the empire east of the Roman empire. The Parthians were feared and respected by the Romans, for they were never conquered. In 40 B.C.E., the Parthians captured Palestine and Jerusalem and were driven out three years later by Herod the Great. In 62 C.E., the Parthian Vologeses defeated Roman forces in the valley of the Tigris River, an event that made an impression on the Romans and especially on their subjects living closest to the Parthian border. It would be natural if our author, anticipating warfare that would result in the overthrow of Roman power, looked to the Parthians to participate in it. Indeed in the sixth trumpet (9:13–21) demonic armies come from the Euphrates River, and in 16:12 the pouring out of the sixth bowl results in the drying up of the Euphrates so that the kings of the east can attack Rome. The fear of armies from the east became associated with legends about the return of Nero after his death, which we discuss in connection with chapter 13.

The victory of the first horseman is emphasized by the repetitive sentence, "He came out conquering and to conquer" (6:2). It is also expressed by his riding on a white horse and being given a crown. This evokes pictures of a triumphant commander riding in the victory parade. The fact that a crown "was given" to him shows that God gives him the victory, since throughout Revelation, the word "to give" indicates God's allowing or causing things to happen through intermediaries of one sort or another.

The Second Seal (6:3–4)

The second seal is opened, and a second horseman is summoned by another of the four living creatures. The second horseman takes peace from the earth, and people "slaughter" one another. The same verb, "slaughter," is applied to the Lamb in 5:6 and to the martyrs in 6:9. The punishment of humanity fits the crime, since those implicated in the slaughter of Christ and the martyrs are themselves slaughtered. The color of the horse matches the blood being shed. Charles (1920, 1:164) interprets the content of the second seal as civil and international strife, based on his comparison with the apocalyptic discourses in the gospels. The precise nature of what the second horseman does is not certain, but it involves more than just normal social conflict. It must at least indicate the sort of radical social breakdown that many Jewish sources expected before the eschaton (Charles 1920, 1:164; see *Jub.* 23:19; *1 Enoch* 56:7; 4 Ezra 5:9; 6:24; 13:31; *2 Bar.* 48:32; 70:3, 6). The role of God in the work of this horseman is implied by the words, "He *was given* a great sword" (6:4). Charles (1920, 1:165) sees this as the culmination of a tradition concerning the eschatological sword which God wields in the Bible (Isa 27:1; 34:5; 46:10; 47:6; Ezek 21:3ff.), which is given to God's people in the Animal Apocalypse (*1 Enoch* 90:19): "A great sword was given to the sheep" (90:34; 91:12) and which is given to God's enemies so that they might destroy each other in *1 Enoch* 88:2 and 100:2. Charles connects this with the sword that Jesus says he has come to cast on the earth (Luke 12:51).

The Third Seal (6:5–6)

The Lamb opens the third seal; another living creature says "Come!"; and a third rider comes forward. This one rides a black horse and carries scales. The scales are an instrument of commerce, and the rider causes economic hardship. The seer hears a voice "in the midst of the four living creatures" which proclaims that wheat and barley will sell for exorbitant prices (a denarius for a quart of wheat or three quarts of barley, eight to sixteen times their normal price [Charles 1920, 1:166–67]), whereas oil and wine will be unaffected. A denarius was a day's wage for a laborer (Matt 20:2). At these prices, a laborer would have just about been able to buy enough grain for himself and would not have had enough to support a family. That oil and wine are unaffected may mean that luxury goods will be as cheap as before, a situation favoring the rich. Some object that oil and wine were not luxury goods in the ancient world, but they were certainly less crucial than wheat and barley.

This seal may have a contemporary reference in a decree issued by Domitian in 92 C.E. Because of a shortage of staple grains and the tendency of farmers to plant the more lucrative vineyards and olive groves, Domitian decreed that no new vineyards could be planted in Italy and that half of the vineyards in the provinces should be destroyed (Charles 1920, 1:167). Domitian was forced to relent. The Roman writer Suetonius reports that cities in Asia in particular objected.

The Fourth Seal (6:7–8)

After the fourth seal is opened and the living creature issues the summons, the last rider comes forth on a "pale green" horse. The color is probably our author's translation of the color of the third horse in Zech 1:8. It is an appropriate color for death. Death is personified here and coupled with Hades, the Greek designation for the underworld, corresponding to the biblical Sheol, where the dead go. Death and Hades are personified and paired in 20:13–14 as well. They also appear in 1:18, where the personification is not clear but can be inferred given the other two passages. Hades is sometimes pictured as having a large mouth with which it swallows the dead. The picture may be of Hades following Death around to swallow its victims. Death is personified in Job 18:13, and death and Hades (Sheol) are personified together in Isa 28:15, 18 and Hosea 13:14 (see 1 Cor 15:55).

Death and Hades "were given" authority over a quarter of the earth to kill its inhabitants (6:8). That they kill only a quarter indicates that this is a catastrophic happening but is not yet the end. Later, the trumpets in chapters 8 and 9 will destroy a third of what they attack, including humankind, signaling an intensification of the destruction of the seals. The verb "to give" occurs here again to indicate that God allows Death and Hades to act. They kill persons "with sword, famine, and pestilence [literally: death], and by the wild animals of the earth" (6:8). These same four elements constitute God's punishment of Israel in Ezek 5:16–17 and 14:21. Jeremiah uses three of them (excluding animals) in a formulaic warning of God's approaching vengeance (14:12; 15:3; 21:7; 24:10; 29:17–18; 42:17; 43:1). In Revelation the four elements tie the first four seals together. The sword is related directly to the second seal and indirectly to the first (warfare); famine recalls the third seal; and pestilence is part of the fourth.

The Fifth Seal (6:9–11)

The opening of the fifth seal marks a shift in focus. No longer does the opening of the seal result in the summoning of horsemen who go forth to wreak destruction on the earth. Instead it reveals a scene in heaven where the souls of the martyrs are seen under an altar in heaven, asking God for vengeance. The author shows the same freedom with respect to his use of temple imagery as with his other images. Charles (1920, 1:226–30) shows that such freedom is typical of apocalypses dealing with heavenly scenes that use temple imagery. He shows that the altar in Revelation combines features of the altar of incense located in the Holy Place in the Jerusalem temple and the altar of burnt offering located outside of the temple building in the court of the priests.

It is the altar of burnt offering that sheds the most light on the scene of the sixth seal. On that altar the priests burned the portions of the offerings God demanded. The blood of the sacrifices was given to God by pouring it at the foot of the altar (Lev 4:7, etc.). The rationale for this is given in Lev 17:11: "For the life of the flesh is in the blood; and I have given it to you for making atonement for your lives on the altar; for, as life, it is the blood that makes atonement." Consuming blood was forbidden, because the life of living creatures belongs to God alone. Gen 9:4 says, "You shall not eat the flesh with its life, that is, its blood." The seer draws on such sacrificial imagery as he pictures the souls of the martyrs under the heavenly altar.

A complex of ideas and images contributes to this scene. Charles points out that the idea of a heavenly altar and/or temple is common in Judaism, and he refers to the extended treatment of the correspondence between the earthly and heavenly sanctuaries in Hebrews. In our treatment of chapter 5 we noted that the idea of the angels fulfilling a priestly role in heaven is also well known. Charles (1920, 1:173–74) adduces several rabbinic parallels for the idea that the souls of the righteous are under the heavenly altar. The portrayal of martyrdom as cultic sacrifice is found in Jewish tradition in *1 Enoch* 47:4 and 4 Macc 6:29 and 17:21–22. Christian martyrs are seen as sacrifices or libations in 2 Tim 4:6 and Phil 2:17 and in Ignatius's *Letter to the Romans* 2:2 (early second century).

The martyrs are "those who had been slaughtered for the word of God and for the testimony they had given" (6:9). We noted in the introduction that there is no evidence for a large-scale persecution of Christianity at the time Revelation was written, late in Domitian's reign, nor does Revelation constitute such evidence. But there was a brutal and wide-ranging persecution of the Christians in Rome by Nero in the mid-sixties, and that experience left a vivid impression on the author. The souls under the heavenly altar undoubtedly consist primarily of those many Christians who died under Nero. They were "slaughtered" as the Lamb was slaughtered (5:6).

The souls under the altar were slaughtered because of their loyalty to God. This is expressed as their having died for "the word of God and for the testimony they had given" (6:9). The NRSV translation hides an ambiguity here. The final words read literally, "For the testimony which they kept [or had]." This recalls the summary of Revelation's content as expressed in 1:2: "The word of God and the testimony of Jesus Christ." The question is whether the reference in 6:9 is to Christ's testimony which the faithful "keep" in some sense, or whether it is a reference to the testimony of the faithful Christians themselves. The seer is aware that both Jesus and Christians bear testimony (12:11). The rhetorical force of Christians' keeping Jesus' testimony is to bind their witness closely to his and to see their witness as continuing his. This interpretation is supported by 1:2; 12:17; 19:10; and 20:4. It also forms another intriguing point of contact between Revelation and the gospel of John, which says concerning Jesus, "He testifies to what he has seen and heard, yet no one accepts his testimony. Whoever has accepted his testimony has certified this, that God is true" (3:32–33; Charles 1920, 1:174). For both the gospel and Revelation, the faithful are those who accept and keep Jesus' testimony, although the context is different. In the gospel, the emphasis is on Jesus, who testifies concerning a world he has seen but to which humans can have access only if they accept him. In Revelation, Jesus testifies to God's sovereignty and pays with his life, a pattern Christians must follow.

The martyrs under the altar "cried out with a loud voice, 'Sovereign Lord, holy and true, how long will it be before you judge and avenge our blood on the inhabitants of the earth?' " (6:10). The psalms supply numerous examples of the oppressed people of God, individuals or community, asking God how long their oppression will continue (Pss 6:3; 13:1, 2; 35:17; 74:10; 79:5; etc.). We noted above that Zechariah's vision of the four horses is followed by the angel's question to God concerning how long he would withhold mercy from Jerusalem (1:12). The martyrs' question in Rev 6:10 causes consternation among Christian readers who fear it may be unchristian in its desire for vengeance. But for the author it is reasonable to expect that those who "slaughtered" the martyrs will have to pay the price. The martyrs are already dead and in heaven. They are not asking to be allowed to return to earth and torture or kill their adversaries. They are asking that justice be done. The word translated "avenge" here is *ekdikeô,* which is derived from the word for "justice." In making this request, the martyrs are in a long line of biblical prayer for the bringing of enemies to justice.

The martyrs address God as "master," stressing God's sovereignty (Schüssler Fiorenza 1991, 64). The martyrs also call God "holy and true." Christ applies these adjectives to himself in 3:7, and holiness is ascribed to God in 4:8; 15:4; and 16:5. It may seem a bit sweeping that the martyrs entreat God to exercise retributive justice on "the inhabitants of the earth," but this phrase is used negatively throughout Revelation. This is the viewpoint of a tiny minority within the Roman empire that feels that everyone else is on the other side. The usage recalls the prologue of the gospel of John, which claims that no one accepted Jesus, Jew or Gentile, but then goes on to discuss those who did accept him (1:10–13). Mounce (1977, 159) summarizes Revelation's view of the inhabitants of the earth:

> "Them that dwell on the earth" is a semi-technical designation for mankind in its hostility to God. In 11:10 they are those who rejoice over the death of the two witnesses. In chapter 13 they are pictured as worshiping the beast (vss. 8, 12), and in chapter 17 as drunk with the wine of fornication of the great harlot (vs. 2). Their names are not

written in the book of life (17:8), and they are subject to the coming hour of trial (3:10; 8:13).

Ultimately, God's response to the martyrs' prayer is what happens in the rest of the book (see Heil 1993). The same combination of words, "judge and avenge" (6:10), found in the prayer also occurs in 19:2, where the heavenly multitude praises God for judging Rome and for "avenging on her the blood of his servants." In chapter 6, it is too early for such rejoicing. Although Christ has already won the victory and the final outcome is not in doubt, certain things must happen before Satan is finally and definitively defeated in chapter 20. God's interim answer to the martyrs is found in 6:11. They are given white robes and told to "rest" awhile longer. White robes symbolize either their resurrection bodies or simply the fact that they belong in heaven (see comments on 3:5). The ultimate consummation is to come, but they already enjoy membership in the heavenly court. They will also reign with Christ for a thousand years in the messianic kingdom before the final consummation (20:4–6).

The full significance of the term "rest" can be gauged by referring to chapter 14. There it is said of the wicked, "There is no rest day and night for those who worship the beast and its image and for anyone who receives the mark of its name" (14:11). Concerning the righteous it says, "They will rest from their labors, for their deeds follow them" (14:13). "Rest" means to be in the presence of the creator, who on the seventh day rested from his labor (Gen 2:2). Hebrews uses the same metaphor in 3:7–4:11.

It takes some ingenuity to reconcile the idea of a great last judgment with the death of individuals. Many ancient Jewish and Christian writers make no attempt to do so (but see *1 Enoch* 22; 4 Ezra 7). In the fifth seal, Revelation discloses the location and state of the martyrs as they await God's judgment on the earth. The purpose of the passage is not so much to convey information about this intermediate state as to make clear that they are in heaven and vindicated and that the eschatological events to follow constitute God's avenging their deaths.

The martyrs are told what must happen before the end. They must wait "until the number would be complete both of their fellow servants and of their brothers and sisters, who were soon to be killed as they themselves had been killed" (6:11). The idea that God's plans preordain a certain number of martyrs grows from the more general idea that God's plans preordain a set number of righteous humans to live, and when that number is reached the world as we know it will come to an end (4 Ezra 4:35–37; *2 Bar.* 30:2).

First Enoch 47 provides a close parallel to Revelation 6:

> "In those days, the prayers of the righteous ascended into heaven, and the blood of the righteous from the earth before the Lord of the Spirits.
>
> There shall be days when all the holy ones who dwell in the heavens above shall dwell [together]. And with one voice, they shall supplicate and pray... on behalf of the blood of the righteous ones which has been shed. Their prayers shall not stop from exhaustion before the Lord of the Spirits... [until] judgment is executed for them." In those days, I saw him—the Antecedent of Time, while he was sitting on the throne of his glory, and the books of the living ones were open before him. (*1 Enoch* 47:1–3)

The passage depends on Daniel 7, where the "Ancient of Days" takes his throne in heaven, books are opened before him, and the Jews' oppressors are judged and destroyed. In Rev 20:11–15, there is a similar judgment scene based on Daniel 7. Where *1 Enoch* combines the idea of a fixed number of righteous with the prayers of the righteous and the heavenly judgment scene, Revelation separates the prayers of the martyrs (6:10) from the final judgment (20:11–15) by means of the bulk of its visions, because the other eschatological events must precede the judgment. But the logic is the same in Revelation and *1 Enoch.* In both there are martyrdoms which lead to prayers of the righteous and the presence of the martyrs' blood before God, a judgment by God on his throne with books being opened, and ultimate punishment of the wicked and reward of the righteous, forcefully expressed in the remainder of each book. Revelation delays the ultimate judgment until chapter 20, but what immediately follows in the sixth seal (6:12–17) contains key elements of the end of God's judgment, and the seventh seal contains the seven trumpets, which bring events right up to the coming of God's kingdom. By placing the martyrs' prayer at the beginning of this process, Revelation makes it clear that it is not only the last judgment that results from the prayer but all the eschatological events that lead up to the judgment as well.

The suffering and death the seer expects the Asian Christians to undergo are critical in God's eschatological plans. Suffering and martyrdom play a central role in the final confrontation between good and evil and help bring about the defeat of evil (see 12:11). This is reminiscent of the *Testament of Moses* 9–10 and 2 Maccabees 7, where the death of the Jewish martyrs brings about God's judgment. This gives Christian suffering meaning, and it also places a tremendous responsibility on Christians to be willing to resist Roman authority to the death. God's kingdom depends on it. The fixed nature of the number of martyrs also brings hope to the sufferers. The end will come when the foreordained number is reached. In Romans, Paul uses a similar sort of argument when he says that "the full number of the Gentiles" must hear the gospel and enter the church, and then all Israel will convert (11:25–26). He uses this as a motivation to intensify his efforts with the Gentiles so as to bring the conversion of Israel closer.

The Sixth Seal (6:12–17)

The sixth seal contains eschatological events whose long tradition in Jewish apocalypses, in prophetic books of the Bible, and elsewhere in the New Testament is well attested. Charles (1920, 1:180–81) compiles the following list of parallels: eschatological earthquakes (Amos 8:8; 9:5; Ezek 38:19; Joel 2:10; *T. Moses* 10:4; 4 Ezra 5:8; 9:3; *2 Bar.* 70:8; see also Rev 8:5; 9:13; 16:18); eschatological darkening of the sun (Amos 8:9; Isa 13:10; 50:3; Ezek 32:7; Joel 2:10, 31; Matt 24:29; Mark 13:24; Luke 23:45; *T. Moses* 10:5; Acts 2:10; Rev 9:2); shaken and torn heavens (Isa 13:13; 34:4; 63:19; Hag 2:6, 21; cf. *Sib. Or.* 3:82; 8:233, 413); falling of the stars (Isa 34:4; Matt 24:29; *Sib. Or.* 3:83). This list is not exhaustive, but it gives a feel for the extent to which Revelation's scenarios are fully a part of Jewish and Christian eschatological thought.

The following parallels to the sixth seal are particularly helpful. Joel 2:30–31 reads, "I will show portents in the heavens and on the earth, blood and fire and columns of smoke. The sun shall be turned to darkness, and the moon to blood, before the great and terrible day of the LORD comes." Isaiah 13 describes the coming of the LORD in anger: "Therefore all hands will be feeble, and every human heart will melt, and they will be dismayed. . . . See, the day of the LORD comes, cruel, with wrath and fierce anger, to make the earth a desolation, and to destroy sinners from it. For the stars of the heavens and their constellations will not give their light; the sun will be dark at its rising, and the moon will not shed its light. . . . Therefore I will make the heavens tremble, and the earth will be shaken from its place, at the wrath of the LORD of hosts in the day of his fierce anger" (Isa 13:7, 9–10, 13). The rolling up of the heavens like a scroll in Revelation's sixth seal (6:13–14) sounds like Isa 34:4: "All the host of heaven shall rot away, and the skies roll up like a scroll. All their host shall wither like a leaf withering on a vine, or fruit withering on a fig tree." The *Testament of Moses,* a Jewish work written in the second century B.C.E. and rewritten around the time of Herod the Great, describes the coming of God's kingdom in a way that is similar to the description in Revelation (*T. Moses* 10:1–5).

In the apocalyptic discourses in the gospels, Jesus says similar things (Matthew 24; Mark 13; Luke 21). Signs that the end are imminent are wars, international strife, earthquakes, famines, pestilence, and persecutions. Signs that the end has come are the following: "The sun will be darkened, and the moon will not give its light, and the stars will be falling from heaven, and the powers in heaven will be shaken" (Mark 13:24–25). Then the Son of Man comes. Charles (1920, 1:181) notes that apocalyptic writers often refer to the unvarying order of the heavenly luminaries (*1 Enoch* 2:1; 41:5; 43:2; 69:16ff.; *T. Naph.* 3:2; *Pss. Sol.* 18:11–14; 4 Ezra 6:45). He continues, "When, then, the sun and moon and stars forsook this order, the end of the world was at hand." He cites as examples *1 Enoch* 80:5–6; 4 Ezra 5:4; *Sib. Or.* 3:801ff.

Distress that the day of the Lord has come is present in the quote from Isaiah 13 above. The particular language in Rev 6:15–16 is influenced by Hosea. As God prepares to punish Israel, "They shall say to the mountains, Cover us, and to the hills, Fall on us" (Hos 10:8). In the gospel of Luke, these words are quoted by Jesus on the way to the cross (23:30). A more elaborate scene of the panic of the wicked on the day of the Lord is in *1 Enoch* 62–63. As in Revelation, it is primarily the mighty of the earth who have cause for dismay, but Revelation includes "everyone, slave and free" (6:15). "Everyone" is like the "inhabitants of the earth" used earlier and throughout Revelation. It does not include the righteous, for they have no reason to fear. What is described in the sixth seal is not their earthly persecution (referred to in the fifth seal), nor is it the general social disruption of the first four seals, but it is the approach of divine judgment, which is bad news only for the wicked.

Revelation develops the words borrowed from Hosea 10 by making explicit what the people wish to avoid. They want to hide "from the face of the one seated on the throne and from the wrath of the Lamb; for the great day of their wrath has come, and who is able to stand?" (6:16–17). Their question echoes that of the prophet Amos who, when he hears of the coming punishment of Israel, asks, "How can Jacob stand?" (7:2, 5; see Joel 2:11; Zeph 2:2; Nah 1:6; Mal 3:2). It is characteristic of Revelation that the Lamb acquires God's eschatological role.

It seems strange that although in 6:17 the people declare that the day of God's and the Lamb's wrath has come, many more chapters follow before the end is consummated. This demonstrates the author's literary genius. Just at the moment of the great climax, on the threshold of the arrival of God and Lamb in judgment, it is delayed. There is yet another seal to be opened which will unleash the seven trumpets, and at its conclusion God's sovereignty will be proclaimed first by "loud voices" in heaven and then by the twenty-four elders in heaven (11:15–18), followed by a theophanic scene (11:19). This would seem to be the end, but even then the seer is not finished. What is described in the visions of the seals and trumpets must be recapitulated in the bowls, but not before still other visions intervene. The sixth seal ends with the question, "Who will be able to stand?" in the face of the wrath of God and the Lamb. Chapter 7 supplies the answer. It is a joyful and magnificent vision of the saved righteous worshiping before God, a proleptic vision of what for the righteous is on the other side of the destruction that permeates these chapters.

Interlude: Sealing and Salvation (Chapter 7)

Chapter 7 is an interlude between the sixth and seventh seals, consisting of two visions. The first (7:1–8) concerns the sealing of the 144,000 and begins with an introduction containing elements not developed elsewhere in the book (7:1–3). The second (7:9–17) is a proleptic vision of an innumerable multitude worshiping before the divine throne. Both visions begin with the familiar formula, "After this I saw." The formula marks off the visions as important new revelations. They are not part of the sixth seal. Because of inconsistencies between the two visions and because 7:1–3 contains elements not found in the rest of Revelation, Charles (1920, 1:188–203) proposes that behind 7:1–3 and 7:4–8 lie two earlier Jewish visions that were reworked by the author, and that 7:9–17 is entirely the work of the author, since it is permeated by his language and ideas. Even within 7:9–17 Charles finds some inconsistencies, so he proposes that the author has reworked one of his own visions to make it fit into its present literary context.

In chapter 7, the onrushing eschatological events of the first six seals are brought to a halt. The sixth seal containing cosmic disturbances ends with the inhabitants of the earth panicking and asking who can stand before the wrath of God and the Lamb. Instead of proceeding immediately to the seventh seal, chapter 7 intervenes. The vision of the 144,000, sealed to protect them from coming calamities, and of the blessed in God's presence at the end of time contrasts sharply with the panic that concludes the sixth seal.

The 144,000 Sealed (7:1–8)

In Rev 7:1–3, four angels are pictured at the four corners of the earth, holding back the four winds that threaten to inflict more damage on the earth. A fifth angel arises from the east and tells the other angels not to release the destructive winds until "the servants of our God" are marked "with a seal on their foreheads" (7:3). The scene recalls Ezekiel 9, where God is about to punish Jerusalem for its idolatry. Six men (really angels) are ordered to act as executioners of Jerusalem's inhabitants. A seventh man (another angel) has a writing case at his side. God says to him,

> "Go through the city, through Jerusalem, and put a mark on the foreheads of those who sigh and groan over all the abominations that are committed in it." To the others he said in my hearing, "Pass through the city and kill; your eye shall not spare, and you shall show no pity. Cut down old men, young men and young women, little children and women, but touch no one who has the mark." (Ezek 9:3–6)

In both Revelation and Ezekiel angels who are about to execute God's wrath are delayed by another angel who receives orders to put a protective mark on the foreheads of the righteous. There are two other possible parallels. In Revelation the angel who delays the destruction comes from the east, whereas the threshold of the temple on which God rests as he speaks in Ezekiel is on the east of the temple. There is a contrasting parallel in that Ezekiel's destructive action centers on Jerusalem and the temple, while in Revelation there follows a scene of salvation in the temple (7:9–17).

The scene in Revelation is inspired by Ezekiel 9, but it also depends on a later tradition that grew out of Ezekiel. In *2 Baruch,* a Jewish apocalypse contemporary with Revelation, Baruch has a vision in which the spirit lifts him above Jerusalem's wall (chap. 6, recalling the spirit's translation of Ezekiel to Jerusalem in Ezek 8:3 and John's translation to heaven in the spirit in Rev 4:1–2). There Baruch sees four angels standing at the four corners of Jerusalem, each holding a torch with which to set the city aflame. Another angel descends from heaven and orders them to wait until he rescues the temple vessels and hides them for safekeeping. Revelation and *2 Baruch* depend on similar developments of Ezekiel 9. Especially striking is the occurrence of four angels standing at four corners about to wreak destruction and the intervention of a fifth angel who must protect something or someone. (A similar pause takes place in *1 Enoch* 66:1–2 to allow Noah time to build the ark.)

The idea that God can punish through the natural elements is common in Jewish tradition. For example, the plagues during the exodus are God's action against Pharaoh (Exodus 7–12). They include water turning to blood, frogs, gnats, flies, disease of livestock, boils, thunder, hail, locusts, darkness, and death. The book of Wisdom says, "Creation will join with him [God] to fight against his frenzied foes," and specifies lightning, hailstones, sea water, rivers, and finally wind (5:20–23). Winds are a common feature of God's wrath (Charles 1920, 1:192–93). Jeremiah says in God's name, "I will bring upon Elam the four winds from the four quarters of heaven; and I will scatter them to all these winds" (49:36). In Dan 7:2, Daniel sees "the four winds of heaven stirring up the great sea," and from the sea arise the four evil monsters representing successive empires that oppress Israel. *First Enoch* 76 is a detailed description of the effects of winds on the earth (cf. *1 Enoch* 34). It says that there are twelve portals at the edges of the earth from which winds blow. The winds from the north, south, east, and west are beneficial. Those from the other directions, which could be considered the "corners," are destructive.

Another way in which Revelation is rooted in Jewish thought is the idea, expressed in several apocalypses, that intermediate superhuman beings, often specified as angels, have charge of the natural elements (e.g., *1 Enoch* 60:11–22; 65:8; 69:22; *Jub.* 2:2). This preserves God's control of the universe but simultaneously guards divine transcendence (Yarbro Collins 1979, 51). Revelation shares this worldview. Here in chapter 7 angels have charge of winds; 14:18 mentions an angel with authority over fire; 16:5 speaks of "the angel of the waters"; and 9:11 speaks of the angel in charge of the abyss.

There is no specific parallel to the fact that the angel who arises to delay the destruction comes from the east (7:2–3), but the east is a natural symbol since it is the place where the sun rises. Ancient temples often faced east, as did the one in Jerusalem. In Rev 7:2–3, the angel from the east cries out to the other four angels — who are now described as those "who had been given power to damage earth and sea" — not to do harm until God's servants are sealed. Seals could mean a variety of things in the ancient world. Later Christian tradition speaks of the seal of baptism. In the New Testament itself, being sealed in the Holy Spirit may refer to baptism (1 Cor 12:13; 2 Cor 1:22; Eph 1:13; 4:30), and Paul speaks of the seal of circumcision (Rom 4:11), which as a ceremony that admits one to a community is analogous to baptism. Some believe that the seer refers to baptism in 7:1–3, but others disagree (Boring 1989, 129, accepts the connection; Mounce 1977, 167, rejects it). Ephesians speaks of sealing by the Holy Spirit to preserve one until the end: "Do not grieve the Holy Spirit of God, with which you were marked with a seal for the day of redemption" (Eph 4:30). This protective, eschatological sealing is close to the idea in Rev 7:3.

The closest parallel to Revelation 7 is Ezekiel 9, where the seal is a mark of loyalty to God and protects its bearer from punishment. This is one of the basic meanings of a seal — a mark to show that something belongs to someone. In the author's world, seals could be placed on persons such as slaves and soldiers to identify their lord. The sealing of the faithful in chapter 7 cleverly ties that chapter into the seven seals, even as it sets chapter 7 off by a somewhat different use of the word "seal." The seals on the scroll do more than show that the contents are secret. They show that the author of the contents is God and that only his authorized agent can open the scroll. The seal applied to the faithful also shows that they belong to God. As the scroll's seals guard its contents, the seals on the humans guard them. Aune comments, "It was widely held in the ancient world that magical sealing could provide protection" (1993, 2318).

For Revelation every human bears one of two seals. Those faithful to "the living God" (7:2) bear his seal on their foreheads (7:2–3; 9:4; 14:1; 22:4), and there is a contrasting seal on the foreheads or the right hands (cf. Isa 44:5; 49:16) of followers of Satan and his beast (13:16–17; 14:9; 16:2; 19:20; 20:4). These seals are another way the author clarifies the central issue of the book—one's loyalty either to God or Satan. The term "the living God" sets up resonances that support this contrast. It appears in Jewish and Christian sources when opposition between idolatry and true worship is at issue (e.g., Jer 10:10; 1 Thess 1:9). Opposing seals are reminiscent of the following passage in the *Psalms of Solomon,* a first-century B.C.E. Jewish text:

> For God's mark is on the righteous for [their] salvation.
> Famine and sword and death shall be far from the righteous;
> for they will retreat from the devout like those pursued by famine.
> But they shall pursue sinners and overtake them,
> for those who act lawlessly shall not escape the Lord's judgment.
> They shall be overtaken as by those experienced in war,
> for on their forehead [is] the mark of destruction.
>
> (*Pss. Sol.* 15:6–9)

As in Revelation, one mark destines one for wrath; another protects the just.

The analogy of the seals in Rev 7:1–3 with those in Ezekiel 9 implies that God's servants are sealed to protect them from harm. But then it is puzzling why they are sealed only now, after the first six seals. Schüssler Fiorenza (1991, 62) suggests that the first five seals describe circumstances in the Roman empire which affected Christians and non-Christians alike, while the fifth seal reflects persecution of Christians. The use of the verb "to give" for each horseman shows that God does allow the actions they take, but he is not their *source,* so the distress of the first five seals does not come from God. The sealing refers to protection from destruction that does proceed from God, much as the marking of Israelite dwellings with the blood of the Passover lamb protected the Israelites from the killing of the firstborn inflicted by God on the Egyptians (Exod 12:21–27).

The sealing does not, however, protect the faithful from martyrdom. The martyrs have already been killed before the fifth seal, whereas the sealing happens after the sixth seal. Other references show that the author expects widespread martyrdom (see 13:15). At a minimum, the sealing must ensure that God will support his own during the terrible happenings to come. Charles (1920, 1:196–99) goes further and proposes that the faithful are protected from the three woes that coincide with the fifth, sixth, and seventh trumpets, which are "demonic." He bases his proposal on 9:4, which is at the beginning of the fifth trumpet (first woe). There the locusts who emerge from the abyss are told not to harm anyone with God's seal. Charles (1920, 1:243) reasonably sees these locusts as demonic, given their origin. The sixth trumpet also releases demonic forces, armies from the east who, although they accomplish God's will, are not on God's side. Charles's suggestion is helpful. It accounts for the facts that God does not protect his own from physical harm, that they do not escape eschatological disasters unscathed, but that they are ultimately rescued from the power of Satan. It also takes the relation between 7:1–3 and 9:4 seriously. Because the sealing takes place not between the fourth and fifth trumpets, but just before the seventh seal, it serves two functions. It delays the seventh trumpet, thus heightening suspense and intensifying expectation—a common delaying device in Revelation—and at the same time it anticipates the demonic plagues to come.

It is striking that we never hear about the angels in charge of the winds again (but see 9:14), nor do the four winds reappear. This supports Charles's theory that underlying 7:1–3 is a Jewish source which is used for its emphasis on sealing, but whose other features are not developed by our author.

Another question concerns the identity of the 144,000 who are sealed (7:4–8). There were twelve tribes in Israel according to the Bible, and Rev 7:4–8 claims that twelve thousand from each of the twelve tribes are sealed. When the ten northern tribes were exiled by Assyria in the eighth century B.C.E., Israel began to look forward to a time when it would be reconstituted as God originally willed, including all twelve tribes. The "lost tribes of Israel" have appeared in legends down through history. Most scholars believe that the reason Jesus had twelve disciples in his inner group was symbolic—his message and mission had something to do with the restoration of Israel.

The list in 7:5–8 raises questions. It does not conform to any of the approximately twenty lists of the twelve tribes found in the Bible. It is unique in beginning with the tribe of Judah, although that is easily explained by the tradition that Jesus was of this tribe (Heb 7:14). The claim that Jesus was of Davidic lineage (Rev 5:5; 22:16) requires that he be of the tribe of Judah. The list omits the tribe of Dan, which is also unusual. This may be explained by the rather bad press Dan gets in several Jewish and Christian traditions (Judges 18; 1 Kgs 12:28–30; Jer 8:16–17; Irenaeus, *Adversus Haereses* 5.30.2). The omission of Dan leaves a gap in the twelve tribes. To fill the gap, the author inserts the tribe of Manasseh. This makes little sense, because the tribe of Joseph split into the tribes of Ephraim and Manasseh. Since Joseph is listed in Revelation 7, it is not logical to include Manasseh in the list, but the author does so to restore the number twelve.

The number 144,000 is obviously symbolic (see Boring 1989, 130). It is twelve squared times one thousand. This is a very large number, since the two largest numbers mentioned in the Bible are one thousand and a "myriad" (ten thousand). We already have seen in Rev 5:11 the immense number of the heavenly multitude expressed by the phrases "myriads of myriads and thousands of thousands," modeled on Daniel 7. Although 144,000 is a very large number, it is limited, in contrast to the multitude seen in the next vision (7:8). The main question concerning 7:4–8 is the identity of the 144,000. One suggestion has been that they represent the righteous of historical Israel, so that the author is saying that the saved will consist of both faithful Jews (limited number) and Christians (unlimited number). This is unlikely, given the probability that our author is a Jewish Christian who now defines faithfulness to God in terms of belonging to Christ (see esp. 2:9 and 3:9).

Another possibility is that the 144,000 represent Jewish Christians, whereas the uncountable multitude in the second part of chapter 7 stands for all Christians, or perhaps just Gentile Christians. But this distinction between Jewish and Gentile Christians is reflected nowhere else in the book. Besides, there seems to be no reason that only Jewish Christians should be protected from the coming catastrophes. Another possibility is that the 144,000 are all Christians who need to be protected, that is, all faithful

Christians who live during the demonic plagues. By the time of the author, Christianity was two or three generations old, and many Christians had already died, some in Nero's persecution. The total number of righteous Christians would in the end be innumerable, according to 7:9. One last possibility is that the 144,000 are martyrs, who form a special group among the total number of Christians. This is probably the best suggestion, for although in 13:15 all who do not worship the beast are killed, they do not represent *all* Christians, since many lived before the crisis described in chapter 13.

Although martyrs represent only one part of the church, potentially all faithful Christians are martyrs, since all must be willing to die rather than be disloyal to God. John sees the church as a whole as the true Israel, the true Jews (2:9; 3:9). John is not alone in seeing the church as the true Israel (see 1 Pet 1:1; Jas 1:1; Gal 3:29; 6:16; Phil 3:3). The church is not only seen as the true Israel — it is the ideal Israel. The number 144,000 (twelve squared) could allude to the combination of twelve tribes and twelve apostles (see Rev 21:12–14), or it may just reflect the ideal nature of the community, as do the cubic dimensions of the new Jerusalem (twelve thousand stadia long, twelve thousand stadia wide, and twelve thousand stadia high [Rev 21:16]). The messages to the churches in chapters 2 and 3 are a realistic view of the church, but now that the author has passed into the eschatological visions, he adopts an idealized apocalyptic view.

The Innumerable Multitude (7:9–17)

The formula "After this I saw" (7:9) introduces the second vision of chapter 7. Charles (1920, 1:199–203) argues that the crowd in the second vision is the same as the 144,000 of the first. He says that the first group symbolizes Christian martyrs as they face the eschatological events and are protected by God from the demonic plagues (the "church militant"). The second are the same martyrs who now stand in God's presence, and to whose number martyrs are continually being added (the "church triumphant"). The visions are of the same group, seen from different perspectives. Charles's explanation does account for the difference that the first group needs to be sealed to protect it from the dangers to come, while the second group has already "come out of the great ordeal" (7:14). The first group is on earth in the present age; the second stands before God and so is either in heaven or in the renewed earth to come. The first group is vulnerable to danger; the second is protected by God from hunger, thirst, heat, and sadness.

However, Charles's reading does not solve the problem that the 144,000 is a large but limited group, whereas the second "no one could count" (7:9), and it also assumes Charles's conviction that the author speaks of universal martyrdom. A more satisfactory solution sees the 144,000 as a subset of all Christians. Elsewhere in Revelation there are Christian groups that are set apart from other Christians, namely, the 144,000 in 14:1–5 and those who rise to rule with Christ in the messianic kingdom (20:4–6), distinguished from the rest, who rise later (20:11–13). We now look at 14:1–5 and 20:4–6 for what they can reveal about 7:1–3, but we shall analyze them more fully in their place.

In the fourth of the seven unnumbered visions that begin in chapter 12, John sees 144,000 persons standing with the Lamb on Mount Zion (14:1–5). They bear the Lamb's and the Father's names on their foreheads. These are the same 144,000 whom we see in 7:1–8, and the names that they bear on their foreheads are the seal the angel applies in 7:3. Revelation 14:5 says that they are already "redeemed from humankind as first fruits for God and the Lamb." This is the same sort of proleptic vision as in 7:9–17. It sees in advance the ultimate fate of this group. "First fruits" is a cultic term and may add a sacrificial tone here, implying martyrdom. The same sort of sacrificial overtones associate the Lamb who was slaughtered (5:6) with the martyrs who were also slaughtered (6:9). Paul applies the term "first fruits" to Jesus in 1 Cor 15:23 because he was the first to be raised from the dead. So it appears that the 144,000 in chapter 14 are martyrs who have the privilege of being raised before others. The overtones of martyrdom are strengthened by the statement in 14:4, "These follow the lamb wherever he goes." This close association with everything the Lamb does is a veiled way of saying that these are killed as Christ was. They stand with the Lamb on Mount Zion (14:1), the hill in Jerusalem on which the temple stood. The scene in 14:1–5 is the mirror image of the one in chapter 13, where the beast is seen with his followers, all of whom have his seal on their foreheads or hands. In chapter 13, all who do not follow the beast are killed (13:15), and the author immediately introduces a scene of their vindication in 14:1–5.

In chapter 20, those "who had been beheaded for their testimony to Jesus and for the word of God" and who "had not worshiped the beast or its image and had not received its mark on their foreheads or their hands" rise with Christ to rule with him for a thousand years. The author explains, "This is the first resurrection," implying that there is a second. The millennial kingdom is in Jerusalem. This becomes clear when the evil armies that attack it at the end of the thousand years surround "the beloved city" (20:9). It is of course in Jerusalem that the 144,000 stand with the Lamb in 14:1–5. In view of these connections, it is best to read 7:1–3, 14:1–5, and 20:4–6 together as referring to the same group. They are martyrs who reign with Christ in the millennium because they, like he, die for God's word.

The 144,000 come from every tribe of Israel, while those who stand before God in 7:9–17 are "from every nation, from all tribes and peoples and languages" (7:9). In the first vision (7:1–8), the author stresses the church's continuity with Israel, or more accurately, his claim that the church is the true Israel. When presenting the victorious church in God's presence (7:9–17), the author underlines its universalism. Most of the early church found no inconsistency between its claim to be the true Israel, on the one hand, and its composition of both Jews and Gentiles, on the other, as is attested in many parts of the New Testament.

In 7:9, John observes "a great multitude that no one could count, from every nation, from all tribes and peoples and languages, standing before the throne and before the Lamb, robed in white, with palm branches in their hands." In 5:9, the seer heard the four living creatures and the twenty-four elders singing a song of praise to Christ who "ransomed for God saints from every tribe and language and people and nation." Now he sees those ransomed saints themselves standing before God, singing praise to God and Christ. Yarbro Collins (1990, 1005) calls this the climax of the seven seals because it states most clearly the reward of the righteous. Mounce (1977, 171) compares the effect of the vision in 7:9–17 to that of the transfiguration in the gospels, where the disciples can for a moment see beyond the suffering Christ is about to endure to the glory that lies beyond it. The fact that the Lamb succeeds in winning people for God "from every tribe and language and people and nation," expressed in chapters 5 and 7, contrasts with the beast's "authority over every tribe and people and language and nation"

(13:7). The same contrasting use of this phrase appears in Daniel (see comments on 5:9).

The multitude is dressed in white, for as the elder's interpretation in 7:14 clarifies, they are the ones who have "come out of the great ordeal," and so they have received what was promised to the faithful ones at Sardis (3:5). Some are martyrs, but since it seems that all Christians are included here, there is no reason to assume that every member of the multitude is a martyr. But each would be ready to die. Although the martyrs do receive white robes in the fifth seal (6:11), white robes do not imply martyrdom, merely worthiness to be in God's presence. The multitude carries palm branches, which some have taken to be a detail from the ceremonies of the feast of tabernacles (Ulfgard 1989). However, palms had a wider usage. They signify joy and victory (see 1 Macc 13:51; 2 Macc 10:7), as in the entry of Jesus into Jerusalem in the gospels.

The assembled multitude cries out "in a loud voice" in 7:10: "Salvation [*sôtêria*] belongs to our God who is seated on the throne, and to the Lamb!" There is some disagreement over the precise meaning of the word translated by the NRSV as "salvation" (*sôtêria*). Yarbro Collins (1990, 1005) thinks that it means "victory" here. She notes that it translates the Hebrew *yeshuʿa,* a word that means "victory" in 1 Sam 14:45; Hab 3:8; and Pss 20:6; 44:5. She reads the song in 7:12 as a victory song on the analogy of Exodus 15 and Judges 5 and suggests that the scene be read in conjunction with chapters 5 and 6, where God's victory results in the opening of the seals on the scroll. It is fitting that there be a victory song at this point. Schüssler Fiorenza thinks that the word should be translated "salvation" here, not "victory." She gives the basic meaning of *sôtêria* as "the total well-being of people" and says that throughout Revelation it means "eschatological, final salvation." She continues, "The official source of such total well-being, peace, and salvation, according to the political ideology of the time, was the Roman emperor. In contrast, those who stand before the throne acknowledge God and the Lamb as the ultimate source of all well-being and salvation" (1991, 68). Although Yarbro Collins and Schüssler Fiorenza opt for different translations for *sôtêria,* their basic points of view are in harmony. The victory of God over God's enemies constitutes final, eschatological salvation precisely because, in the seer's view, allegiance to Satan and to Rome is the main obstacle to general recognition of God's sovereignty in the world.

The acclamation "Salvation belongs to our God" has a close parallel in Psalm 3, whose final verse begins in precisely the same way: "Deliverance [salvation; Hebrew: *yeshu'a;* Greek: *sôtêria*] belongs to the Lord" (3:8). The psalm thanks God for deliverance from oppressive enemies, and so is a fitting parallel with the doxology in Revelation 7.

The praise of the ransomed saints is confirmed by the angels who stand around the elders and four living creatures (7:11–12). They first say "Amen" to the song of the multitude in white, then add their own song praising God, and then conclude their song with another "Amen." They thus frame their own song with the liturgical word of affirmation. Their song is a doxology with seven elements and is like the ones found in chapters 4 and 5, six of the seven elements being found in the earlier doxologies. The seventh is "thanksgiving." It is appropriate that thanksgiving come in this scene, for it depicts the righteous after God has rescued them from all evils.

One of the twenty-four heavenly elders now assumes the role of an interpreting angel, as found in other apocalypses. All of 7:14–17 is the elder's interpretation of the vision. Such a lengthy explanation, when explanations in general are rare in Revelation, indicates the significance of the vision. The elder asks the seer about the identity and origin of those dressed in white. The seer responds, "Sir, you are the one who knows" (7:14). The interchange sounds much like where God asks Ezekiel a question about something the prophet sees, and the prophet replies, "O Lord God, you know" (37:3). Again the seer models himself on the prophets. The elder then explains: "These are they who have come out of the great ordeal [*thlipsis*]; they have washed their robes and made them white in the blood of the Lamb" (7:14). The presence of the definite article plus the adjective "great" makes clear that the ultimate eschatological ordeal is meant. The multitude has left the ordeal behind and has received white robes, signifying it now belongs to the heavenly realm.

There is nothing in 7:9–17 that necessitates the view that these are all martyrs. The scene in chapter 7 corresponds to the one in chapter 5. What is promised in chapter 5, that the Lamb will be able to open the seals, has happened in chapter 6. The sixth seal ends with the question "Who is able to stand?" in the face of the Lamb's imminent wrath. Chapter 7 answers the question. In chapter 5, Christ is praised for redeeming people from all tribes, tongues, peoples, and nations, and the same phrase (with a slight change in word order) describes those who are present before the throne in 7:9. The scene in 7:9–17 proleptically discloses one side of the goal of the six seals—the reward of the righteous. Subsequent chapters develop in more detail the other side—the punishment of the wicked.

As with most images in Revelation, that of the white robe is not entirely consistent. In 3:5, it looks to be a future reward given by Christ for loyalty to God. In 6:11, white robes are given to the martyrs after their martyrdom. But in the present passage the image is that the Christians have washed their robes in the Lamb's blood, implying that they have the robes before the tribulation. Yarbro Collins (1990, 1005) suggests that here the robes symbolize the inner selves of the faithful. This is reminiscent of Psalm 51, which speaks of the true cleansing as being inward.

In speaking of washing garments in the blood of the Lamb, the author is again rooted in Jewish and Christian tradition and metaphors. Clean garments can be a metaphor for preparedness to be in God's presence. In Exodus 19, God commands Moses to tell the people to wash their clothes before approaching Mount Sinai (Exod 19:10, 14). In Zechariah 3, the high priest Joshua stands in the heavenly court wearing dirty garments, which God orders to be removed and replaced with festal apparel (3:4–5). The mental images of the red of blood and the white of the garments bears an intriguing but uncertain relationship to Isa 1:16, 18: "Wash yourselves; make yourselves clean;... though your sins are like scarlet, they shall be like snow; though they are red like crimson, they shall become like wool."

Revelation's author may also have in mind the cleansing value of blood in the Jerusalem cult. Blood purifies sacred places, persons, and vessels defiled by sin or other sorts of impurity. Hebrews is an extensive study in the use of such metaphors to describe the effect of Christ's death. The argument of Hebrews concerning blood is concentrated especially in chapter 9, and the following statement is typical: "If the blood of sheep and goats and bulls, with the sprinkling of the ashes of a heifer, sanctifies those who have been defiled so that their flesh is purified, how much more will the blood of Christ, who through the eternal Spirit offered himself without blemish to God, purify our conscience from dead works to worship the living God" (9:13–14). It later asserts, "Indeed, under the law almost everything is purified with blood, and without the shedding of blood

Figure 3

7:15–17

For this reason they are before
the throne of God,
and worship him day and night
within his temple,
and the one who is seated on
the throne will shelter [*skênoô*]
them.
They will hunger no more, and
thirst no more;
the sun will not strike them,
nor any scorching heat;
for the Lamb at the center of the
throne will be their shepherd,
and he will guide them to the
springs of the water of life,
and God will wipe away every
tear from their eyes.

21:3–4

And I heard a loud voice from
the throne saying,
"See, the home of God is among
mortals.
He will dwell [*skênoô*] with them
as their God;
they will be his peoples,
and God himself will be with
them;
he will wipe way every tear from
their eyes.
Death will be no more;
mourning and crying and pain
will be no more,
for the first things have passed
away."

there is no forgiveness of sins" (9:22). A similar thought lies behind 1 John 1:7: "The blood of Jesus his Son cleanses us from all sin." Revelation hints that Jesus' death is sacrificial in this sense in 1:5 and 5:6, 9. Although there is no direct parallel for saying that Christians have washed their garments clean in the Lamb's blood (7:14), the texts adduced above manifest the sort of contexts and backgrounds from which such notions emerge. The main point is that only through Christ's death can anyone gain access to God.

The last three verses of chapter 7 paint a wonderful picture of harmony between God and God's people. Images of throne and temple come together explicitly, as the faithful worship before God. Like the angelic host, their worship is unceasing (see 4:8), and God reciprocates by sheltering them. The scene has many similarities to the consummation described at the end of Revelation, as is seen in figure 3. Revelation 22:3 says of the new Jerusalem, "The throne of God and of the Lamb will be in it, and his servants will worship him."

The connections of 7:9–17 to scenes at the end of the book show that it is indeed a prolepsis of the final consummation. The author is not yet ready to proclaim that "Death is no more" or

"The first things have passed away." A prolepsis is not yet the end. The main element of the consummation is one taken from the Jewish covenant — God is present among the people, protecting them (Lev 26:11–12; Ezek 37:27–28; 48:35; Zech 2:10), and the people reciprocate with praise and obedience. The Greek verb *skênoô,* translated by the NRSV as "shelter," comes from the word for "tent" and recalls God's dwelling with the Israelite tribes in the desert in a tent. Even when the Israelites entered the promised land, the ark of the covenant, sign of God's presence among the people, was kept for a while in a tent. When David first wishes to build a temple, God objects, "I have not lived in a house since the day I brought up the people of Israel from Egypt to this day, but I have been moving about in a tent or a tabernacle" (2 Sam 7:6). Jewish literature, and especially rabbinic sources, speak of God's presence as the "Shekinah," a term derived from the Hebrew for tent, *mishkan.* John's gospel speaks of Jesus as God's real presence among humans when it says that Jesus "tented" among us (1:14). In Rev 12:12 and 13:6, the verb is applied to those who dwell in heaven.

The ideal circumstances portrayed in 7:15–17 and 21:3–4 rely on Isa 49:10, where similar words describe what God will do for the Israelites returning from exile in Babylonia:

> They shall not hunger or thirst,
>   neither scorching wind nor sun shall strike them down,
> for he who has pity on them will lead them,
>   and by springs of water will guide them.

Revelation uses these words both literally and figuratively. The faithful are promised more than just freedom from physical ills, although that freedom is not unimportant. The central aspect of the salvation depicted here is living in the presence of God. That being true, all else follows. This is the "total well-being of people" of which Schüssler Fiorenza (1991, 68) speaks.

What our author adds to Isaiah's picture is crucial for Christians, for it is the christological element. God does not sit alone on the throne. The Lamb also sits on it. In a clever turnabout, the Lamb becomes the shepherd. The combination of royal and pastoral imagery here is not incongruous, for kings and rulers were often compared to shepherds in the Bible and in other Jewish literature (2 Sam 7:7; Isa 44:28; Jer 3:15; see Charles's list, 1920, 1:217). The classic example is Ezekiel 34, where God, angry with the failure of Israel's "shepherds," himself becomes the shepherd of the sheep. John 10 uses Ezekiel when it depicts Jesus as the Good Shepherd. Like the gospel's author, our author sees Jesus as the one through whom God shepherds his flock.

Jesus leads the flock to water in Rev 7:17, as does God in Isa 49:10. The combination of shepherding and water is a natural one, but the similarity between Rev 7:17 and Ps 23:1–3 makes it possible that the author also has that psalm in mind:

> The LORD is my shepherd, I shall not want.
> He makes me lie down in green pastures;
> he leads me beside still waters;
> he restores my soul.

In Near Eastern cultures situated in dry climates, the promise of water perhaps has deeper resonances than in one where water is more plentiful. In various texts water symbolizes all the good that flows to humans from God (Ps 36:9; John 4:14; 7:38; *1 Enoch* 48:1). In Revelation, it is part of the blessings of the end (21:6; 22:1, 17). In Revelation 7, the Lamb's shepherding is positive, since it is exercised over the faithful, but for the wicked, Christ's shepherding is fearful (2:27; 12:5; 19:15). There, instead of strains of Psalm 23, one hears the more ominous tones of Psalm 2: "You shall break them in pieces with a rod of iron." The Septuagint has *poimaneis* (you will shepherd), where the Hebrew has *tr'm* (break). The allusion to Psalm 2 in Rev 2:27 uses the Greek verb found in the Septuagint. There Christ gives faithful Christians the power to "rule" (*poimainô*) the nations.

Chapter 7 constitutes an interlude between the sixth and seventh seals. In the first part of that interlude John sees some of the faithful prepared for the coming tribulation, and in the second part he witnesses the glory of all faithful Christians after it. Yarbro Collins (1990, 1005) notes that the interlude is necessary to complete the pattern of persecution (fifth seal), punishment of the oppressors (sixth seal), and reward of the righteous (chapter 7). At the end of his experiences narrated in chapter 7, the seer, fully assured of the outcome for faithful Christians, is ready to see the violent and disturbing visions to follow. If John has been so prepared, the same is true for his audience, who share his experience through his narrative. The scene is set for the seventh seal.

The Seventh Seal (8:1–2)

Chapter 8 begins with the opening of the seventh seal. The reader or hearer expects that the great climax will now occur. Instead there is a half-hour of total silence in heaven. This heightens the drama and again injects an element of suspense into the scene. Then there appear seven angels with seven trumpets, and after a short liturgical scene, each of the angels blows his trumpet. Thus the seventh seal contains the seven trumpets. Instead of a quick conclusion when the seventh seal is opened, there begins another lengthy series of seven.

The half-hour's silence that follows the opening of the seventh seal intensifies anticipation of what is to come. The insertion of a period of silence in the action also happens in the Jewish apocalypse 4 Ezra, roughly contemporary with Revelation, where after the four-hundred-year reign of the messiah and before the new world comes, "The world shall be turned back to primeval silence for seven days, as it was at the first beginnings, so that no one shall be left" (4 Ezra 7:30; cf. *2 Bar.* 3:7). But the function of silence in the two texts differs. In 4 Ezra, it signals the end of history and a "clearing of the decks" so that the new creation can come about. The silence that presumably preceded God's creative word in Genesis is analogous to the silence that precedes the coming of the new world in 4 Ezra. This cannot be the case in Revelation, for the silence is only in heaven. It does not affect all creation. In 4 Ezra, furthermore, the silence does not intensify expectation in quite the same way as in Revelation, for it occurs at the end of the messianic reign and before the new world comes. In Revelation, the silence is the direct result of the opening of the seventh seal, so it directly contravenes the reader's or hearer's expectation that the consummation will come immediately.

Better parallels to the silence of Rev 8:1 are found in the prophets. The prophet Habakkuk proclaims, "The LORD is in his holy temple; let all the earth keep silence before him!" (2:20). The prophet Zephaniah commands, "Be silent before the Lord GOD! For the day of the LORD is at hand" (1:7). Zechariah proclaims, "Be silent, all people, before the LORD; for he has roused himself from his holy dwelling" (2:13). Silence is an appropriate response to God's presence in the temple. Silence is still more appropriate when the deity is roused to action. The final result of that rousing, the imminent day of the Lord, is still greater reason to be speechless before the immensity of what is taking place. Because of Revelation's eschatological outlook, the awaited divine visitation is the more awesome because it is the final one. This underscores the dramatic quality of the silence.

After the half-hour's silence, John sees seven angels to whom seven trumpets are given. Although the giver of the trumpets is not explicit, the passive voice suggests that it is God. In any case, everything that happens in the seventh seal is part of God's plan. The angels are "the seven angels who stand before God," implying that they are already known to John. Their standing before God signifies closeness to God and readiness to serve. Jewish tradition frequently attests to God's angelic attendants, and there are particular traditions about specific groups of attendants, among which are a group of seven. In the book of Tobit, an angel identifies himself as follows: "I am Raphael, one of the seven angels who stand ready and enter before the glory of the Lord" (12:15). The angel who appears to Zechariah, father of John the Baptist, says, "I am Gabriel. I stand in the presence of God" (Luke 1:19). The Greek of *First Enoch* 20 lists seven archangels, among whom are Raphael, Gabriel, and Michael (see Rev 12:7), each of whom has particular duties (Charles 1920, 1:225). It may be that the seven trumpeting angels are the same as "the seven spirits who are before his throne" (1:4), the seven stars in the hand of the one like a son of man (1:16) interpreted as "the angels of the seven churches" (1:20), the seven torches before the throne (4:5), and the Lamb's seven eyes, which are "the seven spirits of God sent out into all the earth" (5:6; see commentary on each of these passages). The angels who pour out the seven bowls of God's wrath in Revelation 16 may also be the same. They are called "the seven angels," which also assumes that they are known to the seer. The task of the angels in chapters 8 and 16 is analogous to the task of the four living creatures in chapter 6. They are among God's closest attendants and are agents through whom he sets in motion eschatological events.

Like the opening of the seals, the blowing of the trumpets unleashes eschatological happenings. Since the seventh seal contains the seven trumpets, and since Christ opens the seals whereas the angels blow the trumpets, the angels are subordinate to Christ. Trumpets are used for a great variety of purposes in the Bible. They summon the people for diverse reasons; are used in liturgical functions, including the new year festival and the coronation of kings; order the movements of the Israelite tribes in the desert; and are sounded in warfare, including holy war (Charles 1920, 1:255; Paulien 1988; see Giblin 1991 for an analysis of Revelation in terms of holy war patterns).

The best parallels to Revelation's trumpets are those passages in which the trumpet indicates the presence of God, particularly when that is combined with scenes of impending judgment. The Bible's classic theophany at Sinai combines the familiar thunder, lightning, smoke, and earthquake with the sound of a trumpet. Scenes of eschatological judgment often use such elements. A prophetic example is in Zephaniah:

> The great day of the LORD is near,
> near and hastening fast;
> the sound of the day of the LORD is bitter,
> the warrior cries aloud there.
> That day will be a day of wrath,
> a day of distress and anguish,
> a day of ruin and devastation,
> a day of darkness and gloom,
> a day of clouds and thick darkness,
> a day of trumpet blast and battle cry
> against the fortified cities
> and against the lofty battlements.
> (Zeph 1:14–16; cf. Joel 2:1; Isa 27:13)

Paul twice associates a trumpet with the eschaton (1 Thess 4:16; 1 Cor 15:52), and Matthew says of Jesus' second coming, "He will send out his angels with a loud trumpet call" (Matt 24:31). The Jewish apocalypse 4 Ezra, like Revelation, uses trumpets to signal impending eschatological suffering: "The trumpet shall sound aloud, and when all hear it, they shall suddenly be terrified" (6:23; see Charles 1920, 1:225).

The seven trumpets are both part of a heavenly liturgy and the initiators of cosmic disturbances and punishment of those without God's seal. These two things are intimately connected. Revelation contrasts the imperial cult and public ceremony with proper worship of God. In the heavenly liturgy, things are as they should be, for it is only the Lord of the universe that should be worshiped. It is this very liturgy that brings to an end the false sovereignty of Rome. When the prayers of the saints are included in the heavenly liturgy, as they are in 5:8, 6:10, and 8:3–5, their act of worship is part of the liturgy that brings about Rome's downfall. This makes still clearer why the seer calls Christian witness conquest.

Liturgical Interlude (8:3–5)

"Another angel" appears with a golden censer and stands at the altar. He "was given" (indicating that this is all part of God's will) much incense to offer "with the prayers of all the saints on the golden altar that is before the throne" (8:3). He then uses the censer to take fire from the altar and hurl it to the earth, "and there were peals of thunder, rumblings, flashes of lightning, and an earthquake" (8:5). All of this happens between the giving of the trumpets to the angels and their sounding the trumpets.

The scene echoes 5:8: "The four living creatures and the twenty-four elders fell before the Lamb, each holding a harp and golden bowls full of incense, which are the prayers of the saints" (5:8). It is oversubtle to try to make something out of the fact that in 5:8 the incense *is* the prayers, whereas in 8:3–4 the incense is offered *with* the prayers, or that in 5:8 the elders offer the prayers, whereas here it is an angel. The author is not concerned with such consistency. The point of each of the two scenes is that the prayers of Christians ascend to heaven and are presented by angels to God, an idea rooted in Jewish tradition (see commentary on 5:8). The first offering of the prayers and incense occurs when the Lamb is proclaimed as worthy to open the seals, and the second occurs after he has opened the seventh seal. Thus they frame the seals. This close association of the seals with the prayers of the saints suggests that the seals are a response to the prayers. This impression is confirmed by what follows.

The only other place that prayers of humans are mentioned in the eschatological visions is when the seer observes the souls of the martyrs beneath the altar in heaven in the fifth seal (6:9–11). Those souls pray for vengeance, and there follows the sixth seal in which the cosmos is disturbed and earth's frightened inhabitants realize that the wrath of God and the Lamb is approaching. It is fitting that at the opening of the seventh seal, which unleashes divine and demonic cosmic fury, the saints' prayers are again mentioned. The final events answer their prayer for vengeance. This is made still clearer when the angel who offers the incense and the prayers of the saints now uses the very same censer to take fire from the altar and to cast it on the earth (8:5; Charles 1920, 1:232). Then come "thunder, rumblings, flashes of lightning, and an earthquake," the usual signs of divine activity. These signs are associated with the seventh seal, trumpet, and bowl, as is appropriate for the culminating items of each series (Charles 1920, 1:232; Bauckham 1977).

The throwing of fire onto the earth symbolizes all that is to happen in the first six trumpets. As the author follows Ezekiel 9 in Revelation 7, so he follows Ezekiel 10 here. In Ezekiel 10, the prophet sees the divine chariot-throne and hears an angel being commanded, "Go within the wheelwork underneath the cherubim; fill your hands with burning coals from among the cherubim, and scatter them over the city" (10:2). It is remarkable that Ezekiel uses two images for the punishment God is about to inflict on the sinners in Jerusalem, but neither is narrated. In Ezekiel 9, the six angels are to kill the sinners with their weapons after the seventh angel seals them, but Ezekiel never narrates the slaughter. In chapter 10, Ezekiel has the angel gather fire from beneath the throne to scatter on the city, but the scattering is not explicitly recounted. Ezekiel uses the images of angelic slaughter and the scattering of coals to represent the destruction that comes on Jerusalem at the hands of the Babylonians. One cannot push his metaphors too far or insist too strongly on consistency. The same holds for Revelation, for which Ezekiel is a major model. The image of throwing fire onto the earth is juxtaposed with seven trumpets. Neither is to be taken absolutely literally, but each symbolizes in its own way something that is for the seer undeniable—God and the Lamb are coming in wrath, as the earth's inhabitants fearfully exclaim at the end of the sixth seal (6:16–17).

The liturgical scene in 8:3–5 refers backward to chapters 4–6 by alluding to the altar in heaven, God's throne, the prayers of the saints, the incense, the priestly angel, and the theophanic features. It refers forward to the destruction that the trumpets will do and to the theophanic features to occur in the seventh trumpet. The fact that 8:3–5 is so closely tied to what precedes and to what follows but is itself not the content of one of the trumpets means that it interlocks the seals and trumpets (Yarbro Collins 1990, 1006).

Chapter Seven

The Seven Trumpets (8:6–11:19)

The Seven Trumpets as a Whole

In 8:6, the trumpets are reintroduced by the statement that the seven angels make ready to blow them. This picks up the narrative of 8:2, forming a frame around the liturgical interlude in 8:3–5. The trumpet series is structured like that of the seals in that the first four items form a unit because of similarity of structure and content. The fifth and sixth items in each series are different in kind from the first four. There is an interlude between the sixth and seventh items of each series (chapter 7 for the seals; 10:1–11:13 for the trumpets). Each series is preceded by a heavenly liturgy (chapters 4 and 5 for the seals; 8:3–5 for the trumpets).

Although the two series have several similarities, they are also different in key ways. The trumpets are contained in the seventh seal, so there is a telescoping effect, which means that all of what the trumpets contain is also contained in the seven seals. The two series also differ considerably in their content. The first five seals concern happenings that from one point of view are everyday. War, social dislocation, famine, death through famine, disease, killing, and persecution—all of these would have been regular occurrences in the seer's world. Seen through the eyes of faith, such everyday occurrences can be eschatological, but there is nothing in them that demands such an explanation. The sixth seal is another matter. It concerns cosmic happenings that only God can control. Earth's inhabitants recognize this, for they ask the mountains and rocks to hide them from the wrath of God and the Lamb (6:17). In contrast to the first five seals, every trumpet concerns cosmic events. This is logical, since the trumpets are completely contained within the seventh seal, and in the sixth seal cosmic disturbances have already occurred.

An obvious chronological discrepancy between the seals and trumpets is that in the sixth seal all of the stars fall out of the sky, which is then rolled up like a scroll (6:13–14), whereas the trumpets assume that the stars are still there. A third of the stars cease to give their light in the fourth trumpet (8:12), and individual stars fall from heaven in the third and fifth trumpets (8:10; 9:1). Similarly, in the sixth seal the sun becomes black and the moon red (6:13), whereas in the fourth trumpet a third of their light is darkened (8:12). This last is not necessarily a contradiction, since it is not clear that the change in the sun and moon in 6:12 is permanent, although 6:13, where the sky is rolled up, would imply that. The fact that every mountain and island is removed from its place in the sixth seal (6:14) indicates that the earth is radically changed, but much in the trumpets implies that it remains as before. There are also discrepancies within the trumpets. The most obvious is that in the first trumpet all grass is burned up (8:7), but in the fifth trumpet the demonic locusts are told not to harm the grass (9:4). Charles (1920, 1:218–23) sees this as one among several indications of stages in the text resulting from the author's rewriting, whereas Mounce (1977, 185–86) claims that the destruction of the grass in the first trumpet applies to only one-third of the earth's grass, since it says, "A third of the earth was burned up." Commentators are reluctant to resort to dividing the text up into sources or stages, as Charles does. Mounce's proposal must contend with the explicit statement in the first trumpet that a third of the trees are burned, which makes one suspect that the rather different statement that "all" of the grass is burned means all of the grass on all of the earth.

One could write at length about such discrepancies in Revelation. Charles and others resort to source theories to account for them. In some cases their arguments have convinced scholars, but the trend in interpretation has been against chopping up the text. Whether one is speaking of one author who wrote all of Revelation, or of an author and one or more editors of his work, the fact remains that someone was relatively satisfied with the text as it stands.

A reasonable solution to such discrepancies is twofold. First, there is recapitulation throughout Revelation (see the introduction under "Structure"). It is not systematic in the sense that entire sequences of events are repeated, but one cannot assume a linear progression over the course of the book. This will become still clearer when we look at the seven bowls in chapter 16. Second, the imagery and metaphors in Revelation cannot be taken completely literally. They are evocative, and they present kaleidoscopic variations on ancient mythology, biblical texts, and apocalyptic scenarios. That is not to say that one can reduce them simply to symbolic narrative or even allegory. They reflect real events to some degree and anticipate actual happenings, but not in a simplistic, one-to-one, literal fashion.

The first five trumpets echo the exodus plagues. For the author, the endtime events are analogous to the exodus. Just as God rescued the people from Egypt using plagues, so now he rescues the new people of God using similar plagues. Just as God once punished the Egyptians for their oppression of Israel, so now he punishes the inhabitants of the earth for their persecution of Christians. The bowl sequence in Revelation 16 also echoes the exodus plagues, and so the bowls and trumpets are roughly parallel, supporting the recapitulation theory still further.

The First Trumpet (8:7)

When the first trumpet sounds, hail and fire mixed with blood are "thrown" onto the earth, and a third of the earth, the trees, and all of the grass are burned up (8:7). The verb "throw" is the same used in 8:5 when the angel "throws" fire from the altar onto the earth. The hail and fire mixed with blood recall the hail and fire of the seventh exodus plague (Exod 9:22–26) and the blood of the first exodus plague (Exod 7:20–21). The content of this trumpet is also reminiscent of Joel 1:19: "Fire has devoured the pastures of the wilderness, and flames have burned all the trees of the field," and Joel 2:30: "I will show portents in the heavens and on the earth, blood and fire and columns of smoke." Mounce (1977, 185) points to *Sib. Or.* 5:377–79 as another parallel for such an eschatological occurrence: "For fire will rain on men from the floors of heaven, fire and blood, water, lightning bolt, darkness, heavenly night, and destruction in war, a mist over the slain." Such images elicit suggestions about natural occurrences that may have given rise to them. Hail mixed with fire, for example, might derive from experience of a hailstorm in which there was thunder and lightning. Although such suggestions are possible, they miss the point of the author's imagery. For ancient Jews and Christians, all of nature was in God's power. There was no neat dichotomy between natural laws and God's action, a dichotomy that modern thought depends on to define "miraculous." That only a "third" of the earth and trees burn indicates that although the destruction is massive, it is not final. That there is a progression, or at the least an intensification, over the seals series is implied by the fact that in the fourth seal only one-quarter of earth's inhabitants are killed (6:8). The bowls in chapter 16 go further, speaking of complete destruction. The statement at the end of the sixth trumpet that humankind does not repent in spite of the plagues (9:20–21) implies that the partial nature of the catastrophe is meant to give humans time to repent.

The motif of a "third" is repeated in trumpets two, three, four, and six (cf. 12:4). Two possible backgrounds for the idea of a third are Ezekiel 5 and Zechariah 13. In Ezek 5:12, God says, "One third of you shall die of pestilence or be consumed by famine among you; one third shall fall by the sword around you; and one third I will scatter to every wind and will unsheathe the sword after them" (cf. 5:2). Zech 13:8–9 reads:

> In the whole land, says the LORD,
> two-thirds shall be cut off and perish,
> and one-third shall be left alive.
> And I will put this third into the fire,
> refine them as one refines silver,
> and test them as gold is tested.
> They will call on my name,
> and I will answer them.
> I will say, "They are my people";
> and they will say, "The LORD is our God."

An interesting aspect of this citation from Zechariah is that God's punishment is designed to bring about reconciliation with the people, yet Zechariah is even harsher than our seer, for two-thirds perish, and only one-third is reconciled to God. Given the background supplied by Zechariah, it is less surprising that God uses such extreme measures as are depicted in the trumpets to attempt to bring humanity to repentance (9:20–21).

The Second Trumpet (8:8–9)

The second trumpet causes "something like a great mountain, burning with fire" to be "thrown" into the sea, causing the sea to become blood, killing a third of its creatures, and destroying a third of its boats. This recalls the first exodus plague, where water becomes blood (Exod 7:20–21). A burning mountain thrown into the sea reminds some of volcanic islands or volcanoes located near the sea, such as Mount Vesuvius, which erupted in 79 C.E. and destroyed the city of Pompeii in Italy, south of Rome. Charles (1920, 1:234) notes that in *1 Enoch* 18:13 Enoch sees stars confined in the abyss for dereliction of duty that appear to him as "great, burning mountains" (cf. *1 Enoch* 21:3). Stars are heavenly beings, often thought to be angels (Mounce 1977, 192). The burning mountain in the second trumpet may have this as a background, but the author does not capitalize on the angel connection. In 8:8, the mountain appears to be inanimate.

An interesting parallel is indicated by Mounce (1977, 186) in the *Sibylline Oracles:* "A great star will come from heaven to the wondrous sea and will burn the deep sea and Babylon itself and the land of Italy, because of which many holy faithful Hebrews and a true people perished" (*Sib. Or.* 5:158–61). This comes from a Hellenistic Jewish prophetic collection written at about the same time as Revelation. Here, as in Revelation, "Babylon" is a cipher for Rome, and this author is angry with Rome over Jewish deaths, as Revelation is over persecution of Christians.

The Third Trumpet (8:10–11)

At the third trumpet, a blazing star falls from heaven onto the fresh rivers and springs (8:10–11). The star's name is "Wormwood," and it makes the waters bitter and poisonous. There is a general resemblance between trumpets two and three, especially if the background of the burning mountain in the second trumpet is that of a star. Whereas the burning mountain affects the sea, the falling star affects fresh waters. Wormwood is mentioned several times in the Bible as a bitter plant, but it is not poisonous (e.g., Prov 5:4; Lam 3:15). Our author has been influenced by the parallelism in Jer 9:15, where God says through the prophet, "I am feeding this people with wormwood, and giving them poisonous water to drink" (see also Jer 23:15; cf. Deut

29:17; Lam 3:19; Amos 6:12). In keeping with the motif of one-third, only a third of the fresh waters is affected. "Many died from the water" rather than one-third, but this may be a stylistic variant (Mounce 1977, 188).

The Fourth Trumpet (8:12)

The fourth trumpet results in the striking of the sun, moon, and stars so that "a third of their light was darkened." The end of the verse clarifies that this does not mean that their intensity was reduced by a third but that their length of shining was reduced by that amount. This contrasts with the sixth seal, where the sun completely stops giving its light; the moon becomes as blood; and the sky is rolled up. Darkness is a common feature of eschatological scenarios (see Isa 30:26; Joel 2:30; 3:15; Amos 8:9; see Mounce 1977, 188), and it is reminiscent of the ninth exodus plague (Exod 10:21).

The Three Woes (8:13)

In the seals series the first four form a unit, being different in form and content from the last three, but there is no formal divider between the first four and the last three. The trumpets do have such a divider, one which focuses attention on the final three trumpets. It divides the first four trumpets, which focus on the attack on the cosmic order, from the next two, which speak of demonic plagues that afflict humankind. After the fourth trumpet, the seer sees and hears an eagle (or a vulture, since the words are the same in Greek) crying "with a loud voice" in midheaven, "Woe, woe, woe to the inhabitants of the earth, at the blasts of the other trumpets that the three angels are about to blow" (8:13; cf. *2 Bar.* 77:19–26). At the conclusion of the fifth trumpet, the narrator declares that the first woe is past and the second is to come (9:12), showing that the fifth trumpet is the first woe. After the sixth trumpet and the interlude that follows, the narrator announces that the second woe has passed and that the third is coming soon (11:14), thus identifying the sixth trumpet and perhaps the interlude as the second woe. There is no final statement about the third woe, leaving its interpretation uncertain, but it is probably to be identified with the seventh and last trumpet. Because the phrase "inhabitants of the earth" is negative in Revelation, the coming events are woeful not to Christians but to their enemies.

The Fifth Trumpet (9:1–12)

The fifth angel blows the trumpet, and a star falls from heaven to earth (9:1). In this way the fifth trumpet resembles the third and to a lesser extent the second. The star is not inanimate, for it is given a task to perform. Stars are frequently identified with angels, and the identification applies in this case. Some have taken the word "fallen" to mean cast out of heaven, in the sense of "fallen angel," but Charles (1920, 1:238–39) shows that applied to stars it does not necessarily carry this meaning. Many commentators adduce as parallels Isa 14:12, which uses the metaphor of a star fallen from heaven to speak of the downfall of the king of Babylon, and Luke 10:18, in which Jesus sees Satan fall from heaven. Those parallels are more appropriate for Revelation 12, where Satan is cast out of heaven. This star is God's agent sent to accomplish the first woe. He "was given the key to the shaft of the bottomless pit [literally: abyss]" (9:1). The passive voice of "was given" with no agent specified implies that it is God who gives the key and the task associated with it.

The star opens the pit, and bizarre, otherworldly locusts emerge to torture earth's inhabitants. They are not allowed to harm anyone having "the seal of God on their foreheads" (9:4). This is the first reference to this seal since 7:1–3, leading Charles to conclude that the 144,000 are sealed in order to protect them from these three woes (1920, 1:188–89). The word "abyss" can have several senses in the Bible and in early Jewish and Christian literature (Charles 1920, 1:239–42; Mounce 1977, 193). There is no single definitive cosmology in the Bible or in early Jewish or Christian literature, and thus the precise definition of "abyss" changes. It can mean a place below the earth, perhaps the site where the subterranean waters are, called "the deep" (*tehom*) in the Hebrew Bible. The abyss appears elsewhere in Jewish and Christian literature as the place of temporary or permanent punishment for angels and demons (*1 Enoch* 18–21; Luke 8:31). Charles (1920, 239) offers the following definition for Revelation: "The abyss is conceived of as the *preliminary* place of punishment of the fallen angels, of demons, of the Beast, and the false Prophet, and the prison for 1000 years of Satan. It is referred to in ix. 1, 2, 11, xi. 7, xvii. 8, xx. 1, 3." The "lake of fire" is the final place of punishment for demon and human alike in Revelation (19:20; 20:10, 14–15). In 20:1, an angel comes down from heaven with the key to the abyss and locks Satan there for the duration of the Lamb's thousand-year reign. The angels with the key to the abyss in 9:1 and 20:1 are apparently the same. In the fifth trumpet, the terrifying locusts from the abyss are properly termed demonic because of their origin and description.

When the shaft of the abyss is opened, smoke "like the smoke of a great furnace" pours out and darkens the sun and air (cf. Gen 19:24; Exod 19:18). The smoke indicates that the abyss is a fiery place. Then locusts emerge from the abyss. This locust plague recalls the eighth exodus plague (Exod 10:4–20), but the description has been heavily influenced by Joel 2. The prophet Joel interpreted an invasion of locusts as punishment of Israel. "Locusts" is a name applied to grasshoppers when they come in large and destructive swarms. They are a danger even in the modern world and require steps to keep them in check, including such measures as spraying by airplane. In the ancient world, huge swarms of locusts were disastrous when they descended on farmland and devastated it in a short time, leading to famine and death. This made locusts an apt choice for the eighth exodus plague. The description of the locusts in Revelation is in two main parts. The first (9:3–6) focuses on their effect, and the second (9:7–11) concentrates on their appearance.

The demonic locusts are said to be like scorpions, which inflict a painful sting with their tails but generally do not kill humans. The scorpionlike locusts are allowed to carry on their dismal work for five months (9:5, 10). Some propose that this time period corresponds to the life span of locusts. The strange combination of locust and scorpion can be explained as follows. The author chooses locusts because they are one of the exodus plagues, because Joel uses them to describe a punishing scourge from God and supplies a description the author finds compelling, and because of their military associations (see below). But the author wants this plague to be against people, not against vegetation, as would be natural with locusts. The three woes must attack people directly, for they represent God's fierce punishment meant to lead to repentance. Scorpions, although their main victims would be other insects or small animals, were fearsome and were a useful image for pain that does not kill. By introducing a plague that does not kill in this fifth trumpet, the author is able to escalate to a fatal plague in the sixth trumpet. The extent of the anguish inflicted by these strange creatures is expressed by the assertion that people seek death to escape the pain but do not receive that relief (9:6).

The second part of the trumpet is a detailed description of the locusts (9:7–10). They look like horses equipped for battle, with golden crowns, human faces, hair like women's hair, teeth like lions' teeth, scales like armor; their wings sound like horses and chariots going to battle; and they have tails like scorpions with stingers in them. Joel is a major source for this description. Joel 1:6 compares the locust swarm to a foreign invasion:

> For a nation has invaded my land,
>   powerful and innumerable;
> its teeth are lions' teeth,
>   and it has the fangs of a lioness.

In 1:19, Joel compares the locusts to a fire that burns land and trees (the verse was quoted above as background for the first trumpet). Joel continues,

> Blow the trumpet in Zion;
>   sound the alarm on my holy mountain!
> Let all the inhabitants of the land tremble,
>   for the day of the LORD is coming, it is near—
> a day of darkness and gloom,
>   a day of clouds and thick darkness! . . .
> Fire devours in front of them,
>   and behind them a flame burns. . . .
> They [the locusts] have the appearance of horses,
>   and like war-horses they charge.
> As with the rumbling of chariots,
>   they leap on the tops of the mountains,
> like the crackling of a flame of fire
>   devouring the stubble,
> like a powerful army
>   drawn up for battle. . . .
> The earth quakes before them,
>   the heavens tremble.
> The sun and moon are darkened,
>   and the stars withdraw their shining. (Joel 2:1–5, 10)

Common to Joel and Revelation are the connection of the locust plague to the blast of a trumpet, use of the term "inhabitants of the land [earth]," the comparison of the locusts to an army, the darkening of the sun in Joel by the locust swarm and in Revelation by the smoke from which the locusts come, the comparison of the locusts' teeth to lions' teeth and their sound to the rumbling of chariots. The general resemblance of locusts' heads to those of horses has often been noted in diverse literatures. Mounce notes, "An Arabian proverb is often quoted to the effect that the locust has a head of a horse, a breast like a lion, feet like a camel, body like a serpent, and antennae like the hair of a maiden" (1977, 196). Horse's head, lions, and maiden's hair all appear in Revelation's description. Some see in the locusts' flowing hair reference to Parthian warriors, who are alluded to in the next trumpet. The locusts have what appear to be crowns, possibly a reference back to the first horseman, who wears a crown and who also may recall the Parthians. The claim that the locusts have scales like breastplates is natural, given the appearance of their bodies. They have human faces. This intensifies their demonic aspect, for they are not animals but rational beings (Mounce 1977, 196).

The fifth trumpet closes with the words, "They have as king over them the angel of the bottomless pit; his name in Hebrew is Abaddon, and in Greek he is called Apollyon" (9:11). Charles asserts, "We have no means of identifying the angel of the abyss beyond the statement here. In fact, as a person he does not exist outside this verse" (1920, 1:245). The word "Abaddon" occurs several times in the Bible (Job 26:6; 28:22; 31:12; Ps 88:11; Prov 15:11; 27:20). In Job and Proverbs, it is in synonymous parallelism with Sheol, the Hebrew word for the underworld where people go after death. The basic meaning of Abaddon is "destruction," so the Greek word used to translate it here, "Apollyon," meaning "destroyer," fits. Some detect a reference to the Greek god Apollo, with whom the emperors Nero and Domitian identified. Charles notes that an ancient Greek etymology derived the name Apollo from the same root from which "Apollyon" comes (1920, 246). Schüssler Fiorenza remarks, "If such a pun is intended, then the author ironically asserts that the destructive hosts of the abyss have as their king the Roman emperor who claims to be the divine incarnation of Apollo" (1991, 72). It would be a mistake to identify Abaddon with the angel who descends to unlock the abyss in 9:1 and 20:1, for that angel is on God's side.

Yarbro Collins (1990, 1006) notes that the fifth trumpet foreshadows the scene in 20:1–3, 7–8. In these latter verses an angel descends from heaven with the key of the abyss (as in 9:1) and imprisons Satan there for a thousand years so that the messianic kingdom can come. After the thousand years, Satan reemerges and gathers "the nations at the four corners of the earth, Gog and Magog," and surrounds Jerusalem and the saints (see Ezekiel 38–39). Fire comes from heaven and destroys him.

The Sixth Trumpet (9:13–21)

The fifth trumpet is identical with the first woe, and the next two trumpets correspond to the other two woes (9:12). The fifth trumpet shows the detail and focus that one would expect from an event the author already showcases by the eagle's announcement of the three impending woes. The same holds for the sixth trumpet. It is unique in that the angel who blows this trumpet has a role in the ensuing action. The chain of intermediaries present here emphasizes both God's transcendence and his control of the world: the sixth angel blows his trumpet, which leads to a "voice from the four horns of the golden altar before God," a voice that orders the angel to release four angels held at the Euphrates, who then turn into marauding armies. This chain reaction creates a direct relationship between the heavenly world and the plague on earth but preserves God's distance from what happens on earth. Because the altar is gold, it is like the altar of incense in the Jerusalem temple. Ancient Near Eastern altars often had a "horn" on each corner. The "voice" here is not identified further. Possibly the altar itself speaks. But the author may refer back to the altar under which the martyrs rest (6:9) and at which the angel offers incense and the prayers of the saints (8:3), so that the voice is that of the martyrs. In that case, the altar creates yet another connection between the coming affliction of the Christians' enemies and the prayers of martyrs and faithful Christians.

The four angels bound at the Euphrates River are otherwise unknown, despite the fact that the definite article implies that they are familiar. They are not the same as the four angels in 7:1–3. Charles notes that in chapter 7 they are at the four corners of the earth, but here they are at the Euphrates; there they hold back the destructive winds, but here they themselves are held back from destroying (1920, 1:248). When the angels are released, a huge army attacks and kills a third of humankind. Charles rightly points to *1 Enoch* 56 as containing a scene similar to the one here. In *1 Enoch,* God proclaims, "In those days, the angels will assemble and thrust themselves to the east at the Parthians and Medes. They will shake up the kings [so that] a spirit of unrest shall come upon them, and stir them up from their thrones.... And they will go up and trample upon the land of my elect ones" (*1 Enoch* 56:5–6; cf. *T. Moses* 3:2). As Charles says, *1 Enoch* alters Ezekiel's expectation of marauding eschatological armies from the north (Ezekiel 38–39) and applies it to Parthian and Median armies from the east. The Euphrates River, to the north and east of Palestine, formed the boundary between the Parthian empire and the Roman empire. In our commentary on the first horseman (6:2), we pointed out possible allusions to the Parthians. Like *1 Enoch,* Revelation refers to dreaded Parthian armies from the east. The seer transforms armies that attack Israel (as in Ezekiel and *1 Enoch*) into armies that attack the inhabitants of the earth. Detailed comparisons between the seven trumpets and the seven bowls of chapter 16 await analysis of that chapter, but it should be noted that the sixth trumpet is very similar to the sixth bowl, which refers to "kings from the east" whose way is prepared by the angel who pours his bowl on the Euphrates.

The four angels are released, and the armies from the Euphrates advance to kill a third of humankind. The author says that the angels have been "held ready for the hour, the day, the month, and the year." God precisely ordains all that happens, an idea present in the Bible but especially prevalent in apocalypticism (e.g., *1 Enoch* 92:2; 1QS 3–4). The army from the east is huge, two hundred million strong. The Greek actually says two myriads times a myriad. The number has no special significance except as meaning, for the ancient mind, an almost inconceivably large number (see Ps 68:17; Dan 7:10; Rev 5:11).

The army is a gigantic cavalry, and the horses do the damage, not the riders. The attention to horses recalls Hab 1:8: "Their horses are swifter than leopards, more menacing than wolves at dusk." The riders in Revelation wear "breastplates the color of fire and of sapphire and of sulfur," colors that relate to what comes out of their horses' mouths—"fire and smoke and sulfur" (9:17). Mounce remarks, "Fire-breathing monsters were common in mythology. John's source is probably Leviathan, the sea-monster, of Job 41 ('out of his mouth go flaming torches . . . out of his nostrils comes forth smoke,' vss. 19–20)" (1977, 203). The horses have lions' heads, which makes them otherworldly and fearsome. Fire and smoke are common features of theophanies and judgment scenes. Sulfur, in older translations, is "brimstone." It is a substance found in and around volcanoes, and so it fits the fiery and violent images common in Revelation (for references to brimstone, see 14:10; 19:20; 21:8). In Genesis, "The LORD rained on Sodom and Gomorrah sulfur and fire from the LORD out of heaven" (Gen 19:24; cf. Jude 7).

What comes out of the horses' mouths harms humans, and so does the activity of their tails, which are like serpents with heads that do damage. In this way they are similar to the locusts of the previous trumpet who do damage with their tails. An important difference between the locust army and that of the eastern cavalry is that the former merely tortures, while the latter kills, signaling an escalation in the action.

Revelation 9:20–21 says that the humans not killed by the trumpet plagues do not repent (cf. 16:9, 11, 21). This recalls Pharaoh's repeated refusals to repent in the face of the exodus plagues. It also may be an ironic mirror image of Christians' refusal to "repent" when challenged by Romans in court, as Pliny reports, for example (Boring 1989, 138). The rest of the passage enumerates the sins of which these people were guilty. The list is in two parts, each of which begins with the words, "They did not repent of. . . . "

The sin of the first part of the list is idolatry, and its description is the most detailed of all the sins (9:20). The author considered the Roman empire idolatrous. The author begins by defining idolatry as the worship of demons, a common Jewish and Christian assessment (see Deut 32:17; Mic 5:12; Ps 106:37; 1 Cor 8:5; 10:20). Revelation does not see the worship of idols as serving beings that do not exist. They do exist and are demonic. The worship of demons, be it through the imperial cult or through local guild meetings, is not neutral or meaningless. It is aligning oneself with those superhuman powers that oppose God. It is choosing the wrong side in the great final battle.

The attribution of real power to the demons that idols represent does not prevent the author from drawing on the long Jewish tradition of ridiculing the worship of idols on the grounds that they are lifeless and powerless. That tradition is hinted at when the 144,000 are sealed with the "seal of the living God."

"Living God" is often used to contrast the true God with lifeless idols. As 9:20 says, these idols are made "of gold and silver and bronze and stone and wood, which cannot see or hear or walk." This sort of criticism is also found in such passages as Isa 40:18–20; 41:6–7; 44:9–20; Jeremiah 10; and Ps 115:3–8.

The second part of the list consists of sins of human behavior – murder, sorcery, fornication, and theft. Such lists are common in ancient texts, Jewish, Christian, and philosophical. Jewish and Christian tradition associates idolatry closely with such behavior. In early Christianity it was not unusual to assume that anyone who had the wrong doctrine must of necessity engage in such behavior. This was especially true of idolatry. A classic text is Romans 1, where Paul attributes the vast array of Gentiles' misconduct to their failure to acknowledge the one God. Three of the four sins in Rev 9:21 are of such a basic nature as to be included in the Ten Commandments. The fourth, sorcery, is a broad term encompassing various forms of witchcraft and magic. We already noted a possible antimagic polemic in the messages to the churches in chapters 2 and 3, a polemic pointed out by Aune (1987). In 18:23, Rome is told, "All the nations were deceived by your sorcery." The deceptions of the imperial cult (13:13–15) are excellent examples of what the author may mean.

As in the seals series, there is now an interlude consisting of 10:1–11:13. It is only after that interlude that we get the summarizing statement, "The second woe has passed. The third woe is coming very soon" (11:14). This could be taken to imply that the entire complex of the sixth seal plus the long interlude are all part of the second woe. However, the interlude itself does not describe punishment of the "inhabitants of the earth." Rather it addresses the role of the faithful Christian prophets in the context of the plagues.

Interlude: Prophetic Witness (10:1–11:13)

Just as there is a twofold interlude (chapter 7) between the sixth and seventh seals, so there is a twofold interlude (10:1–11:13) between the sixth and seventh trumpets. Just as the focus of the first interlude is the status and role of the faithful in view of the ongoing and impending plagues, this is also the focus of the second interlude (Mounce 1977, 205). The two visions of the first interlude were closely joined in that the first showed a limited number of faithful who were sealed for the final tribulation (7:1–8), while the second pictured an innumerable multitude safe with God after that tribulation (7:9–17). The second interlude is one vision introduced by a single "And I saw" (10:1). It is in two parts that are closely joined because in the first (chapter 10) the seer receives a new commission to prophesy, and in the second (11:1–13) he performs a prophetic symbolic action (11:1–3) leading into a section dealing with the role of Christian prophets in the last days (11:4–13). The whole interlude can be treated under the heading "Prophetic Witness."

Recommissioning of the Seer (Chapter 10)

The first part of the interlude consists of chapter 10 and includes a recommissioning of the seer as prophet. The chapter contains many parallels with chapter 1, where John is originally commissioned by the one like a son of man, and with chapter 5, where he sees the Lamb commissioned by taking the sealed scroll containing the events about which John is to prophesy. Chapters 5 and 10 both mention a "mighty angel" associated with the scroll that has to do with the commissioning of each figure.

The sealed scroll in chapter 5 holds the content of "what must take place after this" that John is called up into heaven to learn in 4:1. The seals on the scroll are opened in chapters 6 and 8. In chapter 10, John sees "another angel, a mighty one," coming down out of heaven with a scroll in his hand, this one open (10:1–2). The scene in chapter 10 assumes that the seer is now on earth, though his movement from heaven to earth is not recorded. For the rest of the book he sometimes seems to be in heaven, sometimes on earth. He sees everything in each sphere that relates to his message. The angel who comes down is "wrapped in a cloud, with a rainbow over his head; his face was like the sun, and his legs like pillars of fire." This description draws connections between the angel and both God and Christ. It is also reminiscent of the angelic figure in Daniel 10 and 12, which influenced the picture of Christ in Revelation 1.

In Daniel 10, the prophet stands on the banks of the Tigris River and sees "a man clothed in linen, with a belt of gold from Uphaz around his waist. His body was like beryl, his face like lightning, his eyes like flaming torches, his arms and legs [Greek manuscripts have either legs or feet] like the gleam of burnished bronze, and the sound of his words like the roar of a multitude" (Dan 10:5–6). Our author adapts most of these features to describe the one like a son of man in Rev 1:12–16 (see comments there). Among other changes he makes in Daniel, the one like a son of man has a face that shines like the sun (instead of lightning), and it is just his feet (not arms and feet) that are like burnished bronze. The word translated "burnished" here literally means "burned" or "purified by fire." The angel of Revelation 10 also has a face like the sun. His feet (not legs, thus agreeing with Revelation 1 instead of Daniel 10) are like "pillars of fire." The angel is wrapped in a cloud, a detail that recalls Rev 1:7, where Christ is the one "coming on the clouds," a detail derived from the picture of the son of man in Daniel 7. In Revelation 14, the one like a son of man is seen sitting on a cloud.

Two of the features of the angel in Revelation 10 that do not correspond to features of the one like a son of man are his having a rainbow over his head and having feet that are like "pillars" of fire, features that are associated with God. In Rev 4:3, depending on Ezek 1:27–28, a rainbow surrounds God's throne. The word "pillar" when associated with fire and cloud recalls the pillar of fire and cloud that led Israel through the Red Sea and the wilderness at the exodus (Exod 13:21). In Exod 14:19, God and an angel are closely associated in the context of the pillar: "The angel of God who was going before the Israelite army moved and went behind them; and the pillar of cloud moved from in front of them and took its place behind them." Mounce (1977, 207–8) cites Farrer's creative interpretation of the angel in Revelation 10: "The description of the angel fits his message—the affirming of God's fidelity to his covenants (10:7): the bow reminding of God's promise through Noah, the pillar of fire God's presence in the wilderness, and the scroll the tablets of stone." The angel stands with one foot on the land and one on the sea, a colossal figure with a message of great significance to the whole universe. He roars like a lion, another divine touch (Hos 11:10; Amos 1:2; 3:8; Joel 3:16; in 4 Ezra 11:37, the messiah is a roaring lion).

The detail with which the angel is described, unique for an angel in Revelation, and the terms used highlight the importance of this scene, which recommissions the seer. The angel is a powerful and authoritative heavenly figure who is an agent of God and Christ. Boring's reflections on this scene are instructive (1989, 139):

The figure of the angel is thus transparent to the figures of God and Christ who speak through him. As in 1:1–2 and throughout Revelation, the images of God, Christ, Spirit/angel collapse into each other. The ultimate Revealer is God, who defines and represents himself in Christ and communicates with the prophet by means of the angel. Although the figures are kept somewhat distinct, the imagery overlaps in such a way that God/Christ/angel are all presented to the mind's eye by the one picture.

When the angel roars, seven thunders sound. Thunder is a common feature in Revelation, and it is associated with God's presence and action and also represents the voices of heavenly beings. John 12:29 supplies a parallel, where God speaks to Jesus in thunder and it is interpreted by bystanders as an angel speaking to him. A closer parallel is Psalm 29, which has as its theme the voice of God. After an initial exhortation to praise, the psalm continues,

> The voice of the LORD is over the waters;
> the God of glory thunders,
> the LORD, over mighty waters.
> The voice of the LORD is powerful,
> the voice of the LORD is full of majesty. (Ps 29:3–4)

The phrase "the voice of the LORD" occurs seven times in the psalm, leading some to surmise that this very psalm inspired our author to conceive of seven thunders answering the angel's roar.

In the seer's original commissioning, Christ tells him to write down what he sees (1:11, 19). The seer's remarks in 10:4 show that he has been obeying that injunction to this point in the book: "When the seven thunders had sounded, I was about to write, but I heard a voice from heaven saying, 'Seal up what the seven thunders have said, and do not write it down'" (10:4). The injunction to seal the revelation in 10:4 recalls the end of Daniel, where Daniel is told twice that his revelation must remain sealed because it pertains not to his own but to a future time (12:4, 9). At the end of Revelation the seer is told, "Do not seal up the words of the prophecy of this book, for the time is near" (22:10; see comments there), but 10:4 indicates that our seer is privy to heavenly revelation that must be kept secret as well. This heightens the mysteriousness of the other world. Even the seer cannot disclose all of his experience. Similarly, the apostle Paul is not free to make public what he learns on his heavenly journey. Paul says that he "was caught up into Paradise" and "heard things that are not to be told, that no mortal is permitted to repeat" (2 Cor 12:3–4). Our seer hears material that falls into this same category, even though he writes most of what he sees and hears.

Various commentators attempt to guess why the seer is told not to write down what the seven thunders say. Schüssler Fiorenza (1991, 75) suggests that the thunders may have revealed the time of the end. In the New Testament the answer to the question about the precise time of the end is avoided. For example, in Mark 13:32, Jesus says that not even he knows when it is, and various passages indicate that it should not be of concern to Christians (Acts 1:7; 1 Thess 5:1–2). Mounce (1977, 209) thinks that perhaps the seven thunders are seven plagues, on the analogy of the seven seals, trumpets, and bowls. God then omits the seven plagues of the seven thunders because the previous plagues did not cause humanity to repent, so further ones would be futile, and God has decided not to delay the end any longer. Indeed, the next action in the scene is the angel's oath that there will be no more delay (10:5–7). This proposal is bolstered by the statement in Mark's apocalyptic discourse that God shortened the days of the end for the sake of the elect (Mark 13:20).

What happens next in Revelation 10 is clearly based on Daniel. In Daniel 12:5, the angel is asked when the eschaton will come. The text continues, "The man clothed in linen [the same as the angel in Daniel 10], who was upstream, raised his right hand and his left hand toward heaven. And I heard him swear by the one who lives forever that it would be for a time, two times, and half a time" (12:7). Daniel does not understand these words (12:8). He is told later in the chapter first that the end will come in 1,290 days, and then that it will come in 1,335 days. These figures are variant calculations of the three-and-a-half "times" of Dan 12:7, each "time" being a year (cf. Dan 8:14; see Collins 1993). Daniel's three-and-a-half times, or forty-two months, fascinated our seer, as we shall see.

Revelation's scene is strikingly similar to the one in Daniel 12, with the significant difference that the time before the end is extremely short:

> Then the angel whom I saw standing on the sea and the land raised his right hand to heaven and swore by him who lives forever and ever, who created heaven and what is in

> it, the earth and what is in it, and the sea and what is in it: "There will be no more delay, but in the days when the seventh angel is to blow his trumpet, the mystery of God will be fulfilled, as he announced to his servants the prophets." (Rev 10:5–7)

Like Daniel's angel, this angel raises his hand to heaven (with the difference that Daniel's angel raises both hands). For both Daniel and Revelation, this is a gesture of oath-taking. In both Daniel and Revelation, the angel swears by the one who lives forever, and Revelation adds an elaborate threefold reference to God's identity as creator. Charles notes that although reference to God as creator is frequent in the Hebrew Bible, it is far less so in the New Testament (1920, 1:263). Most of the New Testament references are in the book of Revelation. Revelation affirms God's sovereignty over all humanity, and to do this it refers to the beginning and end of everything, a common strategy in Jewish and Christian apocalypticism. God created everything in the beginning, and at the end God will regain complete dominance over it.

The angel's declaration implies that the eschatological events preceding his announcement have delayed the end and that no more such events are pending. The "mystery" to be revealed has been the subject of much discussion. In an apocalyptic context, mysteries are secrets of the other world accessible only to the seer or to those whom the seer enlightens. These mysteries are often of an eschatological nature, as in Rom 11:25–26 and 1 Cor 15:50–57. This corresponds to a view of scripture widely attested in early Christianity that assumes that God hid secrets in the prophets that were only understood later. The same view is found in the Dead Sea Scrolls. The pesher (commentary) on the prophetic book of Habakkuk says,

> God told Habakkuk to write down that which would happen to the final generation, but he did not make known to him when time would come to an end. And as for that which he said, *That he who reads may read it speedily:* interpreted this concerns the Teacher of Righteousness, to whom God made known all the mysteries of the words of His servants the Prophets. (1QpHab 7:1–6)

This passage alludes to Amos 3:7: "Surely the Lord GOD does nothing, without revealing his secret to his servants the prophets." For the community of the Dead Sea Scrolls, the Teacher of Righteousness, its founder, was God's servant, a prophet, who decoded the hidden meanings in scripture. Revelation uses the same passage from Amos (Rev 10:7), this time to indicate that the eschatological events shown to the seer were announced to the prophets. So the author is the one who has been given the key to understand what was promised to the prophets.

Suggestions that limit the mystery's content to one or another element of the events yet to be described in Revelation are unconvincing. An ambiguity in the Greek of Rev 10:7 is retained by the NRSV translation, which leaves open whether the disclosure of the mystery is to come when the seventh angel blows the seventh trumpet or when that angel is *about* to blow the trumpet. The former makes more sense. When the seventh trumpet is blown, it brings about the goal of the seer's entire revelation, the defeat of God's enemies and the permanent and complete establishment of God's kingdom throughout the cosmos (11:15–19). The "mystery" now revealed is the imminent coming of God's kingdom (for other suggestions about the content of the mystery, see Charles 1920, 1:265–66; Schüssler Fiorenza 1991, 75–76).

Questions about whether the prophets mentioned in Amos 3:7 and Rev 10:7 are biblical prophets or Christian prophets are misplaced, because the seer makes no such distinction, just as he does not see Christianity as a new religion. It is the culmination of God's plan, expressed to Israel through the prophets, to reestablish divine sovereignty.

The seer is now told to take the scroll from the angel's hand (10:8). As he does so, the angel tells him to eat the scroll and that it will be sweet in his mouth but bitter to his stomach. The angel then says, "You must prophesy again about many peoples and nations and languages and kings" (10:11). Ezekiel 2–3 is the basis of this scene, just as it contributes to the picture of the Lamb receiving the scroll in Revelation 5 (see commentary on Revelation 5 for a quotation of Ezekiel). In Ezek 2:8–3:3, the prophet hears God telling him to eat what God will give him. God gives him a scroll written on front and back in which are words of woe. He eats the scroll, which is sweet in his mouth and fills his stomach, and is then told to prophesy to Israel. In our comments on Revelation 5, we compare all three passages, Revelation 5, 10, and Ezekiel 2–3. Revelation 5 uses the elements of a scroll in

God's hand that has writing on both sides and the Lamb taking the scroll. Revelation 10 uses the idea that there is a scroll in the hand of a heavenly figure and the eating of the scroll that is sweet, as God's word is sweet (Pss 19:10; 119:103; Jer 15:16, 17). In both Ezekiel and Revelation the eating of the scroll symbolizes that the prophet must internalize the message that comes from God before sharing it.

Common to Revelation 5 and 10 are a heavenly figure with a heavenly scroll in his hand and the taking of that scroll by someone else. Further, in both chapters a "mighty angel" plays a role. In chapter 5, he tells John that the Lamb can open the scroll, and in chapter 10, he brings the scroll down from heaven and gives it to John to eat. The points of contact between Revelation 5 and 10 reaffirm the nature of Revelation 10 as a recommissioning of the seer. In chapter 1, the one like a son of man tells the seer to write down coming events, events contained in the sealed scroll of chapter 5. In chapter 5, the Lamb receives the commission to open the sealed scroll. In chapter 10, as the seventh trumpet is about to be blown that brings to a conclusion the scroll's seventh seal, an open scroll is mentioned that contains what the seer will write for the rest of the book.

The scrolls in chapters 5 and 10 differ in that the former is sealed and the latter is open. This has been read in a number of ways. One possibility is that it is the same scroll in each case (Mazzaferri 1989). The scroll of chapter 5 has now been fully unsealed, and only now can its contents be conveyed to the seer. All of the events recounted to this point are merely accompaniments to the opening of the scroll's seals. Since the trumpets are part of the seventh seal, all of the action since chapter 5 concerns the opening of the seals. Only now can the seer finally disclose the scroll's contents, symbolized by the open scroll.

There is a certain common sense to the observation that the scroll cannot be read until all seven seals are broken. In this reading, the open scroll contains either the rest of Revelation or some portion of it, such as the second part of the interlude (11:1–13), or the seventh trumpet (11:15–19), or the rest of the book, or some combination of those passages (see Mounce 1977, 215–16, for other theories). But we must reject this hypothesis. Our main objection comes from the conviction that as each seal of the first scroll is opened, the eschatological events contained in the scroll occur.

Yarbro Collins finds a solution to the puzzle of the two scrolls in the theory of recapitulation, according to which the book does not unfold in a chronologically unilinear way (1990, 1007). Rather, parts of Revelation review things that happen in other parts and restate them or look at them from different perspectives. By the seventh trumpet, everything that must happen has happened, so the essential contents of the sealed scroll are fully revealed once the trumpet is blown. This means that the second part of Revelation, beginning in chapter 12, recapitulates the first part. This is supported by the fact that there is a complete break between chapters 11 and 12. An examination of chapters 12 to 22 will confirm that they do cover the same material as is treated in the earlier chapters, but they do so in greater detail and with more focus. Yarbro Collins interprets the notice that the second scroll is open in this light. The revelation of chapters 6 to 11, represented by the sealed scroll, is veiled and oblique, and that of chapters 12 to 22, symbolized by the open scroll, is less so. Since the open scroll recapitulates the closed one, the sealed scroll received by the Lamb does contain the fullness of the eschatological events.

The recommissioning scene in chapter 10 interlocks the second part of Revelation with the first. Chapter 10 is an interlude between the sixth and seventh trumpets, but the content of the scroll that it contains is chapters 12–22, and the recommissioning of the seer in 10:11 concerns his disclosure of material that does not begin until chapter 12. The seer is told to prophesy again "about many peoples and nations and languages and kings" (10:11). This is the same fourfold formula found throughout Revelation and based on Daniel (Rev 5:9; 7:9; 11:9; 13:7; 14:6; 17:15). In this case "tribes" has been replaced by "kings." This conforms to the more focused nature of chapters 12 and onward. In these later chapters, the seer speaks frequently of the kings of the earth and their opposition to God and consequent defeat and punishment.

Measuring the Temple (11:1–2)

Chapter 11 continues the interlude begun in 10:1. The continuation of the interlude is in two parts. The first is a command to the seer to measure God's temple, the altar, and the worshipers (11:1–2). The second is about God's two witnesses who will prophesy, die, rise from the dead, and ascend into heaven (11:3–13). The chapter division gives the false impression that

11:1 is a new start in the text, but there is no break in the action. The formula "And I saw" in 10:1 covers the entire interlude (10:1–11:13), which is then a single vision.

Charles (1920, 1:270–73) offers detailed argument for seeing 11:1–2 and 11:3–13 as built on two preexistent and independent visions picked up and adapted by the author. Each vision assumes the existence of Jerusalem, and the first assumes that the temple still stands, so the original visions must be dated to before the destruction of 70 C.E. The material in 11:1–13 has been subject to a wide variety of interpretations, ranging from efforts to discover a close relation between the text and the world outside of the text, to considering the text to be highly symbolic, rendering attempts to find history in it futile. Specific issues are the identities of the temple, the holy city, and the two witnesses. Charles (1920, 1:273) shows that words are used differently in this passage than in the rest of the book, making interpretation of the text still more difficult. He attributes this discontinuity with the rest of Revelation to the author's use of preexistent sources.

Chapter 10 ends with a renewed prophetic commission to the seer. Chapter 11 continues that commission with a command to perform a symbolic action – measuring the temple. Several biblical prophets were ordered to perform symbolic actions as expressions of their prophecy. For example, God tells Ezekiel to symbolize Israel's coming exile by gathering his baggage and digging through his wall. Isaiah is told to go about naked and barefoot for three years to symbolize Assyria's impending conquest and exile of Egypt and Ethiopia. The Christian prophet Agabus binds his own hands and feet with Paul's belt to depict Paul's future imprisonment. The measuring the seer is told to undertake in 11:1–2 is a similar prophetic symbolic action, and so it is part of his recommissioning.

The act of measuring is symbolic in several biblical contexts (Ford 1975, 176; Charles 1920, 1:274–75). The closest parallels to Rev 11:1–2 are Ezekiel 40–42 and Zech 2:2, where measuring Jerusalem signifies its restoration after its destruction by the Babylonians. For our author, measuring implies preservation from destruction. This becomes clear when he is told not to measure "the court outside the temple; leave that out, for it is given over to the nations, and they will trample over the holy city for forty-two months" (11:2). This reflects a common prophetic and eschatological expectation that at some future time Jerusalem will be attacked by the nations (e.g., Isa 63:18; Zech 14:2–3, 12–15; 1 Macc 3:45; Luke 21:24), an expectation that appears in Revelation (16:14; 20:7–10).

The vision in 11:1–2 speaks of the protection of the temple while the city around it is trampled by Gentiles, suggesting that it may have originated in 70 C.E. when the Zealot defenders of Jerusalem were besieged inside the temple by the Romans (Charles 1920, 1:278). The vision prophesies that God will protect the defenders. The image of trampling Jerusalem derives from Dan 8:13 (cf. Dan 7:23; 8:7, 10), where an angel asks how long God will allow the sanctuary to be trampled and is told that it will be for 2,300 mornings and evenings (or 1,150 days). The author may also know the saying of Jesus preserved in Luke's apocalyptic discourse: "Jerusalem will be trampled on by the Gentiles [in Greek 'the Gentiles' is the same as 'the nations'], until the times of the Gentiles are fulfilled" (21:24). This saying reflects the apocalyptic belief that the times are predetermined, so that the time of Gentile domination is foreordained. Revelation and Daniel reflect that viewpoint when they say that Jerusalem will be trampled on for three-and-a-half years or forty-two months (Rev 11:2; see also Rev 12:6, 14; 13:5, and the discussion below of this time period).

Elsewhere in Revelation "temple" refers to the heavenly temple, but here in 11:1–2 it appears to mean the earthly temple. The seer is on earth in 11:1–2, for in chapter 10 the angel has come down to earth from heaven. John must measure the temple to preserve it from destruction by the nations, something that would not be necessary for the heavenly temple. And yet it is difficult to know what the preservation of the earthly sanctuary could have meant for the seer. If our dating is correct, he writes decades after the temple's destruction by the Romans. Even if an earlier dating is accepted, we must account for the fact that nowhere else in the book does the author concern himself with Jerusalem's physical temple, and in 21:22 he explicitly denies that there will be a temple in the new Jerusalem, which may imply a critical view of the temple as such.

Charles is probably right that a preexistent Jewish oracle about the actual earthly temple underlies 11:1–2, but we still need to understand how the author adapts it. Some have thought that such an unusual (for the author) reference to the earthly temple indicates a reference to the Jewish people, so that the entire passage (11:1–13) concerns the Jews (Feuillet 1964; Beagley 1987). In this view, the indication that the city's inhabitants who survive the earthquake in 11:13 give glory to God means that the Jews will be converted. This is speculative and unlikely. In 2:9 and 3:9, the author implies that he considers faithful Christians to be the real Jews, and he shows no interest elsewhere in the conversion of non-Christian Jews.

If the author is not really concerned about the preservation of the earthly temple, and if this does not refer to the Jews, then a more symbolic approach is demanded. The immediate context supplies clues to the author's meaning. In 11:3–13, God's two witnesses are protected as they deliver their prophecy (11:5–6), but then they are opposed by the beast and killed (11:7). The identity of the two witnesses has been the subject of much discussion, but we make the case below that they represent the witnessing church as a whole during the period of tribulation. If so, that means that the church will both be protected and be vulnerable. This recalls our commentary on the sealing of the 144,000 in 7:1–3. There we noted that the sealing was for protection, as 9:4 makes clear, but the sealing does not protect the faithful from harm completely. Christians are not immune from persecution and martyrdom, and indeed they ought to expect it, but they will be protected in a more important way, for Satan will have no real power over them. This recalls the advice of Jesus in the synoptic gospels when he tells his disciples, "Do not fear those who kill the body but cannot kill the soul; rather fear him who can destroy both soul and body in hell" (Matt 10:28; see John 17:15). Rome's persecution may be fierce, but by enduring it and remaining faithful, Christians conquer Rome.

It is best to take 10:1–11:13 as a unit and to interpret each part in the light of the other parts. The seer is recommissioned for his prophetic task in 10:8–11:2, and 11:3–13 is symbolic of what that task holds in store. It entails both suffering and vindication. It means being subject to evil treatment and even death at the hands of unbelievers, but it brings eventual triumph and participation in God's kingdom. Satan "wars against" the faithful, but they are ultimately protected from his power. We interpret 11:1–2 against this backdrop and in light of 11:3–13 in particular. Just as the two witnesses are protected from the beast's power as they prophesy and just as they are vindicated by their resurrection and ascension, so the temple, its altar, and the worshipers around it are preserved from Satan's ultimate power. And just as the beast wars against, conquers, and kills the witnesses, the holy city outside the temple is trampled by the nations for a time. This fits with everything we have learned about the author's view of Christians' place in the Roman empire.

The temple is best seen as the church protected from Satan's onslaughts (in *1 Enoch* 61:1–5, measurement signifies spiritual protection). Other New Testament texts see the church as God's temple (1 Cor 3:10, 16; 2 Cor 6:16; Eph 2:19–22; 1 Tim 3:15), and the community of the Dead Sea Scrolls also saw itself as God's temple (Gärtner 1965). An intriguing New Testament example is 1 Pet 2:5, which combines the idea of church as temple with a reference to Exod 19:6 in portraying the people as priestly and royal. Revelation's seer is in this same tradition when he promises the conquerors that they will become pillars in God's temple (3:12), and like 1 Peter, Revelation also sees the church in the light of Exod 19:6 (Rev 1:6; 20:6).

The temple is a fitting image for Revelation's priestly people (1:6; Schüssler Fiorenza 1991, 77). The temple, altar, and worshipers measured in 11:1 constitute a cultic scene which in its entirety represents the church in union with its God through worship. The temple in 11:1–2 stands for the church's relationship with God, which is protected and cannot be destroyed by the nations' power. Mounce expresses this line of interpretation most cogently (1977, 219–20). He sees the temple and the holy city of 11:1–2 as the church under two different aspects. The church as temple symbolizes the faithful in indissoluble relationship with God, a relationship that the forces of evil cannot affect. The church as holy city is the church under the temporal power of Rome, trampled and suffering. God's seal does not protect from Rome's military and political power, at least not until the messianic kingdom in chapter 20.

It might seem logical to take the area outside the temple, referred to both as "the court outside the temple" and as "the holy city," to mean those who are not inside the church. But this results in the puzzling idea that "the nations" are trampling non-Christians. This is not impossible, since Rome oppresses the whole world, but it would be strange to find the author referring to these oppressed non-Christians as "the holy city," a phrase denoting the new Jerusalem in 21:2, 10 and 22:19. Rather, Revelation is interested in the oppression of Christians.

The time references contained in the passages join the images of temple and witnesses closely. The holy city outside of the temple is to be trampled for forty-two months (11:2), and the witnesses are to prophesy for 1,260 days (11:3). Behind the time references stands the book of Daniel, which was written when Judaism was being persecuted by the Seleucid king Antiochus IV. Antiochus stopped the lawful Jewish sacrifices in the temple and had idolatrous sacrifices performed on the altar. Daniel sees this as an attack not only on God's people but also on God himself and the angels, called the "holy ones" or "saints" in the text (Dan 7:21–22). The interpreting angel tells Daniel that Antiochus's persecution of Judaism was to last "a time, two times, and half a time" (7:25). A "time" means a year, so the persecution was expected to last for three-and-a-half years (cf. 8:14; 9:27; 12:7, 11, 12; Collins 1993, 322). The closing verses of Daniel interpret the three-and-a-half years in two different ways, as 1,290 days and as 1,335 days, perhaps because the prediction of Antiochus's death in Dan 11:45 did not happen when expected.

Daniel's visions in response to Antiochus's attack on Judaism, its temple and cult, and its God and his attendants, had a profound effect on the seer John. Revelation's forty-two months and 1,260 days (11:2, 3) are variants of three-and-a-half years. Since these two time periods are equivalent, it is natural to assume that both events — the trampling of the holy city (the church) and the prophesying of the witnesses — happen simultaneously. Three other events in Revelation are said to last for about the same length of time, God's protection of the heavenly woman in the wilderness (12:6, 14), during which time Satan makes war on her offspring (the church; 12:17), and the beast's making war on the saints (13:5–7). All of these are the same thing seen from different angles.

The Two Witnesses (11:3–13)

The identity of God's two witnesses introduced in 11:3 has been the subject of much discussion, with a large number of possibilities emerging (see Mounce 1977, 223). It is not surprising that Revelation's opaque imagery gives rise to such confusion, but this passage is especially open to multiple interpretations, particularly when some of them are based on the premise that the two witnesses are identifiable historical figures. The multiplicity of suggestions is a clue that they are not actual people but symbols. "Witness" is a word applied to Christ (1:5; 3:14), who died for his testimony, and Antipas, who was also martyred (2:13). The only other use of the noun "witness" is in 17:6, where it applies to everyone killed for the faith. The seer believes that all Christians are in danger of death because of the great tribulation about to engulf the entire world, and some think that he anticipates universal martyrdom of faithful Christians. The book prepares all to become true witnesses unto death. In that sense the two witnesses may represent the entire church on the brink of a great eschatological persecution. However, the witnesses are said to prophesy. Prophecy is not a function the author attributes to all Christians. Prophets are a group within the larger church who have the specific task of relaying God's messages to the church. The context in which that prophecy must be delivered is the hostile environment of the Roman empire, supported by Satan. It is no accident that the passage about the two witnesses forms part of the recommissioning of the seer as an endtime prophet. Revelation 11:3–13 describes the role, context, and fate of the true prophet.

That there are two witnesses may depend on the rule in Torah that the testimony of two witnesses is valid (Deut 17:6; 19:15; see also Matt 18:16; 2 Cor 13:1; 1 Tim 5:19; Heb 10:28). Their sackcloth garments indicate the somberness of their message (Jer 4:8; Zech 13:4; Matt 11:21). The witnesses are modeled on Elijah and Moses, both of whom tradition considers prophets. Revelation 11:5 says that if anyone tries to harm the witnesses, they will consume their attackers with fire from their mouths. This is reminiscent of Elijah's ability to call down fire on his opponents (2 Kgs 1:10, 12), and it may also reflect a verse from Jeremiah, where God says about Jeremiah's prophetic word, "I am now making my words in your mouth a fire, and this people wood, and the fire shall devour them" (5:14; cf. 4 Ezra 13:10, 37–38; 2 Thess 2:8). Jeremiah's use of the image of fire is a warning against taking the seer's words in an overly literal fashion. The witnesses will not literally set their enemies aflame. They will effectively destroy them by the truth that they speak.

Another feature that recalls Elijah is the statement that the witnesses can shut the sky so that there will be no rain while they prophesy (11:6). Elijah opposes the god Baal, thought by his worshipers to control rain. God gives Elijah the power to prevent rain (1 Kgs 17:1) and to make it rain (1 Kgs 18:1) as a sign that Israel's God controls nature. This power of Elijah is noted in Luke 4:25 and Jas 5:17, but whereas 1 Kings says that Elijah shut off the rain for about three years, both Luke and James say it was for three years and six months. The change is due to the influence of the passages in Daniel discussed above that speak of three-and-a-half years and demonstrates the power of that tradition. The witnesses have two traits reminiscent of Moses during the exodus. They are said to be able to turn the waters to blood and to afflict the earth with plagues whenever they wish (11:6). The first plague that Moses inflicts on Egypt was turning the Nile's water to blood (Exod 7:14–25). He follows this with nine other plagues. The two witnesses of Revelation 11 prophesy about repentance, and both Moses and Elijah are pictured as preachers of repentance (e.g., Deuteronomy; Mal 4:5–6).

There are extant traditions that attest to expectations of either Elijah or Moses returning at some future date. The Moses expectation may be built on Deut 18:15 where Moses predicts, "The LORD your God will raise up for you a prophet like me from among your own people." Acts 3 identifies Jesus as the prophet like Moses that Moses predicted. Samaritan traditions contain expectations of a prophet like Moses and may influence the gospel of John (see John 1:21; 6:14; 7:40). Elijah ascended to heaven in a fiery chariot (2 Kgs 2:11–12), so he never died. The last book in the Christian Old Testament predicts that Elijah will return to warn the people before God comes in judgment (Mal 4:5). Mark implies that John the Baptist is Elijah, and Matthew says so explicitly (11:14; 17:12–13). In the transfiguration in the synoptic gospels the disciples see Jesus transformed and conversing with Elijah and Moses (Mark 9:4–5 and parallels), a scene probably influenced by the same eschatological expectations.

In Revelation 11, the two witnesses are not distinct figures, each with his own powers. They are a unit, and each has the range of powers mentioned. This sort of transformation of tradition is typical of Revelation and is common in apocalypses in general. True to form, Revelation is not predicting that the historical Moses and Elijah will return to earth before the eschaton, as Matthew claims for Elijah. Rather the two witnesses are generalized images, employing features from both Moses and Elijah, tapping into the power and resonances of those figures from the past. The same God who acted powerfully through Moses and Elijah is about to act definitively in the present. Just as these two witnesses are not literally Moses and Elijah, neither do they represent other specific persons to come. Rather they stand for the prophetic function of the church.

Revelation 11:4 says that the two witnesses "are the two olive trees and the two lampstands that stand before the Lord of the earth." This reflects Zechariah 4, a passage whose influence we have already discussed several times (see commentary on 1:4, 12, 20; 3:1; 4:5; 5:6). Zechariah sees a lampstand with seven lamps on it, a vision probably originating in the seven-branched menorah in the temple. Then he sees "two olive trees, one on the right of the bowl and the other on its left" (4:3). The trees supply the lamps with oil through two golden pipes (4:12). The interpreting angel explains to Zechariah, "These are the two anointed ones [messiahs] who stand by the LORD of the whole earth" (4:14). For Zechariah, the two trees represent the high priest Joshua and the royal governor Zerubbabel, who may have been descended from King David. Revelation 11 does not call the two witnesses messiahs, but they are described in terms of Zechariah's olive trees. As symbols of Christian prophecy, they are leaders of a church that is both royal and priestly (1:6). This may be the reason our author connects them with Zechariah's two olive trees, symbolizing the priestly and royal heads of Israel. The witnesses are also called two lamps, again an allusion to Zechariah 4.

After the witnesses complete their prophetic activity, the beast comes to make war on them, conquer them, and kill them (11:7). The fact that the definite article is used for the beast implies that he is already known, but this is his first appearance in the book. Like the demonic locusts of the fifth trumpet, he comes from the abyss, which signals his demonic nature. The beast's appearance foreshadows the more detailed description of his coming and its consequences beginning in chapter 13, preceded by the appearance on earth of the beast's patron, Satan, in chapter 12. In 12:17, Satan "makes war" on faithful Christians, and in 13:5–7, the beast "makes war" on the faithful and "conquers" them. The trampling of the holy city (11:2), the prophesying of the witnesses in a hostile environment when the beast makes war on them and kills them (11:3), the dragon's pursuit of the heavenly woman (12:6, 14), Satan's warring against the woman's children who are the church (12:17), and the beast's warring against and conquering the saints (13:5–7) are all the same events seen under different guises. They happen during a length of time based on the time, two times, and half a time of Daniel. That the beast "makes war" on the witnesses in 11:7 as he does on all Christians in 12:17 and 13:7 supports the theory that the witnesses represent not two individuals but the prophetic activity of the church, seen as an aspect of the whole church, especially embodied in Christian prophets and martyrs.

The bodies of the slain witnesses lie in the street of "the great city that is prophetically called Sodom and Egypt, where also their Lord was crucified" (11:8). "Members of the peoples and tribes and languages and nations" refuse to let them be buried for three-and-a-half days, while they celebrate release from the burden of the two troublesome prophets who had been a "torment to the inhabitants of the earth" (11:9–10; the text literally has "who tormented the inhabitants of the earth"). The use of the verb "to torment" also occurs in 9:5, where the locusts torment the earth's inhabitants while God's seal protects the faithful, and in 14:10 and 20:10, where the evil are tormented. A noun derived from the verb appears in 9:5, 14:11, and 18:7, 10, 15, all in reference to torment inflicted on the wicked. The witnesses' prophecy is thus part of a larger picture in which the wicked are punished for their disloyalty to God and mistreatment of the faithful. To be unburied was shameful in the ancient world. Tobit is considered especially pious because he risked his life to bury fellow Jews (Tob 1:16–2:10). The use of the fourfold formula adapted from Daniel and the use of the phrase "inhabitants of the earth" emphasize that the vast majority of humanity rejoices in the witnesses' death and humiliation.

The identity of the city where the witnesses prophesy and meet their end is uncertain (see Charles 1920, 1:287–88), and the question is complicated by the possibility that the author uses sources in chapter 11. The reference to Christ's crucifixion implies that it is Jerusalem, which would imply that its background is the same as that of the holy city in 11:2. The city is "prophetically" called Sodom and Egypt. The word translated "prophetically" is literally "spiritually," which in this case means "symbolically" or "allegorically." Jerusalem is not called Sodom or Egypt in any other text, but the kingdom of Judah, of which Jerusalem was the capital, is called Sodom in Isa 1:9–10 (cf. Rom 9:29); 3:9; Ezek 16:46, 48, and 49. Sodom and Egypt are paradigms of wickedness in Wisd 19:14–15. On the one hand, Jerusalem is called "the great city" in other texts (Charles 1920, 1:287), as it is here in Rev 11:8. On the other hand, the phrase "the great city" elsewhere in Revelation always denotes Rome (16:19; 17:18; 18:10, 16, 18, 19, 21), which is also called "Babylon the great" (14:8; 16:19; 17:5; 18:2). Charles thinks that on the analogy of other apocalyptic scenarios, Jerusalem is a more likely candidate for "the great city" in 11:8 than is Rome. He also notes that the people who survive the earthquake in 11:13 repent, while the inhabitants of Rome do not repent (9:21; 16:9). Charles suggests that the author expects a substantial number of non-Christian Jews to convert before the end (1920, 1:291-92; see Romans 11). This possibility cannot be ruled out, but there is nothing anywhere else in the book to support it.

On the one hand, given the fluidity of this imagery, one could argue that although Jesus was actually crucified in Jerusalem, it was the power of Rome that killed him, so the great city could be Rome (for arguments that it is Rome see Mounce 1977, 226-27). On the other hand, the author may be collapsing both cities into a single idea, representing resistance to God. If so, then although the images of the holy city of 11:2 and the great city of 11:8 have their roots in Jerusalem, they represent two very different things in chapter 11.

The witnesses' humiliation lasts three-and-a-half days, which corresponds to their three-and-a-half-year ministry but is of a substantially lower order of magnitude. Then there is a reversal that vindicates the witnesses. The reversal begins when God's life-giving spirit (or "breath," the Greek word is capable of either meaning) enters the witnesses' corpses and they stand on their feet. The scene recalls Ezekiel 37, where Ezekiel prophesies to dead bones, God's spirit enters them, and they come to life and stand up. Ezekiel's vision symbolizes the revival of Israel after the Babylonian exile. Revelation adapts this to describe the vindication of the prophetic church persecuted by Rome, the new Babylon. This resurrection terrifies those who see it, for it negates their own perceived victory and warns of the power of the God whose witnesses these are. The vindication of the witnesses suggests punishment for those who mistreat them. The enemies see the witnesses ascend to heaven in a cloud. Elijah ascended to heaven at the end of his ministry (2 Kgs 2:11-12), and there is also a tradition that Moses did not really die but ascended to heaven (see Charles 1920, 1:281).

Ascension in a cloud recalls Jesus' ascension in Acts 1:9. The entire career of the witnesses — prophetic activity in Jerusalem including powerful deeds, death, resurrection, and ascension — mirrors Christ's and justifies the application of the name "witness" to them, a title they share with Christ. That the career of the prophetic church mirrors that of Christ is an idea we have already encountered several times in Revelation. The interlude in 10:1-11:13 depicts that career in detail.

After the witnesses ascend, there is "a great earthquake," and a tenth of the city falls (11:13). Seven thousand people perish in the quake (a tenth of the city), and the rest give glory to God. Giving glory to God is precisely what is demanded of all humanity by an angel in 14:7, so this reaction means repentance and acceptance of God's sovereignty.

Eschatological scenarios often contain earthquakes because they are a graphic way of saying that the very stability of the cosmos is disrupted and perhaps even destroyed by the power of the one who created it (Ezek 38:19–20; Hag 2:6–7; Zech 14:15). Earthquakes occur at strategic points in Revelation (see Bauckham 1977). There is an earthquake as part of the cosmic happenings of the sixth seal (6:12), when an angel throws fire from the heavenly altar onto the earth just prior to the blowing of the first trumpet (8:5), at the conclusion of the seventh trumpet (11:19), and when the seventh bowl is poured out (16:18). These are not individual and discrete events. Each recapitulates or anticipates the others. Together they constitute the great eschatological earthquake that signifies the end of the cosmos as presently constructed, in preparation for the definitive establishment of God's sovereignty. Because the cosmos has been disrupted and defiled by human and demonic disobedience, it must be radically reordered. If the city is seen not just as Jerusalem or the Jews but as all humanity that opposes God, then the fact that nine-tenths of its inhabitants repent after the earthquake is remarkable. Caird (1966, 140) says, "There seems then to be a good case for holding that John had wider hopes for the conversion of the world than he is commonly given credit for," and Schüssler Fiorenza (1991, 79) claims, "It is crucial to recognize that Revelation's rhetoric of judgment expresses hope for the conversion of nine-tenths of the nations in response to Christian witness and preaching. Otherwise, one will not understand that the author advocates a theology of justice rather than a theology of hate and resentment." Later passages in Revelation are less optimistic on this point.

The Woes (11:14)

At the end of the interlude the author declares, "The second woe has passed. The third woe is coming very soon" (11:14). The inclusion of so much material between 9:12 and 11:14 makes it difficult to decide just what constitutes the second woe. The matter is further complicated when we observe that there is no final statement that the third woe has happened. This ambiguity has led to the usual plethora of interpretations. What precisely are the three woes? The first is clearly the first trumpet. The second woe must occur between 9:12 and 11:14, but is it the demonic cavalry from the east (9:13–19), or the earthquake of 11:13, or both? Are the sufferings of the witnesses part of the woes, or are the woes just those events that affect the wicked? Is the second woe all that occurs between 9:12 and 11:14, given the fact that even the prophecy of the witnesses "torments" their hearers? Then we must ask about the third woe. Is it the rest of the book? Is it just the seventh trumpet? Is it only the things that Satan does, beginning in chapter 12?

Rather than examine all possibilities, we should look for clues in the text that point to a reasonable reading. The seals and the trumpets are alike in that the first four items of each series differ from the last three in form and content. The eagle in midheaven who says that three woes are coming makes a division between the first four and last three trumpets, so it is probable that it refers to the last three trumpets as the three woes. This is supported by the fact that the first woe and the fifth trumpet are identical. The interlude is not part of any trumpet, although it is associated with the sixth trumpet by the placement of the notice about the woes in 11:14. The author does not place the notice in 11:14 immediately after the sixth trumpet because placing it after the interlude isolates the climactic seventh trumpet more effectively and also adds drama and suspense by functioning as an announcement of the final trumpet.

In our view, the observations above suggest that the seventh trumpet is the third woe. The author does not add a statement declaring the completion of the third woe because the seventh trumpet anticipates everything else that happens in the book, as we shall see. The seventh trumpet concludes all that leads up to it. But the author also does not place too definitive a division between the seventh trumpet and the rest of the book, because the rest of the book is a recapitulation of what has already been described. He chooses therefore to simply begin anew in 12:1, without any univocal statement that things have reached their head or that 12:1 is a new beginning.

The Seventh Trumpet (11:15–19)

The seventh trumpet falls into three parts. The first is a hymn sung by unidentified "loud voices in heaven" (11:15). The second is another hymn, this time sung by the twenty-four elders (11:16–18). The last part is the climax not only of the seventh trumpet but of the trumpet series in general, as well as the entire first half of Revelation. God's heavenly temple opens; the ark of the covenant becomes visible; and there are the usual cosmic manifestations of God's presence and action in lightning, rumblings, thunder, an earthquake, and hail (11:19).

The first hymn proclaims, "The kingdom of the world [literally: cosmos] has become the kingdom of our Lord and of his Messiah, and he will reign forever and ever" (11:15). The coming of God's kingdom is the aim of everything that happens in Revelation, and it implies the defeat of Satan and Rome, so everything that follows in the book must be recapitulation.

The declaration that the world is now God's kingdom echoes many such claims in the Bible, where God's kingship is a common subject (Pss 93:1; 96:10; 97:1; 99:1; etc.). Revelation's hymn claims that the kingdom is not only God's but also the messiah's. This fits Revelation's elevation of Christ to God's level, even to the extent of having them sit on the same throne in 3:21; 22:1, 3 (see Bauckham 1993, 54–65). The hymn recalls Psalm 2, which sings of the rule of God and God's messiah and their overcoming of the opposition of the nations with their kings and rulers. This psalm also finds an echo in the elders' hymn in this chapter, which says, "The nations raged," but God overcame them (Rev 11:18; cf. Ps 2:1–6). Revelation 11:15 says, "He will reign forever." In the Greek there is no expressed subject here, and the verb is singular. It is useless to try to determine whether it is God or Christ who is the subject. They share the reign, as the hymn shows.

The twenty-four elders now respond to the announcement that the kingdom of God and Christ has come (11:16–18). Their hymn gives thanks that this has happened and makes explicit that this has come about only after the nations' opposition has been overcome. As they sing they prostrate themselves before God, a gesture due to God alone, and one which the seer denies both to Caesar and to angelic authorities (19:10; 22:8–9). They praise God with an altered version of the title that he has in 1:4, 8, and 4:8. In the earlier passages, God is the one "who is and who was and who is to come," a variation of the title given to God in Exodus 3. The characterization of God as the one to come points to God's impending action in the eschatological events. In 11:17, the third part of the threefold formula is missing. God is not spoken of as the one who is to come, because God has *already* come. Instead, the hymn says, "You have taken your great power and begun to reign" (11:17).

The seer uses elements of Psalm 2 to articulate God's defeat of human enemies (see comments on 2:26–27; 12:5; 19:15). The Psalm begins,

> Why do the nations conspire,
> and the peoples plot in vain?
> The kings of the earth set themselves,
> and the rulers take counsel together,
> against the LORD and his anointed....
> "I have set my king on Zion, my holy hill...."
> You shall break them with a rod of iron,
> and dash them in pieces like a potter's vessel.
> (Ps 2:1–2, 6, 9)

The elders' hymn follows the same pattern of opposition to God's reign by the nations, followed by God's wrath that destroys that opposition (11:18). The announcement of the establishment of the reign of God and the messiah in the psalm is already present in the first hymn (11:15). The elders' hymn rejoices that God has begun to reign (11:17) and goes on to praise God that the time has now come for judgment (11:18). This anticipates what happens at the end of the book where God sits on the throne and judges all (20:11–15).

Regarding judgment, the hymn speaks first of the reward of "your servants, the prophets and saints and all who fear your name, both small and great" (11:18). The NRSV punctuates the text so as to take "servants" as an all-inclusive term for Christians, so that the church consists of prophets, which is the only church office mentioned in Revelation, and saints, which includes everyone. The addition of the phrase "both small and great" is common in the Bible to indicate full inclusion (e.g., Gen 19:11; 1 Sam 30:2; 1 Kgs 22:31), and it is used with this sense elsewhere in Revelation (13:16; 19:5, 18; 20:12). Then the hymn goes on to speak of punishment of the wicked. The destroyers of the earth receive the treatment they mete out, so that the biblical principle that the punishment fits the crime is maintained (Exod 21:24; Lev 24:20; Deut 19:21; Ps 7:15–16; Wisd 11:15–16).

Revelation 11:1–18 bears remarkable similarities to Psalm 79. The following excerpts from the psalm show the most similarity with Revelation:

> O God, the nations have come into your inheritance;
> they have defiled your holy temple;
> they have laid Jerusalem in ruins.
> They have given the bodies of your servants
> to the birds of the air for food,
> the flesh of your faithful to the wild animals of the earth.
> They have poured out their blood like water
> all around Jerusalem,
> and there was no one to bury them.
> We have become a taunt to our neighbors,
> mocked and derided by those around us.
> How long, O LORD? Will you be angry forever?
> Will your jealous wrath burn like fire?
> Pour out your anger on the nations
> that do not know you,
> and on the kingdoms
> that do not call on your name....
> Let the avenging of the outpoured blood of your servants
> be known among the nations before our eyes.
> Let the groans of the prisoners come before you;
> according to your great power preserve those doomed to die....
> Then we your people, the flock of your pasture,
> will give thanks to you forever;
> from generation to generation we will recount your praise. (Ps 79:1–6, 10–11, 13)

Both the psalm and Revelation 11 begin with the mistreatment of Jerusalem by the nations. Both passages speak of the killing of the righteous, leaving them unburied, and the taunts of their enemies. Both speak of God's wrath toward the nations. In both the enemies do not acknowledge God. Not giving glory to someone (cf. Rev 11:13), not recognizing their proper place in society, is equivalent to not knowing their name or calling on their name (cf. Ps 79:6). Both Revelation 11 and the psalm speak of God's great power (Rev 11:18; Ps 79:11), and in both cases that power is to be exercised to liberate God's people and overthrow their oppressors. Both passages speak of retributive justice, and when the psalm speaks of vengeance for the spilled blood of God's servants, it evokes various passages in Revelation in addition to chapter 11 (see 6:10; 16:5–7; 17:6; 18:21–24; 19:2). Finally, the psalm ends with an expression of thanksgiving, while the song of the elders is also a thanksgiving.

Rev 11:19 is not only the final verse of the final trumpet but the final verse of the first great cycle of visions. The full implications of the opening of the seven seals are now felt. God's heavenly temple is opened, and the ark is seen within it. The ark was the traveling shrine that the Israelites had with them in the desert, and it symbolized God's presence with the people. It bore a special relation with the covenant, for it carried the tablets that God gave to Moses on Mount Sinai when the covenant was established between God and the people. In Solomon's temple the ark was kept in the Holy of Holies, the holiest part of the temple, where God was thought to dwell or at least appear from time to time. It was a windowless cube and was cut off from view by a heavy curtain. Only the high priest could enter the Holy of Holies, and he could do so but once a year, and then only to atone for the sins of Israel.

Given this background, we can appreciate the full implications of the opening of the temple so that God's ark is visible. It is God's temple in heaven that is opened, not the earthly temple. It would probably be too much for the seer to say that God is visible, for even when he sees the heavenly throne room in chapter 4, he can give only a cryptic description of God. Saying that God's ark is visible is the next best thing. It means that the very heart of the temple is now open (cf. Mark 15:38 and parallels). The only way that God's accessibility to human beings could be stated more clearly is as happens at the end of the book when the new Jerusalem comes to earth and God and the Lamb sit on the throne in the midst of the city with humanity gathered before them.

Chapter 11 ends with God still in heaven but with the heavenly temple completely opened. Beginning with chapter 12 the author will review the endtime events with all their violence and struggle, so his vision of the consummation in chapter 11 is reserved and terse. The final battle with evil has not yet been fully described, and this battle will set the tone for how God relates to the world in most of chapters 12 to 19. It is only after the final battle is fully described that the irenic picture of God among the people can be presented (chapter 21). In chapter 11, the seer is more reticent. Rather, he resorts to the usual theophanic elements of lightning, rumblings, thunder, an earthquake, and hail to express the fact that God's power touches the earth. The heavy hail especially calls to mind the plagues, both those in Egypt and the ones already described in Revelation. The list of theophanic elements foreshadows what is to come, the final battle between God and Satan, the winning of which has already been assumed in the seventh trumpet and its hymns.

The heavenly scene in the seventh trumpet (11:15–19) mirrors the one in chapters 4 and 5, and so it forms an inclusio with it. Together they frame all of chapters 4 to 11, which constitute the first "run through" of the eschatological events that will now appear in more detail in chapters 12 to 22. Both heavenly scenes picture God in heaven, duly worshiped and praised by loyal attendants. In both, the sovereignty of God over the entire cosmos is proclaimed. When Revelation's audience experiences such visions, their assessment of their position in the world, in history, and with respect to cosmic powers is adjusted so that they center completely on God on the throne, undeceived by appearances of Rome's domination.

Part III

The Second Major Cycle of Visions (12:1–22:5)

Chapter 12 begins the second half of Revelation. Chapters 4 to 11 are controlled by the image of the first scroll, sealed with seven seals. The interlude between the sixth and seventh trumpets, which is comprised of Rev 10:1–11:13, points forward to the second half of the book. As the sealed scroll, introduced in chapter 5 and gradually opened in chapters 6 to 8, represents the revelations of the first part of the book, the open scroll of chapter 10 symbolizes revelations in the second. The revelations in chapters 12 to 22 cover much of the same ground as chapters 4 to 11, but in greater detail and with clearer connection to earthly referents. The satanic beast who first appears in the trumpets interlude (11:7) and who attacks the prophetic church there becomes a major player in the rest of Revelation. He is the foe of God, the Lamb, and the church. Conflicts with Satan's forces, vindication of the faithful, punishment of the wicked, and arrival of God's kingdom pictured in chapter 11 are laid out much more fully in chapters 12 to 22.

Yarbro Collins divides the visions in chapters 12 to 22 into three sections (1979, xiii). First there is a series of seven unnumbered visions (12:1–15:4); then there are seven bowls (15:1–16:20) followed by an appendix that details Babylon's fall (17:1–19:10); and finally there is another series of seven unnumbered visions (19:11–21:8) followed by an appendix on the new Jerusalem (21:9–22:5). Each section incorporates the three elements of persecution, judgment, and reward found in each major part of Revelation.

•

The first section, 12:1–15:4, is the clearest statement in Revelation concerning the cosmic forces that lie behind the experience of the churches. Boring calls it "the central axis of the book and the core of its pictorial 'argument'" (1989, 150). The section discloses that Roman power and hostility to Christians are truly satanic, for Satan has given Rome its power, and through Rome, Satan attacks the churches. The everyday experience of the churches is part of a cosmic drama. Christians face not just human but superhuman adversaries (cf. Eph 6:12). The section assures its audience that Satan's power will be overthrown, and indeed it has already been overthrown through Christ's death and through Christian witness.

Revelation 12:1–15:4 is a series of visions that is not numbered. Mounce thinks that attempts to find exactly seven visions here are not entirely convincing, because different commentators divide the material differently (1977, 234n.1). Nonetheless, Yarbro Collins (1976, 37–38) presents a plausible division. Vision one (chapter 12) describes the cosmic conflict within which Christian experience must be read; vision two (13:1–10) deals with the beast from the sea; vision three (13:11–18) treats the beast from the land; vision four (14:1–5) depicts the 144,000 with the Lamb; vision five (14:6–13) announces judgment for Babylon and the beast's worshipers; vision six (14:14–20) speaks of the defeat of the earthly powers in a veiled way; and vision seven (15:2–4) shows the conquerors of the beast standing beside the sea of glass.

Chapter Eight

The First Series of Seven Unnumbered Visions (12:1–15:4)

The First Unnumbered Vision: The Woman and the Dragon (Chapter 12)

Chapter 12 is in three parts which are in a ring structure. The first part (12:1–6) concerns a woman about to give birth and a dragon; the second (12:7–12) describes a war in heaven between good and bad angels; and the third (12:13–17) returns to the woman and the dragon. Charles (1920, 1:298–314) argues that behind chapter 12 lie two sources, both of which were Jewish and both of which relied heavily on ancient mythology. One of the Jewish sources has to do with the woman and the dragon, and the other concerns the war in heaven. Charles's arguments are persuasive. As when the author uses sources in chapter 11, chapter 12 is not a completely smooth narrative, but the mythology of the sources taps into deep streams of the ancient imagination, capitalizing on foundational patterns in ancient storytelling and conceptualization, ensuring that the resulting picture is compelling and evocative.

The Woman and the Dragon, Part 1 (12:1–6)

Chapter 12 begins with two great "portents" or "signs" that the seer observes in heaven. The first is a woman and the second a dragon. Generally speaking, "signs" are things that point beyond themselves. In the Bible and in apocalyptic texts, signs can be indications of divine power at work. Here the story of the woman and the dragon has ultimate significance for the state of the world and its fate. The effect of the heavens on earthly events is a given in astrology, which was very popular in the ancient world. A third heavenly sign will appear in 15:1. There are also deceptive signs brought forth by Satan or his helpers (13:13, 14; 16:14; 19:20). The author teaches his audience to read both kinds of signs properly.

The woman John sees is clothed with the sun, has the moon under her feet, and has a crown of twelve stars (12:1). She appears with the trappings of a heavenly goddess and recalls prominent goddesses of the ancient world such as the Egyptian Isis, popular during the Hellenistic and Roman periods. Heavenly bodies — sun, moon, planets, stars — were thought to be supernatural beings. The woman's relationship to these entities shows her dominance over them. She is queen of heaven, wearing a diadem fashioned of twelve stars symbolizing the twelve signs of the zodiac. The woman is pregnant with a son, who is later described in messianic terms as shepherding the nations with an iron rod (Ps 2:9; see comments on the use of that psalm in Rev 2:26–28; 11:18; 19:15).

The seer spies a second sign in heaven, a red dragon with seven heads and ten horns, who sweeps a third of the stars out of the sky with his tail and who stands before the woman to devour her child when she delivers him. But the child is snatched up to God, and the woman flees to the wilderness, where she is nourished for 1,260 days. This concludes the first of the three sections of the chapter. The story of the woman and dragon resumes in 12:13. Between the two sections is another mythological tale — the casting of Satan out of heaven — followed by a hymn that comments on the action (12:10–12). The resumption of the story of the woman and dragon in 12:13–17 entails recapitulation, for it retells the woman's flight to the wilderness. The dragon pursues her, tries to attack her with a river of water from its mouth, is unsuccessful, and goes off to make war on her other children.

Charles makes a strong case that the source behind the story of the dragon and the woman is a Jewish one that draws on Greek and Hellenistic mythology. He posits a Jewish source rather than a Christian one because although the woman's son is portrayed in messianic terms, he is a passive messiah. He is snatched up to God immediately following his birth and plays no further role in the action, though his future reign is mentioned. Charles (1920, 1:308) finds no good parallel in early Christian literature for such a passive messiah, but he does find

Jewish depictions of a passive or hidden messiah. The author's use of this source explains the fact that the story ignores Christ's ministry, passion, and death, even though 12:11 extols those activities.

The Combat Myth

The story of the woman and the dragon recalls a group of stories widespread in the ancient Near East and Mediterranean that falls into the general category of the combat myth (see Yarbro Collins 1976, 61–85, for various versions of this myth; see also Charles 1920, 1:310–14). This myth most clearly influences Revelation 12, but its influence permeates the book. Batto (1992) demonstrates its importance to the entire Hebrew Bible. Yarbro Collins characterizes the combat myth as follows:

> The pattern depicts a struggle between two divine beings and their allies for universal kingship. One of the combatants is usually a monster, very often a dragon. This monster represents chaos and sterility, while his opponent is associated with order and fertility. Thus, their conflict is a cosmic battle whose outcome will constitute or abolish order in society and fertility in nature. (1976, 57)
>
> In some forms of the story, the beast attempts to prevent a young hero from coming to power. In these cases, the attack is directed against the hero's mother while she is pregnant with him or against the hero as a defenseless infant. (1979, 84–85).

Not all of the features of Revelation 12 are accounted for by the author's use of any single known form of the combat myth (Yarbro Collins 1976, 58). The author's use of the myth is free and creative, and he combines motifs from several versions of the myth to come up with an original form. Yarbro Collins (1976, 58) goes so far as to say, "It would seem that the author of Revelation was consciously attempting to be international by incorporating and fusing traditional elements from a variety of cultures."

The closest parallel to Rev 12:1–6, 13–17 is the Greek myth about the birth of Apollo. As with most ancient myths, it occurs in various forms, but the main outline is as follows. Zeus has relations with Leto, Apollo's mother. Zeus's consort, Hera, is angry and engages the aid of Python, a serpent-monster, to pursue

Leto. Zeus orders the north wind to rescue Leto, and the sea-god Poseidon also helps her. She receives shelter on an island. Leto gives birth to Apollo and Artemis, brother and sister. Apollo subsequently slays Python. Revelation and the Leto story share the elements of a woman pregnant with a future prominent ruler who will share in the divine rule of the universe, the mother attacked by a serpentlike monster, the rescue of the woman and therefore of her child, the element of being carried through the air by the north wind or the eagle, and the fact that water plays some role in the story, although it is a different role in the two stories. In the Leto myth, Apollo kills his former attacker. Revelation 12 may hint that Christ will return to deal with Satan in the reference to his rule with an iron rod (12:5), but the clearer attack on Satan is carried out in the inserted passage regarding a heavenly war (12:7–9).

Allusions to the Apollo myth are appropriate in a work that sees Roman power as demonic. Several Roman emperors, including Augustus and Nero, identified with Apollo, interpreted as the ruler of a bygone golden age. Nero's appropriation of Apollo imagery for himself is especially important, for he was the first emperor who persecuted the Christians. Most see the sea-beast in chapter 13 at least partially as representing Nero, and that beast contrasts with the Lamb in several ways. Thus Revelation's use of the Apollo myth is ironic, for it uses the myth to speak of Christ, opposed by the sky-dragon, whereas Nero, who had pretensions to being Apollo, is a sea-monster who is the opposite of Christ.

Another version of the combat myth that involves a hero's mother is Egyptian. The goddess Isis is pregnant by the god Osiris. She gives birth to Horus, and mother and child are then attacked by a god named either Seth or Typhon (in dragon form). They are rescued with divine help, and Horus defeats Seth-Typhon and assumes rule.

In other ancient Near Eastern versions of the combat myth, a god or monster associated with the sea attacks the ruling god or another god closely associated with him and therefore threatens cosmic order. In the ancient Babylonian version of this myth, the battle results in the creation of an orderly cosmos, attained when the god Marduk defeats the sea-monster Tiamat. In ancient Canaanite myth, Baal, often mentioned in the Bible as a rival of the Israelite God, is attacked by the god Yam, a name that means "sea." Baal defeats Yam and builds his royal palace. This is one of a series of Canaanite stories in which Baal conquers a supernatural enemy. Another of these enemies is Lothan, the seven-headed sea-monster.

The influence of versions of this myth is discernible in the Bible, where God's creative activity or action on behalf of his people is depicted in terms of a fight with a dragon or sea-monster. The creation story in Genesis 1 does not contain such mythology explicitly, although one of God's first acts is to set limits to the waters to protect the dry land. There is a famous passage in Isaiah in which God's act of creation and his rescue of the people at the exodus by splitting the Red Sea are used as paradigms for divine action and as the basis of prayers for God's future action:

> Awake, awake, put on strength,
> O arm of the LORD!
> Awake, as in days of old,
> the generations of long ago!
> Was it not you who cut Rahab in pieces,
> who pierced the dragon?
> Was it not you who dried up the sea,
> the waters of the great deep;
> who made the depths of the sea a way
> for the redeemed to cross over?
> (Isa 51:9–10; cf. Ps 89:9–10;
> Job 26:12–13; etc.)

Rahab here is the name of the primeval sea-dragon. God's defeat of Rahab at creation is parallel to his drying up of the Red Sea at the exodus:

> Yet God my King is from of old, working salvation in the earth.
> You divided the sea by your might;
> you broke the heads of the dragons in the waters.
> You crushed the heads of Leviathan;
> you gave him as food for the creatures of the wilderness.
> (Ps 74:12–14)

Leviathan is another name for the primeval sea-dragon. Note that it has more than one head here. Job complains that God treats him like an enemy: "Am I the Sea, or the Dragon, that you set a guard over me?" (Job 7:12). God's enemies, such as Pharaoh (Ezek 29:3–6; 32:2–8) and Nebuchadnezzar (Jer 51:34–36), are portrayed in terms borrowed from dragon or sea-monster mythology. In an eschatological application, Isaiah predicts, "On that day the LORD with his cruel and great and strong sword will punish Leviathan the fleeing serpent, Leviathan the twisting serpent, and he will kill the dragon that is in the sea" (Isa 27:1). These citations demonstrate that the myth of a battle between God and a dragonlike monster was well known in ancient Israel.

All the variations of the combat myth express the basic pattern of the fight of order against chaos, life against death. They all attest to the common human conviction that order and life are vulnerable and subject to attack. They embody the belief that positive forces are stronger than negative ones, but they do not trivialize the power of the negative ones. Such basic patterns have always fed into religious belief and mythological expression, but they are particularly strong in apocalypticism. Yarbro Collins notes that the book of Daniel found the combat myth an appropriate way for expressing a battle between cosmic forces in which righteous humans do not actively oppose God's enemies (1996, 201–2). For the same reason, the myth is especially useful to Revelation's author.

Revelation 12 puts the churches' experience firmly in the framework of the combat myth. Such contextualization is typical of apocalypticism. It allows people to make sense of their experience by relating it to larger meanings and more sweeping narratives.

Revelation's Version of the Combat Myth

Commentators have frequently tried to identify the woman of Rev 12:1–2. Since she is the mother of one described in messianic terms (12:5), she has often been seen as Mary, mother of Jesus. But the pursuit of the woman by the dragon, her protection and nourishment for 1,260 days in the wilderness, her rescue by the earth, and the persecution of the rest of her children are hard to explain if we limit ourselves to this possibility. It is more likely that she represents the messianic community, the community from which the messiah comes. A parallel may be found among the hymns of the Dead Sea Scrolls, where the hymnist sings of the birth pangs of a woman as she brings forth one described in messianic terms (1QH 3:1–11). The woman here may represent the community behind the scrolls. Commenting on this passage, Collins (1995, 66) says, "Birth imagery is often associated with the coming of the messiah." He mentions Revelation 12 and rabbinic parallels.

Israel is depicted several times in the Bible as a woman undergoing birth pains. Isaiah complains that the community suffers like a woman in childbirth, only to give birth to wind (Isa 26:17). In Mic 4:10, Israel's sufferings in the exile are like those of a laboring woman, and in Isa 66:7, Zion gives birth to her children, symbolizing the rebirth of the community after the exile. Charles (1920, 1:317) offers more examples (Isa 13:8; 21:3; Jer 4:31; 13:21; 22:23; Hos 13:13). Mounce (1977, 236) points to passages in which Zion is the mother of the people (Isa 54:1; 4 Ezra 10:7; Gal 4:26). Since the seer does not distinguish between Judaism and Christianity, the woman represents the messianic community both before and after the messiah's birth. But this does not preclude a reference to Mary as well, for the author's symbols are multivalent, as are most apocalyptic images.

The pregnant woman is confronted by a dragon who means to devour her child (12:3–4). The dragon is red and has seven heads and ten horns. Charles (1920, 1:318) traces the dragon's redness and his seven heads ultimately to Babylonian mythology. He also notes that a monster, often a dragon, is frequently God's enemy in the Bible (1920, 1:317). The Canaanite Lothan also had seven heads. Yarbro Collins notes that "the red color of the dragon recalls the adversary of Isis, Seth-Typhon" (1997, 19).

The dragon's seven heads and ten horns also allude to Daniel 7. In that chapter Daniel sees four beasts arise out of the sea. The sea represents the forces of chaos opposed to God and God's creation. The four beasts are later interpreted as four successive empires that oppress Israel. The total number of heads and horns on these beasts are seven and ten respectively. Daniel's author may have made the total number of heads on his beast seven because of the seven heads of the primeval sea-monster. Daniel 7 also heavily influences Revelation 13, where a beast rises out of the sea, a beast to whom the dragon gives authority and power.

Revelation's dragon has seven crowns (12:3), implicitly contrasting with Christ, who in chapter 19 is pictured with "many crowns." There are no crowns in Daniel 7, but there the beasts' horns are said by the interpreting angel to be kings (7:24). One of the horns is Antiochus IV, who persecuted Judaism in the first half of the second century B.C.E. His attack on the temple cult and Torah was considered to be an attack on heaven itself. Daniel

8:10 offers one description of the attack: "It [the horn representing Antiochus] grew as high as the host of heaven. It threw down to the earth some of the host and some of the stars, and trampled on them." This is used by Revelation's author when he says that the red dragon "swept down a third of the stars and threw them to the earth" (12:4). The heavenly luminaries were thought to be supernatural beings. Stars falling to earth recalls apocalyptic scenarios where cosmic disruption is described in this way (e.g., earlier in Revelation: 6:13; cf. 8:10, 12; 9:1; cf. also *1 Enoch* 46:7).

As an aside we note that anyone who has ever dressed as the devil on Halloween has followed the dictates of Revelation, even if unknowingly. Common to all such costumes are undoubtedly the color red, horns on the head, and a tail. This is but a small example of the influence Revelation has had on the imagination of Western civilization.

The dragon confronts the pregnant woman, waiting to devour her child (12:4). The closest parallel to this is Python, waiting to attack Apollo when he is born of Leto. It also recalls Isis being chased by Seth (Yarbro Collins 1997, 20). The woman gives birth to a child who is described in messianic terms: "She gave birth to a son, a male child, who is to rule all the nations with a rod of iron" (12:5). This alludes to Ps 2:7, 9 (see comments on Rev 2:27; 19:15). Once born, the child is immediately taken up "to God and his throne" (12:5).

In a Christian text, the messiah is obviously Jesus, but 12:5 passes over all of his life, his suffering and death, and even his resurrection. It mentions only his ascension and interprets that as being rescued from Satan's power. The view of Christ that this assumes is contrary to what we hear elsewhere in Revelation and even elsewhere in this chapter. Revelation 12:11 claims that Satan is conquered by the blood of the Lamb and by Christian witness, which clashes with the idea that he is rescued from the dragon by being snatched up into heaven before his death is mentioned. Christ does not need to be rescued from Satan, nor do Christians. They conquer Satan precisely by *not* being rescued from Satan's capability to make them suffer and die. Some claim that the author and his audience would read all of this into the brief notice in 12:5. For example, Caird (1966, 150) claims that the dragon's trying to devour the child is equivalent to the crucifixion. Others take the ascension as implying suffering and death. But the fact remains that the statement in 12:5, taken only within the verses that deal directly with the woman and dragon (12:1–6, 13–17), does not adequately express the christology of Revelation. This supports Charles's theory that the author uses a source here.

The woman now flees to the wilderness to a place God "prepared," and she "is nourished" there for 1,260 days. The time period is the same as that during which the "holy city," symbolizing the persecuted Christian community, is trampled (11:2) and the time during which God's two witnesses prophesy (11:3). This suggests that the woman's period of protection from Satan is the same period as the one now being endured by the church, during which it is besieged by Satan but is promised God's protection. Seen in this way, the message is much the same as that of the sealing in 7:1–3 and the temple measuring in 11:1–2. The community's relationship with God will survive. In the gospel of John, Jesus prays, "I am not asking you to take them out of the world, but I ask you to protect them from the evil one [Satan]" (John 17:15; see Matt 10:28). Together, 7:1–3, 11:1–2, and 12:1–6, 13–17 form a triptych which promises spiritual but not physical protection.

The wilderness is a frequent and powerful symbol in Judaism. The Israelites escaped from Egypt into the wilderness at the exodus. There God nourished them miraculously with manna, quail, and water (Exod 15:22–17:7). At Sinai in the wilderness, God forged a covenant with the people and gave them the Torah. For forty years in the wilderness the relationship between God and Israel took shape. Wilderness became synonymous with renewal of the relationship with God in later sources. After his battles with the Baal-worshiping queen Jezebel, Elijah retreats to the wilderness and Sinai to renew his mission (1 Kgs 19:1–18). In Hosea, God says of Israel,

> Therefore, I will now allure her,
> and bring her into the wilderness,
> and speak tenderly to her.
> From there I will give her her vineyards,
> and make the Valley of Achor a door of hope.
> There she shall respond as in the days of her youth,
> as at the time when she came out of the land of Egypt.
> (Hos 2:14–15)

Earlier in Hosea, God complains that Israel, his wife, is disloyal and that she thinks that her nourishment comes from the Baals of the land (2:5). In the wilderness God will bring her back to faithfulness to him and will nourish her (2:21–23). Hosea combines the wilderness motif with the metaphor of Israel as a woman whom God woos, treats as a wife, and nourishes. Revelation 12 also pictures the messianic community as a woman whom God nourishes in the wilderness, and in chapter 19 the community is seen as Christ's bride.

The power of wilderness imagery in the New Testament is illustrated by the fact that John the Baptist preaches repentance in the wilderness, and Jesus prepares for his ministry by spending forty days in the wilderness, recalling the forty years Israel spent there. Like Israel, Jesus battles temptation there. Jesus confronts Satan directly in the wilderness, and when he is successful God sends angels to minister to him.

War in Heaven (12:7–12)

Verses 7 and 8 contain the myth of the war in heaven. Michael and his angels defeat Satan and his angels and expel them from heaven. As usual, the author does not simply adopt wholesale a legend found in another source. Rather the author combines a number of elements into a new narrative. In Job 1–2 and Zechariah 3, Satan appears as a member of the heavenly court whose task is to be the prosecuting attorney. The Hebrew word *satan* means "accuser," and in Job and Zechariah it is not a proper name. "Satan" is used in a neutral way in 1 Kgs 11:14, 23, 25; Pss 38:20; 71:13; 109:4, 20, 29 (Boring 1989, 164–67). Prosecuting attorneys are not popular with those whom they prosecute, and the accuser in heaven is no exception. So as time goes on, the figure of Satan becomes more and more negative. In *1 Enoch* 40:7 it is the task of one of God's attendants to repel the "satans": "And the fourth voice I heard expelling the demons [literally: satans] and forbidding them from coming to the Lord of the Spirits in order to accuse those who dwell on the earth."

Such passages supply the background for the joyful proclamation of 12:10, "The accuser of our comrades has been thrown down." But they do not account for the military imagery here nor for the idea that there is all-out war in heaven resulting in Satan's ejection. For such ideas it is necessary to look at legends of assaults on heaven that are repelled. Daniel supplies such a story. In persecuting Judaism, Antiochus IV is really attacking heaven (Dan 8:10–12, quoted above). In Dan 11:36, it is said of Antiochus, "The king shall act as he pleases. He shall exalt himself and consider himself greater than any god, and shall speak horrendous things against the God of gods." The angel Gabriel tells Daniel that he and Michael are warring against the "princes" of the oppressive empires (10:20–21). "Princes" here means their supernatural patrons, perhaps angelic figures. The defeat of Antiochus and his death occur in Dan 11:45, at which point Michael arises as protector of Israel; there is a period of eschatological woes; and there is a resurrection in which the good join the stars and the evil are punished. Although the word "Satan" never appears in Daniel, Revelation 12 and Daniel share the assault on heaven, the repulsion of that assault which is put in terms of warring angelic forces, the eschatological woes, and a major eschatological role for the archangel Michael. The trampling of the Jerusalem sanctuary in Daniel compares with the measuring of the temple and the trampling of the holy city in Rev 11:1–2, as we noted in that context.

The idea of an assault on heaven that is repulsed is older than Daniel. It appears in the taunt against the king of Babylon preserved in Isaiah 14:

> How you are fallen from heaven,
>   O Day Star, son of Dawn!
> How you are cut down to the ground,
>   you who laid the nations low!
> You said in your heart,
>   "I will ascend to heaven;
> I will raise my throne
>   above the stars of God;
> I will sit on the mount of assembly
>   on the heights of Zaphon;
> I will ascend to the tops of the clouds,
>   I will make myself like the Most High."
> But you are brought down to Sheol,
>   to the depths of the Pit.
> Those who see you will stare at you,
>   and ponder over you:
> "Is this the man who made the earth tremble,
>   who shook kingdoms . . . ?" (Isa 14:12–16)

Charles (1920, 1:324) also cites *2 Enoch* 29:4–5 and the *Book of Adam and Eve* 1:6, where one finds "the statement that Satan once attempted to set his throne on an equality with that of God, and was thereupon hurled down from heaven."

There are stories of the fall of angels that do not include an assault on heaven or an attempt of angels to rise above their station (Gen 6:1–4; *1 Enoch* 6–11). In *1 Enoch* 10, God tells Michael to confine the fallen angels under the earth until the judgment, at which time they go to the fiery abyss (see also *1 Enoch* 54:6; Rev 20:3). Against the backdrop of all these legends, our author's narratives in chapter 12 and subsequent chapters are more comprehensible. The backdrop also helps us understand the related saying of Jesus in Luke 10:18: "I watched Satan fall from heaven like a flash of lightning."

The angel Michael wins the battle against Satan in Revelation 12. We have already encountered several passages in which Michael plays a major role (*1 Enoch* 10:11; 54:6; Daniel 10; 12; see *T. Moses* 10:2). In the *War Scroll* from the Dead Sea Scrolls, Michael aids Israel in the final battle, and in the end he rules among heavenly beings, corresponding to Israel's earthly rule (1QM 17). Michael is also Israel's intercessor (e.g., *T. Levi* 5:6; *T. Dan.* 6:2–3).

A final set of passages providing background for a heavenly battle deals with portents in the sky of impending events. In 2 Macc 5:2, Jerusalem's inhabitants see full-scale battles in the sky over the city that foreshadow the misfortunes connected with Antiochus IV's attack. Josephus tells of similar portents at the time of the Jewish war against the Romans shortly before Revelation was written (*J.W.* 6 §§288–315). A heavenly battle portends the end in *Sib. Or.* 3:796–809. These parallels point to simple omens and not to actual battles fought by superhuman beings, but they attest to the widespread belief in heavenly signs, particularly signs of a military nature.

The author recites a string of names for Satan when he says that he has been thrown down. He is the "great dragon" and "that ancient serpent, who is called the Devil and Satan, the deceiver of the whole world" (12:9). The word translated "devil" is *diabolos,* from which the English "diabolical" comes. It means "slanderer," calling to mind both Satan's deceitful nature and his role as accuser. *Diabolos* translates *satan* several times in the Septuagint. The mention of "ancient serpent" as one whom the audience should know connects directly with Genesis 3, where the serpent tempts Eve in the Garden of Eden. The serpent is not identified with Satan in Genesis, but Revelation makes the identification, as does Jewish tradition. The effect is to have Satan's influence felt from the very beginning of the human race. With this identification Satan goes from being an accuser to being a tempter, a development that already has a precedent in the Bible (1 Chr 21:1). Humans would still be in Eden were it not for him (Wisd 2:24). In Genesis the serpent is crafty and deceitful (3:1, 12), traits that show up in Rev 12:9 when he is called "the deceiver of the whole world" (cf. 2 Cor 11:3; 1 Tim 2:14).

The connection with Genesis 3 also brings to mind the words God speaks when he curses the serpent for having tempted humans and caused their fall:

> I will put enmity between you and the woman,
> and between your offspring and hers;
> he will strike your head,
> and you will strike his heel. (Gen 3:15)

"Offspring" in both the Hebrew and Greek versions of Gen 3:15 is "seed" (Greek: *sperma*), the word used in Revelation 12 when Satan goes off to make war on the rest of the woman's "seed" (12:17). The enmity between the ancient serpent, Satan, and the woman's seed, both as messiah and as messianic community, is evident throughout Revelation. In 13:3, the beast to whom Satan gives his authority is wounded in the head, another connection with Genesis 3. To Eve, God says that he will "greatly increase your pains in childbearing" (Gen 3:16). This may be reflected in that the woman of Revelation not only is said to be pregnant but "was crying out in birth pangs, in the agony of giving birth" (12:2). Our author discerns similarities between the combat myth, particularly when the mother is involved, and the prediction in Gen 3:15 of enmity between Eve's seed and the serpent. Both are versions of the combat myth.

The seer now hears an unidentified "loud voice" in heaven proclaim the defeat of Satan and the coming of the kingdom of God and his messiah (12:10–12). Because the voice speaks of humans as "our comrades" (12:10; literally: "brothers"), some commentators think that the voice is that of the martyrs under the heavenly altar (6:9). Others—pointing to the angel of 22:8–9 who tells the seer that he is but a "fellow servant" of John and the prophets—claim that the voice can be angelic. The author's point is that the voice is reliable and authoritative, for it comes from heaven. This is true of all the heavenly hymns and proclamations throughout Revelation. Their function is similar to that of the chorus in Greek drama, to comment on the action in a reliable way.

The heavenly proclamation is in three parts, each of which is in two sections. The first part declares the coming of God's kingdom and the defeat of Satan (12:10). The second part asserts that Satan has been defeated by the blood of the Lamb and by Christian testimony (12:11). The third part tells the heavens to rejoice but predicts woe for the earth (12:12).

As we shall see repeatedly, the visions from the second major cycle (12:1–22:5) are more detailed than those from the first (4:1–11:19). The first part of the proclamation (12:10) echoes the loud declaration by heavenly voices at the blowing of the seventh trumpet which say, "The kingdom of the world has become the kingdom of our Lord and of his Messiah" (11:15). Here in chapter 12 it is the "salvation and the power and the kingdom of our God and the authority of his Messiah" that have come (12:10). This is immediately associated with the fall of Satan, who is called "the accuser of our brethren." Chapter 11 speaks briefly about the beast from the abyss, his prophetic victims and their vindication, and the subsequent coming of God's kingdom (11:7–18). Chapter 12 digs deeper, looking at the power behind the beast, the dragon, his frustration as he pursues the woman and her child, and his defeat at the hands of Michael and his angels. Where chapter 11 speaks simply of the kingdom of God and the messiah, chapter 12 speaks of the "salvation" (meaning "victory" here since it is a victory that has just been won [Charles 1920, 1:326]), the "power" (just exercised in Satan's overthrow), and the "kingdom" of God that comes. Further, it is the "authority" of the messiah that comes. "Authority" is a common word in Revelation, corresponding to the question of sovereignty that permeates the book. The true view is that all legitimate authority comes from God. Christ is ruler of the kings on earth because of his relationship with God.

The second section of the first part says that the kingdom of God and the messiah have come *because* the accuser of "our comrades has been thrown down, who accuses them day and night before our God" (12:10). In Job and Zechariah, Satan is the accuser of humankind. But in Rev 12:11, this activity is seen as destructive of the relationship between God and humans and as a barrier to God's kingdom. Satan is no longer in the divine court. The second part of the proclamation (12:11) uses trial imagery, for Christians have conquered Satan because of the suffering and death of the Lamb and also because of their own testimony unto death.

There is irony here for Christians who expected to be dragged before Roman courts, accused of crimes against the divine Caesar, and executed. They are told that precisely because they stood up to their accusers on earth, their accuser in heaven has been defeated. Conviction in one court means vindication in the other (Yarbro Collins 1990, 1008). Because they were willing to undergo death in loyalty to God, they are joined to the Lamb who suffered the same fate and now is the messiah to whom God has given authority. The past tense of 12:11 raises a question. Are those who have witnessed in the face of death identical with the martyrs of chapter 6 who are already under the heavenly altar? Or is this a proleptic scene, which anticipates the triumph of future martyrs? Or does victory belong even now, despite appearances, to those who have not yet died but who are willing to do so? Probably all three are true. The author claims victory for all who are willing to bear testimony in the face of death, whether they have already done so or have yet to do so. Christian resistance to Roman persecution is part of the war against Satan embodied in Christ's work and in Michael's victory. The proclamation shows that the myth related in 12:7–8 is but another expression of the victory won in the career of the earthly Jesus and in the churches' witness. Caird emphasizes that the victory is won by the crucifixion, so Michael's victory is the heavenly counterpart of Christ's death (1966, 153).

The third part of the proclamation contrasts the victory in heaven with what is now to happen on earth (12:12). Satan's defeat takes place in stages. His defeat in heaven explains his activity on earth, to which he has now come. He is filled with wrath at his defeat and knows that the time of his final doom is near, so he is all the more dangerous (12:12). Thus the heavens are told to rejoice, an exhortation in biblical language (Isa 44:23; 49:13; Ps 95:11), but the earth and sea are to suffer woe.

Christians must understand that the suffering that Satan inflicts on them signals the *end* of his power. Satan fuels the Roman empire's hostility to Christians. Satan is enraged at those who still recognize the sovereignty of the God who threw him out of heaven. His revenge is to mislead most of humanity into recognizing the counterfeit sovereignty of his puppet, the beast of chapter 13, and to persecute those who do not follow him.

The seer and his audience live in this in-between period, between Satan's ejection from heaven and his final defeat. They inhabit the world that Satan now haunts, and they are in danger from him. This raises the question about when Satan's downfall occurs. Is it at the beginning of time, so that all of history has been under Satan's sway? Does it begin only with Christ's death? If so, does the Roman empire begin to be satanic only at that time? The proclamation in 12:11 says that Satan's defeat has been accomplished by the Lamb's blood and by Christian testimony. The seer does not answer theoretical questions about what circumstances existed before that. His job is to explain what is happening in his own day. Unlike many writers of apocalypses, he does not give a synopsis of all history. For him, what is significant in history has been set in motion by Christ's witness and death.

When the heavenly voice declares woe on the earth and sea in 12:12, it raises the question about whether this is the third woe of the three predicted in 8:13 (see 9:12; 11:14). Mounce (1977, 244) thinks not, because he takes the woe in 12:12 as directed against Christians. There is no doubt that the emphasis in this chapter and the one that follows is on the persecution of Christians, but this is perhaps too narrow a reading of the woe of which the heavenly voice speaks. The events in chapters 12 to 22 certainly affect more than Christians, and they spell doom particularly for the inhabitants of the earth who worship the beast. Although 9:4 shows that Christians are shielded from the demonic plague in the fifth trumpet, there is no reason to assume that *none* of Satan's activities in the woes will affect Christians in any way. We take the mention of woe in 12:12 to confirm our suggestion about the third woe made earlier. The third woe is the seventh trumpet interpreted most broadly as a summary of all that is to happen in the rest of the book. It spells perdition for worshipers of the beast (19:17–18; 20:15) and temporary suffering with eventual vindication for the faithful.

The Woman and the Dragon, Part 2 (12:13–17)

Verse 13 returns to the story of the woman and the dragon. In 12:13–14, the dragon pursues the woman, who is "given the wings of the great eagle, so that she could fly from the serpent into the wilderness, to her place where she is nourished for a time, and times, and half a time" (12:14). But in 12:6, the woman already flees to the wilderness to be protected and nourished by God for 1,260 days. Because of the repetition, some suggest that the author uses two different sources for this aspect of the story. But it is common in ancient documents when there is an insertion into a story for the resumption of the story to repeat what happens just before the insertion. This forms a frame around the insertion. The "time, and times, and half a time" in 12:14 is another reference to Daniel's designation of the time when Antiochus persecuted Judaism. It means three-and-a-half years, approximately 1,260 days. It is the same time period that encompasses the trampling of the holy city (11:2) and the ministry of God's two prophets (11:3). All refer to the time between Satan's ejection from heaven and his final defeat.

The dragon attempts to destroy the woman by spewing forth from his mouth a river by which he hopes to sweep her away. His scheme is frustrated when the earth opens its mouth and swallows the river. In ancient Near Eastern myths, the dragon is associated with water, but this scene has no precise parallel. Water plays a role both here and in the Leto myth, but it is different in the two instances. In the Leto myth, Poseidon uses water to help Leto. In Revelation 12, in contrast, the water is inimical to the woman, and the earth comes to her rescue.

We observed exodus motifs with respect to the woman's flight to the wilderness where she is nourished (12:6). The water in chapter 12 may be part of the author's adaptation of the exodus story here. In the exodus, the Red Sea cuts off the Israelites' escape from their pursuers, but God splits the sea. Our author may intend for the dragon's use of water and the woman's rescue by the land (earth) to allude to the exodus. Of course a river is not a sea, but the splitting of the Red Sea found an echo in Joshua's leading of the people into the promised land, splitting the Jordan River so that they could cross it (Joshua 3). Further, Egypt was closely associated with its river, the Nile. Jeremiah compares Egypt's destructive power to the rising of the Nile (46:7–8). In the Hebrew Bible, Egypt is also spoken of as a dragon or sea-monster. It is Rahab (Isa 30:7; perhaps also 14:4; Ps 87:4), the primeval dragon God defeats to bring about creation. Pharaoh is portrayed as a dragon in Ezek 29:3–5 and 32:2–8. In the passage from Isaiah quoted above, the splitting of the Red Sea at the exodus is compared to the slaying of the dragon Rahab (51:9–11). Another possible exodus allusion (taking the exodus broadly as the escape from Egypt and the wandering in the wilderness) is the earth's swallowing. In Numbers 16, Korah and some others rebel against Moses' authority. The earth opens its mouth and swallows them. In Revelation 12, the earth also serves God's purposes by swallowing the river meant for the woman's destruction.

A final exodus allusion occurs when the woman receives the wings of the great eagle so that she can escape. In the book of Exodus, when the Israelites escape from Egypt into the wilderness and come to Mount Sinai, God tells Moses to say to them, "You have seen what I did to the Egyptians, and how I bore you on eagles' wings and brought you to myself" (19:4; cf. Isa 40:31; Mic 4:9–10). The connection of escape from Egypt with eagles' wings is repeated in the song of Moses in Deuteronomy. Note the collocation of motifs that occurs in Deuteronomy, in the exodus story in Exodus, and in Revelation 12:

> He [God] sustained him [Israel] in a desert land,
> in a howling wilderness waste;
> he shielded him, cared for him,
> guarded him as the apple of his eye.
> As an eagle stirs up its nest,
> and hovers over its young;
> as it spreads its wings, takes them up,
> and bears them aloft on its pinions,
> the LORD alone guided him;
> no foreign god was with him.
> He set him atop the heights of the land,
> and fed him with produce of the field.
> (Deut 32:10–13)

Revelation shares with Deuteronomy the features of the wilderness, escape by an eagle's wings, and nourishment.

In Rev 12:17, the dragon, angry at the woman's escape, goes off to "make war on the rest of her children, those who keep the commandments of God and hold the testimony of Jesus" (cf. 14:12). The rest of the children here are the children in addition to the messiah, that is, faithful Christians. This recalls Gal 4:26 where Paul calls the heavenly Jerusalem the mother of Christians. In 11:7, the beast from the abyss makes war on the prophetic witnesses, conquers them, and kills them. In 13:7, the beast from the sea makes war on the saints and conquers them. All of these references (11:7; 12:17; 13:7) are to the same reality. The period between Satan's fall and his final conquest is marked by his making war on the faithful and conquering them.

The passages recall Dan 7:21 where the horn representing Antiochus makes war on the "holy ones" or "saints" and prevails over them, a situation that endures until Antiochus is overthrown and Michael arises. Revelation is written for Christians in a similar situation.

It is puzzling that the woman is protected during this period while her children are embattled. This is yet another instance of the author presenting the community under different aspects. He presents the ultimate spiritual protection of the community through sealing (7:1–3), measuring of the temple (11:1–2), and protection of the woman (12:6, 13–16; Schüssler Fiorenza 1991, 81). He shows that this does not mean its preservation from persecution when he speaks of the great ordeal Christians must come through (7:14), the trampling of the holy city (11:2), the killing of the two witnesses (11:7–10), and the war Satan wages on the woman's children (12:17).

Boring makes two noteworthy points in connection with Revelation 12 and 13 (1989, 154). The first is that God is a hidden actor here. Although he does not appear as a direct actor (except for his having prepared a place for the woman), his action is hinted at through the use of the passive voice in 12:5, the impersonal "they" in 12:6 (the Greek reads literally, "in order that *they* might nourish her there"), and in chapter 13 through the use of the verb "to give" in the sense of "to allow" (13:5, 7, 14, 15), a usage evident many times in the book. The second point is that although in ancient myth earthly events reflect heavenly ones, that order is to an extent reversed in Revelation 12 and 13 (Boring 1989, 159). The best example of this is that when one compares the defeat of Satan as expressed in parallel fashion in the battle with Michael (12:7–8) and the death of Christ (12:11), it is the latter (an earthly event) that takes precedence and is the real cause of the former (a heavenly event).

Revelation 12 takes a step backward from where chapter 11 finishes. At the blast of the seventh trumpet the consummation is announced (11:15–19). The final victory is won; the kingdom of God and God's messiah is come; and the good are rewarded and the evil punished. The victory announced in chapter 12 is an earlier one, won by Christ on the cross, reflected in Michael's victory in heaven and Satan's descent onto earth. It is the first stage of a victory that will not be complete until Satan, Death, and Hades are cast into the fiery lake (20:7–15). The author has "backed up" so that he can now review Satan's temporary rule and his defeat in more detail and with clearer references to earthly powers and happenings. The rest of the book is dedicated to that review.

Revelation 12:18 is a transition from the story of Satan's fall from heaven to earth to that of the beast who arises from the sea. It reads simply, "Then the dragon took his stand on the sand of the seashore." The proclamation in 12:12 pronounces woe on earth and sea because Satan has come down to them in wrath. In chapter 13, Satan gives his authority to a beast from the sea, supported by a beast from the earth (13:11–18). Chapter 12 ends as the dragon stands on the seashore, awaiting the beast who will be his agent.

The Second Unnumbered Vision: The Beast from the Sea (13:1–10)

Chapter 13 introduces two agents of the dragon. The first is a beast from the sea and the second a beast from the land. In commenting on chapter 12, we traced the background of the primeval dragon or sea-monster. There are also biblical and post-biblical traditions that speak of two primeval monsters. In Job 40–41, God stresses his power by reminding Job of the two great beasts he created. The land-beast is called Behemoth, and the sea-beast is called Leviathan. Leviathan is also the name applied to the single sea-monster in Ps 74:13–14, quoted above. In Job 41, God boasts to Job that only he can approach and fight with Behemoth and Leviathan. The idea of a primeval dragon and the notion that God created two great beasts, one from the sea and the other from the land, are from the same complex of combat myths. Two monsters also appear in *1 Enoch,* a sea-monster named Leviathan and a land-monster named Dundayin (60:7–9). Fourth Ezra speaks of God's creation of Leviathan and Behemoth and says that God has kept them to be eaten by those whom he chooses (6:49–52). A comparison with *2 Bar.* 29:4 clarifies this, showing that the two beasts will be eaten by those who participate in the messianic age. This notion is similar to the one in Ezek 39:17–20, picked up in Rev 19:17–18, where God gives a feast at which the bodies of his defeated foes are the food.

Revelation's symbols operate at several levels simultaneously. They do often refer to earthly events, places, and persons, but they are not reducible to ciphers for them, nor can a simple one-to-one correspondence usually be established between symbol and earthly referent. But, broadly speaking, we take the mainline position that the first beast represents the Roman empire, and perhaps specific emperors within it, while the second beast symbolizes local officials in Asia Minor who are loyal to Rome, and perhaps also more narrowly officials and priests responsible for the operation of the imperial cult. The use of mythology puts those historical entities into a cosmic context, so that they become more than just historical persons.

The beast from the sea in chapter 13 is best interpreted in light of its connections with the dragon of chapter 12 and with its reappearance in chapter 17. An immediate connection is established between the dragon and the sea-beast that comes up from the sea in chapter 13 in that the dragon is standing on the shore of the sea when the beast emerges from it (12:18–13:1). That connection is sharpened when 13:2 says that the dragon, Satan, gave to the beast "his power and his throne and great authority." The beast is therefore an agent of the dragon and derives power and political rule from it. The extent of that authority is demonstrated when it is said that "the whole earth followed the beast" (13:3) and that the world worships both the dragon and the beast (13:4). The people of the world do so because, as they themselves say, "Who is like the beast, and who can fight against it?" (13:4). It is the military strength and brute force of the beast that bring the people to their knees. The phrasing of their amazement at the beast's power is reminiscent of many expressions of praise for God in the Bible (Exod 15:11; Pss 35:10; 89:6; 113:5; etc.), and so it underscores the beast's usurpation of God's status.

When the seer speaks of a sea-beast of great military and political strength to whom the whole earth owes allegiance and who, with the dragon, is worshiped, he refers to Rome and its emperors. The powerful Romans who visited Asia Minor usually came by sea, and the Roman proconsul landed each year at Ephesus. Fourth Ezra pictures Rome as an eagle arising from the sea (11:1).

The dragon, Satan, gives his throne to the beast, Rome (13:2). This forms a contrasting parallel with God and the Lamb. Like God and the Lamb, Satan and the beast share a throne, and like God and the Lamb, they are worshiped. This means that the beast is the Antichrist (although the term "Antichrist" itself does not occur in Revelation [see *Asc. Isa.* 4; Mark 13:6, 21–22]), the one who resembles the Christ but is his opposite, thus fooling many.

Revelation's descriptions of both the dragon and the sea-beast draw on features of the primeval sea-monster. The beast from the sea physically resembles the dragon, for both have seven heads and ten horns (12:3; 13:1). While the dragon has seven diadems on its heads, the beast has ten diadems on its horns. The author uses the same symbol in different ways depending on the context. In chapter 12, he draws connections between Satan and the primeval monster, which has seven heads. Locating the diadems on the dragon's seven heads is natural and indicates its usurpation of God's authority. In chapter 13, the beast's diadems are on its horns, which foreshadows the interpretation of those horns as kings in chapter 17.

The scenario of a beast arising out of the sea brings to mind the similar scene in Daniel 7. In Daniel, four beasts arise from the sea. The sea carries its usual connotation of a force inimical to God. It is chaos, opposed to the order of creation established by God. To create order, God needed to conquer the sea, either explicitly as in non-Israelite creation myths (see Ps 74:13–14; Isa 51:9–10) or more subtly, as in the first account of creation in Genesis. Psalm 77 pictures the battle between God and the waters:

> When the waters saw you, O God,
>   when the waters saw you, they were afraid;
> the very deep trembled.
>   The clouds poured out water;
> the skies thundered;
>   your arrows flashed on every side. (Ps 77:16–17)

This text demonstrates the sort of myth-oriented world in which the writers of the Bible lived. The word for "deep" (it is actually plural: "the deeps") here is the Hebrew *tehomoth,* the same word that describes the deep just before creation in Genesis 1. In the Septuagint this becomes "the abysses." The word "abyss" occurs seven times in Revelation, translated by the NRSV as "bottomless pit." It is the place from which the demonic locusts come (9:1–2), of which Abaddon ("The Destroyer") is king (9:11), from which the beast arises (11:7; 17:8), and the place where the dragon is imprisoned for a thousand years (20:1, 3). The sea and the abyss are interchangeable in Revelation as the place from which the first beast comes (11:7; 13:1; 17:8).

Daniel 7 interprets the four beasts as four kings (7:17) and also as four kingdoms (7:23–24), each of which oppresses Israel and is defeated. Revelation reduces the number of beasts arising from sea from four to one. Our author is not interested in tracing a succession of kingdoms leading to the final, destructive kingdom. Rather, he concentrates on Daniel's fourth beast, now interpreted as Rome, and assimilates the other beasts to it. Revelation is not alone in seeing Rome as the fourth beast of Daniel. The scheme of four kingdoms was known in non-Jewish contexts in the eastern Mediterranean in the Hellenistic period and expresses resistance first to the Greek empires following Alexander the Great's conquests and later to Rome (see Eddy 1961). Various other Jewish and Christian texts also see Rome as the fourth kingdom (see Charles 1920, 1:345–46). Fourth Ezra represents Rome as an eagle that arises out of the sea, and the interpreting angel says to Ezra, "The eagle that you saw coming up from the sea is the fourth kingdom that appeared in a vision to your brother Daniel" (4 Ezra 12:11).

Like Daniel's fourth beast, Revelation's has ten horns. His seven heads are modeled on the dragon of chapter 12, which itself has seven heads, primarily because that is the number of heads possessed by the mythical sea-monster. The total number of heads of Daniel's four beasts is seven as well. This feature of Daniel's picture may itself derive from the seven-headed primeval monster, and our author may have seen the coincidence between Daniel's beasts and the primeval monster. The first of Daniel's beasts is like a lion; the second is like a bear; and the third is like a leopard. The fourth is not compared to any animal, but it has ten horns. Revelation brings all of these features together in the beast, which is "like a leopard, its feet were like a bear's, and its mouth like a lion's mouth" and which has ten horns (13:1–2).

The first beast of Revelation 13 bears blasphemous names on its heads (13:1). This fits his activity later in the chapter:

> The beast was given a mouth uttering haughty and blasphemous words, and it was allowed to exercise authority for forty-two months. It opened its mouth to utter blasphemies against God, blaspheming his name and his dwelling, that is, those who dwell in heaven. Also it was allowed to make war on the saints and to conquer them. It was given authority over every tribe and people and language and na-

> tion, and all the inhabitants of the earth will worship it. (13:5–8)

Here the blasphemous nature of the Roman empire is clearest. What shocks the seer is not just that Rome is powerful, oppressive, and politically supreme. What really tips the scales for our author are the explicitly religious claims for Rome and its emperors, so evident in the environment of Asia Minor.

Rome's religious claims are an affront to God and blaspheme "his name" (13:6). As noted a number of times earlier, names were very important in the ancient world and were thought to carry something of the essence of their owners. To attack God's name is to attack God. The beast also attacks God's dwelling. In 70 C.E., Rome attacked and destroyed the representation of God's dwelling on earth, the temple. Revelation's beast does something analogous, but it attacks heaven itself, where God's attendants and those humans who have already been martyred dwell. Almost every feature of the passage from Revelation just quoted comes from Daniel. The horns on the fourth beast of Daniel 7 represent kings, and one king in particular rebels against God and even attacks heaven itself. At its first appearance this horn was "speaking arrogantly" (Dan 7:8, 11, 20). It "made war with the holy ones [saints, meaning angels] and was prevailing over them" (7:21). Daniel says concerning the horn, "He shall speak words against the Most High, shall wear out the holy ones of the Most High, and shall attempt to change the sacred seasons and the law; and they shall be given into his power for a time, two times, and half a time" (7:25). This horn represents Antiochus IV, persecutor of the Jews.

Like Daniel's horn, Revelation's beast utters arrogant words against God (13:5). Daniel's horn and Revelation's beast both make war on and prevail over the "saints" (Rev 13:7). In Revelation "saints" means faithful Christians, while in Daniel it denotes angels. The difference fades when one realizes that in both Daniel 7 and Revelation 13 an attack on God's people is an attack on heaven and God himself. Both read the troubles of their own times in terms of the combat myth, where rebellion against God is central. In Revelation 12, the dragon sweeps stars, heavenly figures, to the earth with its tail (12:4, based on Dan 8:10) and later makes war on the faithful (12:17), and in 13:6, the beast speaks blasphemies against God's name and dwelling (i.e., those who dwell in heaven). In both Daniel and Revelation the cosmic and earthly struggles are two sides of the same coin. In both books the dominance of forces opposed to God is limited to a symbolic period of time that is variously expressed but amounts to three-and-a-half years. That number is repeated in various forms several times in both books, indicating its importance (Dan 7:25; 8:14; 12:7, 11, 12; Rev 11:2, 3; 12:6, 14; 13:5). It signifies a time determined by God which has a definite end.

Later in Daniel, Antiochus is described as follows: "He shall exalt himself and consider himself greater than any god, and shall speak horrendous things against the God of gods. He shall prosper until the period of wrath is completed, for what is determined shall be done" (11:36; cf. 2 Thess 2:4). This recapitulates Daniel 7 and characterizes the three-and-a-half years of Daniel 7 as a time of wrath that is limited and determined, recalling the statement in Rev 12:12 that the dragon has come down to earth "with great wrath, because he knows that his time is short!"

Both Daniel and Revelation solve the crises facing their communities apocalyptically. The solution depends on revealed knowledge of cosmic struggles that determine what happens on earth. Both contain visions that reveal the supernatural reasons for the hostility of the communities' enemies. In both cases the reason relates to the cosmic rebellious forces that embody themselves on earth in oppressive empires. In both cases the visionaries learn that the time of oppression is limited and short. The purpose of both books is to impart this view to their audiences and thereby make endurance possible.

In Rev 13:7–8, there are three characterizations of people under the sway of Satan and Rome. First, those who follow the beast are from "every tribe and people and language and nation." This is a formula repeated frequently (with variations) in both Revelation (5:9; 7:9; 11:9; 13:7; 14:6) and Daniel (3:4, 7, 29; 5:19; 6:25; 7:14). In both books it usually expresses the extensive following of the rebels against God. But in both books it also supplies a contrasting parallelism, indicating the scope of authority of the one like a son of man in Dan 7:14 and of the Lamb in Rev 5:9 and 7:9. The occurrence of the phrase in Rev 13:7 carries its negative sense, denoting those who oppose God and follow the beast. The second characterization of those under the sway of Satan is "inhabitants of the earth," which in Revelation denotes those who are not among the faithful. Finally, the followers of the beast are everyone "whose name has not been written from the foundation of the world in the book of life of the Lamb that was slaughtered" (13:8). The book of life appears in 3:5; 17:8; 20:12, 15; and 21:27. We discussed its possible background in commenting on 3:5. It is a list of those faithful to God. Those whose names are in the book will enter the new Jerusalem and be eternally in God's presence. Those who follow the beast do not have their names in the book. This reinforces the dualism evident throughout Revelation.

Revelation 17:8 also speaks of names "written in the book of life from the foundation of the world." There is an analogy in Eph 1:4: "He [God] chose us in Christ before the foundation of the world to be holy and blameless before him in love" (cf. Matt 24:24). This may sound like predestination, but Rev 3:5 shows that one may lose one's place in the book as well. Running through Jewish and Christian apocalypticism is a basic tension between God's ordaining everything in advance and free will. It is also found in Paul (see, e.g., Romans 9–11). The basic position of most apocalyptic works is that the eschatological events are determined, but individuals may choose on which side they will be.

Another issue raised by the passage on the first beast needs attention. Speaking of the beast, the text says, "One of its heads seemed to have received a death-blow, but its mortal wound had been healed. In amazement the whole earth followed the beast" (13:3). This verse must be read in light of the vision that follows in 13:11–18. There the second beast makes "the earth and its inhabitants worship the first beast, whose mortal wound had been healed" (13:12), and makes an image "for the beast that had been wounded by the sword and yet lived" (13:14). Finally, the second beast does not allow anyone to buy or sell who does not have as a mark on him- or herself "the name of the [first] beast or the number of its name. This calls for wisdom: let anyone with understanding calculate the number of the beast, for it is the number of a person. Its number is six hundred sixty-six" (13:17–18).

We have already asserted that the first beast represents the Roman empire. In Rev 13:3, one of the beast's heads (kings) receives a deathblow and yet is healed. There is some fluidity of imagery in chapter 13 in that in 13:3 one of the beast's heads is wounded with a deathblow and is healed, whereas in 13:14 it is said that the beast itself is wounded but lives. In 13:18, the number of the beast is said to be the number of a person. Thus the beast itself, which earlier in the chapter signifies the Roman empire as a whole, now symbolizes one of the emperors. The imagery has shifted. Although some commentators object to allowing the interpretation of the beast to shift in this way, the beast imagery in Daniel shifts in precisely the same way. Daniel's beasts represent both kings (7:17) and kingdoms (7:23). Further, the beast and head images meld into one another in Revelation 17. The beast in chapter 17 is the same as the first one in chapter 13. In chapter 17, the interpreting angel tells the seer, "The seven heads are seven mountains on which the woman is seated; also they are seven kings, of whom five have fallen, one is living, and the other has not yet come; and when he comes he must remain only a little while. As for the beast that was and is not, it is an eighth but it belongs to the seven, and it goes to destruction" (17:9–11). Here the beast has seven heads and is itself an eighth head that is at the same time one of the seven! Given the fluid nature of the imagery of both Revelation 17 and Daniel 7, it is best to assume the same for Revelation 13.

There is a parallelism between the Lamb and the wounded beast of chapter 13. A literal translation of part of 13:3 might read, "And one of its heads was as if slaughtered unto death." The phrase translated "as if slaughtered" is the same as occurs in chapter 5 where the seer sees "a Lamb standing as if it had been slaughtered" (5:6; see also 13:8). The similarity with the Lamb is strengthened when in 13:14 the beast is the one "who had been wounded by the sword and yet lived [*ezêsen*]." The same word for "lived" applies to Jesus when he says of himself that he "was dead and came to life [*ezêsen*]" (2:8).

Who then is this individual who receives a deathblow and yet survives and who is set in contrasting parallelism with the Lamb? Some have suggested the emperor Caligula (Gaius), who came close to death through illness but was cured. He went on to insist on divine honors for himself and even ordered that his statue be set up in the Jerusalem temple. Eventually he was assassinated. Caligula's brush with death did not involve a sword, as mentioned in 13:14. Further, the reference to worship in 13:4 need not imply the incident of Caligula's statue in Jerusalem, for the imperial cult in Asia Minor is sufficient reason to speak of worship of the dragon and beast. There is a much better candidate for the wounded beast that survives—the emperor Nero.

Nero was hated by Christians and Romans alike. He was a self-indulgent man who did not shrink from shedding the blood of his own mother. He compared himself to the god Apollo and to other gods and desired divine honors. A great fire devoured much of Rome during his reign, and he blamed the Christians, initiating a brutal persecution in Rome. It was under Nero that the Jews revolted against Rome in 66 C.E. Before his death in 68 C.E., the Roman senate declared him an enemy of the state, and he committed suicide in a villa outside Rome, stabbing himself in the throat. The Roman writer Suetonius says that Nero did retain a few supporters, who "even continued to circulate his edicts, pretending he was still alive and would soon return to confound his enemies" (*Nero* 57). In the same place Suetonius goes on to say, "Twenty years later, when I was a young man, a mysterious individual came forward claiming to be Nero; and so magical was the sound of his name in the Parthians' ears that they supported him to the best of their ability, and only handed him over with great reluctance." Parthia was Rome's rival to the east, and threats of a Parthian invasion often shook the empire (see comments on 6:2 and 9:13–19). The Roman historian Tacitus also says that many refused to believe that Nero had died and that there were several who pretended to be he, leading to various upsets (*Hist.* 1.2; 2.8–9; cf. Dio Cassius 64.9).

The return of Nero is also predicted in *Sib. Or.* 5:93–110, where he comes from Persia (a cipher for Parthia), bringing war and destruction, especially on Asia Minor (see also 5:361–84). In the context of the war of the Jews against Rome (66–70 C.E.), *Sibylline Oracles* 4 speaks of Nero fleeing from Italy to Parthia (4:119–24) and then of his returning at the head of Parthian hosts (4:137–48). *Sibylline Oracles* 5:34 states that Nero claimed that he was equal to God, which recalls the depictions of Antiochus IV in Daniel and of the beast in Revelation.

In a section dealing with the coming of Rome and with eschatological events, another part of the oracles predicts the following:

> Then Beliar will come from the Sebastenoi [meaning Augustus's line],
> and he will raise up the height of the mountains,
> he will raise up the sea,
> the great fiery sun and shining moon,
> and he will raise up the dead,
> and perform many signs for men.
> But they will not be effective in him.

> But he will, indeed, also lead men astray,
> and he will lead astray many faithful, chosen Hebrews,
> and also other lawless men who have not yet listened to the word of God. (*Sib. Or.* 3:63–70)

This passage is especially interesting in that it identifies Nero with Beliar, another name for the leader of the demons. Nero/Beliar will do signs that will lead people astray, just as happens in Revelation 13. The same identification is made in *Ascension of Isaiah* 4, a Jewish work revised by Christians:

> And after it [the world's allotted time] has been brought to completion, Beliar will descend, the great angel, the king of this world, which he has ruled over ever since it existed. He will descend from his firmament in the form of a man, a king of iniquity, a murderer of his mother — this is the king of this world — and will persecute the plant which the twelve apostles of the Beloved will have planted.

The passage goes on to relate the miraculous signs this Nero/Beliar will work, setting up his own image in every city and deceiving even the faithful into thinking that he is Jesus. In other words, this Nero/Beliar is the Antichrist. The expectations in the *Ascension of Isaiah* 4 and in *Sibylline Oracles* 3 go beyond the idea that Nero is not really dead. They transform Nero into a figure of supernatural proportions. They expect him to play a role even after his death. This expectation is frequently referred to as the Nero redivivus myth, that is, the myth of Nero come back from the dead (Charles 1920, 1:350, traces the development of the Nero legends in more detail).

Nero is the likeliest candidate for the Roman emperor who received a deathblow and survived (or perhaps came back to life). The last clue to his identity is that the number of his name is 666 (Rev 13:18). An alternative reading in some manuscripts of Revelation is 616. The author says that "calculating" the number "calls for wisdom," meaning esoteric knowledge. Number symbolism was very significant in the ancient world (see introduction under "Numbers in Revelation"), and words could be turned into numbers and numbers into words because numbers were represented by letters in Greek and Hebrew. It is easy to take a name and turn it into a number. For example, *Sib. Or.* 1:324–30 calculates the value of the name "Jesus" to be 888.

However, it is far more difficult to translate a number into a name, for there will always be a large number of possibilities. As might be expected, this has led to many suggestions about the meaning of 666.

Since we have decided on other grounds that the best candidate for the beast of 13:17–18 is Nero, it is legitimate to see whether his name can be equivalent to the number 666. In Hebrew, the name Nero Caesar can be written *nron qsr,* which is equivalent to the value 666. Further, this option can explain the variant reading 616. In Latin the name Nero would not have a final *n* as it does in Hebrew. The value of the Hebrew letter *n* is 50. If it is dropped, the value of Nero's name is 616. Some object to calculating the number using Hebrew letters, since Revelation is written in Greek (Mounce 1977, 264–65), but the author uses Hebrew words in 9:11 and 16:16 (Boring 1989, 163), and many think that he spoke Hebrew, based on his Greek diction and use of scripture. The calculation (invited by our author in 13:18) of 666 as *nron qsr* does not in itself prove anything, but taken with other indications that Nero is in mind, it is confirming evidence. It is not surprising that the only Roman emperor of the first century who conducted an extensive and notorious persecution of Christians is the model for the oppressive and satanic Roman empire.

Revelation 12–13 is a good example of what Batto calls mythopoeic speculation, or mythmaking. Mythic conceptions about the universe and its origins and structure can address changing circumstances. Christians who found themselves victims of Roman hostility and brutality needed to make sense of their experience. To make sense of their experience, early Christians rewrote the myths with which they had grown up, be they Jewish, Greek, or of other origins. This changed both the way their myths were told and their very perceptions of the world. The man Nero and the human institution of empire took on cosmic proportions and were transformed into otherworldly beasts with cosmic powers. Religious and political claims were seen as attacks on God and heaven. This mythmaking activity puts Revelation firmly in the biblical and ancient Near Eastern context of mythopoeic thinking.

In order to explain the background of the wounded head and wounded beast, we have jumped ahead into the second part of chapter 13 and even into chapter 17. We now return to the end of the first vision of chapter 13. It closes with a prophetic warning whose precise meaning is disputed. The warning reads as follows in the NRSV:

> Let anyone who has an ear listen:
> If you are to be taken captive,
> into captivity you go;
> if you kill with the sword,
> with the sword you must be killed. (13:9–10)

In these verses the author steps out of the mode of narration of his visions to direct prophetic address. The NRSV translation expresses this by using the second person, transferring the warning into a direct address to Revelation's audience, but in the original Greek the warning is in the third person, which makes its addressees less clear.

The warning is introduced with the exhortation to listen in 13:9, like those at the end of each of the messages to the seven churches (chapters 2–3). The formulation implies that not everyone can understand the message. The prophetic warning adapts Jer 15:2 and 43:11. Revelation's warning is meant to strengthen the audience for what they must undergo, for it is followed by the words, "Here is a call for the endurance and faith of the saints" (13:10). Jeremiah prophesies God's punishment to Israel, and his oracle stresses the inevitability of that punishment, which consists of pestilence, sword, famine, and captivity. From those four catastrophes our author chooses captivity and sword as most relevant to his own situation.

The first half of the warning is clear. If captivity awaits one, one must endure it. There is no choice, except to apostasize and therefore lose all hope of eternal life with God in the new Jerusalem. The second half of the warning is more problematic, for there are variant readings in the manuscripts (for analysis of the options, see Charles 1920, 1:355–57). The NRSV adopts the following reading: "If you kill with the sword, / with the sword you must be killed." If this is correct, then the warning is both about something that might happen to one, captivity, and something one might inflict on others, the sword. Other manuscripts have the "if" clause in the passive voice: "If you are killed with the sword. . . ." In this case the two parts would form a better parallel. Christians might be imprisoned and they might be killed, and they must endure whichever comes to them. Yet another reading makes the first part active ("If one leads into captivity") and accepts the active reading in the second part. If this is the text, then it predicts retributive justice for the oppressors. Those who imprison will be imprisoned; those who kill with the sword will be killed with the sword.

Reading the first part of the warning as active ("If one leads one into captivity") is weakly attested in the manuscripts, and it could be a scribe's effort to bring the first part of the warning into line with an active reading in the second part ("If one kills by the sword"). This eliminates the third reading presented in the previous paragraph. This leaves the decision about whether the warning of the second part ought to read "If one is killed" or "If one kills." Both readings have solid attestation in the ancient manuscripts. As noted earlier, in textual criticism the more difficult reading usually gets the nod, for it is easier to explain changing a difficult reading to an easier one than vice versa. The active reading ("If one kills by the sword") is the more difficult in this case, for it results in less perfect parallelism between the two parts and also raises the question of why the author would need to convince his audience not to take up the sword against the Romans, which would seem a rather remote possibility. In the messages to the churches, the seer is far more concerned about the opposite possibility — that Christians will assimilate to the culture of Roman Asia Minor. But given this context, it is more likely that the warning should be passive in both parts, despite the principle of textual criticism to adopt the more difficult reading. The author's purpose is to prepare his audience for persecution and death, imprisonment and the sword. The shift from the passive to the active voice for the second part of the warning may be explained by the influence of Jesus' saying preserved in Matt 26:52: "All who take the sword will perish by the sword."

The Third Unnumbered Vision: The Beast from the Land (13:11–18)

Although the pairing of a beast from the sea and one from the land may be influenced by such passages as Job 40–41, *1 Enoch* 60, 4 Ezra 6, and *2 Baruch* 29, the description of Revelation's land-beast owes nothing to those passages. The land-beast in Revelation "had two horns like a lamb and it spoke like a dragon" (13:11). Although the text does not say that the beast is like the Lamb of Revelation 5, it is hard to imagine that the author does not intend a comparison between the two. Just as the first beast resembles Jesus, so does the second. This is another contrasting parallel, recalling the Antichrist motif, noted in our comments on 13:3. The second beast may look like a lamb, but it speaks like a dragon. The message of the second beast conforms to that of the dragon. The task of the second beast is to serve the first, and the first owes its power and authority to the dragon and carries out its purposes. The picture of the second beast as one who looks like a lamb but speaks like a dragon is one of a deceiver, a picture that is developed in the verses that follow. One is reminded of Jesus' saying, "Beware of false prophets, who come to you in sheep's clothing but inwardly are ravenous wolves" (Matt 7:15).

The activity of the second beast centers on the cult of the first. The description of that activity begins with the statement that the second beast "exercises all the authority of the first beast on its behalf" (13:12). Those who would exercise the authority of Rome in Asia Minor would be the local aristocracy and officials, and they would also have the most at stake in maintaining good relations with Rome. The next information about the second beast's activity is that it "makes the earth and its inhabitants worship the first beast, whose mortal wound had been healed" (13:12). The first beast is worshiped along with the dragon (13:4), and the job of the second beast is to enforce that worship. In a broad sense, this would be the responsibility of the ruling class in Asia Minor. In a narrower sense, it would designate those directly involved in the imperial cult either as priests or in some other capacity. The second beast causes an image of the first beast to be set up by earth's inhabitants (13:14). A major activity of the imperial cult was to set up images of the emperor. Such images were important in the imperial cult. Pliny, writing to the emperor Trajan in the early second century from northern Asia Minor, says that he tests Christians by making them offer wine or incense before the emperor's statue (see introduction under "Christians in the Roman Empire").

The next three verses specify some activities of the imperial cultic officials. They perform great signs, including making fire come down to earth, and by those signs they deceive the earth's inhabitants; they cause the earth's inhabitants to make an image of the first beast; and they give breath to the image so that it can speak (13:13–15). Jesus predicts, "False messiahs and false prophets will appear and produce signs and omens, to lead astray, if possible, the elect" (Mark 13:22; see 13:5–6).

The power of the second beast is real. Its deception consists in the conclusions to which the exercise of that power leads. The earth's inhabitants conclude that the first beast is divine, and they worship it and pledge it allegiance. For our author, a more accurate conclusion would be that the second beast was simply allowed by God to have these powers and that true sovereignty belongs to God. This is conveyed both by the claim that the second beast "deceives" the world and by the use of the term "to give" in the sense of "to allow." It deceives people "by the signs that it is allowed [which are given to it] to perform on behalf of the beast" (13:14).

The author mentions two specific signs of the beast. The first is that it can call down fire "from heaven to earth in the sight of all" (13:13). This is a sign performed by the prophet Elijah (2 Kgs 1:10, 12) and is similar to the power possessed by God's two prophetic witnesses: "Fire pours from their mouths and consumes their foes" (11:5). In the gospel of Luke, Jesus' disciples think they have this sort of prophetic power and offer to use it on his behalf (Luke 9:54).

The false prophet is a contrasting parallel to the two true prophets in chapter 11. The possession of such powers is no guarantee that anyone is of God. These powers can as easily be evidence for being in league with the devil (see the accusation that Jesus is allied with Satan in Mark 3:22). The "lawless one" in 2 Thessalonians is an Antichrist figure: "The coming of the lawless one is apparent in the working of Satan, who uses all power, signs, lying wonders, and every kind of wicked deception for those who are perishing" (2 Thess 2:9–10).

It is unclear precisely what in the imperial cult might correspond to calling fire down from heaven. Ancient literature attests to various sorts of trickery to which Hellenistic cults resorted to impress their audiences (Charles 1920, 1:361; Schüssler Fiorenza 1991, 85; Mounce 1977, 261). What is remarkable in Revelation 13 is that the author does not accuse imperial cultic officials of trickery. God gives them real powers. The deception occurs in the interpretations of the powers. The second beast is also allowed to give breath to the image of the first beast so that it can speak. Ancient sources contain examples of priests using ventriloquism or pipes within statues to create the impression that they could speak, but the author does not claim such trickery. He seems to take the supernatural manifestations of the imperial cult at face value, but he asserts their satanic origins.

The second beast, the false prophet, does not stop at miraculous signs to win over humanity to the first beast's worship. It also resorts to brute force. In 13:15, it causes "those who would not worship the image of the beast to be killed." This implies that the imperial cult was forced on all of the empire's residents and that there would be martyrdom for all faithful Christians. We have examined the idea of universal persecution and martyrdom in the introduction and found it to be a question of the seer's expectation, not founded on any act of Domitian or even of Nero. No emperor of the first century made a concerted effort to enforce emperor worship throughout the empire. But the imperial cult was always present as a dangerous and sinister reminder of Rome's claims, and it could always be used against Jews or Christians. The author sees it as a powerful symbol and a real threat. Since Judaism was an established and protected religion, the imperial cult could be more of a danger to Christians than to Jews, depending on how it was enforced. This would lend urgency to the dispute between some Christians and Jews about who was the true Israel.

Besides the peril of death, the second beast also enforces economic sanctions against those who refuse imperial worship. Revelation claims that those who worship the beast receive a mark on their right hand or forehead, and no one without the mark is allowed to buy or sell (13:16–17). The mark is the name of the first beast or the number of its name (see also 14:11; 15:2; cf. 17:5). This is a contrasting parallel to the fact that the 144,000 receive God's seal on their foreheads in 7:1–3, which consists of the name of God and of the Lamb (see 3:12; 14:1; 22:4). To be marked with the name of God and the Lamb or the name of the beast signifies that one belongs to one or the other. The word for "seal" in 13:16 is *charagma,* the same word used to denote the emperor's seal that marked what was his.

The background of the beast's mark is uncertain. The sealing of the faithful in Revelation 7 is modeled on the same sort of action in Ezekiel 9, and the sealing of the beast's worshipers in Revelation 13 is a contrast to the sealing of the faithful in chapter 7. That much is clear. But there are various possible backgrounds for sealing in the Hellenistic world, as mentioned in our commentary on chapter 7. Suggested backgrounds have been the branding of slaves or soldiers or magical sealings for special protection (see Charles 1920, 1:363 n.1, for other possibilities; Mounce 1977, 262). An odd feature here is that the name is either on the forehead or on the right hand (cf. 20:4). Some suggest that this parodies the Jewish practice of wearing phylacteries, small leather boxes containing a portion of the Torah and tied by leather straps to the forehead and left forearm or hand. It is difficult to see what a reference to phylacteries could mean, for Revelation does not oppose any Jewish practices as such.

It is unlikely that the author actually expects that every person in the world will have an observable mark on his or her body indicating allegiance to God or to Satan, just as it is unlikely that Ezekiel thought he could go to Jerusalem and recognize those who had been sealed by the angel in his vision of Ezekiel 9. The seals are symbolic. But the question arises whether the economic sanctions are real or merely symbolic. The seer is concerned with the degree of engagement of Christians with their surrounding culture. Early Christianity was predominantly urban, and city-dwelling Christians would have to buy and sell in order to survive and would need some occupation entailing buying and selling. If officials of Asia Minor prohibited buying and selling to all except those who worshiped the beast, it could be disastrous for Christians. But we have no evidence that such a prohibition was in force in Asia Minor at this time.

A helpful suggestion is that the reference here is to coinage (Yarbro Collins 1977b, 252–54). Many of the coins of the time bear images of the emperor, his name, and inscriptions honoring him. Some coins imply divine status for the emperor or members of his family. Coinage was a major vehicle of propaganda. It would not be surprising that Christians sharing the strict views of our author would object even to using such coins. A further objection might be that human images of any sort would be offensive to Jews or Jewish Christians who interpreted strictly the Torah's prohibition against images (e.g., Exod 20:4). Attitudes toward this prohibition may lie behind the dispute between Jesus and the Pharisees about paying taxes to Caesar with coins bearing his image (Matt 22:17–21). It is said that the Zealots, rebels against Rome during the war of 66–70 C.E., refused to carry Roman coins because of their idolatrous images (Yarbro Collins 1979, 96). The first-century Jewish historian Josephus tells the story of Pilate bringing military standards bearing the image of Caesar into Jerusalem (*Ant.* 18 §§55–59). The people's response forced him to withdraw the standards. The leader of the Jewish revolt against Rome in 132–135 C.E., Bar Kochba, minted his own coins without human images. Revelation 13:17 may be criticizing the propagandistic value of the very medium of economic exchange, Roman coins.

Chapters 12 and 13 set the stage for the final showdown between God and Satan, the Lamb and the beast, the Christian prophets and the false prophets, and those with the mark of God and the Lamb and those with the mark of the beast. Members of the seer's audience can now analyze their own environment and understand the cosmic forces at play in historical events. They have had their apocalyptic consciousness raised, and with this newfound or reinvigorated perception they can accomplish what the seer demands: to endure hostility and persecution. They can see at a glance the beginning and end of the conflict in which they are participating and have a clear idea of their role in it. They possess the "wisdom" demanded in 13:18, the apocalyptic wisdom necessary to pierce the veil of things as they appear and to arrive at a vision of things as they are.

The Fourth Unnumbered Vision: The 144,000 (14:1–5)

The first three verses of chapter 14 are a vision (14:1–3), which the next two interpret (14:4–5). In the vision John sees the Lamb standing on Mount Zion, and with him are 144,000 with the names of the Father and the Lamb on their foreheads. This is an obvious allusion to the 144,000 who were sealed on their foreheads in 7:1–8. Mounce comments that of those sealed in chapter 7, none has been lost (1977, 268). In our comments on that passage we made the case that the 144,000 are a subset of the total number of faithful Christians. They are the martyrs and will be raised from the dead before everyone else to participate in the messianic kingdom (20:4–6). This does not contradict 13:15, which says that *everyone* who refuses to worship the first beast will be killed. Rather, the author stresses something slightly different in each of these passages because of the context of each. Chapter 13 portrays the absolute sway and totalistic demands of the Roman empire. Rome's idolatrous claims potentially put all Christians (and Jews, for that matter) in jeopardy. In this context, the author seems to anticipate universal martyrdom (13:15). The seer must know, however, that not every faithful Christian who has died in the past was a martyr, and he probably has a more realistic expectation of the extent of any future persecution than appears in 13:15. Therefore in 7:1-8, 14:1-5, and 20:4-6, he presents a special group within the larger group of all Christians, and that special group consists of actual martyrs.

If this interpretation is correct, then the further designation of this group as the ones who "follow the Lamb wherever he goes" (14:4) means that they imitate Christ even to the point of being put to death. The verb "to follow" is a common one in the gospels to denote being Christian, but the added phrase "wherever he goes" may carry the added meaning of undergoing martyrdom. The only other group that is explicitly said to "follow" Christ is the army that follows him to battle in 19:14, whose identity we will discuss in that place. The 144,000 who "follow" the Lamb in 14:1-5 contrast with those who follow the beast (13:3).

Several other features of 14:1-5 indicate that the 144,000 are a special group within Christianity. The strongest evidence is that they "have been redeemed from humankind as first fruits for God and the Lamb." "First fruits" (Greek: *aparchê*) is a technical term for the part of the agricultural produce that must be given to God before the rest is freed for human use (Exod 23:19; Deut 12:6). Charles shows that *aparchê* can also mean simply "offering" or "gift" in the Septuagint, but its use elsewhere in the New Testament justifies the translation "first fruits" (1920, 2:6-7). In 1 Corinthians 15, Paul says that Christ is the first fruits of those who have died, meaning that his resurrection happens before the resurrection of all who belong to him (15:20, 23). In Rom 11:16, Paul uses *aparchê* to contrast potential Jewish converts with the whole body of believers. In Rom 16:5, he says that the convert Epaenetus was the first fruits of Asia for Christ. In Romans, Paul also uses the term to show what we now have in Christ (the Spirit) and what is to come in the future (resurrection; 8:23). In Jas 1:18, Christians are said to be the first fruits of all God's creatures.

These references justify taking *aparchê* in Rev 14:4 as meaning a specific group that is part of the larger group. Furthermore, twice in 14:1-5 the 144,000 are said to be redeemed, once from the earth (14:3) and once from humankind (14:4). To redeem is to buy (used in 13:17 for ordinary commerce), and the price paid is the death of Christ. This applies to all Christians, as 5:9 makes clear: "You [the Lamb] were slaughtered and by your blood you ransomed [redeemed] for God saints from [*ek*] every tribe and language and people and nation." The Greek preposition *ek* denotes origin here, and the idea is that Christians are separated from humanity as a whole through their relation with Christ. In 14:3–4, the 144,000 are redeemed from (*apo*) the rest of humanity, and the Greek preposition again emphasizes separation.

The overall impression of 14:1–5, read in conjunction with chapters 7 and 20, is that the 144,000 are a special group within the body of believers. Their further characterization in 14:4 has been a cause of much puzzlement and consternation: "It is these who have not defiled themselves with women, for they are virgins." These words are in the vision's interpretation (14:4–5). If taken literally, this advocates celibacy. Charles claims that 14:4–5 was inserted by a "monkish interpolator," "who sought by his manipulation of the text to destroy the identity of the 144,000 in vii. 4–8 and the 144,000 in the present passage, and to transform them into a body of monkish celibates" (1920, 2:6). Here as elsewhere we decline to follow Charles in his emendation of the text, but he is correct when he says that if 14:4 advocates cessation of sexual contact between men and women, it is unique in the book. But even if it is meant only figuratively, it still stands out from other figurative uses of sex in the book in that intercourse with women is seen as inherently defiling.

Yarbro Collins thinks that literal virginity is meant here because of the concreteness of the description (1987, 86). If the seer has literal celibacy in mind, and if one takes the 144,000 to mean all Christians, as does Charles, then 14:4 would advocate universal celibacy. If the 144,000 are a special group of Christians, then because of their celibacy they would occupy a higher status than other Christians. This calls for a brief discussion of celibacy in ancient Judaism and early Christianity.

Celibacy for ascetic purposes was uncommon in ancient Judaism, but sexual abstinence for the purpose of ritual purity was well known. Modern readers tend to read terms like "pure" and "impure" as moral categories, but in ancient Judaism they were ritual terms, often with no moral overtone. What was impure was not to come into God's presence. For example, touching a dead body could make one temporarily impure, even though doing so might even be an act of piety, as in the case of Tobit, mentioned in our comments on 11:9. When purity rules dealt with relations between the sexes, they inevitably reflected the patriarchal nature of ancient society. Within that context they were not necessarily intended to be denigrating to women, although from our point of view they were. Thus priests about to participate in certain religious ceremonies and warriors about to engage in holy war (both groups male) in which God was present were commanded to sexual abstinence. It was probably for these sorts of reasons that some of the Dead Sea Scrolls advocated celibacy.

In 1 Corinthians 7, Paul offers a lengthy discussion of sexual abstinence. His views are not ones that make for a healthy theology of marriage. He considers sexual intercourse a necessity for those who cannot control their passions and allows marriage so that they may satisfy their needs without sinning. But he wishes that all could be celibate as he is. His reasons for this are not ascetic. Rather, he thinks that the second coming of Christ is near, and he therefore considers it urgent that as many people as possible be converted, since only those who belong to Christ will be saved. All Christians who have the strength to resist their natural impulses ought to do so for the sake of dedicating their efforts to making more converts and building up the church. It is not clear what Paul's view would be if he did not think that the end was near. Given his low view of human sexuality, he may still have thought it more useful to devote oneself entirely to the apostolate rather than raising a family. There is a saying of Jesus in Matt 19:12 that says with approval that "there are eunuchs who have made themselves eunuchs for the sake of the kingdom of heaven. Let anyone accept this who can." Celibacy for the sake of the apostolate, found in Paul, is probably behind this saying as well, although Daniel Olson suggests that it is because the faithful are like angels that they are encouraged to avoid sexual intercourse (Olson 1997, 503; see Luke 20:34–36). Despite the high view of celibacy in Paul and Matthew, neither author enjoins celibacy on everyone. In following centuries, Christianity began to value celibacy for ascetic reasons, although it was never demanded of everybody.

Given our arguments for seeing the 144,000 as a special group, and given the context of ancient Judaism and early Christianity in which celibacy, when encouraged at all, was for specific purposes like engagement in the cult, in warfare, and in the apostolate, it is highly unlikely that our author advocates universal celibacy or celibacy for ascetic reasons as a condition for being truly Christian. Such a radical view is supported nowhere else in the book. But could the author be encouraging celibacy for the few for other reasons, as do Paul and Matthew? Even this less radical demand is not in evidence anywhere else in Revelation. If the author really desires his audience to abstain from sex, this sole mention would hardly make his case. Furthermore, if we are right to see a connection between 7:1–8, 14:1–5, and 20:2–4, and if these passages are about martyrs, then it is very difficult to interpret them as actual virgins. Our author cannot have thought that the only people martyred were male celibates. In Revelation as a whole the issue is not sexual abstinence but resistance to Rome's idolatry.

If the author is not interested in sexual abstinence in itself, then what could it mean that the 144,000 are virgins and that they have not defiled themselves with women? The book of Revelation is filled with sexual imagery that is figurative. When the seer castigates "Jezebel" for teaching fornication and threatens "those who commit adultery with her," few take "fornication" literally. When John sees a vision of a "great whore" sitting on a red beast, drunk with the blood of the saints, "with whom the kings of the earth have committed fornication," this is a metaphor for alliances with and subjugation to Rome. In the Bible, fornication and adultery are frequent images for idolatry (see especially Hosea). Conversely, faithful Israel is sometimes depicted as a virgin (2 Kgs 19:21; Lam 2:13; Jer 18:13; Amos 5:2; see Mounce 1977, 270). In 2 Cor 11:2, Paul says he has betrothed the church as a "pure bride" to Christ, and in Revelation 19 the church also appears as a pure bride. There seems to be little reason, then, to take 14:4 literally.

Boring (1989, 168–69) makes the case that 14:4 can be interpreted figuratively and fit well into the context of Revelation as a whole. He points out that Christians are portrayed as a priestly people in the book and that Christian life is seen in terms of battle with Rome and Satan. Precedents for sexual abstinence in early Judaism occur in priestly and military contexts, as mentioned above. In such contexts defilement is not a moral category. It means being in a state of ritual impurity with the resulting inability to participate in the cult or in holy war. Sexual abstinence with the goal of taking part in holy war then becomes an image for being ready to join the Lamb in resistance to Rome, so not "defiling" oneself with women means avoidance of ritual defilement and does not necessarily carry the same connotations as does the word "defile" today.

Schüssler Fiorenza (1991, 88) warns against taking 14:4 literally:

> A literal meaning of "women" and of the 144,000 as male ascetics is unlikely since Revelation's language does not function as a cipher with a one-to-one meaning. Moreover, such a misogynist stance appears nowhere else in Revelation. Since Philo (*De Cherub.* 49–50) uses the grammatically masculine term *virgins* similarly in a metaphorical sense for God's people, male and female, such a metaphorical sense has been understood. A metaphorical meaning of the 144,000 is therefore likely. In addition, celibacy is not stressed elsewhere in Revelation. Since in the rhetorical context and sign system of Revelation sexual language is used metaphorically, the phrase "they have not soiled themselves with women" refers to the idolatry of the imperial cult.

This discussion has not solved the puzzle of why the author has used the particular language of virginity and avoidance of defilement with women, as opposed simply to "fornication," as he does elsewhere. It is the unusual nature of this language in Revelation and its specificity that convince Yarbro Collins that literal virginity is meant. Yarbro Collins observes that the ancient Jewish philosopher Philo supplies a parallel to Rev 14:4 when he paints a picture of Moses as a priest and says that "he had to be clean, as in soul, so also in body, to have no dealings with any passion, purifying himself from all the calls of mortal nature, food and drink and intercourse with women" (*On the Life of Moses* 2:68–69; translation of F. H. Colson in LCL, as quoted by Yarbro Collins 1987, 88). Although Philo, unlike the author of Revelation, is influenced by a metaphysical dualism derived from his study of Greek philosophy, Yarbro Collins suggests that both authors dissociated "earthly things" from heavenly. She notes another important parallel, this time from a Jewish apocalypse, in the *Book of the Watchers,* preserved in *1 Enoch* 1–36. The book tells a version of the fall of angels (called watchers) from heaven, who then ask Enoch to intercede for them. When Enoch does so, God says to tell the angels that they ought to be interceding for humans, instead of a human interceding for them. God then accuses them of defiling themselves with women (*1 Enoch* 15:2–4). The angels belong to the heavenly world, not the earthly, and they fulfill a priestly role there. Their intercourse with women means a blurring of categories that is abhorrent to the priestly outlook. In *1 Enoch,* the fallen angels may represent actual priests of whom the book disapproves (Suter 1979).

Olson (1997) builds on Yarbro Collins's suggested parallel with *1 Enoch* and the fallen watchers and finds the key to the puzzle of Rev 14:4 in that allusion. He rejects the parallels adduced above to sexual abstention by soldiers and priests, for neither were expected to remain virgins (1997, 495). But the angels of the *Book of the Watchers* were supposed to maintain their virginity. Olson emphasizes that the priestly function assigned to the watchers—that is, intercession—is now taken up by the human Enoch (1997, 501). He sees the depiction of the 144,000 in Revelation 14 as also having priestly characteristics, for they sing a new song before the throne (a priestly function—1 Chronicles 25), as do God's angelic servants in Rev 5:8-10, who sing a new song and offer incense—priestly tasks. Indeed those angelic servants praise the Lamb for having formed a priestly people (5:10). Olson interprets the fact that no one but the 144,000 can learn the new song (14:3) as priestly privilege. By such allusions, he takes the seer to be suggesting a contrast between the unfaithful priestly angels of *1 Enoch* and the 144,000. He also reads Revelation as part of a larger set of traditions in Jewish apocalypses and early Christianity that see the faithful as angels or equal to them (1997, 501-7). No conclusions about actual virginity ought to be drawn from Revelation 14. Rather, it is likely that "John is merely portraying the church as a 'kingdom of priests' replacing the fallen angelic priesthood" (1997, 509).

Chapter 7 says that the 144,000 are sealed, but it does not say exactly what the seal is. Chapter 14 discloses that it consists of the names of God and the Lamb, recalling 3:12, where the Philadelphians learn that Jesus will write on them the names of God, the new Jerusalem, and Jesus' own new name (cf. 9:4; 22:4). Christians are a priestly people, and the high priest of the Jewish cult wore God's name on the front of his turban, on his forehead (Exod 28:37). The 144,000 are with the Lamb, who stands on Mount Zion, where the temple stood. The scene draws on liturgical images, and it contrasts with chapter 13, where the dragon stands on the shore of the sea, representing forces against God from which the beast arises. People worship the beast and the dragon, and each of the beast's followers wears its name, not God's, on his or her forehead or hand.

The seer tells us that he sees the Lamb standing on Mount Zion, but it is not clear whether this is in heaven or on earth, before the great tribulation or after. Although Revelation images a temple in heaven, nowhere in the book does it state that there is a Mount Zion there, so we ought to take it as being on earth. If this is so, then the seer may be thinking of the locus of the messianic reign of 20:4-6. It is not explicit in chapter 20 that the messianic kingdom is centered on Mount Zion, but that would be its logical center (Charles 1920, 2:1), for in many Jewish and Christian scenarios of the end, Jerusalem and Zion are central (e.g., Isa 2:2-4; Joel 2:32). In 4 Ezra 13, one like a son of man, who is also God's son and the messiah, stands on Mount Zion and conquers the nations (see Rev 20:7) and then gathers a multitude about him (4 Ezra 13:5-13).

The scene in Rev 14:1-5 probably takes place in the seer's future. The 144,000 are the complete number of martyrs expected in 6:11, who have come through the impending ordeal (see comments on 6:11 and 7:1-8). Since the scene of salvation in 14:1-5 is limited to the 144,000, it must refer to the millennial kingdom of Rev 20:4-6, where a select group reigns with Christ for a thousand years. The special nature of the group is underlined by their being the only ones able to learn the "new song" sung in heaven that sounds as if it is sung by heavenly harpists (cf. 5:9-10). The sound of the hymn is compared both to mighty waters (see 1:15; 19:6; cf. Ezek 43:2) and to loud thunder (cf. esp. 6:1; 10:3-4). The sounds of mighty waters and thunder are also combined in Ezek 1:24, where they describe the sound of the wings of God's cherubim. This stresses the hymn's heavenly origin. It is mysterious, powerful, and majestic, fitting tribute to the supreme sovereign offered by his most faithful servants.

The final two qualities of the 144,000 mentioned are that there is no falsehood in their mouths and that they are "blameless." The first quality fits with the ongoing motif of truth and falsehood in Revelation. God is the true sovereign; the beast is false. True prophets are to be found in the Bible and in the faithful Christian communities; the false prophet serves the seabeast (16:13; 19:20; 20:10). At the end of the book, liars are excluded from the new Jerusalem and end up in the fiery lake (21:8; 22:15). As God's ultimate witnesses, the 144,000 are completely without falsehood. They are "blameless" in this essential way. The term "blameless" is often found in the Hebrew Bible in a cultic context, where it describes the only sacrifice worthy of

God. It is applied to Christ as a sacrifice in Heb 9:14 and 1 Pet 1:19. This fits with the sacrificial terminology of "first fruits," applied to the 144,000 in 14:4.

The Fifth Unnumbered Vision: The Three Angels (14:6–13)

This vision consists of announcements by three angels flying in midheaven. The first angel calls upon the earth's inhabitants to give glory to God, for the time of judgment has come. The second proclaims Babylon's fall. The third predicts punishment for those who bear the mark of the beast. The vision is a logical conclusion to what has gone before in this vision cycle. Visions one and two present the cosmic dragon and his earthly agent, both of whom receive glory from the earth's inhabitants in their worship. The third vision speaks of the first beast's earthly agents who enforce this worship. Vision four reveals the blessed fate of those who resist. The present vision, vision five, depicts the punishment of those who do not. With this vision the pattern emphasized by Yarbro Collins (1979, xii–xiii)—persecution, punishment, and reward—is complete. The final two visions of the series present another punishment scene (14:14–20), followed by another scene of reward (15:2–4). The effect of the entire series is to make clear the choice facing humans and the results of that choice.

The first angel flies in midheaven and cries out with a loud voice (14:6–7). The next two angels follow him in midheaven, and the third angel also cries with a loud voice (14:8–9). This threefold proclamation is thus accessible to the whole earth. To stress further its universal application the seer uses the familiar formula, "To every nation and tribe and language and people" (14:6). The first angel's message, termed an "eternal gospel," is an imperative to fear God and give him glory. The term "gospel" or "good news" was used by imperial propaganda to tout the emperor's accomplishments. But our author demands that earth's inhabitants imitate those of heaven who repeatedly give God, not Caesar, glory. Those who taste God's wrath in chapter 11 also give God glory (11:13). The angel's "eternal gospel" in Rev 14:6–7 demands recognition of God's sovereignty, particularly in the face of the fraudulent demand for recognition by the beast and its agent, the second beast. Humans have made their choice in chapter 13, but final judgment is now prefaced with this call to decision. It is a demand for unconditional surrender issued to earth's inhabitants before God's final onslaught and inevitable victory.

From chapter 12 the dragon is known as the one who was thrown out of heaven, not before wreaking some havoc among the stars; and from chapter 13 the beast is known as the one who arises from the sea, locale of chaotic forces disruptive to God's creation. Now, in chapter 14, the angel commands the earth to worship the one "who made heaven and earth, the sea and the springs of water." Charles (1920, 2:14) observes that although references to God as creator are common in the Hebrew Bible, they are not common in the New Testament. The angel's call in Rev 14:7 for the earth to worship God is based on God's status as creator. The beast and the sea from which it arises are subordinate to God, for God is the creator, and they are but his rebellious creatures. God is the creator of the heaven from which the dragon fell, the earth to which he falls, the sea from which the beast emerges, and the springs of water that give life to the earth and which themselves are affected by God's wrath (8:10).

A second angel follows the first. His proclamation is full of biblical resonances: "Fallen, fallen is Babylon the great! She has made all nations drink of the wine of the wrath of her fornication" (14:8). The announcement foreshadows the extended treatment of Babylon's fall in chapter 18. Revelation 14:8 is the first mention of Babylon in Revelation. Judah was for a time part of the Babylonian empire. The Babylonian king Nebuchadnezzar destroyed Jerusalem and its temple in 586 B.C.E., a traumatic event that lived on in the Jewish imagination. The temple was rebuilt at the end of the sixth century B.C.E. When the Romans destroyed the second temple in 70 C.E., Babylon and the first destruction served as figures to describe the second destruction (4 Ezra, *2 Baruch*, *Sibylline Oracles* 5, 1 Peter, and Revelation; see Murphy 1985a).

For John's audience, Babylon's, that is, Rome's, fall is future, but the seer's vision allows them to hear the angel announce the event as if already past. This echoes announcements of the fall of Babylon in Isaiah and Jeremiah. Isaiah's wording is closer to that of the first half of Rev 14:8. Isaiah hears from horsemen who ride in pairs, "Fallen, fallen is Babylon; and all the images of her gods lie shattered on the ground" (Isa 21:9). Jeremiah combines the idea of Babylon's fall with a cup of punishment given by God: "Babylon was a golden cup in the Lord's hand, making all the earth drunken; the nations drank her wine, and so the nations went mad. Suddenly Babylon has fallen and is shattered" (51:7–8). The phrase "Babylon the great" in Rev 14:8 may come from Dan 4:30. It is a favorite phrase in Revelation (14:8; 16:19; 17:5; 18:2, 10, 21).

The second half of 14:8 is confusing, since Babylon's cup is full of both wrath (*thymos*) and fornication. Throughout the Bible fornication and adultery are symbols of disloyalty to God and idolatry. The motif of fornication is frequent throughout Revelation, and it symbolizes illicit engagement with Hellenistic and Roman culture. Loyalty to Rome, including participation in the imperial cult, is fornication. In chapter 17, Rome appears as "the great whore . . . with whom the kings of the earth have committed fornication, and with the wine of whose fornication the inhabitants of the earth have become drunk" (17:2). That Babylon (Rome) gives people a cup of fornication to drink in 14:8 fits naturally into the way this sexual metaphor is used throughout the book.

The problem arises with the addition of the word "wrath" to "fornication" in 14:8, so that the cup contains both fornication and wrath. The cup of God's wrath is a biblical image (e.g., Ps 75:8; Isa 51:17; Jer 25:15; 51:7). In Rev 14:10, the wine is unmixed, at full strength, not diluted with water (see, e.g., Ps 75:8). The same combination of fornication and wrath in connection with wine occurs in 18:3, where it again refers to the relationship between Rome and the nations. Some have suggested that *thymos* does not mean "wrath" in 14:8 but "passion," a possible meaning for the word, but it certainly means "wrath" in 14:10, where it is in parallel with "anger," and that is its most likely meaning throughout Revelation (12:12; 14:8, 10, 19; 15:1, 7; 16:1, 19; 18:3; 19:15). Others have proposed that since engaging in fornication with Rome inevitably leads to one drinking the cup of God's wrath (as in 14:10; 16:19; 19:15), the two are brought together here.

A third angel appears who pronounces judgment on "those who worship the beast and its image, and receive a mark on their foreheads or on their hands" (14:9; cf. 13:16). Chapters 13 and 14 are remarkable for the close juxtaposition of the crime and its punishment, leaving no room for doubt about the results of engagement with Rome. Their punishment is that "they will also drink the wine of God's wrath, poured unmixed into the cup of his anger [*thymos*]" (14:10). This is further defined as being tortured by fire and sulfur (brimstone) in the presence of the angels and the Lamb. "The smoke of their torment goes up forever and ever," and "there is no rest day or night for those who worship the beast and its image and for anyone who receives the mark of its name" (14:11; cf. 13:4, 12, 15–16).

Fire and sulfur are frequent instruments of punishment, starting with the destruction of Sodom and Gomorrah, where God rains fire and sulfur on them (Gen 19:24). When Abraham looks at the destroyed cities, he sees "the smoke of the land going up like the smoke of a furnace" (Gen 19:28). Speaking of the punishment of Edom, Isaiah says that its soil will be turned into sulfur and burning pitch and that "night and day it shall not be quenched; its smoke shall go up forever" (Isa 34:9–10). In Revelation, the punishment takes place in the presence of the angels and the Lamb. God's sovereignty has been challenged, and it is appropriate that God's agents witness the retribution inflicted on the beast's followers.

Many are distressed at what seems to be a vengeful attitude on the part of the author here (see also 18:7, 10, 15; 19:20; 20:10, 14–15; 21:8). Some see such scenes as being unchristian. Unfortunately, few see them as "un-Jewish"! The fact is that both Judaism and Christianity have had a place for such retributive justice (see Himmelfarb 1983). Scenes of punishment of the wicked as a spectacle for the righteous occur throughout *1 Enoch,* for example, and in 4 Ezra 7:93 one of the rewards of the righteous is to see the distress of the wicked. In *2 Baruch* 51 there is a general resurrection in which people recognize each other, ensuring that everyone will know who is rewarded and who is punished. This increases the suffering of the damned. But the severity of these scenes is matched by Jesus' shocking sayings concerning cutting off of bodily members lest one sin, for it is better to enter heaven maimed than to go to hell (Matt 5:29–30), or his threat of continuous torture inflicted by the Father on those who do not forgive (Matt 18:34–35; see also Matt 10:28; 25:30, 46).

Although 14:9–10 does expect vengeance to descend on the beast's followers, the vision does not end on that note. The final two verses (14:12–13) bring attention back to the faithful. Revelation 14:12 is remarkable in that the seer steps out of his role as mere recorder of visions and speaks directly to his audience, as he did in 13:10. The message in both places is the same: a call to the saints to endure (see also 1:9; 2:2, 3, 19; 3:10). This is the "bottom line" of the book. Those who endure "keep" or "hold fast" God's commandments and the faith of Jesus. This echoes 12:17, where those who are pursued by the angry dragon are the woman's children, "those who keep the commandments of God and hold the testimony of Jesus." They must remain faithful despite the dragon's onslaughts, lest they worship the dragon and the beast and so be punished with the rest of humanity.

The warning is followed by a promise of reward. A voice from heaven says, "Write this: Blessed are the dead who from now on die in the Lord" (14:13). This is the third of seven beatitudes in Revelation (1:3; 14:13; 16:15; 19:9; 20:6; 22:7, 14; see comments on 1:3). The command to write (see 1:11, 19; 2:1, 8, 12, 18; 3:1, 7, 14; 14:3; 19:9; 21:5; cf. 10:4) emphasizes the beatitude's importance. Beatitudes disclose what action or attitude brings true happiness and blessedness. In Rev 14:13, right action is dying in the Lord. Humans can follow the beast and receive temporary advantage but be eternally punished, or they can remain loyal to God and so die in the Lord at the hands of the second beast but end up truly "blessed." The phrase "from now on" indicates that the great ordeal is about to begin, and those who die in it are especially blessed.

The choice Christians face is so crucial that the Spirit intervenes to confirm the truth of the beatitude (14:13). He says, "Yes," and adds that for the righteous their death results in "rest," for "their deeds follow them." The Spirit speaks directly to the churches here, as he does in chapters 2 and 3. He is heard again at the end of the book when he prays to Christ to come again (22:17). The rest that the righteous receive contrasts with the fate of the beast's followers, who receive "no rest day or night" from their torment (14:11). One's "deeds" or "works" determine one's ultimate fate.

The Sixth Unnumbered Vision: The Eschatological Harvest (14:14–20)

This vision is another judgment scene, this time presented through two images of harvesting, one of grain and the other of grapes. The double image is inspired by Joel 3:13:

Put in the sickle, for the harvest is ripe.
Go in, tread, for the wine press is full.
The vats overflow, for their wickedness is great.

The sixth vision opens with "one like a son of man" sitting on a white cloud, wearing a golden crown, and holding a sharp sickle (14:14). The NRSV has "one like the Son of Man." The translators chose to insert a definite article and capitalize "Son of Man" to show that this is the same figure as appears in chapter 1, whom the seer and his audience know to be identical with Jesus. Certainly the ancient hearers and readers would make that connection. But since the Greek lacks the definite article, it is better to translate simply "one like a son of man." This makes the vision more vivid. The seer is deluged with a multitude of visions, and he reports them as he sees them with a minimum of interpretation. He does not explicitly interpret the son of man here, so the ambiguity should also appear in the translation. Some take the author's lack of identification of the one like a son of man to mean that we should not necessarily identify the one here with the one in chapter 1. Since the ones portrayed as being sons of men in Daniel are angels, the figure in Rev 14:14 may also be an angel. This is unlikely, given the prominence of the title Son of Man in gospel tradition, the importance of the figure in Revelation 1, and the fact that the figure wears a crown here.

The one like a son of man sits on a cloud. This is a feature taken from the son of man of Daniel 7, a passage that also influenced Rev 1:7. Since the one like a son of man wears a crown, the cloud is like a throne for him. The sharp sickle that he carries indicates that he is about to harvest the earth. The harvest is an image for judgment (Joel 3:13; Hos 6:11; Matt 13:30, 39). Matthew's last judgment scene portrays the Son of Man as a king and judge who sits on a throne (25:31–46). Mark speaks of the Son of Man as judge coming with clouds and gathering his elect from the ends of heaven and earth (13:26–27; see also 8:38; 14:62). All of these elements — harvest as judgment, the Son of Man coming on or with clouds, the Son of Man as king and judge, and the Son of Man as gatherer of the elect — feed into the picture in Revelation 14. The one like a son of man is structurally central to visions five and six because he is preceded by three angels (14:6–11) and followed by three angels (14:15–20). There are thus seven heavenly figures in all, the one like a son of man being the central one (Schüssler Fiorenza 1991, 90). That the one like a son of man in Revelation 14 is accompanied by angels recalls Mark 8:38; 13:27; 14:62; and Matt 25:31.

An angel now comes out of the heavenly temple, calling in a loud voice to the one like a son of man to put in his sickle and reap (14:15). Some find it inappropriate that an angel commands Christ in this way, but that is to misconstrue the angel's role. The angel carries the message from the temple, where God resides. The scene emphasizes what the book regularly stresses, that God initiates the judgment just as God initiates the endtime events in general. Despite the high christology of Revelation, it remains theocentric, centered on the Father.

In the verses that follow there are two harvests, a grain harvest by the one like a son of man (14:14–16) and a gathering of grapes by an angel that are then thrown into the wine press (14:17–20). The grain harvest can be a symbol for judgment (Hos 6:11; Matt 13:30, 39) or the ingathering of the righteous elect (Matt 9:37–38; John 4:35–38). Since the grain harvest is sometimes used to present the positive side of judgment (the saving of the good grain), and the wine press is more frequently used to symbolize God's negative judgment on the wicked and their punishment (Isa 63:1–3; Joel 3:13; Rev 19:15), some commentators see the double harvest here to refer to the positive and negative sides of judgment. That is an attractive hypothesis, and it has the advantage that it accounts for both the interpretation of the grape harvest as punishment in 14:17–20 and for the final scene of victory and salvation in the seventh vision of this series (15:2–4).

In the grape harvest in Rev 14:17–20, the harvester is "another angel," who comes from the heavenly temple and who also has a sharp sickle. As in the first harvest scene, an angel brings news that it is time to reap (14:18). The messenger angel in this case comes from the altar and is the angel of fire (see comments on 7:1). Fire is especially associated with judgment in Revelation, as in other apocalypses, Jewish and Christian. That it is the angel of fire who comes from the altar in 14:18 recalls the brief scene at the beginning of the trumpet series, where the angel takes fire from the altar and throws it on the earth (8:5), a scene that summarizes the destruction that results from the seven trumpets that follow. In our comments on 8:5 we noted that the collocation of the altar and the prayers of the saints points back to the prayer for vengeance of the martyrs under the heavenly altar in 6:9–10. Revelation 14:18 resumes those two earlier scenes and again connects the judgment of the wicked with the prayers for vengeance of the martyrs.

The angel with the sickle gathers the ripe grapes from the earth and throws them into "the great wine press of the wrath of God. And the wine press was trodden outside the city, and blood flowed from the wine press, as high as a horse's bridle, for a distance of about two hundred miles" (14:19–20). This scene is subsumed in the later scene of the coming of Christ as rider on a white horse to do battle with the nations. There Christ "will tread the wine press of the fury of the wrath of God the Almighty" (19:15). There is no real difference between drinking the cup of God's wrath (14:10) and being thrown into the wine press of God's wrath (14:19). These are not different judgments or stages of judgment. They are representations of the final judgment of those who follow the beast. The image of treading grapes to symbolize God's wrath comes from Isaiah 63 (cf. Lam 1:15), a passage that influences the scene of Christ as rider in chapter 19. The detail that the blood from the wine press is as high a horse's bridle is a military image, again connecting to Christ as warrior in chapter 19. It recalls a detail from a Jewish scene of judgment: "The horse shall walk through the blood of sinners up to his chest; and the chariot shall sink down up to its top" (*1 Enoch* 100:3). The city "outside" of which the wine press is located is probably Jerusalem (see 14:1). Jesus was crucified outside of Jerusalem, so there may be an allusion to his death here, indicating that the punishment fits the crime. There are Jewish traditions to the effect that the final judgment will occur in the environs of Jerusalem (e.g., Joel 3:2, 12; *1 Enoch* 53:1; Zechariah 14).

The blood from the wine press spreads out to a distance of sixteen hundred stadia or furlongs. The symbolism of this number is uncertain, but it is unlikely that the author would use a number with no symbolic value. A plausible solution is that it signifies the whole world. The world has "four corners" and the number ten can mean completeness. The number sixteen hundred is four squared times ten squared (Schüssler Fiorenza 1991, 91; see also Charles 1920, 2:25–26).

The Seventh Unnumbered Vision: The Conquerors and Their Hymn (15:2–4)

The end of the first series of unnumbered visions is similar to the end of the seals series in the way that it leads into the subsequent series. The seventh seal contains the seven trumpets, introduced by 8:1, 6. Embedded in that introduction is a liturgical interlude (8:3–5) which refers both to what comes before and to what will come after, thereby interlocking the trumpets series still more tightly with the seals. Similarly, the seventh unnumbered vision contains the seven bowls, introduced by 15:1, 5–8. Embedded in that introduction is a heavenly scene with liturgical features. Because the scene is a seventh unnumbered vision, but is framed by the introduction to the bowls, it interlocks the bowls series with the unnumbered series.

The vision of 15:2–4 pictures "those who had conquered the beast" in heaven singing a song of praise to God. They stand in heaven beside a sea of glass mixed with fire. The salvation scene recalls similar ones in 7:9–17 and 14:1–5. All three passages depict salvation in terms of heavenly worship (Yarbro Collins 1979, 107). The glassy sea in 15:2 refers back to chapter 4, where before God's throne is a sea of glass, like crystal (4:6). In the commentary on chapter 4 we noted that it is not unusual in Jewish apocalyptic texts for there to be a sea in heaven. In several ancient Near Eastern texts creation takes place or is defended in a battle between a major god and the sea or a sea-monster, and the sea often stands for disruptive forces opposed to creation's order. The presence of a sea before God's heavenly throne indicates God's control of the sea. Since triumphant faithful have conquered Rome, the beast that arises from the sea, it is fitting that they now appear beside a sea in heaven.

The sea is mixed with fire (15:2). Later in the book the damned are cast into the fiery lake, but it is a different place (19:20; 20:10, 14, 15; 21:8). A different word is used to designate it, and it is not in heaven. Some think that the fire in 15:2 symbolizes God's judgment, which may be true, since it is such a common element in judgment in this book and many others. It is more likely that fire is present here primarily to accentuate the awesomeness of the scene. Fire is often associated with God's presence and with God's throne (e.g., Ezekiel 1; 10:6–7; Dan 7:9; *1 Enoch* 14:8–25; Rev 4:5).

Another important reason for mentioning the glassy sea in this vision is the prominence of the sea in the exodus tradition. As we have seen, God's conquest of the sea at creation and his splitting of the sea during the exodus are brought together in Isa 51:9–11. An exodus association is made explicit when the faithful sing the song of Moses and the song of the Lamb in Rev 15:3. This does not mean that they sing two songs. The conquest of the Red Sea (Exodus 14) and the song that Moses and the Israelites sing to celebrate it (Exodus 15) are but a foreshadowing of the victory won by the Lamb and the faithful at the end of times and the song that the faithful sing. The exodus is a paradigm through which the author interprets the anticipated conquest of the beast and vindication of the faithful.

The song in Rev 15:3–4 is full of language reminiscent of the Hebrew Bible (Deut 32:4; 1 Sam 2:2; Pss 86:9, 12; 92:5; 95:17; 98:1, 2; 111:2; 139:14; 1 Chr 16:9; Jer 10:7; Amos 4:13; Mal 1:11; see Charles 1920, 2:36). The hymn is the most explicit reference to the exodus in Revelation, and it alerts the reader to the exodus allusions in the bowls that follow in chapter 16 (Schüssler Fiorenza 1991, 91). Exodus 15 and Rev 15:3–4 are broadly similar in that both celebrate the awesome exhibition of God's power on behalf of his people and his rescue of them. A difference is that the enemies in Exodus 15 are either destroyed (Egyptians) or in terror (inhabitants of Philistia, Edom, Moab, Canaan), and their conversion is not contemplated. Revelation 15:3–4 anticipates the acceptance by all nations of God's sovereignty. This contrast must be qualified, however, for the nations' fear in Exod 15:14–16 is a recognition of God's power, and non-Christians are not treated so benignly elsewhere in Revelation.

Revelation 15:3 employs synonymous parallelism, a common feature of Hebrew poetry. In synonymous parallelism, the same thing is said in two different ways, thereby enriching the statement being made:

> Great and amazing are your deeds,
>   Lord God the Almighty!
> Just and true are your ways,
>   King of the nations!

God's universal sway is indicated by the title "Almighty" (Rev 15:3), a favorite title in Revelation (see comments on 1:8). The parallel assertion is that God is "King of the nations." To the unaided human eye, Caesar is king of all nations. Any nation or individual that sees things differently soon tastes Rome's wrath (see chapter 13). But the faithful who are in heaven after the final harvest know that Rome's power is counterfeit (15:3–4).

The song of 15:3–4 is precipitated by God's saving the faithful who now sing. God's deeds, which are "great and amazing," are most clearly manifested by the eschatological events in which the good are rewarded, the evil punished, and the power of Satan broken forever. The parallelism between "Great and amazing are your deeds" and "Just and true are your ways" asserts that God's deeds are amazing not just because they are awesome but because they are just. Justice is a major theme in Revelation, and God's actions establish justice, while Rome's rule is a rule of injustice. Truth and justice are equivalent in 15:3, and God's action throws light on the meaning of truth itself, another major theme of Revelation. Truth is not merely abstract, a matter of doctrine with tenuous connection to real life. Truth manifests itself in the establishment of justice on earth. Those who worship the beast are dedicated to falsehood, because Satan's rule through Rome is by definition false. Schüssler Fiorenza remarks, "Like the chorus in a Greek drama, this hymn interprets the meaning and intention of the preceding and following visions of cruel judgment. Their goal is justice and salvation" (1991, 92).

This hymn, which puts God at the center of everything, claims that God alone is holy. Holy means wholly other, majestic, powerful, mysterious. It is a term that should be applied to God alone and to what belongs to God—persons, times, places. Because of God's holiness, all nations will be forced to acknowledge him as supreme in a way that negates Rome's claims (15:4). As a result, the entire world, which in chapter 13 follows the beast, now acknowledges God as the one true God (cf. 13:3 to 15:4). In 13:4, the whole earth exclaims, "Who is like the beast, and who can fight against it?" In 15:4, the faithful sing,

> Lord, who will not fear
>   and glorify your name?
> For you alone are holy.
>   All nations will come
>   and worship before you,
> for your judgments have been revealed.

Revelation 21:24–25 and 22:2 also expect the conversion of the nations. Revelation draws on the Israelites' tradition that at the end of time all nations will acknowledge their God as the one true God (e.g., Ps 86:9; Isa 2:2–4; 42:1–9; 49:6; 52:13–53:12; Mic 1:1–4; Mal 1:11). It is the revelation of God's judgments that makes this happen. It is clear from the context that "judgments" means more that judicial decrees. God's judgments have been enacted in the preceding visions, especially 14:14–20, and their fulfillment will be described in still more detail in the following chapters.

The visions in this series of unnumbered visions fall into two groups. The first consists of the first three visions (chapters 12–13) and the second of the last four visions (14:1–15:4). This distinguishes it from the seals and the trumpets, in which the first four visions belong together structurally. In the present series the first three visions unmask the true nature of the Roman empire. Behind the empire stands Satan (first vision, chapter 12). The empire itself is best represented by a supernatural beast of chaos (second vision, 13:1–10). The Asian ruling class committed to Rome is symbolized by another beast (the third vision, 13:11–18). The last four visions begin and end with scenes of salvation (vision four, 14:1–5, and seven, 15:2–4), which flank two visions of judgment (vision five, 14:6–13, and six, 14:14–20). Altogether these seven visions form an effective introduction to the more detailed descriptions of the fall of Babylon (Rome), the final battle, the defeat of Satan, the last judgment, and final salvation or punishment that occupy the rest of the book.

Chapter Nine

The Seven Bowls (15:1; 15:5–16:21)

Liturgical Interlude Introducing the Bowls (15:1, 5–8)

John sees "another portent in heaven" (15:1). The new portent consists of "seven angels with seven plagues, which are the last, for with them the wrath of God is ended." These seven plagues are the ones contained in the bowls of chapter 16. The only other entities to which "portent in heaven" applies in Revelation are the woman and the dragon in heaven (12:1, 3), so the term "portent" ties the bowl series to the first unnumbered series. This new portent is "great and amazing," the same adjectives used in 15:3 to describe God's deeds, deeds that are also "just and true." The bowls are themselves God's deeds, and in the third bowl an angel appears who declares God's acts of judgment to be "just" (16:5–6). The word "plague" recalls the ten exodus plagues (Exod 7:14–12:32), and the bowl plagues contain several clear allusions to the exodus plagues.

The seer says that with the bowls God's wrath is ended (15:1). But the seven bowls take up only chapter 16, whereas the book continues for six chapters more. This problem is only apparent, for Revelation does not tell its story in a linear fashion. Chapters 17 and 18 elaborate on the fall of Babylon, a fall already announced in 14:8 and implied in the fifth and seventh bowls. Similarly, the following chapters (19–20) play out explicitly what the last four (14:1–15:4) of the seven unnumbered visions imply. Seen in this way, the bowls are the climax of God's wrath. Yarbro Collins notes that the unnumbered series concentrates on persecution while the bowls focus on judgment (1990, 1010).

Revelation 15:5–8 is a scene similar to the one at the beginning of the seven trumpets (8:3–5). In 8:3–5, an angel offers incense mixed with the prayers of the saints at the heavenly altar. He then takes fire from the altar and throws it onto the earth, and there is thunder, lightning, rumblings, and an earthquake. The scene connects God's wrathful judgment on the earth to the prayers of the saints by alluding to the prayer of the martyrs under the altar in 6:9–11 and the offering of the prayers of the saints as bowls (*phialê*) of incense in 5:8. It also confirms that the trumpets' events originate with God. Revelation 15:5–8 is also a heavenly liturgy which stresses the divine origin of the impending judgments and subtly associates the plagues with the prayers of the saints. The plagues, also said to be "the wrath of God," are contained in bowls (*phialê*), as are the saints' prayers in 5:8. The smoke that fills the temple in 15:8, caused by God's glory and power in wrath, recalls the smoke of the incense of 5:8 and 8:4, which is connected with the prayers of the faithful. The seven angels in chapter 15 are suitably dressed in priestly clothing of linen robes and golden sashes (cf. the description of the one like a son of man in 1:13).

In 15:5, John sees the temple in heaven opened. This recalls the last trumpet, where God's heavenly temple is opened (11:15–19). Revelation 15:5 is not a second opening of the temple but is a recapitulation of the opening in 11:19, leading to the ultimate consummation of God's wrath. The designation of the temple is awkward: "The temple of the tent of witness in heaven" (15:5). This phrase has no precise parallel. Elsewhere in Revelation and in Jewish and Christian apocalypticism it is a heavenly temple that is at issue, not a tent (Charles 1920, 2:37). In the Bible, the tent is the form the sanctuary takes during the desert wanderings following the exodus. The tent as focus of God's presence with Israel receives more attention in the Pentateuch (first five books of the Bible) than any other object. It is called the tabernacle, the tent of meeting, and sometimes the tent of witness (e.g., in Num 17:7; 18:2; see Friedman 1992). It is called the tent of witness because in it is kept the ark of the covenant, which contains the tablets of the law, called the "tablets of witness" in Exod 32:15 and 34:29 (see Deut 10:5; Mounce 1977, 289). The tablets and tent witness to the covenant between God and the people. The awkward phrase in Rev 15:5 results from the author's wish to associate the heavenly temple idea with the tent that recalls the exodus and desert wanderings. The term "tent of witness" also reflects the importance of the theme of witness in Revelation.

The introductory scene concludes as the temple fills with "smoke from the glory of God and from his power," so that no one can enter the temple until the plagues are over. Smoke or a cloud is often associated with God's presence in the Bible, and the cloud of God's presence in 1 Kings 8 makes it impossible for the priests to remain in the temple (see Exod 19:18; 40:34; Isa 6:4). Such passages emphasize the majesty and otherness of God and human inability to endure God's unmediated presence. Revelation's bowls are concerned with God's wrath, so the author uses smoke rather than cloud, and he limits the time of inaccessibility of the temple to the carrying out of God's wrath. Mounce suggests that this means that no more intercession before God is possible now (1977, 290). Ultimately all barriers between God and humans will vanish, so that even the temple becomes unnecessary (Rev 21:22–23). But God is unapproachable while the powers of evil persist and until God completely and wrathfully destroys them. It is this overwhelming divine onslaught on the forces of evil that is embodied in the seven bowls.

The Seven Bowls as a Whole (Chapter 16)

A "loud voice from the temple" tells the seven angels to pour onto the earth the "seven bowls of the wrath of God." This recapitulates earlier passages in Revelation. In 14:9–11, it is announced that the followers of the beast will drink the wine of God's wrath from the cup of his anger. The pouring out of the bowls is just another way of saying this (see the parallel between cup and bowl in Isa 51:17, 22). The bowls of chapter 16 bring about what in the sixth seal is feared by the earth's inhabitants, who recognize that the day of God's and the Lamb's wrath has come (6:16–17). The seventh seal refers to the punishment of sinners (11:18).

The bowls parallel the trumpets closely, recapitulating their content, intensifying and making more specific what the trumpets contain. While the trumpets describe partial destruction (one-third; 8:7, 9, 10, 11, 12; 9:18; cf. 9:4; 11:13), in the bowls the destruction is total. The first four trumpets (8:7–12) are directed against parts of the cosmos, and although they affect humankind (8:9, 11), this is not stressed, nor are their human targets specified. The target of the demonic plague in the fifth trumpet is more specific. It is all of those who do not have God's seal on their foreheads (9:4). But such specificity does not recur in the sixth trumpet, which simply affects a third of humanity.

The last trumpet is again more specific, mentioning the destroyers of the earth (11:18). In the bowls the targets of God's wrath are much clearer throughout.

The bowls of God's wrath are followed by scenes that treat Rome's fall (chapters 17–18), the final battle (19:11–20:3), the messianic kingdom (20:4–6), Satan's final defeat (20:7–10), the final judgment (20:11–15), and the new Jerusalem (21:1–22:5). In other words, this time it is really the end. The seals, trumpets, and the unnumbered visions also speak of the end, and the bowls recapitulate them, but the bowls represent the clearest and most specific expression of God's wrath so far. The bowls series is set in motion by a loud voice from the heavenly temple (16:1). This is God's voice, since only God is in the temple until the plagues are ended (15:8). This recalls Isa 66:6: "A voice from the temple! The voice of the LORD, dealing retribution to his enemies" (see Mounce 1977, 293).

It is instructive to compare the trumpets and the bowls, since they have so much in common. They are parallel even to the order of the specific elements mentioned in each item. Figure 4 reveals this commonality and also shows how each series draws on the exodus plagues of Exod 7:14–12:32. Exodus imagery occurs several times in Revelation before the bowls, but the explicit reference to the song of Moses in the seventh unnumbered vision (15:2–4) prepares the way for the extensive exodus imagery of the bowls. God's action on behalf of his people in the exodus is a paradigm for his impending action. Just as God rescued the people from Egyptian oppression through a series of plagues, so God will rescue those loyal to him from Roman oppression.

The First Bowl (16:2)

Both the first trumpet and the first bowl are directed against the earth. The first trumpet does not mention a direct effect on humanity, but the first bowl says that painful sores come upon "those who had the mark of the beast and who worshiped its image" (16:2). This specificity marks the bowls as a whole. The trumpet draws on the seventh Egyptian plague (thunder and hail) and the bowl on the sixth (boils). The first trumpet affects only a third of the earth. No such limitation is mentioned in the first bowl, although its effects are limited to the beast's followers.

Figure 4

Trumpets **Rev 8:7–11:19**	**Bowls** **Rev 16:1–21**	**Egyptian Plagues** **Exod 7:14–12:32**
1. On the earth; hail and fire mixed with blood; a third of vegetation burned	1. On the earth; painful sores on humans	First plague: water turns to blood; Sixth plague: boils; Seventh plague: thunder and hail
2. On the sea; a third of sea turns to blood	2. On the sea; sea turns to blood	First plague: water turns to blood
3. On rivers and springs; a third of rivers and springs become bitter	3. On rivers and springs; rivers and springs turn to blood	First plague: water turns to blood
4. On the sun, moon, and stars; a third of their light darkened	4. On the sun; it scorches humans	Ninth plague: darkness
5. Abyss opened; smoke rises and darkens sun and air; locusts come from abyss and torture humans with stings	5. On the beast's throne; darkness and sores on humans	Sixth plague: boils; Eighth plague: locusts; Ninth plague: darkness
6. Angels held at Euphrates River released; demonic cavalry attacks humankind; fire, smoke, and sulfur come out of horses' mouths and kill a third of humankind	6. On the Euphrates River; dries up river so kings from east can come; frog demons come from mouths of dragon, beast, and prophet and assemble kings for battle against God	Second plague: frogs
7. Kingdom of God and messiah come; punishment of wicked and reward of righteous; destruction of destroyers of earth; lightning, rumblings, thunder, earthquake, great hail	7. On the air; lightning, rumblings, thunder, earthquake, great hail; destruction of Babylon	Seventh plague: thunder and hail

The Second Bowl (16:3)

Both the second trumpet and the second bowl turn the sea to blood. This recalls the first Egyptian plague, where the Nile is turned to blood. The trumpet affects only a third of the sea, and a third of its creatures die, while the bowl turns the entire sea to blood, and all its creatures die. The sea becomes like the blood of a corpse in the third bowl, increasing the repulsive power of the image.

The Third Bowl (16:4–7)

Both the third trumpet and the third bowl are directed against the fresh waters, rivers and springs. The trumpet turns a third of them bitter and poisonous, killing many. The bowl turns all of them to blood. Both recall the first Egyptian plague. The third bowl is markedly different from the third trumpet in that an angel intervenes to proclaim God's justice (16:5–6) and the altar confirms the angel's words (16:7). The intervention serves the same purpose as do the hymns throughout the book. The angel provides reliable commentary on what happens in the third plague, which is applicable to the entire bowls cycle. The angel's words resume those of the righteous before the glassy sea in 15:2–4. Both declare God's judgments to be just, and both declare God's holiness. It is important that these declarations take place at this point, lest it be thought that God's judgments are arbitrary or disproportionate. The hymn of the righteous in chapter 15 calls God "the Almighty," stressing divine sovereignty. The title applied to God by the angel here carries similar connotations (16:5). In addition to calling God just and holy, he says that God is the one who is and was. This recalls the formula in 1:4, 8, and 4:8, where God is the one who is, was, and is to come. The third part of this formula is missing in 16:5, for God has now come in his wrath. We observed the same change in the climactic hymn of the second trumpet (11:17–18).

The angel of the third bowl makes explicit the object of God's judgment, those who "shed the blood of the saints and prophets" (16:6). The angel interprets God's action as giving blood to drink to those who shed Christian blood. The angel's comments occur here because they fit the particular plagues of the second and third bowls. Those who shed blood must drink blood, so the punishment fits the crime. The designation of the martyrs as "saints and prophets" corresponds to how the seer speaks of the churches in general. The only office he mentions is that of prophet, and all Christians qualify as "saints." Because the followers of the beast have shed Christian blood, they "deserve" the plagues now being inflicted on them. The text says literally that they are "worthy" of what they receive. The same word is applied to the righteous in 3:4. In God's justice, people get what they deserve. This is in marked contrast to what happens in Roman courts.

The altar responds to the angel's words by saying, "Yes, O Lord God, the Almighty, your judgments are true and just" (16:7; cf. 9:13). We noted in commenting on 6:9–11 and 8:3–5 that the heavenly altar is associated with the martyrs and the prayers of the saints, as well as with judgment. The altar thus connects Christian suffering with divine retribution. When the angel declares in 16:7 that God's wrath is rightly directed at those who shed the blood of the martyrs, the altar itself testifies to the truth of that assertion. In so doing it resumes the words of the faithful in 15:2–4. It uses the same title for God as is found in 15:3, "Lord God, the Almighty." The faithful say, "Just and true are your ways" (15:3; ways are then defined as "judgments" in 15:4), and the altar says, "Your judgments are true and just" (16:7). It is significant that "the angel of the waters" defends God's justice. The very angel whose element has been destroyed, the angel of the waters, testifies to the justice of God's action.

The Fourth Bowl (16:8–9)

Both the fourth trumpet and the fourth bowl affect the sun. The fourth trumpet draws on the ninth Egyptian plague, so that the result on the earth is darkness, but only a third of the shining of the heavenly bodies is affected, in keeping with the partial nature of the trumpets. In the bowls the darkness motif is put off until the fifth bowl. Instead, the fourth bowl causes the sun to increase its heat, and it scorches humans. Their reaction is not repentance, but anger. They curse God, "who had authority over these plagues," and they do not "repent and give him glory" (16:9).

The intransigence of earth's inhabitants recalls that of the Egyptians at the exodus. God afflicts the Egyptians with ten plagues, but they achieve at best temporary cooperation. Egyptian resistance is mentioned repeatedly in Exodus. Similarly, human refusal to honor God is mentioned three times in the bowls cycle (16:9, 11, 21; cf. 9:20-21). The plagues serve only to increase their opposition, for they "cursed the name of God" (16:9). The text literally reads they "blasphemed" God's name. The same verb is used in 16:11 and 16:21. The use of this verb ties those who are afflicted by the bowls, already identified as those who have the mark of the beast and worship its image (16:2), still more closely to the beast symbolizing Rome, since in 13:1 the beast has blasphemous names on its head (see also 17:3) and speaks blasphemy (13:5, 6).

The Fifth Bowl (16:10–11)

The fifth trumpet and the fifth bowl both involve darkness, so they both recall the ninth Egyptian plague. The angel pours the fifth bowl directly on the beast's throne and plunges his kingdom into darkness and brings pains and sores on its subjects. This is the throne Satan gave to the beast in 13:2, making it clear that more than a physical throne is in question. Satan is behind the power and dominion of the Roman empire. The fifth bowl directly assaults that power and dominion. Its local manifestations are the persons (land-beast) and places (throne of Satan in Pergamum, 2:13) through which Rome and Satan exercise their authority. The fifth bowl thus comes close to the center of the problem, but it is only in chapter 20 that the deepest root of the problem, Satan, is definitively eliminated. Even the assault on the beast's throne fails to convert the beast's subjects. Instead of repenting of their deeds, they curse God.

The Sixth Bowl (16:12–16)

Both the sixth trumpet and the sixth bowl build on the Roman fear of the Parthian empire to the east of the Euphrates (see commentary on chapter 13 and on 9:13–19). The blowing of the sixth trumpet causes the altar to command that the destructive angels held at the Euphrates be released (9:13–19). This causes a demonic cavalry to descend on humankind. Out of the cavalry's horses' mouths come fire, smoke, and sulfur that kill a third of humankind.

The pouring of the sixth bowl dries up the Euphrates so that the kings of the east can invade the Roman empire (16:12). The drying up of the Euphrates echoes several incidents in the history of God's dealings with the world. At the creation God creates dry land so that earth creatures can flourish (Genesis 1). There are hints in the first Genesis creation story of the combat myth in which God conquers the sea to make room for creation. At the Red Sea, God splits the sea so that the Israelites can escape Egyptian oppression (Exodus 14). Isaiah 51 sees God's conquest of the waters in the creation and exodus as analogous, so here again there are echoes of the combat myth. In Joshua 3, God dries up the Jordan, itself an allusion to the exodus, so that the Israelites can cross over to attack the Canaanites and take possession of the land. Now, at the end of time, God again dries up a body of water (Rev 16:12). This time it is the Euphrates, and he dries it up so that Rome's enemies can cross and attack it. In 4 Ezra 13:43–44, God dries up the Euphrates to allow the exiled Israelite tribes to return home. This uses the drying-up-of-water motif in an eschatological context, as does Revelation, but with quite different results.

There is disagreement about the relation of 16:13–16 to 16:12. As mentioned, 16:12 draws on the traditions about an attack on Rome from the east, and so it concerns Rome's demise. But 16:13–16 is closer to Jewish traditions concerning a final eschatological attack on Jerusalem (see below). We analyze 16:13–16 first, and then return to the question of how it relates to 16:12. John sees three "foul spirits" come from the mouths of the dragon, the beast, and the false prophet (16:13). As fire, sulfur, and smoke come from the mouths of the horses in the sixth trumpet and harm humanity (9:17–18), here evil spirits come from the mouths of these three figures to harm humanity. The dragon is the dragon from chapter 12, and the beast is the beast from the sea in chapter 13. Since chapters 12 and 13 deal with three major evil figures (the dragon, the sea-beast, and the land-beast), just as does 16:13 (the dragon, the beast, and the false prophet), it is natural to suppose that the false prophet and the land-beast are the same. This is confirmed when in 19:20 the false prophet is defined as the one who did wonders before the beast and his image and who deceived those who received the beast's mark. This description matches that of the land-beast in chapter 13.

The phrase "foul spirits" is the same as is usually translated "unclean spirits" in the gospels. As part of Jesus' ministry of preaching and inaugurating the kingdom of God, he casts the unclean spirits—enemies of God and humanity—out of people whom they possess. In Rev 16:13–14, these spirits come from the mouths of the dragon, beast, and false prophet and go out into the world performing signs and gathering all the kings of the earth for battle "on the great day of God the Almighty" (16:14). The "day of the Lord" in the prophets signifies the day on which God intervenes in history to punish those who oppose him, and belief in such a day was common in early Christianity (e.g., 1 Cor 5:5; 1 Thess 5:2; 2 Thess 2:2; 2 Pet 3:10). It was a common notion in Jewish eschatology that at the end of time God's adversaries would gather for a final attack at Jerusalem (e.g., Ezekiel 38–39; Zechariah 14; 4 Ezra 13). This passage in Revelation brings together the notion of evil spirits associated with the dragon, the beast, and the false prophet, with the notions of the day of the Lord and that of the eschatological attack on Jerusalem.

This final battle is resumed in 19:11–20:3, where Christ rides out at the head of a heavenly army to meet the foes and defeats them. Given the connections between 16:13–16 and 19:11–20:3, it is clear that both passages concern the final showdown between forces loyal to God and those loyal to Satan. This brings us back to the relation between 16:12 and 16:13–16. Since 16:12 is an attack on Rome and 16:13–17 a battle between God and his enemies, some suggest that the latter passage is an interlude coming between the sixth and seventh bowls (Schüssler Fiorenza 1991, 94). The destruction of Rome implied in 16:12 is then narrated in the seventh bowl (16:17–21), while the final battle between good and evil prepared for in 16:13–16 is carried out in chapter 19. This suggestion has much to commend it, for it makes sense out of the contrasting allusions in 16:12 and 16:13–16 and supplies an interlude between the sixth and seventh bowls, as there was between the sixth and seventh seals (chapter 7) and the sixth and seventh trumpets (10:1–11:13). It also takes into account the introductory formula "And I saw" in 16:13. Mounce objects that this theory would shorten the sixth bowl to a single verse, and so break the pattern established in the seals and trumpets of the fifth and sixth elements being longer and more developed than the first four (1977, 299). This objection is not strong, since his suggestions would mean there is no interlude as in the other cycles. One way or the other the pattern changes.

A more important observation is that the blurring of the distinction between the assault on Rome (16:12) and the final battle between the forces of good and evil (16:13–16) also happens in chapters 17 to 19. In chapter 17, Rome and the kings of the earth band together and make war on the Lamb (17:12–14), and then the beast and its allies, the ten kings, attack the great whore (17:16). Chapter 18 describes Rome's fall, and chapter 19 reverts to a final battle between the dragon, beast, false prophets, kings, and their followers against Christ. We cannot neatly disentangle the two strands in these chapters. Rome's fall and the final battle between the forces of good and evil are part of the same process. Rome's fall means the end of Satan's power. The neat lines drawn by modern commentators between the two battles visible in the sixth bowl would not make sense to the seer.

The unclean spirits who gather the kings together for battle come from the mouths of the three evil figures. Mounce makes the interesting suggestion that this symbolizes Roman propaganda (1977, 299). This should be compared to the fact that in 1:16 and 19:15 a sharp sword comes from Christ's mouth. Revelation deals with a clash of claims made by Rome and by Christians. It is a war of words and myths more than weapons. The unclean spirits go about performing signs, and an implicit connection is drawn between their doing signs and their ability to gather the kings (16:14). In chapter 13, the land-beast performs miraculous signs and by these signs convinces people to worship the beast and its image (see our comments there).

A famous problem in this passage is where the kings of the earth are gathered: "They assembled them at the place that in Hebrew is called Harmagedon" (16:16). Harmagedon, usually spelled Armageddon in English, has received about as many different interpretations as has the enigmatic 666 of Rev 13:18. For a discussion of scholarly opinions, see Paulien (1992). The apparent specificity of these two references combined with an inability to determine their precise referents have made Harmagedon and 666 fruitful texts for those who read their own contemporary meanings into Revelation. The same traits make interpretation difficult for those whose goal is to decide what the text meant in its original context. The author offers a hint when he says that "Harmagedon" is Hebrew. But even given this help, scholars do not agree on its meaning. The most common solution is that Harmagedon is a combination of the Hebrew word for "mountain" (*har*) and Megiddo, the name of a fortress town guarding the pass between the coastal plain of Palestine and the Jezreel Valley, between Samaria and Galilee. Because of its strategic location, the town was the scene of key battles though history (e.g., Judg 5:19–21; 2 Kgs 23:28–30).

Others object that there is no "Mount Megiddo" ever mentioned in ancient sources, and Megiddo itself is not located on a mountain but on a plain. In fact the phrase "plain of Megiddo" occurs in the Bible. However, Megiddo is close to Mount Carmel on the coast and to the ridge of highlands to the north that is the beginning of Galilee. The author may be looking at the region as a whole, at the same time alluding to traditions about a final battle on a mountain, usually Zion (e.g., Ezekiel 38; Zechariah 14; 4 Ezra 13; Rev 20:9). Other suggestions include taking *magedon* as a form of the Hebrew word for "abundance," or alternatively for "assembly." Still others derive *har* from the Hebrew word for "city" so that Harmagedon means "city of Megiddo."

There is one more verse to be analyzed in the sixth bowl, namely 16:15. It is not part of the vision. The NRSV recognizes this, printing it within parentheses. Although not explicitly identified as such, it is a statement by Christ about his second coming, and it is the sort of statement one would expect from a Christian prophet: "See, I am coming like a thief! Blessed is the one who stays awake and is clothed, not going about naked and exposed to shame" (16:15). Since this verse seems out of place, Charles resorts to his usual remedy of rearranging the text (1920, 2:49). He finds that the saying fits much better into the message to the church at Sardis, in which Christ says, "If you do not wake up, I will come like a thief, and you will not know at what hour I will come to you" (3:3).

Charles is right to point to the similarity between 16:15 and 3:3, but one can make good sense of the verse in its present context. A quotation from Paul's first letter to the Thessalonians reveals how the collocation of elements found in Rev 16:12–16 is traditional for early Christian eschatology:

> For you yourselves know very well that the day of the Lord will come like a thief in the night. When they say, "There is peace and security," then suddenly destruction will come upon them.... So then let us not fall asleep as others do, but let us keep awake and be sober.... For God has destined

> us not for wrath but for obtaining salvation through our Lord Jesus Christ. (1 Thess 5:2–3, 6, 9)

Revelation and Paul share the expectation of wrath for God's enemies, the expectation that Christ will come like a thief in the night, and the exhortation to stay awake for Christ's coming.

Because the author uses the form of direct prophetic pronouncement in 16:15, the verse seems like an intrusion, but it is perfectly at home in its eschatological context (see Matt 24:42–44; Luke 12:39–40; 2 Pet 3:10). The form of a prophetic pronouncement makes the saying more vivid and catches the attention of the audience. Schüssler Fiorenza observes that the inclusion of this prophetic warning in 16:15 shows that the author does not wish to encourage speculation about the coming of the eschaton (1991, 94). No one knows when it will come. Rather the purpose of the scenes described in the bowls is to encourage the audience to be always ready for the end and to resist oppression.

The Seventh Bowl (16:17–21)

It is striking that the seventh bowl is poured out on the "air." Yarbro Collins notes that the first four trumpets are aimed at the earth, sea, rivers and fountains, and heavenly bodies, respectively (1977a, 374). These are traditional biblical constituents of the world (see especially Prov 8:23–24, 27, 29). The first three bowls are directed toward the earth, sea, and rivers and springs. The fourth bowl is poured on the sun, which then scorches with fire (16:8), and the seventh bowl is poured on the air (16:17). Thus fire and air are worked into the presentation. In Hellenistic cosmology it was commonly thought that the cosmos was composed of the elements earth, air, fire, and water. Yarbro Collins suggests, "It seems that the old cosmology, which is the only one evident in the vision of the trumpets, is still the fundamental one for the vision of the bowls, but that it has been modified so that it reflects the Hellenistic motif of the four elements as well" (1977, 376). She goes on to demonstrate that the Hellenistic influence probably took place at the level of a source used by the author, since the four elements do not appear in Revelation outside of this passage (378). Revelation's author "seems to have preferred traditionally Jewish ways of referring to the cosmos as a whole" (376).

When the seventh angel pours out his bowl, a loud voice comes out of the temple and says, "It is done [from the verb *ginesthai*]!" The author brings his audience to the brink of the end at the conclusion of each of the preceding series, but it is only in the bowls series that such a clear, terse statement of the completion of the endtime events appears. The verb *ginesthai* means "to be" or "to take place." It is the same verb used in 1:19 when John is told to write down "what is to take place after this" and in 4:1 when he is called up to heaven to be shown "what must take place after this." The announcement in 16:17 signals the completion of what John was to be shown, and it comes from the temple and from the throne, so it is a statement of God. God repeats the pronouncement in 21:6, after the endtime events have been recapitulated in more detail in 17:1–21:4. The fact that Revelation continues for another six chapters does not negate the finality of the statement in 16:17, for what follows recapitulates what goes before.

The parallel with the trumpet series continues into the seventh bowl, for the seventh trumpet is equally final (11:15–19). The prominence of God's temple and ark in the seventh trumpet is matched in the seventh bowl by the loud voice coming from the temple and from the throne. The bowl series begins and ends with references to the temple (16:1, 17), framing the bowls and making it clear that their origin is God. Each element of the storm theophany in the seventh trumpet (11:19) is taken up again in the seventh bowl (16:18; see also 4:5; 8:5). Hail and thunder together recall the seventh exodus plague (Exod 9:13–35). God uses hail to attack Israel's enemies in Josh 10:11 as well. Mounce says, "Hail was part of the accepted arsenal of divine retaliation" (1977, 305).

In keeping with the intensification represented by the bowls, the earthquake and the hail are emphasized more in 16:18 and 21 than in the seventh trumpet. The earthquake is considerably embellished in the seventh bowl. The trumpet merely includes the earthquake in the list of theophanic elements (11:19). The bowl says that it was a "violent [literally: great] earthquake, such as had not occurred since people were upon the earth, so violent was that earthquake" (16:18). This language recalls Dan 12:1, where the eschatological time is spoken of as follows: "There shall be a time of anguish, such as never occurred since nations first came into existence" (cf. *T. Moses* 8:1; Exod 9:18). All islands and mountains disappear with this tremendous earthquake (16:20). As is conventional in apocalyptic scenarios of the end, the cosmos in general and the earth in particular come undone in the execution of God's wrath (cf. 6:14). This is undeniably the end, and it is incomparable. No effects of the earthquake are enumerated in the seventh trumpet, but in the seventh bowl the effects are quite specific. The "great city" is split into three parts, and the nations' cities fall. The "great city" is Babylon, as is the "great city" in 18:10, 16, 18, 19, 21 (cf. 14:8). Babylon, as cipher for Rome, is the political center of the world, and when it falls the entire empire dissolves. All cities of the empire fall with Babylon (16:19). The fall of Babylon is repeated in other terms when the city is forced to drink "the wine-cup of the fury of his [God's] wrath." The fall of Babylon in the seventh bowl recapitulates the angel's announcement of its fall in 14:8, and the mention of God's cup of wrath resumes the angel's prediction of punishment for followers of the beast in 14:10 (cf. 19:15).

The hailstones of the last bowl, called "heavy [literally: great] hail" in the seventh trumpet, are embellished in the seventh bowl, becoming "great hail," each weighing a "talent," a somewhat variable measure of weight that is usually around a hundred pounds. These gigantic hailstones come down from heaven onto humans, who curse God because of the plague's severity.

The bowls cycle is unrelievedly negative. Nowhere does one find the equivalent of the rest given to the righteous in the fifth seal (6:9–11), the protection of the righteous in the fifth trumpet (9:4), the repentance of humans at the end of the interlude after the sixth trumpet (11:13), the reward of the righteous and the coming of God's and the messiah's kingdom in the seventh trumpet (11:15–18), or the scenes of salvation of the fourth and seventh of the unnumbered visions (14:1–5; 15:2–4). God's wrath must come quickly and without more delay, as the angel of chapter 10 predicts. Chapter 16 is remarkable for the violence of its images and for the speed with which it passes. It is like the grand finale in a fireworks display, in which all previous parts of the display are taken up and redisplayed in one last, tumultuous series.

Chapter Ten

The Babylon Appendix (17:1–19:10)

Vision of the Great Whore and the Beast and Its Interpretation (Chapter 17)

Overview

Revelation 17:1–19:10 is a unit and is a development of the bowls series in chapter 16. Chapter 17 presents the fall of Rome, and 18:1–19:10 describes responses to Rome's fall. Chapter 17 is closely tied to the bowls series, for it begins with the appearance of "one of the seven angels who had the seven bowls," who tells John to come and see the vision and then explains it. Angelic interpreters are common in apocalypses. The vision in chapter 17 is of a woman, "the great whore," representing Rome, seated on a beast. The climax of chapter 17 is the fall of that woman, so it elaborates the fifth and seventh bowls.

Chapters 17 and 18 are sometimes called the "Babylon Appendix," a usage we follow here, but this should not give the impression that the passage is less central than it is. Since the focus of the entire book is the defeat of Rome and Satan and the establishment of God's kingdom, chapter 17 elaborates on one of the most important themes of Revelation. The relationship between the defeat of Rome and the consummation of the church's relationship with Christ is conveyed by the fact that the fall of Rome in chapters 17 and 18 leads to the announcement of the marriage feast of the Lamb, where the bride is the church (19:6–9). This implies a contrast between the whore and the bride. The contrast is made clearer still in 21:9 when a vision of the Lamb's bride is introduced in precisely the same way as is the vision of Babylon in chapter 17.

Rome is represented by a prostitute depicted in lurid terms. This recalls the depiction of the Christian prophetess with whom the seer disagrees as Jezebel, who engages in adultery and fornication (2:20–23). The use of sexual imagery denigrating to women is not unique to Revelation's writer (Mounce 1977, 307–8). Ezekiel 23 calls the northern and southern Israelite kingdoms whores unfaithful to God. Ezekiel also depicts Jerusalem as an unfaithful wife in graphic terms in chapter 16. Similarly, God orders the prophet Hosea to marry a prostitute to symbolize God's marriage to the unfaithful Israel. The image is common in the Bible (see also Isa 1:21; Jer 2:20–31; 13:27). Cities were depicted as women in the ancient world and in the Bible (Isa 1:21; 66:7–16; Jer 15:9), and both the Assyrian capital of Nineveh and the Phoenician city of Tyre were portrayed as seductive prostitutes by the prophets (Nah 3:4; Isa 23:16–17). The author is also capable of depicting women positively, as the bride in chapters 19 and 21 and as the mother of God's people in chapter 12, for example. Although the positive value of these images is not to be ignored, even they restrict women to the traditional roles of wife and mother, and in Revelation these roles are fairly passive and dependent on males — God, the Lamb, and the dragon. The alternatives of whore or docile bride and mother have been used throughout history by patriarchal cultures to control women, their sexuality, and their social roles. Revelation's author did not invent this, but he is fully involved in the tradition (see Pippin 1992a, 1992b, 1992c).

Chapter 17 can be treated in three sections (for possible source analysis, see Charles 1920, 2:54–62). The first is the angel's command to come see the vision (17:1–2). The second is the vision itself (17:3–6). The third is the angel's lengthy interpretation of the vision (17:6–18). We begin by examining the chapter's biblical background.

Biblical Precedents for Revelation 17

Revelation 17 is deeply rooted in the Bible, as is the rest of the book. Two biblical passages, Nahum 3 and Jeremiah 51, are especially important as background for this chapter. We cite them here at the beginning of our analysis so that they are available for comparison as we proceed (cf. also Isa 23:16). Parallels to Revelation are cited within the quotations. The parallels are not meant to be exhaustive, nor is it necessary to trace every possible parallel to appreciate the extent of the similarities between Revelation and these prophetic texts.

Nahum lived during the downfall of the powerful Assyrian empire, which destroyed the northern kingdom of Israel and dominated the southern kingdom of Judah in the eighth century B.C.E. Assyria's fall is depicted graphically throughout Nahum. Nahum 3 contains particularly close parallels to Revelation 17. Speaking of Nineveh, Assyria's capital, God says,

> Ah! City of bloodshed,
> utterly deceitful, full of booty—
> no end to the plunder! . . . [cf. Rev 17:4, 6; 18:11–13, 16–17]
> Because of the countless debaucheries of the prostitute,
> gracefully alluring, mistress of sorcery,
> who enslaves nations through her debaucheries,
> and peoples through her sorcery, [cf. Rev 17:1–5; 18:23]
> I am against you,
> says the LORD of hosts,
> and will lift up your skirts over your face;
> and I will let the nations look on your nakedness
> and kingdoms on your shame. . . . [cf. Rev 17:16]
> Then all who see you will shrink from you and say,
> "Nineveh is devastated; who will bemoan her?" [cf. Revelation 18]
> Where shall I seek comforters for you?
> Are you better than Thebes
> that sat by the Nile,
> with water around her,
> her rampart a sea,
> water her wall? . . . [cf. Rev 17:1, 15]
> You also will be drunken,
> you will go into hiding; [cf. Rev 17:6]
> you will seek
> a refuge from the enemy. . . .
> There the fire will devour you,
> the sword will cut you off. [cf. Rev 17:16]
> It will devour you like the locust. . . . [cf. Rev 9:3–11]
> You increased your merchants
> more than the stars of the heavens. [cf. Rev 18:11, 15]
> (Nah 3:1, 4–5, 7–8, 11, 15, 16)

As is clear from the references, almost every element from these selected verses has a corresponding element in Revelation 17 or elsewhere in Revelation.

Jeremiah's lengthy harangue against Babylon in chapter 51 offers numerous parallels to Revelation 17 and 18. We have already referred to Jeremiah 51 several times for imagery parallel to that in Revelation. The citation that follows selects elements from the chapter that are most clearly reflected in Revelation 17–18 in particular:

> Flee from the midst of Babylon,
>   save your lives, each of you! [cf. Rev 18:4]
> Do not perish because of her guilt,
>   for this is the time of the LORD's vengeance;
>   he is repaying her what is due. [cf. Rev 19:2]
> Babylon was a golden cup in the LORD's hand,
>   making all the earth drunken;
> the nations drank of her wine,
>   and so the nations went mad. [cf. Rev 14:8; 17:4; 18:3;
>   see also Jer 25:15–29]
> Suddenly Babylon has fallen and is shattered;
>   wail for her! . . . [cf. Rev 18:10, 16–17, 18–20]
> You who live by the mighty waters,
>   rich in treasures, [cf. Rev 17:1, 15]
> your end has come,
>   the thread of your life is cut. . . .
> I will repay Babylon and all the inhabitants of Chaldea
>   before your very eyes for all the wrong that they have
>   done in Zion, says the LORD. . . . [cf. Rev 18:6]
> Raise a standard in the land,
>   blow the trumpet among the nations; [cf. Revelation
>   8–11]
> prepare the nations for war against her,
>   summon against her the kingdoms. . . .
> Prepare the nations for war against her,
>   the kings of the Medes, with their governors and
>   deputies,
>   and every land under their dominion. . . .
>   [cf. Rev 16:12–16; 17:16]
> "May my torn flesh be avenged on Babylon,"
>   the inhabitants of Zion shall say.
> "May my blood be avenged on the inhabitants of Chaldea,"
> Jerusalem shall say. . . . [cf. Rev 6:9–11; 16:5–6; 17:6; 18:24]
> How Babylon has become
>   an object of horror among the nations! . . .

Her cities have become an object of horror,
  a land of drought and a desert. . . . " [cf. Rev 17:1]
Come out of her, my people!
  Save your lives, each of you,
  from the fierce anger of the LORD! . . .
    [cf. Rev 18:4]
Then the heavens and the earth,
  and all that is in them,
shall shout for joy over Babylon. . . . [cf. Rev 19:1–5]
Babylon must fall for the slain of Israel,
  as the slain of all the earth have fallen because of
    Babylon. . . . [cf. Rev 6:9–11; 16:5–6; 17:6; 18:24]
    (Jer 51:6–8, 13, 24, 27, 28, 35, 41, 43, 45, 48, 49)

Jeremiah tells one of the exiles going to Babylon to take the scroll containing his words. He continues, "When you finish reading this scroll, tie a stone to it, and throw it into the middle of the Euphrates, and say, 'Thus shall Babylon sink, to rise no more, because of the disasters that I am bringing on her' " (Jer 51:63–64; cf. Rev 18:21–24).

Other elements in Jeremiah 51 that find an echo in Revelation are destructive wind (51:1; Rev 7:1), archers (51:3, 11; Rev 6:2), Babylon's judgment that goes up to heaven (51:9; Rev 14:9–11), troops like locusts (51:14; Rev 9:1–11), God's voice like the tumult of waters (51:16; Rev 1:15), God as creator (51:15–19; Rev 21:5), Babylon as destroyer of the earth (51:25; Rev 11:18), Babylon as a woman (daughter; 51:33; Revelation 17–18), the king of Babylon as a monster (51:34; Revelation 13 and 18), the drying up of Babylon's sea (51:36; Rev 16:12), Babylon's images as an offense against God (51:47; Rev 13:14–15), and Babylon's blasphemy in presuming to "mount up to heaven" and her subsequent punishment (51:53; cf. Revelation 13).

The Angel's Command (17:1–2)

The angel's command to the seer to come see the vision is lengthy. He declares that John will see "the judgment of the great whore," and he then describes her in detail through several relative clauses. Although the author uses the definite article with "whore," this is her first appearance; but Rome, whom the whore represents, has already appeared as the beast and as Babylon. The author has already employed the image of fornication to describe lack of faithfulness to God (2:20-22; 9:21; 14:8). Although the angel promises to show the seer the whore's judgment, most of the chapter does not describe the judgment but is devoted to explaining the vision of the woman seated on the beast. God's judgment is present in the statement that the Lamb defeats the beast and its allies and in the attack of the beast and its allies on the woman, an attack said to be in accord with God's purpose (17:14, 16-17). Since 18:1-19:10 consists of an announcement of Babylon's fall and reactions to it, 17:1-2 is really an introduction to the whole unit.

The angel says that the great whore John will see is seated on many waters. This fits the situation of Babylon, as Jer 51:13 notes. Babylon was located on the Euphrates River and was surrounded by canals (Charles 1920, 2:63). Rome, in contrast, was a bit inland, its port being Ostia. Of course our author was not constrained by such literalness, and the angel later explains, "The waters that you saw, where the whore is seated, are peoples and multitudes and nations and languages" (17:15). The image is appropriate for Rome and the empire over which it ruled, situated around the Mediterranean and dependent on sea transportation for many of its functions – economic, political, and social. In that sense, Rome is indeed seated on many waters. The universal sway of Rome's power is expressed by the familiar fourfold formula that can also denote the Lamb's sphere of influence (5:9).

The angel further characterizes the woman as the one "with whom the kings of the earth have committed fornication, and with the wine of whose fornication the inhabitants of the earth have become drunk" (17:2). This recalls the angel's announcement in 14:8: "Fallen, fallen is Babylon the great! She has made all nations drink of the wine of the wrath of her fornication" (cf. Jer 51:7, 39, 57). The specification "kings" in 17:2 fits the concern of the chapter with political entities and especially with rulers. The angel in chapter 10 who carries the open scroll symbolizing the more detailed and specific revelation of the second half of Revelation tells the seer, "You must prophesy again about many peoples and nations and languages and kings" (10:11). The substitution of "kings" for "tribes" in the familiar fourfold formula also signals the interest of the second half of the book in political rulers. The political system, with Caesar at the top and client kings beneath him, is responsible for what is wrong in the world, for Satan uses the system and empowers it to undermine God's sovereignty. There is no real distinction between religion and politics.

The involvement of kings in the eschatological events is foreshadowed when in the sixth seal the kings and all inhabitants of the earth despair in the face of the coming of the wrath of God and the Lamb (6:15–16). The kings' role in the final events is described briefly in the sixth bowl (16:12–16), which parts of chapter 17 elaborate. The author's audience must see all of this in the broad framework of the book as a whole, which at its very beginning calls Jesus Christ "the ruler of the kings of the earth" (1:5; see also 17:14; 19:16). Similarly, the actions of the kings in chapter 17 are determined by God (17:17). It is really God and the Lamb who rule, not the kings of the earth or Rome.

Revelation 17:2 recalls the angel's announcement of Babylon's fall in 14:8, and so in both places it is the engagement of Rome with the nations, characterized as fornication and as drunkenness, that leads to Rome's downfall. The cup image is frequent in the Bible. It is especially reminiscent of Jer 51:7, where Babylon itself is a cup God gives to the nations to make them drunk and worthy of divine wrath.

The Vision (17:3–6)

The angel carries the seer in the spirit to the wilderness, where he sees the vision (17:3). In 1:10, the seer says that he receives his vision while in the spirit, which we take to mean a prophetic trance. The seer's trip to heaven in chapter 4 is somehow associated with the spirit (4:2). The only other mention of transport in the spirit in Revelation is 21:10, in the vision of the Lamb's bride that parallels the vision of the great whore here. These mentions of the spirit thus occur at strategic points in the narrative: at the beginning of the whole vision contained in Revelation (1:10), at the beginning of John's eschatological visions that make up the bulk of the book (4:2), at the beginning of his vision of Babylon's fall (17:3), and at the beginning of his vision of the union of the Lamb and his bride (21:10). This structure underscores the importance of these four moments in the narrative.

John is carried to a wilderness. Wilderness can have several meanings in Jewish and Christian texts. Here it contrasts with the site of the parallel vision beginning in 21:9, where John is transported to a high mountain to observe the descent of the new Jerusalem. Jerusalem symbolizes God's dwelling with humans; the wilderness is the place inhabited by evil spirits. This meaning for wilderness is assumed also in the gospel narrative when Jesus is led by the spirit into the wilderness to spend forty days there with the wild beasts, tempted by Satan (Mark 1:12–13).

In the wilderness John beholds a woman sitting on a scarlet beast covered with blasphemous names and having seven heads and ten horns (17:3). This is the same beast that John sees rise out of the sea in chapter 13, a beast which also has seven heads and ten horns (13:1). Whereas the beast of chapter 13 has blasphemous names on its heads, the one in chapter 17 is covered with (literally, "full of") blasphemous names. The difference may be purely stylistic, but it may also indicate a shift of emphasis. Where the names on the first beast emphasize the idolatrous claims of the emperors, the position of the names on the second beast stresses the spread of Rome's idolatry throughout the empire. Both the beast in chapter 13 and the one in chapter 17 share the number of heads and horns with the dragon of chapter 12, so they are in its image. It is no real contradiction that the woman, who earlier was said to sit on the waters, here sits on the beast. The author is not so literal. Besides, the beast is associated with waters in chapter 13.

The color of the beast of chapter 13 is not mentioned, but in chapter 17 it is said to be scarlet (17:3), a color similar to that of the red dragon in 12:3. The woman is dressed in purple and scarlet, ostentatious and expensive colors, which may allude to her royalty (see Matt 27:28; Mark 15:17, 20; John 19:2, 5). Her gold, jewels, and pearls indicate both her wealth and her seductive nature. In 18:9–19, the earth's merchants and seafarers who profited from Rome's taste for such luxuries mourn Rome's passing, for it means the end of their trade in luxury items. The woman holds in her hand a golden cup that contains "abominations and the impurities of her fornication" (17:4). The word "abomination" is frequent in biblical cultic texts, meaning anything that is abhorrent to God and that should not exist among God's people or should be carefully kept away from God's cultic presence. "Abomination" goes well with fornication to denote what is repulsive to God and contrary to divine sovereignty.

The woman wears her name, called a "mystery," on her forehead (17:5). Charles (1920, 2:65) notes that Roman prostitutes wore their names on their foreheads, but there are closer parallels within the book of Revelation itself. Both the followers of the Lamb (7:3; 9:4; 14:1; 22:4) and those of the beast (13:16; 14:9; 20:4) wear names on their foreheads. The names they bear signify whether they belong to the Lamb or the beast and place them on one side or the other of the great eschatological divide that runs through Revelation. When the author calls the woman's name a mystery, he does not mean simply that it is a puzzle to be decoded. In apocalyptic contexts, the word "mystery" means insight about the true nature of things possible only through revelation (cf. 10:7). "Mystery" in apocalyptic contexts often concerns eschatological realities (e.g., Rom 11:25; 1 Cor 15:51). In the case of the woman, her true nature is knowable only through revelation. The Roman empire has deceived the world about its true nature. The inhabitants of the earth go by appearances in chapter 13 and therefore worship the beast. An accurate appraisal of Rome would make them see that the majesty and power of Rome are grotesque imitations of divine power and majesty, just as prostitution is a distortion of marriage. Rome's true nature is revealed in its name, a "mystery": "Babylon the great, mother of whores and of earth's abominations" (17:5).

The name of the whore is in striking contrast to the name of the Lamb, revealed when the beast and its allies clash with him in 17:14: "He is Lord of lords and King of kings." These titles are repeated when Christ rides out to the eschatological battle in chapter 19: "He has a name inscribed that no one knows but himself.... His name is called the Word of God.... On his robe and on his thigh he has a name inscribed, 'King of kings and Lord of lords' " (19:12, 13, 16). To all appearances, Rome reigns supreme and is worthy of all honor, and Christ is but a criminal executed by Rome. But seen from God's point of view, Rome is a distorted parody of divine power, and Christ embodies the majesty and sovereignty of God. To name is to define and control. On an earthly level, Rome has the authority to name. Our author, by renaming things, changes the world for his audience.

Revelation 17:6 goes to the heart of the seer's concerns. He sees "that the woman was drunk with the blood of the saints and the blood of the witnesses to Jesus" (17:6). It is Rome's persecution of Christians, God's faithful, that most fully embodies its opposition to God. Rome not only mistreats Christians or fails to be converted by them; it wages war on them. Combined with the vision of a whore holding a cup of abominations and fornication, decked out in seductive finery, 17:6 completes a picture of consummate debauchery and alienation from God. Rome slaughters Christians and does so while reclining at ease and enjoying luxuries. This picture expresses forcefully the author's view of Roman power and culture. It demonstrates his extreme alienation from that power and culture, an alienation not shared by Paul before him, or indeed by many Christians of his own day, as the messages to the seven churches attest. But for the author, this is Rome's essence. This is the mystery, the insight, that comes from direct access to the true meaning of things. Such a vile institution can only exist if supported by Satan, and it cannot survive God's wrath for long.

The Angelic Interpretation of the Vision (17:7–18)

The angel's interpretation of the vision takes up most of chapter 17. It concentrates on the beast. The structure and content of chapter 17 as a whole recall Daniel 7, in which Daniel sees four beasts arise from the sea and then receives an angelic interpretation of the vision. John's reaction to the vision of the woman is to be amazed (17:6). Ironically, this is the same reaction that the inhabitants of the earth have to the beast in 13:3–4, a reaction that causes them to worship the beast and the dragon, and their amazement is noted again in 17:8. Clearly this is the wrong reaction. The angel challenges the seer, asking him why he marvels and saying he will disclose "the mystery" of the woman and the beast.

The angel begins with a general interpretation of the beast as a whole and explains specific aspects of the beast later in the chapter. The angel says that the beast "was, and is not, and is about to ascend from the bottomless pit and go to destruction." This explanation is packed with meaning in the context of Revelation. It shows the beast to be a parody of both God and the Lamb. God is the one who is, was, and is to come (1:4, 8; 4:8; cf. 16:4). This identifies God as both the eternal one (was and is) and the one who will intervene in history (is to come). Revelation shows that God's coming results in Babylon's destruction. When applied to the beast, the threefold title is modified in its third member to say that the beast is going to destruction. The title also makes clear that when the beast comes, it is not from heaven, where God comes from, but from the bottomless pit, the abyss, which makes its demonic character evident. This is the same beast that emerges from the abyss in 11:7 to make war on the prophetic church.

The beast is also a parody of the Lamb. In chapter 13, it is said that one of the beast's heads had a mortal wound that was healed (13:3) and then that the beast itself had a mortal wound from which it recovered (13:12, 14). This creates a parallel between the beast and Christ, who identifies himself in 2:8 as the one "who was dead and came to life" and who in 5:6 appears as the Lamb who stands "as if it had been slaughtered." The verb "slaughtered" is applied to both the Lamb and beast in chapter 13 (13:3, 8). The references in chapter 13 to the beast that received a mortal wound but was healed are allusions to the Nero redivivus legend – that is, the legend that Nero died and then came back to life. The tripartite title of the beast in 17:8, which says that he "was, and is not, and is about to ascend from the bottomless pit and go to destruction," is also inspired by the Nero myth, and so it restates what is said about this same beast in chapter 13. He once reigned, is not now present, and will come again when he emerges from the abyss, at which time he will be finally destroyed.

Although this formulation is inspired by the Nero myth, it also sets up resonances that go beyond Nero. The Neronian persecution is vivid in the author's imagination, and he anticipates another, still broader persecution to be pursued by a Roman emperor yet to come, who as persecutor is equivalent to another Nero. But as we have frequently observed, the author also sees this as part of a larger cosmic struggle that defines history and that will soon be resolved in a definitive battle. His conceptions are deeply influenced by the ancient combat myth, in which the forces opposed to God and to God's order were subdued at creation, but still exist. They must be held in check throughout history, and they occasionally attempt to rise again, endangering God's order.

The threefold title of the beast also tells us something about the seer's circumstances. He is less concerned about individual Roman emperors for their own sake than he is about emperors as expressions of satanic power and opposition to God's people. Nero is the paradigm of such emperors because of his persecution of the church in the 60s. That is in the author's past. The beast "was." Presently, there is no ongoing persecution matching the seer's expectations, so the beast "is not." The seer says that a great ordeal is about to come upon the entire world (3:10), and this will be when the beast arises from the abyss (Boring 1989, 181).

The angel's attention now turns to the beast's followers. They, like the seer, are amazed at the beast. Their amazement is because the beast "was and is not and is to come" (17:8), just as in chapter 13 their amazement was because the beast's head received a mortal blow but was healed (13:3). The subtle change of the third member of the description back into "is to come" from "is about to ascend from the bottomless pit and go to destruction" may reflect the deluded faith of those who follow the beast, who are unable to distinguish between divine and satanic power. Their amazement causes them to worship the dragon and the beast in 13:3, and in 13:8 the one who worships is the one "whose name has not been written from the foundation of the world in the book of life of the Lamb that was slaughtered." In 17:8, the amazed inhabitants of the earth are those "whose names have not been written in the book of life from the foundation of the world." This does not imply predestination. It is possible, for example, to be blotted out of the book (3:5); various passages suggest that repentance is at least possible even for earth's inhabitants (see 11:13); and in the end there is provision for "healing of the nations" (22:2). Nonetheless, in chapters 13 and 17, the seer's focus is on the necessity of choosing sides, of belonging to the Lamb or the beast, and social dualism comes to the fore.

Revelation 17:9–14 explains the beast's heads and horns. The explanation begins with the notice, "This calls for a mind that has wisdom" (17:9). This recalls the similar notice when the number of the beast, 666, was divulged (13:18). The wisdom in question is not human wisdom that is the fruit of thoughtful reflection on experience and tradition. Rather it is apocalyptic insight available only through direct revelation. The interpretation entails the same combination of apparent specificity and basic ambiguity as we encountered when looking at the number 666. This opens the door to multiple conflicting interpretations. We are not concerned here with interpretations through history that attempt to relate Revelation's images to contemporary persons and events in the interpreters' environments. Our basic view of Revelation sees such interpretations as futile and well beyond the author's intentions.

The angel first explains the beast's heads. He offers two separate explanations. The first is that "the seven heads are seven mountains on which the woman is seated" (17:9). It was a commonplace at this time that Rome was the city built on seven hills, so this was a reference that would have been understandable to the audience (Charles 1920, 2:69). The woman is Rome, or perhaps the goddess Roma, and she sits on Rome's seven hills. The second explanation is that the seven heads are seven kings, five of whom "have fallen"; the sixth reigns; and the seventh is yet to come but will "remain only a little while" (17:9-10). The angel adds that the beast is an eighth, but belongs to the seven, and goes to destruction. Commentators like Charles (1920, 2:68-69), who are disposed to see apparent disjunctions in the text as pointers to sources, explanatory glosses, and the like, do not think that these two explanations of the seven heads come from the same hand. However, the book of Daniel offers just such a double interpretation when it deciphers the four beasts of Daniel 7 first as kings (7:17) and then says that the fourth beast represents a kingdom and its ten horns stand for ten kings (7:23-24). Revelation demonstrates the same flexibility when in chapter 13 it sees the beast from the sea first as Rome and then as one of its emperors. In 17:9, the explanations of the beast's seven heads as Rome's seven hills and as kings are related in that both relate the heads to imperial Rome.

The angel's statement that five kings have fallen, one lives, and the seventh is to come is continually tantalizing for commentators. This seems so concrete and specific that we should be able to establish a one-to-one correspondence between the seven kings and actual emperors. But the variety of solutions that have been proposed show that, even more than with the number 666, the impulse to "decode" the seven kings is doomed to failure. Aune supplies a chart that outlines no fewer than eight different ways of relating the seven kings to the early Roman emperors (see introduction above). Options in the counting include beginning with Julius Caesar or Augustus; beginning with Nero as the first emperor to persecute Christians; including or omitting three emperors who ruled immediately after Nero for very short periods of time; counting only emperors who were killed (this is based on the strength of the word "fallen" in Rev 17:10); starting with Gaius (Caligula) because of his evil treatment of Jews and his attempted blasphemy of setting up his statue in the Jerusalem temple; including only emperors who were deified by the senate; and so forth. Choices made by commentators often reflect attempts to make the numbering fit their notion of when Revelation was written, but even that criterion can be misleading if the author incorporates a source here and does not adapt it to fit his own time perfectly.

Given the uncertainty about which real emperors the seven represent, we must question whether we should attempt to relate the seven to actual emperors at all. The fact that there are precisely seven kings is hardly a coincidence. It is likely that the author is less interested in numbering real kings than in having the total number be seven. Seven is too symbolic a number throughout Revelation for it not to be symbolic here. It likely means the proper number of emperors that God has determined. Apocalypses are full of examples of periodization of history, such as Daniel's four kingdoms in Daniel 7 (see Mounce 1977, 315-16, for more examples). It is a common device to signify that God controls history and that all happens according to God's plan. A function of these periodizations is to provide a chronological map for the audience, showing them that they live near the endtime (Hartman 1976).

Some observations about the seven kings can be made here that shed light on the function of the angel's interpretation. The author writes to tell his audience where they fit in history and to warn them of what is to come. For that reason, what is most important for them is that the beast from the abyss, already familiar from 11:7 and chapter 13, has appeared in the person of a Roman emperor and will do so again as the eighth in a series of emperors. Since the eighth is also one of the seven, the future emperor amounts to a reincarnation of the earlier demonic emperor, whether taken as a literal reincarnation or a symbolic one. The emperor under whom they live, the sixth, is not this demonic incarnation. In our judgment, this is Domitian. Nor will the seventh emperor be the one. The seventh will reign but a short time, and then the beast will rise again as the eighth emperor, but he is doomed to defeat. He will go to destruction.

The next section involves the beast's ten horns (17:12-14), interpreted as ten kings. The ten kings come ultimately from Dan 7:24. The angel says that these ten kings have not yet received their kingdom (17:12). This has led to all sorts of speculation down through history about just who these kings are. That they are in the seer's future has been taken as license to identify them with whatever entities contemporary with the interpreter that strike his or her fancy. Recent commentators have identified the kings with the nations of the European Economic Community, for example, or the oil-producing nations belonging to OPEC. Such identifications are gratuitous and serve merely to lend supposedly divine sanction to individuals' judgments about their own times.

In 17:14, the angel says that the ten kings will cede their power and authority to the beast and become his allies against the Lamb, who will conquer them. This is a reference to the final eschatological battle between the Lamb and God's adversaries. We have already noted that Jewish eschatology attests to the idea of a great final battle in which the nations ally themselves against Israel or against the righteous (see comments on 16:12–16). Since that battle is future for the author and occurs only after the great ordeal, the kings themselves must be future. We note in our comments on the demonic cavalry from the Euphrates (9:13–19) and on the invasion of kings from the east who assemble for battle at Harmagedon (16:12–16) that such images draw both on the idea of a final battle between Israel and the nations and on the Nero legends that picture the emperor returning at the head of Parthian hordes to conquer Rome (Charles 1920, 2:76–87).

The ten kings reign for only a short time with the beast, a symbolic "hour" (17:12). Their reign is brought to an end when they unite against the Lamb and make war on him (17:14). The Lamb wins victory because he is "Lord of lords and King of kings." These same titles are applied to Christ in chapter 19 as he rides out to battle against "the beast and the kings of the earth with their armies" (19:16, 19). Charles shows that they are applied to God in other texts, so in the final battle Christ represents God (1920, 2:75; e.g., *1 Enoch* 9:4; 1 Tim 6:15). The battles in 17:13–14 and 19:11–21 are the same. The battle is ultimately between the Lamb and all adversaries of God, characterized broadly in chapter 19 as the beast and the kings of the earth (Mounce 1977, 317).

Those who are with the Lamb when he fights the beast and its allies "are called and chosen and faithful" (17:14). The precise identity of these figures and their role is uncertain. This is the only occurrence of "called" and "chosen" in Revelation. Aside from its application to those with Christ in 17:14, "faithful" is applied to Christ (1:5; 3:14; 19:11), the martyr Antipas (2:13), and to the words of Revelation itself (21:22; 22:6). Christ and

Antipas carried their witness to the point of death. In 2:10, the Smyrneans are exhorted to be "faithful" unto death. It is possible, then, that those present with Christ at the last battle are the martyrs. In 19:14, the armies of heaven, dressed in white linen, follow Christ into that battle. In 6:9–11, the martyrs in heaven have already received white garments. All of this is quite imprecise, but it is possible that the groups in 6:9–11, 17:14, and 19:14 are the same. Charles (1920, 2:74–75) cites passages in Jewish apocalypses where the righteous take part in the final battle, and the *War Scroll* from Qumran supplies another example. Whether this means that the author actually expects the martyrs to fight or whether this is just symbolic is disputed.

The angel's attention now shifts back to the woman seated on the beast. If there is any doubt that the woman symbolizes Rome, it is dispelled by the pronouncement, "The woman you saw is the great city that rules over the kings of the earth" (17:18). For one living in the Roman empire, this could mean only Rome. After briefly identifying the waters on which the woman sits as "peoples and multitudes and nations and languages," showing the universality of her sway (17:15), the angel goes on to say that the beast and the ten horns will hate the whore, and "they will make her desolate and naked; they will devour her flesh and burn her up with fire" (17:16; see Nahum 3 and Jeremiah 51). All this they will do because God has "put it into their heart . . . until the words of God will be fulfilled" (17:17). As is usual in Revelation, this scenario should be seen against several backgrounds, all of which are drawn upon by the author to set up resonances in his audience. One version of the Nero legend had it that Nero, at the head of Parthian armies, would attack Rome. This would explain the actions of the beast and the kings in 17:16. The scenario also fits the idea, present in the concept of holy war, that God's enemies would turn on each other. This is transposed into an eschatological key in Ezek 38:21 and Zech 14:13.

Another background against which the scenario must be viewed is the motif of harlotry as giving to other gods and nations what God alone merits. We previously mentioned biblical passages in which the harlotry theme surfaces. A good parallel to the scene in Rev 17:16 is Ezekiel 23, where the northern and southern kingdoms, Israel and Judah, are portrayed as harlots, unfaithful to God because of their foreign alliances. God angrily declares, "I will rouse against you your lovers from every side" (23:22). The prophet continues, "They shall cut off your nose and your ears, and your survivors shall fall by the sword. They shall seize your sons and your daughters, and your survivors shall be devoured by fire. They shall strip you of your clothes and take away your fine jewels" (23:25–26). A bit later God says, "I will deliver you into the hands of those whom you hate" (23:28). Then God says that he will punish Judah as he has Israel, saying that he will give Israel's cup to Judah. He says, "You shall be filled with drunkenness and sorrow" (23:33).

The parallels between Revelation and Ezekiel are clear. Both speak of stripping the woman (cf. Nah 3:5); both speak of hatred; in both the woman's flesh is mutilated; and in both fire plays a role in the punishment (cf. Nah 3:15). Such imagery is repulsive to modern ears. A reading of Ezekiel 23 makes Revelation seem mild; the former is so graphic and lengthy. Ezekiel 16 contains the same sort of detailed description of a harlot who is punished brutally, thus furnishing another parallel to Rev 17:16. Some commentators see Jezebel as another harlot who is punished in ways "suitable" to her supposed sexual crimes, since she is thrown on a bed in 2:22, while those who commit adultery with her are thrown into distress. In that case the reference is less sure, since the reference to a bed may be to a sickbed.

As in the sixth bowl, there are two different battles alluded to in chapter 17. In 17:14, the beast and its allies make war on the Lamb and are conquered by him, and in 17:16, the beast and its allies attack the woman and destroy her. The first of these, the battle between the Lamb and his adversaries, is also reflected in 11:15–19, 14:14–20, 16:13–21, and 19:11–20:4, and is anticipated in 6:12–17. The second, the battle between Roman armies and forces from the east, is reflected in 9:13–21, 16:12, and perhaps 6:1–2. As we noted in our comments on the sixth bowl, these two strands do not separate neatly. Logically, the battle with the Lamb must come after the one between Rome and the east, but the order is the reverse in chapter 17. In any case, the two battles are closely related in the author's mind. Boring (1989, 184–85) thinks it best to recognize that these two are inconsistent with each other and cannot be reconciled chronologically. Rather, they are two different aspects of the downfall of evil. One stresses God's conquest of evil in the death of Christ, and the other emphasizes the self-destructive nature of evil.

By the end of chapter 17 the audience has experienced vicariously, through the seer's account of his visions, the inexorable downfall of Rome, under the guise of Babylon. In this second part of Revelation, which begins with chapter 12, the references to Rome's downfall are clear and detailed. Rome's fall is predicted in 14:8, described in the fifth and seventh bowls (16:10–11, 17–21), and elaborated in chapter 17, particularly in 17:14, 16–17. The beast's destruction is also seen as inevitable, for it goes to destruction (12:12; 17:8, 11). This scene leads into chapter 18, a lengthy description of different reactions to Rome's downfall.

Reactions to Babylon's Fall (18:1–19:10)

Chapter 18 is in three major parts, each of which is a reaction to Babylon's (that is, Rome's) fall (for an analysis of the chapter's structure, see Yarbro Collins 1980). The first is a twofold reaction from heaven, one by an angel who descends from heaven and one by a voice from heaven (18:1–8). The second is a series of laments over Babylon's fall by kings, merchants, and seafarers (18:9–19). The third is a symbolic action and prophetic announcement by an angel (18:21–24). Angelic comments thus begin and end the chapter and frame the reactions of kings, merchants, and seafarers. The effect is one of contrast: joy from the angels that God's justice has been done, and sorrow from Babylon's inhabitants that its prosperity and theirs are at an end. The angels' words are emphasized both by their position in framing the dirges and by their parallel content. Each of their pronouncements (18:2–3, 21–24) contains an announcement of Babylon's fall, a description of its results, and a reason for its judgment.

Reasons for Babylon's Fall: The Seer's Critique of Rome

The reactions to Babylon's fall in 18:1–19:10 are more specific about why God judges it than are most other parts of Revelation. Taken together, they sketch a picture of how John sees the Roman empire and why he thinks it deserves annihilation. We begin by collecting together those verses that make concrete the charges against Rome. They fall into two main categories: those that involve economic matters and those that concern Rome's persecution of Christians.

In 18:3, an angel speaks in a familiar metaphorical way of Babylon's relationship with the nations as fornication, and he then says, "The merchants of the earth have grown rich from the power of her luxury." Another voice from heaven later says,

"As she glorified herself and lived luxuriously, so give her a like measure of torment and grief" (18:7). In the same context, Rome is taken to task for its arrogant confidence in its own invincibility (18:7–8). The merchants of the earth are those who "lived in luxury with her" in 18:9, and in 18:11 they weep "since no one buys their cargo anymore," a cargo enumerated in verses 12 and 13 and consisting largely of luxury goods. The merchants go on to mourn that Rome has lost its "fruit" and all its "dainties and splendor" (18:14). In 18:15, the merchants are those "who gained their wealth from her," and they lament that Rome has lost its wealth, its adornment with fine linen, gold, and jewels (18:16–17). Seafarers lament, for "all who had ships at sea grew rich by her wealth" (18:19).

Verses in the preceding paragraph indict Rome for its wealth and luxury. To some this might seem to be simply a case of envy (Lawrence 1988). But this is not simply a question of members of a secure middle class wishing that they had what the wealthy have. In the Roman empire a tiny proportion of the population was very wealthy; there was a small "middle" class which consisted mainly of retainers and merchants who serviced the wealthy; and the great majority of the people lived poorly or even in destitution. The cost of Rome's luxuries and of the wars necessary to preserve them fell to the lower classes, those who tilled the earth, whose "surplus" was siphoned off through taxes and confiscation. Most of the texts that come from the ancient world are from members of the upper classes, so they seldom give an adequate picture of how the economic and political system was perceived by those on the lower end of the scale. Viewed from the bottom of society, the excesses and luxuries of the ruling classes must have seemed to some divine and to others demonic. A common interpretation sees the third seal (6:5–6) as reflecting a situation where subsistence items like wheat and barley were subject to terrible inflation, while luxury items were not affected, putting still more pressure on the poor.

When one adds to economic factors Rome's brutality toward the groups to which our author belongs—Jews and Christians—one senses the moral outrage underlying Revelation. The author probably came from a country (Jewish Palestine) devastated by the Roman legions. Revelation's focus on liturgy and cult, and particularly on the temple and Jerusalem, can be seen in the context of the destruction of Jerusalem and its temple by the Romans in 70 C.E. From 18:20 on, the text centers on Rome's "slaughter" of Christians, particularly the shedding of blood. In 18:20, saints, apostles, and prophets are told to rejoice because God has given judgment for them against Rome. In 18:24, Rome is told that within her has been found the blood of prophets, saints, and all who have been "slaughtered" on the earth. In 19:2, a heavenly chorus declares that God has avenged the blood of his servants on Rome.

Such a dire picture of Rome's oppression must be balanced by the observation that the seer perceives things in dramatic and oppositional terms, as is common in someone with an apocalyptic view of the world. As terrible as Rome's brutality was, Augustus brought relative peace to the world for a time, and the single overarching authority that Rome embodied sometimes helped to deflect potential disasters, such as wars, economic instability, and arbitrary local rulers. Paul has a positive view of Roman administration, even seeing it as God-given (Romans 13), and the messages to the seven churches in Revelation 2–3 attest to the existence of Christians in Asia who did not share the seer's antipathy to Roman rule and culture. Furthermore, we have made the case in the introduction (under "Christians in the Roman Empire") and in our discussion of the messages to the churches that there was no systematic, widespread persecution against Christians or Jews during most of the first century. Nonetheless, the seer had a clear vision of Rome's evils, and his condemnation of Rome's economic exploitation and political and religious repression was based on real abuses in the Roman order.

Heavenly Reaction to Babylon's Fall (18:1–8)

"Another angel" now appears (18:1). Since 17:1–19:10 is a unit, this angel is distinguished from the angel who leads the seer to the vision of the woman on the beast (17:1). The way in which his advent is described leaves no doubt that he is of the heavenly world and that his reaction is a reliable reflection of the divine reaction. Not only is he said to come down from heaven; he also has "great authority," and "the earth was made bright by his splendor [literally, glory]" (18:1). The word "authority" is frequent in Revelation, occurring twenty-one times. The overall pattern of its use reinforces the idea that all authority comes ultimately from God, even if it be the authority of the demonic locusts to torture the earth's inhabitants (9:3, 10). The angel who comes down from heaven with "great authority" speaks for God.

The earth is illuminated by the angel's glory. The idea is common in ancient Jewish and Christian documents that heavenly beings shine and that those who are from the heavenly world or come in contact with it glow with its "glory" (e.g., Moses in Exod 34:29; Jesus in Matt 17:2–3). The closest parallel to Rev 18:1 is Ezek 43:2, where God returns to Jerusalem at the end of the Babylonian exile: "The glory of the God of Israel was coming from the east; the sound was like the sound of mighty waters; and the earth shone with his glory." In Revelation the angel's glory is also to be seen against the backdrop of the frequent repetition of the idea that glory must be given to God, because it is only to God that glory is due. This is an implicit criticism of those who glorify the Roman emperor or the empire. Only when the heavenly being descends is the earth made bright.

The angel's pronouncement is an elaboration of the angel's proclamation in 14:8: "Fallen, fallen is Babylon the great! She has made all nations drink of the wine of the wrath of her fornication." The angel in 18:1–3 reproduces the first words of 14:8: "Fallen, fallen is Babylon the great!" Both pronouncements echo Isa 21:9: "Fallen, fallen is Babylon." In both 14:8 and 18:2 the angels announce Babylon's fall as if it were already past. This is because the seer sees the future. Chapter 18's angel elaborates on Babylon's fall by describing its results. Babylon is in ruins, home only to demons, foul spirits, foul birds, and hateful beasts. The scene of desolation echoes in a general way the picture of the fall of Babylon in Jeremiah 51, but the language more closely reflects Isaiah's oracle against Babylon:

> Wild animals will lie down there,
>   and its houses will be full of howling creatures;
> there ostriches will live,
>   and there goat-demons will dance.
> Hyenas will cry in its towers,
>   and jackals in the pleasant palaces. (Isa 13:21–22)

This picture is in stark contrast to Babylon's previous prosperity, presented graphically in the person of the whore on the beast in chapter 17, and remembered in the dirges of Babylon's collaborators later in chapter 18.

The angel now takes up the second half of the pronouncement of the angel of 14:8 by saying, "For all the nations have drunk of the wine of the wrath of her fornication, and the kings of the earth have committed fornication with her" (18:3). The strange phrase "the wine of the wrath of her fornication" is exactly the same as in 14:8 and 18:3. As in chapter 14, the phrase constitutes a play on words, for the word translated "wrath" (*thymos*) is often used of God's anger in Revelation, but it can also simply mean "passion." The nations engage in passionate "fornication" with Rome, and by so doing they incur God's wrath. The symmetry is clear in chapter 14 where the same ones who drink Rome's wine from her cup will drink God's anger from his cup (14:8, 10). The symmetry is also clear in 18:6. The causal connection between fornication with the nations and Rome's fall is grammatically expressed in verse 3, which begins with the word "for" or "because." Babylon has fallen "because" of her corruption of the nations and her luxury.

The seer detests Rome's effect on the world. As is typical of the second half of Revelation, and particularly of 17:1–19:10, the political and economic system is highlighted. The angel explicitly mentions the "kings of the earth" who fornicate with Rome (18:3), while the angel of 14:8 speaks only of the nations. Verse 3 goes on to say that the earth's merchants have grown rich through supplying Rome with luxuries (cf. 18:15). Persecution of Christians is not the seer's only concern. That persecution is one symptom, even if a crucial one, of an unjust system opposed to God. The political and economic characteristics of the empire are another crucial symptom.

The second part of this first heavenly reaction to Babylon's fall is supplied by "another voice from heaven" (18:4). The second voice speaks before Babylon is destroyed, for it exhorts the faithful to abandon Babylon both to avoid participation in its sins and to escape its punishment. The pronouncement has three parts. The first addresses the faithful who live in Babylon, telling them to depart before God's anger descends on it (18:4–5). The second is to an unspecified agent of God, commanding that Babylon be punished for its deeds (18:6). The third is a prophetic section stressing that Babylon's punishment is appropriate and in proportion to her misdeeds (18:7–8).

The voice commands, "Come out of her, my people, so that you do not take part in her sins, and so that you do not share in her plagues" (18:4). This sounds like God speaking, but in the following verse God is in the third person (18:5). Perhaps the voice is that of Jesus, although one would expect Jesus' statements to be marked as such. Another possibility is that an angel speaks for God here. What is important is that the voice comes from heaven and so reflects God's viewpoint. The words again allude to Jeremiah's long oracle on Babylon's fall (Jeremiah 51), where God says, "Come out of her, my people! Save your lives, each of you, from the fierce anger of the LORD!" (Jer 51:45). Isaiah has a similar passage exhorting the Jewish exiles to leave Babylon: "Depart, depart, go out from there! Touch no unclean thing; go out from the midst of it, purify yourselves" (Isa 52:11). Jeremiah tells the people to leave Babylon so as to avoid the effects of God's anger (called plagues in Revelation), and Isaiah tells them to leave so as not to join in Babylon's uncleanness (called sin in Revelation). Revelation 18:4 combines the two reasons. Separation from Babylon's sins and their consequences is necessary because its sins have become so numerous and heinous that they "are heaped high as heaven," and God "has remembered her iniquities" (18:5; cf. 16:19). The author does not mean that God ever forgot what Babylon was doing. "Remember" in the Bible is often applied to God in the sense that he has finally decided to take action.

The language of Babylon's sins being heaped up sounds a bit like Jeremiah's statement in chapter 51:

> Suddenly Babylon has fallen and is shattered;
>   wail for her!
> Bring balm for her wound;
>   perhaps she may be healed.
> We tried to heal Babylon,
>   but she could not be healed.
> Forsake her, and let each of us go
>   to our own country;
> for her judgment has reached up to heaven
>   and has been lifted up even to the skies.
> The LORD has brought forth our vindication.
> (Jer 51:8–10)

Here it is Babylon's judgment, not its sins, that reaches to heaven, but our author often changes the application of images from his sources. The way that the author reinterprets these verses from Jeremiah 51 is intriguing. We have made the case that the seer is dismayed at the extent to which Christians from several of the Asian cities were willing to compromise with the culture around them, while his stand toward the surrounding culture is one of prophetic opposition. In Jeremiah 51, the prophet and his contemporaries try to "work within the system." They attempt to compromise with Babylon for a while. But God's judgment on Babylon is undeniable. Even after Babylon falls, the people try to make compromises, but it is futile. Therefore God, through Jeremiah, orders the people to separate themselves from Babylon. They must also recognize that the punishment of Babylon is their own vindication. The dynamics of Jer 51:8–10 must have caught our author's attention. The tension in Jeremiah between trying to help Babylon and separating from it becomes absolute opposition between points of view in the Asian churches. No compromise is possible. There is but one course for Christians: separation.

The second part of the heavenly voice's speech orders Babylon's punishment in terms that assert its fairness: "Render to her as she herself has rendered" (18:6). That the punishment fits the crime is a common theme in the Bible, and it occurs in Revelation repeatedly. The voice's next words seem contradictory in that they order God's agent to "repay her double for her deeds." This is a rhetorical flourish based on such passages as Isa 40:2 and Jer 16:18. It does not mean that God's punishment does not fit the crime. The same is true of the following words, "Mix a double draught for her in the cup she mixed." As Babylon did to others, it shall now be done to her.

The third section of the heavenly voice's pronouncement is in two parts, each of which states first Babylon's sin and then its punishment (18:7–8). The first part resumes the theme of Babylon's luxurious living, adding now that she "glorifies" herself (18:7). "Glory" belongs only to God (see comments on 14:7). As is true in the real world of Roman politics and economics, economic exploitation and political claims go hand-in-hand. Because Babylon claims a certain status for herself, a status the seer considers a challenge to God, she confiscates the world's resources to support her own extravagant lifestyle, a lifestyle parodied in the whore of chapter 17. In proportion to her self-glorification and luxury, the voice declares, "So give her a like measure of torment and grief" (18:7). The punishment fits the crime.

In poetic parallelism, the author again states Babylon's crime and declares the retribution (18:7–8). Babylon's arrogant confidence now comes under fire. The voice says, "Since in her heart she says, 'I rule as a queen; I am no widow, and I will never see grief,' therefore her plagues will come in a single day." The verse recalls Isaiah's indictment of Babylon's arrogance:

> Now therefore hear this, you lover of pleasures,
> who sit securely,
> who say in your heart,
> "I am, and there is no one besides me;
> I shall not sit as a widow
> or know the loss of children" —
> both of these things shall come upon you
> in a moment, in one day. (Isa 47:8–9; cf. Ezek 28:2)

For her arrogance, plagues come upon Revelation's Babylon suddenly. The plagues are further enumerated as "pestilence and mourning and famine," a trio two of whose members occur in the fourth seal (6:8). The voice also says that Babylon will be burned by fire, a common element of judgment in Revelation and throughout Jewish and Christian literature. The voice's speech ends with a reminder that the God who judges Babylon is powerful (18:8). This picks up on the notice at the beginning of the speech that plagues are coming upon Babylon because God has remembered her iniquities. Although appearances say that Rome is supreme and the Jewish and Christian God is powerless, Rome in fact is subject to God.

It is common in Jewish literature that God rebukes or punishes those, especially rulers, whose position makes them proud and unmindful of God's supremacy. For example, Daniel tells the Babylonian king that God will afflict him "until you have learned that the Most High has sovereignty over the kingdom of mortals, and gives it to whom he will" (Dan 4:25; cf. *1 Enoch* 63:4). For the seer, this translates into the attitude a Christian should have toward the unjust society around him or her. Engagement with that society and financial success within it undermine faithfulness to God. As Christ says in the message to the church at Laodicea, "You say, 'I am rich, I have prospered, and I need nothing.' You do not realize that you are wretched, pitiable, poor, blind, and naked" (3:17).

Revelation 17:16 depicts Babylon's fall as due to the attack of the beast and the ten kings. In chapter 18, her fall is due to God. There is no real contradiction here. In apocalypticism, what happens in the unseen world determines what happens on earth (Yarbro Collins 1990, 1013). To say that God accomplishes Babylon's fall is complementary to saying that her earthly enemies did it. In both cases, fire is a major element in Babylon's judgment (17:16; 18:8, 9, 15, 18).

Dirges by Kings, Merchants, and Seafarers (18:9–20)

The next section of chapter 18 contains laments over the fall of Rome, first by the kings of the earth, then by the merchants of the earth, and then by seafarers. Taken together, the laments illustrate how Rome's fall implies the dissolution of the world's political and economic system. The engine of that system is Rome's lust for power and pleasure, and when that engine begins to break down, the entire system falls apart. The dirge of the kings, merchants, and seafarers is modeled broadly on Ezekiel's dirge over the city of Tyre in Ezekiel 27. In Ezekiel's dirge, each of the three groups of Revelation 18 is represented. Ezekiel describes the wailing of seafarers (27:29), the horror of kings (27:35), and the gasping of merchants (27:36) at Tyre's fall. The three sections containing the three dirges in Revelation 18 are to some degree parallel to each other in structure, but the structure varies somewhat.

The kings' section is 18:9–10. The structure of this section is the simplest of the three. The kings are described in terms of their relations with Babylon; it is said that they will weep and mourn, that they stand far off because they fear Babylon's torment, and that they will utter a lament that begins with the words "Alas, alas." The dirge itself portrays Babylon's previous glory and laments her fall. The kings are characterized as those "who committed fornication and lived in luxury with her" (18:9). The economic circumstances of kingship are critiqued here. The kings weep when they see "the smoke of her burning" (cf. 14:11; 19:3). They stand at a distance, symbolizing their desire, now too late, to be separated from Rome. God's faithful chose to be separated at an earlier time (18:4–5). The kings lament that Babylon, the great and mighty city, has fallen "in one hour" (18:10). This recalls the swiftness of Babylon's fall in Isa 47:8–9.

Each group of mourners in chapter 18 mentions that Babylon's fall takes but one hour, a figure emphasizing the suddenness of the destruction (as does the "one day" of 18:8), a suddenness that demonstrates God's tremendous power. What took so long to build up, God destroys in short order. The "one hour" also recalls 17:12, where the ten kings reign and are allied with the beast for one hour. In 17:16, that royal alliance turns against the whore and destroys her. The phrase "one hour" is thus another connection between God's judgment in chapter 18 and the action of earthly entities in chapter 17, showing them to be two aspects of the same reality.

The next section belongs to the merchants (18:11-17) and is in two parts. The second of the parts (18:15-17) is in strict parallelism with the lament of the kings, for it tells of the merchants' relationship to Babylon and pictures them standing at a distance for fear of Babylon's torment, weeping and mourning, and it quotes their words, beginning with "Alas, alas." Like the kings, they briefly recall Babylon's lost glory and then lament that it has all perished in one hour. Whereas the kings are those who shared in Babylon's luxury, the merchants are those who "gained wealth from her" because they sold Babylon her coveted luxury items. Their description of Rome's glory focuses on those items. They remember that Babylon was attired in fine linen, purple, and scarlet, and wore gold, jewels, and pearls. The picture recalls that of the great whore at the beginning of chapter 17.

The lament in 18:15-17 is introduced by 18:11-14, which says that the merchants mourn because there is no longer a buyer for their luxurious cargo. The text supplies a long list of the content of cargo the merchants once brought to Rome—gold, silver, jewels, pearls, fine linen, purple, silk, and so on. Many items in the list correspond with items on Ezekiel's list of products that flowed into Tyre from its many trading partners (Ezek 27:12-24). Revelation's list concludes with "bodies, and souls of human beings" (18:13). This is a reference to Rome's dependence on slavery. Bodies and souls may indicate Rome's complete mastery of its subjects, body and soul, but they may be merely two ways of referring to slaves, both of which are attested (Charles 1920, 2:104-5). The latter is more likely. The treatment of humans as commodities brings the list to a climactic close. The list is followed by a direct address to Rome. The address exclaims that Babylon has lost and will never regain its "dainties" and "splendor," for which it "longed."

The third and last part of the lament of Rome's clients is that of the "shipmasters and seafarers" (18:17-19; whether verse 20 is part of their lament is disputed). Like the other two groups, these stand far off, observe the smoke of Babylon's burning, and utter a lament. There is a variation on the patterns of the previous two sections in that inserted into the narrative description of their mourning and before the main lament beginning "Alas, alas," the seafarers say, "What city was like the great city?" (18:18). This sounds a bit like the question in Ezekiel's lament over Tyre, "Who was ever destroyed like Tyre?" (Ezek 27:32). It also recalls better days for the empire, when the whole earth worshiped the dragon and the beast saying, "Who is like the beast, and who can fight against it?" (13:4). When the seafarers lament, "they threw dust on their heads" (18:19). The seafarers in Ezekiel's dirge do the same thing (27:30). This lament does not begin with a description of the seafarers' relation with Rome, but they later themselves admit why they mourn Babylon's passing. They say, "All the ships at sea grew rich by her wealth" (18:19). Like the other two groups, the seafarers marvel that Babylon is destroyed in a single hour.

The fall of Babylon, representing Rome, means disaster for those with a vested interest in the political and economic system of which Rome is the center. The wealth, status, and power of kings, merchants, and seafarers depend on Rome's hunger for luxury, a luxury that must be paid for by the lifeblood of Rome's subjects. The ones who mourn Rome's destruction are those who profit from its injustice.

Verse 20 is a direct address to heaven and to saints, apostles, and prophets, telling them to rejoice, "for God has given judgment for you against her." There is nothing here to indicate a change of speaker, so one might take the words as coming from the seafarers. On the one hand, that would be striking, since one would expect them to be more concerned with their own misfortune than with the vindication of the faithful. On the other hand, putting these words in their mouths makes the message the more powerful. It is more likely, however, that this is another interjection by the narrator, on the order of 13:9–10 and 14:12. The exhortation to rejoice is in marked contrast to the despair and grief of Babylon's clients in the foregoing dirges. It shows that the author does not share the clients' sorrow at Rome's fall. The command to rejoice in 18:20 echoes Jer 51:48: "Then the heavens and the earth, and all that is in them, shall shout for joy over Babylon." Revelation 18:20, like Jeremiah 51, speaks of heaven rejoicing. Instead of speaking explicitly of earth rejoicing, as does Jeremiah, Revelation substitutes saints, apostles, and prophets, thus adapting Jeremiah to the circumstances of the church. At the end of the chapter, Rome is accused of having within her the blood of the prophets and saints (18:24). Verses

20 and 24 frame the mighty angel's condemnation of Babylon, emphasizing that the cause for Rome's fall is its treatment of Christians.

The Mighty Angel's Symbolic Action and Prophetic Pronouncement (18:21–24)

In Jewish and Christian prophetic texts, symbolic actions are physical actions performed by prophets that embody prophetic messages. Such actions are common among the prophets. Jesus' attack on the moneychangers in the temple is just such a symbolic action. The third section of Revelation 18 begins when a "mighty angel" performs a prophetic symbolic action by taking up a heavy millstone, casting it into the sea, and delivering a judgment oracle against Babylon. The angel's interpretation of his own action is contained in the oracle, especially its opening words: "With such violence Babylon the great city will be thrown down and will be found no more" (18:21). This scene is inspired by Jeremiah 51, the chapter quoted at the beginning of our commentary on Revelation 17 because of its great influence on Revelation 17–18. After Jeremiah delivers his long judgment oracle against Babylon in chapter 51, he gives the scroll containing his oracle to a Jewish official traveling to the exiled Jews in Babylon. Jeremiah tells the official to read the scroll in Babylon. He then says, "When you finish reading this scroll, tie a stone to it, and throw it into the middle of the Euphrates, and say, 'Thus shall Babylon sink, to rise no more, because of the disasters that I am bringing on her' " (Jer 51:63–64). It is fitting that our author includes such a symbolic action and interpretation toward the end of this unit (17:1–19:10), which is so affected by Jeremiah 51. It completes the analogy the author sees between his own situation as a prophet facing Rome and that of Jeremiah, the prophet who condemned Babylon.

In verses 22–23, the angel predicts, in the form of a direct address to Babylon itself, the desolation of Babylon that will follow its downfall. No more will there be in Babylon the sounds of musicians, artisans, millstones, or of bridegroom and bride; nor will there be the light of a lamp in it anymore. Again it is Jeremiah who provides the best prophetic parallel. Speaking again of the judgment of Jerusalem at the hand of Babylon he says, "I will banish from them the sound of mirth and the sound of gladness, the voice of the bridegroom and the voice of the bride, the sound of the millstones and the light of the lamp" (25:10). The sounds missing from Babylon in Revelation 18 are significant. Music represents joy, now gone. Artisans care for the daily upkeep of the physical city, no longer necessary. Millstones grind grain for food, but people no longer live in the city. Bridegrooms and brides stand for human society and human reproduction, so their absence means that humans no longer inhabit Babylon. Lack of light also means absence of human presence and activity. There may be a subtle contrast here with the new Jerusalem, which has no need of sun or moon because God is its light (21:23).

The litany of sounds and sights of human life now absent from Babylon is followed by the words, "For your merchants were the magnates of the earth, and all nations were deceived by your sorcery" (18:23). The word "for" or "because" introduces the reasons for Babylon's punishment. Babylon makes rich the merchants with whom it deals. They become the great ones of the earth. In the seer's view, this is not because they fulfill legitimate needs but because they cater to Babylon's extravagant and wasteful desires. This is but a part of Babylon's deception of the entire world, a deception mentioned frequently, but most forcefully presented here and in chapter 13 when the Roman empire appears as the beast from the sea, in league with the demonic dragon. This deception is also called "sorcery" here, an unusual word in Revelation. Its only other occurrence is in 9:21, where it appears as a sin of humanity. The presence of sorcery in 18:23 can be attributed to the influence of Nahum's picture of the seductive prostitute. Nahum 3:4–5 reads,

> Because of the countless debaucheries of the prostitute,
> gracefully alluring, mistress of sorcery,
> who enslaves nations through her debaucheries,
> and peoples through her sorcery, I am against you,
> says the LORD of hosts. (see Rev 17:1–6)

Note also Isa 47:12, a passage that comes just after Isaiah's critique of Babylon's arrogance and that serves as the model for Rev 18:7–8 (see above), which says to Babylon, "Stand fast in your enchantments and your many sorceries, in which you have labored from your youth."

As we noted above when we looked at the seer's indictment of Babylon (Rome) in this chapter, the other side of Rome's oppressive and exploitative rule is its persecution of the faithful. In

18:24, the indictment is widened. Now Rome is held responsible not only for Christian martyrs but for all who are "slaughtered" on the earth. Schüssler Fiorenza (1991, 95) sees 18:24 as "the theological key to the whole Babylon series of judgments." Rome's guilt is so deep that it subsumes the guilt for all murders. Following somewhat the same logic, Matthew's Jesus says to scribes and Pharisees, "Therefore I will send you prophets, sages, and scribes, some of whom you will kill and crucify, and some you will flog in your synagogues and pursue from town to town, so that upon you may come all the righteous blood shed on earth" (Matt 23:34–35).

The judgment delivered against Babylon in 18:21–24 comes through a "mighty angel." This phrase appears only three times in Revelation. The first such angel asks in 5:2 who is worthy to open the sealed scroll containing the contents of the eschatological visions in 6:1–11:19. The second descends from heaven in chapter 10 with an open seal in his hand containing the eschatological visions of 12:1–22:5. It is fitting that the third in the series announces the final punishment of Babylon, a goal toward which all the visions in the book lead.

Hymns of Praise (19:1–8)

The exhortation to rejoice directed to heaven and to saints, apostles, and prophets in 18:20 is obeyed in 19:1–8. The passage is a liturgy consisting largely of two hymns, the first by "a great multitude in heaven" (19:1–3), answered by the twenty-four elders and the four living creatures (19:4). There follows an exhortation to praise God addressed to all God's servants (19:5), praise contained in the second hymn (19:6–8). The three groups here — heavenly multitude, elders and creatures, all God's servants — balance the three groups that mourn Babylon's fall in chapter 18 (Schüssler Fiorenza 1991, 101; Mounce 1977, 336).

Each of the two hymns begins with the word "hallelujah," an acclamation derived from the Hebrew words *halal,* meaning "praise," and *yah,* the short form of God's name, Yahweh. "hallelujah" means "praise God." It occurs in biblical psalms of praise (it begins Pss 106; 111–13; 117; 135; 146–50). The first hymn is in two sections, since there is a fresh narrative start in 19:3 ("Once more they said . . ."). The second section of the hymn also begins with the word "hallelujah." The response of the elders and creatures to the first hymn contains the word "hallelujah" as well. The fourfold occurrence of "hallelujah" expresses the exuberant joy of all creatures, heavenly and earthly, at God's judgment of Babylon, and it praises God in biblical language for that liberating action. This liturgical scene which celebrates God's salvation is one of a series of such scenes (7:9–17; 11:15–19; 20:4–6; 21:1–22:5; Yarbro Collins 1990, 1013). Together with a scene between the seer and the angel in 19:9–10, this liturgy concludes the entire section 16:1–19:10, which consists of the bowls series (chapter 16) and the Babylon appendix (17:1–19:10), which elaborates on the fall of Babylon in the seventh bowl.

First Hymn and Response (19:1-4)

The first hymn is uttered by "the loud voice of a great multitude in heaven" (19:1). The scene recalls 7:9, where the great multitude from every nation stands before God and the Lamb and acclaims them, saying that "salvation" belongs to them. In chapter 7, we found this to be a foretaste of God's final victory. The hymns in 19:1–8 respond to a major stage in the final victory, Babylon's defeat (the defeat of Satan is yet to come). The first hymn begins, "Hallelujah! Salvation and glory and power to our God" (19:1). "Salvation" means victory here, as in 7:9. Salvation also means victory in 12:10, when God's angels throw the dragon out of heaven. In chapter 18, to which the hymns in chapter 19 respond, God punishes Babylon, the dragon's agent on earth. The inclusion of the word "power" in the acclamation of 19:1 is appropriate, given God's overthrow of powerful Babylon. Revelation, after all, is about power. The inclusion of "glory" is fitting, too, for it implies the theme of sovereignty that permeates the book. By overthrowing Babylon, God proves his sovereignty and demonstrates that only he has the status and position in the cosmos that demands honor and glory.

The first hymn follows a twofold pattern typical of hymns of praise. First, praise is expressed, and then the reasons for that praise are given. The acclamation in 19:1 constitutes the praise, and 19:2 contains the reasons for praising God. The reasons are in three parts. The first is a general assertion that God's judgments are just. The second is God's judgment on Babylon as corrupter of the earth. The third is God's avenging the persecution of the faithful. The heavenly multitude's declaration that God's judgments are "true and just" echoes the same assessment by the altar in the third bowl where it uses the same words: "Your judgments are true and just!" (16:7; cf. 15:3). The similarity of the statements in 19:2 and 16:7 is so striking that Charles rearranges the text to bring 16:5–7 to this spot in chapter 19. Charles is right in pointing to the apparently intrusive nature of the praise of God in the third bowl (16:5–7), as he is when he points to the fact that the command in 18:20 to rejoice over Babylon's fall unexpectedly follows the three dirges in chapter 18. But Charles's rearrangements are due to his conviction that when such apparent disruptions occur, they are evidence of the activity of a clumsy editor who did not understand the seer's work. Rather, such disruptions are frequently due to the author's intention to present his audience with stark contrasts, often suddenly introduced, that force the audience to compare worldviews and to choose God's viewpoint. Revelation 16:5–7, as unexpected as it is in that context, forces just such a choice. The sudden appearance of 18:20 at the end of the dirges fulfills the same function. Both passages show the proper reaction to Babylon's punishment. The fact that both have contacts with 19:1–2, a hymn that occurs in a more "logical" spot, coming after Babylon's defeat, shows that the author anticipates the final victory several times throughout the book.

The double indictment leveled against Babylon in 19:2 is that it is a prostitute who has "corrupted the earth with her fornication" and has persecuted God's servants. The previous chapter, chapter 18, opens with an angel charging Babylon with fornication with the kings of the earth (18:3) and ends with the second angel accusing Babylon of spilling the blood of prophets and saints (18:24). The Bible furnishes numerous examples of idolatry associated with political alliances. This mixture of politics and religion characterizes Revelation as well and is typical of the ancient world. This unholy system of alliances with Rome at its center and Asia as a prime example is hostile to the faithful. The hymn's statement that God "has avenged on her the blood of his servants" (19:2) recalls Deut 32:43, which states that God "will avenge the blood of his servants."

The first hymn makes a new start in 19:3 when the narrator says, "Once more they said. . . . " The heavenly multitude again begins with the acclamation "Hallelujah" and goes on to say, "The smoke goes up from her forever and ever." These words recall the punishment of those loyal to the beast in chapter 14: "The smoke of their torment goes up forever and ever" (14:11) and the punishment of Babylon in 18:8, 9, 18 (cf. Isa 34:8–10). This raises again the question of whether the book of Revelation is vindictive. Suffice it to say here that such statements are well within a long biblical tradition in which God's people rejoices in its rescue from the hands of its enemies. Within that tradition, the defeat of the enemies is often portrayed.

The hymn in 19:1–3 comes from the multitude in heaven. It is fitting that the twenty-four elders and the four living creatures confirm it, responding with the liturgical assent "Amen" and with the familiar "Hallelujah" (19:4). We first meet the elders and creatures in chapters 4 and 5, where they take part in a heavenly liturgy that is the source of all eschatological events narrated thereafter. They make their last appearance in this passage (19:4), confirming heaven's praise of God for bringing those events to their proper climax by ending the rule of Babylon. As in the earlier liturgy, they prostrate themselves before God and worship him, thus embodying the proper relationship of creatures to God.

Second Hymn (19:5–8)

Now a voice comes from the throne itself, bidding all of God's servants, defined as "all who fear him, small and great," to praise God (19:5). The second great hymn of chapter 19 is in 19:6–8. It is an obedient response to the voice from the throne in 19:5. The singers are described in terms quite like the singers of the first hymn, "the voice of a great multitude," but this time it does not say that the multitude is in heaven. This leaves open the possibility that the chorus includes earthly voices. The sound of the second chorus appears to be more awesome than that of the first. The first utters a "loud voice," but the second is "like the sound of many waters and like the sound of mighty thunderpeals, crying out" (19:6). In 14:1–5, John sees the 144,000 on Mount Zion with the Lamb, and he hears a hymn that is "a voice from heaven like the sound of many waters and like the sound of loud thunder" singing a new song before God (cf. 1:15). Only the 144,000 can learn this hymn. What 14:1–5 anticipates, chapter 19 delivers. This mighty chorus is the final hymn of the book, and it is introduced in a way that stresses its magnificence and its definitive character.

The multitude's hymn begins with "Hallelujah," which in this hymn constitutes the exhortation to praise (19:6). The rest of the hymn is made up of the reasons to praise God. There are two reasons given, closely related to each other. The first is "For the Lord our God the Almighty reigns" (19:6). The second reason is that the Lamb's marriage has come (19:7–8). The first reason makes the second possible, and the second is a full implementation of the first. The verb for "reign" in this verse is in the simple past tense. That tense, usually used to describe an action in the past as a whole or in a "snapshot" mode, can also be used in what is called an "ingressive" sense, as the past beginning of an action or state that then continues. The frequent assertions in the book of Psalms that God reigns use the perfect tense in Hebrew in the same way. When the psalms or Revelation state literally that "God reigned," they mean that at some definite point in the past God took control of things and that now his reign is recognizably expressed in events. For Revelation, this means that God has defeated Satan's proxy on earth, Babylon, and that this is the beginning of Satan's definitive end and the coming of the kingdom of God. The coming of that kingdom is celebrated by the song of those loyal to God, so they can call the Lord of the universe "our God" and give to him the title that states clearly God's power over everything and everyone, "the Almighty" (19:6). Revelation 19:6 resumes the proclamation in 11:15, and it is now heard by an audience that has experienced the fall of Babylon in its clearest and most detailed form.

In verses 7–8, the singers exhort each other to "rejoice and exult and give him the glory" because the Lamb's marriage has come. The Lamb's bride "has made herself ready; to her it has been granted to be clothed with fine linen, bright and pure." The bride's "fine linen" is then interpreted as "the righteous deeds of the saints" (19:8). In some versions of the ancient combat myth, the victory of the good god over the rebellious god is marked by the assumption of kingship, marriage to a goddess, and the building of a temple (Yarbro Collins 1990, 1013). Revelation 19:6 declares the beginning of God's rule; 19:7–8 speaks of the wedding of the Lamb; and chapters 21 and 22 describe the new Jerusalem in which the temple is replaced with the presence of God and the Lamb. On one level the bride is the church, and the marriage symbolizes the close union that now exists between Christ and the faithful. In the Bible, Israel is spoken of as God's wife (Isa 54:6; Ezekiel 16; Hos 2:16), and in the New Testament marriage represents the relationship between Christ and the church (2 Cor 11:2; Eph 5:25, 32; see Matt 22:2ff.; 25:1;

Mark 2:19; John 3:29; see Charles 1920, 2:126–27). The union with Christ is both a gift of God to humanity ("to her it has been granted...") and a result of human action in remaining loyal to God in heart and deed (the bride has "made herself ready," and her attire is composed of the deeds of the righteous). The victory is won by Christ's death, but Christians profit from that victory only if they are willing to imitate Christ in his witness to God in a hostile world to the point of death.

The bride of the Lamb is in marked contrast to the prostitute (Babylon) of chapters 17 and 18. The latter is dressed in purple and scarlet, colors of the Roman imperial order and symbolic of luxury and decadence (17:4; 18:16). The Lamb's bride wears white, pure linen symbolizing purity, a purity contrasting with the prostitute's fornication. White is also characteristic of the heavenly world. The faithful in the churches are promised white garments (3:18); the martyrs receive their white garments as they wait to be avenged (6:11); the multitude of the faithful singing before God's throne are "robed in white" (7:9, 13); and the armies that follow the heavenly warrior later in this chapter wear "fine linen, white and pure" (19:14). The prostitute wears gold and precious stones, but the bride has only her linen as an ornament, and that linen represents the righteous deeds of the faithful. The stereotypes here are also found in 1 Tim 2:9–10: "Women should dress themselves modestly and decently in suitable clothing, not with their hair braided, or with gold, pearls, or expensive clothes, but with good works, as is proper for women who profess reverence for God."

We said above that the bride is the church "on one level." As with other images in Revelation, this one does not operate on only one level. Even though the bride can be thought of as the church, the beatitude in 19:9 declares blessed those invited to the Lamb's marriage feast. In the beatitude members of the church are those invited to the feast, so they are not identified with the bride. In 21:9–10, the bride is the new Jerusalem, which descends from heaven. The new Jerusalem is also depicted as a woman in 4 Ezra 9:38–10:59. In a broader view, the bride is part of the atmosphere of peace and fertility that accompanies the restoration of creation, elements taken from the combat myth (Yarbro Collins 1979, 131). It is the opposite of the absence of bridegroom and bride that Babylon faces (18:23).

A Beatitude and the Seer's Attempt to Worship the Angel (19:9–10)

In 19:9–10, an angel utters the fourth of Revelation's seven beatitudes, then declares it to be the true words of God, and then the seer falls down to worship the angel but is rebuked. The angel tells the seer to worship only God. Revelation 19:9–10 is very similar to a later passage, 22:6–9. In chapter 22, an angel says, "These words are trustworthy and true"; then comes a beatitude; and then the seer falls down to worship the angel and is rebuked by him and told to worship God. The angel in both cases is one of the angels of the bowls (see 17:1 and 21:9). The scene between angel and seer in chapter 19 marks the end of the Babylon appendix, and the corresponding scene in chapter 22 marks the end of the new Jerusalem appendix, thus underlining the contrasting parallelism between these two appendices.

In 19:9, the angel says, "Blessed are those who are invited to the marriage supper of the Lamb." After the beatitude the angel says, "These are the true words of God." Commentators do not agree on the precise referent of this sentence. Some think that the angel refers only to the preceding beatitude, while others see a wider referent. But if the beatitude is understood rightly, it encompasses all of what has gone before in Revelation. True to its roots in the apocalyptic worldview, Revelation divides all of humanity into those who are faithful to God and those who are followers of the beast. There are only two camps to which one can belong. When one considers those camps, things are not as they appear. An "objective" observer would pronounce members of the beast's camp blessed or happy. They enjoy earthly success and prosperity. They participate in a system that brooks no opposition. Those who do not submit to the beast's order are killed. "Obviously" the members of God's camp cannot be happy, for they are persecuted. But the angel's beatitude reiterates and summarizes the message of the entire book that those who are really blessed are the enemies of the Roman order; its supporters face torment and eternal punishment. This is truth. Anything else is by definition false.

The seer now falls before the angel to worship (*proskyneô*) him. The word for worship here is frequent in Revelation, occurring twenty-four times. One's loyalty, whether to God or to the dragon and beast, is apparent in whom one worships. The vast majority of the earth's inhabitants worship the dragon and the beast (13:4, 8, 12, 15; cf. 14:9, 11; 16:2; 20:4). Not only is it idolatrous to worship the dragon and the beast; the angel of chapter 19 says that it is not even permitted to worship an angel (some see here a polemic against angel worship in Jewish circles or the early church; see Boring 1989, 194; Krodel 1989, 103–4). The angel puts himself on the same level as God's human servants: "You must not do that! I am a fellow servant with you and your comrades who hold the testimony of Jesus. Worship God!" (19:10). Angels appear to be exalted figures, but as servants of God they are not above humans. Conversely, righteous humans often become equal to angels in Jewish and Christian texts (Yarbro Collins 1990, 1014).

The angel makes himself equal to those "who hold the testimony of Jesus." He follows this with the enigmatic statement, "For the testimony of Jesus is the spirit of prophecy" (19:10). The phrase "testimony of Jesus" is used several times in Revelation (1:2, 9; 12:17; 19:10; 20:4). Discussion of the phrase's meaning centers around whether the possessive (genitive) form "of Jesus" is subjective or objective. A subjective genitive would mean that Jesus is the subject of the testimony, that he *does* the testifying. An objective genitive would mean that Jesus is the object of the testimony, that the testimony is *about* Jesus. Although this distinction makes sense to modern scholars, it is doubtful whether it would make sense to our author. Jesus' testimony consists of his unwavering affirmation of God's sovereignty even in the face of his own death at the hands of the hostile Romans. Christians must be willing to bear the same witness in the face of the same threats (see 6:9; 11:7; 12:11, 17; 19:10; 20:4). In that sense, the witness of both is to God's sovereignty. But God's sovereignty has been definitively revealed and established on earth only through Christ's witness, a witness most fully implemented in his death. So to witness to Christ is at the same time to witness to God's sovereignty, which is the essence of Christ's own witness. The two cannot really be distinguished.

Chapter Eleven

The Second Series of Seven Unnumbered Visions (19:11–21:8)

The Second Unnumbered Series as a Whole

These visions lead us through the final eschatological events. The first vision depicts Christ's second coming, this time as a warrior; the second and third visions deal with the struggle between Christ and Satan's forces that results in Christ's victory; the fourth narrates the binding of Satan for a thousand years; the fifth deals with the thousand-year messianic kingdom and the subsequent final defeat of Satan; the sixth is the last judgment; and the seventh portrays the coming of a new heaven and a new earth and the descent of the new Jerusalem. Just as the bowls are elaborated by the Babylon appendix, so this final series is elaborated by the new Jerusalem appendix (21:9–22:9). Both appendices are revealed to the seer through one of the angels of the bowls, a device that helps tie together all of chapters 16 and 22. Here in 19:11, the final events (one is tempted to say, the *final* final events) begin with heaven itself opened. Mounce sees a progression from 4:1 where a door is open in heaven, to 11:19 where the heavenly sanctuary is opened, to 19:11 where heaven itself is open (1977, 343).

The First Unnumbered Vision: The Advent of the Warrior Christ (19:11–16)

Revelation 19:1–10 celebrates the fall of Babylon, but defeat of the dragon, the beast, and the false prophet (same as the land-beast) is narrated in the second unnumbered series of visions. In this ultimate series, Christ himself appears, reasserting divine sovereignty over the earth. The defeat and destruction of God's enemies have already been anticipated by each of the preceding series, and they are recapitulated and spelled out in more detail in chapters 19 to 20. In particular, Rev 17:14 anticipates a battle between the Lamb and the alliance of the beast and kings in which the Lamb will be victorious. It is this final battle that the final series of visions concerns.

True to his usual practice, the seer does not say clearly who the warrior appearing in 19:11–16 is. He rides a white horse, as does the figure in the first seal (6:2), but efforts to see the two figures as the same have not won acceptance. All that the two have in common is that they both ride a white horse and are both military (see comments on 6:2). It is clear to any reader of Revelation that the warrior in chapter 19 is Christ, since there are numerous connections between the description of the warrior in 19:11–16 and earlier descriptions of Christ. When he appears in chapter 19, his advent is the climax of everything that has gone before. The appearance of Christ himself can only mean that this is the last narration of the end.

The detail with which Christ is described supports the conviction that the portrayal of the final events has come. The rider "is called Faithful and True, and in righteousness he judges and makes war" (19:11). In the message to the church at Laodicea, Jesus refers to himself as "the faithful and true witness." In 1:5, he is "the faithful witness," and in 3:7, he calls himself "the holy one, the true one." For Revelation, faithfulness is a virtue demonstrated by loyalty to God in the face of persecution. Christ is the ultimate example of that faithfulness. It is by Christ's ultimate witness, his death, that the power of the dragon is broken. It is this same Christ who now comes to finish the job of defeating Satan and his forces. He is "true" precisely because he is of the heavenly world, God's realm, locale of the true creator and sovereign.

Where Christ's earlier advent was as the one who witnessed and died, he now comes as a mighty judge and warrior, recalling God's numerous appearances as warrior in the Bible. The song of Moses celebrating the exodus says, "The LORD is a warrior; the LORD is his name" (Exod 15:3). Now it is Christ who is the divine warrior. The notion of a warlike messiah was well known in Jewish and Christian circles (see Mounce 1977, 343; Charles 1920, 2:131). Christ judges and makes war "in righteousness," which constitutes yet another assertion of the justice of

God's judgment (see especially 16:7; 19:2-3). In Isaiah 11, it is expected of the messiah that "with righteousness he will judge the poor." The messianic passage in Isaiah 11 also influences the images later in this vision of the sword protruding from Christ's mouth and the rod with which he strikes the earth (see below on 19:15).

The rider has eyes like fire, as does the one like a son of man in 1:14, a feature modeled on the angel in Daniel 10 (see Dan 10:6). That feature alludes to Christ's ability to see all and his fiery condemnation of that upon which he looks. He wears "many diadems" on his head, referring to his universal sovereignty, in contrast to the fraudulent claims of the dragon, who wears seven diadems, and the beast, who wears ten. He has a name that no one knows but himself (cf. 2:17; 3:12). Some have seen Christ's titles later in the passage to be the name hidden here. But there is no indication in the text that is the case. In the ancient world, the name of an entity was thought to reveal its essence. To name was to know and to have power over someone or something. When Adam names the animals in Genesis, he exercises lordship over them (Gen 2:18-23). Christ's secret name indicates that he is ultimately mysterious, incapable of being fully understood. He belongs to another realm.

The meaning of the next verse is disputed. The rider wears "a robe dipped in blood" (19:13). Later in the passage it says, "He will tread the wine press of the fury of the wrath of God the Almighty" (19:15). Taken together, these two predicates derive from the picture of God in Isaiah 63. In Isa 63:1-6, a voice asks who it is who comes from Edom (one of Israel's traditional enemies) with clothes "stained crimson" and splendidly dressed. The one coming from Edom, clearly God, replies, "It is I, announcing vindication, mighty to save." The voice asks further, "Why are your robes red, and your garments like theirs who tread the wine press?" God answers:

> I have trodden the wine press alone,
>   and from the peoples no one was with me;
> I trod them in my anger
>   and trampled them in my wrath;
> their juice spattered on my garments,
>   and stained all my robes.
> For the day of vengeance was in my heart,
>   and the year for my redeeming work had come....

I trampled down peoples in my anger,
I crushed them in my wrath,
and I poured out their lifeblood on the earth.
(Isa 63:3–4, 6)

The dispute about the meaning of Rev 19:13 centers on whether the blood on Christ's robe is his own or that of his enemies. On the analogy of Isaiah 63 it would be that of his enemies, although we see repeatedly how the seer is not bound by the original application and configuration of his images. When the image of a wine press is used for God's judgment in 14:18–20, the blood is clearly that of sinners. Some think that because the reference to treading the wine press comes later in the passage (19:15), the blood on the garment cannot be caused by treading the wine press. This cannot be decisive, since the author shows no great love for chronological order, even within passages. Those who think the blood is Christ's note that there are several references to Christ's blood earlier in the book, starting at the very beginning when Christ is described as the one who "freed us from our sins by his blood" (1:5) and continuing in the heavenly scene where he appears as a slaughtered lamb, praised by God's attendants as the one by whose blood a people is ransomed for God (5:6, 9).

Our own view is that the blood on Christ's robe is that of his enemies. However literally one should take the warrior aspects of Christ, it seems clear that his enemies will be killed and consigned to eternal torment. Their blood on his garments states clearly that their fate is due to him, and their suffering is his judgment on them. The whole scene recalls a passage from the Palestinian Targum on Genesis, which is a free translation of Genesis into Aramaic, as quoted by Charles (1920, 134): "How beauteous is the king Messiah, who is about to arise from the house of Judah. He hath bound his loins and gone forth to war against those that hate him: kings and princes shall be slain: he will make red the rivers with the blood of their slain.... [H]is garments will be dipped in blood."

The rider is now called "the Word of God." This is strikingly reminiscent of the gospel of John (1:1, 14). In John the phrase expresses John's christology, which focuses on Jesus as the ultimate revelation of God and as the only way one can reach the Father. In Revelation the focus is less on Jesus' nature or revelatory function and more on his role as God's ultimate agent, come to judge the earth. A suggestive passage for comparison is Wisd 18:15–16:

> Your all-powerful word leaped from heaven, from the royal throne,
> into the midst of the land that was doomed,
> a stern warrior
> carrying the sharp sword of your authentic command,
> and stood and filled all things with death,
> and touched heaven while standing on earth.

God's word is also seen in a context of judgment in Hebrews: "The word of God is living and active, sharper than any two-edged sword.... It is able to judge the thoughts and intentions of the heart" (Heb 4:12). As word of God, the rider does not act on his own, but as God's agent. Jesus' judgment and God's judgment are the same.

The rider is followed by a heavenly army dressed in "fine linen, white and pure," and riding on white horses. As usual the heavenly color is white. The white and pure linen garments connect this army to the bride of 19:7–8. The word for "linen" here (*byssinon*) occurs only four times in Revelation. It is found as an item sold to Rome by merchants (18:12) and as part of Babylon's clothing (18:16). In those two instances it is not modified by any adjective. Only the Lamb's bride and heavenly army following Christ are said to wear linen (*byssinon*) that is "clean." The bride wears "fine linen, bright and pure" (19:8), and the army wears "fine linen, white and pure" (19:14). In 19:8, it is said that the bride's "fine linen" is her deeds.

This raises the question of whether the heavenly army is made up of angels or humans. In most Jewish texts that speak of a battle involving a heavenly army, that army is made up of angels, but the *War Scroll* from Qumran envisages a final battle in which God's army is composed of both angels and humans. In the preview of the final battle found in Rev 17:14, the Lamb is accompanied by those who are "called and chosen and faithful." It is unlikely that angels would be described in this way. In 2:26–27, Jesus says that he will share with Christians "authority over the nations; to rule them with an iron rod, as when clay pots are shattered." It is quite possible, then, that the heavenly army includes humans. Presumably they would be only those faithful who had already received their heavenly white garments, and the only group this applies to is the martyrs (6:9–11). Since they are later singled out as those who will rise and rule with Christ for a thousand years (20:4–6), it would be natural for them to be mentioned here.

Verse 15 consists of three parallel statements. The first is that a sharp sword protrudes from the rider's mouth "with which to strike down the nations"; the second is that he "will rule them with a rod of iron"; and the third is that "he will tread the wine press of the fury of the wrath of God the Almighty" (19:15). These are hardly peaceful images. They are as forceful as the biblical holy war passages from which they are drawn. The sword coming from the rider's mouth is found in the mouth of the one like a son of man in 1:16. Its purpose is not stated there. Here it is to strike down the nations, and it is said later, "The rest were killed by the sword of the rider on the horse" (19:21). The feature of the sword is influenced by the words Isaiah the prophet speaks of himself: "He made my mouth like a sharp sword" (Isa 49:2).

That the rider will rule the nations with a rod of iron recalls Rev 2:26–27, where Jesus shares with the faithful "authority over the nations; to rule them with an iron rod, as when clay pots are shattered." This in turn depends on the picture of God's messiah in Psalm 2, to whom God says he will give the nations, continuing, "You shall break them with a rod of iron, and dash them in pieces like a potter's vessel" (Ps 2:9). In Rev 19:15, the juxtaposition of the descriptions of the sharp sword coming from Christ's mouth and the rod of iron recalls the messianic passage in Isaiah 11, which includes the following: "With righteousness he shall judge the poor, and decide with equity for the meek of the earth; he shall strike the earth with the rod of his mouth, and with the breath of his lips he shall kill the wicked" (Isa 11:4). This passage also influences the assertion of the righteousness of the rider's judgments in 19:11. Psalm 2 and Isaiah 11 are also behind the picture of the warlike messiah in the Psalms of Solomon:

> See, LORD, and raise up for them their king, the son of David,
> to rule over your servant Israel in the time known to you, O God.
> Undergird him with the strength to destroy the unrighteous rulers,
> to purge Jerusalem from Gentiles who trample her to destruction;

> in wisdom and in righteousness to drive out the sinners
> from the inheritance;
> to smash the arrogance of sinners like a potter's jar;
> to shatter all their substance with an iron rod;
> to destroy the unlawful nations with the word of his
> mouth;
> at his warning the nations will flee from his presence;
> and he will condemn sinners by the thoughts of their
> hearts. (*Pss. Sol.* 17:21–25)

The last of the three statements in 19:15 is that the rider "will tread the wine press of the fury of the wrath of God the Almighty." This image comes from Isaiah 63. The emphatic expression "the fury of the wrath" stresses God's anger. God is genuinely enraged at the usurpation of his authority by Babylon and at its reign of injustice, oppression, and persecution. In 14:18–20, the treading of the wine press results in a flow of blood "as high as a horse's bridle, for a distance of about two hundred miles" (14:20; cf. *1 Enoch* 100:3).

The first vision ends with the application of two titles to the rider: King of kings and Lord of lords. In the anticipation of this final battle found in 17:14, the Lamb is also called Lord of lords and King of kings. In 1:5, Christ is said to be "ruler of the kings of the earth." The fact that the name is on Christ's robe and on his thigh is puzzling. Mounce probably has the best suggestion when he interprets this to mean the name is written on the part of the robe that falls across the rider's thigh (1977, 347–48).

The Second Unnumbered Vision: Invitation to God's Great Supper (19:17–18)

The beatitude at the end of the Babylon appendix declares blessed those who are invited to the "marriage supper of the Lamb" (19:9). God's feast in 19:17–18 is quite a different affair. This is another case of contrasting parallelism. The feast of the present vision is announced by an angel in the sun to the birds that fly in midheaven (19:17). The location of the angel and birds indicates that what is announced concerns the whole earth. This recalls 8:13, where an eagle in midheaven announces the three woes to come on the inhabitants of the earth, and 14:6–11, where three angels in midheaven demand submission to God, announce Babylon's fall, and predict the torment of the beast's followers.

The fare at God's great feast is gory indeed. It consists of "the flesh of kings, the flesh of captains, the flesh of the mighty, the flesh of horses and their riders—flesh of all, both free and slave, both small and great" (19:18). This inclusive list encompasses all of the empire, rulers and ruled. Kings and the mighty merit a place at the head of the list of the doomed, but everyone, even the slaves and the small, who collaborates in the imperial system is condemned. The general image of a feast made up of the conquered derives from Ezekiel's eschatological battle in chapters 38 and 39, a reference made still clearer in Rev 20:8. In Ezekiel's battle, a mythological king, Gog, from a mythological land, Magog, wars against Israel and is defeated by God. At the conclusion of the battle God says,

> Speak to the birds of every kind and to all the wild animals: Assemble and come, gather from all around to the sacrificial feast that I am preparing for you, a great sacrificial feast on the mountains of Israel, and you shall eat flesh and drink blood. You shall eat the flesh of the mighty, and drink the blood of the princes of the earth—of rams, of lambs, and of goats, of bulls, all of them fatlings of Bashan. You shall eat fat until you are filled, and drink blood until you are drunk, at the sacrificial feast I am preparing for you. And you shall be filled at my table with horses and charioteers, with warriors and all kinds of soldiers, says the Lord God. (Ezek 39:17–20; cf. Isa 34:1–7)

Ezekiel speaks only of the flesh and blood of rulers and the mighty. Revelation includes the lowly subjects of the empire. Even they have no excuse, for by submitting to the beast they oppose God, and they also will be part of the fare at this grisly banquet (Mounce 1977, 347–48).

The Third Unnumbered Vision: War between Christ and His Enemies (19:19–21)

Revelation 19:19 says, "Then I saw the beast and kings of the earth with their armies gathered to make war against the rider on the horse and against his army." This picks up where the sixth bowl left off, for that bowl closes with the notice that the dragon, the beast, and the false prophet gather together the kings of the earth to do battle at Harmagedon on "the great day of the Almighty" (16:12–16). At that point the bowl ends, and the seventh bowl concerns the fall of Rome, the "great city." The same sequence occurs in 17:14–16, where the final battle between the Lamb and the alliance of the beast and kings is mentioned (17:14) before the attack of the beast and kings on Rome (17:16). In 19:19, the beast and kings are arrayed for battle against the rider and his army, just as they are in 16:16 and 17:14.

This time the battle is carried through. The battle is over quickly, for the beast and his minions are no match for Christ. The beast and the false prophet are immediately captured. The false prophet is identified by recalling the deeds of the land-beast in chapter 13. He is the one who performed signs by which he deceived those who received the beast's mark and worshiped its image. The two are thrown "alive into the lake of fire that burns with sulfur." This is the place of ultimate punishment. It recurs in 20:10 and 14, and in 20:14 it is called the second death. This does not mean, however, that those who end up there go out of existence. In 20:10, the devil is thrown there and is "tormented day and night forever and ever." We have repeatedly encountered fire as an element of judgment in Revelation, a role fire plays in many other apocalypses. Sulfur is also a common commodity in Revelation. It is a foul smelling, combustible substance that makes its first appearance in the sixth trumpet, which is also the second demonic plague (9:13–19). The fifth of the first series of unnumbered visions depicts the judgment of the beast's followers as follows: "They will be tormented with fire and sulfur in the presence of the holy angels and in the presence of the Lamb. And the smoke of their torment goes up forever and ever" (14:10–11).

Of the three leaders of the evil army, two have now gone to eternal torment. Now the rider attacks "the rest," meaning the rest of the enemy army except for the dragon, who will be dealt with in the next vision. "The rest" are killed by the sword of the rider and comprise the promised meal for the birds at the "great supper of God" (19:21). The vision ends with the words, "All the birds were gorged with their flesh" (19:21; cf. *1 Enoch* 46:4–6).

The Fourth Unnumbered Vision: Satan Is Bound (20:1–3)

Now Satan must be dealt with. An angel descends from heaven with the key to the abyss and a great chain. He seizes Satan, binds him, and casts him into the abyss for a thousand years. As we discover in the next vision, this is so that he is not present during the millennial messianic kingdom. The scene is the opposite of that in the fifth trumpet (9:1–11), where an angel (there called a star) descends from heaven with the key to the abyss and opens it, unleashing on the earth the plague of demonic locust-like figures, although in both cases divine control over the abyss and its inhabitants is asserted. The claim of the one like a son of man in 1:18 that he possesses the keys of Death and Hades is also relevant, since Hades and the abyss are related concepts that can overlap. After a thousand years Satan must be released for a short time (20:3). The binding of Satan is a victory for Christ, but the fact that it is temporary emphasizes that Satan is powerful and can reemerge, even after the messiah's reign.

The scene in Rev 20:1–3 draws upon traditions common in ancient Jewish literature. A passage in the Isaiah Apocalypse (Isaiah 24–27) speaks of the imprisoning of sinful angels and humans:

> On that day the LORD will punish
> the host of heaven in heaven,
> and on earth the kings of the earth.
> They will be gathered together
> like prisoners in a pit;
> they will be shut up in a prison,
> and after many days they will be punished.
> (Isa 24:21–22)

Striking parallels to Rev 20:1–3, 10 occur in *1 Enoch.* In *1 Enoch* 10 the name of the leader of the fallen angels is Azaz'el:

> The Lord said to Raphael [an angel], "Bind Azaz'el hand and foot [and] throw him into the darkness!" And he made a hole in the desert which was in Duda'el and cast him there; he threw on top of him rugged and sharp rocks. And he covered his face in order that he might not see light; and in order that he might be sent into the fire on the great day of judgment. (*1 Enoch* 10:4–6)

Other passages in *1 Enoch* reflect this same scenario (e.g., *1 Enoch* 53–54; see Charles 1920, 2:141–42). In both Revelation and *1 Enoch* an angelic evil force is imprisoned in some sort of underworld until the day of judgment, at which time it is cast into a fiery place of punishment. In both Revelation and *1 Enoch* that angelic force is accused of deceiving earth's inhabitants.

The seer refers to Satan in the same fourfold way used in 12:9. He is "the dragon, that ancient serpent, who is the Devil and Satan" (20:2). He is bound "so that he would deceive the nations no more, until the thousand years were ended" (20:3; cf. 12:9). This establishes a connection between the scenes in chapters 12 and 20, and so it highlights the stages in the progressive defeat of Satan. First he is thrown out of heaven by angels; then he is bound in the abyss by angels. In 20:10, he will be thrown into the lake of fire, which will be his final and definitive defeat. He will not be allowed to deceive the nations during the messianic kingdom (20:3). Deception is an issue throughout Revelation (2:20; 12:9; 13:14; 18:23; 19:20; 20:3, 8, 10). For the seer, the majority of humanity is deceived by Roman claims. But the faithful are not fooled, for they know where true authority resides. And in the messianic kingdom, Satan cannot deceive. But he still lurks in the background (or rather the underworld), waiting for one last chance, for then "he must be let out for a little while" (20:3).

The use of the word "must" in 20:3 deserves attention (see Boring 1989, 208–9). Apocalypses in general and Revelation in particular view history as unfolding according to God's plan. They use such techniques as periodization of history and visions of the endtime to demonstrate God's control of history. God's plan is frequently presented as inevitable. It "must" happen. But we can inquire further about why God includes the binding of Satan and the coming of the temporary messianic kingdom in the divine plan. Why not just have Satan defeated completely in 20:1–3 and bring in the final consummation described in chapters 21 and 22 immediately? The author uses this opportunity to assert once again the resilience of Satan and the difficult and complicated process by which he is annihilated. At the same time, this is held in creative tension with the idea that divine power is such that it can conquer demonic power swiftly and without sustaining any casualties (19:20–21; 20:1–3, 10). The millennial kingdom also supplies an opportunity for those who actually lose their lives in resistance to

Rome to receive a special reward, co-ruling with Christ for a thousand years.

The Fifth Unnumbered Vision: The Messianic Kingdom (the Millennium) and the Final Defeat of Satan (20:4–10)

This vision is in two parts. The first (20:4–6) concerns the thousand-year reign of the messiah, whose reign the martyrs share. The second concerns the release of Satan at the end of the thousand years and his assault on Christ and his people, followed by Satan's defeat and ultimate punishment (20:7–10). Because the messianic reign lasts a thousand years, it is often called the millennium, which, as stated earlier, comes from the Latin words for "thousand," *mille,* and "year," *annus.*

Considering the amount of attention the thousand-year reign of Jesus has engendered, one might think that it is the most important part of Revelation. Yet it occupies only three verses out of the entire book. This reign is not the book's climax. It is only a step along the way to the true climax, contained in chapters 21 and 22. The millennial kingdom has received an amount of attention disproportionate to its place in Revelation (Boring 1989, 202). At the same time, the millennium does play an important role in the sequence of events leading to the final consummation. Crucial to its interpretation is that it is an *earthly* kingdom and that the martyred faithful share in its rule. It serves as an assertion of God's sovereignty through Christ within the realm of *this* world. Later the present heaven and earth will go out of existence and a new universe will come about in which the boundaries between heaven and earth are effectively abolished (20:11; 21:1–4). Before this happens, God takes control in a definitive manner. Martyred Christians are vindicated for their refusal to accept the counterfeit authority of Rome. Because they rejected Rome's rule, they become the real rulers even before the present world passes away.

As the vision begins John sees thrones. Those sitting on them have authority to judge (20:4). Then he sees those "who had been beheaded for their testimony to Jesus and for the word of God" (20:4). They are further characterized as those who "had not worshiped the beast or its image and had not received its mark on their foreheads or on their hands" (20:4). These are two sides of the same coin. To hold the testimony of Jesus (see commentary on 1:2, 9; 6:9; 12:11; 19:10) is to resist Roman idolatrous claims. In chapter 13, those who refuse to worship the beast and its image are killed (13:15). Those who do suffer martyrdom deserve special recognition, even in the course of the eschatological events. They "came to life and reigned with Christ a thousand years" (20:4). The verb for "came to life" is the same as that used to allude to Christ's resurrection in 2:8, and to Nero redivivus in 13:14.

The judges sitting on thrones come before the mention of the martyrs in 20:4. That leads some to see these as two different groups. If so, then perhaps the unnamed judges judge the martyrs themselves. Although the actual judgment is not narrated, its result would be evident in that they share Christ's rule. The simple juxtaposition of judges and the result of judgment without an intervening narrative describing the judgment follows the pattern of Daniel 7, a chapter that influences this scene. There Daniel sees thrones set in heaven, then sees God take his fiery throne with all of his attendants around him, and then "the court sat in judgment, and books were opened" (7:9–10). In Daniel as in Revelation there are multiple thrones, but it is not specified who sits on them. In Daniel the result of the judgment (defeat of the beast) is simply juxtaposed with the statement about judgment, as in Revelation.

Alternatively it may be that the martyrs themselves sit on the thrones. True, they are mentioned after the thrones, but that is hardly definitive, given the enigmatic way the author's imagery operates. To juxtapose figures on thrones with the martyrs may imply that the martyrs are those figures. This raises the problem of whom they judge. Many commentators suggest a relation to Jesus' prediction to the disciples, "Truly I tell you, at the renewal of all things, when the Son of Man is seated on the throne of his glory, you who have followed me will also sit on twelve thrones, judging the twelve tribes of Israel" (Matt 19:28; cf. 1 Cor 6:2–3). Although this saying could refer to the last judgment, one recent commentator interprets "judge" in Matt 19:28 more broadly, seeing as a possible background the "judges" of Israel in the book of Judges whose "judging" is not so much forensic as general governance (Horsley 1993, 199–208). In this case the martyrs judging is simply another way of saying what is asserted later in the passage, that they reign with Christ. Whom they judge then becomes the same question as whom they rule. The question of who is judged is sharpened by the observation that in 19:21 all of the evil army is killed. If that army consists of all who are not faithful Christians, and if Christians other than the resurrected martyrs are not raised until the second resurrection (see below), then there is no one left to judge in the millennial kingdom. There is also the possibility that Christians who are not martyred survive into the millennial period, despite 13:15 (Yarbro Collins 1990, 1014). This entire line of reasoning may be overly literal, and we have seen repeatedly that such questioning leads to unanswerable questions. One must strike a balance between reading individual visions and cycles of visions in terms of one another and reading them as semi-independent pictures of the same things seen in different ways. Our author is quite capable of asserting, on the one hand, that all of God's enemies, who seem to be defined as everyone who is not a faithful Christian, are wiped out, and of maintaining, on the other hand, that in the messianic kingdom the martyrs rule the world or that the nations come to worship God in the end (15:4; 21:24–26; cf. 22:2).

Revelation 20:5 makes clear that those who rise to reign with Christ for a thousand years are a special group, even among Christians. "The rest of the dead" must wait until the thousand years end (20:5). The martyrs' resurrection at the beginning of the millennium is "the first resurrection." Those who think that all of the faithful are martyred see this resurrection as including all of the faithful and the resurrection of 20:12–13 as consisting of just the unrighteous. But the mention of the book of life in the later judgment (20:12) indicates that the later judgment also involves righteous ones. It is best to see those who reign with Christ during the millennium as martyrs and as a special group among the faithful.

The first half of this vision ends with the fourth of Revelation's beatitudes: "Blessed and holy are those who share in the first resurrection" (20:6). The specialness of this group is indicated by the addition of the adjective "holy" to the beatitude here, which makes it unique among the seven beatitudes. They belong in a special way to Christ. As is customary in beatitudes, the announcement of blessedness is followed by its grounds. Here they are in three parts. First, the risen do not fall under the power of "the second death," defined in 20:14 as consignment to the lake of fire, the place of ultimate and unending punishment (see 2:11). The second and third grounds for their blessedness are that "they will be priests of God and of Christ, and they will reign with him a thousand years." The description of the martyrs and of all the faithful as both priests and kings derives from Exod 19:6. They are the part of humanity that is fit to come into God's presence, and they are the locus of God's effective sovereignty in the world. The special rule of the martyrs with Christ lasts for a thousand years. What the martyrs now receive (priesthood and kingship) is already posited of the faithful in 1:6 and 5:10, so the thousand-year reign is a special instance of the reign of the righteous in general. The tension between the present reign of the faithful and their future reign points to the "already/not yet" aspect of Christian eschatology in general. What the churches already have in a proleptic or partial way, they have fully and definitively only at the end.

There are ample examples of the idea of a temporary messianic kingdom in ancient Jewish literature (Charles 1920, 2:184). Prophetic and apocalyptic scenarios of God's intervention in history are legion, and there is great variety in such scenarios. In his studies of Jewish eschatology, Charles sees a major shift in around 100 B.C.E. (2:142). In the postexilic prophets (beginning in the late sixth century B.C.E.), there is the notion that God will set matters straight on earth, and the new situation will be permanent. At around 100 B.C.E., the view shifts to the idea that a more radical reordering of creation is necessary, one that involves going beyond history. In many texts the idea of an earthly messianic rule is preserved, but it is to be temporary and will be succeeded by a more profound change in the universe.

As with most such sweeping characterizations, Charles's view can be debated with respect to specific texts, but his broad insight is well founded. Scholars often distinguish between prophetic and apocalyptic eschatology by saying that the former expects a continuation of history, while apocalyptic eschatology anticipates a more radical change and is often described as the end of history as we know it. It is "deliverance out of the present order into a new transformed order" (P. D. Hanson 1976, 30). Collins pinpoints the transcendence of death as the specific feature of apocalyptic eschatology that distinguishes it from what precedes (1974), which shows that the rectification of the world must be on the other side of death. Things have become so bad that a more fundamental dividing line must be drawn between the present age and the age to come. For Revelation, the absolute nature of that dividing line is represented by the annihilation of Satan's forces and influence and the passing out of existence of the present heaven and earth.

Revelation is one of several apocalyptic texts that reconciles the expectation of an earthly messianic kingdom with a more fundamental change in the universe. For example, 4 Ezra 7 says that the messianic kingdom will last for four hundred years. Then the messiah will die, and the world will return to its primeval silence for seven days. Then there will be a general resurrection of the dead and the last judgment, resulting in eternal reward in God's presence or punishment in the fiery abyss. This sequence is close to that in Rev 20:4–15 (see also *2 Baruch* 29–30; *Sib. Or.* 3:652–701; see Charles 1920, 2:142–43). Revelation is unique in saying that the messianic kingdom will last for a thousand years. Other Jewish documents opt for different lengths of time or do not specify it. It is possible that the author merely chooses an even measure of time that is extremely long, and one that indicates the importance of the millennium and the superiority of messianic to Roman rule, but a time that is nonetheless limited (see Yarbro Collins 1990, 1014, for other possibilities). An intriguing suggestion combines Genesis 1 and Ps 90:4. In Genesis 1:1–2:3, the creation of the universe takes six days, and on the seventh day God rests. In Ps 90:4, it is said that to God a thousand years are like a day. Second Peter refers to this psalm when, in trying to understand the delay of Christ's second coming, it says, "With the Lord one day is like a thousand years, and a thousand years like one day" (2 Pet 3:8). If Revelation depends on Psalm 90 and Genesis, then the millennial kingdom corresponds to the seventh day of creation, the day of God's rest. This speculation is made more likely when in *2 Enoch* 32–33 the length of history is determined by treating each of the days of Genesis 1 as a thousand years. It is further supported by the fact that Hebrews 3–4 presents God's "rest" as the goal of a Christian, equivalent to heaven.

The author of Revelation is clearly influenced by traditions concerning the binding of antidivine powers until the end of time and by the notion that a temporary messianic kingdom will precede the last resurrection, last judgment, and ultimate rewards and punishments. Ezekiel influences the author deeply, and it contains these same elements. The general scheme informing Ezekiel 37–48 is visible in this section of Revelation. In Ezekiel 37, the restoration of Israel after the Babylonian exile is described in terms of a resurrection of dead bodies. This corresponds to the messianic kingdom in Rev 20:4-6, which begins with the resurrection of the martyrs. In Ezekiel 38-39, there is an eschatological war against Jerusalem and the restored community. The enemy is the mythological enemy from the north, Gog from the land of Magog. Gog is destroyed by fire from heaven (38:22), as is Magog (39:6). This corresponds to Rev 20:7-10, where Satan is released, gathers the nations of the earth along with Gog and Magog (now seen as two individual leaders) against the messiah and his people, and is defeated by fire from heaven. Ezekiel 40-48 concerns a new Jerusalem, built on a mythological scale, in which God is present. Revelation 21-22 contains a similar description of a new Jerusalem in which God and the Lamb are present among the people.

As mentioned, the millennium has received a great deal of attention throughout history. Interpretations of it fall into various categories. "Premillennialists" believe that Christ will come before the millennium and be present on earth during it. "Postmillennialists" think that he will come only afterwards. "Amillennialists" do not take the millennium literally as an earthly kingdom. Most of the earliest interpreters of Revelation were "chiliasts," meaning that they believed in a literal thousand-year rule of Christ to come. Augustine was influential in establishing another view—that the millennium is a way of speaking about the church on earth, in which Satan has been conquered and Christ rules. It is always difficult to decide just how literally to take Revelation's images, but there is little reason to deny that our author expects a reign of Christ on earth that will precede the final consummation. The figure of a thousand years is symbolic, but the messianic kingdom itself need not be. Keeping in mind that the seer is dealing with a real and concrete political situation which he is interpreting, to make the millennium only symbolic would depoliticize his point of view somewhat.

The second half of this vision depicts Satan's last efforts at rebellion (20:7-10). He is released from the abyss, much as the demonic locusts were released in chapter 9. He immediately engages in his characteristic activity, deceiving the nations. As before, that deception leads to their opposition to God, this time expressed through their gathering with mythological enemies known from Ezekiel, Gog and Magog, against "the camp of the saints and the beloved city." The transformation of Gog from the land of Magog into two eschatological enemies of God, Gog and Magog, is also attested in the *Sibylline Oracles* and in rabbinic literature (Charles 1920, 2:188). In Rev 20:9, they come against Jerusalem, as Gog does in Ezekiel. This is a specific instance of the common tradition that at the end of time the nations will attack Jerusalem and be defeated (e.g., Zechariah 14; 4 Ezra 13; see Charles 1920, 2:188–89). The reference to "camp" is another connection between the faithful and the Israelites of the Bible, for throughout their desert wanderings the Israelites live in a camp, and when they are engaged in military campaigns, they also live in a camp.

As goes the battle of chapter 19, so goes this final battle. Satan's forces cannot inflict harm on their adversaries. God decides the battle by destroying Satan's army with fire from heaven. Satan is thrown into the same fiery lake as were the beast and the false prophet (19:20; 20:10). The author cannot resist the impulse to say one last time that Satan is the one "who had deceived" the final army into attacking the faithful (20:10). The fiery lake does not mean annihilation for the beast, the false prophet, and Satan. Rather, "they will be tormented day and night forever and ever" (20:10; cf. 14:11). Finally Satan is defeated for good. In what follows, there is no more possibility of rebellion against God. The universe has now changed absolutely. Indeed, heaven and earth themselves will pass away shortly.

The Sixth Unnumbered Vision: The Last Judgment (20:11–15)

The last judgment is concise. The author is anxious to move on to a lengthy description of the splendid future God has in store for the faithful. But a last judgment scene is necessary. Despite the importance of military imagery throughout Revelation, the seer is deeply concerned about individual conduct. He may conceive of the faithful and unfaithful as two armed camps led by cosmic forces, but he also stresses human choice. It is now necessary to narrate a judgment scene in which each person is judged for his or her deeds (20:12).

As do other judgment scenes in ancient Jewish and Christian literature, this one begins with a picture of a throne on which the king sits as judge (20:11; cf., e.g., Daniel 7; Matthew 25; *1 Enoch* 62). The throne is imposing and is the color of heaven, white. The one who sits on the throne is not identified, leading Boring to speculate that the author is purposely vague so that one will not distinguish between God and Christ, even in this function of judging (1989, 211). It is frequently Jesus who is the judge elsewhere in the New Testament, as in the famous last judgment scene in Matthew 25. But Jesus never sits on the throne alone in Revelation. Where it is not specified that Christ shares God's throne, God alone sits there. In the great throne room scene of chapters 4 and 5, the Lamb is not on the throne, even though in 3:21 Jesus says that he already sits on the throne with God. In the judgment scene of chapter 20, only one sits on the throne, and it must be God. God's presence in Rev 20:11 is awesome. Earth and heaven flee from him. This is equivalent to the passing of the first heaven and earth mentioned later in 21:1. It is significant that it happens at the appearance of God as judge. The old heaven and earth are in fact no longer fit for God and his faithful and must be replaced. Human and angelic sin have defiled heaven and earth beyond repair, and when God appears as judge, the old heaven and earth know that their time is expired.

All stand before the throne to be judged (20:12). The phrase "great and small" again indicates that all humanity is present, although presumably the martyrs who have already risen in 20:4 are not judged here. It is not until the next verse that the dead emerge from Hades and from the sea (20:13), but narrative dislocations are common in Revelation. Verse 13 emphasizes the completeness of the resurrection, which, although it does not say so explicitly, must be the second resurrection that the "first resurrection" implies (20:6). Even those lost at sea and therefore unburied must rise and come before God. Death and Hades are a duo here, as when the one like a son of man claims authority over them in 1:18, and as in the fourth seal when they receive authority to kill a quarter of the earth (6:7–8). The resurrection and judgment involve righteous and unrighteous alike. There are Jewish and Christian texts that refer to places where people are kept between death and the last judgment (Charles 1920, 2:196–97).

Resurrection is an idea that seems to have entered Judaism through the medium of apocalypticism. The first clear reference to resurrection in Jewish literature is in Daniel 12, written in the second century B.C.E. Already in that passage resurrection is connected to judgment: "Many of those who sleep in the dust of the earth shall awake, some to everlasting life, and some to shame and everlasting contempt" (Dan 12:2; see Nickelsburg 1972). Thus resurrection is a Jewish idea adopted by Christianity. It signifies a continuity of persons pre- and postdeath, and it makes it possible for the risen righteous to participate in a renewed and reformed world and for the wicked to be suitably punished.

Individual responsibility is stressed as the author twice says that people will be judged according to their deeds (20:12 and 13; cf. 2:23). This is of course an idea frequent in the Bible and in Jewish and Christian literature (e.g., Ps 62:12; Prov 14:14; 24:12; Jer 17:10; Rev 2:23; Rom 2:6; 1 Pet 1:17). For John, one's decision to resist Rome and one's environment determines one's fate. As in many other judgment scenes, record books play a role (Dan 7:10; *1 Enoch* 47:3; 90:20; 4 Ezra 6:20; *2 Bar.* 24:1; *Asc. Isa.* 9:22; see Charles 1920, 2:194). Here there are two sorts of books. One sort records deeds by which humans are judged (20:12). Also consulted is the book of life, the list of those who belong to God rather than to the emperor (see 3:5; 13:8; 17:8). The presence of one's name in the book is necessary for ultimate salvation (see commentary on 3:5 and 13:8).

Death and Hades are thrown into the lake of fire. As in the fourth seal, they are personified, as elsewhere in Jewish and Christian texts (see commentary on 1:18 and 6:7–8; cf. 1 Cor 15:26). Revelation reveals that the lake of fire into which Death and Hades are thrown is the second death from which Jesus promises to save the faithful (2:11) and from which the martyrs are protected (20:6). Jewish sources contemporary with Revelation that speak of the abolition of Death and Hades or at least of their being rendered unimportant are 4 Ezra 8:53 and *2 Bar.* 21:23.

The vision of the last judgment ends with the casting into the lake of fire of "anyone whose name was not found written in the book of life" (20:15). Again, being consigned to this lake does not mean that one perishes entirely. At least for Satan, the beast, and the false prophet it means eternal torment (20:10). This illustrates the social dualism of the seer. There are two sorts of people in the world—those who are loyal to God and everyone else. Repentance is possible, as are apostasy and backsliding, but in the end there are only two possibilities. The final separation of good and bad in the judgment of 20:11–15 contradicts later passages that assume the continued existence of the nations and their conversion to God later (21:24–26; 22:2). Again, the way the author uses traditions depends on his needs in any given passage. He wants to say that all who are loyal to Rome will pay, and at the same time he anticipates that the nations will recognize the true God in the end. He says both, without regard to the problems that this causes modern interpreters.

The Seventh Unnumbered Vision: Descent of the New Jerusalem (21:1–8)

This vision together with its elaboration in 21:9–22:5 is the most complete and detailed description of the final consummation in Revelation. It begins with John seeing a new heaven and a new earth, because the first heaven and earth have passed away (21:1). In the previous vision, the first heaven and earth flee before the presence of the divine judge (20:11). Creation has become so alienated from God that it must be profoundly transformed. The transformation is so complete that it can be spoken of as a new creation, which is the meaning of God's pronouncement in this vision, "See, I am making all things new" (21:5).

The idea that at the eschaton there will be a radical transformation of creation is not an invention of our author. Chapters 40 to 55 of the book of Isaiah, written at the end of the Babylonian exile, express their author's anticipation that Israel will be rescued from exile by God and brought back to the land of Israel, where Jerusalem will be rebuilt and God will again dwell among the people. Several times Isaiah calls what God is about to do a "new thing," requiring a "new song" of praise to God (Isa 42:9–10; 43:18–19; cf. Rev 5:9; 14:3). The newness is expressed radically in 51:6:

> Lift up your eyes to the heavens,
>   and look at the earth beneath;
> for the heavens will vanish like smoke,
>   the earth will wear out like a garment,
>   and those who live on it will be like gnats;
> but my salvation will be forever,
>   and my deliverance will never be ended.

In a passage perhaps written after the return to the land, God declares:

I am about to create new heavens
  and a new earth;
the former things shall not be remembered
  or come to mind.
But be glad and rejoice forever
  in what I am creating;
for I am about to create Jerusalem as a joy,
  and its people as a delight.
I will rejoice in Jerusalem,
  and delight in my people;
no more shall the sound of weeping be heard in it,
  or the cry of distress. (65:17–19)

The picture of renewal that Isaiah presents uses the language of cosmic transformation, but the renewal itself remains within the limits of prophetic eschatology. The cosmic transformation is more poetic than literal, and there is no idea of the transcendence of death. There is no resurrection from the dead, and people live healthy, long lives. No afterlife is mentioned.

Although Isaiah remains within the limits of prophetic eschatology, the book furnishes later prophets and seers with language for describing the profound change needed to reconcile the cosmos to God. A new heaven and earth are now required. That heaven and earth can pass away is attested to in the quote from Isaiah above and in Ps 102:25–26. The renewal of creation is mentioned in later Jewish apocalypses (e.g., *1 Enoch* 45:4–5; 91:16; 4 Ezra 7:75; *2 Bar.* 32:6; see the list in Charles 1920, 2:203). The passing away of heaven and earth becomes a commonplace in New Testament texts heavily influenced by apocalypticism. In Mark 13:31, Jesus says, "Heaven and earth will pass away, but my words will not pass away" (see 1 Cor 7:31; Rom 8:19–23). The idea in 2 Peter seems to be that the present world is corrupted and that righteousness must have a new home:

> But the day of the Lord will come like a thief, and then the heavens will pass away with a loud noise, and the elements will be dissolved with fire, and the earth and everything that is done on it will be disclosed. . . . But, in accordance with this promise, we wait for new heavens and a new earth, where righteousness is at home. (2 Pet 3:10, 13)

Revelation belongs to this long tradition when it declares that the first heaven and earth have passed away, and there is now a new heaven and earth. The seer adds, "And the sea was no more" (21:1). The sea is where the dragon goes when he is cast out of heaven (12:18). It is the locale from which the beast, the dragon's agent, arises (13:1) in imitation of the four beasts of Daniel 7. Such passages assume the notion of the sea in ancient Near Eastern mythology as the place of chaos, opposed to divine order. There is no place for the sea in a new order that fully conforms to God's will. The absence of the sea in the new creation is another way of saying what the author has already claimed in describing the ultimate defeat of Satan in 20:10 and of Death and Hades in 20:14. The rebellion against God is finished forever. The same idea is expressed in strikingly similar terms in the *Testament of Moses:*

> Then his kingdom will appear throughout his whole creation.
> Then the devil will have an end.
> Yea, sorrow will be led away with him. . . .
> And the sea all the way to the abyss will retire,
> to the sources of waters which fail.
> Yea, the rivers will vanish away. (10:1, 6)

Now that there is a new cosmos, God can come again, not as judge but as the God of the covenant, guarantor of life and protection, joy and security. John describes the new Jerusalem "coming down out of heaven from God" (21:2; cf. 3:12). Like the many other images and metaphors in Revelation, the new Jerusalem image is fluid and draws upon many biblical passages and postbiblical traditions (see Boring 1989, 214). Ever since Jerusalem was destroyed by the Babylonians in the sixth century B.C.E., visions of a rebuilt Jerusalem appeared in Jewish sources. Even after Jerusalem was rebuilt under Persian auspices at the end of the sixth century, such visions were useful to those who were dissatisfied with the second temple or who were living when the second temple was under attack, was damaged, or was destroyed.

It is simplistic to decide either that the seer expects a new Jerusalem that conforms precisely to his fantastic description or that this is but an allegory for enduring truths, such as the relation of God to his people. There are both literal and allegorical aspects here, and they cannot be neatly disentangled. One cannot take this vision as a simple prediction of future events; nor can one reduce it to general truisms. The seer expects real, concrete changes in the world. It is not simply a matter of changing humanity's attitude or of a transfer of political power. The seer does believe in cosmic powers that stand behind social realities such as church and empire, and their struggle is real and has observable effects on the world. Big changes are coming. But in describing those changes, the seer uses any elements at his disposal, especially those that come from the Bible. These elements are expressive and evocative, not simply predictive.

The new Jerusalem that descends from heaven in 21:2 is called "the holy city," the city that belongs to God. It now falls completely within the realm of the sacred, as the vision and its elaboration will show. The new Jerusalem is "prepared as a bride adorned for her husband" (21:2). Her husband is the Lamb (see 21:9–10). This image picks up on the conclusion of the Babylon appendix, where the bride is the church (19:7–8). But such a one-to-one identification does not do full justice to the rich image of the bride. There are also echoes of the combat myth where the conquering hero is married and receives kingship (see comments on chapter 19). The new Jerusalem as a woman has a parallel in 4 Ezra 9–10, where a woman appears to Ezra as he mourns the destruction of the temple by the Babylonians (Romans). The woman is then transformed into the Jerusalem built by God. Of course even in the Hebrew Bible, Jerusalem symbolizes the unity between God and people.

Because of the alienation between God and creation, it is necessary for the old heaven and earth to pass away and for a new creation to come. Similarly the Jerusalem that descends in 21:2 is a *new Jerusalem.* It is not a rebuilt or restored Jerusalem, but a new one, and its origin is heaven, that is, God. The Jewish apocalypse *2 Baruch,* written in response to the destruction of the temple by the Romans in 70 C.E., explains that God's promise through Isaiah to protect Jerusalem was directed not toward the earthly Jerusalem but toward the heavenly one (*2 Baruch* 4; see Murphy 1985a). In 4 Ezra, the angel explains to Ezra that he must go out into the fields to see the new Jerusalem: "Therefore I told you to go into the field where there was no foundation of any building, because no work of human construction could endure in a place where the city of the Most High was to be revealed" (10:53–54).

The idea that there is a heavenly Jerusalem is found in the New Testament in Gal 4:26 and Heb 12:22 (cf. Phil 3:20). In each case the image stresses continuity between the church and Israel (i.e., Christians are heirs of Israel's heritage), but at the same time it emphasizes discontinuity between Israel and the church.

Paul contrasts the earthly Jerusalem, mother of non-Christian Jews, with the heavenly Jerusalem, the mother of Christians (Gal 4:21–31). The new Jerusalem in Revelation also maintains a tension between continuity and discontinuity, a tension that is also apparent in the combination of messages to the churches which imply that it is faithful Christians who are the true Jews, not those who belong to the "synagogue of Satan" (2:9; 3:9).

The essential meaning of the descent of the heavenly Jerusalem is conveyed by "a loud voice from the throne" (21:3–4). As in 19:5, the voice speaks of God in the third person, so it is not God's voice, but because it issues from the throne it carries God's authority. The first part of the voice's proclamation speaks of God's presence with humans and the covenantal relationship he therefore has with them. The second part speaks of the advantages humans derive from that relationship. The first part reads:

> See, the home of God is among mortals [humans].
> He will dwell with them as their God;
> they will be his peoples,
> and God himself will be with them. (21:3)

This is covenantal language. The special relationship between God and Israel is frequently expressed in the Bible by saying that they are his people and he is their God (e.g., Lev 26:11–12; Jer 31:33; Ezek 37:27; Zech 8:8). The supreme expression of that relationship is God's presence with the people. In the desert wanderings, a tent traveled with the people to which God would come to confer with Moses. The ark of the covenant, symbol of God's presence, was kept in the tent. After David made Jerusalem his capital city, his son Solomon built a temple which symbolized God's relationship with the people (1 Kings 8). The priestly book Leviticus records these divine words: "I will place my dwelling in your midst, and I shall not abhor you. And I will walk among you, and I will be your God, and you shall be my people" (26:11–12). In that context God's presence with the people brings them numerous blessings, such as victory over their enemies and abundant crops. Ezekiel, contemplating Israel's return from the Babylonian exile to a rebuilt Jerusalem, sees the essence of that restoration in God's presence in the temple in the midst of the people. God promises, "My dwelling place shall be with them; and I will be their God, and they shall be my people. Then the nations shall know that I the LORD sanctify

Israel, when my sanctuary is among them forevermore" (Ezek 37:27–28). The very last words of Ezekiel express this same idea: "And the name of the city from that time on shall be, The LORD is There" (Ezek 48:35).

The Greek manuscripts differ on whether "peoples" in 21:3 is singular or plural. In biblical covenantal contexts, Israel is differentiated from "the nations," so it is the "people" in the singular who belong to God. Weighing the relative reliability of the manuscripts does not yield a clear preference for one reading or the other. If "peoples" is correct (as in the NRSV) this may be another instance where the author stresses that the church contains people from various nations.

The second part of the proclamation from the throne lists benefits accruing to humanity because of God's presence. Tears are wiped away; death goes out of existence; and "mourning and crying and pain will be no more." God brings this about, "for the first things have passed away" (21:4). According to Genesis, before Adam and Eve sinned things were very different in the world. Tempted by the serpent, they disobeyed God's command not to eat of the tree of the knowledge of good and evil. As a result, God decreed ongoing enmity between the serpent and the seed of the woman (a story that influenced Revelation 12), death for humanity, pain in childbearing and subjection to the man for the woman, hardship and toil for the man, and difficulty in fertility for the earth. It is this old creation that has now passed away. Satan, the ancient serpent (12:9; 20:2), is gone, and death is no more (20:14; 21:4).

The absence of tears in 21:4 recalls the salvation scene in Revelation 7, where the blessed stand before God's throne and are sheltered by him. They do not hunger and thirst; nor does the heat of the sun scorch them; they are guided by their shepherd the Lamb to "springs of the water of life," and God wipes all tears from their eyes (7:15–17). Behind both Revelation 7 and 21 stands Isaiah, who in a salvation scene says that God will make for all peoples a rich feast on the mountain, and "he will swallow up death forever. Then the Lord GOD will wipe away the tears from all faces, and the disgrace of his people he will take away from all the earth" (Isa 25:6–8; cf. 35:10; 51:11; 65:19). This is how the gracious God acts toward his people. For the seer, Isaiah's words are about to be fulfilled. The disappearance of death recalls Rev 20:14 (cf. also 1 Cor 15:54; 4 Ezra 8:53; *2 Bar.* 21:23).

The rest of this vision consists of a declaration by God. As usual, he is identified simply as "the one who was seated on the throne" (21:5). This is one of only two times in Revelation that God speaks directly. The previous time God speaks is at the very beginning of the book, where he proclaims, "I am the Alpha and the Omega" (1:8). In that same verse God is given the titles "Lord God," the one "who is and who was and who is to come," and "the Almighty." Now, toward the end of Revelation, God speaks again. First he says, "See, I am making all things new" (21:5). The old heaven and earth are gone (20:11; 21:1). What comes now is a new creation. Then God says to the seer, "Write this, for these words are trustworthy and true" (21:5). Revelation's audience has known from the very first verse that John's witness is true, for it comes ultimately from God. He is told by Jesus several times to write (1:11, 19; 2:1, 8, 12, 18; 3:1, 7, 14). But 21:5 contains the only time that the seer is told to write directly by God. The divine command comes at a climactic point. It is the last vision of the last vision cycle, and it is after all God's enemies are vanquished. The old creation has passed and the new has come. The new Jerusalem has descended to earth, and God makes his dwelling with humans. This is how creation was meant to be from the beginning.

It is unclear just what God commands the seer to write. But it makes no real difference whether he is to write simply the words, "See, I make all things new" (21:5), or whether he is being told once again to write the entire book of Revelation, for the whole book is contained in this simple declaration of God in 21:5. For God to say that he is now bringing about the new creation implies the defeat of his enemies, the saving of the righteous, and the descent of the new Jerusalem. And "these words" which the seer is to write are "trustworthy and true," whichever they refer to. Truth resides in the sovereignty of God over all creation, witnessed to by Christ, the martyrs, and all of the faithful. The words describing this and the ones who are witnesses to it are by definition "trustworthy" (elsewhere translated "faithful"; Greek: *pistos*).

God speaks again to the seer (21:6–8). He begins by saying, "It is done!" (21:6). The words echo those of the loud voice from the temple in the seventh bowl, which also declares, "It is done!" (16:17). The seventh bowl contains the destruction of Rome, elaborated by the Babylon appendix, which, after Rome falls and is mourned by her collaborators, contains the great hymn of the great multitude exclaiming, "Hallelujah! For the Lord our God the Almighty reigns" (19:6). In other words, both God's declaration of 21:6 and that of the voice from the throne in 16:17 refer to the same events when they say "It is done!" The new creation has come. God reigns. This supplies content to God's next assertion: "I am the Alpha and the Omega, the beginning and the end" (21:6). God makes this assertion about himself in 1:8 and here in 21:6, so in a literary sense God speaks for himself at the beginning and end of the book. This literary device underlines the fact that God as the creator is the source of all and that he is also the goal of all. As God's own words frame the book of Revelation, occurring at the beginning and end, so God himself is the beginning and end of the cosmos. The goal of all history is God's reassertion of his sovereignty and the cosmic and social harmony that results. But it is significant for Revelation's christology that the titles God applies to himself here Christ applies to himself in 22:13, and the throne on which God sits is also occupied by Christ (3:21; 22:1, 3).

God offers to "the thirsty," that is, those who seek him (see Pss 42:2; 63:1; 143:6), water from "the spring of the water of life" (21:6). This recalls the salvation scene of 7:9–17, where the Lamb leads the faithful "to springs of the water of life" (7:17). Attempts to find here references to baptism or to the gift of the Spirit interpret this image too narrowly. Water is always a potent metaphor, more so in a culture where water is scarce. In such cultures, the connection between water and life is vividly apparent. This connection makes water an apt symbol for physical and spiritual life, and it is God who gives and sustains life in all of its manifestations and levels. Only God can offer this water, and only as the supreme agent of God and as God's co-regent can the Lamb lead the faithful to this water (7:17). God's offer echoes the divine invitation in Isa 55:1: "Everyone who thirsts, come to the waters." In Jer 2:13 and 17:13, God bemoans Israel's abandonment of him, the "fountain of living water." In Rev 21:6, God offers this same water to the thirsty as a "gift." God's invitation recalls that of Jesus in John 7:37–38. God's wisdom is associated with the satisfaction of thirst in Sir 24:21 and 51:24.

Verses 7 and 8 conclude this climactic vision with a promise of reward for those who conquer and a warning of punishment for sinners. Combined with an allusion to persecution (since the righteous are those who "conquer" —resist to the point of being willing to give up their lives), these verses contain the pattern of persecution, reward, and punishment that permeates Revelation.

God says, "Those who conquer will inherit these things, and I will be their God and they will be my children" (21:7). At the end of each of the messages to the seven churches in chapters 2 and 3, a promise is made to the one who conquers. The picture of the final consummation in chapters 21 and 22 contains, explicitly or implicitly, the fulfillment of each of these promises. God's declaration here encompasses all of those fulfillments, for God promises that the conquerors will "inherit these things," referring to all of the blessings available in God's presence. This is restated in covenantal terms when God says that he will be their God and they will be his children. The more usual expression in a covenantal context here would be that they will be God's "people." The change to "children" may reflect Jewish and Christian ideas that God's people are his children (e.g., Isa 1:2; 43:6; Hos 11:1; Rom 8:29; Gal 4:1–7). The same combination of the covenantal promise to God's "people" and the use of "children" terminology is found in 2 Cor 6:16–18, which loosely combines several biblical passages into a single quote:

> I will live in them and walk among them,
>   and I will be their God,
>   and they shall be my people.
> Therefore come out from them,
>   and be separate from them, says the Lord,
> And touch nothing unclean;
>   then I will welcome you,
> and I will be your father,
>   and you shall be my sons and daughters,
>   says the Lord Almighty.

God speaks not only of reward for the righteous (21:7) but also of punishment for the wicked (21:8). Eternal punishment awaits sinners in the lake of fire. This is defined as the second death, not because sinners so condemned go out of existence (see 20:10) but because although all participate in the first death, which is physical, the second death means being deprived of the life-giving presence of God forever. In 2:11, Jesus promises that those who conquer will not undergo the second death. Revelation 21:7–8 fulfills that promise.

The list of sinners in 21:8 resembles the many lists of sins found throughout the New Testament (e.g., Gal 5:19–21; 1 Tim 1:9; Jas 2:11). In the Hellenistic world, such lists were teaching devices to exhort to good behavior. The list in 21:8 is generally appropriate to Revelation and to its concerns. The first group on the list, the "cowardly," are those who lack the courage to remain faithful in the face of hostility. The "faithless" (*apistos*) are the opposite of the "faithful" (*pistos*), who are loyal to the true sovereign of the universe and refuse to worship his counterfeit, Caesar. The "polluted" is a cultic term designating that which is hateful to God and which should not come into his presence. The great harlot in chapter 17 holds in her hand a cup full of "pollutions," and she is called "Babylon the great, mother of whores and of earth's abominations [pollutions]" (17:5–6). Cultic language expressing the incompatibility between devotion to God and to Rome fits the seer's situation in Asia, where he is surrounded by cultic reminders of Rome's claims. "Murderers" is a term the seer may find well suited to describe those who bring violence to bear on faithful Christians. Sexual language symbolizing unfaithfulness to God permeates Revelation, so it is not surprising to find "fornicators" on the list. "Sorcerers" is a bit more difficult. The only other occurrence of the root in Revelation is in 18:23, where Babylon is accused of deceiving all nations by its sorcery (see comments there). "Idolaters" are next on the list. Idolatry, concretely expressed as loyalty to Rome, is the prime sin in Revelation. "Liars" bring up the rear in the list. Opposition between truth and falsehood is a theme that runs through Revelation. God is the true sovereign of the world, and true words are those that witness to this. Rome is by definition false, and it can win over adherents only by deception.

With this vision Revelation reaches its logical conclusion. There remains only the new Jerusalem appendix and a short epilogue. The new Jerusalem appendix is an elaboration of the new Jerusalem whose descent is already described in 21:2 and whose implications have already been elucidated in 21:3–4. It is significant that God, sitting on the throne, has the last word in 21:5–8. Throughout the book God is transcendent, identified usually as the one sitting on the throne, symbolizing his power and authority. God now discloses the meaning of what has transpired. It is the new creation in which things are as they should be. The righteous are rewarded, not persecuted, and the sinners are punished, not honored. Finally things are as they appear, and it is God who announces the new state of affairs.

Chapter Twelve

The New Jerusalem Appendix (21:9–22:9)

The bowls series (chapter 16) is followed by the Babylon appendix (17:1–19:10), which elaborates on the seventh bowl (16:17–21), the fall of Babylon (Rome). In the same way, the second unnumbered vision series (19:11–21:8) is followed by the new Jerusalem appendix (21:9–22:9), which elaborates on the seventh unnumbered vision (21:1–8), the descent of the new Jerusalem. The two appendices, the Babylon and the new Jerusalem, begin in the same way:

> Then one of the seven angels who had the seven bowls came and said to me, "Come, I will show you the judgment of the great whore who is seated on many waters.... So he carried me away in the spirit into a wilderness, and I saw a woman. (17:1, 3)
>
> Then one of the seven angels who had the seven bowls full of the seven last plagues came and said to me, "Come, I will show you the bride, the wife of the Lamb." And in the spirit he carried me away to a great, high mountain and showed me the holy city Jerusalem coming down out of heaven from God. (21:9–10)

The appendices also end the same way. At the conclusion of each there are (in slightly different order in each) a beatitude, an attestation by the angel to the truth of the words either of the beatitude or of the whole vision, after which the seer falls down to worship the angel, who rebukes him and tells him to worship God (19:9–10; 22:6–9). Revelation 22:6–9 serves as a conclusion both to the Jerusalem Appendix and to Revelation as a whole, so we treat it separately. The parallelism of the two appendices highlights the contrasting parallelism between the great harlot and the pure bride. This falls into the long tradition of contrasting the whore and the virgin, a contrast that looks at women in terms of stereotyped categories determined by patriarchal cultures and worldviews. Biblical examples include the contrast between Folly and Wisdom, both of whom are portrayed as trying to entice men with their attractions (e.g., Proverbs 8-9), and the portrayal of Israel as faithful or unfaithful wife.

For the seer, humanity faces only two alternatives. One can be loyal to God or to Caesar. There is no middle ground; nor can the two be combined. They are as opposite as are the two women in Revelation 17 and 21. Both women are "adorned" (17:4; 21:2), but the harlot is adorned so as to seduce her illicit lovers, whereas the bride is adorned for her husband. Whereas the harlot wears purple and scarlet, symbolizing Rome's fraudulent claims to sovereignty as well as its decadence, the bride wears pure white linen, symbolizing her connection to heaven. The bride is the betrothed of the Lamb; the harlot is mistress to the nations.

Since the second unnumbered series is the final series in the book, the seventh vision—the new Jerusalem—is climactic. The new Jerusalem vision with its elaboration is in contrasting parallel with the vision of the fall of Babylon and its elaboration. The new Jerusalem appendix takes up almost every element of the new Jerusalem vision. Schüssler Fiorenza notes the following correspondences: 22:1-5 corresponds to 21:1; 21:9-11 to 21:2; 21:22-23 and 22:3 to 21:3; 22:2 to 21:4; 22:1 to 21:6; 22:4 to 21:7; 21:26-27 and 22:3 to 21:8 (1991, 109). That both appendices are introduced by one of the angels of the "seven last plagues" contained in the bowls indicates the climactic nature of these two visions. The final plagues in the bowls lead directly to the downfall of the harlot and the elevation of the bride.

This is the fourth time that John mentions being in the spirit (21:10). The first two times are at the beginnings of the book as a whole (1:10) and the beginning of the eschatological visions (4:2), and the last two are at the beginning of the Babylon and the new Jerusalem appendices (17:3; 21:10). These are key points in the narrative, and the mention of the spirit underlines the authority by which John speaks.

Both Ezekiel and Revelation end with visions of a magnificent, cosmically proportioned Jerusalem that is God's dwelling place with humans. Revelation draws on Ezekiel's vision as well as on other traditions of Jerusalem's restoration. Ezekiel's vision of the new Jerusalem (chapters 40-48) begins with the seer being brought by the hand of God from Babylon to Palestine. "He brought me, in visions of God, to the land of Israel, and set me down on a very high mountain, on which was a structure like a city to the south" (Ezek 40:2). This passage is the model for Rev 21:10. The same passage from Ezekiel stands behind Rev 17:3 (see our comments there), but the parallel is closer in 21:10 because of the presence of the city on the mountain in each. Mountains in the Bible are often places of revelation, as was Mount Sinai, and it was on a mountain (Mount Zion) that Jerusalem and its temple were built. Therefore to see the heavenly Jerusalem descend to earth, the seer is brought to a high mountain. As in the seventh of the unnumbered visions (21:2), the seer observes the heavenly Jerusalem descend to earth (21:10).

Before proceeding to specific features of the city, the seer characterizes it in a general way—it "has the glory of God and a radiance like a very rare jewel, like jasper, clear as crystal" (21:11). Throughout Revelation we find hymns and doxologies that give "glory" to God (1:6; 4:9, 11; 5:13; 7:12; 11:13; 19:1, 7). In 14:7, an angel in midheaven commands all inhabitants of the earth to "give God glory," a command set in synonymous parallelism with "fear God." It is an acknowledgment of God's status. The "glory of God" in 21:11 deals with that same status from the other side. Whether or not humans give God glory, he has it. God's position does not depend on human recognition, as does Rome's (see chapter 13). Thus we have a contrasting parallel. God does not depend on humans for his glory, but if they give him glory, they receive salvation. Rome does depend on humans for its glory, but if they give it glory, they receive condemnation.

In the Bible, the glory of God becomes a way of speaking of God's presence in power. It is especially prominent in the priestly tradition, which speaks of God's glory present in the temple (e.g., 1 Kgs 8:11) and in the events of Israel's history. God's glory can sometimes be conceived of as light. Even people and objects that come in contact with God's glory can take on this illumination, as when Moses' face shines when he returns from meeting with God on Mount Sinai in Exodus 34. In Rev 21:11, God's glory illumines the entire heavenly Jerusalem, which then shines "with a radiance like a very rare jewel, like jasper" (see 21:24-26; 22:5). Jewels, including jasper, are also used in the heavenly throne room scene of Revelation 4 to describe God and his surroundings. In 21:11, the city's radiance is "like jasper, clear as crystal." Such clarity is a recurring image in Revelation, especially in this vision. In chapter 4, there is a sea of glass, like crystal, before God's throne.

Revelation 21:12-22:5 describes the new Jerusalem. The description is in four parts. The first (21:12-14) associates the city wall with the Israelite tribes, the apostles, and angels. The second (21:15-21) deals with Jerusalem's measurements and adornment with precious stones. The third (21:22-26) speaks of God's presence in the city and who is allowed to enter it. The fourth part (22:1-5) sees the city as the place where the tree of life is, which, together with God's presence, benefits the city's inhabitants, particularly God's servants.

The first part of the description deals with the city wall, which is said to be great and high (21:12-14). In the ancient world, any city worthy of respect had a wall. Without it, the city would be prey to any attacker. In Revelation angels stand at the wall's twelve gates as watchmen. We learn in 21:16 that the city is square, so its wall consists of four equal sides. The sides are perfectly oriented, facing north, south, east, and west. There are twelve gates, three in each wall. Each gate bears the name of one of the twelve tribes of Israel. This corresponds to Ezekiel's vision, in which each of the four walls has three gates, each one assigned to an Israelite tribe (Ezek 48:30-34). Revelation adds that there are twelve foundations of the wall, each bearing the name of one of the "twelve apostles of the Lamb" (Rev 21:14). The wall symbolizes continuity between Israel and the church. The letter to the Ephesians uses a similar image when it speaks of the church as a temple with the prophets and apostles as its foundation (Eph 2:20).

The second part of the description (21:15-21) begins with the observation that the angel showing John the city has a golden measuring rod with which to measure the city, gates, and walls. This depends on Ezekiel's vision, in which the "man" (angel) who shows him the vision of Jerusalem has a measuring rod with which to measure it (Ezek 40:3). Revelation's city is in the shape of a cube, its length, width, and height being the same (Rev 21:16). This shape represents perfection. The innermost part of the historical Jerusalem temple – the Holy of Holies – had the shape of a perfect cube. The square shape that appears in Revelation also appears throughout Ezekiel's description of the ideal restored Jerusalem (40:47; 41:21; 43:16, 17; 45:2; 48:20), as it does in the idealized picture of the temple in the *Temple Scroll* from the Dead Sea Scrolls. Charles notes that the Greek historian Herodotus describes ancient Babylon as a square, each side of which was 120 stadia, and he cites passages from Plato and Aristotle implying that a square is a shape of perfection (1920, 2:163).

The measurements of the ideal Jerusalem are exaggerated in Ezekiel's vision, but they are far more so in John's vision (cf. *Sib. Or.* 5:423–24). The city is twelve thousand stadia to a side. A stadium was a unit of measure equivalent to about 607 feet, so the city is close to fifteen hundred miles to a side. This is indeed a cosmic city, capable of containing the innumerable multitude of the saved and of being God's dwelling. The wall is 144 cubits high, which would be around 75 yards. Although this is a gigantic wall by normal standards, it is small compared to the city as a whole. Various solutions have been proposed to this problem. Some think that the wall, bearing the names of the Israelite tribes and of the apostles, represents those who belong to the people of God before the eschaton. According to this theory, in the end many more will be included in the new Jerusalem, since all nations now come to worship (21:24–26; 22:2). The city would represent the whole of the saved; the wall would represent the more select group who belong to earthly Israel or the church. Another theory interprets the proportionally tiny wall as signifying that the new city does not need the sort of protection required before evil was defeated. In 21:25, the seer says that its gates are never shut. Whatever the solution to this puzzle, the measurements of the city and wall have symbolic dimensions. Not only are they perfect as squares or as a cube; the wall is also twelve times twelve cubits high (perhaps a combination of the twelve tribes and twelve apostles), and the city is twelve times a thousand stadia to a side, which is the number twelve taken to a much higher order of magnitude.

Now the building materials are specified (21:19–21). The wall is jasper, the precious stone especially associated with God (4:3; 21:11). The city itself is gold, the most precious metal, so pure as to be transparent like glass. The twelve foundations of the wall are adorned with twelve precious gems. The word "adorn" here is the same as used to describe the great harlot and the bride (17:4; 21:2). In chapter 17, the great harlot is adorned with jewels, as is the city here. The author of Revelation is not advocating asceticism, even though he disapproves of the luxury and decadence of the Roman empire. It is not gold and jewels that are evil; it is the empire that hoards them and uses them to adorn itself as the outward expression of its claims to mastery over the world and its peoples. Riches ought to belong to God and God's people. The new Jerusalem is a city of immense richness, but it is a pure and proper wealth.

The image of a city adorned with jewels is found also in Second Isaiah (Isaiah 40–55) in a passage that looks forward to the restoration of Jerusalem after the Babylonian exile. God says:

> I am about to set your stones in antimony,
> and lay your foundations with sapphires.
> I will make your pinnacles rubies,
> your gates of jewels,
> and all your wall of precious stones. (Isa 54:11–12)

A similar picture of the restored Jerusalem appears in the book of Tobit:

> The gates of Jerusalem will be built with sapphire and emerald,
> and all your walls with precious stones.
> The towers of Jerusalem will be built with gold,
> and their battlements with pure gold.
> The streets of Jerusalem will be paved
> with ruby and stones of Ophir. (Tob 13:16–17)

The author did not originate the idea of a restored, ideal Jerusalem built of gold and adorned with jewels, but he did combine this idea with the twelve stones fastened to the breastplate of the high priest (Exod 28:17–20). Those stones represent the twelve tribes of Israel. In Rev 21:19–20, they adorn the foundations of the wall of the new Jerusalem. A comparison of lists of such stones from text to text is difficult, since the names are not precise and could refer to different stones for different authors, and the names could shift as the names were translated from one language to another. Charles notes that the twelve stones that appear in Rev 21:19–20 were each associated with a different sign of the zodiac (1920, 2:167–68). The first-century C.E. Jewish writers Philo and Josephus associate the stones on the priest's breastplate with the zodiac. Other ancient cultures had the notion of a heavenly city with twelve gates corresponding to the twelve signs of the zodiac, and with the Milky Way as its main street (Yarbro Collins 1996, 133). According to Charles's coordination of stones and constellations, following the order of gems in Revelation 21 would mean proceeding through the signs of the zodiac in the opposite direction from that taken by the sun. This may signify the same sort of continuity-discontinuity tension that we have observed elsewhere in Revelation. The new creation is like but unlike the old. In Rev 21:21, each gate of the city is a single pearl. Charles cites a rabbinic tradition that says the gates of the eschatological Jerusalem will be single pearls of immense proportions — ten by twenty by thirty cubits (1920, 2:170).

This section of the description closes with the words, "The street of the city is pure gold, transparent as glass" (21:21), the same substance from which the city as a whole is constructed in 21:18. This is the purest of the most precious metal (21:18, 21). Following the image of the heavenly city, the street may correspond to the Milky Way.

The third part of the description of the new Jerusalem (21:22–27) deals with God's presence in the city and who is privileged to be there, which picks up on 21:3–4 (cf. 22:3–5). Verses 22 and 23 consist of two assertions, each of which is composed of a negative statement grounded in a positive one:

21:22: I saw no temple in the city, for its temple is the Lord God the Almighty and the Lamb.

21:23: And the city has no need of sun or moon to shine on it, for the glory of God is its light, and its lamp is the Lamb.

It is remarkable that the city has no temple, especially in view of the fact that the author's Jewish models feature a restored temple. Ezekiel spends more time on the temple than on the city. The temple is sign and instrument of God's presence within Israel. The importance of the cult of the Jerusalem temple is demonstrated by its centrality not just in priestly texts but also in the worldview of important postbiblical groups such as the Pharisees and later the Rabbis, as well as its symbolic value in the New Testament, particularly in Hebrews and in Revelation itself. Revelation was written after the temple was destroyed in 70 C.E. Our author expects no restoration of that temple, contrary to Jewish thought as evidenced in many other sources (see Charles 1920, 2:171).

The author's rejection of the idea of a third temple is the more remarkable in that not only does he use general cultic imagery throughout the book, but he also mentions the temple itself in several places. Two of the most striking of these references are when he speaks of a temple in heaven in which the glorified faithful enjoy the presence of God (7:15) and of the opening of the heavenly temple at the blowing of the seventh trumpet, revealing the ark of the covenant (11:19). Apparently, when God is in heaven he has a temple there, but when the heavenly Jerusalem descends to earth at the consummation it contains no temple. The next section of the description (22:1–5) discloses the reason for the temple's absence. Although the temple represents God's *presence* with the people, it simultaneously symbolizes God's *separation* from the people. The temple is part of a symbolic system that divides the world into the sacred and the profane, clean and unclean (see Douglas 1966; Murphy 1991, 71–91; K. C. Hanson 1993). The temple is a space which makes possible interaction and interchange between the two realms, by means of a special class of persons who can go from one realm to the other (priests) and who can then act as mediators between the two realms. For Revelation, the faithful have all been made priests through Christ's redeeming death. At the final consummation, the ability of the faithful to enter into the presence of God is expressed in a definitive way. Nothing separates them from God, not even the temple structure and ceremony. As is stated in the next part of the description, they "worship him," and "they will see his face" (22:3–4).

For John, the temple is unnecessary not only because God is in the city but also because the Lamb is there (21:22). Jesus says in 3:21 that he sits on his Father's throne. In chapter 7, the glorified multitude stand before "the throne and before the Lamb" worshiping (7:9), and the Lamb is "at the center of the throne" (7:17). God is still central and supreme in Revelation, but he shares his sovereignty with Christ. Christ is the ultimate agent through whom God exercises sovereignty in the world. Even after Christ accomplishes his mission of conquering Satan through his own death, through his continued witness within the church, and through the eschatological events in which he has a major role, he continues to share God's sovereignty. This contrasts with Paul's view in 1 Corinthians 15, where after Christ conquers all his enemies as Lord of the universe, he then hands over the kingdom to the Father so that the Father is supreme over all. At the end of Revelation, God and Christ are co-regents. But, as we shall see, this does not detract from the book's theocentrism.

The second statement containing a negative declaration followed by its reason is in verse 23: "The city has no need of sun or moon to shine on it, for the glory of God is its light, and its lamp is the Lamb." God is the source of all as the creator. It is God who created sun and moon. The presence of the ultimate source of light makes the created sources of light redundant. The restoration of the people in the land of Israel is spoken of in the same terms in Second Isaiah:

> The sun shall no longer be
> your light by day,
> nor for brightness shall the moon
> give its light to you by night;
> but the LORD will be your everlasting light,
> and your God will be your glory.
> Your sun shall no more go down,
> or your moon withdraw itself;
> for the LORD will be your everlasting light,
> and your days of mourning shall be ended.
> (Isa 60:19–20; cf. 24:23)

In the fourth part of the description of the new Jerusalem (22:1–5), the image of God replacing sun and moon recurs (21:5; cf. 21:24–26). In Rev 21:23, the city needs neither sun nor moon not only because God is its light but also because the Lamb is its lamp. It is unclear whether "light" and "lamp" are meant to claim implicitly that God is superior to the Lamb. It is more likely that the parallelism here is complete. Just as God and the Lamb together replace the temple, so they together replace the sun and moon.

God's glory as the source of light in the new Jerusalem affects not just the church but all humanity. "The nations will walk by its light, and the kings of the earth will bring their glory into it. Its gates will never be shut by day—and there will be no night there. People will bring into it the glory and honor of the nations" (21:24–26). Since sun and moon have been replaced by God and the Lamb in Jerusalem, the nations have no choice but to walk by Jerusalem's light. This fulfills the prediction in the "song of Moses" in Rev 15:3–4: "All nations will come and worship before you." The question of where these nations come from, if all of God's enemies have been destroyed in chapters 19 and 20, is overly literal. In chapters 19 and 20, the point was to express the absoluteness of God's victory. Here in chapter 21 the point is to show the universal recognition of God's sovereignty. That the nations will come to the new Jerusalem and acknowledge its status as God's dwelling place is a common feature of biblical and postbiblical visions of Jerusalem's eschatological restoration. Charles supplies a list of texts which speak of the nations' conversion (1920, 172). Again, Isaiah provides excellent examples. The prophet says to Jerusalem:

> For darkness shall cover the earth,
> and thick darkness the peoples;
> but the LORD will arise upon you,
> and his glory will appear over you.
> Nations will come to your light,
> and kings to the brightness of your dawn....
> Your gates shall always be open;
> day and night they shall not be shut,
> so that nations shall bring you their wealth,
> with their kings led in procession.
> (Isa 60:2–3, 11; cf. 66:12, 18–23)

This passage is the model for Rev 21:24–26. Both passages contain the elements of God as Israel's light, Jerusalem as the light even of the nations, the coming of the nations and their kings to Jerusalem's light, the gates of Jerusalem always open, and the nations bringing their glory and honor. The picture of the nations and their kings being led into the blissful light of God in Jerusalem contrasts with the grim sight of Satan, the beast, and the false prophet leading the nations and kings into a suicidal battle with the Lamb in chapter 19.

The gates of a city would normally be closed and guarded at night and at times of danger. Since there is no threat to the eschatological Jerusalem, there is no need to shut the gates (21:25). The very nations that previously surrounded the "beloved city" to attack it (20:7–9) now stream in at the gates to bring homage (glory and honor) to Jerusalem (21:24). This contrasts with the views of the beast in chapter 13 and the great harlot Babylon in chapters 17 and 18, for the beast and the harlot drain off the wealth of the nations for Babylon's own indulgence. In Rev 21:24–26, nations bring not wealth, of which God in his incomparably rich city has no need, but rather homage to God. In return they can enter into Jerusalem and walk in God's eternal day (21:25).

The book of Tobit offers a similar collocation of images in its last two chapters. We quoted Tob 13:16–17 above for its depiction of the eschatological Jerusalem as built of gold and adorned with jewels. In the same chapter, speaking to the restored Jerusalem, Tobit says,

> A bright light will shine to all the ends of the earth;
> many nations will come to you from far away,
> the inhabitants of the remotest parts of the earth to your holy name,
> bearing gifts in their hands for the King of heaven.
> (Tobit 13:11; cf. 14:5–6; Zech 14:14)

The nations will stream into Jerusalem, but at the same time nothing "unclean" shall enter it (Rev 21:27). The classification of things, places, and persons as clean and unclean creates a symbolic system in which everything has its place and which distinguishes clearly between sacred and profane, between what belongs in a special way to God and what is part of the rest of the universe, and between what is pleasing to God and what is hateful to him (see Douglas 1966; Murphy 1991, 71–91; K. C. Hanson 1993). The general characterization of what is unclean as "abomination" and "falsehood" here conforms to Revelation's general use of these terms. Together they characterize Satan, the beast, and the false prophet. Their fraudulent claims to loyalty and worship, and the deception with which they obtain those from humanity, constitute the core of the rebellion against God that is Revelation's main subject. The author divides humanity into those who practice such abomination and falsehood, namely, all who do not recognize God's sway, and those who are written in the book of life (21:27). Charles cannot conceive how there would be "unclean" people outside the walls of Jerusalem once the final consummation has taken place and God dwells on earth. He thus assigns this verse and others like it to the description of the millennial kingdom preceding the portrayal of the descent of the heavenly Jerusalem. But the seer does not exactly claim that there *are* such sinners present at the end. He simply claims that of all the nations (non-Jews) streaming into Jerusalem at the end, there is no one who is still rebellious against God or engaging in uncleanness.

Revelation claims that *nothing* unclean will enter the new Jerusalem. This absolute cleanness of the entire city appears in other scenarios of the eschatological city. The influential treatment of the eschatological Jerusalem contained in Zechariah 14 says that the whole city, even down to the bells on the horses and all the cooking pots in the city, will be clean at the consummation (14:20–21). Isaiah 52:1, personifying Jerusalem as a woman, says,

> Awake, awake,
>   put on your strength, O Zion!
> Put on your beautiful garments,
>   O Jerusalem, the holy city;
> for the uncircumcised and the unclean
>   shall enter you no more.

The reference to Jerusalem's garments here and their contrast with uncleanness recall the bride of Rev 19:7–8. The difference between Isaiah's scene and that of Revelation is that the nations stream into Jerusalem in Revelation, whereas they are excluded in Isa 52:1.

The final section of the description of the new Jerusalem is in 22:1–5. This section concentrates on the benefits to the nations and to the faithful Christians in the new Jerusalem. The section begins with a scene of marvelous fertility whose origin is the throne of God and the Lamb. The angel shows the seer "the river of the water of life, bright as crystal," flowing from the throne (22:1). This idyllic scene is in marked contrast with the scene of judgment in 14:19–20, where blood flows deeply from the wine press of God's wrath outside the city. In Rev 22:2, the tree of life is located "on either side" (i.e., on both sides) of the river (or perhaps between the river and the street, depending on the translation). The tree bears twelve kinds of fruit, producing fruit each month (either one fruit a month or all twelve fruits continuously). The leaves of the tree "are for the healing of the nations" (22:2). The water here corresponds to the water of God's promise in 21:6.

A close parallel to Revelation 22 is found in the author's main model for the Jerusalem appendix, Ezekiel. Ezekiel 47 presents a scene in which water flows from the temple to the east, the direction the temple faces (see Zech 14:8). An angel with a measuring rod leads the prophet along the water, measuring it as they go. The farther they go, the deeper the water gets, until it was "a river that could not be crossed" (47:6). The angel and prophet return to the temple, and as they go along the river bank the prophet sees "a great many trees on the one side and on the other" (47:7). The angel explains the life-giving properties of the river, concluding with the following words: "On the banks, on both sides of the river, there will grow all kinds of trees for food. Their leaves will not wither nor their fruit fail, but they will bear fresh fruit every month, because the water for them flows out of the sanctuary. Their fruit will be for food, and their leaves for healing" (47:12).

Both Revelation and Ezekiel present pictures of a Jerusalem inhabited by God, who is the source of fertility for the world. Both use the image of water flowing from Jerusalem and trees growing by that water, giving forth fruit for nourishment and leaves for healing. The texts differ in several respects. Whereas Ezekiel focuses on the temple as the source of fertility, for Revelation there is no temple in the city. Rather, the water flows directly from the throne of God and the Lamb. The author's high christology is expressed in the Lamb sharing God's throne. The idea that the messiah sits on God's throne is present in other Jewish and Christian texts, but God and the messiah never sit on the throne together (*1 Enoch* 45:3; 51:3; 55:4; 61:8; 62:2–3, 5; 72:2; cf. Matt 25:31; see Charles 1920, 2:175–76).

Another important change the author makes in his model is that while Ezekiel has many trees growing beside the river, Revelation has but one, the tree of life. Other Jewish texts attest to the idea that the tree of life from the Garden of Eden (Gen 2:9; 3:22) will be available to the saved at the end (4 Ezra 8:52; *1 Enoch* 24:4; 25:4–6; *2 Enoch* 8:3–4; *T. Dan.* 5:12). In the Genesis story of the garden, God forbade Adam and Eve to eat of the tree of knowledge of good and evil. When they did so in spite of the divine command, God feared that they would then eat of the tree of life and so live forever (3:22). To prevent this, God ejected them from the garden. In the endtime, when there is no more sin and all hint of rebellion against God has been banished, it is appropriate that the faithful eat of the tree of life and so share forever in the bliss of God's presence. Our author combines this idea with Ezekiel's marvelous picture of the new Jerusalem as the source of fertility. A final change made by our author to Ezekiel's picture is that the leaves of healing from Ezek 17:12 are now for the nations. This would have been impossible for Ezekiel, who thought that after the exile Israel could only survive through renewed efforts at separating itself from the profane world and from foreigners in particular. For our author the population of the new Jerusalem will be made up of every ethnic and national identity. The availability of the tree of life to the righteous fulfills the promise to the conqueror in 2:7: "To everyone who conquers, I will give permission to eat from the tree of life that is in the paradise of God."

The author next says, "Nothing accursed will be found there any more" (22:3). This may have something to do with the nations, for earlier when their presence in Jerusalem is mentioned in 21:26 the author immediately states, "Nothing unclean shall enter it" (21:27), so the presence of the nations does not defile the city. But given the references to the tree of life, it is more likely that this indicates the lifting of the curses God utters in Genesis 3 in response to the sin of Adam and Eve, who surrendered to the serpent's deceptive temptations.

The final words of the Jerusalem appendix concentrate on the relationship between God and God's people in the new Jerusalem. The author repeats that the throne of God and the Lamb is in Jerusalem and adds, "And his servants will worship him" (22:3). The singular "him" does not exclude the Lamb from the servants' worship, but it again reminds us that despite its high christology Revelation remains theocentric. God's servants "will see his face, and his name will be on their foreheads" (22:4). The assertion that God's servants will see his face is striking, particularly for a book that jealously guards God's transcendence. Most often in Revelation God is referred to simply as the one who sits on the throne. The reservation in describing God contrasts with the substantial descriptions of the one like a son of man in Revelation 1 and the Lamb in Revelation 5. Christ, as God's agent, is more accessible than God. But now the righteous see God face-to-face. The reservation in describing God earlier in the book makes this even more powerful.

In Israelite and Jewish tradition, seeing God is dangerous for humans, and it is sometimes said that one cannot see God and live, although the traditions are not completely consistent on this. In Exod 33:18, Moses asks to see God's glory. God replies, "You cannot see my face, for no one shall see me and live" (33:20). God then allows Moses to see his back but not his face (33:23). The people of Israel are frightened when they witness the theophanic phenomena that accompany God's presence on Sinai, and they say to Moses, "You speak to us, and we will listen; but do not let God speak to us, or we will die" (Exod 20:19).

There are in fact other traditions not entirely compatible with these. For example, the end of Deuteronomy says, "Never since has there arisen a prophet in Israel like Moses, whom the Lord knew face to face" (Deut 34:10). Nonetheless, the statement in Rev 22:4 should be read against the background of the more conservative tradition, especially given Revelation's reluctance to describe God and the efforts to guard his transcendence. At the consummation, God's faithful will receive the ultimate reward: the sight of God. Fourth Ezra is similar, for the greatest reward the righteous receive after death in 4 Ezra is that they behold God's face (4 Ezra 7:98; cf. Matt 5:8; 1 Cor 13:12; 1 John 3:2).

There are now no barriers between God's servants and their God. Their reaction is worship. This one statement contains the goal of the book, acknowledgment of God's sovereignty. If humanity as a whole had worshiped God, the battles and suffering in Revelation need not have taken place. But the inhabitants of the earth did not heed the warning of the angel in midheaven: "Fear God and give him glory, for the hour of his judgment has come; and worship him who made heaven and earth, the sea and the springs of water" (14:7). The closeness of the servants to God in chapter 22 reminds us of their priestly nature, for in Israel it is the priests who are privileged to come close to God. The faithful have God's name on their foreheads, as does the high priest who enters the Holy of Holies. They choose to have God's name rather than the beast's on their heads (see 3:12; 7:3; 13:16; 14:1). They worship God and not Caesar.

The promise from chapter 21 that God will be the light of the new Jerusalem replacing the sun and moon (21:23) is now repeated with specific application to God's servants. Like the city itself, they now exist in unending light in which the darkness of night has no place. God is their light, "and they will reign forever and ever" (22:5). These words conclude the vision that began with 4:1, for everything that follows 22:5 has the character of an epilogue and forms an *inclusio* (frame structure) with elements in chapter 1. The promise of an eternal reign for the righteous picks up on the characterization of Jesus as the one "who made us to be a kingdom" in 1:6, and so it is one of the many points of contact between chapter 1 and the end of the book. These words also signal the fulfillment of Jesus' promise in 3:21 that the one who conquers will rule with him. Those who share God's sovereignty now truly reign on earth, in appearance as well as in reality. The cosmos itself attests to the new state of affairs, for there is unending day. The theocentrism of this last section of the description of the new Jerusalem is evident in that while the faithful stand before a throne on which sit both God and the Lamb, the rest of the closing verses deal only with God. Although in 21:23 both God and the Lamb are the source of light, 22:5 says, "The Lord God will be their light." This is not to deny Revelation's high christology or the role Christ plays in the book. Rather it shows that although our author goes beyond Paul in the status he attributes to Jesus, he essentially agrees with Paul, "So that God may be all in all" (1 Cor 15:28).

Mounce points out the importance of Revelation's having the final consummation take place on earth (1977, 368). An alternative would be to have the righteous go to heaven. By picturing a renewed earth on which everyone enters the fabulously rich new Jerusalem and partakes of the tree of life which was originally in the Garden of Eden, the author affirms this life and its goodness. The author does not seek to escape the earth or the body. God originally intended for humans to live, body and soul, on an earth that supplied their needs, and on which God himself walked and associated with humans. Now that goal is achieved. In a sense the end is like the beginning. This is common in apocalyptic works. God created the world good, but it was corrupted by sin (sometimes human sin as in Genesis, and sometimes angelic sin as in *1 Enoch*). At the end, things will be as God intended at the beginning. But this does not entirely negate human history. The consummation does not mean returning to the Garden of Eden, although it contains features of the garden before sin (e.g., the tree of life, the absence of a curse). Rather it means a new Jerusalem to which the nations stream and in which they worship God along with God's servants.

At the end of the new Jerusalem appendix there is a passage that contains all of the elements found in a similar passage at the end of the Babylon appendix (19:9–10; 22:6–9). An angel declares the words to be true; there is a beatitude; the seer tries to worship the angel; and the angel rebukes the seer (see the commentary on 19:9–10). This can be taken as the conclusion of the appendix as in chapter 19, but its scope is broadened, so that it also serves as one of the several sections through which Revelation as a whole comes to a close. Since it cannot be treated only as the conclusion of the appendix but must be taken as part of the closing of Revelation, we treat it as part of the next section under the heading "Epilogue."

Chapter Thirteen

Epilogue (22:6–21)

Prophetic Sayings (22:6–20a)

Throughout the epilogue there is some question of who speaks. When the voice says, "I am coming soon" (22:7, 12, 20), it is Jesus who speaks; in 22:13, Jesus identifies himself with titles elsewhere applied to God; in 22:16, Jesus explicitly identifies himself. So it is clear that the main speaker in the epilogue is Jesus. But in 22:9, the speaker must be the angel, who forbids John to worship him. At the end of 22:20, there is a prayer that Jesus come, spoken perhaps by the entire church. Verse 21, the last in the book, is a final epistolary blessing, corresponding to the letter form at the beginning of the book (1:4–6). But aside from the angel's words in 22:9, the brief prayer at the end of 22:20, and the epistolary ending in 22:21, the rest of the words can be read as coming directly from Jesus. This balances the section at the beginning of the book where Jesus speaks at length to the churches (chapters 2–3), as well as the portions of the vision of the one like a son of man where Jesus speaks to John (1:11, 17–20). Jesus' words thus form yet another frame for the book. It is particularly suitable that Jesus speaks so much in the epilogue, one of whose major functions is to legitimate Revelation, for the book is, after all, the "revelation of Jesus Christ" (1:1).

These verses can seem like a loose collection of sayings with minimal connection to one another, but together they form an appropriate ending to the book and have a logic in their arrangement. The first section (22:6–9) is both the end of the new Jerusalem appendix and the beginning of the epilogue. It parallels the ending of the Babylon appendix (19:9–10). Although the order is slightly different between the two endings, both passages contain an attestation of the prophetic words, a beatitude, and a brief narrative where the seer attempts to fall down to worship the angel but is rebuked by the angel, who tells him to worship God.

At the end of the book of Daniel, Daniel is told to seal up his revelation because the time for its fulfillment is far off. In contrast, John is told *not* to seal his revelation, "for the time is near" (22:10). Given the nearness of the endtime, the author seems to have little hope for conversion of sinners. Sinners and the righteous will simply continue in their respective ways until the end comes (22:11). Having mentioned the nearness of the end, the author now inserts an oracle of Jesus, who identifies himself and says that he is coming soon to judge (22:12–13). This is followed by a blessing for the righteous and a warning for sinners (22:14–15). To bolster the authority of Revelation, whose purpose is to prepare the faithful to endure until the end, which is imminent, Jesus attests to the book (22:16). Since the one who is about to come has been mentioned again, there are now two prayers that Christ come, followed by an invitation to all to come themselves to benefit from Christ's coming. There follows a warning not to alter Revelation in any way (22:18–19). There is then yet another oracle by Jesus saying that he, the one who has testified to the truth of the book, is coming soon (22:20). The response is "Amen" and a prayer that Jesus come, perhaps meant to be uttered by the hearers of Revelation in the seven churches where the message is read (22:20). The book closes with an epistolary blessing (22:21) corresponding to the epistolary opening of 1:4–6.

Read in this way, the seemingly loosely connected final verses of Revelation have a certain logic in their flow. Themes which tie the entire passage together are that of the imminent coming of Jesus (22:7, 10, 12, 17, 20), the reliability and sacred nature of the book's revelation (22:6, 16, 18–19, 20), and reward for those who hold fast to the revelation and punishment for others (22:7, 11, 12, 14–15). The epilogue has several elements that refer back to the opening of Revelation, thus forming an *inclusio* for the entire book. We will note those elements as we proceed. The formal element tying the end of the book to its beginning is the epistolary ending (22:21).

The end of the new Jerusalem appendix is also the opening of the epilogue (22:6–9). Because it performs both functions, it is broader in scope that the ending of the Babylon appendix, to which it is parallel (19:9–10; 22:6–9). Both begin with an attestation to the truth of "these words" and with a beatitude

(19:9; 22:6–7). In 19:9, the beatitude comes first, while in 22:6 the attestation precedes. Whereas in 19:9 the speaker is the angel who showed John the vision of Babylon's fall, in 22:6–7 the speaker seems to be Christ himself. This follows from the fact that in 22:6 the angel is spoken of in the third person, and in 22:7 Christ speaks without further introduction, saying, "I am coming soon!"

Revelation 22:6–7 is in three parts: an attestation of the truth of the words that precede, in this case meaning the entire book of Revelation; an oracle of Christ, indicating that he is coming soon; and a beatitude pronounced on the one "who keeps the words of the prophecy of this book." Aune (1983b, 332–33) notes that at the end of prophetic revelations there are often legitimation formulas, which confirm the truth of the revelation "by identifying the divine speaker, by appealing to the inspired state in which the oracle was uttered, or by utilizing conditional threats and curses." Biblical prophetic oracles often end with the words "an oracle of the Lord," or some such phrase (see 1 Cor 14:37; Rev 22:18–20 [see below]; see Aune for other examples). Aune sees Rev 22:6–7 as such a legitimation formula. Christ is the speaker, and he declares the truth of the revelation. The beatitude shows the positive results of holding fast to the revelation and implies negative consequences for the one who does not accept it. In fact the whole of the epilogue serves a legitimizing function for Revelation. The seemingly disjunctive nature of the epilogue has a cumulative effect on the audience. It is as if one salvo after another is fired, each of which is aimed at the same target. That "target" is any possible doubt that Revelation is the ultimate and final communication to humanity about God's intent and plans.

When the angel in chapter 19 attests to the truth of Revelation's words, he does so as follows: "These are true words of God" (19:9). The attestation in 22:6 is far fuller: "These words are trustworthy and true, for the Lord, the God of the spirits of the prophets, has sent his angel *to show his servants what must soon take place.*" There is a clear allusion to the beginning of Revelation, where it is said that the revelation contained in the book came from God to Christ, who sent his angel "*to show his servants what must soon take place,*" the angel being sent via Christ's servant John, who then "testified to the word of God and to the testimony of Jesus Christ" (1:1–2). The words we have italicized in the two passages are precisely the same in Greek.

In 22:6, God sends the angel, whereas in 1:1, Christ sends the angel. This is not a contradiction, in view of the blurred lines between the functions of the Father and Jesus. Where in 19:9 the words are pronounced "true," in 22:6 the fuller phrase "trustworthy [literally, "faithful"; Greek: *pistos*] and true" appears. In 3:14 and 19:11, these same two adjectives are applied to Christ, and Christ is the only person to whom both adjectives are applied in the book. It is fitting that the faithful and true Christ declares the words of Revelation faithful and true. In 21:5, God himself declares, "These words are trustworthy and true." The parallel declarations of God and Christ lend to Revelation a legitimacy that is absolute. The identification of God in 22:6 as "the God of the spirits of the prophets" emphasizes the author's consciousness of being in the line of the prophets. He makes no distinction between biblical prophets and Christian prophets. The phrase "the spirits of the prophets" denotes not a multifaceted divine Spirit, but rather the individual spirits of prophets, as in 1 Cor 14:32.

Christ's oracle proclaiming his imminent coming (22:7) introduces a theme repeated in 22:10, 12, 20. The occurrence of this theme four times in sixteen verses demonstrates its centrality to Revelation's conclusion. The seer's visions do not apply to some time in the distant future. Christ is to come soon. This conforms to the characterization of the book's contents as "what must soon take place," which appears at the beginning (1:1) and the end (22:6) of Revelation, thus framing the book. Christ's second coming is central to the eschatological events depicted throughout Revelation.

The beatitude in 22:7 is also broad. In the corresponding beatitude at the end of the Babylon appendix, the one invited to the marriage feast of the Lamb is pronounced blessed (19:9). That beatitude is context-specific, since in the immediately preceding verses a voice announces the marriage of the Lamb (19:7). In 22:7, the beatitude is pronounced upon "the one who keeps the words of the prophecy of this book." These words point to the self-conscious nature of Revelation as a complete and self-contained written prophecy. It is reminiscent of the book of Deuteronomy, where Moses repeatedly makes reference to "this book," meaning Deuteronomy itself, as the supreme depository of divine law (see Deut 28:58, 61; 29:20–21, 27; 30:10; 31:24, 26). The unalterable nature of both books also makes them similar (see below on Rev 22:18–19). The necessity of abiding by the book of Revelation appears in 22:7, 9, 10, 18–19, and is supported by Christ's confirmation of "this testimony" (22:16) and by his testifying to "these things" (22:20).

The beatitude alludes to the book's very first beatitude: "Blessed is the one who reads aloud the words of the prophecy, and blessed are those who hear and who keep what is written in it; for the time is near" (1:3). Although the word "book" is not used in 1:3, Revelation's contents are called "prophecy." The prophecy is "written," and it refers to imminent events. Those who read and hear the book must "keep what is written in it." The essence of the beatitudes in 1:3 and 22:7 is the same, and so they also serve to frame Revelation and provide a context within which to read it. They make the reading and "keeping" of Revelation a matter of ultimate importance.

The next section of the epilogue (22:8–9) also echoes the end of the Babylon appendix (19:10). In both passages the seer falls down to worship the interpreting angel, but the angel rebukes him and tells him to worship God. The scene in chapter 22 differs from the earlier one in that John adds, "I, John, am the one who heard and saw these things. And when I heard them and saw them, I fell down to worship" (22:8). John transforms the simple "then" of 19:10 into another legitimation formula.

The scenes where the seer tries to worship the angel underline God's absolute sovereignty. In 19:10, the angel declares himself a "fellow servant with you and your comrades who hold the testimony of Jesus." In 22:9, the angel declares himself on the same level with "you and your comrades the prophets, and with those who keep the words of this book." Holding the testimony of Jesus and keeping the words of the book of Revelation are equivalent. Later in the epilogue it is asserted that Jesus himself sent his angel with "this testimony for the churches" (22:16) and that Jesus "testifies to these things" (22:20). The angel singles out prophets in 22:16, which is fitting in an epilogue that confirms Revelation's status as prophecy. The same emphasis accounts for the change from "testimony of Jesus" in 19:10 to "the words of this book" in 22:9.

The next section of the epilogue alludes to the book of Daniel. Most scholars think that Daniel was written around 165 B.C.E., but the fictional setting of the book is hundreds of years earlier. The device of attributing one's work to a hero who lived much earlier is common in apocalypses. The question would naturally arise for the readers of Daniel in the second century B.C.E. why a book of such import had remained unknown for centuries. The solution is found at the end of the book, where the revealing angel instructs Daniel, "Keep the words secret and the book sealed until the time of the end" (12:4; cf. 12:9; Charles 1920, 2:221, points also to *1 Enoch* 1:2; 93:10; 104:12; *2 Enoch* 33:9–11; 35:3). Since the real author of Daniel lived at "the time of the end," the contents of the book were no longer sealed in his time. Our author did not use the device of pseudonymity. Widespread prophecy and eschatological fervor were common features of early Christianity. In that context, there would be a greater openness to a contemporary seer who claimed to possess knowledge about an imminent eschaton. But in the cases of both Daniel and Revelation, the knowledge in the book is really meant to be available to all contemporaries who are willing to hear it.

The fact that the angel tells Daniel to seal the prophecy allows our author to stress the nearness of the eschaton by deliberate contrast with Daniel: "Do not seal up the words of the prophecy of this book, for the time is near" (22:10). Since the time is short, the author holds out little hope that sinners will repent. The evil will continue in their ways, as will the righteous (22:11): "Let the evildoer still do evil, and the filthy still be filthy, and the righteous still do right, and the holy still be holy." This verse may be the author's interpretation of Dan 12:4, which says, "Many shall be running back and forth, and evil shall increase." In other words, the coming judgment does not deter evildoing. It goes on as usual until the end.

The next section consists of a prophetic/apocalyptic pronouncement by Jesus that he is coming soon (22:12) and a self-identification of Jesus (22:13). Jesus' statement that he is coming soon is followed by the reason for his coming. He says, "My reward is with me, to repay according to everyone's work" (22:12). This echoes Isaiah, who anticipates the coming of God to conquer and judge his enemies: "His reward is with him and his recompense before him" (Isa 40:10; cf. Wisd 5:15). Mention of judgment follows appropriately after Rev 22:10–11, which predicts an imminent end and says that evildoers and righteous will continue to act as they have. Ultimately Revelation is concerned with what one does (see chapters 2–3; 20:13–14). The coming of Jesus will mean the separation of humanity into two parts, either for reward or punishment, based on human deeds.

Jesus now identifies himself, using titles previously applied to

God (22:13). He says that he is the Alpha and Omega, a phrase applied to God in 1:8 and 21:6. In 21:6, that title is defined as meaning "the beginning and the end," as it is also by Christ here in 22:13. Jesus has already called himself "the first and the last" in 1:17 and 2:8, as he does here. Revelation's high christology is stressed in these final chapters, where Jesus shares the throne of God (22:1, 3) and the divine titles (22:13). God himself judges in 20:11–15, while here (22:12) Jesus comes to repay each according to his or her deeds. Again the line between the functions of the Father and the Son are blurred.

The next two verses follow naturally on the theme of judgment. The first is the seventh and final beatitude of Revelation, pronounced on the righteous (22:14). The second states that sinners will be excluded from reward (22:15). The verses are probably spoken by Jesus, who is clearly the speaker in the sections preceding (22:12–13) and following (22:16) them. The beatitude promises those "who wash their robes" that "they will have the right to the tree of life and may enter the city by the gates." This picks up on the picture of the new Jerusalem (21:12–13, 21, 25; 22:2). Membership in the city where God dwells with humans is restricted to those who "wash their robes" (see 7:14). Everyone else is "outside" (22:15). Charles (1920, 2:148–49) thinks it strange that at the time of final consummation, when all evildoers are supposedly in the lake of fire or have been converted, there are such sinners "outside" the new Jerusalem. He therefore assigns this to the earlier period of the millennial kingdom. But this is to try to fit Revelation's images into too tight a scheme. The author's point here is the same as in 21:27. Sinners are excluded from God's presence in the end. Nothing unclean enters God's city.

The list of sinners in 22:15 corresponds largely to those whom God consigns to the lake of fire in 21:8. They are now contemptuously called "dogs." The list of sinners concludes with "everyone who loves and practices falsehood." Adherents of the beast are deceived, and imperial officials perpetuate the deception (chapter 13).

Verse 16 is yet another legitimation formula: "It is I, Jesus, who sent my angel to you [plural] with this testimony for the churches. I am the root and the descendant of David, the bright morning star." "This testimony" refers to the entire revelation contained in the book. Jesus' words echo the opening words of the book, where the "revelation of Jesus Christ," given to Jesus by God, is made known by Jesus, who sends his angel to John, who bears testimony to everything that he sees. What he sees is the "testimony of Jesus" that is identical to the "word of God" (1:2). The revelation must be shared with all of God's servants, as chapters 1 to 3 make clear, so the plural "you" in 22:16 makes sense. Jesus again applies titles to himself, once again stressing his status and ability to convey the will and plans of God. He is the Davidic messiah (see 3:7; 5:5). The term "root" of David alludes to Isa 11:1, a messianic passage. Jesus also calls himself the "bright morning star." In the message to the church at Thyatira he promises the morning star to the conqueror (2:28). The morning star is Venus, symbol of victory. As we noted in our commentary on 2:28, the juxtaposition of the word "star" with other messianic references brings to mind Num 24:17, a passage taken messianically in both Jewish and Christian sources of this period: "A star shall arise out of Jacob, and a scepter shall arise out of Israel." Revelation 22:16 makes the Davidic associations of the star explicit.

The precise meaning of the beginning of Rev 22:17 is unclear. The imperative "come" is uttered first by the Spirit and the bride and then by "everyone who hears." It is not certain whether the imperative "come" is addressed to Jesus or is an invitation to individual humans to come to Christ. What follows in 22:17 suggests the latter, for it is an invitation to the thirsty to come and "take the water of life as a gift." God himself offers this water to the thirsty in 21:6. Since Christ is the focus of chapter 22, this continues the parallelism between God and Christ we have already seen with respect to judgment (22:12) and titles (22:13). It is possible, however, that the Spirit, bride, and everyone who hears pray to *Christ* to come, since there is such a prayer at the end of 22:20 as well.

The next section warns against tampering with the contents of Revelation (22:18–19). The author claims an authority for his work equal to that of the Bible. In Deuteronomy, Moses says, "You must neither add anything to what I command you nor take away anything from it" (4:2). The same demand for preservation from alteration is made for the Greek translation of the Bible in the *Letter of Aristeas* 311. This attitude toward the sacredness of scripture is forcefully stated by Josephus: "We have given practical proof of our reverence for our own scriptures. For, although such long ages have now passed, no one has ventured either to add, or to remove, or to alter a syllable" (*Ap.* 1 §42).

Revelation's author ties the warning not to alter the book closely to the content of the book by saying that if anyone adds anything to Revelation then the book's plagues will be "added" to that person, and if anyone "takes away" anything from the book then the book's rewards will be "taken away" from that person. The word "book" occurs four times in these two verses, emphasizing Revelation as a sacred entity in its own right, equal to scripture. The word "prophecy" is used twice, placing Revelation firmly in the line of the writing prophets (see Ruiz 1989).

For the last time Jesus declares that he is coming soon (22:20; cf. 22:7, 12). He identifies himself as "the one who testifies to these things," an appropriate designation for the end of the book for which he is the origin and guarantor. Aune (1983b, 332–33) considers two elements — the curses in 22:18–19 and the self-identification of Christ in 20:20 as the one who guarantees the revelation — as constituting another legitimation formula. By the end of the epilogue, the audience has heard Revelation's message confirmed by God (22:6), Jesus (22:7, 16, 20), and John (22:8).

Epistolary Closing: Prayer and Final Greetings (22:20b–21)

Following the curses pronounced on anyone who alters the book, Jesus' identification of himself, and his statement about his imminent coming is the prayer, "Amen. Come, Lord Jesus!" (22:20), and then the final epistolary blessing (22:21). The first letter of Paul to the Corinthians ends in similar fashion. There Paul identifies himself and writes in his own hand to authenticate the letter, pronounces a curse on anyone with no love for the Lord, prays in Aramaic, *Marana tha* (which means, "Our Lord, come!"), and ends with an epistolary blessing: "The grace of the Lord Jesus be with you. My love be with all of you in Christ Jesus" (1 Cor 16:21–24). The author of Revelation models his work on the Pauline letter form. This is the more obvious in view of the contents of the blessing: "The grace of the Lord Jesus be with all the saints. Amen" (22:21). The word "grace" occurs only twice in all of Revelation, both times in the epistolary framework (1:4; 22:21), whereas Paul uses the word frequently, often as part of his epistolary greeting at the beginnings and ends of letters. The author directs his final blessing to "all the saints." "Saints" throughout Revelation designates faithful Christians (5:8, 9; 8:3, 4; 11:18; 13:7, 10; 14:12; 16:6; 17:6; 18:20, 24; 19:8; 20:9).

Revelation is the last book in the Christian Bible. Given Revelation's worldview and the apocalyptic bent of much of early Christianity, it is fitting that it concludes with Jesus' promise that he is coming soon, a prayer for his second coming, and a wish that the grace of the Lord Jesus be with all faithful Christians.

Conclusion

To Change the World

Despite its enigmatic language and images, Revelation was written by a real person facing a concrete historical situation. He lived in the Roman empire, a political and cultural system that many Christians saw as good, but that he saw as satanic. He saw both Christian and non-Christian Jews coming to terms with that system in different ways. For fellow Christians who shared his views, who rejected the culture around them and longed for God's transformative intervention in history, he had a message of hope and encouragement. They would soon be vindicated by the coming of Christ, who would defeat God's enemies and enable God to dwell with humans on earth. For Christians who did not share his views and who sought to coexist peacefully with the Roman empire and its political and religious manifestations in Asia Minor, he offered warnings of God's wrath and commanded them to repent. He saw Jews who did not believe in Jesus, who opposed Christianity, and who were comfortable with their Hellenistic surroundings as allied with the same Satan who stood behind Roman power. For the majority in the seer's world, who submitted to Rome and expressed their loyalty to it, even to the extent of participating in the imperial cult, the author expected condemnation and destruction.

Revelation's author wished to change the world of his audience, to convince them that things were not as they appeared. To all appearances, it was Rome that was powerful, honored, and glorious. Rome ruled the world, and anyone who opposed it condemned themselves to oppression and suffering. But the author was convinced that reality was the opposite. Rome's power derived from Satan, whom the forces of heaven had already defeated. It was Satan's consciousness of his own defeat and impending ruin that motivated him to give his power to Rome and to use Rome as an instrument to harass and persecute faithful Christians. To understand that was to see why Christians, in John's view the only true adherents of the creator and true ruler of the universe, were oppressed in this world. Christian suffering was then seen as part of a larger battle between the forces of God and those of Satan in which God's victory and Satan's defeat were assured.

The warrant that the seer claimed for his way of looking at the world was powerful—he had visited heaven, and he had seen God and his Christ setting the eschatological events in motion. His imparting of this knowledge to Christians was urgent, for their eternal fate depended on it. Their perception of the world must conform to the truth that Christ had revealed to the seer, for the entire universe was about to have the reality of its own everyday world changed radically to conform to God's reality. Only then would appearance and reality coincide. John believed that only Christians who accepted his message saw the earth as it truly was.

The author's aim was not to write predictions of things to happen in the distant future, but rather it was to provide his audience with the key to understanding their own time and to preparing for the imminent coming of Christ. Christians must understand the Roman empire as satanic and themselves as God's priests. They must refuse to engage in accepted expressions of loyalty to Rome, despite the consequences. They must stand ready to die rather than to deny the supreme sovereignty of God and his Christ. This alone would allow them to escape God's wrath that was coming on the whole world. Revelation's viewpoint was not the only possible one for Christians of this time. Paul, 1 Peter, and Acts of the Apostles furnish alternative ways for looking at Rome. The author stood ready to condemn "Jezebel" for her compromises with Roman Asian culture, but the church of Thyatira, whose works the author recognized as "love, faith, service, and patient endurance," saw in her a prophet of God (2:18–29).

Revelation's author was one among many voices in earliest Christianity. Not all Christians agreed on all things then, any more than they do now. Indeed, the book of Revelation did not find acceptance into the canon of the New Testament easy. It was one of the books whose entry into the canon encountered the most resistance. But its presence there is testimony to the apocalyptic beginnings of Christianity and to the struggles the emerging religion faced in finding its place in the world. It reminds us that as Christianity sought to understand its relation to the world in which it lived and by which it was influenced, at the same time it changed that world.

Revelation's author's discourse seems strange to many living near the turn of the twenty-first century. The book raises many questions, not just historical ones, but also ones about how the book should be read by believing Christians in the modern world. Historical and literary study can supply us with an important control for interpretation and can aid us in being self-critical in our own reading. John's world was very different from our own. No amount of background information or historical and theological analysis will make this world entirely familiar, but the more we know about his environment, the more likely we are to understand him and his message accurately. As an inhabitant of the Roman-Hellenistic world, he was touched by its mythologies and images, and he lived with its realities. When he responded to his own specific situation, he did so as a person of his own time.

Although John was willing to label institutions and persons as being in Satan's camp, we ought to resist such condemnation of others. Surely it is problematic to label any human or human institution satanic. Even many Christians of the author's own time did not agree with his judgments. Evil is real and powerful, but when we categorize people and institutions into divine and demonic, we risk mistaking human judgments for God's, something which other New Testament passages firmly warn against (e.g., Matt 7:1–5; 13:24–30, 36–43; Luke 6:37). One can heed the seer's call to render absolute loyalty to God alone without being too anxious to consign those who disagree to the fires of the second death.

It is ironic that the Rome that the seer so vehemently opposed adopted Christianity as its official religion at the beginning of the fourth century. Whether the seer would have seen this as victory is debatable. On the one hand, it is doubtful that he would have recognized it as the new world that he anxiously awaited. On the other hand, it is probably safe to say that those Christians who were more at home in their environment would have preferred this transformation of Rome to the dire scenes that the seer envisioned.

Works Cited

Ashton, John. 1985. "The Identity and Function of the *Ioudaioi* in the Fourth Gospel." *NovT* 27:40–75.

Aune, David E. 1981. "The Social Matrix of the Apocalypse of John." *BR* 26:16–32.

———. 1983a. "The Influence of Roman Imperial Court Ceremonial on the Revelation of John." *BR* 28:5–26.

———. 1983b. *Prophecy in Early Christianity and the Ancient Mediterranean World.* Grand Rapids, Mich.: Eerdmans.

———. 1987. "The Apocalypse of John and Graeco-Roman Revelatory Magic." *NTS* 33:481–501.

———. 1990. "The Form and Function of the Proclamations to the Seven Churches (Revelation 2–3)." *NTS* 36:182–204.

———. 1993. Notes to "The Revelation to John (Apocalypse)." In *HCSB,* 2307–37. New York: HarperCollins.

Barr, David. 1984. "The Apocalypse as a Symbolic Transformation of the World: A Literary Analysis." *Int* 38:39–50.

Batto, Bernard F. 1992. *Slaying the Dragon: Mythmaking in the Biblical Tradition.* Louisville: Westminster/John Knox.

Bauckham, Richard. 1977. "Eschatological Earthquake in the Apocalypse of John." *NovT* 19:216–25.

———. 1993. *The Theology of the Book of Revelation.* New Testament Theology. Cambridge: Cambridge University Press.

Beagley, A. J. 1987. *The Sitz im Leben of the Apocalypse with Particular Reference to the Role of the Church's Enemies.* BZNW 50. New York: de Gruyter.

Beale, G. K. 1992. "The Interpretive Problem of Rev. 1:19." *NovT* 34:360–87.

Bell, A. A. 1979. "The Date of John's Apocalypse: The Evidence of Some Roman Historians Reconsidered." *NTS* 25:93–102.

Berger, Peter, and Thomas Luckman. 1963. *The Social Construction of Reality: A Treatise in the Sociology of Knowledge.* Garden City, N.Y.: Doubleday.

Bloom, Harold. 1988. *The Revelation of St. John the Divine.* New York: Chelsea House.

Boismard, M. E. 1965. "The Apocalypse." In *Introduction to the New Testament,* ed. A. Feuillet and A. Robert, 693–722. New York: Desclée.

Boring, M. Eugene. 1986. "The Theology of Revelation: 'The Lord Our God the Almighty Reigns.'" *Int* 40:257–69.

———. 1989. *Revelation.* Louisville: John Knox.

———. 1992. "Prophecy (Early Christian)." In *ABD* 5:495–502.

Bornkamm, Günther. 1937. "Die Komposition der apokalyptischen Visionen in der Offenbarung Johannis." *ZNW* 36:132–49.

———. 1969. *Early Christian Experience.* New York: Harper and Row.

Brown, Raymond E. 1958a. "The Pre-Christian Semitic Concept of 'Mystery.'" *CBQ* 20:417–43.

———. 1958b. "The Semitic Background of the New Testament *Mysterion.*" *Bib* 39:426–48.

———. 1979. *The Community of the Beloved Disciple: The Life, Loves, and Hates of an Individual Church in New Testament Times.* New York: Paulist.

Caird, George B. 1966. *The Revelation of St. John the Divine.* London: Adam and Charles Black.

Charles, R. H. 1920. *A Critical and Exegetical Commentary on the Revelation of St. John.* 2 vols. Edinburgh: T. and T. Clark.

Charlesworth, James H. 1992. "Paradise." *ABD* 5:4–55.

———, ed. 1983–85. *The Old Testament Pseudepigrapha.* Garden City, N.Y.: Doubleday.

Clifford, Richard J. 1975. "History and Myth in Daniel 10–11." *BASOR* 220:23–26.

Collins, John J. 1974. "Apocalyptic Eschatology as the Transcendence of Death." *CBQ* 36:21–43.

———. 1977. "Pseudonymity, Historical Reviews, and the Genre of the Revelation of John." *CBQ* 39:309–28.

———. 1984. *The Apocalyptic Imagination: An Introduction to the Jewish Matrix of Christianity.* New York: Crossroad.

———. 1993. *Daniel: A Commentary on the Book of Daniel.* Hermeneia. Minneapolis: Fortress.

———. 1995. *The Scepter and the Star.* New York: Doubleday.

———, ed. 1979. *Apocalypse: The Morphology of a Genre.* Vol. 14 of *Semeia.* Missoula, Mont.: Scholars.

Collins, John J., and Michael Fishbane, eds. 1995. *Death, Ecstasy, and Other Worldly Journeys.* Albany: State University of New York Press.

Douglas, Mary. 1966. *Purity and Danger: An Analysis of the Concepts of Pollution and Taboo.* London: Routledge and Kegan Paul.

Downing, F. Gerald. 1988. "Pliny's Persecutions of Christians: Revelation and 1 Peter." *JSNT* 34:105–23.

Dunn, James D. G. 1991. *The Partings of the Ways: Between Christianity and Judaism and Their Significance for the Character of Christianity.* Philadelphia: Trinity Press International.

Eddy, Samuel K. 1961. *The King Is Dead: Studies in the Near Eastern Resistance to Hellenism.* Lincoln: University of Nebraska Press.

Elliott, John. 1981. *A Home for the Homeless: A Sociological Exegesis of 1 Peter, Its Situation and Strategy.* Philadelphia: Fortress.

Farrer, Austin. 1949. *A Rebirth of Images: The Making of St. John's Apocalypse.* Westminster, England: Dacre.

Fekkes, Jan, III. 1994. *Isaiah and Prophetic Traditions in the Book of Revelation.* JSNTSup, 93. Sheffield, England: Sheffield Academic.

Feuillet, A. 1964. *The Apocalypse.* New York: Alba House.

———. 1965. "The Twenty-Four Elders of the Apocalypse." Trans. Thomas E. Crane. In *Johannine Studies,* 183–214. New York: Alba House.

Ford, Josephine Massyngberde. 1975. *Revelation.* AB 38. Garden City, N.Y.: Doubleday.

Fowler, A. 1982. *Kinds of Literature: An Introduction to the Theory of Genres and Modes.* Cambridge, Mass.: Harvard University Press.

Friedman, Richard Elliott. 1992. "Tabernacle." *ABD* 6:292–300.

Gager, John. 1975. *Kingdom and Community: The Social World of Early Christianity.* Englewood Cliffs, N.J.: Prentice-Hall.

Gärtner, Bertil. 1965. *The Temple and the Community in Qumran and the New Testament.* Cambridge: Cambridge University Press.

Giblin, Charles Homer. 1991. *The Book of Revelation: The Open Book of Prophecy.* Collegeville, Minn.: Michael Glazier (Liturgical Press).

———. 1994. "Recapitulation and the Literary Coherence of John's Apocalypse." *CBQ* 56:81–95.

Gruenwald, Ithamar. 1980. *Apocalyptic and Merkavah Mysticism.* Leiden: Brill.

Hanson, K. C. 1993. "Blood and Purity in Leviticus and Revelation." *Listening* 28:215–30.

Hanson, Paul D. 1976. "Apocalypticism." In *IDBSup,* 28–34. Nashville: Abingdon.

Hartman, Lars. 1976. "The Function of Some So-called Apocalyptic Timetables." *NTS* 22:1–14.

Heil, John Paul. 1993. "The Fifth Seal (Rev 6,9–11) As a Key to the Book of Revelation." *Bib* 74:220–43.

Hemer, Colin J. 1986. *The Letters to the Seven Churches of Asia in Their Local Setting.* Sheffield, England: JSOT.

Himmelfarb, Martha. 1983. *Tours of Hell: An Apocalyptic Form in Jewish and Christian Literature.* Philadelphia: Fortress.

———. 1993. *Ascent to Heaven in Jewish and Christian Apocalypses.* New York: Oxford University Press.

Hodgson, R. 1992. "Superstition." *ABD* 6:239–41.

Horsley, Richard A. 1993. *Jesus and the Spiral of Violence: Popular Jewish Resistance in Roman Palestine.* Minneapolis: Fortress.

Horsley, Richard A., and John S. Hanson. 1985. *Bandits, Prophets, and Messiahs: Popular Movements at the Time of Jesus.* New York: Seabury.

Jones, D. L. 1980. "Christianity and the Roman Imperial Cult." In *ANRW* 2.23.2, 1023–54. New York: de Gruyter.

Knibb, Michael. 1976. "The Exile in the Intertestamental Period." *HeyJ* 17:253–72.

Krodel, G. A. 1989. *Revelation.* Minneapolis: Augsburg.

Lambrecht, J., ed. 1980. *L'Apocalypse Johannique et l'Apocalyptique dans le Nouveau Testament.* Louvain: Louvain University Press.

Lawrence, D. H. 1988. "Apocalypse." In *The Revelation of St. John the Divine.* Ed. Harold Bloom. New York: Chelsea House.

Lévi-Strauss, Claude. 1963. "The Structural Study of Myth." In *Structural Anthropology.* New York: Basic Books.

MacMullen, Ramsay. 1966. *Enemies of the Roman Order.* Cambridge, Mass.: Harvard University Press.

Malina, Bruce J. 1995. *On the Genre and Message of Revelation: Star Visions and Sky Journeys.* Peabody, Mass.: Hendrickson.

Martin, Luther H. 1987. *Hellenistic Religions: An Introduction.* New York: Oxford University Press.

Mazzaferri, Frederick David. 1989. *The Genre of the Book of Revelation from a Source-Critical Perspective.* New York: de Gruyter.

McDonald, Patricia M. 1996. "Lion as Slain Lamb: On Reading Revelation Recursively." *Horizons* 23:29–47.

Meade, D. G. 1987. *Pseudonymity and Canon: An Investigation into the Relation of Authorship and Authority in Jewish and Earliest Christian Tradition.* Grand Rapids, Mich.: Eerdmans.

Metzger, Bruce G. 1972. "Literary Forgeries and Canonical Pseudepigrapha." *JBL* 91:3–24.

Michaels, J. Ramsey. 1991. "Revelation 1.19 and the Narrative Voices of the Apocalypse." *NTS* 37:604–20.

Mounce, R. 1977. *The Book of Revelation.* Grand Rapids, Mich.: Eerdmans.

Moyise, Steve. 1995. *The Old Testament in the Book of Revelation.* JSNTSup, 115. Sheffield, England: Sheffield Academic.

Murphy, Frederick J. 1985a. *The Structure and Meaning of Second Baruch.* Atlanta: Scholars Press.

———. 1985b. "*2 Baruch* and the Romans." *JBL* 104:663–69.

———. 1991. *The Religious World of Jesus: An Introduction to Second Temple Palestinian Judaism.* Atlanta: Abingdon.

———. 1994a. "Apocalypses and Apocalypticism: The State of the Question." *Currents in Research: Biblical Studies* 2:147–79.

———. 1994b. "The Book of Revelation." *Currents in Research: Biblical Studies* 2:181–225.

———. 1996. "Introduction to Apocalyptic Literature." *NIB* 7:1–16.

Mussies, G. 1980. "The Greek of the Book of Revelation." In *L'Apocalypse Johannique et l'Apocalyptique dans le Nouveau Testament,* ed. J. Lambrecht, 167–77. Louvain: Louvain University Press.

Nickelsburg, George W. E. 1972. *Resurrection, Immortality, and Eternal Life in Intertestamental Judaism.* Harvard Theological Studies, 26. Cambridge, Mass.: Harvard University Press.

Olson, Daniel C. 1997. " 'Those Who Have Not Defiled Themselves with Women': Revelation 14:4 and the Book of Enoch." *CBQ* 59:492–510.

Overman, J. Andrew. 1990. *Matthew's Gospel and Formative Judaism: The Social World of the Matthean Community.* Minneapolis: Fortress.

———. 1996. *Church and Community in Crisis.* Philadelphia: Trinity Press International.

Paulien, Jon. 1988. *Decoding Revelation's Trumpets: Literary Allusions and Interpretations of Rev 8:7–12.* Berrien Springs, Mich.: Andrews University.

———. 1992. "Armageddon." *ABD* 1:394–95.

Pilch, John. 1993. "Visions in Revelation and Alternate Consciousness: A Perspective from Cultural Anthropology." *Listening* 28:231–44.

Pippin, Tina. 1992a. *Death and Desire: The Rhetoric of Gender in the Apocalypse of John.* Louisville: Westminster/John Knox.

———. 1992b. "Eros and the End: Reading for Gender in the Apocalypse of John." In *Ideological Criticism of Biblical Texts,* ed. Tina Pippin, 193–210. Decatur, Ga.: Scholars Press.

———. 1992c. "The Heroine and the Whore: Fantasy and the Female in the Apocalypse of John." In *Fantasy in the Bible* (vol. 60 of *Semeia*), ed. George Aichele and Tina Pippin, 67–82. Decatur, Ga.: Scholars Press.

Potter, D. S. 1992. "Smyrna." *ABD* 6:73–75.

Price, S. R. F. 1984. *Rituals and Power: The Roman Imperial Cult in Asia Minor.* Cambridge: Cambridge University Press.

Ramsay, William M. 1904. *The Letters to the Seven Churches of Asia and Their Place in the Plan of the Apocalypse.* London: Hodder and Stoughton.

———. 1994. *The Letters to the Seven Churches.* Updated Edition. Ed. Mark W. Wilson. Peabody, Mass.: Hendrickson.

Ricoeur, Paul. 1969. *The Symbolism of Evil.* Boston: Beacon.

Roloff, J. 1993. *The Revelation of John.* Minneapolis: Fortress.

Ruiz, Jean Pierre. 1989. *Ezekiel in the Apocalypse: The Transformation of Prophetic Language in Revelation 16,17–19,10.* Frankfurt am Main: Peter Lang.

Saldarini, Anthony J. 1994. *Matthew's Christian-Jewish Community.* Chicago: University of Chicago Press.

Satake, A. 1966. *Die Gemeindeordnung in der Johannes-Apokalypse.* Neukirchen-Vluyn: Neukirchener Verlag.

Schüssler Fiorenza, Elisabeth. 1985a. *The Book of Revelation: Justice and Judgment.* Philadelphia: Fortress.

———. 1985b. "The Quest for the Johannine School: The Book of Revelation and the Fourth Gospel." In *The Book of Revelation: Justice and Judgment,* 85–113. Philadelphia: Fortress.

———. 1991. *Revelation: Vision of a Just World.* Minneapolis: Fortress.

Sherwin-White, R. N. 1964. "Why Were the Early Christians Persecuted?—an Amendment." *Past and Present* 27:23–27.

Silberman, L. H. 1963. "Farewell to O AMHN." *JBL* 82:213–15.

Smith, Morton. 1983. "On the History of APOKALYPTO and APOKALYPSIS." In *Apocalypticism in the Mediterranean World and the Near East,* ed. David Hellholm, 9–20. Tübingen: J. C. B. Mohr (Paul Siebeck).

St. Croix, G. E. M. de. 1963. "Why Were the Early Christians Persecuted?" *Past and Present* 26:6–38.

———. 1964. "Why Were the Early Christians Persecuted?—a Rejoinder." *Past and Present* 27:28–38.

Stendahl, Krister. 1968. *The School of St. Matthew and Its Use of the Old Testament.* 2d ed. Philadelphia: Fortress.

Stone, Michael E. 1990. *Fourth Ezra.* Minneapolis: Fortress.

Stuckenbruck, Loren T. 1995. *Angel Veneration and Christology: A Study in Early Judaism and in the Christology of the Apocalypse of John.* WUNT, 70, 2d ser. Tübingen: J. C. B. Mohr (Paul Siebeck).

Suter, David W. 1979. "Fallen Angel, Fallen Priest: The Problem of Family Purity in 1 Enoch 6–16." *HUCA* 50:115–35.

Sweet, J. P. M. 1979. *Revelation.* Philadelphia: Westminster.

Theissen, Gerd. 1982. *The Social Setting of Pauline Christianity: Essays on Corinth.* Trans. John H. Schütz. Philadelphia: Fortress.

Thompson, Leonard. 1990. *The Book of Revelation: Apocalypse and Empire.* New York: Oxford University Press.

Trites, A. A. 1973. "*Martys* and Martyrdom in the Apocalypse: A Semantic Study." *NovT* 15:72–80.

Ulfgard, H. 1989. *Feast and Future: Revelation 7:9-17 and the Feast of Tabernacles.* Stockholm: Almqvist and Wiksell.

Vanni, Ugo. 1991. "Liturgical Dialogue as a Literary Form in the Book of Revelation." *NTS* 37:348–72.

van Unnick, W. C. 1962–1963. "A Formula Describing Prophecy." *NTS* 9:86–94.

Wainwright, Arthur W. 1993. *Mysterious Apocalypse: Interpreting the Book of Revelation.* Nashville: Abingdon.

Wallace, Howard N. 1992. "Tree of Knowledge and Tree of Life." *ABD* 6:656–60.

Yarbro Collins, Adela. 1974. "Numerical Symbolism in Jewish and Early Christian Apocalyptic Literature." *ANRW* 2.21.3.

———. 1976. *The Combat Myth in the Book of Revelation.* Missoula, Mont.: Scholars Press.

———. 1977a. "The History-of-Religions Approach to Apocalypticism and the 'Angel of the Waters' (Rev. 16:4–7)." *CBQ* 39:367–81.

———. 1977b. "The Political Perspective of the Revelation to John." *JBL* 96:241–56.

———. 1979. *The Apocalypse.* Wilmington, Del.: Michael Glazier.

———. 1980. "Revelation 18: Taunt-Song or Dirge?" In *L'Apocalypse Johannique et l'Apocalyptique dans le Nouveau Testament,* ed. J. Lambrecht, 185–204. Louvain: Louvain University Press.

———. 1984. *Crisis and Catharsis: The Power of the Apocalypse.* Philadelphia: Westminster.

———. 1987. "Women's History and the Book of Revelation." *SBLSP* 26:80–91.

———. 1990. "The Apocalypse (Revelation)." In *The New Jerome Biblical Commentary,* ed. Raymond E. Brown, Joseph A. Fitzmyer, and Roland E. Murphy, 996–1016. Englewood Cliffs, N.J.: Prentice Hall.

———. 1996. *Cosmology and Eschatology in Jewish and Christian Apocalypticism.* Leiden: Brill.

———. 1997. "Pergamum in Early Christian Literature." In forthcoming work, ed. Helmut Koester. Valley Forge, Pa.: Trinity Press International.

———, ed. 1986. *Early Christian Apocalypticism: Genre and Social Setting.* Decatur, Ga.: Scholars Press.

Index of Ancient Sources

APOCRYPHA

OTHER EARLY CHRISTIAN SOURCES

GRECO-ROMAN SOURCES

JOSEPHUS

PHILO

RABBINIC SOURCES

DEAD SEA SCROLLS

Index of Ancient Persons

Index of Gods and Goddesses

Index of Modern Authors

Frederick J. Murphy is Professor of Religious Studies at the College of the Holy Cross in Worcester, Massachusetts, and the author of *The Structure of Second Baruch, The Religious World of Jesus,* and *Pseudo-Philo: Rewriting the Bible.*

CPSIA information can be obtained
at www.ICGtesting.com
Printed in the USA
LVOW01s1923010316
477332LV00010B/269/P